THE RESEARCH PROCESS IN EDUCATION

DAVID J. FOX

The City College of the City University of New York

With a chapter
on Electronic Data Processing
by SIGMUND TOBIAS
The City College of the City University of New York

Holt, Rinehart and Winston, Inc.
New York / Chicago / San Francisco / Atlanta / Dallas
Montreal / Toronto / London / Sydney

Dedicated to Louise

PREFACE

For the past twenty years I have enjoyed the double life of conducting research in psychology and education and teaching introductory and advanced courses in research at the graduate level. This book is a direct reflection of that joint exposure to the theoretical-academic and practical-field sides of research, for I have attempted to provide a thorough overview of the conceptual aspects of the research process as it functions in the reality of the educational setting.

The book is directed to three audiences. The first is comprised of students taking a first course in research, typically given now at the master's as well as at the doctoral level, and which some institutions are considering introducing in the undergraduate years. Since most of these students have had no previous coursework or experience in research, I assume that the reader begins knowing nothing of the concepts or language of research or statistics. Moreover, since students in these introductory courses are more likely to be research consumers than practitioners, I have considered the research process in terms of the skills and knowledges needed to critically evaluate and use research as well as those needed to conduct research.

The second audience is the individual graduate student faced with the necessity to complete a research project or paper without adequate training in research, who comes to his adviser with the question, "What book can I read to tell me how to _____?" Whether the blank is completed with "review the literature," or "know which measure of central tendency to use," or "construct a questionnaire," the adviser is faced with the problem that few of the current texts emphasize how to do research in the reality of school settings. For that reason, the emphasis in this text is on providing the background for understanding the various stages of the process and providing specific guidance in how to implement each stage.

The third audience is the increasing number of educators faced with the responsibility to evaluate programs and study problems through the research approach. This audience has needs similar to the second, except for even greater pressure of reality. With this audience in mind, I have tried to consider the practical as well as the theoretical aspects of each stage of research, and to make suggestions which can be implemented in a real setting.

In addition to a concern with meeting needs of the potential user, several basic concepts have guided the preparation of these materials. The first is that while research in the social disciplines does consist of a series of stages beginning with the identification of a problem and culminating in the production of a report, it must also be seen as an ongoing process in which several of the stages are underway simultaneously, and in which decisions made at early stages in the process have irreversible implications for later stages.

This perception of research as a total process has several direct expressions in the nature, and the order, of the material presented. The book begins with the presentation of a complete research project conducted in the New York City public schools in the early 1950s. This material is intended to provide the reader with a sense of what the entire research process is like in the reality of the public school setting. The second chapter presents a model of that process in terms of the several stages of research, with the dynamics underlying each stage, and the outcomes, the focus of the discussion. The chapter concludes with an illustration of how a student might use the model to develop his own problem.

By this point it is hoped that the reader without previous experience or course work in research will have sufficient understanding of the total process so that the chapters devoted to specific stages will be seen and understood in context, that is, in terms of how any one stage is affected by decisions made in earlier stages and in turn affects the stages which follow.

To further the orientation to research as a total process the projects discussed in the first two chapters are used throughout the book for the majority of the illustrative comments and examples. Other studies are mentioned only when they offer a more precise or relevant illustration than was available from these two basic studies. It is hoped that this practice will help the reader see the illustrative point being made in the context of a total project he has previously considered, more effectively than would brief, out-of-context reference to isolated studies. The inevitable consequence of this practice is that the book contains fewer references to the research literature than might be expected. I believe the gains derived from seeing examples in context more than compensates for the loss of contact with the literature.

The combination of the concern with process and the assumption of neither experience nor course work on the part of the audience has led to the placement of material on the nature of data and statistical concepts early in the book. Intelligent research understanding must be based upon a full understanding of the nature of data and of data analysis, particularly statistical concepts. The emphasis here is on concepts, not computations, for I am deeply convinced that in our teaching of statistics we have tended to overemphasize derivations and computations at the expense of concepts. For that reason, the consideration of this material is placed early in the book, before the consideration of data-collection techniques and procedures. Thus, the student is encouraged to see these concepts as fundamental components of research *planning,* about which he must be sophisticated before he considers collecting data. Furthermore, these chapters are written from a research, rather than a statistical point of view, centered about the nature of data and the descriptive and inferential statistics appropriate for each kind of data. This has made it possible to cover a much wider set of statistical concepts than typically is covered in a research text, and it also continually emphasizes the interrelationship between the data and the statistics. This approach obviously minimizes the computational aspects of statistics. This book contains few computational techniques or formulas, for I believe statistical computation and theoretical thinking are separate issues from research application of statistical concepts. Since many excellent books exist totally devoted to this issue it does not seem useful to attempt to treat computational techniques in one or two chapters.

A significant aspect of this text is the concern with ethics, the point being made that as social scientists we must do our research in accordance with ethical principles. Essentially we use people as the subjects of social research, and I believe there are real and partially unrecognized limits to what can be done ethically with and to people in the name of research. Moreover, there are specific responsibilities researchers have too often ignored, such as the responsibility to feed back the results of research to those who have cooperated in the research process. Limits and responsibilities are considered throughout the text.

A final referent in developing this book is the belief that for research in the social sciences to achieve any meaningful results, it must be a rational process. We must know why we do what we do, and why we do it in the way that we do, and we must also know what ways we have considered and rejected and why. In view of the severe limits to our available methods and instruments and the practical difficulties in sampling, we must choose within these limits in as knowledgeable a way as possible. Thus, a heavy emphasis has been placed on making research decisions and on developing the ability to recognize the alternatives available and to choose rationally between them.

In summary then, I have attempted to find a middle level at which to teach research, a level which is abstracted and generalized above the "cookbook" approach of how-to-do-it, yet is more concerned than the theoretical text with the pressures and limits of a realistic setting. I hope that this middle way will help eliminate the current gap between the researcher and practitioner in education, and enable us to realize more fully and more quickly the potential contribution of the research approach to current efforts to evaluate and improve the quality of educational programs.

Several people made significant contributions at appropriate stages in the development of this book. The several versions of the text were efficiently and insightfully typed by Rita Roth assisted by Anne Goldstein and Janet Leibman. The index was prepared by Sophie Colten. Dale Harris provided a critical reading of the entire manuscript, which was an immense help in identifying aspects in need of clarification, revision, or expansion. Working with him was a stimulating intellectual experience. Obviously the responsibility for the final manuscript remains with the author.

A book which has a gestation period of several years, as this one did, is an immense burden on the author's family. I am grateful to my children who, young as they are, tried to understand why Daddy was forever at the typewriter. I am grateful for, and in awe of, my wife's understanding throughout these years. Always encouraging, always confident that it would one day be finished, and graciously abandoning an infinite series of family plans to the book, she was the personal support an author needs to work on one set of material for twelve years! For this, and for her many suggestions and insightful reading of the manuscript, it is a pleasure to be able, at last, to dedicate this book to her.

New York, N. Y.   D. J. F.
January 1969

CONTENTS

PART I
Introduction and Basic Concepts

Chapter 1

A CASE STUDY IN RESEARCH DESIGN

Research is difficult to discuss in the abstract, and so to illustrate the research process as it actually functions in education, as well as the different aspects of this process to be discussed in detail in subsequent chapters, this first chapter will present the history of an actual research project in which the author participated a few years ago. We shall begin with a description of the original concern which prompted the project, and follow it through the various stages in the development and design of the research to the actual way in which the project was conducted.

THE PUERTO RICAN STUDY

The project to be used as the illustration was carried out in the early 1950s in New York City. Its purpose was to determine the best method of teaching English as a second language to children who were non–English-speaking Puerto Rican language learners. As many readers will remember, there was a heavy inmigration of Puerto Rican families to the continental United States in the 1950s. More than 90 percent of the Puerto Rican inmigrants first settled in New York City, and so schools in many neighborhoods were faced with the problem of developing educational programs for children whose first language was Spanish. A basic part of any such program was to teach the children English as a second language. But how best to do it? Rather than rely on opinion, the Puerto Rican Study, a research group established through funds provided by the Ford Foundation, was asked to provide a research answer.

The nature of the question to be answered—what is "the best method"—implied evaluation of methods in terms of specific criteria so that the "best" could be determined. This meant that those given responsibility for the research set off on two immediate searches: (1) to identify methods of teaching English as a second language; (2) to see if data were already available on the basis of which a "best" method could be identified.

The Historical Approach

We began, as all research begins, with a search of the literature, in this case a search for evidence of the effectiveness of previous programs in the teaching of English as a second language. The historical approach is always the logical first step in research, as the researcher wishes to be certain that the research question being raised has not already been answered. Even if it has not been definitively answered, he may find that it has been studied and that he can use the experience of the previous studies in planning his own study. For this particular research question there was good reason to embark on the historical phase with some optimism.

This was not the first time that school systems of large metropolitan areas in the United States had had influxes of large numbers of non–English-speaking children. In fact the opposite was true; the event which precipitated the research had happened several times before, and presumably schools in New York, Boston, Chicago, and Philadelphia had used and/or developed methods of teaching English as a second language to children whose first language was German, Italian, Polish, or Russian. But as so often happens in education, the methodological experiences of these previous generations of teachers were never written down, and so were lost as a source of methodology for the contemplated study. We faced the frustrating fact that innumerable creative approaches of generations of teachers faced with this problem died with these teachers because they had never been recorded. The closest we came to a treatise on methodology was *The Education of Hyman Kaplan*,[1] and while wonderfully amusing it had little to contribute to our research planning. Obviously, in view of this lack of any recording of methodology, we found no data comparing various methods. Therefore, we had the other frustrating experience of knowing that data relevant to our problem had undoubtedly existed at some point or points in the historical past, but that since they had never been recorded they might as well never have happened.

In addition to searching the literature for previous research, we searched it for material written by experts in our problem area presenting their ideas, opinions, or theories. This nonresearch literature proved more rewarding. Two clearly defined methods of teaching English as a second language were identified. One, which we shall refer to as the vocabulary-oriented method (more widely known as Basic English), had been developed by I. A. Richards of Harvard. He argued that the essence of

[1]Leonard Q. Ross, *The Education of Hyman Kaplan* (New York: Harcourt, Brace & World, Inc., 1937).

second-language teaching was teaching the words of the language and so developed a basic vocabulary of 850 English words through which he believed any thought or phrase could be expressed in English. We found a somewhat contrary methodological argument which had been advanced by Charles Fries of the University of Michigan, who argued that the essence of language teaching was to teach the structure of the language, that is, how it ordered nouns, verbs, adjectives, or how questions are asked in the language. He analyzed the structure of English and developed a full series of lessons for teaching these structural patterns from what he believed to be the simplest to the most complex. A further aspect of Fries' methodology of interest in the research was his belief that the problems of teaching English as a second language had to be studied in the context of the original language spoken by the student. Fries had developed materials especially for the student whose first language was Spanish.

However, this success in finding in the nonresearch literature two well-developed methods did not provide the basis for answering our research question because the advocates of the methods had no data to offer comparing their method to other methods under controlled conditions, and so we had no basis for making a judgment of "best."

Survey of the Present

While this search of the past through research and nonresearch literature was going on, a parallel study was under way surveying the present. In this survey we were seeking to determine if the answer to the research question existed in some educational setting other than those with which we were familiar, and which had not yet been reported in the literature. As in the search of the historical past, the survey of the present had two goals: (1) to seek comparative data on methods, or if no data were available, then (2) to seek methods other than the two we had already identified.

The survey, conducted on a variety of sites, found no comparative data but did find a third method. First we sent teams of observers and interviewers into the New York City schools to learn what methods teachers could identify as the basis for their educational planning. We found that most teachers did not have a specific method to which they could point or to which they could attribute their lessons. While they had developed their own techniques and materials, these were not in the context of formal methodology. A second part of the survey was to learn what was being done in Puerto Rico, where English as a second language was taught regularly beginning in the second grade. Here, however, we found that the

Fries method and materials had been adopted, and so this part of the survey too added nothing new. We also surveyed activity in other areas of the United States, since the problem of teaching English as a second language to children whose native language was Spanish was a problem which had been faced by school systems in states such as Arizona, Texas, Florida, New Mexico, and California. The children involved were of Mexican rather than Puerto Rican background, but the methodological problems were the same. The survey of these school systems provided us with no comparative data but did provide us with advocates of a third methodological approach to the teaching of English as a second language: those who believed that the key to success was to provide the child with a variety of language-needing experiences. Advocates of this method believed that children provided with these experiences would indirectly learn the language. This method, which we called the experiential, could be considered an indirect approach to language teaching in contrast to the direct methods of instruction suggested by both the vocabulary approach of Richards and the structural approach of Fries.

As we concluded our survey of the present, we had identified a third possible method but still had identified no data which could help answer the original research question. This placed the burden of providing such data on the staff of the Puerto Rican Study, and meant that we had to utilize the experimental approach, the third major research approach. This sequence—attempting to answer research questions through historical, then survey or descriptive research, utilizing experimentation only in those instances when the research question cannot be answered by the other approaches—is the proper sequence of considering approaches in the social sciences. This process of identifying all that has already been studied and all that is now underway makes it possible to identify when experimentation is necessary as well as identifying the specifics of what we should experiment with.

Thus in the present instance the lack of any data comparing the effectiveness of methods highlighted the necessity for experimentation, while the historical and survey phases spelled out with what we should experiment: the vocabulary, structural, and experiential approaches to second-language teaching. Assuming that both the search of the literature and the survey were thoroughly done we could be confident that these three were the only ones fully developed enough to use in the contemplated experiment. But note the word that introduces the previous sentence: "assuming." As we planned the experiment involving these three methods, we could only assume that there was no other method with which we should be concerned. There was also a second assumption in this plan, that one of these three methods would be the answer to the research question. An obvious question that came up at this point was what about some combination of the methods? The question of combinations was tabled to be revived again after the experiment was completed, because a moment's reflection will indicate that an infinite number of combinations could have been developed—such as one hour of vocabulary and one hour of structure for every experience, or one half hour of each, or one hour of structure to one half hour of vocabulary, and so on. There would have been no end to the combinations, and so we decided to experiment with each method in a relatively pure sense and then see if the data suggested possible combinations at the conclusion of the research. We abandoned the question of new methods on the simple grounds that there was no reason to believe that in a few months we would produce something significantly different from the methods produced to date by the best experts in the area of second-language teaching. We decided to evaluate experimentally the effectiveness of the three methods we had identified: the vocabulary approach, the structure approach, and the experiential approach.

In a sense, this decision rewrote the research problem, so that it now was more specific: Which of three—vocabulary, structure, and experiential—is the best method of teaching English as a second language to children who are non–English-speaking Puerto Rican language learners?

DEFINITION OF TERMS

The first task was to define our terms. Most people with whom the story of this project is discussed reach this point without realizing that both the general research problem presented at the beginning of this chapter, and the specific problem listed above, are stated ambiguously from a research point of view. Who, for example, was a non–English-speaking Puerto Rican language learner? Were children born in Puerto Rico but who came with their parents to the continental United States before school age to be included if they were non–English-speaking? Were children born in New York whose parents took them to Puerto Rico at an early age and who then returned unable to speak English to be included? For that matter, what did we mean by non–English-speaking? Unable to speak a word? Able only to state name and address?

Similarly, we had to define the criteria we would use to decide on the "best" method. Would it be the single criterion of teaching the originally non–English-speaking child to speak English? Or should we include the three other modalities of language—reading, writing, and understanding?

Continuing to analyze the research problem, note that each of the three methods to date has been referred to only in terms of its particular orientation or emphasis on vocabulary, structure, or experience. For an experiment, each must be "defined" in terms of classroom practice and materials. Finally (but in practice the first definition we developed) what did we mean by children—elementary school, junior high school, or senior high school students? All three were possible, since at the time that the study was contemplated, large numbers of non–English-speaking children were transferring into all three levels of the school system.

To define all of these terms we had to make several decisions, some based on academic aspects of the problem, some on the realities of the school system within which the study would be conducted, and some arbitrary in the sense they reflected only our hunches or feelings about the research.

Let us consider the problem of defining "children." In what grades should the study be done? To make this decision involved two issues: identifying the grade in which the problem was first considered serious, and then identifying in how many educationally different ways the problems appeared above that grade. Discussions with administrators and teachers made it clear that in kindergarten and first grade few were troubled by the problem of second-language teaching. Teachers pointed out that these are grades in which all children are language learners and grades in which they learn language rapidly. They felt no need for special lessons or materials for Puerto Rican children. Teachers of the second and third grades did feel that second-language teaching was one of their problems, particularly as they began direct teaching of reading. By the fourth grade it was clear that second-language teaching was the paramount problem, since instruction in content areas like science, art, or social studies was now impeded by the lack of fluency in English. Considering all of these views we decided that when we defined the term "children" for the study, it should be defined minimally in terms of third or fourth grade. There seemed no educational rationale to define it to include preschool or early elementary grades.

Now we turned to deciding how many educationally different problems we had. For example, if the study was conducted in the fourth grade, would fifth-grade teachers accept the results as applicable to them as well? Or would they feel that there were so many aspects of the educational process which were different in fourth and fifth grades that they would not accept the results? If fifth-grade teachers would accept the results, would sixth-grade teachers? What would happen when we moved on to the junior high school teachers, or the senior high school teachers?

The gross limits of the educationally different settings were simple to identify. Everyone agreed that teaching English as a second language was an entirely different methodological question for a fourth-grade and a twelfth-grade teacher. Similarly, most experts agreed that it was much the same methodological problem for the fourth- and fifth-grade teacher. Thus, the findings of a study conducted in the fourth grade only would generally apply to the fifth grade, but not to the twelfth.

Where is the line drawn? Even more important, how many lines must be drawn? We finally decided, after consultation with language teaching experts, that the upper elementary, junior high, and senior high schools presented educationally different settings for second-language teaching and so we could not assume that the results obtained at any one of these levels could be applied to the others. However, they felt that within each level, we could assume that the separate grades presented sufficiently similar problems of second-language teaching so that we could apply results from one grade to the other. This meant that to completely cover the school range we had to repeat the study three times, once in upper elementary grades, once in the junior high school grades, and the third time in the senior high school grades.

Notice that, while based upon the best information we could obtain, these decisions nevertheless had large elements of assumption and/or arbitrariness within them. If some educator had challenged us to *prove* that fourth and fifth grade presented essentially the same methodological problems we could not have done it. This in itself would have required research, and since the research was not available we had to rely on expert opinion as the basis of our assumption that the problems were essentially the same. Moreover, we decided to do the study in the fourth grade only, and so our own research would provide no data to test the assumption. Yet, this assumption *had* to be true for our research to be applicable to the fifth and sixth grades. These are the two attributes which characterize all assumptions in research: They must be true for the research to be sensible, and the research itself will provide no basis for demonstrating their truth.

Having selected the fourth grade as the elementary grade in which the study would be done, we also selected the seventh and tenth grades as the setting for junior and senior high replications. To some extent these decisions were arbitrary, but they had a rational basis as well. The key decision was the junior high school decision, because it was the middle grade. We decided on grade 7 in large part because the school drop-out problem first appeared severely in grade 8 and we wanted the maximum number of children available to us. Once grade 7 was chosen, this established the selection of grades 4 and 10, as it was felt that we should choose elementary and senior high grades at least three years away from the junior high school grade selected. The selection of grade 4 as opposed to grade 3, however, was arbitrary.

We then turned to the issue of defining non–English-speaking. The obvious way to define non–English-speaking was to use some measure of the children's ability to speak English and establish some cutoff point, defining all children who scored below this point as non–English-speaking. The problem we faced, another one which typifies much educational research, was that no such measure existed. To use this empirical definition we would have to develop the measure. We considered other possibilities which would not require developing the measure. For example, we considered defining non–English-speaking as "lack of any formal instruction in English," but decided that this was too imprecise and treacherous. We considered using teacher judgment, but this, we felt, would be too unreliable for research purposes. There seemed no acceptable substitute for developing some objective measure to use as the basis of this definition.

Allied to this problem of developing so.ne measure of English-speaking ability was the issue of developing the measures with which we would ultimately decide which method was "best." We decided to define "best" in terms of all four language modalities—reading, writing, speaking, and understanding. Standardized tests were available for measuring ability to read English, but there were none which would measure ability to write English or to understand spoken English. Therefore, the test development phase of the research involved not only the development of a measure of ability to speak English, but also of measures of ability to write English and to understand spoken English.

As a matter of fact, as work on these measures got under way, we decided to use the test of ability to understand spoken English as the criterion measure to identify non–English-speaking children, even though this meant defining non–English-speaking in terms of the understanding modality rather than the speaking modality. The reason for the change was simply that the measure we developed to test understanding of spoken English was a group test, whereas the measure of speaking ability was an individual test. The group test of ability to understand could be given to thousands of children in the amount of time the individual test could be given to a hundred. Again, this illustrates the interaction of academic concerns and the realities of the field situation in making research decisions.

Deciding whom we would call a Puerto Rican language learner was a simpler matter, involving no measurement but rather agreement among the researchers. We decided to use a combination of birthplace and schooling and recency of arrival in the United States, defining a Puerto Rican language learner as a child born in Puerto Rico, who had attended school there and had arrived for the first time in New York City within the previous six months. Defining a Puerto Rican language learner in this way meant that we would eliminate from the research a variety of children who had presented special educational problems, such as children who entered the fourth grade without ever having attended school in Puerto Rico, children who had shuttled back and forth between the mainland and Puerto Rico, and children who had been in New York for more than six months and still scored below the cutoff point on our criterion of ability to understand spoken English.

The methods were defined in consultation with experts in the teaching of English as a second language, who advised that in grade 4, 30 minutes a day be devoted to the experimental method while instruction during the remainder of the day consist of the regular curriculum for the grade. In grade 7, they advised that one period be devoted to language instruction, while the rest of the school day be devoted to the regular curriculum.

We were now in a position to reconsider the research problem with all of the previously ambiguous terms defined specifically enough for research purposes. The research problem could now be stated as: Which of three methods, vocabulary, structure, or experiential, was the best (in terms of ability to read, write, speak, and understand spoken English) for teaching English (with one-half hour or one hour of direct instruction daily) to children (in grades 4, 7, and 10) who are non–English-speaking (who score below the cutoff on a test of ability to understand spoken English) Puerto Rican language learners (born and schooled in Puerto Rico who have arrived in New York within the past six months).

PLANNING THE EXPERIMENT

With all of these decisions made, we could turn now to planning the details of the experiment. Because this study was intended to provide a basis of estimating the effectiveness of methods of teaching, we needed an estimate of the ability of the children before and after exposure to the methods, so that we could know what, if any, change occurred. Furthermore, because the research question was a comparative question, that is, asking which method was better, we needed three groups of children, one for each of the three methods. Thus we had need of what we will call a "three group" before and after design for the research.

Notice that for this particular study we had no need of a control group. In fact it would be difficult to conceptualize what a control group would be in this type of study, unless we were willing to permit a group of non–English-speaking Puerto Rican children to attend school without any instruction in English. This type of control group would have permitted us to estimate how much learning takes place in the absence of any formal instruction in school and so would provide us with a basis for estimating how much more takes place with the three methods. While data like these would have been of research interest, establishing this kind of a control was ethically unthinkable. This illustrates a problem more often faced by the social than the physical scientist: the necessity to alter designs, or to delete aspects of a design because of the ethical considerations involved in doing research with people.

With the design selected, we turned to the issue of selecting the schools, children, and teachers for the study.

Selecting Schools

Typical of most research in the social sciences, we had available far more schools than it was necessary to use for our research, and so we had to select a sample of schools to participate. This posed three research problems: what criteria to use in selecting schools, how many schools to select, and finally how to select them. Let us consider the experiment to be conducted in the fourth grade as an example. As we began to consider possible criteria, the obvious one of the proportion of Puerto Rican pupils in the school stood out. After considering the different enrollment patterns in the school system, we decided that there were four significant ones for the purposes of our study: (1) schools with less than 20 percent Puerto Rican enrollment; (2) schools with between 20 percent and 50 percent Puerto Rican enrollment; (3) schools with between 50 percent and 75 percent Puerto Rican enrollment; and (4) schools with more than 75 percent Puerto Rican enrollment. But how many to select of each type? We decided that one school of each type would be sufficient for the research. This decision was based on the interaction of research need with availability of staff. The availability of staff limited the total number of schools with which we could work, but of course it would have been better to have done one thorough study at the fourth grade than three weak studies at grades 4, 7, and 10. The fact which made for the decision was that we also believed that one school of each type was enough to provide us with the meaningful research answer.

What of all of the other characteristics of schools? What about characteristics like facilities, learning atmosphere, language atmosphere, or neighborhood atmosphere and facilities? These characteristics typically are difficult, if not impossible, to measure. Moreover we had no data available about the school system on the basis of which we could decide how many significant variations there were for each of these characteristics. For example, how many different neighborhood atmospheres are there? How many different types of school facilities are there? There was simply no way to answer questions like these, and so we could not treat these variables the way we had treated the variable "proportion of Puerto Ricans in the school." However, we still were able to equate the experimental groups for a wide variety of the variables involving neighborhood and school facilities, climate, and atmosphere by the simple process of establishing all three experimental variations in each school selected. For example, for each elementary school we selected to participate in the study we asked for three fourth-grade classes; one class would be assigned to the vocabulary, one to the structure, and one to the experiential method. Thus if school A had unusually fine educational facilities, these would be available to children in each experimental variation. Similarly, if school B was in a neighborhood where Spanish was the predominant language, this too would hold for children in the three experimental classes in school B. Notice that we are not arguing that schools A and B have the same facilities, or are in neighborhoods with similar language climates. Nor are we arguing that school facilities and language climate have no effect on language learning. What we are arguing is that by establishing all three variations of method in each participating school we are minimizing any *differential* effect of factors like school facilities and language climate. Realistically, this is often the best degree of control that can be achieved in the social sciences in relation to certain variables. We must so design a study that whatever effect the variable does have on our results, it has the opportunity to affect all experimental conditions equally.

Having decided to select four elementary schools using the single criterion of the proportion of Puerto Rican pupils, we turned to the last sampling question involving schools: How were the four actually to be selected? For example, from all of the schools in the city with fewer than 20 percent Puerto Rican enrollment, we now had to pick one. One way was to place the numbers of the schools in a hat and draw one. This process, called "random selection," is the classic way to sample. It has the virtue of being bias-free in that the researcher has no influence on the selection process. But this study was being done within the setting of a functioning school system, and the administrative authorities felt that some schools were more likely research settings than others. In view of this, we used a different selection process, called "deliberate sampling" in which we selected the participating schools from a list drawn up by the school system.

Selecting Children

With the schools selected we could turn to the question of establishing the experimental classes and populating them with children. Since we were using the experimental approach, we set out to achieve the essential goal in designing experimental research: that the separate groups within the experiment differ from each other only on what are called independent variables. In this instance, we had only one independent variable, the method of teaching. This meant that ideally our three experimental classes in each school would be comparable in every other aspect relevant to the educational process, specifically in the characteristics of the children, the schools, the neighborhoods, material, and the teachers. Anyone familiar with the current state of measurement in the social sciences will recognize what an ambitious level of aspiration that sentence established!

As we considered characteristics of children on which the experimental classes should be equated, we considered our language learners and nonlanguage learners separately. For the language learners, we compiled a list of characteristics like intelligence, socioeconomic status, language spoken at home, sex, learning climate at home, previous school achievement, or facilities for study at home, to name only a few of those which would be expected to be relevant for any study of school learning. Some of these characteristics, such as learning climate at home or intelligence, we had to eliminate from consideration because we had no ability to measure them.

However, there were factors such as sex, previous school achievement, language spoken at home, and socioeconomic status for which data could be obtained and which previous research and/or expert opinion suggested were relevant to the problem. The issue was which of these to use and how many. Again, reality played a part in the research decision. Let us think of school A, where we have 150 fourth-grade children, and let us assume that school A is our 33 percent Puerto Rican school so that 50 of these children are of Puerto Rican background. Finally let us assume that of these 50, 15 score below the cutoff point on our test of ability to understand spoken English. We now wish to distribute these 15 children into three classes, placing five each in the vocabulary, structure, and experiential class, and wish to place them so that the three sets of five have comparable ability on the criterion test of ability to understand spoken English. But on how many other variables can we realistically equate these sets of five? The answer is, very few. For what happens is that as the sets of five are manipulated to equate them on language spoken at home, we find that we have destroyed the balance on language ability. We then rejuggle to rebalance on language ability, attempting to hold the balance on language spoken at home, and find that one set consists of five boys and so the balance on sex is gone. Here we have an example of the researcher knowing more about the research process than he is actually able to implement. We could have, and did, spell out the list of significant social, educational, psychological, and personal characteristics on which it would have been desirable to equate the experimental classes. In practice we were able to use only two, the child's ability to understand spoken English and the sex of the child.

Why then bother to spell out the list? There are three reasons. First, because to select intelligently the one or two variables on which we *will* equate the groups involves knowing the full list of variables we might possibly use. Second, if research is to be a rational process we should be fully aware of what we *cannot* do, that is, the limitations of our research plan and design. The third reason is that recognizing the limits of any one research plan, particularly in identifying those characteristics for which measures do not exist, creates a pressure within the fraternity of researchers to develop such measures. One researcher may even decide that one particular measure is so critical to his study that he must go off on a tangent and develop it himself. This is what happened within our study when we went off on the tangent to develop the test of ability to understand spoken English, to speak English, and to write English, after deciding that these measures were essential to the successful completion of the study.

When we turned to the question of the nonlanguage learners in these experimental classes we decided that all we could hope to do was to equate the classes in terms of the proportions of children of three different types of nonlanguage learners: (1) Puerto Rican–born children who scored above our cutoff point and so would not be defined as non–English-speaking; (2) mainland-born children of Puerto Rican parentage; and (3) mainland-born children of other than Puerto Rican parentage. Notice that for other research purposes this third group could have been split into several subgroups depending on the child's parentage, just as we singled out the second group on the basis of Puerto Rican parentage. Similarly, the first group of Puerto Rican–born children could have been broken into subgroups on the basis of the level of language ability in English, rather than being combined on the single criterion of scoring above the cutoff score established on the test of ability to understand spoken English. But for this particular study, we were interested in the gains achieved by our non–English-speaking language learners and interested in the numbers of the other children in the experimental classes only to keep "class composition" as a variable on which the three experimental classes within any one school could be equated.

Summarizing these sampling decisions, we now had decided to select four elementary schools in each of which we would establish three classes, peopled with sets of non–English-speaking Puerto Rican children comparable in terms of proportions of boys and girls and ability to speak English, and of children of our other three groups.

The reader familiar with school systems and how classes are organized will recognize that to achieve this equating of classes involved an unusual degree of cooperation from the school system and particularly from the principals of the participating schools. The school system in which this study was done, like most others, organized its classes in June for the coming September and then adjusted the classes in September on the basis of late admissions and transfers. But this organization had no relevance for the research. What we needed to do was to come into the school in September when all the children were there, give our test of ability to understand spoken English to all Puerto Rican children who had arrived in the previous six months, and also determine the birthplace and parentage of all other children in the fourth grade. Then, using these data we had to create three new classes with similar proportions of the four types of children listed earlier[2] and with the group of non–English-speaking Puerto Ricans in each of the classes matched by sex and for ability to understand spoken English. In other words, for the research we needed to reorganize the fourth grade in September. The problems imaginable in terms of clerical chores, teacher resistance, children resenting being pulled out of established classes were all present, but this was the only way we could have any confidence that the classes were comparable on the two factors we had decided to use: ability to understand spoken English, and sex.

Selecting Teachers

The next aspect on which we had to equate the experimental groups concerned the teachers to be assigned each class. The process used was the same as in assigning the children, and so we set out to list the characteristics of teachers which are related to children's learning. We faced another typical problem in educational research—no one really knows which characteristics of teachers are related to children's learning, and so we had to turn once again to a logical analysis of the problem. As was true of the characteristics of the children, there were characteristics of teachers, such as attitude toward Puerto Rican children, which we considered relevant but which we could not measure. But there were other relevant characteristics which we could handle relatively easily, such as experience in the teaching of English as a second language, knowledge of Spanish, and interest in participation in the study. The first two characteristics were handled by taking teachers who spoke no Spanish and had no experience or training in the teaching of English as a second language. The third characteristic was handled by taking only teachers who truly

---

[2]In practice, no school had more than three of the four types of children.

volunteered for the study (as opposed to the military concept of volunteering!).

Taking teachers without experience was realistic because we knew there were few teachers in the entire school system who had been so trained. Even more important it had an important public relations aspect. We were thinking ahead to the time when the study was completed and reported to the profession where it, hopefully, would be accepted. But if the study had been done using teachers who were expert in the teaching of English as a second language, most principals would have little interest in the results for in all probability they would have no such teachers available. In research terms, this would have imposed a severe limitation, and it was one we were not willing to impose. A similar line of reasoning was followed in the decision to use only teachers with no knowledge of Spanish, although this was not as clear-cut a decision as the language-teaching decision, for teachers who spoke Spanish were more frequently available than teachers trained in teaching English as a second language.

Finally there was the question of teacher ability. In one sense, this was another characteristic for which there was no accepted measure, and yet this was one which could not be ignored because it was so critical to equating the experimental groups. Again, all we could do was seek to eliminate any consistent bias by the following procedure exemplified by school X, in which we had three volunteers. We asked the principal to rank the three in order of ability, and then arbitrarily assigned the best of the three to the vocabulary method, the second-best to the structure method, and the one ranked third to the experiential method. We then moved on to school Y, asking the principal to rank his three volunteers. But since the vocabulary method had been assigned to the best teacher in school X, we assigned it to the second-best in school Y. We then had the first- and third-ranking teachers in school Y available, and since the experiential already had the third-ranking teacher in school X we assigned that method to the first-ranking teacher in school Y, with the third teacher in school Y assigned to the structure method. Of course, when we moved on to school Z we completed the cycle, so that each method had one teacher ranked first, second, and third.

It is important to note that the procedure did not equate the methods for teacher ability. A moment's thought will indicate that in school X all three of the volunteers might have been far more able teachers than the best of the volunteers in school Y. Lacking any abstract measure of teacher quality, we would never know whether or not this was so. However, we did assure that teacher quality would not of itself produce a consistent difference between the methods. This might have happened if, for example, in the absence of some plan like the one used, the best teacher in each school had been assigned to the vocabulary method by chance.

Now that the classes were peopled with children and teachers had been assigned, we had only one other problem of experimental control, and that was to control the nature of the material to be taught. Two issues were involved; assuring that all fourth-grade teachers assigned to any one method used the same procedures, and assuring that except for the 30 minutes per day of language instruction, classes were comparable in instruction. There was only one way to assure this, and that was to prepare detailed daily lesson plans, and train the teachers in their use. This is exactly what was done. Detailed guides were prepared for each of the three variations of method, and teachers were relieved of their regular teaching responsibility so that they could attend special training institutes conducted by the staff of the study. At the same time, detailed lesson plans were prepared for the rest of each school day, other than the experimental period. Thus when all three classes received a science lesson on the fourth day of the third week of the study, it was, within limits set by variations among children, the same science lesson. The training institute prepared the teachers for using these materials as well.

The reader untrained in research may wonder how long all these preparations took. From the time that the decision was made to pursue this study, until the time the classes were organized and the experiment was ready to begin, took a professional staff of about 15 people the major part of a year. Even this is an underestimate, because the test development part of the project, that is, developing the measures of ability to understand spoken English, to write English, and to speak English had been accomplished in a previous year. Remember that the few sentences above in which we noted the fact of preparing guides to the use of each method represent a huge professional undertaking, as does the preparation of the units of content to be taught the children. Recognize also, that ideally this would not be the researcher's responsibility, in the sense that wherever possible the researcher uses materials already available. Unless absolutely necessary he does not stop along the way to develop tests, units, or guides to language teaching. But in this instance we had no choice if the study was to be done properly. We could have avoided developing a measure of ability to understand spoken English had we been willing to use teacher ratings despite their known unreliability and inadequacy. Similarly, we could have avoided developing complete units had we been willing to assume that once we had structured the 30 minutes of language instruction, the units of instruction for the rest of the school day could be left to the teachers and presumably would not be too different. These points are stressed because only rarely have educational researchers been willing to stop "along the way" and take the time to remedy lacks in instrumentation and material development so that they might more thoroughly conduct their research.

Stating the Hypotheses

As the study was ready to get under way, we began to wonder about the outcome. We had defined "best," that is, had selected as the criteria of evaluation four tests: of ability to read, write, speak, and understand English. Which of the three groups would score highest on each of the criterion measures?

It seemed sensible to expect the two direct instruction methods, the vocabulary and structure, to have more of an effect on reading ability than the experiential, and since the early reading materials in use in the schools were essentially word-oriented, using simple patterns, it further seemed reasonable to expect the vocabulary group to do better in reading than the structure group. These expectations of the research result are called hypotheses. This brief consideration of the results with the reading criterion led to three hypotheses:

1. Children taught by the vocabulary method will read significantly better than children taught by the experiential method.
2. Children taught by the structure method will read significantly better than children taught by the experiential method.
3. Children taught by the vocabulary method will read significantly better than children taught by the structure method.

As will be discussed in more detail in a later chapter, these hypotheses, like all well-stated hypotheses, are specific predictions of a single research outcome.[3] Since they are specific and refer to a single outcome, once the study is completed and the data collected it is possible to make a definite judgment on each hypothesis, stating either that the data did or did not support it.

Just as we had these hypotheses for the reading criterion, we could have had parallel sets of three with the other criteria, provided we had some basis for making each prediction. They would not all have been the same. For the writing criterion, we might have decided that writing was a basic aspect of the experiential method of language learning, since after an experience the children often dictated what they did and saw to the teacher, who wrote it on the board or on an experience chart, after which

---

[3]Note that the researcher may state an expectation of a difference without specifying the amount of that difference. Thus here we are stating the expectation that after the experimental period the vocabulary children will read "better" than the experiential children, but we are not saying how much better.

the children copied it. In view of this habitual contact with writing we could have expected the experiential children to do best in this modality. This would have led to two hypotheses:

1. Children taught by the experiential method will perform significantly better on the writing test than children taught by the vocabulary method.
2. Children taught by the experiential method will perform significantly better on the writing test than children taught by the structure method.

But what difference did we expect between the vocabulary and structure-method classes in ability to write English? Neither set of materials emphasized writing, and there was nothing in the literature to suggest that one led to any more increased ability to write than the other. Thus, there seemed to be no reason to expect one group of children to do better than the other, and so here we phrased the hypothesis in what is called the null form, that is, we hypothesized no difference:

3. There will be no significant difference in ability to write English between children taught by the vocabulary and structure methods.

Through this same procedure we developed the hypotheses for the three possible comparisons in ability to speak English and in ability to understand spoken English, so that we had 12 hypotheses in the area of language learning. But this was only one aspect of evaluation. We might have decided to evaluate the study using other objective criteria such as children's attendance or more subjective criteria like children's expressed attitude toward school. We might have gone on to the teacher, considering the teacher's liking for teaching English as a second language as a criterion. All the criteria by which the outcome of a study is evaluated are called the "dependent variables." The general rule is that there must be *at least* one hypothesis for each dependent variable, although, as in this instance, it is possible to have more than one for any one dependent variable.

Anticipating Outcomes

With the hypotheses stated, all of the preparatory activities were completed. A good last step in research planning is for the researcher to think ahead to the possible outcomes of the research. He does this to make certain that he has designed the research in such a way that he can satisfactorily explain any possible outcome. It is seldom difficult to explain results if what is hypothesized actually does come true. The theoretical or practical considerations which motivated the research should explain these positive findings. But the researcher also wants to be certain that he can adequately explain the results if what is hypothesized does *not* come about.

Every study has a finite set of possible outcomes, and one way for the researcher to recognize weaknesses in his research plan is to assume that each possible outcome has occurred and then try to explain how these results happened or to criticize the experiment in the light of the outcome.

For example, as we anticipated outcomes we felt there were four. One outcome, and the most disappointing outcome, would be for none of the methods to effect any change. A different kind of outcome would be for all of the methods to effect change, but without any difference among the methods. The third possible outcome would be for some methods to effect change, but not others, so that we would have differences among the methods. The fourth outcome would be for all three to effect change but with a clear single best method.

If none effected change this finding could be interpreted to mean that none were effective or else that none were effectively implemented. These are obviously two quite different interpretations. We felt that it would be woefully weak if, to counter the interpretation of poor teaching, all we could offer was our belief or assumption that each method was effectively implemented. A far stronger argument would be some evidence to demonstrate that the methods *were* effectively implemented. Similarly, if all three experimental groups did show change, but without any differences among them, two interpretations of the null finding were possible. One would be that each was effective but to the same extent. The alternative explanation would be that leakage had taken place and so all three groups were exposed to essentially the same composite method created by teachers discussing their materials with each other. Again, we felt that for us to say we assumed that each teacher had remained methodologically "pure" would not be an adequate basis for ruling out the second interpretation. Only evidence that the teachers had in fact remained methodologically pure would rule out this explanation of this possible outcome.

These considerations pointed up the necessity for us to obtain data, during the experiment, proving that the teachers had in fact adhered to the method to which they had been assigned and moreover that they had effectively taught this method. With this evidence we could rule out any explanations of the null findings based on ineffective teaching or methodological contamination.

To gather this evidence, we decided that we would recruit a team of experts in the teaching of English as a second language, have them observe the classes during the experiment, and make two judgments: one about the effectiveness of the teaching, the second about the methodological consistency or "purity" of the teaching. As is true of so many phases of research planning, this too was easier said than done. For observational data to have merit, they must be obtained as close to the real situation as possible. This meant that the observers would have to be able to enter schools and classrooms unannnounced and unexpected. Moreover, for their judgments as to methodological purity to have any meaning, the observers could not know the method to which the teacher had been assigned. We knew well how efficient school "grapevines" are, and so to keep the observations "surprise observations" each observer could make only one each day in any one school. To insure that the observations were true tests of methodological consistency we assigned observers only once to each teacher and moreover assigned them to see the teacher at different points during his school day, not only during the language period. Thus a teacher who was methodologically a "pure" structure teacher during the language period, and was unofficially supplementing this structure instruction with a vocabulary drill in the afternoon, would have been seen at both times by this plan and would have been discovered.

With the addition of the observation plan, we felt that we had strengthened the research as much as possible and could satisfactorily explain any outcome of the research. Thus all advance preparations were completed and the study was ready to begin. This meant that we now should simply carry out all of the decisions which had already been made earlier. This phase of the research process is not a decision-making phase at all but rather one in which the researcher does all that he had earlier intended in the way planned. This orientation of the "doing" phase of research as a phase which is not a decision-making, but rather a decision-implementation, stage is critical to the philosophy of this book. If research is to be a rational process with the maximum degree of precision and control, then all of the possible decision points must be anticipated and thought through before data collection begins. In this way alternative solutions can be considered and one selected at relative leisure in terms of the research problem and purpose. If decision making is delayed until after data collection has begun then decisions are often made under the pressure of schedule, and doing "something" becomes the primary goal, rather than doing what is best for the research.

Of course, we are working with people in the social sciences and so can never aspire to the degree of control that the physical scientist can achieve. Inevitably, things happen which force some revisions of the research plan. But many of these events can be anticipated and planned for. For example, in the Language Study, the major problem was one of the experimental teachers falling seriously ill, but we had anticipated this type of problem and had trained extra teachers who had been kept informed of the progress of the study. One of these was ready to step in on little notice.

Another factor which we had also anticipated but which we could do little to control was pupil mobility. Throughout the course of the experiment, children in the experimental classes transferred out of the school as their families moved to other school districts. This mobility was beyond our power to control, and reflects the perils of doing research in a free country! The opposite mobility, of pupils transferring into the experimental schools, we could handle somewhat better. We assigned a teacher in each experimental school who tested all new arrivals with our criterion test of ability to understand spoken English and assigned the children to the experimental classes so as to keep them equivalent in terms of our definition of non–English-speaking.

RESULTS

Although irrelevant to the purpose of this chapter, let us briefly consider the results of the study, so that the reader has some closure on this topic before we move on. In the fourth grade all three methods achieved gains in pupil's ability to understand, speak, write, and read English, with little difference between them. The pattern was similar in the seventh grade, although here none of the methods achieved a significant gain in ability to read. The general pattern of the results however did suggest the greatest strengths of each method: For the experiential it was in the child's ability to understand; for the vocabulary it was in his ability to speak; and for the structure it was in his ability to write. This pattern suggested that each variation had some positive contribution to overall methodology and that no one was completely "best." Thus the conclusion was drawn that a composite method seeking to capitalize on the identified strengths of each variation, supplemented by instruction in reading which no method did well, should be developed for use in the schools.

With the study completed, the researchers could then turn to the problem of reporting these results and suggesting ways of implementing the findings. Note that we consider reporting and implementation basic aspects of the researchers' responsibility. It is not sufficient to do research: One must report it to the relevant possible audiences if it is to serve any function and make any professional contribution. In the same sense, suggesting possible implementation of findings and doing whatever is possible to expedite implementation is also a critical aspect of the researchers' responsibility.

In the Language Study a formal report of the results was prepared,[4] but even more important, two series of materials were prepared to help

[4]*The Puerto Rican Study, 1953–1957.* Board of Education, City of New York, 1958, 265 pp.

implement the finding that direct instruction in both vocabulary and structure in the context of regular content units did result in significant improvement in the children's language ability. One series coordinated the separate language teaching guides for the structure and vocabulary experimental sections.[5] The other series was based on the content units used in the experiment.[6] Both of these series were adopted by the New York City Board of Education, and as this is written continue to provide the basis for teaching English as a second language to non–English-speaking children in the New York City public schools.

[5]*Language Guide Series.* Board of Education, City of New York, 1956–1957, 4 vol.
[6]*Resource Unit Series.* Board of Education, City of New York, 1955–1957, 9 vol.

Chapter 2

A MODEL OF THE RESEARCH PROCESS

As the reader has seen in Chapter 1, the process of planning, implementing, and writing up a piece of research in the social sciences is multidimensional in that many of the stages, although different and beginning at different points, overlap in time so that several are being carried on at the same time. Nevertheless, each stage does have primary importance at some one point in the research process, and so in this chapter we shall discuss this process as a series of 17 sequential stages. These stages will be considered in detail in the chapters that follow; here each will be considered only briefly. The purpose of this chapter is to provide a model of the entire process, so that it can be seen how the specific chapters fit into this process. The reader planning his own project is cautioned that for any one specific research project, not only may the order vary, but so will the relative importance of each stage. In the course of this overview, the basic conceptual terms used in research will be defined and illustrated by showing how they operated in the Language Study just discussed. At the end we shall show how the several stages operate in a hypothetical project we shall develop ultimately entitled "The Effect of Daily Phonics Instruction in Small Groups upon the Reading Level of Fourth Graders at Least Two Grades Retarded in Reading."

The model is presented in Figure 2-1. As can be seen, the model has been developed at three levels: the stage itself, the dynamic forces underlying the stage, and the outcomes of the stage. The model is to be read from the bottom up. Along the bottom row are the *underlying dynamics* of each stage, defined as all the forces which operate during the stage. These forces include aspects of the researcher such as his motivations, and aspects of the situation such as cost in time and money, or the needs and demands of respondents or others cooperating in the research. All these provide the criteria which guide the researcher's functioning during the stage. While they are all dynamic forces, typically they are not the researcher's overt or direct concern during the stage, and so they are here

Figure 2-1

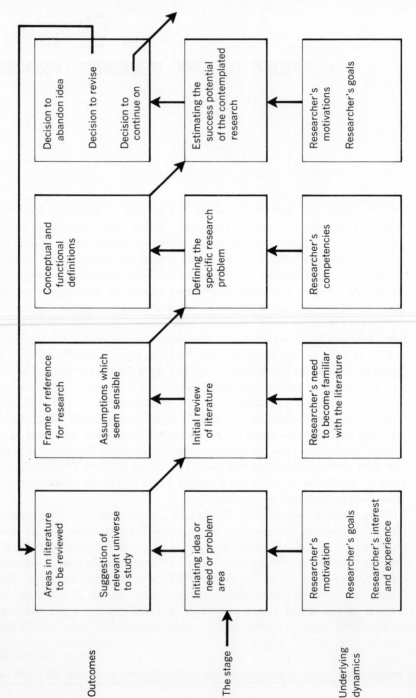

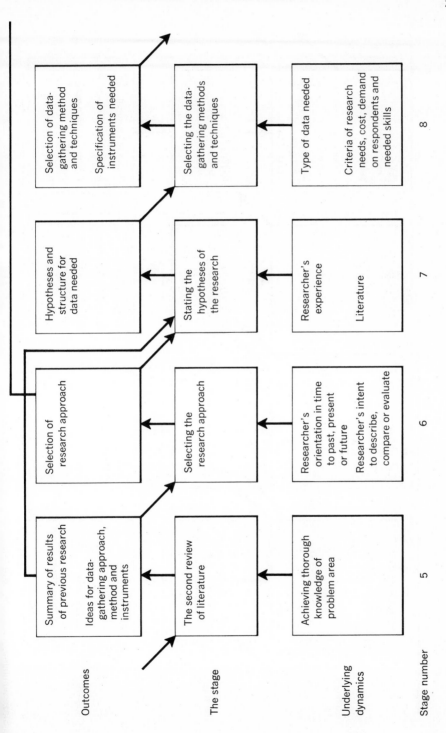

Outcomes	Summary of results of previous research Ideas for data-gathering approach, method and instruments	Selection of research approach	Hypotheses and structure for data needed	Selection of data-gathering method and techniques Specification of instruments needed
The stage	The second review of literature	Selecting the research approach	Stating the hypotheses of the research	Selecting the data-gathering methods and techniques
Underlying dynamics	Achieving thorough knowledge of problem area	Researcher's orientation in time to past, present or future Researcher's intent to describe, compare or evaluate	Researcher's experience Literature	Type of data needed Criteria of research needs, cost, demand on respondents and needed skills
Stage number	5	6	7	8

Figure 2-1 continued

28

Outcomes	Instruments to be used	Descriptive statistics to be used Inferential statistics to be used Level of significance Layout of tables	Data-gathering plan	Delineation of population Selection of method of sample selection Decision on sample size Identification of those to be invited to participate
The stage	Selecting and developing data-gathering instruments	Developing the data-analysis plan	Designing the data-gathering plan	Identifying the population and invited sample
Underlying dynamics	Needs of research problem Commitment to the adequacy of instruments	Demands on researcher's skills Needs of research problem Hypotheses	Needs of research Needs of respondents Criteria of cost, personnel, and time Research approach	Needs of research Acceptance of research Realities of research setting Practical needs of researcher
Stage number	9	10	11	12

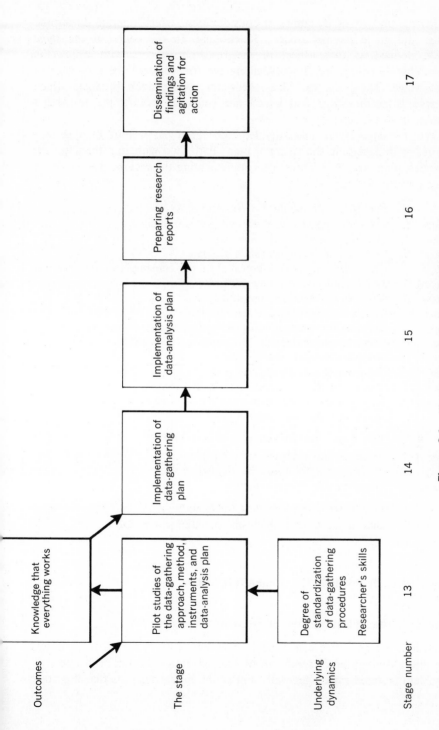

Figure 2-1 Illustration of the research process.

called the underlying dynamics or considerations which operate during the stage and guide the researcher's functioning. In the center is the *stage* itself, defined as that aspect of the research process with which the researcher is concerned. Finally, along the top row are the *outcomes* of each stage. These are the ideas, decisions, or research products which emerge from the stage and which are necessary before the researcher moves on to the next stage.

The 17 stages have been divided into three parts. Part One is concerned with designing the research plan, Part Two with implementing the research plan, and Part Three with implementing the results. The stages in each part are as follows:

Part One: Designing the Research Plan

Stage 1. The initiating idea or need and problem area
Stage 2. The initial review of the literature
Stage 3. Defining the specific research problem
Stage 4. Estimating the success potential of the contemplated research
Stage 5. The second review of the literature
Stage 6. Selecting the research approach
Stage 7. Stating the hypotheses of the research
Stage 8. Selecting the data-gathering method(s) and technique(s)
Stage 9. Selecting and developing data-gathering instruments
Stage 10. Designing the data-analysis plan
Stage 11. Designing the data-gathering plan
Stage 12. Identifying the population and invited sample
Stage 13. Pilot studies of the data-gathering approach, method and instruments, and the data-analysis plan

Part Two: Implementing the Research Plan

Stage 14. Implementing the data-gathering plan
Stage 15. Implementing the data-analysis plan
Stage 16. Preparing the research reports

Part Three: Implementing the Results

Stage 17. Dissemination of findings and agitation for action

PART ONE: DESIGNING THE RESEARCH PLAN

Stage 1: The Initiating Idea or Need and Problem Area

Research begins either with a need experienced by those active in a field or with a description of some sort of problem in a field. Often this need or problem is stated rather generally and so the model suggests that this stage need not define more than a problem area, or the general body of knowledge within which the research shall be done. For example, the problem area of the Language Study was "teaching English as a second language."

Most often our thinking in research begins with a consideration of the problem area. This is subsequently narrowed down through early stages of the research process until it becomes the highly specific research problem of Stage 3. Later stages of research, such as the collection of data, must be within the context of the specific research problem, but the initial stages require no more than the problem area. We do not need to, and actually should not, specify a highly specific research problem until we have done some reading within the area and our thinking has developed.

To plan a research project generally means translating a rather vague interest in a particular problem area or curiosity about some specific hunch or idea into a specific problem which can be researched. However, the model indicates that the process can start at either point, that is, from an *initiating idea or need*, or from a *problem area*. It always ends at the problem area, because it is from this that we move on to later stages. In the Language Study, for example, we began with the initiating need to develop a program for teaching English to non–English-speaking Puerto Rican children. This need was placed into the problem area of second language teaching and the literature in this area was reviewed. However, the study could as easily have been developed by a researcher interested in the problem area of instruction in a second language.

UNDERLYING DYNAMICS   The model suggests that three dynamics underlie this first stage: the researcher's motivation in doing research, his goals for this particular piece of research, and his interest and experience. Spelling these out as underlying dynamics is intended to highlight the importance of clearly understanding all three before venturing into a problem area, and certainly before venturing into the later stages.

Why do people do research? The primary purpose should be because of curiosity about the research result. We could almost paraphrase the response of the mountain climber who says he climbs a mountain "because it's there" and say a researcher studies a question "because it's a question and we don't know the answer." But this is only one of the possible motivations. Another is the desire to learn about, or from, the research process. Some even do research to learn a way of thinking or of approaching problems. There is the realistic reason, particularly for students, of the "partial fulfillment" of the requirements for a course or a degree. In recent years this has been a motivation for faculty too, as research has come to be considered partial fulfillment of the requirements for promotion. Finally, there are those who do research because they have been hired to do research. Generally, although these are professionals who carry out problems developed by others, if they are to be more than technicians they must be curious about the research result as well, and so we need to consider only the three motivations.

They are not mutually exclusive, and ideally can all be combined. It is perfectly possible to find a problem where the potential results intrigue us, which will partially fulfill whatever requirements we face, and the execution of which will teach us a great deal about the research process. In fact, since almost any well-planned research project will teach us more about the process than all of the courses we might take, or books we might read, this third motivation is the simplest to realize. When conflict arises, it is usually between curiosity and partial fulfillment, typically when a student is told that a project which has aroused his curiosity will not meet requirements.

Faced with this conflict, a student has little choice but to attempt to revise the idea or find a new one which will meet requirements. But this need not mean abandoning the curiosity motivation, for students can continue exploring an idea which intrigues them. Successful research demands tremendous personal involvement, and if the researcher has little or no interest in the project other than completing it and obtaining a grade or a degree, this will inevitably be reflected in the caliber of the project. Moreover, it will turn what should be an exciting intellectual experience into academic drudgery of the worst sort. It is a basic part of the research philosophy underlying this book that research is best done by people genuinely curious about the content area. Stated simply, the best research is done by people who care what the results are.

Allied to the curiosity aspect of motivation is the second dynamic of interest and experience. The researcher can select a problem area in which he already has interest, experience, and even expertise. In this case, of course, he is working in a familiar area and obviously this affects the handling of later stages. For example, the review of literature in Stage 2 is entirely different for the researcher who is working in an area of previous interest and for the researcher entering a new area. A second possibility is that the problem area can be of interest, although the researcher has no previous work in it or related to it. Then the two parallels exist for lack of interest: He can have no interest but experience, or neither interest nor experience.

Obviously, interest is preferable to lack of interest. But it does not follow that experience is preferable to inexperience. There have been instances when a researcher new to a problem area brought a fresh insight free of the "facts" and "beliefs" which experience brings. Thus, the inexperienced researcher may design his study to test some of these facts and beliefs and thus challenge, and even alter, previously fully accepted material.

The third dynamic in the model, the researcher's goals, refers to the question of whether the researcher's primary goal is to produce a defendable document within a finite period of time or to produce findings that contribute to knowledge in some way. The two goals are not necessarily mutually exclusive, but the student is usually primarily concerned with the first goal, and the professional researcher should be concerned with the second. However, the professional, too, is often like a student in his concern with the goal of a defendable document. That these statements can be made in the late 1960s reflects two facts. The first is that colleges and universities have not been willing to accept theses and dissertations if they fail to meet certain stereotyped standards of successful research, and so students have had to be concerned with the nature of the final document. The second fact is that fund-granting agencies have made parallel demands of professional researchers, typically demanding fully detailed plans for data collection and analysis before being willing to consider an application for funds. Both of these demands operate to steer research into the study of stereotyped and well-defined areas and away from the study of obscure and ill-defined areas. They also operate to pressure researchers toward techniques and approaches reasonably certain of providing relevant, even if unexciting, data within a finite period and away from innovative or creative approaches or techniques where there is a high risk of data not being relevant or not being analyzable within that finite period. Of course, over the years, the researcher who makes the spectacular breakthrough in a discipline typically has a long history of both spectacular and unspectacular failures. In the social disciplines, particularly education, we have so structured the demand that the primary goal of research be a complete, defendable document that we have had few spectacular failures, few unspectacular failures, but also no spectacular successes. Instead we have a long succession of unspectacular "successes" in the sense of projects which accomplish what they set out to do within a specific period of time, but which do not vividly extend the bounds of knowledge.

What has been painfully lacking in educational research has been the study which might be called the *productive failure*. This is a research study which does not achieve its original goal, but during which the researcher learns or develops something of significance which will enable others to move research forward. He may learn that a long cherished assumption does not stand up when challenged or tested. Or he may develop some new approach to measurement of a critical characteristic which did not fully work in his own study, but which others can pick up and refine further. He may only learn that some yet untried idea or approach does not work, and so have to look elsewhere for a new instrument or approach to measurement. In all of these the study may have failed in the sense of not producing the data needed to answer the research question which motivated it, but it was productive in the sense that we learned something from it. This is far better than the study which successfully produces its expected data and from which, even with those data, we learn nothing.

The classic story of what is meant by this concept of productive failure involves Thomas Edison's search for a filament for his incandescent bulb. The story goes that after the five thousandth substance had failed, a friend asked Edison how he could continue to work when he was learning nothing. Edison's response was that he *was* learning, that he now knew 5000 different substances which did not work. The key to his learning from failure, of course, was the use of different substances each time. He would not have learned much from 5000 tests of his first substance. Yet in education, we seem to do that more often than we try 5000 different ideas. For example, consider the question of teaching through television. In the early 1960s Wilbur Schramm reviewed 100 studies of this problem.[1] All of them were essentially the same in design, comparing the achievement of groups of college students taught by television to the achievements of those taught by traditional classroom lecture and discussion. Of the 100, 84 reported no significant difference in achievement! Despite this clear finding of no differences such studies are still being conducted and more are being planned. To this author, it would seem to be time to accept the conclusion of no difference, conclude that the success potential of another such study was low, if not nonexistent, and so move on to some new aspect of the problem area.

OUTCOMES   With all the underlying dynamics understood and either the initiating idea or problem area identified, the model suggests that there are two outcomes to Stage 1: First, the problem area should delineate the areas in the literature to which the researcher should go for his initial review of the literature in Stage 2; second, the problem area should begin to suggest the *relevant universe* for the proposed study. By universe I mean those entities to which the researcher wants his findings to apply. Thus, in the Language Study, once we were oriented to the problem area of teaching English as a second language to Puerto Rican children, this delineated a universe of non–English-speaking children whose first language was Spanish.

[1]Wilbur Schramm, "Learning from Institutional Television," *Review of Educational Research*, vol. 32, no. 2 (April 1962) pp. 156–165.

With these outcomes, we move on to the second stage—the initial review of the literature.

Stage 2: The Initial Review of the Literature

During the initial review of the literature we attempt to discover relevant material published in the problem area under study. Two kinds of literature are reviewed. The first kind will be called the *conceptual literature* and consists of articles or books by authorities giving their opinions, experiences, theories, or ideas of what is good, bad, desirable, and undesirable within the problem area. The conceptual literature is particularly useful in delineating needed research in the problem area as well as in developing the researcher's understanding and background. Second, we review the *research literature* which covers actual research studies done previously within the problem area. These studies may be similar to the one contemplated or they may be different, if they have in common that they were directed toward gathering information and insight in the same problem area.

UNDERLYING DYNAMIC   The model notes that the one underlying dynamic to Stage 2 is the researcher's need to become familiar with the problem area. This is intended to indicate that an overview is needed now rather than the thorough knowledge to be developed at Stage 5. How extensive a review will be needed here depends upon how familiar the researcher already is with the problem area. Obviously, the more familiar he already is, the more easily he can assume that he can move quickly through this stage.

OUTCOMES   The basic outcome of this initial review of literature is what shall be called a *frame of reference* for the research. By this, we mean to develop an understanding of the basic body of facts in the area, the major issues or controversies, as well as an awareness of the underlying theories which have attempted to explain behaviors and interactions in the problem area. If we successfully develop a frame of reference we are much better able to specify our own research problem in a meaningful context. Ideally, every research project fits somewhere into some larger frame of reference. Admittedly, research on any one specific problem provides a small bit of information, but these bits of information can best be brought together to form larger generalizations and conclusions provided they are all conducted within the same theoretical framework and directed toward the same end. Only through several small research enterprises do we advance knowledge at all, and this advance is possible only if each research enterprise has been developed with an understanding of where we already are in our knowledge and understandings within the problem area. Therefore, it is the responsibility of the researcher himself to sufficiently review and know the relevant literature so that he may place his own project within the scope of current understanding and in this way advance understanding through his research. In the Language Study, it was the review of literature which made us aware of the conflicting schools of thought as to the best way to teach English as a second language. Awareness of this conflict between major language theorists made us decide to place the study in the frame of reference of the relative effectiveness of emphases on different language elements like vocabulary and structure.

A second outcome from this review of literature is an awareness of the points in the problem area which have been sufficiently demonstrated to be true by previous research, or if not demonstrated by research have been so widely accepted by authorities in the field that we can assume that they are true and plan our research so that it departs from these assumptions. Obviously, no one researcher is expected to demonstrate anew those facts or relationships or findings which others have already done. If we are to progress at all, we must in new research be able to assume that the truth of certain points has been amply demonstrated. These points form part of our assumptions (the other parts will be discussed later in this chapter), and should begin to be identified in this initial review of the literature.

In the Language Study we learned from the literature that we could assume that the problem of second-language teaching was not critical in the early elementary grades. Moreover, we learned we could assume that for research purposes grades 4 and 5 could be considered comparable. There was sufficient material in the nonresearch literature for us to assume materials for each language emphasis could be developed within realistic time limits. Perhaps most critical, we came upon enough anecdotal reports of successful teaching for us to assume that children could be taught English as a second language. This assumption meant that any failure of our experimental methods to produce progress could be attributed to the method and not to the impossibility of teaching English as a second language.

Stage 3: Defining the Specific Research Problem

Once we have completed the initial review of the literature we are ready to go to the third stage of research, defining the specific research problem.

In the course of reading the literature, we should acquire enough information to enable us to decide on the specifics of what we shall do. It often helps in delineating the specific research problem to ask what is the specific question that we hope the research will answer. The specific research problem should be directed to answering this question, and may in fact be a direct or paraphrased statement of the question. The reason this is designated a separate stage is to make clear the need for specificity. For example, in the Language Study we began with what might seem like a specific research problem: What is the best method of teaching English as a second language to newly arrived, non–English-speaking Puerto Rican children?

Yet, as we saw in Chapter 1, this seemingly specific statement had considerable ambiguity in it. We considered how we had to ask what we meant by "English"—reading, writing, speaking, or understanding when spoken to? What did we mean by "newly arrived"? Who was a "non–English-speaking Puerto Rican"? The necessity to answer all of these questions means that the first step in delineating the specific research is to set down the *definitions* of the terms used in the statement of the problem area. In the process of making decisions as to who a Puerto Rican is or what we mean by newly arrived, we inevitably turn the problem area into the specific research problem.

In research we use words with a far greater precision than usual. This is particularly true of the jargon which we use in the everyday practice of our profession. Every word that has more than one possible meaning must be defined as it will be used in the research. Often we define the words at two levels, a *conceptual definition* and a *functional definition*. The conceptual definition provides the academic concept while the functional definition states how the concept will be applied in a specific study. Thus several studies may use the same conceptual definitions, but they are comparable only if they use the same functional definition.

For example, many studies in reading use the same conceptual definition of a retarded reader, using the *Dictionary of Education* definition, "A child reading below his capacity to read."[2] But if one study functionally defined a retarded reader as "three years below grade level or more," another as "below grade level by any amount," and a third as "at least two years below grade level," it would be difficult to synthesize the results of the three studies.

Good sources for conceptual definitions are standard reference works like the *Dictionary of Education*, the *Encyclopedia of Education*, or the *Comprehensive Dictionary of Psychological and Psychoanalytical Terms*.[3] If the reference works do not help, a second good source is to

[2]Carter V. Good, ed., *Dictionary of Education* (New York: McGraw-Hill, Inc., 1959), p. 442.
[3]These and similar references are discussed in detail in Chapter 4.

turn to the conceptual literature and study the latest published work of the leading authorities in the field. In contrast, the best source for a functional definition is previous research, particularly if a proposed study is to fit into the framework of specific previous studies. Thus, in the Language Study we found that most relevant previous studies involving remedial techniques used daily instructional periods of 30 minutes. Our desire to have the conditions of our evaluation of the effectiveness of the language emphases parallel these other studies helped us decide to define the period of instruction as 30 minutes every day. Other functional definitions are suggested by procedures that others found useful or problems that arose in previous research. Included among the scanty research in the area of second-language teaching with Puerto Ricans was a study[4] which suggested that Puerto Rican children had difficulty learning English when segregated in classes of all non–English-speaking children, but did better in heterogeneous classes. This encouraged us to define our "classes" as heterogeneous classes, containing both language learners and native speakers of English.

In the absence of any structure in the reference works or in the literature the researcher may have to state a purely personal functional definition. Thus, in the Language Study, there was no agreement on what a non–English-speaking child was or knew. Therefore, we had to functionally define it in terms of a score on a test we had specifically developed for the research.

UNDERLYING DYNAMIC   The model notes one critical dynamic underlying this third stage: the researcher's competence, including his research skills, knowledge, and experience. This dynamic is included here in the model to highlight the fact that different research problems demand different competencies. Therefore, there are problems which are appropriate for the beginner or for the student without previous research experience or technical skills, and similarly there are problems which are inappropriate.

Perhaps the most important help the experienced research consultant can provide is to help the inexperienced person evaluate the skills which will be required for any specific problem. Students, particularly, should discuss this point specifically and directly with their faculty adviser. The discussion, to be useful, should involve both analysis of the problem to identify the skills needed, and a candid self-appraisal by, and of, the student in terms of how many and which of the needed skills he has. Only

[4]Irving Lorge and Frank Mayans, "Vestibule vs. Regular Classes for Puerto Rican Migrant Pupils," *Teachers College Record*, vol. 55, no. 5 (February 1954), pp. 231–237.

some of the skills can be provided through consultation or faculty assistance.

Essentially skills can be categorized into five areas: research design, instrument development, data collection, data analysis, and research writing. Consultation can help the inexperienced person design research. Instrument development, in contrast, is a complex technical skill, and so the inexperienced person is well advised to select a problem area in which he will be able to use standardized or previously developed instruments. If none are available, then the problem should be phrased in such a way as to require only the simplest kinds of instruments. The third skill, data collection, involves minimal demands upon the researcher, and is one in which the researcher can directly supplement his own skills with those of more highly skilled persons. Therefore, it is not critical to consider in selecting a problem area.

Data analysis, in contrast, is highly demanding and an area in which help is often sought by the inexperienced person. It is not fully recognized, however, that a vicious circle often begins with help at this stage: Utilization of help in data analysis often demands a level of sophistication that would make the help unnecessary! Thus, many students with limited understanding of statistical concepts seek faculty or outside help in the analysis of their data. However, the very lacks which make them seek the help often make them unable to fully understand or appreciate it, and so they parrot a technique or a procedure. The author well remembers a student who asked a colleague how to analyze a set of data and was told to "test for the significance of the difference between two percents." She was grateful for the advice and went on her way. Then in her outline for the research, she wrote that her statistical analysis would involve "testing for significance of the difference of 2 percent." Thus it is well to recognize that the data-analysis demands of a problem area, like the instrument-development demands, should be planned in terms of the skills and knowledges appropriate for the researcher, and should not be based on supplementing these with the skills of others.

The final area, research writing, is also one in which there is no substitute for experience, but in which consultation can be useful. If an experienced person is available and willing to react to the written report as sections of it are completed, and particularly *if there is sufficient time* for this reaction to be utilized, then the inexperienced person can produce a sound research report. But the key phrase in the sentence is the italicized one: if there is sufficient time. Students typically are preparing reports against the pressure of an impending deadline and so either resent suggestions that a report be rewritten, or if they do not resent the suggestion, do not have the time to consider the suggestions, absorb them, decide which they agree with, and then rewrite the material. But it is only in this way that an inexperienced researcher can meaningfully use more experienced persons for help in writing. Otherwise the inexperienced person, who is usually a student receiving suggestions from faculty, rewrites to order. Thus he makes the changes suggested without discrimination as to his agreement or disagreement, in the hope that the document will be acceptable. This is not what is meant here when it is said that an experienced research writer can help the inexperienced.

OUTCOMES   Conceptual and functional definitions are developed and listed as an outcome of Stage 3. For example, for the Language Study we would have included within the working set of definitions, the conceptual and functional definitions of method:

1. *conceptual:* a systematic plan followed in presenting material for instruction.[5]
2. *functional:* the relative emphasis on vocabulary, structure, or language pattern, and experience in the teaching of English as a second language.

The necessity to define functionally terms like "children" also forces us to take a second look at our delineation of the universe of the research, that is the group to which we wish our conclusions to apply. If we have not previously delineated the universe we *must* do so at this stage. As in developing our other specifications, we utilize the literature, the research area, and the research setting to clarify the nature of the universe.

To illustrate the interaction of these factors, let us consider for a moment our problem area, "identifying the best method of teaching English as a second language." As we review the literature we find general agreement among experts that formal second-language instruction is not necessary in the lower elementary grades, but no consensus as to whether it should begin in grade 2, or 3, or 4. A general universe of children in the middle elementary grades is then suggested by the literature. Our desire to work with the modalities of reading and writing would generally eliminate grade 2, as children could not be sufficiently advanced in reading or writing by then. We ultimately decided to use grade 4 rather than grade 3, so that we would be assured of enough advanced subjects for the research. Thus, through this interaction of the literature, the researcher's desires, and the reality of research needs we delineate a universe of fourth graders who meet our definitions of newly arrived non–English-speaking Puerto Ricans.

Through the definitions and the interaction of literature and researcher

[5]*Webster's Seventh New Collegiate Dictionary* (Springfield, Mass.: G. & C. Merriam Company, 1961), p. 533.

interest, the problem area is thus developed into the highly structured statement that is the specific research problem. Assuming we have a specific problem which is feasible in terms of the researcher's skills, we are ready to move to Stage 4.

Stage 4: Estimating the Success Potential of the Contemplated Research

With the initial review of the literature completed, the researcher should now be aware of both the research studies completed in the problem area, and the nature of the conceptual writings. From the conceptual literature he should have learned the critical questions that need study and testing through research, and can thus estimate the need for the study he is contemplating. From the research literature reviewed he has an estimate of the profoundness of the contributions of previous research as well as some idea of how much he can utilize already existing instruments. Thus he has a basis for estimating the technical advances he must make to carry out the specified project. These two estimates—the need for his project and the technical advances needed to do it—provide the basis for the difficult judgment which comprises Stage 4, estimating the success potential of the contemplated research.

UNDERLYING DYNAMICS   The ideal combination of a clearly demonstrated need and fully available instruments and techniques is rare, for most of these problems have been studied. Most often the researcher is faced either with a clear need but little available in the way of instrumentation, or a weak need but good instrumentation. Here is a good example of how the various stages affect each other, for Stages 4 and 1 share two underlying dynamics—motivation and goal. The student who in Stage 1 has identified a primary motivation of partially fulfilling the requirements for a degree and a primary goal of a completed defendable document will prefer the problem with available instrumentation even if the need for the study is not overwhelming. This preference is understandable, and most faculty advisers will agree with the perception. But while acceptable for a student, this is an indefensible choice for the professional researcher or for the faculty member doing his own research for the motivation of intellectual curiosity and the goal of meaningful findings. These researchers should move into the areas of high need where the available instrumentation and thinking are weak.

The pity is that colleges and universities have not encouraged doctoral students, too, to study small bits of new areas by indicating a willingness to give degrees for productive failure. For it is critical to recognize that when we speak of "success potential" at this stage of the research process we mean that either there is reason to believe that the study will yield positive results or that it will be a productive failure, in the sense that we shall have learned something which did not work.

OUTCOMES The model (Figure 2-1) indicates three outcomes, or paths open to the researcher at this point: (1) he can decide that the success potential is good and proceed on without alteration in his specific research problem; (2) he can decide that some revision is necessary; or (3) he can decide to abandon the idea and area because the success potential is so poor that even revision will not suffice.

The first path takes him on through the process, which we will be discussing below. The third path takes him out of the process entirely, for this problem or problem area, and so needs little additional comment. The little that does need saying is the author's personal belief that researchers do not follow this path often enough. Just as theatregoers and reviewers often wonder, after seeing a particularly disastrous play, how the play ever got far enough along to be produced and presented, so do serious readers of research literature often wonder how a project ever got past the planning stage and was approved and carried out. If there is little or no prospect of a meaningful professional contribution the idea should be abandoned, or revised.

The path of revision, the model notes, takes one back to Stage 1 and may involve a second trip through the literature. It involves a return to Stage 1 since a substantially revised problem should be reconsidered in the light of the researcher's interests, goals, and motivations, just as the original problem area was. Similarly, if the revision involves some shift in the problem area, a second run-through of the literature may be required, since some new literature might be involved. It is particularly important to reconsider interests, goals, and motivations if the revision has come about because of the interaction of researcher and consultant. For example, revision often comes as a student presents an idea or problem area to a faculty adviser who responds in terms of his own interests and goals for the project. This is a traditional process, and if the goal is a defendable document, the student may welcome the guidance in the belief it will move the project a long way toward the goal. But it may represent a shift which moves it away from the student's interests, or in a direction where the student is unwilling to go.

With revision, these first four stages may develop into a cyclic process of idea, initial review, and low success potential, followed by revision and re-review of literature and improved potential but still further revision. This is neither unusual nor unproductive. This stage is essentially a trial-and-error part of the process, particularly if the research is directed toward a new and relatively unexplored aspect of the discipline. Do not begrudge the time required to develop an idea with good potential for a meaningful contribution. The 13 stages beyond this point are tremendously demanding of time and energy, and any effort we can make to make this personal investment worthwhile is important. The author recognizes the anxiousness of many doctoral students who see time passing them by, and periods of candidacy running out, and who are told by faculty advisers that their idea needs further work. But this *is* justifiable advice, for even by the practical criteria of time and cost, a month spent on Stages 1, 2, 3, and 4 can save several months in the later stages of the process, to say nothing of making the difference between a useful and useless project. So move on to Stage 5 only when all persons involved in the research are satisfied that the potential for success is good and the problem is consistent with the researcher's goals, interests, skills, and motivations.

Stage 5: The Second Review of the Literature

With the research problem specified it is advisable to return to the literature for a second and highly focused review of previous research. For this second review the researcher applies a much more stringent definition of relevance. He now reads only those studies which are similar to his in one of the major dimensions of research—the problem, the universe, or the research variables. He would review a study which parallels his in one dimension even if it differed in another, because he is seeking ideas for design and data collection as well as some understanding of previous, directly relevant, results. For example, at this stage of the Language Study we reviewed previous studies comparing methods of second-language instruction (our problem) no matter what the language, or how or to whom it was taught. We also reviewed previous studies involving Puerto Rican children (our universe) and studies involving any of the variations of emphasis with which we had decided to experiment. Of course, at this stage, as he searches for previous research, the researcher seeks relevance but not identity, because if he found a previous study similar in all three dimensions (problem, universe, and variable), he has found his study. In this case he must decide if the prior study is sufficiently definitive to rule out further work, or if replication would make a meaningful professional contribution.

UNDERLYING DYNAMIC   The model notes that the underlying dynamic in Stage 5 is achieving thorough knowledge of the problem area. To be certain that this has been achieved, even the researcher working in an old familiar area should spend some time in the library. He will want to read the most current literature to be certain that recent developments have not occurred which make him less knowledgable than he believes. In both the written research report and any oral defenses of the project, the researcher can legitimately expect to be asked to demonstrate the thoroughness of his knowledge in the problem area, and so this dynamic must be recognized fully.

OUTCOMES   The model indicates that the major outcomes for this second review of the literature are a summary of the results of the previous research, and ideas for the data-gathering approach, method, and instruments. The summary of results will be used as the data context for the new study, almost as foundation in fact upon which the new study will be developed. Equally important is the possibility that the review of relevant previous research will yield clues to the techniques of research. The researcher would hope to gain help in deciding how to do his own project by seeing how others have studied in the area, and the success they have achieved with different research approaches, methods, and techniques. One specific piece of information sought is the instruments which have been used in previous studies, and the data available about the characteristics of these instruments, such as reliability and validity.

This second review of the literature may only make dramatically clear to the researcher that if he is to move on he will have to develop much of what he needs, as happened in the Language Study. What we did learn from this second review was that the traditional design of methods studies was a multiple-group design in which comparable groups were established and taught by the different methods. In the area of instrumentation, we did find that several standardized tests of reading ability were in existence, with varying amounts of data available on the characteristics of these instruments.

This is not much information to gain from Stage 5, and is about the low extreme which a researcher would obtain. In fact, instead of a review *of* the research literature we conducted more of a search *for* research literature. Because we found so little, we did have a guide to the research approach we would use: We were forced to experiment. However, we had no reassurance from the literature that our experiment would work. We had no clues to method, and in three of the four language modalities (writing, speaking, and understanding spoken English) we had no clues to previously developed instruments.

Typically, this second review of the literature provides the researcher with more help than in the Language Study. But a researcher must be prepared to function even when little help is available, and so no matter what Stage 5 produces we move on to Stage 6.

Stage 6: Selecting the Research Approach

With the research problem specified and the second review of literature completed, we turn to the selection of the *research approach* through which we shall actually gather our data.[6]

UNDERLYING DYNAMICS   In considering the research approach, we must consider two separate and independent underlying dynamics or dimensions, along which we can structure our research thinking. The first dimension is a kind of time line reflecting whether we believe the answer to the research question is in the past, present, or future. The second dimension is an intent dimension reflecting what we intend to do with the completed research.

In the time dimension, if we believe the answer is in the past, we resort to what is called the *historical approach*, a research approach in which the effort is made to cast light on current conditions and problems through a deeper and fuller understanding of what already has been done. If we believe the answer exists somewhere at present, we use the *survey approach*. In this approach we seek to cast light on current problems by a further description and understanding of current conditions. In other words, we seek more fully to understand the present through a data-gathering process which enables us to describe it more fully and adequately than now possible.

If, on the other hand, our interest is in predicting what will happen in the future, that is, if we undertake something new and different, or make some changes in the present condition, we have the *experimental approach*, which is experimental in that it seeks to establish on a trial (or experimental) basis a new situation. Then, through a study of this new situation under controlled conditions, the researcher is able to make a more generalized prediction of what would happen if the condition were widely instituted.

The second dimension along which we might structure or classify research approaches is the intent dimension, which reflects what we want to be able to do with the completed research. There are also three parts to

---

[6]Data is used here to mean anything systematically collected in the process of implementing the research project. The data can be numbers gathered through a test or some other paper-and-pencil device. They may be words obtained through a questionnaire or through interview or through a variety of projective or semiprojective techniques; they may be pictures drawn by children in response to a stimulus; in short, anything systematically collected and systematically analyzed.

the intent dimension. The first part will be called *description*. This is a research approach which is intended essentially to describe a limited set of conditions in terms of measures applied to the constituent elements of these conditions, and which is expected to make no judgments, statements of quality, or evaluations; this first part is only to describe.

The second point on the intent dimension is *comparison*. Here interest is in obtaining information about more than one condition or group of subjects, that is, in obtaining more than one set of data, and comparing the multiple sets of data. The intent in comparative research is to be able to make judgments of difference, or no difference, or of larger or smaller or, in other words, to make a comparative judgment.

The third point on the intent dimension is *evaluation*. Evaluative research, while often done in conjunction with comparative research, is unique in that it applies some criterion or standard to make possible an evaluative judgment, like good or bad, successful or unsuccessful. The interaction of these two dimensions is illustrated in Table 2-1. The time dimension extends across the different columns; in other words, interest in the past is indicated in column 1, in the present in column 2, in the future in column 3. The three rows refer to the intent dimension: descriptive research in row 1, comparative research in row 2, and evaluative research in row 3. Once the researcher or student has made the two decisions of

Table 2-1 Interaction of Time and Intent Dimensions To Consider in Selecting the Research Approach

Dimension 2: *Intent of Research*	*Dimension 1:* *Time in Which Interest Lies*		
	Past: Historical	Present: Survey	Future: Experimental
Description	Simple Historical	Simple survey Case study	Single-group experiment
Comparison	Parallel Historical	Multiple-group survey Correlational survey	Multiple-group experiment
Evaluation	Historical and criterion measure	Single-group or multiple-group survey *and* criterion measure	Single-group experiment with criterion measure

(1) where in time his interest is focused, and (2) what he wants to be able to do with the research, he can easily determine what demands this interaction makes for a research approach. For example, in the Language Study we wished to generalize about what might happen if we instituted one of the new methods. In the time dimension of Table 2-1 this put us in the column concerned with the future which suggested, therefore, an experimental approach. Moreover, we were interested in learning how each method compared to two other methods. In the intent dimension, this put us in the row for comparative research. In Table 2-1, the cell corresponding to the interaction between "future" and "comparison" suggests a multiple-group experiment. This research approach, a multiple-group comparative experiment, is consistent with our desire to generalize about the implications of putting one of three methods into practice in the future.

On the other hand, assume we had been interested in showing that the vocabulary method would guarantee a certain percentage of newly arrived non-English-speaking Puerto Rican pupils reading at grade level within a year of their arrival. In time we would have still been concerned with the future, but our intent now would be evaluative and this suggests a single-group experiment with a criterion measure or standard. For example, if experts agree that the needs of schools are met if 50 percent of students achieve grade level in reading within a year, this standard of 50 percent could function as the criterion measure in the evaluative experimental approach. The vocabulary method would be considered successful if at least 50 percent of the students taught by the method read at grade level within a year; it would be considered unsuccessful if fewer than 50 percent did.

OUTCOME   The outcome of Stage 6 is the selection of the research approach. In the Language Study, as we noted above, our interest in the future and our intent to compare methods suggested that the research approach for the study should be a multiple-group experiment.

Therefore we decided to establish on a small scale, that is, on an experimental basis, the emphases in which we were interested, study the results of the experiment, and use these results to predict what would happen if we applied the "best" experimental methods not just to our sample of children, but also to the population about which we wished to generalize: all newly arrived non–English-speaking Puerto Rican children.

Stage 7: Stating the Hypotheses of the Research

With the problem specified, the literature reviewed, and the research approach selected, the researcher is ready to state his *hypotheses*. This stage of the research process devoted to the hypotheses is meant to provide the researcher with an opportunity, in advance of the actual data collection, to predict the results of the study. These predictions of results are called the "hypotheses of the study." Hypotheses serve several functions. First, the necessity to predict specific results forces a level of thinking which helps structure the next stage, involving selection of the data-gathering method, technique, and instruments. Second, they ultimately help structure the statistical analysis. Third, the hypotheses often provide the skeletal structure of the written report of the data analysis and results. Finally, they provide the reader of the report with an understanding of the researcher's expectations before he began his study.

The three research approaches differ once again in the importance of research hypotheses. Historical research and purely descriptive survey research are often hypothesis-free. In these instances, the researcher would be seeking information which does not exist and may have neither a reason nor a basis for predicting what he will find.

However, historical and descriptive survey research can have hypotheses, and comparative survey and experimental research generally do. An example of historical research which did have an hypothesis is a recent student project concerned with determining the educational level of the men who attended the Constitutional Convention. The student conducting this project was convinced that these men represented the educated people of the time, and so he hypothesized that "A majority of the men attending the Constitutional Convention were well-educated in terms of the educational standards of the period." Of course, in the definitions section of his outline, this student had previously defined what he meant by "well-educated" and "educational standards."

In comparative survey research and in experimental research, the researcher should state what he expects the comparison to show, or what he expects the experimental results to be. He may expect differences. In the Language Study, for example, had we asked Professor Fries, who developed the structure method, what he expected to happen, he undoubtedly would have said that he expected children taught by the structure method to show greater improvement than children taught by the other methods. Part of this expectation stated as an hypothesis would be: "Non-English-speaking children taught by the structure method will show significantly greater improvement in understanding spoken English than non–English-speaking children taught by the vocabulary method."

In other instances, the researcher may expect to find no differences. In the Language Study we had no reason to expect differences in attitudes toward school between students taught by three different methods. Since this was so, our hypotheses on attitudes toward school would have indicated this expectation of no difference. When stated in this form, they are called *null hypotheses*. These hypotheses stated as a series of null hypotheses would read:

1. There will be no differences in attitudes toward school between children taught by the vocabulary method and the structure method.
2. There will be no differences in attitudes toward school between children taught by the vocabulary method and the experiential method.
3. There will be no differences in attitudes toward school between children taught by the structure method and the experimental method.

Note that the hypothesis about the comparison between the vocabulary and structure groups is stated separately from the hypothesis about the comparison between vocabulary and experiential groups even though they are verbally redundant. We always state each specific aspect of the expected results in a separate hypothesis, because we want to be able to demonstrate that the data we obtain either do or do not support each hypothesis. This type of either-or judgment is possible only if each aspect of the results is stated as a separate hypothesis. For example, let us suppose that in the Language Study we discovered that vocabulary students did not differ in attitude toward school from structure students but did differ from experiential students. Since we have separate hypotheses for each comparison, we can then conclude that the data support hypothesis 1, but do not support, and in fact contradict, hypothesis 2.

But assume we had decided to eliminate the verbal redundancy, and state one hypothesis: "There will be no differences between vocabulary, structure and experiential students in attitude toward school." With the data we obtained we would have to conclude that we have partial support for the hypothesis but also partial contradiction. This unnecessary confusion about partial support is never wanted, and so each aspect of the results should be specified as a separate hypothesis.

This suggests that complex research will have a multiplicity of hypotheses, and this is true. A simple rule of thumb is that there will be at least one hypothesis for every subproblem, and/or for every data-collection device that is used. There is no upper limit on the number of hypotheses, other than the practical fact that each hypothesis must be tested by the research and the results reported so that, as the hypotheses increase, so does the scope of the research and the research report. The author's experience in teaching research students has been that, consistently, students err on the side of too few hypotheses, principally because they attempt to combine several comparisons in one hypothesis. Remember that several brief, specific hypotheses are to be preferred to one lengthy, complex one, and will serve the purposes of the research far better.

Since hypotheses are predictions, they are stated in advance of the data collection and in the future tense. But they are only predictions and, as such, may or may not be supported by the data, without this in any way reflecting on the quality of the research. Because the hypotheses *are* supported does not make a study a good piece of research. Similarly, if the hypotheses are *not* supported, this does not negate the value of the research. In fact, some of our most important theoretical thinking has resulted from research that did not support its hypotheses. The lack of support in the research data forced a rethinking to understand where and why the rationale for the hypotheses was faulty. A common fear of students is that for a project to be successful, the data must support the hypotheses. This can be stated categorically to be untrue. The hypotheses serve a variety of functions in helping concretize the researcher's thinking, and in structuring the data analysis and research report—but the degree to which they are or are not supported by the data does not provide the basis for evaluating the research project.

UNDERLYING DYNAMICS   The model indicates two dynamics which structure hypotheses: the researcher's previous experience and the literature. The term "prediction" includes a wide variety of concepts ranging from wild guesses based on nothing to reasoned estimates of the future based on a knowledgeable acquaintance with the past and extensive experience with current conditions. Hypotheses belong at the reasoned end of this continuum. They should never be wild guesses, and if there is no basis in the literature or in the researcher's experience on which to estimate the outcome of a study, it is preferable to state no hypotheses. Moreover, the researcher should be able to state the rationale for each hypothesis—using the overview of the conceptual literature obtained in Stage 2, the summary of research results obtained in Stage 4, and his own professional experience—to support his prediction of each specific result.

If the hypothesis came out of thin air or the researcher's intuition, the only reaction to support, or for that matter to contradiction, is to wonder why the researcher expected that result. This is no contribution at all. In contrast, when each hypothesis has such a foundation in the previous theoretical writing and research results of a discipline, then either support or rejection of it becomes a meaningful contribution. If it is supported, this indicates that the previous thinking was sound and led to a reasonable prediction, and this ability to predict future results is one of the basic characteristics of sound theory. If the results do not support the reasoned hypothesis, then they suggest a need for re-examination of the theory or previous research.

OUTCOME   The important outcome of stating the hypothesis at this point is a concretization in the thinking about the data to be collected and analyzed; this concretization helps guide the choice of data-gathering method and technique. The researcher now sets out to select data-gathering methods and techniques that will enable him to test each hypothesis directly. Specifically, we scan each hypothesis we stated and ask ourselves what data we need to come to a definite conclusion about each hypothesis. For example, in the Language Study, to answer the original research problem on language learning, all we needed were the data on achievement in the language modalities. However, had we expanded the problem and phrased hypotheses about attitude toward school, we would need data to test these hypotheses as well.

Stage 8: Selecting the Data-Gathering Method(s) and Technique(s)

With the research approach specified by the interaction of the time and intent dimension, the researcher turns next to the selection of his data-gathering method and technique.

DATA-GATHERING METHODS   There are three methods available in the social sciences for data gathering: *observation,* in which the researcher gathers data by watching the respondent function in the research situation; *measurement,* in which the researcher applies some device to the respondent; and *questioning,* in which the researcher poses a verbal question or series of questions for the respondent. All three methods are available to the researcher in each of the research approaches, but in different ways and to different degrees. For example, in the historical approach the researcher can only "observe" retroactively by looking at historical artifacts. In contrast, the researcher using the survey approach can watch a natural situation as it unfolds, but is troubled by the knowledge that the fact of his observing may affect the situation. The experimenter too can observe directly, but he is watching only a prototype of some future reality.

In the use of measurement, the survey and experimental approaches both permit direct measurement of all relevant aspects of the needed data. The historical approach permits direct measurement only of the physical aspects of the data. There is no way in which the historical researcher can directly measure aspects like knowledge, attitude, or interest, even if relevant to his problem. He may be able to infer them from other data, but he cannot directly measure these affective or cognitive aspects of his data. Finally, in the use of questioning, again the historical approach is different in that *all* questioning must be retroactive and rely on memory. In contrast, the survey and experimental approach may involve questions about past actions and activities, but not necessarily.

DATA-GATHERING TECHNIQUES   Within each of the three methods there are various techniques available for the actual collection of the data. Table 2-2 lists the major techniques within each method. These are discussed in detail in the chapter on data-gathering techniques.

UNDERLYING DYNAMICS   The model in Figure 2-1 notes that several dynamics operate at this point. Basically, the data-collection technique is selected by specifying the type of data needed to answer the problem posed by the research, considering the available methods which might provide these data, and choosing the one most appropriate in terms of criteria, like the needs of the research, the cost in time and money of the different methods, the demands each method makes upon the subjects of the research, and the skills and knowledges needed to analyze the data.

At this point, the previously determined motivations of the researcher and the goals of the research will help in deciding which of these various criteria will be given greatest weight. A student most concerned with what he will learn from doing the research may deliberately select a technique with which he is unfamiliar, even though it will take him longer to do the research. A student pressed for time may select a familiar method and

Table 2–2 Summary of Data-Gathering Techniques Available within Each Method

Observation	Measurement	Questioning
Direct—known	Physical	Structured questionnaire
Direct—not known	Objective testing	Unstructured questionnaire
Participant—known	Performance and work-sample testing	Check list
Participant—not known	Projective techniques	Structured interview
Indirect—known	Inventory techniques	Unstructured interview
Indirect—not known	Sociometric techniques	Critical incident
	Rating scales	
	Semantic differential scale	
	Rank-order scales	
	Q-technique	
	Paired-comparison scale	

sacrifice the possibility of new learning. A professional researcher, of course, should make the choice in terms of the research question, the resources and facilities he has available, and the demands of the different techniques.

For example, within the questioning method, the interview technique involves face-to-face interaction in which the questions are posed verbally between researcher and respondent. The questionnaire technique, in contrast, involves a paper-and-pencil instrument completed by the respondent. Since this is so, there often is no direct contact between researcher and respondent. The questionnaire may involve little writing or it may involve considerable writing. In contrast, the check list as a technique is like the questionnaire in terms of the researcher-respondent interaction and the paper-and-pencil aspect, but it never involves more marking than a simple check to indicate the response chosen. At the opposite extreme in terms of demand on the respondent is the critical incident technique, which requires that the subjects of the research write extensive free-response descriptions of situations. Obviously, it can only be used with literate subjects. But these free-response descriptions are more difficult to analyze and take much longer to analyze than data from more objective methods.

Selecting the data-collection methods for the Language Study illustrates the process well. The basic method had to be the measurement method, and the obvious technique we needed was objective testing to estimate the change in children's ability to read and write. But how would we estimate children's ability to speak, or to understand spoken English? Here we decided on a performance test, in which children were placed in a standardized situation involving an examiner who conducted a conversation with the child along predetermined lines. As we shall see in the chapters on method and technique, the objective tests could be administered easily to groups of children and so could be given to all participants. The performance test had to be given individually and so could be given only to some children.

Thinking ahead to the final report, we recognized that we would also want an estimate of the teacher's perception of pupil progress and some insight into the children's opinions of, and reactions to, the program. In terms of method, the information on the teacher's perception of the children or on the children's perception of the program called for different methods and techniques. One of the scaling techniques within the measurement method, such as a rating scale, would be appropriate for the data from teachers, whereas the interview or simple questionnaire within the questioning method would be more appropriate for the data from children. Finally, we also decided we needed to know the nature of the rest of the school day in the experimental classes. This information could be obtained either through the questioning method by asking the teachers or through the observation method by sending observers into the classrooms for sufficiently long periods to obtain a picture of what happens. The questioning method would have been far less expensive, but we were uneasy about the accuracy of these data. Thus, we decided on direct observation on a sampling basis.

Note that any one project may use all three methods and several techniques. Even one specific type of data may require more than one method.

OUTCOME   As the model notes, the outcome of Stage 8 is the selection of the data-gathering methods and techniques and the specification of the instruments needed for the study. In this instance, we know that we need objective tests in reading and writing, performance tests in speaking and understanding, a rating scale for teachers to rate each child's progress, an interview guide (assuming we chose this technique for questioning in preference to the questionnaire) to obtain the data on the children's perceptions of the program, and an observation guide for our classroom observers to obtain the data on the remainder of the school program.

The next stage, therefore, is instrument selection and development.

Stage 9: Selecting and Developing
Data-Gathering Instruments

Once the method is selected, the choice of selecting an available instrument or developing a new one is often made on the basis of the review of the literature. This review should have provided awareness of available instruments and the basis for deciding, first, if any of these meet the general criteria for acceptable research instruments and, of those which do, if any will serve the specific purposes of our research. If the answer to either question is no, we will need to develop new instruments.

The general criteria referred to are *reliability*, or the accuracy, stability, and repeatability of the data produced by the instrument, and *validity*, or the extent to which the instrument does what it purports to do. These are discussed at length in Chapter 12. What should be noted here is that the researcher using an instrument developed by someone else must determine from the data available in previous studies that the instrument in general is both reliable as an instrument, and valid for the uses to which he intends to put it. Then he must be able to defend his sample as coming from the same universe as the sample or samples used to provide the reliability and validity data. This is particularly true for validity. Thus in the Language Study we might have found an inventory which a previous researcher had shown to be a valid measure of aspirational level and occupational preference for mainland-born children from middle- and high-income homes. To assume that this instrument had the same validity for Puerto Rican–born children in low- or middle-income families would be an assumption the researcher would have to examine thoroughly and carefully before deciding whether to accept or reject it.

If he rejected it, the instrument might still be useful, but he now would have to take on the responsibility of revalidating it for the sample (or universe) on which he intended to use it.

UNDERLYING DYNAMICS   Instrument development is such a difficult and time-consuming process that researchers prefer to avoid it whenever possible. This is particularly true for students. Unfortunately this desire has been so emphatically reinforced by faculty and professional researchers that we have had little advance in instrumentation in the social disciplines in the last decades. Instead, once an instrument is developed in an area, researcher after researcher continues to use it even when study after study demonstrates that the instrument has functioned with partial or limited effectiveness.

It is to highlight this point that the model lists two underlying dynamics. The first is obvious: The needs of the research problem as expressed in the data-gathering methods and techniques clearly structure the instrument-selection stage. In the Language Study, for example, our planning to date has pointed the way to the need for several tests, attitude scales for children, a rating scale for teachers, and an observation guide.

But the second dynamic is one researchers do not fully recognize: This stage of instrument selection or development involves a commitment to the adequacy of the instrument. The author insists that his students understand that once a researcher decides to select an instrument (his own or someone else's) he is committed to that instrument and must be willing to defend it as adequate. Thus, if the expected or desired research results are not obtained, he *cannot* blame the instrument. If he has insufficient faith in the instrument and concludes that there is no substantial instrument available for his research, then he should either abandon the project or consider altering the project to an instrument-development project. If this were done more often, and particularly if universities were willing to support doctoral projects of this sort, we would have less research for a while, but more significant research ultimately.

OUTCOME   The outcome, then, of Stage 9, is a set of instruments which will meet the needs of the research, and which the researcher is willing to defend as adequate and reasonable for his purposes.

Stage 10: Designing the Data-Analysis Plan

Once we have selected the data-collection method, technique, and instruments, we should think ahead to our plans for analyzing the data before we actually do the study. In fact, the plan should be so thorough that the researcher can block out the tables he will use in his written report. The function of the actual research, in other words, is not to learn what kinds of analyses can be done, but only what numbers are to be filled into the analyses already planned. There is nothing further from sound research than the person who comes to a research consultant with data and in essence says, "I think there is a study buried somewhere in these data; help me find one."

For any one research problem and purpose, there is a maximally efficient combination of data-collection method, instrument, and analysis techniques, and no one phase of the research is more critical than the researcher's efforts to find this combination.

UNDERLYING DYNAMICS   The same data will permit of different methods of analysis; therefore, as soon as a method of data collection is tentatively selected, the researcher should carefully consider how these data will be analyzed. In the chapters on statistical concepts and procedures this point will be explored at length, but now let us note that data-analysis techniques differ widely in the skills which they require, in the time which they consume, in the statistical techniques which they permit, in the statistical sophistication which they demand, and, most important, in the nature of the generalizations which can be made from them. The time to consider these issues is at this early stage, *before* the research data have been collected. Considering data analysis now makes it possible to reconsider and, if necessary, revise the choice of data-collection method or, a more usual case, to revise the data-collection instrument.

While practical considerations like the researcher's skills and costs must be considered at this stage, the primary dynamic must be the research problem, as stated in the hypotheses. The data analysis must be planned so that each hypothesis will be directly tested by the data and so answer the questions which precipitated the research. Nothing in research is more frustrating than to realize, after all data have been collected, that information needed for testing a specific hypothesis is not available, or that some data were not collected in a form permitting use of a statistical procedure needed to answer an aspect of the research question. There is no way to atone for these errors short of redoing the study, so too much emphasis cannot be given to the importance of considering data analysis in terms of the research problem, as expressed in the hypotheses, at this stage in the research process, prior to data collection.

There are three aspects of the data-analysis plan which should be complete before the study is actually begun: selecting the *descriptive* and *inferential statistical procedures* to be used, selecting a *level of significance* to guide the data analysis, and reviewing the *assumptions* and *limitations* of the project.

The first aspect of the data-analysis plan to be considered at this stage is the statistical analysis to be done. Almost all research, no matter which approach is used, utilizes what are called *descriptive statistics*. These statistics tell the reader characteristics of the data, like their range, central tendency (average), and variability. Even historical research, which is generally the most data-free approach, often utilizes descriptive statistics. In addition to descriptive statistics, comparative and evaluative research use a second set of statistical procedures called *inferential statistics*. Inferential statistics enable us to determine the probability that any differences we observe in our data are attributable to chance fluctuations.

In education, as in social science research in general, we always must live with the fact that the measures we use are not perfect and the phenomena we study not always finite and stable. This instability and imprecision may produce observable differences in data. Therefore, we have evolved a set of statistical procedures whose function is to estimate the likelihood that chance factors alone produced the result we have observed. Let us assume that in the Language Study we tested the hypothesis about difference in improvement by comparing the average change in score on the writing test for three groups of students: the experiential group, the vocabulary group, the structure group. The average improvements were 11, 7, and 17 points respectively.

To help us determine if these observed differences are real ones or are a product of chance variation like imprecision in the data-collection instrument or other research procedures, we apply one of the inferential statistical procedures.[7] Assume that this procedure tells us that differences of the magnitude we observed would happen by chance twice in 100 times. Restated, this means if we did our study 100 times and there really was *no* difference between students taught by the three methods, nevertheless, we would obtain our observed differences (or even larger ones) in two of the hundred studies, that is, 2 percent of the time.

Now we are faced with deciding if 2 percent of the time is often or seldom. If we consider it "often," we are saying chance factors could produce our observed differences or larger ones often, and then these

---

[7]These procedures will be discussed in detail in Chapters 9 and 10.

specific observed differences are better attributed to chance. In this case, then, we conclude that there really was no difference in improvement in writing between children taught by the three methods. If we consider it "seldom," then we would conclude that the observed differences are more wisely attributed to the research conditions and so conclude that the methods did differ in effectiveness.

So that we make this decision consistently and in an unbiased way, as we develop our data-analysis plan we define the dividing line we shall draw between "often" and "seldom." This dividing line is called the *level of significance*. Figure 2-2 illustrates how the level of significance serves us as this dividing line between chance producing the observed results of "seldom" and "often."

In our example had we decided on 5 percent as the dividing line, we would have noted that 2 percent is less, and so our result falls on the "seldom" side, that is, the difference was *not* sensibly attributable to chance. Had we selected 1 percent as the dividing line, however, 2 percent is greater and so falls on the "often" side, and therefore the results are better attributable to chance.

Thus, depending on what we had selected as the level of significance, our research conclusions, although based on the *same* data, would have been different. Because the level of significance can affect conclusions in this way, it must be chosen and stated *prior* to data collection, when the data-analysis plan is being established.

In theory, the level of significance chosen is arbitrary, but the conventional level in educational research is the 5 percent level of significance, with the more stringent level of 1 percent used less often. In any one study, which of these levels is used should reflect the precision of the methods and instruments used and the nature of the research.

The final stage of the data-analysis plan is for the researcher to review the *assumptions* and *limitations* of his research plan. At this point in the

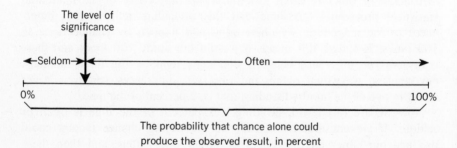

Figure 2-2   Illustration of level of significance.

process, he has committed himself in all of the aspects of research for which he must make assumptions or which will limit the findings and generalizations. Thus, he has made assumptions and accepted limitations involving the research approach; the data-gathering method, techniques, and instruments; the selection of his population and sample; and the often subtle and unrecognized area of data analysis—particularly statistical techniques.

The assumptions and limitations of each of these stages will be discussed in the chapters devoted to each aspect. In this discussion of the model, we want to note that it is critical for the researcher to recognize and review both the assumptions and limitations at this stage before he is irrevocably committed to them. It is still possible to redesign the research plan to avoid either a specific assumption or limitation, if it is seen as incompatible with the acceptance of the research.

OUTCOMES   The outcome of this stage is a thorough data-analysis plan including the selection of the descriptive and inferential statistics to be used, the level of significance, and prototypes of all tables for reporting data. The final outcome is the researcher's recognition of and acceptance of the assumptions and limitations of the research.

Stage 11: Designing the Data-Gathering Plan

We are now ready for the eleventh stage, designing the data-gathering plan. This stage has two aspects to it, the *data-collection process*, or the mechanics of the plan whereby we shall administer our data-collection instruments, and the *research situation*, or the situation in which the respondents of the research will function and in which we shall study their functioning.

In later chapters we shall consider in detail two aspects of the data-gathering process: the *nature of the researcher-respondent contact*, and the *frequency of researcher-respondent contact*. Here we shall simply identify them and note that they have immediate implications for the stage of sample selection, since some people will be willing to participate in research under one type of researcher-respondent interaction but not another.

The researcher-respondent interaction will be considered in two dimensions. The first dimension determines if there is *personal contact*, on a face-to-face basis, or *impersonal contact*, typically with the researcher represented by a piece of paper. The second dimension is concerned with whether or not the respondent is known by name or is anonymous. The two dimensions interact in all four possible combinations: There is personal contact when the respondent is known or unknown and impersonal interaction with the respondent known or unknown. The least likely is personal contact with the respondent unknown. Even when attempted, this is difficult to achieve. For example, one project the author conducted tried for this type of interaction. We planned face-to-face interviews with nursing students, but we assured the students that they would remain anonymous since the interviewers would never know the names of the students they were seeing. The process changed, however, because nursing students all wear name plates on their uniforms, and most of the students did not remove these for the interview!

The second aspect, frequency of contact, simply indicates that at this point in the research process the researcher must decide how often he needs to collect data to accomplish the purposes of the research. This is no problem in historical research, where the collection of data is an on-going process. In survey and experimental research, data are *always* collected at what is perceived as the terminal point of the research so that the only questions which arise concern whether the data need to be collected at the beginning of the research and/or at one or more intermediate points as well. The decision, of course, should be made in terms of the needs of the research, although factors like feasibility, cost, and the cooperation of the respondent must be taken into account as well.

As for the research situation, the primary decision here also involves survey and experimental research and concerns the circumstances under which the respondents will be functioning at the time of data collection. The possibilities include *individual, small-group,* and *large-group* research situations and, like the researcher-respondent interaction, should be chosen in terms of the needs of the research. However, the data-gathering instruments and the types of respondents here intervene strongly as well.

In the Language Study, for example, we learned in the pilot studios that the newly arrived Puerto Rican child did better when tested in small groups than he did in large groups and did even better when tested individually, even if the instruments were developed for use with large groups. This phenomenon apparently reflected a lack of experience in school[8] in group-testing situations. We then were faced with a conflict between the instrument (intended for group use), the research need (to obtain the most accurate data), the feasibility criterion (the tremendous increase in costs and in time which individual or even small-group testing would entail), and the needs of the respondents (best met in individual testing). We decided that the research need was to provide an estimate of the children's ability to function in school and, because school was a group

[8]At the time of the Language Study, the Puerto Rican school system was first beginning a formal testing program.

situation, this need could not be met by individual testing. We also felt an obligation to meet the children's needs as well, however, and so reorganized our testing plan to provide smaller groups than originally intended and also more proctors to assist the children who needed help on issues like how to answer and how to proceed through the test.

UNDERLYING DYNAMICS   The preceding discussion has referred to two of the dynamics which are involved at this stage: the needs of the research and the practical considerations like cost, personnel, and time. They must be reconciled, usually through some compromise like the example just cited. There are two additional dynamics involved at this stage: the needs of the respondents and the research approach.

In planning his data gathering the researcher should be aware that he is intruding into the on-going life process of his respondents, whether they be children, adults, or institutions. Therefore, he should consider what this interruption means to them, and what the act of participating in the research may mean to them. He should specifically consider their motivation, the possible anxiety they may feel, and their need and right to know the nature of the research, what they will be asked to say or do, and the use to be made of the data, before they make a decision whether or not to participate. Finally, those who do participate have a need to know the outcomes of the research. All of this means that in planning for his data gathering the researcher should consider what he should communicate to the respondents before, during, and after the actual data-gathering sessions.

Each research approach (historical, survey, or experimental) makes different demands for a data-gathering plan. The historical approach is least demanding, permitting flexibility in both the data-collection process and the research situation. In this approach our purpose is primarily the collection of information from the past, and as long as we have established a sound framework to guide this search for information, we must feel free to try different ways to collect the data, and to move forward and backward within the research situation, often going off on spontaneous tangents in the pursuit of promising leads. At the research-writing stage, we integrate the material we have collected within the framework that guided its collection, so that the research report is presented as a cohesive and fluent whole. Thus, in the historical approach, as long as the framework for the research is sound, the data-gathering plan can, and indeed must, be flexible and fluid.

The survey approach, however, permits no such flexibility in the data-collection process, which should be controlled or standardized by the researcher so that any one instrument is consistently administered in the same way. This must be done so that we know that any differences we find in the variety of research situations we survey are not a function of differences in the data-collection process. Obviously, however, in the survey approach, the researcher does not seek to control the nature of the situation he surveys other than to let it proceed normally.

The experimental approach requires the most rigorous data-gathering plan, since it demands control of both aspects, the data-collection process and the research situation. Remember that in the experimental approach the research situation has usually been established, for the purposes of the experiment, to enable us to predict the consequences of implementing the experimental conditions on a wider scale. To make such prediction possible and accurate, the researcher must control as many aspects of the research situation as possible and certainly all those aspects most relevant to what is being studied. Thus in the Language Study, not only did we have to make certain that the test data were obtained under comparable conditions, but we also had to make certain that the various methods were implemented as we planned.

Since the three research approaches differ so in the data-gathering plans they require, the importance and difficulty of this stage also differs. It is a relatively unimportant stage in the historical approach which requires control of neither the data-collection process nor the research situation. It is a vital but relatively simple stage for the survey approach which requires control only in the data-collection process. Since this process is usually established by the researcher, it is one he can standardize. It is a vital but tremendously difficult stage in the experimental approach. This is because this approach requires control not only of data-collection process but also of the research situation. Since the research situation in the social sciences generally involves working with people, achieving sufficient experimental control runs counter to the human tendency to function freely and individually. This is a fine characteristic in many respects, but wreaks havoc with experimentation, as we shall discuss at length in Chapter 16.

OUTCOME   The outcome of Stage 11, of course, is the decision on a data-gathering plan. Just as any one study might involve varied approaches, methods, and techniques of data collection, so it might involve different data-collection processes and research situations. For example, if we were developing a data-gathering plan for the Language Study, the data on children's reading ability must be obtained at least twice: before and after the experimental instruction. These data could undoubtedly be obtained without any personal contact between researcher and respondent, other than the test, but the respondent would have to be identified. When it comes to the teacher rating of the children, we could use some combination of impersonal contact followed by selective personal interviews about some children, and we would need these data only after the study had been completed. The process for obtaining the children's ratings of the experience would be difficult to decide. On the one hand we would feel that we would obtain a fuller and franker evaluation if we used impersonal anonymous contact. However, to do this would eliminate any possibility of relating the rating to the child's ability and/or improvement.[9] The choice would have to be made in terms of our knowledge of and perception of the situation and the data we wanted to assure. If we felt that we must have frank ratings, and nothing should endanger these, we would use the impersonal anonymous interaction. If we felt that the ability to relate attitude to achievement was so critical that we were willing to risk the loss of some frankness by some children, we would decide on an interaction with an identified source.

Stage 12: Identifying the Population and Invited Sample

The researcher has tentatively identified the universe of interest in Stage 1 and has specified it in detail in Stage 3. Now he turns to the realistic problem of deciding what portion of the universe is available to him, and how he shall select specific elements to invite as participants.

A researcher seldom has access to the entire universe, which is defined as all possible elements of a certain kind. Rather, the researcher typically has available a *population*, defined as that portion of the universe to which the researcher has access. Rarely in research do we have the time, money, or even the facilities to study an entire population. Think for a moment of the scope of a research project that even within one large city would seek to identify and study every fourth grader who is retarded at least two years in reading. For this reason the great majority of research projects do not study the population of interest, but rather a part of the population or what is called a *sample*. This is feasible because, if properly selected, a sample can provide meaningful and accurate information about the entire population. Obviously, proper sample selection involves creating a sample which simulates the population as closely as possible.[10]

UNDERLYING DYNAMICS   Nowhere in the research process do the underlying dynamics interact more dramatically and in opposition to each other than in the identification of the population and selected sample. The

[9]Note that we are ruling out as completely unethical any procedure which would tell the child he was anonymous, but by some coding procedure enable the researcher to identify the child. The ethics of this are discussed at length in Chapter 12.

[10]Specific techniques for selecting samples and determining sample size are discussed in Chapter 11.

model lists four underlying dynamics: the needs of the research, the ultimate acceptance of the research, the realities of the research setting, and the practical needs of the researcher.

The first dynamic, the needs of the research, should be the only one which structures population and sample selection. It is obvious that in some ideal research world, we would consider the relationship of universe to research problem and decide how large a portion and which portions of the universe should be included in the population. Then from this population we would decide the same questions about the sample: how large, and which portions of the population need to be represented. With these decisions made, it would be relatively simple to use the basic techniques of sample selection to identify the selected sample.

But the other three dynamics interfere with realizing this idealized state. First, when the researcher considers the ultimate acceptance of the research, he finds in some instances that this moves him toward a narrower population; in other instances he may find influences which move him toward a broader population than the needs of the research strictly demand. For example, in the Language Study, the needs of the research suggested that the problem of second-language teaching be studied in varied aspects of the universe where there were significant numbers of Puerto Rican children. This would have included school systems in Chicago, Boston, Philadelphia, Newark, and other cities throughout the United States. However, to achieve the maximum likelihood of the research being accepted and utilized by the New York City school administrators and teachers, we decided it was wisest to limit the population to be studied to schools in New York City. But even within that limit, the research needs would have been met more fully had we studied the problem in both public- and private-school settings, and so defined the population in this way. Again, the public-acceptance criterion was considered more important, and this dictated a population of New York City public schools.

This dynamic of research acceptance can also operate to expand a population beyond the limits set by the research need, when the researcher realizes that for full acceptance he should include in the population elements of the universe not demanded by the research. Thus, in the Language Study, the decision to include schools with fewer than 20 percent Puerto Rican pupils was not a function of the needs of the research but rather a reflection of the large proportion of such schools in New York City at the time of the study. We wanted the administrators and teachers in those schools to believe that the study had direct relevance and applicability for them as well. The most dramatic way to maximize the likelihood of their acceptance was to include them in the population to be sampled.

The third dynamic, the practical needs of the researcher, almost always operates to reduce the population. These practical needs usually involve keeping expenses down, minimizing traveling, and obtaining the data as quickly as possible. These considerations have special impact on student research, for in addition to all of the other considerations, students often have regular responsibilities, such as class schedules, which restrict their freedom of movement for data collection even if financial considerations do not. Therefore, this dynamic operates to specify the population as a limited, conveniently accessible portion of the universe. Of course, these are not research criteria, and so when the researcher's practical needs dominate population and sample selection, the research suffers, particularly the generalizeability of the results. We may understand why students damage their research at this stage, but there is no excuse for professional researchers to make the decision about population and sample in provincial terms, reflecting their personal preferences or reluctance to travel.

The fourth dynamic, realities of the research setting, primarily operates at the level of sample, rather than population selection. This dynamic can function in two entirely different ways. The first way, stated simply, is that the researcher is permitted access only to parts of the population. There is no implication intended here that this is necessarily an attempt to thwart research or prevent discovery of truth. For example, while educators may be reluctant to have research conducted in schools which they know to be weak, they may be equally reluctant to add a research burden to their best schools which already have varied enrichment projects and student activities. Whether the motivation is laudable or not, the result for the researcher is the same: He cannot include some elements of the population he has identified in the group from which he will select his sample.

This dynamic can operate in the opposite direction as well. The authorities who control the population may be particularly anxious that certain elements of the population *are* included in the research. In education, this often reflects the fact that while the authorities are curious about new programs or courses of study they have implemented, they seldom establish evaluation studies on their own. Therefore when a researcher arrives and requests access to their schools as part of his population, they see this as a wonderful opportunity to obtain some evaluation data as a by-product of their cooperation. So they agree to cooperate, provided schools A, B, and C can be included.

How serious this particular dynamic is depends in part on the research-needs criterion and the ultimate-acceptance criterion. If the research needs can be met within the limits of reality established by the setting, there is no serious problem. However, if they cannot be met, then this impasse forces a re-evaluation of the research plan and problem.

One particular research need which is involved whenever there is deliberate exclusion and/or inclusion of certain elements in the population is the statistical analyses planned. Many of the most pertinent statistical techniques available are based on the assumption that the sample can be considered to have been selected by *random-sampling procedures*. Since the definition of a random-sampling procedure in part is that every element in the population has an equal probability of being selected, it is obvious that deliberate sampling is not a random procedure.

Moreover, this loss of randomness has its implications as well for the ultimate acceptance criterion. In many instances research is fully accepted as valid only if the reader or consumer can accept the sample selection as unbiased. Convincing the research public that a particular sample selection *was* unbiased is most easily achieved through random-sampling procedures. When some other process has been used, the public naturally suspects the possibility of bias. Thus, if the criterion of public acceptance is critical, this alone can move the researcher to the use of random-sampling methods.

OUTCOME   The outcome of this stage is the delineation of the population, the selection of a method of sample selection, a decision on sample size, and the identification of those to be invited to participate in the study. The final outcome is the identification of those not to be invited who are therefore available for the pilot studies of Stage 13.

Stage 13: Pilot Studies of the Data-Gathering Approach, Method and Instruments, and the Data-Analysis Plan

The stage of pilot studies or testing is one which is more typical of professional than of student research. True, it is not always necessary, but when students omit this stage, it is more often on grounds of time and expense than on research needs. A pilot study is generally a miniature of some part of the actual study in which the intended instrument is administered to subjects drawn from the same population as the sample, but subjects who are *not* in the sample.

The pilot study generally has several purposes. It may be designed to provide a trial run of the data-collection approach. It may be intended to test out the data-collection method or an instrument to see if it is in need of revision. It may be done to provide some pilot data to test out the data-analysis techniques planned. It may be intended to see if the subjects of the research can handle the data-collection instruments, or it may be intended to give the research staff experience in working with the subjects of the research, in administering the data-collection instruments, and analyzing the research data.

UNDERLYING DYNAMICS   How necessary a pilot study is depends on the interaction of the demands implied in the data-collection approach, method, instrument, and procedure, and the skills of the researcher. If the techniques are standard and familiar to the researcher, and particularly if the instrument is a standard one which has been used before with the universe of the research, then there may be no need for a pilot study. If any one of these conditions is not true—if the approach or method are unfamiliar, and/or if the instrument is newly constructed, and/or if it has not been used before with the universe of the research—then some pilot work is in order.

In many instances, one pilot study may be sufficient to provide the needed data and/or experience. In other instances, several may be needed. Thus, in the Language Study we spent several months testing out the new measures developed, trying out the experimental curricula, and evaluating different data-gathering processes like individual versus small-group versus large-group test administration.

Obviously, pilot studies like these require a large investment in time and money, but this investment inevitably is a wise one. Revisions of the instrument, clarification of instructions, development of a smooth technique of data administration—all repay this investment in the outcome of the actual study.

OUTCOME   The critical outcome of this stage is the researcher's knowledge that everything works. The approach, method, and instrument are appropriate for his sample, yield reliable and valid data which he can analyze to test the hypotheses and thus, hopefully, answer the research questions.

PART TWO: IMPLEMENTING THE RESEARCH PLAN

With the pilot studies, if any, concluded, we have completed the planning and decision-making stages of the research. We are now faced with the implementation stages, that is, implementing the data-gathering plan, implementing the data-analysis plan, and, finally, preparing the reports of the research. If all goes well, these stages involve putting into effect all of the previous decisions and so qualitatively represent a quite different aspect of the research process. Throughout these stages the model notes one critical dynamic, the research problem. Just as all of the earlier stages were devoted to obtaining data to shed light on the research problem, the implementation stages are devoted to realizing the possibilities in the data.

In practice, of course, planning is seldom so complete and respondents seldom so cooperative that this part of the process is truly decision-free. However, the decisions to make now, as unexpected things happen, are always made with the aim of realizing as fully as possible the original data-gathering and data-analysis plans.

Stage 14: Implementing the Data-Gathering Plan

This stage, in which the data-gathering plan is implemented, is the most controlled stage of the research process. As noted earlier, the three research approaches—historical, survey, and experimental—differ in the degree of control to be exerted here, but in each this is the stage where the researcher has least freedom. Except for unexpected exigencies (which are almost inevitable in research involving people), this is not a decision-making stage. Even in the event of unexpected happenings, such as subjects being absent or material not arriving on time, the decisions made are always within the context of the already established data-gathering plan, and each decision should be made in such a way as to carry out that plan as fully as possible. In short, this is not the stage to improvise, make up, or implement sudden insights!

OUTCOME   The obvious outcome of Stage 14 is to provide the data needed for the research, which will be analyzed in Stage 15. These two stages can and often do overlap, so that data analysis can begin as soon as the first logically complete unit of data is available.

Stage 15: Implementing the Data-Analysis Plan

This stage, too, is largely a matter of putting a previously established plan into effect. But unlike Stage 14, the researcher does have the freedom to deviate from that plan, and *can* implement sudden insights. With good research planning, most if not all of the data analysis planned at Stage 10 will now be put into effect. However, in the course of actually analyzing the data, or in the course of the continued thinking and reading in the problem area during the course of Stage 15, the researcher may have new insights, hunches, and ideas for tangential data analyses. This means the decision must be made whether or not to pursue these analyses. If they can be done in addition to those originally planned, this is a simple decision, and most researchers would gladly expand the research to include new analyses. If, however, the new analyses can only be done if some of those originally planned are eliminated, this is a quite different decision. For now, let us just note that the decision is made by reference to the specific research problem and by asking which analyses will contribute most to the provision of data to answer that problem.

OUTCOME   The outcome of Stage 15, the analyzed data, comprise the results or findings of the study. In descriptive research, that is sufficient. In comparative and evaluative research an additional outcome comes from the application of the inferential statistical procedures to the data. This outcome is expressed in conclusions such as difference or no difference, change or no change.

Stage 16: Preparing the Research Reports

The next stage of the research process is to prepare the reports of the research. This stage may overlap many of the others in time, and placing it here is not intended to suggest that report writing be delayed until all data are collected and analyzed. Quite the contrary, report writing should begin very early in the process. In fact, once the second review of the literature is completed, the section of the report based on the review should be written. Similarly, as the data-gathering approach, method and instruments are selected, the researcher should write out the rationale for these selections while they are fresh in his mind. He continues writing as the pilot studies are completed, setting down the record of what was done, why it was done, and the outcomes. Then as the data-gathering plan is implemented, he writes the report of exactly how the research data were collected in sufficient detail for another researcher to replicate his study. Thus, the only part of the actual writing which follows the data-analysis plan is the writing of the results and implications of the study. We like to believe that this part of the report requires the data, and so delay it to this point!

OUTCOMES   The model notes that there are three outcomes to this stage: the research reports, suggestions for further research, and implications for change or action in the problem area.

The research report serves two major purposes. As indicated above, it recapitulates for the reader the researcher's actions and thoughts throughout the several stages of the research process. A good research report takes pains to explain the several decisions which have been made and the rationale for these decisions. Second, it presents the results of the research *in the context of the specific research problem.* In other words, we write the results section in such a way as to present our obtained data as the answer to the problem which stimulated the research, showing the extent to which we have or have not answered the questions posed by the research problem.

With the research report presented in this way, researchers who follow us in the problem area will be able to know what we did, why we did it the way we did, how successful we thought we were in our methods and procedures, and what the results of the research were. Through a series of such projects and reports we profit from each other's experience, build on the research already conducted, and so advance our knowledge and understanding.

The second outcome is the identification of new research suggested by the results. This has been a much misunderstood outcome in two respects. First, it has been considered an academic exercise having little practical application. And so in many instances this is a stereotyped section in which the researcher routinely says that the finding needs verification with larger and/or other samples, or with other instruments. In short, he sees the suggestions for further research as simply suggestions as to how to do his project over again, cleaning up some of the defects in the process. Instead, he should be thinking in terms of the problem area, and see the suggestions as based on those aspects of the problem area he has clarified to a sufficient degree that we can now ask intelligent questions and structure further research.

The second misinterpretation is reflected in the cliché that all good research raises more questions than it answers. This is then taken to mean that research always leaves us in a state of unreadiness for action, and the only logical outcome of research is more research. This is not true. While good research may indeed raise more questions than it answers, this does not mean that it does not answer *some* questions. And therefore the outcome of good research is not only suggestions for more, but also suggestions for change and action.

This third outcome must be considered and included in any sound report of research. In education particularly, we do not do research in a vacuum but in a context which has a strong flavor of reality. Therefore, in his report, the researcher has the responsibility to translate his findings into action terms for the reader, and, an even greater responsibility than this, to work for these changes as discussed in Stage 17 below.

DEVELOPING THE PROBLEM STATEMENT

The model developed here can be used as a guide in the development of the problem statement. When that is done, only the 13 stages of Part One are involved. To assist the reader in the use of the model in this way, two things have been done in the following pages. First, in Table 2-3 these first 13 stages have been listed, with the underlying dynamics and outcomes for each stage also indicated. If these stages are completed, one by one, with the researcher taking each underlying dynamic into account and achieving each outcome, the research outline will emerge. As an example of how to use the model in this way, Table 2-4 illustrates its use by a hypothetical student. The stages, dynamics, and outcomes are printed in Table 2-4. What the student wrote as she developed her outline appears in the column headed "Researcher's Application to Proposed Study." Finally, at the bottom of each page appear this author's comments on how the student handled each stage.

PART THREE: IMPLEMENTING THE RESULTS

Stage 17: Dissemination of Findings and Agitation for Action

The model in Figure 2-1 notes that the researcher's responsibility does not cease when the report has been completed. Instead he should move on to actively disseminate the findings of his research and agitate for whatever changes in program, policy, or organization are suggested by the findings.

The first aspect of Part Three, dissemination of findings, can be achieved in many ways. The publishing of complete research reports is one way. Publishing summaries or sections of reports in professional journals is another. A third and often neglected aspect of the researcher's responsibility for dissemination is to inform the lay public, in terms they can understand, of the nature and significance of the findings. The dissemination responsibility holds for both students and professional researchers. In fact, some universities now insist that together with the doctoral dissertation a student submit an article based on the study. In this way, once the dissertation is approved, the article is ready for submission to an appropriate journal.

The dissemination-responsibility aspect of Part Three has been well recognized as part of the researcher's role, if for no other reason than the "publish or perish" atmosphere in academic circles. The agitation-for-action aspect has not only not been recognized, but has been considered almost as ill-mannered and unbecoming as cheering at a tennis match once was. Moreover, in the United States, by structuring the financing of research on a project-by-project basis, we have forced most researchers to abandon their identification with a project a year or two before completion so that they can begin the process of obtaining a grant to do the next project. Even if they maintain identification with the first project once it is completed, little of their time and energy is free to devote to agitation for implementation of the results, as they are now absorbed in their next project.

We have even managed to create an atmosphere in which the researcher is not expected to be concerned with outcomes and implementation, but only with his study and the questions it raises for further studies. But we know from research and study of the process of social change, that change does not take place simply by making available to people the news that a

Table 2-3 The Thirteen Steps in the Developmental Stages of Research Planning

The Stage	Underlying Dynamics of the Stage	Outcomes of the Stage
1. Identifying the problem area or initiating idea	Researcher's motivation Researcher's interest, experience Researcher's goal	Universe of interest Literature to be read
2. Initial review of literature	Need to become familiar with problem area	Frame of reference Initial assumptions
3. Defining the specific research problem	Researcher's competence, that is, skills, knowledge, and experience	Definitions Statement of specific problem
4. Estimating success potential of the research	Researcher's motivation Researcher's goal	Decision as to whether to a. proceed without revision b. revise, then proceed c. abandon idea or area
5. The second review of the literature	Need to become thoroughly knowledgeable in problem area	Summary of previous results Ideas for data-gathering approach, method, instruments
6. Selecting the research approach	Orientation in time Researcher's intent	Selection of research approach
7. Stating the hypotheses of the research	Literature Researcher's experience	Researcher's prediction Formal statement of hypotheses
8. Selecting the data-gathering method and technique	Data needed to answer research problem or test hypotheses	Selection of data-gathering method and technique

The Stage	Underlying Dynamics of the Stage	Outcomes of the Stage
	Method and technique suggested by this data need Feasibility of techniques under consideration	Instruments needed
9. Selecting and developing data-gathering instruments	Needs of research Commitment to adequacy of instruments	Instruments to be used
10. Designing the data-analysis plan	Research problem or question Hypotheses	Selection of descriptive statistics Selection of inferential statistics Decision on level of significance Prototypes of tables Statement of the assumptions and limitations
11. Designing the data-gathering plan	Needs of the research Needs of the research approach Practical considerations	Design of the data-gathering plan
12. Identifying the population and invited sample	Needs of research Acceptance of research Practical needs of researcher Realities of research setting	Population, sample
13. Pilot studies of approach, method, technique, instruments, and data-analysis plan	Degree of standardization of data-gathering instruments Extent to which instruments have previously been used with universe for research	Reasonable conviction study will produce data relevant to the problem and hypotheses and capable of analysis

Table 2-4 Application of Model to Designing a Research Project

Stage	Underlying Dynamics and Outcomes	Researcher's Application to Proposed Study
1. Identifying the problem area or initiating idea	A. Underlying dynamics:	
	1. Motivation	Identifying a technique to improve reading ability of retarded readers. Curiosity about results. Doctoral dissertation.
	2. Researcher's interest and experience	Teacher of elementary grades for five years, puzzled by extent of retardation in reading.
	3. Researcher's goal	Useful contribution which will be a defendable study.
	B. Outcomes:	
	1. Universe of interest	Elementary-level children retarded in reading but normal in intelligence so that remedial instruction would be appropriate.
	2. Literature to be read	Methods for remedial instruction in reading.
2. The initial review of the literature	A. Underlying dynamics:	
	1. The need to become familiar with problem area	Emphasize literature on nature of methods for remedial instruction because weak there.
	B. Outcomes:	
	1. Frame of reference for research	Importance of structural elements in learning to read. Belief of some experts that relative de-emphasis on phonics has produced large part of retardation. Conclusions that direct remedial instruction in phonics would help.
	2. Initial assumptions	Remedial instruction can be successful with retarded readers. Reading level can be measured reliably. Instruction material in phonics exists.

This doctoral candidate, seeking to capitalize on her interest in reading in the elementary grades and her curiosity about ways to alleviate retardation, wishes to develop a project in the general problem area of improving the reading ability of retarded readers. Her own experience in the elementary grades orients her to a universe of elementary-school children, and the problem specifies that these be children retarded in reading but normal in intelligence. Table 2-4 illustrates how the initial review of literature specified calls her attention to the importance of structural elements in the teaching of reading and how she sees merit in the arguments of those in the field who argue for direct instruction in phonics as a way of alleviating retardation. Moreover, she finds enough in the literature to make her decide that she can assume that remedial instruction can be successful, that reading grades can be estimated accurately, and that materials for this direct instruction already exist and would not have to be constructed for a potential study.

3. Defining the specific research problem

A. Underlying dynamics:
1. Researcher's competence, that is, skills, knowledge, and experience

As teacher, has developed skills and experience in remedial teaching and testing.

B. Outcomes:
1. Definitions and their source or rationale

(a) Phonics method: "a method of teaching reading based on the analysis of words into their basic speech sounds" (*Dictionary of Education*, p. 396).

(b) Children: students in regular classes in fourth grade, with an IQ between 90 and 110. Rationale. Fourth grade selected because researcher wishes to work with children retarded at least two years but does not wish to work with children who have been badly retarded for long. Normal range of IQ selected since researcher wishes to rule out mental retardation as cause of reading retardation.

(c) Retarded in reading: a reading level at least two grades below that appropriate, in this study a reading grade of 2.0 or less.

Table 2-4 continued

Stage	Underlying Dynamics and Outcomes	Researcher's Application to Proposed Study
		Rationale: Desire to work with children who have not gone beyond initial levels of reading.
		(d) Instruction: direct teaching of phonics for 30 minutes each school day, by trained remedial reading specialist.
		Rationale: Experts' belief that this is maximum period for effective remedial work.
		(e) Small group: five children or fewer.
		Rationale: Previous studies which show that this is optimum size for remedial instruction.
2. Statement of the specific research problem		The effects of 30 minutes of daily phonics instruction in groups of five or fewer on the reading level of fourth graders at least two grades retarded in reading.

Comment

Reading further she begins to sense some consensus that these periods of instruction should be given daily for brief periods of about 30 minutes, and that this type of remedial work is most effective if given in small groups of no more than five children. Finally, her reading concretizes that the children of most interest to her are those with considerable retardation who have not been frozen in their retardation. All of these points are expressed in the definitions she develops and states in the worksheet. From all of the reading and thinking comes the highly structured statement of the specific research problem. Note the extent to which it has been developed and refined from the initial vague interest in improving the reading ability of retarded readers. Of course, placing all of this in the few columns of this worksheet is deceptive, as underlying these few entries are hours and weeks in libraries, in thought, and in conferences with advisers as the general interest in the problem area is developed.

4. Estimating the success potential of the research	A. Underlying dynamics:	
	1. Researcher's motivation	To test whether or not phonics instruction will help.
	2. Researcher's goal	A meaningful study and a defendable dissertation.

B. Outcomes:
  1. Decision as to whether to
     (a) proceed without revision
     (b) revise, then proceed
     (c) abandon idea or area

Decision to proceed without revision.
  (1) If results are positive, study will be successful, for data will have been obtained to support use of phonics instruction.
  (2) If results are negative, study will be a productive failure, for data will indicate a logical method does not work.

Comment

With the specific research problem stated, the researcher can now make an initial estimate of the success potential of the proposed project. Note that in doing this she considers both the possibility of positive as well as negative outcomes.

In this instance, she concludes that the proposed study would make a contribution to knowledge, *whether or not* the data come out supporting the idea that the direct instruction in phonics helps.

5. The second review of the literature

A. Underlying dynamic:
  1. Need to become thoroughly knowledgable in problem area

Reread literature on nature of reading, and on remedial techniques. Review studies similar in:
  (a) Problem—other studies concerned with remedial instruction.
  (b) Universe—studies of middle elementary-grade children severely retarded in reading.
  (c) Research variable—studies involving direct instruction in phonics.

B. Outcomes:
  1. Summary of previous results

Research contradictory. Some studies show gains from instruction in phonics, others do not. No previous study has used small-group instruction contemplated in current study. Contradictory results characterize studies of other methods. Most popular "other" method has been "look-say" method.

Table 2–4 continued

Stage	Underlying Dynamics and Outcomes	Researcher's Application to Proposed Study
	2. Ideas for data-gathering approach, method, and instruments	Previous studies in similar areas with similar populations typically have used the experimental approach, and the measuring method. The most popular research design is to establish comparable groups of children and provide remedial instruction to one group by the technique "traditional" in the school and to another group by the new technique. Evaluation of method based on objective testing of ability to read. Several standardized tests of reading ability exist with satisfactory reliability and validity, for example, Metropolitan, Stanford.

Comment

With the decision made to go on, the researcher returns to the literature. She finds her particular study has not been done, and other studies have produced contradictory results. In these studies she finds typical design for research like that she is planning, as well as several standardized measures of reading ability. This review also provides the basis for selecting an alternate method for study, the "look-say" method.

Stage	Underlying Dynamics and Outcomes	Researcher's Application to Proposed Study
6. Selecting the research approach	A. Underlying dynamics: 1. Orientation in time	Study concerned with future, that is, with ultimate effect of introducing new remedial approach.
	2. Intent	Study concerned with comparing direct remedial instruction in phonics with remedial instruction in other methods.
	B. Outcome: 1. Approach required	Study will require a multiple-group experiment. Decides to compare phonics and "look-say" method, selecting "look-say" on basis of literature reviewed in Stage 5.

7. Stating the hypotheses of the research

A. Underlying dynamics:
   1. Literature

   Contradictory; some experts argue in favor of phonics, others in favor of less structured techniques like "look-say" method. As noted earlier, research contradictory as well.

   2. Researcher's experience

   Has found "look-say" not fully satisfactory. Has noticed children seem to lack awareness of formal elements of language.

B. Outcomes:
   1. Researcher's prediction

   Phonics will be more successful than "look-say."

   2. Formal statement of hypothesis

   Fourth-grade children retarded two years in reading given direct remedial instruction in phonics will gain significantly more in reading than comparable children given direct remedial instruction in the look-say method.

Comment

A consideration of her orientation in time and intent (Stage 6) makes her decide on the comparative experimental approach. Although the literature she reviewed was contradictory in terms of the relative effectiveness of different methods for remedial instruction, her own experience makes her believe that children taught by the phonics method will do better than those taught by the look-say method, leading to the hypothesis stated as the outcome of Stage 7.

8. Selecting the data-gathering methods and technique

A. Underlying dynamics:
   1. Data needed to answer research problem or test hypothesis

   Estimate of gains in ability to read.

Table 2–4 continued

Stage	Underlying Dynamics and Outcomes	Researcher's Application to Proposed Study
	2. Method and technique suggested by this data need	Measurement method, objective-testing technique for formal estimate. Measurement method, scaling technique for informal teacher rating.
	3. Feasibility of techniques under consideration	*Criterion*

Technique	Cost	Researcher's Time	Demand upon Subjects	Skills Needed in Data Analysis	Other Considerations
Objective tests	$6.50 per class	45 minutes per class testing time 3–4 hours per class to score	Minimal	Accuracy in scoring test	Want to test before and after study
Scaling techniques	Nominal cost of reproducing scale	Few hours to tally	Each teacher must fill out scale for 30 to 40 children	Simple tallying	

B. Outcome: Instruments needed	Reading test, available in at least two alternate forms for testing before and after study. Rating scale must be brief so as not to make excessive demand on teachers.

With the research problem as stated in Stage 3 and the hypotheses stated in Stage 7, the data needed are clearly estimates of the changes in the children's ability to read. Thus in Stage 8 the researcher considers two possible bases for estimates,	objective tests and teacher ratings. By the varied criteria outlined in that stage, both techniques are feasible, and so she leaves the stage seeking instruments of these two types.
9. Selecting and developing data-gathering instruments	
A. Underlying dynamics: 1. Needs of research	Standardized reading test. Rating scale for teachers: (a) Use one from literature. (b) Develop own.
2. Commitment to adequacy of instruments	Selects reading subtest of Metropolitan Achievement Battery. Reported reliabilities of .88 to .94. Normative sample discussed in manual considered reasonable for population for current study. Omit rating scale. None in literature of sufficiently high reliability; no reason to believe one could be developed in time.
B. Outcome: 1. Forms chosen	Study will use Forms A and B of reading subtest of Metropolitan Achievement Battery.

Table 2–4 continued

Stage	Underlying Dynamics and Outcomes	Researcher's Application to Proposed Study
		Comment
		The objective test in reading which meets acceptable standards of reliability and validity is simple to find. Her problem is to choose from among the several available, and she selects one based on its good reliability but even more because its normative data include children like those she is planning to use. However, the rating scale proves to be more of a problem. The researcher finds none in the literature that she feels is fully acceptable, to which she is willing to commit herself. Specifically she fears that if the rating data did not corroborate the test data, she would begin to question the rating data. Given that low level of faith in the instrument, she is better off without the rating data. She also decides that she lacks the skills needed to develop an adequate one in time for use in the research. Thus, she concludes Stage 9 having selected the reading test, but having reluctantly abandoned the use of a teacher rating scale. Since the objective-test data are the data needed to test the hypothesis, the loss of the rating data is not considered sufficient for her to abandon the study.
10. Designing the data-analysis plan	A. Underlying dynamics: 1. Research problem and hypotheses	Research problem calls for description of the reading levels of the children before and after the study. Hypotheses require a basis for determining if methods achieved differential amounts of change.
	B. Outcomes: 1. Descriptive statistics	Separate summary frequency distribution of reading grade equivalents for pre- and posttest data, including means and standard deviations in reading.
	2. Inferential statistics	Analysis of variance to test for significance of difference in gains, by method and by sex.

4. Prototypes of tables

For descriptive statistics:

Summary Frequency Distribution, before and after Study, that is

Reading Grade	Boys		Girls	
	Phonics	Look-Say	Phonics	Look-Say
6.5–6.6				
6.3–6.4				
6.2–6.3				
↓				
1.0–1.1				
Mean				
S.D.				

For inferential statistics:

Summary of Analysis of Variance for Sex and Method

Source of Variation	Sum of Squares	df	Mean Square	F
Sex				
Method				
Interaction				
Error				
Total				

Table 2–4 continued

Stage	Underlying Dynamics and Outcomes	Researcher's Application to Proposed Study
	5. Assumptions and limitations	The full set of assumptions and limitations cannot be stated until the full details of the study are decided upon. On the basis of what has already been stated in this outline, this researcher would include among her assumptions: (a) Teachers are comparable in ability, interest, and dedication to method. (b) Materials used in two methods are comparable. (c) Period of time experimental instruction to be given is fair to both methods and sufficient for change to take place. (d) Metropolitan Reading Test sufficiently sensitive. Among the limitations would be things like: (a) Study was limited to two classes in one school. (b) Remedial instruction was limited to that provided by regular classroom teachers. (c) Instruction was limited to that provided in groups of five. (d) Study involved only fourth-grade children of normal intelligence but retarded at least two years in reading.

Comment

The researcher thinks ahead to her needs in data analysis by listing the statistics needed to test her hypothesis and provide data for her research problem, and selecting the 5 percent level of significance. To complete Stage 10 thoroughly, she blocks out two major tables needed to present her re-search data, covering both the descriptive and inferential procedures. Finally, the assumptions and limitations of the study, as it has been finally designed, are formally stated so that the researcher comes face to face with them at this final point.

11. Designing the data-gathering plan

A. Underlying dynamics:

1. Needs of the research

Since change is to be estimated, children must be identified as individuals.

Data on reading ability should be collected under standardized conditions.

Evidence needed that methods implemented as intended.

2. Needs of the research approach

Since this is the experimental approach, standardization is needed in both data-gathering process and research situation. Groups to be exposed to different methods should be comparable in terms of children, teachers, materials, facilities, and so on. Researcher must be able to verify integrity of experiment.

3. Practical considerations

Researcher wishes to minimize cost and time in travel. Researcher wishes to avoid necessity to train teachers.

B. Outcome:

1. Design of the data-gathering plan

Ideal data-gathering plan will involve school with two comparable classes, with comparable teachers available already trained in phonics and look-say method. Researcher should collect pre- and posttest data, with tests to be administered in groups. Children will put on names. Periodic observations will be made to be certain that methods will be implemented as intended.

Comment

She then moves on to design her experiment in Stage 11. The work sheet notes only the bare outlines in this stage, since in Chapter 1 we have outlined the variety of step involved in planning a comparative experiment in methodology. From this stage, the researcher emerges with a simple plan involving a pretest, a period of instruction given to comparable classes by comparable teachers, with periodic observations to verify that the method is being implemented. This will be followed by a posttest.

Table 2–4 continued

Stage	Underlying Dynamics and Outcomes	Researcher's Application to Proposed Study
12. Identifying the population and selected sample	A. Underlying dynamics:	
	1. Needs of the research	Suggest broadly based sample of children retarded from variety of causes.
	2. Acceptance of research	For any one group of teachers, the more homogeneous the sample, the more likely the study is to be considered relevant by them.
	3. Practical needs of researcher	To do study in one city, in as few schools as possible.
	4. Realities of research setting	Principal of school X, known to researcher, willing to have study done in his school. Asserts that comparable classes and trained teachers available.
	B. Outcomes:	
	1. Population	Native-born children from intact families with no evidence of retardation or sociopersonal problems, residing in cities of less than 25,000.
	2. Sample	School X, in city Y.

Comment

Through the analysis of the dynamics in Stage 12 the researcher settles on her sample of two classes in school X.

13. Pilot studies

A. Underlying dynamics:

  1. Standardization of data-gathering instruments

  2. Extent to which instruments have been used previously with universe capable of analysis

Metropolitan Reading Test well standardized and fully accepted.

Extensive prior use.

B. Outcome:

  1. Reasonable conviction study will produce data relevant to the problem and hypotheses and capable of analysis

In view of the standardized instruments being used for data collection and the basic statistical procedures to be used in data analysis, no pilot studies are considered necessary to achieve this conviction.

Comment

In Stage 13, in view of the standardized instruments to be used for data collection and the simple statistics planned for data analysis, she concludes that no pilot study will be necessary.

better way exists. Rather it takes place when the people involved in the discovery of the better way take the responsibility for implementing it in their own settings and agitating for others to do the same.

Therefore, if the researcher and participants in any specific project do not accept as one of their roles responsibility for implementation and agitation for change, *change based on research* will not occur. Note that this is change based on research. We have ample change in American education: change in curricula, in patterns of school organization, in class organization, in sequence of content, in methods of teaching, in aids to teaching, in teacher-preparation programs, and so on down an endless list. We also have ample research in some of these areas, although little research in others. But the intriguing thing is how seldom the changes are *based* on the research, and how seldom the research stimulates change, or how seldom change is delayed until there is a research basis for deciding if and how change should occur.

This pattern will not be broken unless and until researchers assume the responsibility for agitation as well as for dissemination, and so this is noted in Figure 2-1 as the final stage of the research process.

Chapter 3

TYPES OF RESEARCH

In Chapter 2, the overview of the research process, we presented three different approaches to research: the historical, survey or descriptive, and experimental approaches. Before beginning the consideration of the specific stages involved in applying these approaches to research, let us consider research itself, as an approach to problem solving. For research is only one of many ways in which problem solutions can be sought. In the social disciplines, and particularly in education, it has been one of the less frequently employed ways.

APPROACHES TO PROBLEM SOLVING

Let us consider how a person faced with a problem might solve it. He might simply try the first idea to come to mind and see if it worked. If it did not work then he might try the second idea he thought of, and the third, until one worked sufficiently well. Or he might seek to determine what others have done before him in similar situations. He might ask someone who had faced the problem and was considered to have handled it well. Finally, he might first try to identify all possible relevant solutions and systematically try each out under comparable conditions to determine which is best.

These four possibilities typify four different approaches to problem solution or resolution: trial and error, reference to precedent, reference to authority, and research.

Trial and Error, Precedent, and Authority

The oldest of the techniques is *trial and error*. This is the procedure whereby the person faced with a problem attempts a solution, sees its effects and evaluates them, and if the effects are reasonably satisfactory, adopts the trial solution. If the first way tried is not satisfactory, then another possible solution is tried, studied, and its effects evaluated. The process is continued until a satisfactory resolution or solution is obtained.

Undoubtedly trial and error was man's earliest approach to problem solving, since it involves no prior experience with the problem. However once trial and error has been used and produced solutions with some degree of success, then another approach to problem solving, *reference to precedent* becomes available. At least it becomes available as soon as men become sufficiently civilized to remember the results of trials. If they do remember, those faced with a problem can refer to what others have tried, that is, use the precedents of earlier trials. In a sense this is the beginning of education, and even preliterate primitive societies use this approach. For example, the teaching of routines and techniques for hunting or farming is simply a way to transmit the results of previous trials by word of mouth from one generation to the next. As more and more applications and trials are made, a third approach usually comes into being, *reference to authority*. By virtue of success, age, experience, or some combination of these, some persons become known and accepted as a good source of information about the consequence of the different trials. Again, even preliterate societies use this approach. However when preliterate societies use precedent and authority, because of the absence of a written record, the initial trials and their consequences are usually forgotten over the passage of time. Therefore, the solution tends to become routinized and even ritualized and so accepted without evidence or rationale. Under these conditions a particular solution may persist long after the conditions which produced it have changed. Moreover, once established, authorities have the opportunity to offer solutions on their own in the absence of evidence from trial and error. In fact, the historical evidence is that sufficiently well-established authorities can offer suggestions which do *not* work, and societies will search for explanations of the failure without questioning the authority. Moreover, the primitive authority is typically so reinforced by magic, ritual, and tradition that it becomes increasingly difficult for anyone to question him and survive. Only after both continued failure and continued inability to explain failure will the authority himself be questioned successfully.

LITERATURE AND ITS USE   As societies become literate, both precedent and the opinions of authority begin to be written down. This has the advantage for posterity of more permanently, and hopefully more accurately, preserving the actions taken and their consequence. It also makes the record available on a far-wider scale than before. With a written record, a person interested in a problem can now call on all of the authorities of the past, and all of the precedents of the past which have been recorded, before acting in his own situation.[1]

We noted in the preceding chapter the fact that knowledge of precedent- and authority-opinion through reference to the literature is the basic foundation of sound research planning. This use of the literature in research in education is in sharp contrast to the almost total avoidance of the literature by the practitioner in education. For example, how many teachers faced with a new and difficult problem will turn to the literature to see what others before him have done? The typical teacher will try some idea which comes to mind (trial and error) or ask some colleague down the hall what he has done in a similar situation (verbally transmitted precedent). In this use of precedent one could argue that the practicing teacher functions almost as if teachers were a preliterate primitive culture without a written record!

Unfortunately, in many areas of teaching practice, this is an accurate analogy of the situation. For example, in the Language Study discussed in Chapter 1, we noted our frustration in finding no written record of the methods used by the generations of teachers who had taught previous groups of non–English-speaking children, successfully or unsuccessfully. This is but one of many areas in which the rich history of successful teaching has been lost because it was never written down.

It is interesting to compare the use of the literature in what might be called the theoretical professions like physics, chemistry, biology, anthropology, sociology, or psychology with the practicing professions like medicine, law, nursing, or teaching. In the theoretical professions, the literature is the basis of all work, and a concept or finding has no status until it reaches the literature. Similarly, a new entrant to the profession, or an experienced professional faced with a new problem, will immediately turn to the literature for advice and guidance.

Among the practicing professions a similar pattern of use of the literature holds for law and somewhat less for medicine. We have noted how little the pattern holds for teaching, and much the same point could be made about nursing. Hopefully, educational research will be one route by which the educator will learn about the use of literature during problem resolution, and eventually come to both enrich and use it.

Research as an Approach to Problem Solving

The next stage, after precedent and authority become literature, is the development of research as a way of solving problems.

[1]Writing down the record, of course, can have the same disadvantage as authority in giving specific solutions a status and permanence long after conditions have changed sufficiently to require new and different solutions.

Research as an approach to problem solution has two basic characteristics which distinguish it from trial and error and reference to precedent or authority. First, it considers a wide variety of alternatives. Second, it uses criteria for identifying the alternative which produces the best solution. For example, consider Figure 3-1, in which five separate possible solutions are available for a problem. Let us assume that solutions number 2 and 4 do not work, that number 3 is adequate but barely so, number 1 is good, and number 5 is excellent and clearly the best. Assuming trial and error, we might try the solutions in a variety of orders, but let us assume, for purposes of this illustration, that we try them in this order: 2, 4, and 3. We would reject 2 and 4 because they do not work. Obviously we would stop at 3 for it does work. Moreover, 3 would become widely used, for when others asked our advice we would suggest solution 3. Thus, we would never get to the two best solutions through trial and error, precedent, or authority.

In contrast, the research approach would be to identify *all* possible solutions, identify relevant criteria on which to compare them, and then try each out under comparable conditions so that they could be compared in terms of the criteria. Through the research approach, then, if all five approaches were known, we would identify both solutions 1 and 5 and be in a position to adopt 5, the best solution.

RELATIVE ROLE OF TRIAL AND ERROR, PRECEDENT, AUTHORITY, AND RESEARCH

Although the four approaches to problem resolution represent different stages in the development of mankind, they each still have a place in educational practice today. The place of trial and error is the most limited. It is properly used in the instance when the practitioner must do something immediately, with no time available for consulting literature, doing research, or even consulting the authority next door. Given this set of circumstances, obviously he must do whatever comes to mind, and to persist in trying solutions until something works. However, he should not generalize from the trials and equate what he has done with research, concluding that he has found the best of all possible solutions.

Precedent and authority have somewhat wider roles today, for they are valid and useful sources of action when the current problem situation parallels previous such situations in all relevant details and the solution offered by precedent or the authority was itself derived from research. For research is clearly the fundamental source of new knowledge. Alone of the approaches it considers all relevant possible solutions, and thus, it

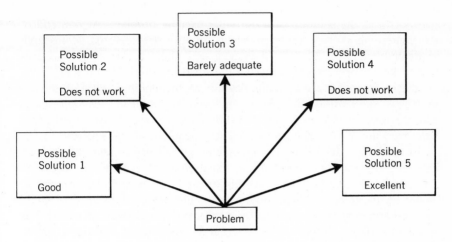

Figure 3-1   Conceptualization of research approach to problem resolution.

alone produces a solution which can be called "best" with any degree of confidence.

But there is a danger with research as well. It too can become fixed, routinized, and ritualized, and action can be taken on the basis of research findings that are no longer applicable. Therefore the same rule stated above for the use of precedent and trial and error applies to research: Results are applicable only so long as the situation in which they are to be applied parallels in all significant aspects the situation from which the research results were derived.

THE VARIED NATURE OF RESEARCH

There are many ways to conceptualize research, but here we shall consider three: (1) the distinction between pure and applied research; (2) the distinction between fundamental and action research; and (3) the characteristics of research done by students as part of their candidacy for a degree.

Pure versus Applied Research

Referring to the distinction between pure and applied research makes it sound as if we were dealing with a dichotomy, but in reality it is a continuum being treated as a dichotomy. The terms pure and applied research refer to the extent to which the research is directed toward, or has relevance for, the solution of a currently existing problem. At one end of the continuum is pure research which, in its extreme form, is research motivated solely by intellectual interest and directed toward the acquisition of knowledge for knowledge's sake. In this extreme form, there is no known or intended practical application of the findings, even if the research is successfully completed. In contrast, applied research in its extreme form would be directed toward solving a specific practical problem, even though no new knowledge was acquired in the process.

For example, if we were to conduct an historical research project designed to identify the familial and social circumstances which motivated Pestalozzi's interest in education, this research, if successfully completed, would be an interesting contribution to the history of education but would have no apparent practical effect or application whatsoever. It would thus be characterized as relatively pure research. In contrast, consider a survey being conducted in a town of 31,000 people on the attitude of parents of children between six and ten toward increased local taxes for school construction, with special reference to their reasons for and against such taxes. This research, if successfully completed, would have many practical applications for the local school board, but probably would add nothing to our fundamental knowledge of group opinion and attitude in general or on taxes for school building. Thus, it would be applied research in a rather extreme sense.

The physical scientist has long distinguished between pure or basic research and applied research. The distinction between them has become increasingly critical as larger and larger proportions of research support come from public funds. In fact, as this book is being written in the 1960s, the scientific community is deeply concerned about the Federal government's and the public's recognition of the importance of pure or basic research. For example, in a speech to the National Academy of Sciences in 1964, Leland Haworth, then director of the National Science Foundation, noted his perception of the public's orientation to the value of science:

> We . . . know the great cultural and intellectual value of science. But we are not good salesmen. The cultural argument, of course, competes with similar arguments for other fields of learning. And we would, in my opinion, be hard put to prove uniqueness for science in this sense. Large federal sums for culture's sake can only come when all culture is heavily supported. So for the present our best drawing card for financial support is the ultimate usefulness of science. I do not defend that this is so; I simply state it as a fact.[2]

What is relatively new is that parallel concern has emerged in the social sciences as well. In fact, at the 1967 convention of the American Educa-

[2]*Science,* vol. 156, no. 3775 (May 5, 1967), p. 625.

tional Research Association, Dr. Louis Bright, associate commissioner of research of the United States Office of Education declared his dissatisfaction with applied research in education.

"Basic research can be extremely valuable; development can be very valuable, but I'm beginning to be dubious about applied research," he said. Just a year ago, said Mr. Bright, he felt applied research had an important role in education.[3]

In the same year, quite the opposite point of view was voiced in a report[4] prepared for the House of Representatives Subcommittee on Research and Technical Programs. Too much federally sponsored research, the study said, has been divorced from issues actually confronting the citizen and society. Such research has been "too often trivial or irrelevant; usable, but not used; valuable, but buried in scholarly journals or government filing cabinets." Then referring to the pure–applied question the study criticizes federal agencies and university scholars as tending to be more interested in knowledge for its own sake than in the use of research to evaluate or improve programs directed to the nation's major social problems.[5]

Actually, research in education and other social disciplines in the years after 1950 had both "pure" and "applied" aspects, rather than representing either extreme. But tendencies could be seen, in that historical research was more often pure, survey more often applied, and experimental research most often a true hybrid with a "pure" intellectual or theoretical aspect and "applied" practical implications.

However, there is little doubt that in the social disciplines, the ultimate application of research has important philosophical implications. For example, one could raise the issue of whether or not any significant proportion of researchers should be encouraged or financed to study anything but social problems with immediately applicable results in a society and world with so many vast and unsolved problems involving human behavior and human relations. Specifically, in Education, we have such a multiplicity of critical problems and know so little of the basic processes of teaching and learning that we might ask how anyone can seriously consider devoting his time to studying Pestalozzi's motivations or the use of different writing styles in the work of Horace Mann.

There is no easy answer to these questions. We can properly defend the point of view that a society must decide how best to spend its financial and professional resources and that when there are critical immediate

[3]*The Chronicle of Higher Education,* vol. 1, no. 8 (March 8, 1967), p. 9.
[4]*The Use of Social Research in Federal Domestic Programs* (Washington: Government Printing Office, 1967).
[5]*The Chronicle of Higher Education,* vol. 1, no. 12 (May 3, 1967), p. 1.

problems to be solved, a sensible society will put its energies and funds to the solution of these problems. To a considerable extent, in the utilization of federal funds in financing research in the social disciplines, we have tended to follow this point of view. It has been easier to secure funds for the study of practical problems like developing or evaluating a particular method or machine than for the study of more theoretical problems like the processes in learning.

But it is also possible to argue from the other point of view, and begin by saying that it is impossible to know the ultimate application of any piece of research. For example, a researcher never knows at the beginning of a project what the actual findings will be or what someone else will do with those findings. Therefore, a researcher can never know for certain whether or not the results of a specific project will be of practical value. Moreover, we could go on and note that no one knows how the world will develop and change, and so needs for information are not static but also change. Therefore, at any one time, all one can say about a particular piece of information is that it has no apparent practical value *at that time*. A third consideration is that creative research often develops as a by-product of some other piece of research, that is, as the researcher starts out in search of an answer to a particular problem he may, along the way, find and go off on some intriguing tangent which no one anticipated. Fleming's discovery of the antibiotic properties of molds, which ultimately led to the development of penicillin, is a recent and profound example of this type of tangential discovery. Fourth, we can argue that no one knows how a researcher will develop, and so the researcher who initially works with esoteric pure problems may himself be stimulated by the experience in such ways that he eventually turns to problems with greater possibilities of application and so makes profound practical contributions as well.

These reasons are all hedging, of course. The direct answer is to say that knowledge for its own sake *is* a value, that a truly intellectual society *is* concerned with learning for the sake of learning, and so the acquisition of knowledge is an appropriate end in and of itself for research and study. President Johnson made this point strongly in 1967 in his letter to Congress accompanying the 16th annual report of the National Science Foundation:

> . . . perhaps most important, we intend to maintain this pool of basic knowledge and understanding because of the stimulus it provides to our young minds in this challenge of ideas. Knowledge, as we have learned from our rich experience, is not a laboratory curiosity. It is a critical tool for our national health, our national growth, and the sound education of all of us.[6]

[6]As quoted in *Science,* vol. 156, no. 3775 (May 5, 1967), p. 625.

For doctoral students, the distinction being made here is reflected in the differences between the two most frequently earned doctoral degrees, the Ph.D. and the Ed.D. The dissertation for the Doctor of Philosophy degree in most universities must have a "pure" aspect, in that it should be a test of, or a contribution to, theoretical knowledge in the area of the project. In contrast, the project for the Doctor of Education degree need not have this pure aspect, but typically can be oriented to the applied end of the continuum. Thus, in the early stage of selecting and specifying a problem, the student must take into account the degree toward which he is heading and the implications of this for the nature of his research.

Fundamental versus Action Research

The pair of terms *fundamental research* and *action research* are used to make a distinction between research which is motivated by a specific local problem and is designed only to resolve that problem in that setting (action research), as contrasted to research which is motivated by interest in a general problem and which is actually done in specific settings because they seem to offer appropriate sample sites for the populations and universes of interest (fundamental research). The consequence of this distinction is that with action research the findings are considered limited to the settings actually studied, whereas in fundamental research the findings are considered applicable to the populations and universes sampled.

The similarities and differences between fundamental and action research are summarized in Table 3-1. As can be seen, in the great majority of aspects, the two research approaches are identical. Both require precise definition of terms, recognition of assumptions and limitations, appropriate methodology, rigorous instrumentation and sound data-gathering techniques. For both, hypotheses are appropriate and desirable. The differences occur in five aspects, the focus and purpose of research, the group to whom the generalizations are applicable, the research situation, and the basis for determining whether or not a significant result occurred.

Fundamental research is conducted within a general problem area and its purpose is to add to knowledge about the problem area studied. The results should be applicable to the population (and ideally, the universe) sampled. To make this possible, the researcher must have sufficient cooperation so that he can manipulate the educational conditions to achieve the degree of control needed for research purposes. Given that degree of control, it is appropriate to use statistical significance as the primary criterion for determining if a significant result occurred.

In contrast, in action research, the focus is on the local situation and the

Table 3-1   Comparison of Action and Fundamental Research on Selected Aspects of Research Process

Aspect of Research	Need for or How Aspect Functions in Fundamental Research	Need for or How Aspect Functions in Action Research
Focus of research	Done within a problem area	Done to resolve a specific problem
Purpose of research	Acquisition of new knowledge about problem area	Acquisition of, or evaluation of, solution to problem
Group to which generalizations are intended to apply	Population and universe sampled	Group which furnished data
Hypotheses	Should be stated, reflecting researcher's expectation of outcome	Same as in fundamental
Assumptions	Must be identified and stated	Same as in fundamental
Limitations	Must be identified and considered in interpreting results	Same as in fundamental
Definitions	Must be stated precisely	Same as in fundamental
Research situation	Researcher must be free to manipulate educational conditions sufficiently to establish needed degree of control for research	Educational conditions must be fully established with research conducted within these pre-established conditions
Research approach	Must be appropriate to problem	Same as in fundamental
Data-collection methods	Must be appropriate to problem	Same as in fundamental
Data-collection instruments	Must be reliable, valid, appropriate, objective and sensitive, and should be ethical	Same as in fundamental

Descriptive statistics	Must reflect the nature and level of data	Same as in fundamental
Basis for deciding if significant result occurred	Inferential statistics and statistical significance	Observed data and practical significance

purpose is to solve a specific local problem or evaluate a tentative local solution. The results are intended to apply to that local situation and, at most, to future replications of the local situation. To assure relevance in that situation, the educational conditions must be established first, and the research planned or even adjusted to meet the educational conditions. In view of this, the observed data themselves, together with the criterion of practical significance, provide the only basis needed for deciding if a significant research result has been obtained.

Note that these are the only differences: the aim and generalizing intent and, therefore, the requirements for the research situation and the basis for decision making. In all other respects, we make the same demands of the action-research approach that we do of the fundamental research approach. Action research, if it is to be considered research, must have the same rigor as fundamental research in all of the foundational aspects of the research process. This is stressed because too often practitioners, encouraged by some journals, act as if action research had easier standards in many aspects of the research process like instrumentation and method. If standards at this stage are eased it ceases to be research and becomes some game or illusion, and can be the basis for seriously wrong conclusions and actions.

IMPLEMENTATION   The distinction between action and fundamental research is also of concern for educators and researchers since it relates to the implementation of research findings. We have already noted that in all the settings other than those which generated the actual data, the findings of action research cannot be generalized, whereas the findings of fundamental research can be generalized to the population and universe sampled.

But generalizing the findings is not implementation of the suggestions for program or policy which follow from the findings. The history of education provides ample evidence that members of a population or universe can read a piece of fundamental research, recognize that in research terms the findings apply to them, and proceed to act as they always have—ignoring the implications for action.

However, if we consider the specific settings in which the research was done, implementation of the findings is more likely to happen as a consequence of action research. Not only were the findings generated by that setting, but the well-planned action-research project involves *both* practitioner and researcher. The practitioner has seen the research at all stages, and if the research was successful he knows this and is generally willing to accept the research findings. Moreover, since he has been involved with the research process, he usually feels identified with the findings. Similarly, if these findings suggest change or support innovation the practitioner is identified with those changes and innovations rather than threatened by them.

In contrast, fundamental research typically is planned independently by a researcher. Once that plan is complete he then uses research principles to select a sample of settings in which he would like to do his research. But the research is his, the practitioner is there to function as directed, and is often seen as "the enemy" who can thwart the researcher by not functioning in accordance with the research needs. Therefore, the practitioner, even in those settings in which fundamental research has been done, typically sees it as an abstract and even threatening phenomenon. Rather than being identified with the project and the findings, he often is hostile to the project and resistive to the findings. Moreover, if the findings suggest change or innovation, he often sees these as casting aspersions upon his current functioning, and so feels betrayed by the research.

In the effort to combine the best of both possible worlds, the sequence of fundamental research followed by local demonstration has evolved. In this sequence, a fundamental research finding of sufficient importance is demonstrated through replication by the action-research model. It is hoped in this way the local practitioner will be more likely to accept and implement the finding generated through fundamental research.

Characteristics of Student Research

At a different level than the distinctions between pure and applied research, or between action and fundamental research, is the distinction between student and professional research. In Chapter 2, both similarities and differences were noted in comparing student and professional motivations, goals, interests, and experience. Here, in the final section of this chapter, we shall review the criteria for evaluating a potential research problem with the aim of establishing criteria for a student research problem. We shall consider six criteria: the significance of the problem, the researcher's interest in the problem, the scope of the problem, technical standards for research, feasibility of the project, and the originality of the research.

SIGNIFICANCE   The basic criterion for evaluating any potential research problem is its significance as a contribution to knowledge, or practice, or both. This is true of both professional and student research,[7] or perhaps it would be more accurate to say that this *should* be true of both professional and student research. Without repeating what was said in Chapter 2 about the stereotyped and banal nature of much of educational research, it is sufficient to note here that the educational researcher at all levels of preparation has left to other disciplines the most challenging and significant research areas. For example, it is the psychologist who studies the learning process and who has developed theories about how children learn, and who is concerned with research into motivation or development. It is the sociologist who has studied the school as an institution, or who has looked at the area of attitudes as related to schools. In recent years it has been the anthropologist who has moved into educational research to study the newly emerging problems of the schools as a separate culture or as the focus of cultural clash and conflict.

Without developing a monologue on this point, it is possible to note that other disciplines moved in because educational research was not sufficiently oriented to the study of the basic and significant problems connected with the teaching-learning process and with the school as a social institution. Otherwise much of this research would have been, and could have been, conducted by educational researchers with the representatives of other disciplines as consultants. The issue is important, because when a psychologist goes into a school to perform an experiment on learning he is primarily concerned with learning as a psychological process, not an educational one. Similarly, the anthropologist who studies a school boycott is studying it as an application of anthropological processes in a school setting. Neither their initial orientation, nor their ultimate interpretation, is primarily educational, and there is no reason why it should be. For this reason much of psychological, sociological, and anthropological research and thinking, although on topics of educational significance, has had little impact on the schools.

[7]The one exception to this statement is research conducted as partial fulfillment of the requirements of one specific course. Such a project belongs in the family of term papers, and should be evaluated in this light. Even if the term paper is for the increasingly common required research course on the master's level which has replaced the thesis, it is, nevertheless, *not* a thesis but a term paper. The main objective is student learning, and there is generally little expectation that the results will have professional significance or meaning. Thus in evaluating a potential research problem at this level, more concern should be placed on the learning the student will derive from the research than the usefulness of the results to the profession. Similarly, when research at this level is completed, it should be evaluated in this same context, not with the meaningfulness of the results, but rather with the quality of the attempt and the learning derived.

If research on these topics is to have actual impact on schools, then these areas of educational significance must be studied by persons whose primary orientation is to education. In short, until the educational researcher moves into the study of problems of educational significance, educational research will not have a more dramatic impact on the educational process. This is as true for the student as it is for the professional researcher.

SCOPE A second criterion for evaluating potential student research is the criterion of scope. Here student and professional researchers differ sharply, and it is the difference in scope which often becomes confused with the difference in the significance of the problem. The professional researcher, operating a funded project, should so design the project that its scope is sufficient to accommodate some reasonably definite conclusion[8] about the problem under study. His conclusion should not be the suggestion that the specific research problem he worked on needs further study, although he may legitimately offer suggestions for further research in the problem area. In contrast, the student operating under limitations of resources and time usually will have to limit the scope of his project to a smaller part of the problem area. Thus he usually will not produce a study with definitive results, and will have to suggest that corroborating studies are needed to make clear the ultimate significance of the results.

Thus while both professional and student should be working on significant problems, the scope of what the student attempts is legitimately narrow and specifically defined. Both, of course, face the same responsibility to provide a definitive answer to their research question, once it is stated.

INTEREST Closely allied to the criterion of significance is the criterion of the researcher's interest in the problem under study. It is this author's opinion that interest in the problem area and specific research problem is an absolute prerequisite for a meaningful piece of research. This holds true both for the student and professional researcher, but with greater strength for the student. The professional researcher, particularly the one who sees himself primarily as a technician, can do research to order. It will be technically sound, but will not have the spark of life which characterizes good research any more than the painting done to order, because a patron wanted "something orange to go over the couch," will have the spark of life which characterizes creative art. For the student who is often learning research as he does a project at the master's or doctoral level, doing research suggested by someone else is a lost opportu-

[8]Of course, there will be instances in which professional researchers will legitimately do limited studies of a pilot or exploratory nature.

nity for significant learning. There are few activities in which the student will engage at any point in an educational program as time-consuming and personally involving as a research project. If the problem is one in which the student has no particular interest, the project itself becomes a tedious affair. Completing it all becomes doubtful, and completing it with any significant outcome becomes even more doubtful.

If, on the other hand, the student is interested in what he is doing, intrigued by the area under study, and concerned and curious about the outcomes of the specific project, then the research enterprise can be a fascinating and worthwhile educational experience. The project is likely to make a significant contribution, and the requirements for the degree of the program will be partially fulfilled.

One further specific should be considered here. Often students will discuss a research idea or interest with a faculty member who shares that interest. This is both a desirable and helpful step in developing the research. It has long been common practice on the doctoral level and is becoming increasingly widespread on the master's and bachelor's level. One danger in the practice is that the faculty member, either subtly or directly, steers the development of the idea in terms of his own interests, rather than serving as a resource person for the student to use in developing the idea in terms of his, the student's, interests. When student and faculty interests are identical, there is no problem. When they are not, there may be a problem. The student may be unaware of what is happening, other than to feel a slowly but steadily diminishing interest in the research and a steadily diminishing identification with it. Or—and this may be even worse—he may be aware of what is happening but feel that it is wiser to go along and do the research as the faculty member seems to wish it done. The author is not unaware of the nature of pressure sometimes exerted on students to do research which is of particular interest to specific faculty members, but personal experience has convinced him of two things. First, students who do research which only the faculty advisor wants done generally do uninspired research. Second, a student who knows what he wants to do, and why he wants to do it, can successfully defend *his* conception of a research proposal.

Interaction of Significance, Scope, and Interest

The three criteria of significance, scope, and interest often interact for student research. The interaction comes as the problem area is narrowed down into the specific research problem to be studied. The interaction of these criteria should be recognized by the student for, as was noted before, the student will have more narrowing to do as he is concerned with problems of more limited scope. The dual criteria of significance and interest provide a sensible basis for the delimiting of the problem area.

Let us assume that in the planning stage of the Language Study it became clear that doing the study at more than one grade level was beyond the resources available. The researcher then would have to face the question of what grade level to study, first considering the significance of doing the study at different grade levels. As we noted in the first chapter, in the early elementary grades there was general agreement that the problem was not severe, because all children were language learners in a sense. One significant grade level would be the middle-elementary grades, for it is here that children begin serious work in the content areas, and language barriers become barriers to content learning as well. A second grade level of significance would be the early secondary grades, where equal concern with and even broader range of content make language fluency critical, and where school drop-out becomes a serious concern. Having identified two grade levels of educational significance, the researcher could now use his own interests in elementary or secondary education to determine the focus of his specific project.

TECHNICAL STANDARDS   Another criterion of student research to consider is the standard for the technical aspects of the research process. This is particularly critical in the areas of sampling and characteristics of data-gathering instruments. The professional researcher is expected to sample well, using the principles of stratification and random selection so that his findings can be considered unbiased and generalized to relevant populations. The student is generally permitted to use deliberately selected samples to which he has access, and so the generalizability of his findings is more limited. In terms of this criterion, professional research parallels fundamental research and student research parallels action research.

A similar easing of demands and standards characterizes student research for instrument characteristics like reliability and validity. Because the process of instrument development is time-consuming and often demands special technical skills, some institutions permit and even encourage students to use existing instruments for data-collection purposes even if they are not 100 percent relevant. Furthermore, where students do develop their own instruments for a project, the standards for adequate reliability and validity are often eased. It is easy to understand why this happens, but nevertheless impossible to accept and encourage. The data produced by a research project can be no better than the instruments used to produce those data, and if the instruments are irrelevant, unreliable, or not valid, then the data are impossible to evaluate and, even worse, may lead to completely erroneous and misleading interpretations.

What is even more unfortunate is that students can legitimately claim that when they ask for lenient standards for evaluating the quality of their data-collecting instruments, they are only seeking privileges educational research now extends to the professional researcher. For, as this book is written in the late 1960s, we must admit that we have not demanded that the professional researcher in education meet high standards of instrument quality. We have financed research which is based on the use of instruments of demonstrated insensitivity and doubtful reliability and validity, or which is based on new instruments without adequate provision for first demonstrating reliability and validity. As long as we continue to be content with low standards for the professional researcher in this area, it is difficult to expect a dramatic upgrading of student research.

What we can expect with student research, and what should be encouraged far more than it is, is the recognition that a creative effort in the area of instrument development, in and of itself, may be the most productive project a student can undertake in a particular problem area. Graduate faculties could move research in education forward if they would consistently support this idea. If a student is stymied in working on a particular problem because of instrument limitations, it is far more sensible to encourage the student to devote his time, energies, and abilities to the effort of trying and evaluating some new approach to instrumentation in the problem area than it is to sympathetically accept his use of the instrument with recognized inadequacies. This author firmly believes that if the efforts which graduate students have devoted in the past 15 years to studies doomed from their beginnings by inadequate instrumentation had been devoted instead to the instrumentation problem itself, we would be far better able today to conduct studies of educational significance.

FEASIBILITY   Cutting across many of the criteria already discussed is the criterion of feasibility of the project. It is worth considering separately, because many students magnify this criterion to the point of its becoming the major one they consider. The feasibility criterion has different meanings in the context of selecting a problem and in the context of aspects of the research process like instrument development, data collection, and data analysis.

In terms of problem selection, it is the author's judgment that one of the reasons we have not progressed further in research in education and the social sciences is that the criterion of feasibility has dominated our evaluation of research problems far out of proportion to its relative importance. In part, this reflects the fact that so much of the research[9] has been done

---

[9]In Chapter 2 it was noted that the process whereby we fund educational research places a similar constraint on the professional researcher as well. The need to submit a fully developed proposal with all stages thoroughly detailed forces the professional researcher to seek funds for problems sufficiently well defined for him to be able to state all of these details in advance.

by doctoral candidates who feel the tremendous pressure to select a "do-able" problem, that is, a problem that will certainly be completed successfully.

It is appropriate to reiterate here what was stated early in Chapter 2, that there is a place, and a great empty place, in educational research for the productive failure. Selecting a problem that will be completed successfully does not mean that we must select one which is so stereotyped and predictable that the nature and direction of the outcome is guaranteed. It means only that we select one from which we can learn something useful no matter how the results come out.

The author is not so naive as to suggest that doctoral students ignore these real considerations of feasibility and go off onto ephemeral research problems. That is not really the choice. The preceding discussion indicates that a professionally and intellectually honest way to implement the feasibility criterion in problem selection is to limit the scope of the project attempted, while retaining the criteria of significance and interest. In other words, the student should identify the problem area on the basis of the significance of research in that area and his own interest in doing that research. Once an area of significance and interest has been identified the student should then sketch out a project of sufficiently limited scope so that it is feasible for him to complete it within the limits of his time, resources, and skills.

Applying the feasibility criterion to the later stages of the research process is a more complex matter. Throughout the later chapters in this book, it will become clear that different approaches, methods, and techniques place quite different demands upon the researcher's time, resources, and skills. No general advice can be given which will have more meaning to different students than to remind them that the primary criterion is the significance of the research. Therefore while feasibility must realistically be considered in determining how a specific project will be studied, it cannot be the only, or the prime, consideration. It is not valid to ignore the best way of studying a problem because that way involves a data-gathering method with which the student is unfamiliar or will provide data difficult to analyze. In making decisions at this stage, the student and faculty adviser must work together closely so that an intellectually honest and defendable plan is developed which the student can complete within the limits he faces.

A final word on feasibility concerns the time it requires to prepare a research report. If there is error in research planning common to students and professionals, it is underestimating how long it takes to prepare a sound and complete research report which reads well. We will have much to say on this subject in the chapter devoted to research writing, but here, as we discuss feasibility, we want to add this caution: In considering how much time will be required for completing a project, be overly generous in allocating time for report writing. Allocate time for editing and revision, and then double this overly generous allotment!

ORIGINALITY   If research is being conducted in partial fulfillment of the requirements for a degree, an additional criterion must be considered: the extent to which the initiating idea is an *original contribution.*

This concept, that the thesis or dissertation be an original contribution, has come to mean different things to different institutions, and even to different departments within the same institution. In its historic and most rigorous sense it means that the project must be unique, that is, must be something that has not been done before. It must look at some new aspect of a problem, seek to clarify an ambiguous point of theory, seek to test some new interpretation of data from other studies. It must be original as defined in Webster: "not copied, imitated, reproduced or translated; underived; not dependent or secondary; new, firsthand. . . ."[10]

The second and somewhat less rigorous concept of "original" is that it does not mean that the problem need never have been studied before, or even that it has never been studied in the way that we intend to do it. Rather it means that we are adding some element to the study of the problem, and so our study, while not unique, should nevertheless make an original contribution to knowledge. By this perception of original, we may extend research someone else has begun by replicating it with a different (but relevant) group of subjects or with different experimental conditions.

The third perception places an even heavier emphasis upon "contribution" than upon "original." In this view, a study may make an original *contribution* even if it is a direct replication of an earlier study. This would be true if a long time has elapsed since the study was first done and there is legitimate relevance in raising a question as to whether the findings still hold. It may also apply to current work, provided there is a legitimate professional reason for replication such as the need for further data on the problem or questions about the validity of the original findings. In fact, one of the key features which distinguishes research in the social sciences from research in the physical sciences is the relative lack of replication. Granting all of the difficulties involved in replicating research in which people are involved, there are, nevertheless, many more opportunities for fruitful replication of research than are currently being realized.

A simple estimate of whether or not any single piece of research makes

---

[10]*Webster's New International Dictionary.* Second Edition (Springfield, Mass.: G. & C. Merriam Company, 1961), p. 1721.

an original contribution can be obtained by asking: "If it is successfully completed, will we know anything significant that we do not know now?" If the answer is yes, then the piece of research can be considered an original contribution. If no, we have what can be called "so what" research—it has been conducted and completed, but so what? This is bitter truth to face after the investment of time, energy, and self that research demands. It can be avoided if these questions about value are asked early in the development of the problem, before a commitment has been made to a project and before time and effort are heavily invested.

The criterion of originality characterizes all research projects that are acceptable for doctoral dissertations whether they be for Ed.D. or Ph.D. degrees. As stated previously, projects for the Ph.D. generally must meet an additional criterion of making a contribution to theoretical knowledge. When the project originates from a practical situation or interest, the theoretical aspect is often applied as an afterthought. While this is often intellectually ingenious, these studies seldom make important theoretical contributions. This suggests that candidates for the Ph.D. degree should make every effort to develop their problems from theory rather than from everyday practice or their own curiosity. Their study will be the stronger for it.

SUMMARY

The preceding discussion noted some instances in which student and professional research differ. Student research is more often limited in scope, conducted with deliberately selected samples, and concerned with the realistic demands upon the student to make an original contribution within the period of his candidacy. However, it was also noted that both student and professional research share basic characteristics. They are both done on problems of educational significance in which the researcher is genuinely interested, using instruments and procedures technically sound in terms of reliability and validity. Otherwise the enterprise, whether conducted by a student or a professional researcher, becomes an academic exercise unworthy of being considered research.

PART II

Foundations
of Research Planning

Chapter 4

REVIEWING THE LITERATURE

Every research project should be based on all of the relevant thinking and research that has preceded it. When completed, it becomes part of the accumulated knowledge in the field and so contributes to the thinking and research that follow. For any specific project to occupy this place in the development of a discipline, the researcher must be thoroughly familiar with both previous theory and research. To assure this familiarity, every research project, whether in the social or physical sciences, has as one of its early stages a review of the theoretical and research literature.

In survey and experimental research, the review of the literature serves a variety of background functions preparatory to the actual collection of data. In these research approaches, the literature is reviewed to create the context from the past for the new study to be conducted with new subjects and newly obtained data. In the historical approach, however, we never leave the past and, in a sense, the review of the literature is the method of data collection if "literature" is used in the broadest possible sense. In this sense the sources used are the "subjects" of the research and the material reviewed, the "data." Therefore, the primary function of the review of the literature in historical research is to provide the research data.

This function means that the very words "review" and "literature" have quite different meanings in the historical approach. In fact, it might be argued that the meanings are so different that these words do not apply. In historical research, the researcher does much more than review already published material—he seeks to discover new information never before reported, or seeks to integrate material never before considered together, or to put material into a context in which it has never been before. Since the concept and process implied in the term "review of the literature" have such different meanings in historical as compared to survey and experimental research, they are best considered separately. This process of historical research will be considered in Chapter 14 in its proper place as a research approach. In this chapter, we shall consider the review of the literature in survey and experimental research, considering first the nature of a review, then the functions of the review, and, finally, how it is done.

THE NATURE OF THE REVIEW OF THE LITERATURE IN SURVEY AND EXPERIMENTAL RESEARCH

Through a process of integration of past research and thinking with current research and thinking, we move knowledge forward. For this process to function successfully, each researcher must know the past so that he can design research to build on what is already known and study what is not. There are times when researchers lack this knowledge. We see research being done on matters which have been demonstrated sufficiently so as not to need further replication. When this is done the research becomes an academic exercise of little interest or consequence to the discipline involved. We also see research into the unknown which does not build on the known. In a sense, this is the greater professional loss. Needless repetition is only a waste of the researcher's time, but new research which is unconnected to previous thinking and research is a lost opportunity to move knowledge forward. When new research is not based on a thorough review of the literature, it becomes an isolated entity bearing at best accidental relevance to what has gone before. When it *is* based on the literature, we can hope for cohesive and integrated approaches to our problems and for resolution and solution of them through research.

Reviewing the literature has two phases. The first phase involves identifying all the relevant published material in the problem area and reading that part of it with which we are not thoroughly familiar. As we read what others have done and/or thought about the problem area, we gradually develop the foundation of ideas and results on which our own study will be built. The second phase of the review of the literature involves writing this foundation of ideas into a section of the research report.[1] This section includes summaries of the major points of view in the field and the major research findings relevant to the current study, and the researcher's critical analysis of both previous thinking and research. This section on the literature provides the reader with the context needed to understand the study and so appears early in the research report, generally immediately after the introductory statement.

A distinction must be made between the literature that is reviewed, that

---

[1]Many universities require the doctoral student to complete the review of literature early enough to include it in his write-up in the outline for a thesis or dissertation.

is, read by the researcher, and that which is discussed in the study itself, that is, referred to in the section or chapter headed "Review of the Literature." The amount that any one researcher needs to read on any one problem is determined by the unique combination of the problem, which delimits the total amount of knowledge needed, and how familiar the researcher may be with none, some, or even all of that knowledge. The section in the research report discussing the literature is a different matter. This section is for the joint benefit of the researcher *and* reader. For the researcher, it establishes the framework or background in the field and thus provides the setting in which he reports the new study. For the reader, the section provides a summary of the thinking and research necessary for him to understand the study. It also gives the reader a good estimate of the researcher's scholarliness. One basis for this estimate is the researcher's ability to distinguish the relevant from the irrelevant. For this chapter is not written to provide other researchers with an annotated bibliography, nor to summarize all of the field for the reader. There are separate articles which do nothing other than review literature, and so serve these functions. The review of the literature in a project is study-bound. This means that the selection of what is to be reviewed in the project is made in terms of what is relevant and necessary to understand the *present* study. Much that was background for the researcher, but is not needed to understand the present study, can and should be eliminated from the section of the report reviewing the literature.

How important this stage will be in the development of the researcher's thinking depends, of course, on the richness of the literature. There are problem areas in education, psychology, and sociology, and in all branches of knowledge in both the social and physical sciences in which there is little literature. The researcher's obligation is to search the literature, find what exists, and review it. He is not responsible for previous generations' disinterest or neglect of a problem area, and so if his search yields little, he is entitled to say this. In this case, the written section will simply be a brief statement, identifying the extent of the search, naming the sources consulted, and reporting how little was found.

But let us assume that there *is* a literature in the problem area. Then the amount of time devoted to this stage of the research depends upon how well the researcher knows the problem area and literature. If he knows the area well and has kept his knowledge current, then he will need only a once-over-lightly review to be certain that he is aware of the latest research and thinking. In all other instances, where a researcher has less than complete current knowledge, a thorough review of the literature is needed, ranging to the deep and extensive review needed by the researcher working in a problem area new to him.

In this chapter we shall refer to two different kinds of literature: what we shall call *research literature* and what we shall call the *conceptual literature*. The term research literature is used to refer to published reports of research studies which present data. All other published material will be referred to as the conceptual literature. Thus, this term includes texts, books, or articles giving opinions, reports of experiences, presentation of theory—any piece of published material whose primary function is something other than the presentation of research data.

Admittedly, this is a gross and all-inclusive category which encompasses a wide range of material. The material is combined, however, because it is usually data-free, and so does not have the same meaning as the research literature for the researcher developing a problem or project statement. This is not to imply that one type of literature is more important than the other, but only that they serve different purposes.

THE FUNCTIONS OF THE REVIEW OF LITERATURE

In previous chapters, a variety of purposes were noted for the review of the literature. In this chapter, these purposes will be discussed according to five major functions of providing: (1) the conceptual frame of reference for the contemplated research; (2) an understanding of the status of research in the problem area; (3) clues to the research approach, method, instrumentation, and data analysis; (4) an estimate of the probability of success of the contemplated research and the significance or usefulness of the findings; and, assuming the decision is made to continue, (5) specific information needed to state the definitions, assumptions, limitations, and hypotheses of the research.

Conceptual Frame of Reference

The first function, providing the conceptual framework of the research, involves both the research and conceptual literature, but primarily the latter. If the contemplated research is to contribute to the relevant discipline in the way discussed at the beginning of this chapter, then the researcher must know and understand that discipline. The most direct way of doing this is to read the basic writings in the field, as well as the recent writings of key thinkers. The researcher must feel fully satisfied when he has completed this phase of his review that he is aware of all the points of view in the field, and particularly that he has devoted himself diligently to learning about the points of view which differ from or are opposite to his own. Furthermore, in the section of the written research report in which this literature is reviewed, the researcher must convince the reader that he has devoted equal attention and care to reviewing and understanding the literature that differed from his own point of view.

This does not mean that the researcher cannot have and express a point of view. It does mean that, in his presentation of the literature, he will make a careful distinction between his summaries of the thinking of others and his critical analysis of that thinking. All points of view relevant to the research problem should be presented as strongly as the most devoted proponent of that point of view would wish. After this, the researcher is free to, and certainly should, present his own reaction and critique.

For the review of the literature to serve this first function, and provide a sound conceptual framework, the researcher must saturate himself in the basic writings in the problem area until such time as he feels that he is conversant with all of the ramifications of all points of view. He should feel that, in a debate, he could represent any point of view fully, in the sense that he has come to understand the arguments for that point of view, even if he does not accept them.

Status of Research

The second function of the review of the literature is to provide an understanding of the status of research in the field. This comes from reviewing the research literature. This phase of the review actually has several specific subfunctions, which can be delineated in terms of the question words, *what, when, where, who,* and *how.* These five words provide basic information needed for intelligent planning of a piece of research which will utilize and build on the successful experiences of previous researchers, profit from their unsuccessful experiences, and avoid unnecessary repetition of errors, both of omission and commission.

First, through his review of the research literature, the researcher learns *what* research has already been undertaken and completed in the problem area, and the results that this research has already achieved. If the researcher has any questions as to whether or not his contemplated research will be an original contribution to the field, then identifying what has been studied in his problem area through a review of the research literature will be one of the first things he will do. If he is planning a doctoral dissertation, which must be an original contribution, he will want to learn about research in progress as well as completed research. In this way he will be protected against the unhappy eventuality of research appearing and pre-empting the problem while he is at some intermediate point in his own project.

Learning about research in progress is difficult, time-consuming, and frustrating, in the sense that no matter how thorough our search there is the ever-present feeling that someone, somewhere, is doing our study and is one step ahead of us. While we cannot eliminate the feeling, we can minimize the probability that this is so. Within a specific university, of course, there will be a central office where approved thesis or dissertation topics are listed. Since other universities have similar central offices, check them as well. Rather than attempting the imposing and unnecessary task of checking with all universities, check with those at which work in your problem area has been done. In fact, as one by-product of our review of the literature, we should cumulate a list of places and people recurring frequently in the conceptual and research literature. In addition to writing to these places, write directly to these people. Typically, these are faculty members at a college or university, and most will respond to a letter explaining contemplated research and asking if they or any of their students or associates are at present doing such research.

In addition to these personal inquiries, there are formal sources to consult. Phi Delta Kappa publishes a listing of research in progress,[2] and the *Bibliographic Index*[3] occasionally also lists research in progress. The Department of Health, Education and Welfare publishes an index of the research it is supporting.[4] This index also lists the principal investigators of each project, providing another list of people to whom we could write. Some of the psychological journals now publish sections listing articles and research reports which they have received and plan to publish in the future, which provides as much as a two-year preview of what is coming in these journals. Finally, your own committee should be able to provide names of researchers with whom to verify the uniqueness of your own project.

By diligent use of all of these sources it is possible to obtain a feeling for what research is now underway or contemplated but not reported in the problem area. From this we should be able to make a reasonably sound prediction as to the probability of our own study being, and remaining, an original contribution when it is finally completed.

The other aspect of *what*, learning the results of previous research, is the best-known purpose of reviewing the literature. As we shall see, we are interested in learning more about previous research than the results, but this does not diminish our interest in them. Learning results means becoming aware of the specific findings of each study, but also of gradually gaining an overview of the total picture of research results within the

[2]Research Studies in Education (1953–   ) (Bloomington, Ind.: Phi Delta Kappa, International Office).
[3]*Bibliographic Index* (New York: The H. W. Wilson Company).
[4]*Research Grants Index*. United States Department of Health, Education and Welfare (Washington, D.C.: Government Printing Office).

problem area. This means identifying whether the area is one in which there are relatively consistent generalizations which can be made, supported by the majority of the studies, as opposed to an area in which the research studies are inconclusive or even contradictory.

This latter condition, an area with inconclusive and/or contradictory results, is a particularly fruitful intellectual challenge. After intensive review of the conceptual and research literature in such an area, a researcher may believe that he has an explanation for the inconsistencies. An insight like this is an exciting basis upon which to design a research project. For example, a colleague recently felt that he had such an insight into some of the inconclusive results in studies of the learning consequences of programmed instructional material. His insight was that the previous research was not selective in its consideration of the learner, specifically ignoring the possibility that there were different styles of learning. If so, different learners might be receptive to different types of programmed materials. This insight is testable, and so he designed a research project in which he would first identify the learning styles of a group of students, and then study their functioning with different types of programmed materials.

Notice that this study will make a useful professional contribution no matter how the results come out. If they are positive and support his insight, then he has provided a possible explanation of the previous inconsistency. If the results are negative and do not support his insight, then we have learned that learning style is not the missing key to reconciling the results in this problem area.

In addition to learning *what* has been done, the researcher seeks to identify *when* the research has been done, specifically how current research in the problem area is. Research often runs in cycles, and thus there are periods of time in which a great deal of research is done in a problem area, then interests change, and there is an hiatus of years in which little or nothing is done. Learning *when* previous research has been conducted has several meanings for the researcher. First, it will determine how far back chronologically his review of the literature will go. When there is a wealth of recent research in the problem area, he will go further back in time only to establish the historical basis of the research. The relevant parallel findings will be the recent ones. When there has been a recent lack of interest in the field, he will need to go further back until he comes upon the research. Of course, in this instance the further back he goes the more acute the problem of diminished relevance of the previous findings. On occasion, he must go back so far as to wonder if the findings are relevant at all. When this happens, this opens the possibility of replicating previous research. *Replication* is sensible when a research study has provided the basis of some current belief, or the research foundation of some current practice, but so much time has elapsed or conditions have changed so much that there is reason to doubt that the findings still hold true. When this happens, then a legitimate research project is to replicate the earlier one: that is, to redo it as exactly as possible, to see if the same findings will be obtained again and the same conclusions drawn.

With *what* and *when* considered, let us consider the importance of *where*, that is, identifying the geographic areas in which the previous research has been completed. The major categories within this classification are national, regional, and degree of urbanization. Typically, educational research reviewed by students in the United States is limited nationally, in that it consists of previous research done in this country. Foreign research—such as the work of the Swiss psychologist, Piaget, in the area of the development of thinking in children—is ignored unless it is basic to an area. Fortunately, this national limitation is diminishing and in the future will undoubtedly diminish further. The researcher concerned with the Phonics Study, like all current and future researchers in methods of teaching reading, will have to read and review Downey and Pitman's research in England with the Initial Teaching Alphabet. Similarly, those concerned with research in the quality of schools and schooling will have to consider Robert Thorndike's research in the 1960s on comparative educational achievement in several countries.

The importance of the second category, region, depends on the problem area. For some areas, primarily those in educational psychology, studying human characteristics and basic behavior, region would seem irrelevant. For example, in research in the learning process, it seems sensible to ignore region of the country, and, instead, to accept the assumption that people learn through the same psychological processes in Idaho as they do in Georgia. However, when the research moves into areas involving attitude, opinion, likes and dislikes, achievement, curriculum, staffing patterns, administrative policy or educational history, despite the large common areas, it is not possible to assume that the regions of the United States present relatively the same research settings. They differ in such varied areas as the origin and tradition of the schools and, reflecting climatic and economic differences, in the length of the school semester, as well as in the months which children spend in school. They differ also in levels of achievement, as reflected in the different regional standards of national competitive examinations like the Merit Scholarship Examination. For this reason, when reviewing research in these areas, the researcher will take careful note of the regions of the country in which the previous research has been conducted. Then he will have to decide whether or not this research applies to the region of his own research and use it accordingly.

It is important to recognize that research of national scope is now feasible to a much greater extent than was possible only a few years ago. This is true both because of increased knowledge and facilities for obtaining research data from a broad geographic area and because of increased facilities for processing masses of data quickly and inexpensively. The establishment of the National Opinion Research Center in Chicago in 1962 makes available a resource for data gathering on a national basis. Similarly, the establishment at many colleges and universities of computer centers utilizing the latest electronic computing methods makes it possible for students and faculty to consider mass-data collection for their research, for these computers can process mass data in less time and at less expense than previously required to process limited amounts of data by hand or desk calculator.

Much the same set of arguments can be applied to the third category, degree of urbanization. This, like region, is a characteristic whose importance depends upon the problem area. The degree of urbanization of the community in which research is done may vary from rural communities at one extreme to large metropolitan centers at the other extreme. The most cursory review of the educational literature will indicate that the preponderance of research in every problem area has been done in metropolitan settings. Thus, the researcher designing a project to be conducted in metropolitan centers will find similar research settings in the literature; the researcher designing a project with a rural setting will find little. This preoccupation with the urban setting can be seen in process as this book is being written. Perhaps the most discussed area at present is the education of the culturally disadvantaged child. Reading the literature one would assume that culturally disadvantaged children live only in urban centers. In fact, the educational problems they pose have a much longer history in rural settings.

Ironically, the shift in the 1950s of large numbers of culturally disadvantaged children into metropolitan school systems has made large sections of the literature obsolete even to the researcher interested in metropolitan schools. If his population consists of metropolitan schools with large proportions of disadvantaged children, the researcher will find little of relevance even in the literature which *was* similar in degree of urbanization, that is, which was also concerned with metropolitan schools.

The solution to this, of course, is to consider not only where previous research was conducted, but *who* was studied. This means identifying the universes and populations which have previously been studied, how they were sampled, and the extent of the sampling. Here the researcher is interested in the broad general levels of universes studied, as well as in the specific populations sampled. For instance, the researcher in education will seek to determine how much of the research in the problem area involves pupils, teachers, parents, administrators, or the lay public. He will also want to identify which groups of pupils: elementary or secondary? first graders, second, or third? Finally, he will want to note the size of the samples used. Has the research in the problem area typically used small samples or large samples? Is there a study which had an unusually broad population and substantial sample size? To what extent have populations been stratified on variables like socioeconomic background, intelligence, sex, interest, and achievement in the problem area? Finally, if he has even tentatively identified his own population, he will be interested specifically in the extent to which there has been previous research on that population.

One purpose of this consideration of the *who* of previous research is to enable the researcher to make a judgment as to the relevance of a universe and population for his own research. Theoretically, we could advise students not to plan to study those universes or populations which have already been sufficiently studied in the problem area, either at the general or specific level. In reality, with the current status of research in most problem areas in education and the social disciplines, this is not a difficulty as there are no problem areas in which populations have been sufficiently studied.

Research Approach, Method, Instrumentation, and Data Analysis

The last of the question words to be considered in the review of the literature is *how*. In the context of this discussion, this word refers to identifying what has and has not been tried in regard to research approaches, and research methods, and what already exists in terms of data-gathering instruments. This aspect of the review will serve the third function of providing clues to methodology and instrumentation. Specifically, the researcher will want to learn the extent to which previous research in the problem area has utilized the historical, survey, or experimental approaches, because this will help guide his own choice of research approach. For this same reason, he will want to identify the research methods which have been used so that experience with these can help him select his own. Finally, he seeks to become familiar with the data-gathering instruments which have been used so that if an already existing instrument is appropriate, it can be used intact or adapted for his own research.[5]

For this consideration of the *how* of previous research, the researcher

---

[5]Whether we are adapting or adopting an existing instrument we must obtain the permission of the individual or company who developed the instrument.

should be as interested in identifying the rationale for the selection of a particular approach, method, or instrument as he is the approach, method, or instrument itself. Furthermore, he should also be interested in what alternative approaches, methods, and instruments were considered and/or tried out and why these were rejected. Unfortunately, the rationale for the selection of research approach, method, and instrument, and the thinking that motivated the rejection of alternatives, is generally omitted from the research literature in every branch of the social sciences. Therefore, while we are alerted to the importance of learning previous research thinking, realistically we must not expect to find it stated very often.

In addition to learning rationales for method as fully as possible, to completely serve the third function of the review of literature, providing clues to methodology and instrumentation, the researcher should know what methods and techniques have been used in his problem area and the success achieved with each. Depending on his purpose in doing research he may decide to use a technique which has been shown to function successfully, or to try one which has not been used before in the problem area. He would not try techniques which have been *unsuccessful* unless he had specific reasons to believe that his use of the method was significantly different from previous attempts.

In the third function of the review of literature, the review of instruments parallels the review of techniques in that here, too, the researcher is seeking to learn what has worked and what has not. If he is fortunate enough to discover a successful instrument which he can use this is preferable to developing a new instrument for two reasons: It establishes continuity between the new research and the previous research and it spares the researcher the time-consuming and difficult job of instrument development. Even finding an instrument which can be adapted to the needs of research is a tremendous advantage.

Again, we must put in a realistic qualification. Most journals which report research do not print the actual instruments. Often these do appear in the appendix of the complete research report or thesis or dissertation on which many journal articles are based, or else can be obtained directly from the author of the article. The simplest procedure is usually to contact the author (or senior author, if more than one) directly, since in any event he will have to be contacted for permission to use or adapt any instruments he has developed.

It is important to distinguish between what are generally considered standardized instruments and those specially developed for some previous research project. Standardized instruments are those which have been used widely enough for normative data to be available. The process of standardizing instruments also provides data on the reliability, and sometimes on the validity, of the instrument. The availability of these three kinds of data—norms, estimates of reliability, and estimates of validity—make standardized instruments attractive to researchers, particularly to students doing research. These attractions are quite real. Using an instrument with norms and established reliability does have great advantages when these data have been obtained from samples from the same universe as we plan to study. For example, evaluative research becomes possible, using the norms as criteria. Even more of an advantage is the probability that we will be able to quote the existing reliability and validity data and not need obtain our own.

However, these advantages are not sufficient to justify the use of an instrument in situations where it does not fully apply, for example, with samples of a universe other than the one for which the instrument was intended. Where this happens most often in educational research is in using instruments developed for one age-group (adults) with a different age-group (early adolescents) or switching the instrument from one sociocultural group (the stable urban middle class) to another (the transient rural lower class). Another instance where the availability of normative data is not enough of an advantage to use an instrument is when the literature indicates that, although standardized data are available, the previous research provides little hope that the instrument will produce meaningful data. Far too often in the literature we find studies which use standardized instruments in instances where it was obvious they would not function.

The discussion above on these first three functions of the review of the literature for survey and experimental research should also imply what it is that the researcher is seeking as he reads. For the first, or overview function, he is concerned with identifying each point of view and supporting arguments and evidence for that point of view. This is a review of ideas and concepts, no matter how those concepts came into being. For the second function, the status of research, he will do a much more structured and specific review, concerned with identifying what was studied, the outcomes of each study, how the outcome of the several separate studies relate to each other, who was studied and where, and when the research was done. For the third function, clues to methodology and instrumentation, he is concerned with how the previous research was done and why it was done the way it was.

In a sense, it is the combination of these first functions which yield the fourth and fifth functions of the review of the literature: (4) the estimate of the success and significance of the contemplated research and, if the decision is to continue, (5) the definitions, assumptions, limitations, and hypotheses of the new project.

Probability of Success and Significance of Findings

With the full body of the previous research literature reviewed, the researcher is in a position to evaluate the success which others have had doing research in the problem area and the usefulness of their findings. If others have been successful, and the findings useful, then the prognosis for his own research is good, and the decision to continue on with the research is clear and simple to make. However, if others have been unsuccessful and produced inconclusive research or research of little value, then the researcher has a more difficult decision to make. He must ask himself whether there are specific reasons to believe that he can succeed where all others have failed. For the literature truly to serve this function of providing an estimate of the success potential of the contemplated research, the researcher must be willing to make the negative decisions to abandon or alter the project, as well as the positive ones to continue on as intended. All too often in research, only lip service is paid to this function. Researchers do review the literature and do seek to determine the success potential of their contemplated research, but never truly entertain the possibility of altering or abandoning their plan. If no one has ever succeeded in doing what they plan, they argue that they may be the first. This author would say more power to them, and would be the first to cheer their courage *provided* it was based on something more substantial than hope.

It has been stated earlier, but is worth reiterating here, that "successful" is used to include any study which produces positive results and any study which produces a negative result that was not previously known. For example, imagine a study which set out to test whether or not teaching by television resulted in greater achievement gains than classroom lecture. Assume that the expected differences in achievement did not materialize. This adds nothing to the literature or our knowledge, for we have hundreds of studies that have produced this identical finding. However, had the researcher tried something new, such as individual receivers with provision for student feedback and supplementary questioning to a teacher at a central transmitter, and *still* found no differences, then he would have made a contribution. We would have another instance in which the finding of "no difference" holds.

If the researcher has some new idea, some new method, some new instrument, which leads him to believe he will succeed where all others failed, then he has every right to proceed. However, if he only intends to try again what has never worked before, then he should seriously consider whether he can reasonably expect to do any better than his predecessors. If not, he should devote his time, energy, and ability to a research problem in which there is a greater likelihood of his making a positive professional contribution.

In the same spirit, each researcher must ask himself what contribution his research will make to our understanding of theoretical issues and basic processes, as well as to the improvement of practice. If this kind of evaluation were consistently and conscientiously made early enough in the research process, and if a greater proportion of researchers were willing to change when faced with the clear prognosis that, in view of the literature, the research they contemplated will have little utility, then we would have less "so what" research done in the social sciences. We have too much research completed after great labor and expense, but so what? No theory is reinforced or challenged, no practice is empirically substantiated or questioned, no ripple created on the seas of educational thought. The research might as well never have been done, and this same time and energy should have been channeled into productive research.

Definitions, Assumptions, Limitations, and Hypotheses

Let us consider the happier alternative that, after considering the literature, the researcher can honestly conclude that there is a reasonable expectation that he will successfully complete the contemplated research with results that will make a contribution to his field. Then he will use the material from the literature as the basis for stating his definitions, assumptions, limitations, and hypotheses. Having read the works presenting opinion and theory in the problem area, and having reviewed the relevant research as well, the researcher should be thoroughly familiar with the way in which terms have been used, both in the theoretical sense in the conceptual literature, and in the more functional sense in the research literature. Thus, he should be able to formulate the definitions for his contemplated project. Where possible and sensible, he should use the definitions which have previously been used in the literature, because this is one way of making old and new research comparable. Where necessary, however, he is free to adapt previous definitions or formulate new ones. The essential point is that this be a knowledgeable decision made with full awareness of how key terms have been used previously.

In the same way that the review of research makes the researcher aware of how terms have been used, it (and the conceptual review as well) should have made him aware of those aspects of the problem area which have been so well demonstrated by previous research that they are widely accepted as true. These he can use as the assumptions of his own research. Finally, he should have become sufficiently attuned to the controversial or open-to-question aspects of the problem area. Then, as he plans his research, he can be alert to which of these aspects he can and which he cannot handle in his own project. Those he cannot handle will form the basis for the statement of limitations of the research.

His awareness of the results of previous research, and his knowledge of the current thinking in the field, can now be combined with his own experience to produce the statement of the hypotheses, or expected results of the research. In addition to identifying the expected outcomes of his study, the researcher should identify the bases in the literature for each specific belief. In this way in both the outline and the report of his project, he can state the rationale for each hypothesis, identifying the theorist, previous research study, personal experience, or combination of these which leads him to expect this particular result.

In addition to the five direct functions discussed above, we can identify one indirect function of the review of the literature: to serve as a sounding board to help the researcher know when his research problem has been sufficiently specified. This function can best be described in terms of two different feeling tones. The first feeling tone is one in which the researcher finds that, simultaneously, all of the literature seems relevant and none of it seems relevant. This is the feeling tone characteristic of the early stages in problem development when the research problem is insufficiently specific. As the problem is specified, however, and the researcher continues to read, a subtle change takes place. He now finds that certain articles or studies have a striking and exciting relevance; others, while possibly in the same problem area, are not directly related. When he experiences this feeling as he reviews the literature, then he knows that the research problem is approaching sufficient specificity. We can restate the general rule mentioned earlier: As long as this judgment of relevance is difficult to make, the literature is reflecting insufficient clarity and/or specificity in the research problem.

HOW TO CONDUCT THE REVIEW OF THE LITERATURE

The place to begin a review of the literature varies, depending upon how familiar the researcher is with the problem area. As we stated earlier, the thoroughly well-read researcher will need to complete only a brief review of the latest writings and research. Since this researcher will also know the major thinkers and sources of research in the field, he does not usually need help in conducting this brief review. This section, then, will assume that the researcher is not an expert in the problem area and discuss how the nonexpert[6] reviews the literature.

The nonexpert should begin by reviewing the conceptual literature, for it is more comprehensive than the research literature and will provide a better overview of issues. An excellent place to begin is with a general text in the problem area or the appropriate material on the problem area in an encyclopedia or review of recent works. In education, we have excellent general texts in almost all areas as well as general encyclopedias like the *Encyclopedia of Modern Education* and the *Encyclopedia of Educational Research*, and more specific works like the *Encyclopedia of Child Care and Guidance* or the *Yearbooks* of the *National Society for the Study of Education*. In the same way, the *Annual Review of Psychology* provides summaries of recent work completed in the major psychological areas. Following is a list of the major encyclopedias and yearbooks of relevance in education and related disciplines.

1. *Annual Review of Psychology.* Palo Alto, Calif.: Annual Reviews, Inc.
   Critical summaries of recent research in several areas of psychology.
2. *Encyclopedia of Child Care and Guidance.* Sidonie M. Gruenberg. New York: Doubleday and Company, Inc., 1954.
   Brief treatment of many "popular" topics.
3. *Encyclopedia of Educational Research.* Walter S. Harris, ed. New York: Crowell-Collier and Macmillan, Inc., 1950.
   Critical syntheses and interpretation of problems in education, including bibliographical references.
4. *Encyclopedia of Modern Education.* Harry N. Rivlin, ed., and Herbert Schueler, asst. ed. New York: Philosophical Library, Inc., 1943.
   Short articles in various areas of education.
5. *Handbook of Research on Teaching.* Norman L. Gage. Chicago: Rand McNally and Company, 1963.
   Summaries of research in the several areas of education.
6. *National Society for the Study of Education Yearbooks.* Chicago: National Society for the Study of Education. (Started in 1902 and published annually.)
   Each volume includes invited papers on topics of current interest.
7. *Review of Educational Research.* Washington, D.C.: American Educational Research Association.
   The *Review* is published five times a year, each issue dealing with one topic from a list of fields of educational research listed on the back cover of each issue. There is one issue of the *Review of Educational Research* especially worth noting: *Twenty-five Years of Educational Research,* vol. 26, no. 3 (June 1956).

---

[6]Any student who has the slightest doubt as to whether or not he should consider himself an expert in this instance is advised *not* to do so and should review the literature as thoroughly as, if somewhat faster than, the naive nonexpert.

8. *The Sixth Mental Measurements Yearbook.* Oscar K. Buros, ed. Highland Park, N.J.: Gryphon Press, 1966.
   Critical reviews of tests in many fields; issued periodically.

Of course, reading a general text or an encyclopedia article will provide only a first overview of the problem area. The researcher must go on to a survey thorough enough to satisfy the first requirement of the review of the literature, that he know all points of view in the problem area. To this end, he will read all relevant aspects of the variety of materials we have lumped under the label "conceptual literature"—texts, theoretical treatises, classic and recent books that develop a particular point of view, or journal articles that do the same thing. One accessible guide to this reading will be provided by the bibliographies at the end of the encyclopedia articles or in the *Bibliographic Index* listed below. A second guide is provided by the indexes to published literature, like the *Education Index,* whose use is discussed below.

1. *Guides to the Literature*

   A Guide to Literature of Education. Shirley Katherine Kimmence. London: Institute of Education, University of London, 1963, 86 pp.
   Guide to Reference Books. Seventh Edition. Constance Winchell. Chicago American Library Association, 1951, 645 pp.
   How To Locate Educational Information and Data. Fifth Edition. Carter Alexander and Arvid Burke. New York: Teachers College Press, 1965, 419 pp.

2. *Indexes and Abstracts to Professional Literature*

   Bibliographic Index (1937–   ). New York: The H. W. Wilson Company.
   A listing of bibliographies in 1500 periodicals, by subject area, published annually since 1943.
   Child Development Abstracts and Bibliography (1927–   ). Chicago: Society for Research in Child Development, Inc.
   Abstracts of articles and bibliographies in area of child development; published three times a year.
   Dissertation Abstracts (formerly Microfilm Abstracts) (1938–   ). Ann Arbor, Mich.: Edwards Brothers.
   Now published monthly. Starting with volume 16, 1957, issue number 13 is both an annual index to *Dissertation Abstracts* and a continuation of *Doctoral Dissertations Accepted by American Universities.*
   Education Index (1929–   ). New York: The H. W. Wilson Company.
   Most comprehensive guide to articles in educational journals. Gives a classified listing of titles.
   International Index (1907–   ). New York: The H. W. Wilson Company.
   An index to American and foreign periodicals in the social sciences and humanities, with a heavy emphasis on political science, history and sociology. and little on education or psychology.

Masters Theses in Education (1953–   ). Cedar Falls, Iowa: Iowa State College, Bureau of Research.

Published annually.

Psychological Abstracts (1927–   ). Lancaster, Pa.: American Psychological Association, Inc.

Nonevaluative summaries and abstracts of American and foreign books and periodicals in psychology and related disciplines. Prior to 1927, consult the *Psychological Index,* which started in 1894, issued monthly.

Research Studies in Education (1953–   ). Bloomington, Ind.: Phi Delta Kappa, International Office.

Published annually; includes completed research and research underway.

Sociological Abstracts (1952–   ). New York: Eastern and Midwestern Sociological Societies.

Abstracts of American and foreign books and periodicals in sociology, political science and related disciplines.

3.   *Indexes to Popular Literature*

Cumulative Book Index (1928–   ). New York: The H. W. Wilson Company.

A topical index of books published in the English language, published biannually at present.

New York Times Index (1913–   ). New York: New York Times Company.

Summaries of news by subject, person, and organization.

Reader's Guide to Periodical Literature (1900–   ). New York: The H. W. Wilson Company.

A topical index to popular periodicals with extensive listings in education and psychology.

We are reading for ideas in this stage of the review of literature and so we read generally and extensively. The nonexpert is as much concerned with developing his own thinking as in transcribing what others have said, and so notes taken at this stage are usually directed toward capturing quotations relevant to identifying the points of view of the different authors, and the different aspects of the theoretical framework as we see it developing. It is desirable to concentrate on the conceptual literature until this framework is well developed and until, as discussed in Chapter 2, the problem area has been narrowed down to the relatively specific research problem.[7]

When the research problem has been specified, the researcher should take stock of his reading to date, particularly appraising its relevance in the light of the newly specified research problem. He will want to ascertain whether the conceptual literature already reviewed provides a thorough conceptual framework for the specific problem that he has now decided upon, or whether further work is needed in the conceptual

---

[7]The review we have been discussing to this point corresponds to the Initial Review of the Literature, discussed as Stage 2 of the model presented in Chapter 2.

literature. In either event, however, he will also want to move on now to the research literature, and begin to see the *what, when, where, who,* and *how* of previous research on his specific research problem.

In the course of reading the conceptual literature, he will have come upon references to research studies. These may be a good first set of studies to locate and read, preferably as complete reports. But usually at some point, his list of references is exhausted and the nonexpert will seek other references from the mass of the published literature. We are fortunate in education in having available several basic tools to use for reviewing professional literature, such as the *Education Index, Child Development Abstracts, Psychological Abstracts, Sociological Abstracts,* and parallel tools for the lay literature such as the *Cumulative Book Index,* the *Reader's Guide to Periodical Literature,* and the *New York Times Index.* In fact there are two guides to reference books and a book on how to locate educational information. These, and the most frequently used indexes and abstracts are listed above, with a brief summation of the main function, purpose, and organization of each. The researcher not already familiar with all of these resources should make it a point to become familiar with each of the sources listed, since at some point in most research, any or all of them might be useful.

The nonexpert begins this phase of his review by using the index or abstract most relevant to his problem area. For example, for the researcher interested in developing a research project in the area of phonics instruction in the elementary school, the most relevant index is the *Education Index.* As noted in the list above, this is an alphabetical topical index issued monthly which lists under each topic recent relevant books and journal articles. To use the *Education Index* in the review of the literature for the Phonics Study, the nonexpert would take the specific problem "phonics," also listing several related terms like "remedial reading," "retardation," and "reading improvement," and go to the *Education Index,* pick up the most recent bound volume, look under these headings, and copy every title appearing there which seems to have relevance for the problem.[8] It is also a good idea to check the other topical headings which the index suggests.

The list below has excerpts from two recent volumes of the *Education Index* for the heading "Phonic Method."

Excerpts from *Education Index* under Heading, "Phonic Method"
A. Excerpt from Volume 14, July 1963 to June 1964, p. 397
   1. Agreements about phonics. R.C. Staiger. El Engl 41:204—6+ Mr '64
   2. Are the schools teaching phonics? H. Heffernan. Grade Teach 81:60+ 0 '63

[8]Obviously, if the list is extensive and the library has photocopying machines, it will be simpler to make copies of the relevant pages.

3. Fascination of phonics. J. F. Travers. bibliog f Ed 84:19–22 S '63
4. Phonics: a boon to spelling? W. P. Hahn. El Sch J 64:383–6 Ap '64
5. Phonics and success in beginning reading. A. V. Olsen. J Develop Read 6:256–60 Sum '63
6. Research comparing phonic and combination methods. H. M. Robinson. El Sch J 63:421–4 My '63
7. Sound, the basis of language. J. M. Veto. Ed 84:17–18 S '63
8. Spelling improvement; the result of multi-sensory phonics. T. G. Bogda. Minn J Ed 44:12–13 Ap '64
9. What schoolmen should know about phonics. D. Durkin. Nations Sch 73:72+ Ap '64
10. When phonics is functional. A. D. Cordts. El Engl 40:748–50+ N '63
11. Why not teach phonics in the middle grades? T. P. Hedden, Ill Ed 52:166–8 D '63

Research

12. Phonics or look-say or both? P. Russell. Nations Sch 73:73 Ap '64
13. Two methods of teaching phonics: a longitudinal study. D. E. Bear. El Sch J 64:273–9 F '64

B. Excerpt from Volume 15, July 1964 to June 1965, p. 461
14. Artificial orthography as a transitional device in first-grade reading instruction. S. L. Sebesta. J Ed Psychol 55:253–7 O '64
15. Common sense about phonics. J. A. Piekarz. Read Teach 18:114–17 N '64
16. Easier way to learn to read: I.T.A. W. D. Boutwell. il PTA Mag 59:11–13 S; 11–13 O '64
17. Effective phonics. R. M. Simmons. Sch & Com 51:10+ Ja '65
18. Frequency approach to phonics. E. Fry. El Engl 41:759–65+ N '64
19. Fundamental approach to education; a report on the reading program at Oakley. W. A. Hendrickson. Calif Ed 1:1–2+ Je '64
20. How to eliminate the non-reader. R. Stewart. il Sch Mgt 8:97–8+ O '64
21. Initial teaching alphabet. il N Y State Ed 51:15 Je '64
22. Innovations in beginning reading. J. Chall. Instr 74:67+ Mr '65
23. Instruction in phonics and success in beginning reading. D. L. Cleland and H. B. Miller. bibliog El Sch J 65:278–82 F '65
24. Phonetic keys to reading as a basal reading program. H. B. Knipp. Conf. on Read Univ Pittsburgh Rep 19:125–33 '63
25. Phonetic-linguistic view of the reading controversy. A. J. Bronstein and E. M. Bronstein. Speech Mon 32:25–35 Mr '65
26. Phonics and spelling. R. C. O'Reilly, El Engl 42:126–7+ F '65
27. Phonics on a shoestring. F. P. Cohen. il Grade Teach 82:28–9+ D '64
28. Sight, sound, and meaning in learning to read. M. Rudisill. bibliog El Engl 41:622–30 O '64
29. Teaching letters C and K effectively. Sister Phillip Ann. Cath Sch J 65:54 F '65

30. Value of ITA; opinions differ. J. Downing and I. Rose; W. G. Cutts. il NEA J 53:20–2 S '64
31. Visual motor phonic program for the experience approach to language arts. V. C. Frasier. Claremont Read Conf Yrbk 28:161−7 '64
32. Whole-word and phonics methods and current linguistic findings. R. Rystrom. bibliog El Engl 42:265–8 Mr '65

Research

33. Note on teaching children to hear separate sounds in spoken words. J. D. McNeil and J. Stone. J Ed Psychol 56:13–15 F '65
34. Phonics: an evaluation. M. K. Hill. bibliog Conf on Read Univ Pittsburgh Rep 19:167–76 '63

In the first 11 references listed, the combination of information provided by the title, where the article was pubished, and the length of the article make it possible to obtain some idea of whether or not the reference has relevance for the study. The subheading "Research" would be the first point of reference. Reference 12 sounds like a study of direct relevance, but our initial enthusiasm is tempered by the fact that it is a one-page article.[9] We would consult it despite this, because the one page could be a summary of or reference to a longer study. Reference 13 would be another we would consider immediately, although it is limited to different methods of teaching phonics. In the second volume, under "Research," reference 33 has no overt relevance, but reference 34 would attract us both for the possibility that it contains a summary of recent thinking on the teaching of phonics and for the bibliography referred to. Scanning the other entries, we would add reference 6 to the list of articles to consult first, for it appears to review research even though it is not listed under the research heading. As we scan the list beyond 6, the other references which would hold promise as research references would be 23 and 32. These might or might not refer to research studies, but the title of reference 32 sounds like an overview of research and the article is long enough to be an overview. Several other references would be of interest as part of the conceptual literature, such as 25, particularly interesting in view of its length, and 31, of interest because it is published in the yearbook of a reading conference and because of its length. Some of the references which are intriguing as titles, such as numbers 1, 9, 10, and 17, lose some interest because they are one or two pages in length. Others, such as numbers 3, 4, 7, and 29 would seem to have little relevance on the basis of the title.

In deciding whether to enter a reference into a working bibliography, remember that any index and abstract provides only the barest hint of

[9]The actual references are not numbered. The numbers in the excerpts from *Education Index* have been added for convenience in referring to them here.

what an article is about. The indexes, particularly, based as they are on titles only are suggestive at best, and one generalization that the new researcher will soon make is that titles often provide a very misleading basis for deciding what an article is about and if the article is or is not relevant. So, at this stage of the review, it is better to include any title that seems even remotely relevant. In a good library, the time involved in tracking down a particular reference in a journal or in a book is not great, so we can afford to expand our initial list of references to be consulted, at least until we have developed some feeling for the field and for what is available in the particular area of our interest.

After using these entries under the major heading "Phonic Method" we would then, in these same volumes of the *Education Index,* move on to other major headings. For example, under "Reading" we would find additional references under such subheadings as "Remedial Teaching," "Teaching," "Teaching Methods," and each of these, like the heading on "Phonic Method," has a subdivision: "Research." After completing the most recent volume, we would go back in time to the preceding volume and repeat the same searching process.

However, we continue searching the index under the different headings of the problem area only until we have accumulated about 15 references which seem to have good potential. At this point we call a halt to the search of the index and begin to read some of the articles. The reason for this halt is simply that many articles and most research studies include a bibliography of related research and conceptual literature, and we can use these bibliographies to gradually build up our own, for the earlier chronological periods. There are few more frustrating experiences than to spend hours and hours copying titles from an index or abstract only to find in the first or second reference actually read, essentially the same 40- or 50-item bibliography just compiled. For this reason, the process of reviewing the literature should be one of constant reference to, and shuttling back and forth between, index and library shelf, between copying down titles of books and articles to be read and actually reading some of these. Bibliographies are printed for this purpose. There is no advantage, personally or professionally, in each researcher digging every reference out of an index. Therefore, we use the work of those who have worked in the problem area before to expedite the review of the literature.

On the other hand, we cannot rely entirely on this process of developing our bibliography from the bibliographies of others. Therefore, periodically, we should refer to the indexes for earlier years, crosschecking the index entries against our cumulative working bibliography and adding all references in the index that we do not already have. In keeping with this philosophy of using others' bibliographic work to help, but not to replace our own, when we find a reference discussed in some earlier researcher's article, we should *read* the original source and not base our comments on someone else's interpretation. Therefore, if we are reading Jones's article and he refers to a study by Smith which seems relevant to our research, we *find the study by Smith* and read it. We do *not* base our comments on what Jones has said about Smith's study. We read it to make our own interpretations and evaluations, because Jones may have had different interests and so may have written about only a part of the study. Different aspects, and even much more, in Smith's study may be relevant for us.

In the unhappy event that the search of indexes and abstracts yields little or nothing that we consider directly relevant, this dearth of research should be reflected, also, in the conceptual literature. There we should find statements about the need for research, the lack of research, or evaluative statements as to the weak state of research in the field. Do not be surprised if, despite the most detailed and involved search, we turn up little or nothing directly relevant. There are, unfortunately, many problem areas in education like the area of the Language Study, in which little research has been done. When our own research interest is in one of these areas, the returns from even the most diligent review of literature will be very limited. In these areas, of course, the researcher has the advantages and disadvantages of the pioneer—the disadvantages of not being able to profit by previous experience and so having to make all the mistakes, the advantages of having the excitement of opening a new area of information or knowledge.

However, there are areas of research in which we have an embarrassment of riches. Educational research projects in the general area of reading, like the phonics example used here, have a problem concerning material—it is not the problem of finding something of relevance in the literature but rather of selecting from the mass of material available that which is most relevant for the particular project under consideration. Obviously, when little is available we have to be most flexible in defining what is "relevant" for our study. We define relevance loosely and include titles of articles that seem to have at best potential relevance to our particular topic for a cursory "once-over." When there is much material in the literature relevance can be defined much more rigidly, and only those titles selected for inspection that seem to contain good promise of fruitful leads.

There is often confusion in the beginning researcher's mind as to when previous research can be considered *related* research. Again, the five question words provide a useful structure to answer the question. Research which is related to all five words, that is, which is the same as our contemplated research in terms of what was studied, how it was studied, who was studied, and close in terms of where and when it was done, would be our study and usually would rule out the possibility of repetition. Generally, we hope to find research in which *what* was studied was the same as what we hope to study, but in which there was variation in one of the other four question words. The best variation is when either the research approach or method (*how*) or research subjects (*who*) were different. Here we have commonality in the research problem, so that the results will contribute to knowledge of the same problem area, but variation in method or subjects, which means that knowledge is extended either to another group of people or that current beliefs are either substantiated or challenged when the problem is studied by a different approach or method. Less important, generally, are the instances in which *what, how,* and *who* are the same, and in which the variation is in *where* or *when.* We discussed earlier the circumstances under which variation is useful, but note that, in either instance, the researcher must be ready to defend the proposition that the difference in locale of the research or the passage of time has been sufficient to merit redoing the same problem in the same way on the same kinds of subjects.

For the Phonics Study, the researcher will, as we said before, find a wealth of literature. He will then be able to hold *what* was studied directly relevant, concerning himself only with other research on raising the reading level of retarded readers. He will also be able to hold *who* was studied relatively constant, looking at studies concerned with children in the middle elementary grades of similar sociocultural background as his population. With this wealth of recent material, he will not go too far back chronologically, except to obtain some historical perspective, and even this he may obtain from the conceptual literature. What he will review, then, are recent studies using different methods of improving the reading level of retarded readers in the middle elementary grades, done in a variety of geographic locales.

Now a few final miscellaneous hints on how to review the literature. First, additional library sources will be helpful, such as specialized dictionaries[10] and biographical references. The dictionaries, of course, are most useful in formulating the research definitions, but also of value in making certain that we understand all of the concepts that we discover in the literature. It is a good policy to verify our understanding of all important terms and concepts, even those which are familiar. We may have enough grasp of the term to use it in conversation, yet not understand it well enough to use it in research. The listings of theses and dissertations

[10]Directly relevant is the *Dictionary of Education,* Carter V. Good, ed. (New York: McGraw-Hill, Inc., 1959).

provide the most complete and current contact with a large part of the research done in colleges and universities, much of which is not published and so never indexed or abstracted.

A second hint is to realize that reviewing the literature is essentially the library phase of the project, and so we must become thoroughly conversant not only with the way in which libraries in general function, classify, and catalogue, but also with the way in which the specific library in which we work does these things. Obviously, we must become thoroughly familiar with the general catalog and Library of Congress cataloging system. Individual libraries differ. For example, if a book has joint authorship, some libraries will index both authors, others only the first author. Even in alphabetizing, they will differ on issues like whether "news" precedes words beginning with "newa..." or whether "New York" precedes "newborn." Therefore, the simplest procedure is to thoroughly familiarize ourselves with the rules and techniques of the libraries in which we shall do our bibliographic research. Most libraries have staff available to give an overview of the procedures and rationales by which the library material is cataloged and organized, and we should take advantage of this advice. Trial and error at this stage is needlessly wasteful of that precious research commodity, time, and so is to be avoided.

A third hint is to recognize that there are only two criteria for good bibliographic research: accuracy and consistency. Therefore, from the very beginning of the review of the literature it is sound practice to begin recording the essential information accurately and in exactly the same way. A simple device to assure both accuracy and consistency is to use

---

Bibliography Card	Library Call No.

Author:_____
      Last Name   First Name   Middle Initial
Full Title:_____
Series Title:_____Edition_____Price_____
Publisher:_____City:_____State:_____Year:_____
Pages of book   Bulletin, yearbook, report,
(Whole, and part used):_____or survey document number:_____
Name of Periodical:_____
      Volume:_____Pages:_____Month:_____Years:_____
Enter specific comments on back.

Figure 4-1   Sample bibliography card.

bibliography cards such as the one in Figure 4-1. Many college bookstores have them for sale; if not, it is a simple matter for the researcher to reproduce his own. Whatever the way of recording the information, it is essential to record the following information for every book that is read:

1. The author's first and last name and middle initial, if any
2. The complete title of the book
3. The publisher
4. The year and city of publication
5. The total number of pages in the book

If the reference is a journal article, we need:

1. The author's full name
2. The title of the article
3. The full name of the journal
4. The volume number
5. The month and year of publication
6. The total pages covered by the article from the first to the last page on which it appears

A fourth hint is to copy direct quotations and not paraphrases of an author's remarks on the bibliography cards. It is impossible at the early stage of the research to know in what form we will want to use an idea abstracted from the literature. If we have it transcribed directly, we can use it later in our report either as a quotation or paraphrased. If, however, we have only paraphrased it and later want to use the quotation, we must make a wasteful and unnecessary trip to the library. When a quotation is put down on the bibliography card, be certain to note the page number of the book or journal on which it appears, for this will be needed in referring to the quoted remark.

Consistently, throughout this library phase of the research, we should be overcompulsive in our notetaking. If we err, it is far better to err on the side of writing too much than on the side of writing too little. The one thing we wish to avoid is the necessity, later in the project when time is precious and needed for activities like data analysis and report writing, of having to return to the library to amplify some brief note or verify a half-remembered quotation. In keeping with this thinking, at every stage of the project we should also make a note and keep a record of every information-seeking activity in which we engage. This includes correspondence, conversations, and discussions on appropriate techniques or methodology with consulting experts. Remember that until the research project is completed and the report written, it is impossible to know what will and will not ultimately prove to have relevance.

We should also be aware throughout the review of the functions of the review of the literature and organize our material under these different functions. This means that as we read we keep in mind that we seek seven major areas of information:

1. Support for the need for our study, its success potential, and its potential significance
2. Delineation of the major theoretical points of view
3. Summary of research results
4. Clues for the hypotheses of the proposed study
5. The rationale for each hypothesis
6. The definitions, assumptions, and limitations of the proposed study
7. Clues for methodology and instrumentation

The final stage of the review of literature is to write that section of the research outline or report based on the review.[11] There are two reasons why at least a draft of this material should be written at the point in time when the review is completed. First of all, our thinking is fresh and complete; it is astonishing how much we forget when we delay writing. Second, the review will be the foundation on which we build the structure of our study, and we should achieve the precision and closure which come only with writing. With this achieved, we are ready to move on to the next step of the research process.

[11]Detailed suggestions for writing the review of the literature appear in Chapter 24.

Chapter 5

THE NATURE OF VARIABLES AND DATA

We are ready to turn to the several aspects of designing the research plan, beginning with the nature of variables and data and statistical concepts. As noted in the Preface, these are being discussed early in this book because they are basic to all intelligent planning of methodology.

This discussion of the nature of variables is founded on applying a general principle to education. The general principle is that anything which exists does so in some form or some quantity, and therefore it is theoretically possible to classify or to measure it. To apply this principle in education and the social disciplines we need to state that we deal with, and study, real phenomena which exist, and so it is therefore theoretically possible to classify or measure the phenomena that we study. The key word is "theoretically." Since it modifies "possible," this suggests that we should consider variables and data at two levels: what is theoretically possible and what is actually attainable in view of the current state of development of research techniques for classification and measurement.

In this chapter we shall consider the nature of variables first, then the two processes involved, classification and measurement, and conclude with a consideration of the nature of data produced.

THE NATURE OF VARIABLES

In this discussion, by *variable* we mean a characteristic which in a given research project can have more than one value.[1] When a characteristic lacks this capacity, that is, when in a given research project it can have only one value, we call it a *constant*. Note that these definitions are tied to specific research projects, which allows for a characteristic to be a variable in one research and a constant in another. In the Language Study, for example, grade in school was a variable because the study was conducted

[1] Value is used here to include qualitative (blonde, brown, or black hair) as well as quantitative (twenty, twenty-one, or twenty-two years old) gradations.

138

in grades 4, 7, and 10. However, in the Phonics Study, grade in school was a constant, because all children were fourth graders.

There are two kinds of variables, *discrete* and *continuous*. The basis for the distinction is whether we can classify or measure the variable only in whole units (discrete) or whether fractional units are possible as well (continuous). Thus the number of students in school is a discrete variable, for there are either 311 or 312 but not 311½ students. In contrast, the age of these students is a continuous variable because we can speak of a student who is seventeen and one-half years old.

A discrete variable then is one for which classification or measurement is possible only in whole units. A continuous variable is one in which measurement is possible in both whole and fractional units. These definitions also reflect a point to be discussed later in this chapter: For discrete variables *both* classification and measurement are available processes, but for continuous variables, only measurement is an appropriate process. This is because discrete variables sometimes have a quantitative aspect, as in the number of children in a class, and sometimes do not, as in sex or marital status. For the quantitative discrete variables we can apply the process of measurement; for the qualitative ones, the process of classification. Continuous variables in contrast always have a quantitative aspect, and can always be *conceptualized*[2] as representing a continuous progression from the smallest possible amount of the variable to the largest possible amount. Because these variables can be thought of in terms of a continuous progression, it becomes both possible and sensible to speak of them in fractional units and to apply the measurement process. Thus continuous variables like height, weight, or annual income can all be measured, and reported using partial units, such as 58½ pounds, 5¼ feet, $5500.75.

Because fractional measurement at varying levels of precision is possible for continuous variables, they have an infinite number of possible responses. Some discrete variables, too, have thousands and even millions of potential responses, such as the number of books in a college library. Most discrete variables, however, have finite numbers of possible responses, such as sex with two responses, undergraduate year in college with four, number of elementary- and secondary-school grades completed with 13 (kindergarten through grade 12), or number of senators voting for a bill with 100.

For research use, and particularly for statistical analysis, it is useful to distinguish among these discrete variables. All books in research and statistics single out the two-category, or dichotomous, discrete variable for special study, but generally group all others. This author has found it

[2]The reader is reminded that even if at present the conceptualization cannot be realized, this does not alter the *nature* of the variable.

useful to distinguish four levels of discrete variables, using the number of possible gradations of response as the criterion.

The simplest possible discrete variable is the *dichotomous variable*, in which only two gradations are possible. This is the simplest possible since if there were only one gradation we would be considering a constant, rather than a variable. Examples of *dichotomous discrete variables* include whether or not one voted in the last election (yes–no), life status (living–dead), or presence at school (present–absent). The second type of discrete variable we shall distinguish is the one with three, four, five, or six gradations of response, the *limited-category variable*. Marital status (single, engaged, married, separated, divorced, or widowed) and highest school level completed (elementary, secondary, college undergraduate, postgraduate) are examples of the limited-category discrete variable. The third type of discrete variable we shall consider is the type with more than six, but fewer than 20 gradations of response, the *multiple-category variable*. Examples of this type include such discrete variables as religion, or number of elementary and secondary grades completed. The final type of discrete variable is the *infinite-category variable*, which has at least 20 gradations of response and which has no upper limit. Country in which a respondent was born or number of students in a school are examples of this type of discrete variable.

For most infinite-category, and many multiple-category, variables the number of categories is considered large enough for research and statistical purposes to treat the variable as if it were continuous. For example, the number of people in a nuclear family, which is a discrete variable ranging from one on up to largest possible family by units of one, would be an infinite category variable since the largest possible nuclear family is more than 20. Yet we often see statistics reported telling us that the average family consists of 4.6 people, a statistic which would be completely correct only if it referred to a family of four, one of whom was pregnant in the sixth lunar month! We shall discuss this convention of treating some discrete-infinite and multiple-category variables as continuous variables at several points again; for now the reader is simply alerted to the phenomenon as well as to the practice in this book of referring to such variables by their proper designation, recognizing that the infinite-category variables represent the extreme instances of the discrete concept.

Illustration of Nature of Variables

As an example of this distinction between discrete and continuous variables, Table 5-1 lists ten variables on which data were collected for some purpose during the Language Study. Before reading on, we can verify our

understanding by classifying each variable as either discrete and dichotomous, limited-category, multiple-category, infinite-category, or continuous,
in the column provided.

Of the ten variables, three—the child's *age, weight,* and *psychological
adjustment*—are continuous variables, for all three can be conceptualized
as varying along a continuum with measurement *theoretically* possible at
any point along the continuum. Thus we can refer to a twelve-and-
one-half-year-old child who weighs 98¾ pounds. Psychological adjustment
may make us pause as we try to express the continuum for this variable,
but again note that when we classify variables by their nature, we are
talking only about theoretical possibilities. Therefore for the nature of
variable 8 to be considered continuous we need only accept two concepts:
First, that people vary in adjustment, and second, that if person X and
person Y differ to some degree in adjustment it is possible that there is a
person Z who occupies some fractional intermediate point, that is, is
somewhat better adjusted than X but not as well adjusted as Y. These two
concepts would make the variable theoretically continuous even if, at
present, we could not precisely measure the adjustment of X, Y, or Z.

All the other variables are discrete because even theoretically they can
only be measured in whole units. Two of them, "number of books at
home" and "state in which the child was born," are discrete infinite-
category variables in that more than twenty gradations of response are
possible. "Number of books at home" is an extreme infinite-category
variable because there are hundreds of thousands of possible gradations of

Table 5–1   Exercise on Nature of Variables

Variable Number	Variable	Nature of Variable
1	Age	
2	Number of books at home	
3	Highest grade in school reached by father	
4	Whether or not family receives welfare assistance	
5	Number of times late previous week	
6	Weight	
7	Whether or not child attended kindergarten	
8	Psychological adjustment	
9	Handedness	
10	State in which child was born	

response, so many in fact that it is an example of the infinite-category variable which would be treated like a continuous variable for research purposes. "State in which the child was born," while not having the huge number of possible categories of response as number of books, does have fifty possible responses and so it, too, is an infinite category variable.

The one discrete multiple-category variable in Figure 5-1 is the highest grade in school reached by the child's father. Whether we count the conventional twelve elementary and secondary grades or add four more for college, there are more than six and fewer than twenty gradations of response, so it is a multiple-category variable.

There are two examples of discrete limited-category variables in the list—variables 5 and 9. Variable 5, "number of times late the previous week," has six gradations of response (0 to 5) and no intermediate measurement and so is a discrete limited-category variable. Variable 9, "handedness," has three possible responses of left, right, and ambidextrous, and so it too is a discrete limited-category variable.

Finally, there are two dichotomous discrete variables listed above in number 4, "whether or not the family receives public welfare assistance," and number 7, "whether or not the child attended kindergarten." In both of these instances there are only two possible responses (yes or no) and so these are dichotomous discrete variables.

THE PROCESSES BY WHICH DATA ARE OBTAINED

In the social sciences, as in the physical sciences, we obtain information about variables through the two major processes of classification, which is not quantitative, and measurement, which is. In this section we shall consider the basic attributes of these two processes and the various ways in which they are found in research.

Classification

Classification is a process whereby the researcher places each observation he makes or response he obtains into one or more of a set of categories, so that he can learn the frequency of occurrence of each category.

For research purposes it is desirable that a set of categories possess four properties: homogeneity, inclusiveness, usefulness, and mutual exclusiveness. By *homogeneity* we mean that all the categories bear a logical relationship to the variable under consideration and to each other. If we were categorizing people on the basis of eye color, "blue, brown, black, grey, and violet" would be a homogeneous set of categories. The homogeneity would be destroyed by the addition of a category "near-sighted," for this category belongs to another variable, abnormalities of vision, and bears no relationship either to the other categories being used or to the variable eye color.

Inclusiveness means that the total set of categories allows for all possible variations and so permits every observation to be classified. This is achieved through a full understanding of the variable being measured, so that all of the relevant dimensions are expressed in a category. In a practical sense, inclusiveness can always be insured by using one category as a catch-all, labeling it "miscellaneous" or "all others." Generally, this is sound practice. For example, adding the category "all others" to the five different eye-color categories above would have made an inclusive set of categories. However, these catch-all categories defeat their purpose if they begin to catch too many of the observations; it is far better to have all important dimensions of the variable being studied expressed in a separate category. During the actual process of data analysis, whether or not we have achieved inclusiveness is always obvious, because either we have a category in which to place every observation or we do not. If we do not, then the set of categories must be expanded if inclusiveness is to be achieved. Similarly, if our miscellaneous category attracts more than 10 percent of our responses, we need further specification of categories.

The third desirable characteristic of a set of categories is that they all be *useful*, a characteristic allied to the inclusiveness just discussed, but which specifically refers to the fact that each category serves a purpose and provides a meaningful dimension of the variable under study. This characteristic protects against one inadequate way to achieve inclusivity: by proliferating categories to such an extent that many cease to have any meaning, and too precise and petty a level of discrimination is achieved. For just as having too great a proportion of observations classified as miscellaneous is poor category development, so is having two-dozen categories, several of which have no or few observations and so are not useful. Thus, in the eye-color example, had we delineated several shades of brown, blue, and grey many of these categories would involve such a meaningless level of precision and would probably occur so seldom as to serve no useful purpose.

The fourth characteristic, *mutual exclusiveness*, means that each category represents one unique dimension of the variable under study so that any one observation can be classified into one and only one category. In contrast, we have non-exclusive categories where each observation can be classified into more than one of the categories. If the categories are nonexclusive, this is symptomatic of an error in the set, typically a lack of homogeneity in that more than one dimension is included within the set, or else that there is ambiguity between at least two categories. Thus, if the eye-color categories included both "hazel" and "green-brown" we might feel a specific child could be classified in both categories. But this reflects the ambiguity between these two categories.

Mutual exclusivity is also desirable in and of itself since when each observation is classified only once the total set of categorizations is equal to the total number of observations.

A Priori and a Posteriori Category Development

When it comes time to develop categories, a researcher may develop the categories himself or he may use categories which already exist. Similarly, he may identify the categories before he obtains his data or he may not develop them until he has had an opportunity to see his data. We call these a priori and a posteriori category development, referring to developing the categories before and after data collection. For example, in the Language Study the variable "Puerto Rican" illustrates the process of a priori classification.

To be able to stratify schools in terms of the proportion of Puerto Rican children, we had to define what we meant by a Puerto Rican child. To do this we developed a set of categories for classifying children as Puerto Rican based on whether the child was born in and attended school in Puerto Rico or not, and the parents' birthplace. Using this information we classified each child as "Puerto Rican born and schooled," or "Puerto Rican born, mainland schooled," or "mainland born and schooled, of Puerto Rican parents." Since we developed the categories prior to collecting any data, this was a priori category development.

To illustrate a posteriori category development, let us take the variable eye color, which we have discussed before. Some data on this variable are presented in Table 5-2 to illustrate how in a posteriori category development the concepts of inclusiveness and usefulness interact with the actual data. In Category Set I, the researcher has tried to analyze data for the variable *eye color* using a limited set of five categories. He has achieved inclusiveness by including as the fifth category, one which reads "all others." While this set of categories is inclusive in the sense that all 100 children in each class could be categorized, the researcher would be disturbed that 26 children in class B were classified in the "all others" category, too high a proportion. To remedy this he might develop the much more precise multiple-category classification schema, presented in Category Set II. Again, the set is inclusive through the use of an "all others" category, but now the proportions in that category are appropriately low. However, he now would be troubled by the fact that some of the new categories are not useful, that is, only one child of the 200 was classified as having either olive, light blue, or hazel eyes, and only three in the medium blue or light brown category. Therefore, he would evolve Category Set III, an all-inclusive set in which every category also serves a useful function, and in which the proportion in the "all others" category is reasonably low. He achieved this by combining all the blues, retaining two rather than three gradations of brown, and moving the olive- and hazel-eyed children back into the "all others" category.

Table 5–2 Examples of Possible Classification Schema for the Variable, Eye Color

Category Set I				Category Set II		
Eye Color	Class A	Class B		Eye Color	Class A	Class B
Blue	20	10		Light blue	1	0
Brown	48	33		Medium blue	2	1
Gray	15	26		Dark blue	17	9
Black	9	5		Light brown	2	1
All others	8	26		Medium brown	36	29
	100	100		Dark brown	10	3
				Hazel	0	1
				Olive	1	0
				Green	4	15
				Gray-green	0	16
				Gray	15	18
				Black	9	5
				All others	3	2
					100	100

Category Set III		
Eye Color	Class A	Class B
Blue	20	10
Brown—light and medium	38	30
Brown—dark	10	3
Green	4	15
Gray-green	0	16
Gray	15	18
Black	9	5
All others	4	3
	100	100

This illustration is typical of the trial-and-error aspect of the a posteriori system of category development and illustrates its great advantage: flexibility in terms of the actual data.[3]

Interaction of Variable Type and Classification Level

In addition to considering the characteristics of the set of categories and when they are developed, we also need to consider the number of categories in the set. Here we parallel the system discussed earlier on the different kinds of discrete variables. Thus we shall speak of dichotomous classification, limited-category classification, multiple-category classification, and infinite classification, meaning a two-category classification, three-four-five- or six-category classification, seven- to nineteen-category classification, and twenty-or-more category classification respectively.

It is here that we first come to face an issue raised at the beginning of this chapter, the difference between the theoretical nature of variables and the actual way in which they are handled in any particular research project. One obvious match-up is to classify discrete dichotomous variables with a dichotomous set of categories, each limited-category variable with limited-category classification and multiple-category variables with multiple-category classification. This is often done. We can also take variables and classify them at a less complex level than could be achieved by the nature of the variable. For example, the state in which a person was born, as we have seen earlier, is an infinite-category variable. Yet if in a specific research project we were doing separate data analyses for families born east and west of the Mississippi River, we might decide to collect data on this infinite-category variable using only the dichotomous category set "east of Mississippi," "west of Mississippi." In practical terms, this means not only can we use dichotomous classification for dichotomous variables but that, *depending on the research instance and purpose,* we can also use it for limited-category, multiple-category, and infinite-category variables. Similarly we can use limited-category classification for limited-category, multiple-category, and infinite-category variables and multiple-category classification for multiple-category and infinite-category variables, when appropriate.

We come to the first example of a conflict we shall see often, the conflict between collecting the strongest possible data and collecting data in a way which will simplify data analysis as much as possible. What resolves the conflict is the basic principle that we attempt to collect data exactly at that level necessary to accomplish the purpose of our research.

[3]A further consideration of classification appears in Chapter 22, where its use in content analysis is discussed.

Either of the two possible errors would be wasteful. The first possible error, collecting data at a weaker level than necessary, will mean failing to accomplish the research purpose. Thus, if during the data-analysis stage, we discovered a need to know how many children were born in New England, the dichotomous category "east of Mississippi" would not provide this information. This possible data analysis would be lost unless we went back to the respondents once again. However, the second possible error, collecting data at a stronger level, is also wasteful, not of possible data analysis, true, but of time—often both in data collection and particularly in data analysis, when time is critical. Collecting the birthplace data with the multiple category set of New England, Middle Atlantic, South Atlantic, North Central, South Central, Southwest, Mountain, Northwest, and Far West would be wasteful if ultimately we would have to combine the first few and last few categories.

It is obvious, however, that these two errors are not of the same quality—one loses data analysis, the other loses only time, and so many researchers, particularly students, prefer to err by collecting data at a more specific level than necessary, as a kind of insurance policy against later insights. The more sensible procedure is first to identify the nature of the variables with which the research is concerned. This sets the maximum level of precision to which we can aspire. Then, considering the measuring instruments available and the needs of the research, decide how close to this maximum level we can and need to achieve. This paradoxical advice to obtain the measure as close to maximum theoretical strength as possible, and to obtain it at the simplest level needed for our research, can only be resolved if we have thought through the research, particularly the data-analysis stage, so thoroughly that while planning our measuring instruments we can decide the level of precision we will need; that is, do we need to know the actual birthplace or the region or only if it was east or west of the Mississippi River?

An example of what can be done through the interaction of nonquantitative discrete variables and different classification plans is seen in Table 5-3. This table presents, for each of four nonquantitative discrete variables, the different levels of classification possible, and illustrates how the data would be collected to have the variable function at that classification level.

We have already noted the first example in Table 5-3, how the state in which the child was born, although by nature an infinite-category variable, could be classified using any of the other three classificatory levels.

Handedness is by nature a limited-category variable and could be classified at this level. However, as Table 5-3 notes, if we were to need only the information as to whether the child was exclusively right-handed

Table 5-3   Possible Interactions of Type of Nonquantitative Discrete Variable with Type of Classification

Variable	Type of Variable, by Nature	Classification Type			
		Infinite Classification	Multiple Classification	Limited Classification	Dichotomous Classification
State in which child was born	Infinite-category	By state	By region, if more than six, that is: Northeast, Middle Atlantic, Southeast, North Central, South Central, Midwest, Mountain, Southwest, Northwest, Far West	By region if less than six, that is: North, East, South, West	By region according to single criterion so yields two regions, that is: East or West of Mississippi River
Hair color	Multiple-category	X	By major colors with sufficient subclassification to have more than six but fewer than twenty categories, that is: dark brown, medium brown, and so on.	By major color only, that is: black, brown, gray, blonde, red	By single criterion, that is: blonde, not blonde
Handedness	Limited-category	X	X	By all possibilities: right-handed, left-handed, ambidextrous	By single criterion, that is: exclusively right-handed, not exclusively right-handed
Whether or not receives welfare assistance	Dichotomous-category	X	X	X	By single criterion, that is: yes, no

or not we could also use dichotomous classification. Finally, the table illustrates that for dichotomous variables we have no choice but to use dichotomous classification.

The other generalization to be made from Table 5-3 is that while we can treat a variable at a grosser level of classification than its nature would permit, we *cannot* treat it at a more precise level. Thus we can treat a limited-category variable with dichotomous classification, but cannot reverse the process and treat a dichotomous variable with a set of limited-classification categories. In short, if it is consistent with his research purpose, a researcher can always choose to lose possible precision but has no ability to inject artificial precision into his classification schema.

The Nature of Data Obtained through Classification

If we reflect for a moment we realize that this process of classifying nonquantitative discrete variables is a way of labeling or naming the data for later use, and so we call this kind of data *nominal data*. There are two generalizations to remember: (1) nominal data are nonquantitative; and (2) nominal data are appropriately derived only from applying the classification process to nonquantitative discrete variables. However, not all discrete variables are nonquantitative. Some, like family size, are quantitative. For these discrete variables and for all continuous variables, measurement rather than classification is possible, and so let us turn to that process.

LEVELS OF MEASUREMENT

If we are working with variables which do have a quantitative aspect we can use the data-collecting process of *measurement*. In this process we attempt to achieve some quantitative estimate of the variable or, more realistically, of the amount of the variable which each of our research subjects has. We can aspire to three different levels of measurement—ordinal, interval, and ratio—and these are listed from the weakest level (ordinal) to the strongest level (ratio).

ORDINAL MEASUREMENT   The simplest level of measurement, *ordinal measurement,* seeks to place each observation in its relative position to every other observation but does not attempt to determine how far apart any two adjacent observations are. If, for example, we aspired to ordinal measurement of two children's psychological adjustment we would only seek to determine which child was better adjusted. We would not seek to determine how much they differed in adjustment. If we extended this to several children we would continue to seek only the ability to order them in terms of relative adjustment. Ordinal measurement then is always in terms like "more–less," "higher–lower," or "faster–slower" and not in terms of quantitative units. For this reason it is the weakest of the three levels of measurement, but also for this reason, the simplest level to achieve, and for many educational, psychological, and sociological variables, the most realistic level to which we can aspire.

We can achieve ordinal measurement in two ways: through verbal descriptions of the different points on an ordinal scale or through numerical delineation of the points on a scale. With numerical ordinal measurement, as with verbal, we argue only that one numerical point is higher than the point immediately below, but do not state how much higher. As an example of verbal ordinal measurement, let us consider the problem in the Language Study of estimating each child's interest in learning to read. We might have asked the child's teacher to rate him on a verbal ordinal scale such as:

1. Extremely interested
2. Interested, but not extremely
3. Uninterested but not extremely
4. Extremely uninterested

Let us ignore until Chapter 19 the problems of developing such scales like the problem of having "extremely" mean the same degree of interest to all teachers. Instead, let us assume that we have developed the scale, and that the words do mean the same thing to all raters. We would now have verbal ordinal data.

Note that with these data we could tell that the children rated as "extremely interested" were considered by their teachers to be more interested in learning to read than those rated as "interested, but not extremely." We could not deal with the question of how much more interested they were, for ordinal data do not tell us.

Verbal ordinal data are used for whole sets of characteristics like interests, attitudes, personality attributes, and social or socioeconomic status. With these types of variables, all we can hope to do realistically is to make verbal judgments about which respondents have most of what we are measuring, which less, and which least. In other words we can put our respondents in order on the variable by verbal ordinal measurement.

We simply have not yet developed measures of these characteristics sufficiently precise to tell us how far apart any two respondents are. Thus if we had teachers rate each child's adjustment on a four-point scale from "excellent" to "good," "fair," and "poor" adjustment, this discrete-limited category variable would provide us with verbal ordinal data in the sense that children whose adjustment was rated "excellent" could be considered better adjusted than children rated "good" and both groups could be considered better adjusted than children rated "fair" and so on. However, these verbal ordinal data do not provide us with any estimate of how *much* better adjusted children rated "excellent" are than children rated "good."

The most frequently encountered example of numerical ordinal data is ranking. As an example, let us assume that we had asked each teacher involved in the Language Study to rank her language learners in terms of their potential for learning English. For each child we would than have a number, beginning with the "1" assigned to the child each teacher felt had the most potential, the "2" she assigned to the child with the second most potential, and so on. As with the verbal ordinal data, we know that the child in the highest category (in this case the number "1") was the one with the most potential, and more potential than the child ranked second, but we do not know how much more. Moreover, we can make no assumptions about the relative difference in quality or quantity between any sets of ranks, or the comparability of several sets of ranks.

For example, let us consider the children ranked first by the teachers of classes 4–1, 4–2, and 4–3. Each of these children has the number 1 next to his name. But these are ordinal "1's," and so we have no basis for knowing if the children are comparable in ability. It may be that class 4–3 has a large proportion of academically able children with excellent potential for learning English, and any of the first twelve children in 4–2 have more potential than the first-ranking child in 4–1.

But not only are different sets of numerical ordinal data not comparable, there is no basis for discussing differences within any one set of such data. For example, in class 4–1, consider the difference between those ranked second and sixth (a difference of four ranks) compared to the difference between those ranked tenth and fourteenth—also a difference of four ranks. We cannot make the comparison because numerical ordinal data do not tell us anything about the amount of differences any more than verbal ordinal data do. In short, we cannot make *any* judgments about the amount of differences based upon ordinal data. To visually illustrate this point let us assume that eight students obtained scores on a test, and based on the scores the students were ranked from 1 to 8, as below.

Score:	90	89	88	87	85	63	62	58
Rank:	1	2	3	4	5	6	7	8

If we only had the numerical ordinal data available, that is, the ranks, we would know only the relative position. But notice that for these data, the person ranked fifth has actually achieved a score much closer to the person ranked first than to the person ranked sixth, and that the person ranked sixth is only one point better than the person ranked seventh but twenty-two points worse than the person ranked fifth. It is because they can be so deceptive in this way that we stress the limits of the ordinal level of measurement so heavily.

INTERVAL MEASUREMENT   The second level of measurement, *interval measurement,* is achieved when we have developed a measure sufficiently precise for one unit of the measure to have the same quantitative meaning at any point in the scale of measurement. Thus one inch represents the same difference in distance whether it is the inch between 1 and 2 inches or between 11 and 12 inches. A pound is the same weight whether it is the pound difference between 76 and 77 pounds or between 89 and 90 pounds, and reading-grade improvements from 4.2 to 4.4 and from 4.7 to 4.9 represent the same degree of improvement, two-tenths of a grade.

It is obviously a long way in the social sciences to move from ordinal to interval measurement, and in most areas this is what we are at present attempting to do and have only to a small extent already done. The point could readily be defended that the inconclusive and contradictory nature of much of our research in education, psychology, and sociology is in part due to the unwillingness of researchers to accept this, and instead treat ordinal measures as if they were interval. When they do, they are apt to make the errors just discussed involving the scores of the eight students, and equally serious statistical misconceptions, as we shall see later.

The precision needed for interval measurement requires, first, an understanding of the phenomena being studied sufficient to delineate meaningful equal dimensions along a scale of measurement and then a measuring instrument which can accurately delineate these dimensions. Looking back over the attempts in recent years to achieve interval measurement in the social disciplines, we seem to have forgotten the first point and concentrated instead on the direct development of instruments. But it is no monumental achievement to create a measure which appears to represent equal units. For example, such a scale of interest in reading appears below.

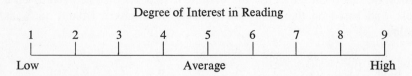

Degree of Interest in Reading

1   2   3   4   5   6   7   8   9

Low   Average   High

The fact that this scale goes from the point 1, meaning low interest, to the point 9, meaning high interest in equal apparent units of one, does not make it an interval measure. It becomes an interval measure only if we could defend the proposition that each of the one-point intervals represents exactly the same difference in interest. Of course, to do this we would first need to define the phenomena of interest in reading and describe meaningful gradations of interest which are equidistant and *then* attempt to develop a measure of these equidistant gradations. Since this has not been done, our scale, despite its equal-appearing intervals, only produces numerical ordinal measurement.

RATIO MEASUREMENT   If we achieve interval measurement, we can then aspire to the highest level, *ratio measurement*. Ratio measures are interval measures, that is, have the same quality of equal intervals, but also have one other quality. They begin from a *true zero* point, representing the total absence of the quality being measured. Here, we should be clear that we are referring to the concept of true zero representing absence of the quality and not to the artificial zeroes which some measures have. Thus the Fahrenheit scale has a zero point but it does not represent absolute zero. The point at which thermal activity ceases in fact does not occur until we reach −460 degrees. On the other hand this true zero need be achieved only at the conceptual level for us to claim ratio measurement. A person's height and weight, for instance, are generally correctly accepted as variables which can be measured at the ratio level. Yet who has *no* height? Who weighs nothing? Obviously in these instances the true zero is only a conceptual or a theoretical referent point, not a physical reality, but that is all it need be for us to have ratio measurement.

Rare as interval measurement is in the social disciplines, ratio measurement is even rarer, occurring most often with the measures we employ of physical characteristics like height and weight, but occasionally available for other characteristics like income.

Possible Treatments of Quantitative Variables

Just as it was possible to treat nonquantitative discrete variables at grosser levels of classification than their nature made possible, so is it possible to treat quantitative variables less precisely than their nature merits or reality makes possible. Table 5-4 illustrates this by listing four quantitative variables from the Language Study and various ways in which data on these variables could be measured.

The first variable listed in Table 5-4, age of mother, is by nature a continuous variable for which ratio measurement is possible. Column 3 indicates that age is to be collected in years and months. In this case, the

Table 5–4 Possible Treatments of Continuous and Quantitative Discrete Variables

Variable	Nature of Variable	Treated as				
		Continuous	Discrete Infinite-Category	Discrete Multiple-Category	Discrete Limited-Category	Discrete Dichotomous
				Data To Be Collected		
Age	Continuous	By years and months	To nearest year	In 10 categories of 5 years each, that is: 16–20, 21–25, and so on	In 5 categories of 10 years each, that is: 16–25, 26–35, and so on	In 2 categories, (a) 30 and under (b) over 30
Number of books at home	Discrete Infinite-category	X	In number of books	In 15 categories of 20 books each, that is: 0–19, 20–39, 40–59, and so on	In 4 categories: (a) less than 50 (b) 51–250 (c) 251–500 (d) more than 500	In 2 categories: (a) less than 50 (b) 50 or more
Highest grade in school reached by child's father	Discrete multiple-category	X	X	In 17 categories: 0 through 16	In 3 categories: (a) elementary (b) secondary (c) college	In 2 categories: (a) less than high school graduate (b) high school graduate or beyond
Number of days of after-school activity	Discrete limited-category	X	X	X	In 6 categories, 0 to 5	In 2 categories: (a) none (b) 1 or more

continuity is maintained and the ratio measurement achieved. In column 4, with age collected to the nearest year, the variable has been treated as a discrete infinite-category variable, but ratio measurement is still achieved. In columns 5 and 6 age is collected through 10 and 5 intervals respectively, and so is being treated as if it were a discrete multiple-category variable or a discrete limited-category variable. Interestingly enough, if we are willing to approximate the age of each respondent with the midpoint of each interval, we have still retained the ratio measurement. However, in column 7, where age is collected as "30 and under" and "over 30," it is treated as a dichotomous variable; we have nothing more than numerical ordinal data.

This last instance is of particular research and statistical interest, for it creates what we call a *false dichotomy*, that is a two-option situation which is an extreme generalization of an underlying continuum. Thus beneath the two ordinal categories, "30 and under" and "over 30" lies the continuous variable, age. Other examples more frequently encountered in education are the ordinal categories "fail" and "pass." Beneath these lie actual test scores, and so these too represent a false dichotomy. In fact, whenever we see quantitative dichotomies, they are false dichotomies. The word "false" is used in this context without any negative connotation, but only to distinguish these dichotomies, which actually come from more complex variables, from the *true dichotomy* like sex, in which there are only two discrete categories.

Just as a continuous variable can be treated as if it were any of the levels of discrete measurement, so can each level of discrete measurement be treated at any of the lower levels. Table 5-4 illustrates this as well, showing how the discrete infinite-category variable, number of books at home, can be treated at its own level or as a multiple-category variable, limited-category variable, or dichotomous variable; how the multiple-category variable, highest grade in school completed by the child's father, can be treated at its own level or as a limited-category or dichotomous variable, and finally, how the limited-category variable, the number of days of after-school activity, can be treated as a limited-category or dichotomous variable.

Approximation in Measurement

Although the process of measurement is possible both with quantitative discrete variables and with continuous variables, there is one basic difference. With the quantitative discrete variable, measurement is by increments of one, for by definition, if the variable is discrete no fractional measurement is possible. Thus when we speak of a nuclear family which consists of four people, we mean exactly four and not somewhere between four and five or between three and four. Similarly, if a child is noted as having 21 books at home, we mean exactly 21 books. However, measurement for continuous variables is possible at fractional levels which means that an infinite set of gradations is possible, although by convention for continuous variables, too, we frequently use one as the smallest increment. Here the "one" is an approximation. For example, if we were to describe the child as having not 21 books, but a brother twenty-one years old, the twenty-one would cover the age range from twenty years, six months, to one day less than twenty-one years and six months of age. Insurance companies, for example, treat age in this way.

Some degree of approximation is inevitable with continuous measurement. There are two conventional ways to approximate in measuring continuous variables. The more frequent way is to treat the number assigned as the midpoint of the interval it represents as we did with age. Thus the number 1 is considered to include the interval from .5 up to 1.49, while the number 2 would go from 1.5 to 2.49, and so on. By this convention the number 0 represents the interval from -.5 to +.49. This use of the concept of the minus troubles some researchers, particularly when it is not logical in terms of the variable under study to conceptualize a negative amount of the variable. Therefore, some prefer to consider the number as representing the upper end of the interval. By this system, the number 0 represents no amount of the variable, and the number 1 represents the interval from some of the variable (that is, .01 or .1) up to and including one unit, while the number 2 represents more than one unit and up to two units. For most research purposes the two procedures are equally sound, provided that the researcher is consistent and adopts one and uses it throughout his research and makes it clear to the reader which convention he has adopted. On the other hand, it should be noted that considering the number to be the midpoint is more widely used and the preferred convention.

In addition to this kind of approximation which is implicit in measuring continuous variables, there are two other kinds of approximation which are usual in measuring both continuous and quantitative discrete variables.

The first approximation occurs because we seldom need to measure variables by units of one, and so measure by larger increments. Instead of asking a respondent how old he is, to the nearest year, we may ask him only to indicate his age somewhere within five-year increments, that is, asking him to indicate if he is "between twenty and twenty-four" or "twenty-five and twenty-nine," and so on. This approximation, if properly done, need not affect the level of measurement. Thus, if, as with age, we had the possibility of ratio measurement with increments of one year, we can retain that level of measurement even though we measure by increments of five years. However, this kind of approximation, or summarization, does lose some precision and so must be carefully thought through before data are collected. It should not be arbitrarily done under the illusion that any set of categories will work as well as any other. The specific caution to which we should be alert is that the summarization retain sufficient precision to accomplish the research purpose. Be particularly alert to any specific point in the variable which it is important to retain. For example, let us say that we wish to measure the number of years of teaching experience of the teachers in schools of the Language Study. We decide that we do not need to know the amount of experience by year, and so decide to use summarization categories. We consider setting up the categories by ten-year increments but reject these as too broad since they make no distinction between beginning teachers and those with eight, nine, or ten years of experience. Therefore we settle on five-year increments, that is, one to five years experience, six to ten years experience, and so on. However, if the school system had a three-year probationary period, so that until the fourth year a teacher did not achieve tenure, the five-year increment loses this particular point in time and we could never distinguish the probationary teachers from those with tenure. However, if we think of this during our planning we can establish our summarization categories to retain this distinction, by using three-rather than five-year increments, such as one to three, four to six, and seven to nine years.

The second kind of approximation in measurement occurs at the extremes of variables and reflects the fact that we may have no interest in similar precision over the full range of a variable. This is particularly true of multiple-category discrete variables or infinite-category discrete variables which often extend far beyond the point at which we need precision. For example, if we were measuring the variable "number of people in the nuclear family" we could enumerate family sizes up to the largest nuclear family known, whatever size that may be. A simpler solution is to decide the point beyond which *we have no further need for precision.* Suppose we decide that for our research purposes we need make no distinction between families of 10 or more, that is, that whether there are 10, 11, 14, or 34 people in the family has no research meaning. We could then make the last category what we call an *open-end category,* letting it read "10 or more." This same procedure can be done to handle this problem for continuous variables. Age, for example, is often measured using an open-end category as the uppermost category, such as letting the last interval read "seventy and older."[4]

[4]The student is cautioned that these are illustrative examples only and are *not* suggestions for handling variables like family size or age in other studies.

An open-end interval may be used at the lower as well as the upper end of a measure. If we wished to learn how many siblings the children in the Language Study had, and also wished to know the age of the school-age siblings, we might use age increments on one or two years from the age of five up ("five or six"; "seven or eight"; "nine or ten") but use only one open-interval for all ages below five ("under five").

Just as the selection of the increment of summarization must be rational and not arbitrary, so the point at which to place the open-end category should be rational. It should be placed one category beyond the point at which the need for precision stops. Seeing the category "ten or more" used in a study suggests that the researcher needed precision up to the number nine and then felt free to generalize.

THE NATURE OF DATA OBTAINED THROUGH MEASUREMENT

Three levels of data can be obtained through the measurement process, corresponding to the three systems of measurement. Thus we can obtain *ordinal data, interval data,* and *ratio data.*[5] The three levels of data differ in function in ways directly related to the characteristics of the measurement which produced them. Thus ordinal data are properly perceived as providing a basis for relative judgments, but no basis for performing any arithmetic operations like addition or multiplication. Interval data, however, can be added or subtracted sensibly, for they do come from an equal interval measure. However, we cannot establish meaningful ratio of one point on an interval scale to another. This final arithmetic operation is limited to ratio data. For example, if it was 60° yesterday, and the weather report notes that 30° was the low for this date and 90° the high, we could appropriately comment that we were halfway between the low and the high. This is appropriate since temperature is an interval measure, and therefore the 30° from 30° to 60° is comparable to the 30° from 60° to 90°. However, we would not be justified in saying that it was twice as hot today as it was on the low for the date. Temperature is not a ratio scale, beginning as it does at 32° Fahrenheit, and 60° is not twice as far from the true zero of −460° as 30° is. But notice that if we retain the same three numbers, 30, 60, and 90, but apply them to a ratio measure like weight, we can make the ratio statement: A child who weighs 60 pounds is twice as heavy as one who weighs 30 pounds, and a 90-pounder three times as heavy.

[5]These three kinds of data, together with the previously discussed nominal data produced from nonquantitative discrete variables, comprise the four types of data it is possible to obtain.

Just as with classification, in measurement too we must distinguish sharply between the level of data it is theoretically possible to achieve for a variable and the level which is actually achievable at any one point in time. For example, in this chapter, we have often referred to the characteristic interest in reading. This has properly been discussed as a continuous variable by nature, and it is one for which theoretically interval data should be obtainable. Moreover, if we conceptualize a point of total absence of interest, that is, a zero point of interest, we can make the stronger statement that ratio data should be obtainable. Remember, this zero point of interest need have no greater reality than the point of zero weight. But at present, whether we should aspire to interval or ratio data for interest is an interesting intellectual issue, but no researcher faces it, for we currently have the ability to produce no more than a gross level of verbal ordinal data. Thus we might develop a five-point limited-category verbal scale ranging from some estimate of little or no interest to some estimate of above-normal interest. But most psychologists, teachers, and researchers would not feel any ability to go beyond this level of measurement. Some, in fact, would feel uncomfortable even attempting a five-point limited-category ordinal scale, preferring a three-point scale ("less than average," "average," "more than average") or a dichotomous ordinal scale ("below average," and "average or above").

Even if we cannot now produce any better than gross ordinal data, there are two reasons why it is important to consider not only what we *can* achieve but what we *should* be able someday *to* achieve. First, only in this way will we constantly recognize where we are in the development of our ability to measure, and how much further we have to go. Second, the researcher must take any discrepancy between the possible and his actual level of data into account when he discusses and interprets his results. To take one specific example, based on verbal ordinal data a finding of no difference between two experimental conditions must allow for the fact that more precise interval measurement might have reflected a difference. So the researcher must always be aware of the level of measurement he can achieve and also of the level which the variable, by its nature, makes possible.

There is no simple guide to the interaction of the nature of the variable and the level of measurement which is possible. Only two consistent rules can be stated. First, continuous variables always have the *potential* for interval measurement and usually for ratio measurement as well. Second, among the quantitative discrete variables, dichotomous variables typically yield ordinal measurement only. But limited-, multiple-, and infinite-category discrete variables may have the potential for interval or ratio measurement, as well as for ordinal measurement. This means that the researcher must decide in each instance what he can achieve with variables of these types.

REVIEW OF CLASSIFICATION AND MEASUREMENT

Now let us review this discussion on measurement by noting in Table 5-5 how, for quantitative variables, the nature of the variable and the nature of the measurement interact to produce data at different levels. To use Table 5-5 as a review, complete the blank spaces before reading further. For each variable, indicate in column 2 the *nature* of the variable as continuous or one of the discrete levels. Then in column 3 indicate whether classification or one of the levels of measurement would be the most appropriate process, and in column 4 the level of data (nominal, ordinal, interval, or ratio) to which we would *aspire*. In column 5 we are told how the data are to be obtained. In view of this, in column 6 indicate how the variable is being *treated* (continuous or one of the discrete levels) and in column 7, the level of data actually to be achieved (nominal, ordinal, interval, or ratio).

Considering columns 2 and 3 first, nine variables are discrete: numbers 1, 4, 5, 7, 8, 9, 10, 13, and 14. Of these, numbers 5, 7, and 9 are nonquantitative, and therefore classification is the appropriate process. For the quantitative discrete variables (1, 4, 8, 10, 13, and 14) and for the five continuous variables (2, 3, 6, 11, and 12), measurement is the appropriate process.

Now let us consider each variable, beginning with variable 1, the number of interests each child has outside of school. By nature this is one of the extreme infinite-category variables with so many categories it can, for all practical purposes, be considered continuous. Theoretically, it should be possible to achieve ratio measurement, for we can conceptualize a point or person with no interests and equal increments of interest. In this study we learn interest will be measured by a list of 50 interests to be given to the child, who will be asked to check all those items in which he is interested. The child then can check anywhere from none to 50 interests, by increments of one. When we come to the process and level we have achieved, it would seem obvious that we have measured, rather than classified. We might hesitate a bit when deciding the level of measurement we have achieved, for now we find we must make some decisions and assumptions.

Let us start at the bottom and work our way up. To claim that we have achieved ordinal measurement, we must be able to argue that the child who checked four interests has fewer interests than the child who checked eight, and both have fewer than the child who checked nine. This seems like a simple assumption to accept. Yet if we think a moment we can easily state a criterion, such as expense, in which two interests like stamp-collecting and model-building may be "more," that is, involve more expense, than four like autograph-collecting, bird-watching, running cross-country, and reading. But if this is true, we may not have measured at all but simply classified the children according to which interests they have. Viewed in this way, we have only nominal data telling us which interests each child has and how many children have each interest. However, let us say we decide to argue that while interests may vary somewhat in expense and other criteria, the variation is not so pronounced as to violate the ordinal assumptions for our particular research purpose.

If we accept this, we may feel it is a short step to interval measurement. But to take this step we must be willing to assume that each of the 50 interests is identical to each other, so the child who checked four interests is exactly as far in number of interests from the child who checked eight as the child who checked eight is from the child who checked twelve. If this argument is acceptable, then what about aspiring to ratio measurement? We do have a zero point, the child who checked no interests on the list. For this to be ratio measurement, however, we would have to interpret a lack of checks to mean that the child has no interests, or, stated another way, we must be willing to assume that our list of 50 interests is all-inclusive, that there are no other interests a child might have. This is not a very tenable assumption, since there are more than these 50 things in which a child might be interested. A compromise we might make is to interpret the data as reflecting ratio measurement within the limits of these 50 interests. Once we do this, however, notice that this immediately requires a restatement of the variable being measured. It no longer is "number of interests" but now becomes "of 50 specified interests, the number of interests." Whether or not this is sensible, of course, depends on the research purpose and illustrates why this consideration of variables must be done early in the research process.

Variable 4, size of the nuclear family, is also an infinite-category discrete variable by nature. Theoretically interval measurement is the maximum possible if we accept the sociologists' concept that family "involves more than two persons."[6] We can claim interval measurement as long as we assume each family member is as important as each other. If, as Table 5-5 indicates, data are to be obtained through five categories, we are treating this infinite-category variable as a limited-category variable.

[6]Arnold W. Green, *Sociology* (New York: McGraw-Hill, Inc., 1952), p. 346.

Table 5-5 Review Exercise for Classification and Measurement

Column 1	Column 2	Column 3	Column 4	Column 5	Column 6	Column 7
Variable	Nature of Variable	Process To Use	Maximum Level Theoretically Possible	Data To Be Obtained as Below	How Treated	Level of Data To Be Obtained
1. Number of out-of-school interests				Child given list of 50 interests, asked to check all he has		
2. Age				To nearest birthday		
3. Reading ability				Reading grade on standardized test		
4. Size of nuclear family				(a) 2-3 (d) 8-9 (b) 4-5 (e) 10 or more (c) 6-7		
5. Whether or not family unit intact				Yes No		
6. Arithmetic ability				(a) Above grade (b) At grade level (c) Below grade level		
7. Birthplace of mother				By continent		
8. Number of times late previous week				By number 0 to 5		

9. Language method to
   which child is
   assigned

   (a) Vocabulary
   (b) Structure
   (c) Experiential

10. Highest grade in
    school reached by
    father

    (a) Elementary
    (b) Secondary
    (c) College

11. Psychological
    adjustment

    (a) Excellent
    (b) Good
    (c) Average
    (d) Poor
    (e) Severely maladjusted

12. Father's income

    (a) more than $7500
    (b) $7500 or less

13. Number of resi-
    dences from birth to
    current attendance
    in grade 4

    (a) 1–3   (e) 13–15
    (b) 4–6   (f) 16–18
    (c) 7–9   (g) 19–21
    (d) 10–12 (h) 22–24

14. Number of child-
    hood illnesses

    (a) 4 or fewer
    (b) 5 or more

Moreover, the use of increments of two up to an open-end category of "10 or more," while it retains the process of measurement, weakens the level of data from interval to ordinal. Those of us who, in doing the exercise, indicated that ratio or interval data had actually been obtained could not answer the question of how much larger the family with 10 or more members is than the family with 8 or 9 members. Since the question is unanswerable, we have lost the possibility of interval data at that point, although we had retained it to that point. We shall see in the next chapter how loss of precision through an open-end final category has serious implications for statistical analysis.

Variable 5, whether or not the child is living in an intact family unit, is a dichotomous discrete variable as stated. In terms of this statement there are only two possible response categories, "yes" and "no," and since both of these are being recorded, the variable is being treated as dichotomous discrete and will provide nominal data.

Variable 7, mother's birthplace, is sufficiently vague for us to consider it an infinite-category variable by nature, as we allow for the possibility that it might be collected as a country or as a city. Upon learning that we are going to collect the data at the gross level of continent, we see that it is being treated as a limited-category variable, which will provide nominal data.

The next discrete variable, variable 8, the number of times the child was late the previous week, is by nature a limited-category discrete variable with ratio measurement possible. Since we are measuring this variable in increments of one, we are capturing its full potential and will have achieved ratio data provided we are willing to assume that absence on any one day is equivalent to any other day. For example, in schools where Friday is routinely used for weekly tests, this assumption may be one the researcher would not wish to make with this variable. This reflects the basic need for a researcher to consider these kinds of questions and assumptions early in the research process.

Variable 9, the language group to which the child has been assigned, has three response categories: vocabulary, structure, and experiential, and so is a limited category variable by nature. Note that this variable illustrates the fact that some variables are study-bound even by nature, in the sense that they have no identity beyond the particular research project. Since data are to be obtained using these three responses, the variable is being treated as a limited-category variable, and will provide nominal data.

Variable 10, the highest grade in school reached by the child's father, is another multiple-category discrete variable where ratio measurement was theoretically possible. Since we are only securing information as to whether or not this highest grade was at the elementary, secondary, or college level, we are treating it as a limited-category variable and are losing considerable precision. This reduces the potential ratio data to ordinal data. Variable 13 is the infinite-category variable, "number of residences," for which ratio measurement is possible, if we accept each residence as equal to each other for research purposes. Here we see that summarization has been done in eight categories. We are treating it as a multiple-category variable. Since the categories have been spelled out beyond the upper limit to be expected, and all categories are closed and equal, we have retained the maximum level of data, ratio data. The final discrete variable in Table 5-5, number 14, is the number of childhood illnesses each child has had. Here the questions involved parallel those for interests, except that probably we would argue that childhood illnesses are so different in their seriousness and health implications that at best we would aspire to ordinal data. Even though this is to be measured as a dichotomy, and even though the second category is an open-end category, we still have a very gross level of ordinal measurement possible, in that we know that the children who have had four or fewer diseases did not have as many as those who had five or more. This gross ordinal measurement is all we shall have, since the data will not distinguish children within each of the two categories.

Let us now consider the continuous variables in Table 5-5. Age, by nature permitting ratio measurement, is to be measured as a multiple-category variable to the nearest birthday. However, since this is being measured in equal increments of one, the full potential will be realized. Variable 3, reading ability, is also a variable where ratio measurement is theoretically possible. Measuring it by deriving a reading grade from a standardized reading test will produce only continuous interval data, since reading grades are not measured from a true zero but often from a grade of about 2.2, the point in the second grade where we begin to teach reading. Since no one is expected to read before this, a child who cannot read at all is usually assigned this or some lower grade equivalent.

As an example of a different interaction between variable and process of data collection, let us consider variable 6, the child's arithmetic ability, measured in this study as "below grade level," "at grade level," or "above grade level." By nature, ability in arithmetic is similar to ability in reading in that it is a continuous variable for which ratio measurement is possible. However, in this study it is being treated as a limited-category variable and being measured at the ordinal level. As a result, considerable precision is being lost, particularly because the ordinal gradations are rather gross.

The last continuous variable, number 12, father's income, is another continuous variable where ratio measurement is possible. Here it is treated as dichotomous in terms of whether or not the income is over $7500, and so we shall have dropped from the ratio potential down to ordinal measurement.

This chapter and these examples hopefully have made clear the importance in research planning of: (1) clearly identifying the variables for which data are needed; (2) understanding the nature of each variable; (3) identifying the maximum strength of data it is possible to achieve in view of the nature of the variable; (4) thinking ahead to the nature of the data analyses contemplated and the research purposes to be served by the variable, to decide the level of precision and the level of data which will be needed; and (5) selecting the process and level appropriate to the nature of the variable and sufficient to serve the research purpose without wasteful precision.

Chapter 6

DESCRIPTIVE STATISTICAL CONCEPTS

As we turn now to statistical analysis of data, the reader is reminded of two points made in the Preface in regard to this and the next chapter. First, these chapters are *not* primarily intended to teach statistical computation, but rather to teach statistical concepts. Because of this emphasis on concepts, the second point holds: These chapters are placed early in the book to simulate their proper place in our research thinking—prior to any final consideration of data collection.

There are two major functions served by statistical analysis: description and inference. Description means exactly what it implies, that we seek to describe to the reader of our research report the characteristics of the data we have obtained. One primitive way would be to tell him every separate piece of data collected, but this way would be both laborious and ineffective. Another approach is to summarize our data through descriptive statistical procedures to enable the reader to learn the highlights of our findings. Even though this sacrifices some of the specificity obtained by informing him of every observation, it is a far more efficient means of communicating research results.

But descriptive statistics do no more than reflect the nature of the data, and in that sense are data-bound. Often, however, while interested in the data per se, we are as interested or even more interested in being able to make inferences beyond the data. For example, if we had instituted our experimental phonics program, we would be interested in knowing the reading ability of the children prior to and after the experiment and would want to employ descriptive statistics to communicate their ability. However, we would also want to know if the children read better after the experiment and, perhaps most important, would want to know if our data suggest that other children would improve if the experimental program were widely implemented. These last two questions, however, are inferential questions in the sense that the data we obtain and can observe do not in and of themselves tell us if improvement took place or if the program would function well if more widely implemented. They do, however, provide a basis on which we can make inferences about change and success. To enable us to make these inferences consistently, objectively, and with a known risk of error, we have the second set of statistical procedures known as inferential statistics.

There are varied systems available for both descriptive and inferential statistics. The choice among them is determined by the nature of the variable being studied, how it is treated in the particular study, and the level of data which is then obtained. Thus there is relatively little freedom involved in the choice of a statistical technique. Once the researcher has clarified his statistical purpose, the nature of his variables, and level of data, the statistical technique which is appropriate is clearly indicated. Therefore, these chapters on statistics will be organized in terms of the preceding discussion in Chapter 5 on the nature of variables and level of data.

Inferential procedures will be discussed in Chapters 8 and 9. For now let us consider the available descriptive procedures.

FUNCTIONS OF DESCRIPTIVE STATISTICS

There are five major functions of descriptive statistical procedures, and the sequence of events in research thinking highlights these different functions. Typically in research we identify a universe and population of interest and from the population select a sample. Then we apply the data-collection instruments to the sample, and thus it is sample data we have to analyze statistically. But of course the focus of our interest is not only the sample but is even more strongly the population and universe. Thus we need a set of procedures to enable us to describe the statistics or characteristics of our particular sample. We also need procedures to enable us to use these statistics to estimate the characteristics of the population, called *parameters*.

For example, in the Language Study, we discussed how we identified the universe of interest, newly arrived Puerto Rican children in the fourth grade. We then went on to identify a relevant population, those Puerto Rican children in the New York City public schools, and from this population selected a sample of the children in the fourth grade of four elementary schools. Let us say we then give this sample of fourth graders, reading at the third-grade level or below, a 20-item vocabulary test. Our first statistical problem is to learn the vital statistics or characteristics of this set of sample data. For example, we might want to know the highest and lowest scores and also the arithmetic average or mean. This function of describing the salient characteristics of a set of sample data is the first function descriptive statistics serve. Our second problem would be to learn what these sample statistics tell us about the parameters or characteristics of the population. Thus, if the sample mean was seven words correct, what insight does this provide into the nature of the population mean? Obviously it provides some insight, but equally obviously since sampling is seldom if ever perfect, there is also some error in this estimate, and so the population mean may not be exactly seven. But how likely is it that it is six, or eight, or somewhere between six and eight? This is a second function descriptive statistics serve: to provide a basis for estimating population characteristics.

If the researcher has collected two sets of data, he can pose a third descriptive question: What is the relationship, if any, between the two sets of data? Estimating the nature and magnitude of the relationship between two sets of data is the third function of descriptive statistics, and involves procedures called *correlational procedures*. Thus, in the phonics example a legitimate and interesting correlational question to pose would be whether or not the scores on the vocabulary test were in any way related to the child's reading grade.

If the researcher has more than two sets of data available on the same sample, he can seek to describe their interrelationships. We shall discuss several ways in which this can be done, ranging from the consideration of all possible pairs of relationships to seeking to isolate the smallest number of underlying characteristics or factors which would explain all of the overt relationships among several variables. Exemplified by the Phonics Study, let us assume the researcher has not only reading grade and vocabulary, but also IQ, mechanical aptitude, space-perception ability, number of out-of-school interests, arithmetic ability, and digital-dexterity score. He would first be interested in how each of these correlates to the others and would present all the correlations in a *correlational matrix*. He might go on to wonder how many separate factors must be posited to explain the child's functioning in all these areas. Thus he might perform a descriptive statistical procedure called *factor analysis*, the results of which would permit him to conclude that if he allows for a verbal-fluency factor, a physical-functioning factor, and a numerical-fluency factor, he can satisfactorily account for the relationships expressed in the correlational matrix. This effort to explore the relationships among, and/or underlying structure of, more than two variables, is the fourth function of descriptive statistics.

Finally, given the understanding of relationship among variables provided by correlations and factor analysis, it should become possible to develop a basis for predicting the functioning of future groups of children.

Thus, at the end of the Phonics Study, when the researcher knows not only all the data he collected about the children at the beginning of the study, but also how much they improved during the course of the study, it should be possible for him to tell us what kinds of improvement we might expect from a child entering the program if we know his reading grade, vocabulary score, IQ, mechanical ability, space-perception ability, and so on through the data he has found relevant. This effort to develop a data-based mathematical formula for predicting future performance is the fifth function of descriptive statistics, and is called regression.[1]

We shall consider these five descriptive functions in this and the next chapter, beginning with the procedures intended to identify the characteristics of single sets of data.

CHARACTERISTICS OF SINGLE SETS OF DATA

Nominal Data

Nominal data are obtained whenever the researcher collects information about discrete nonquantitative variables. Column 1 of Table 6-1 presents a set of such data, the state of birth for each of 27 children in class A of the Phonics Study. The raw data in the table do not serve an effective communication function, and so it is the researcher's task to organize these in ways which will expedite communication yet remain consistent with the nonquantitative character of the data.

One immediate step which can be done is to combine identical information, so that the repetition of state names in column 1 is avoided. This has been done in column 2 in Table 6-1, in which the distribution of the different states represented is listed alphabetically, and the number of children from each state indicated. This procedure is called a *simple-frequency distribution*. The simple-frequency distribution reduces to 14 the 27 separate bits of data reported in column 1 and does this without any loss of precision. In this sense it is the ideal statistical procedure, in that it expedites communication without any loss of information. Of all the procedures we shall consider in this and the next chapter, it is the only one which fully achieves this ideal state!

---

[1]This is one of the more unhappily named statistical procedures, since the term "regression" has the educational and psychological connotation of going backward in time, whereas the statistical procedure enables us to predict future performance. It is called regression for perfectly sound mathematical reasons, but nevertheless is confusing.

Table 6-1 Raw Data, and Simple- and Summary-Frequency Distribution for State in which born, for Class R

	Raw Data	Simple-Frequency Distribution		Summary-Frequency Distribution	
Child	Column 1 State	Column 2 State	Column 3 No. of Children	Column 4 States	Column 5 No. of Children
1	Pennsylvania	Alabama	2	New Jersey, New York, Pennsylvania	8
2	New York	Arizona	1	Illinois, Michigan, Ohio	5
3	New Jersey	California	4	California	4
4	Illinois	Connecticut	1	Alabama, Florida, South Carolina	4
5	South Carolina	Florida	1	Connecticut, Massachusetts	3
6	Alabama	Illinois	2	Arizona, Texas	3
7	Texas	Massachusetts	2		
8	Ohio	Michigan	2		
9	New Jersey	New Jersey	2		
10	California	New York	3		
11	Michigan	Ohio	1		
12	Florida	Pennsylvania	3		
13	New York	South Carolina	1		
14	Pennsylvania	Texas	2		
15	Michigan				
16	Alabama				
17	Illinois				
18	Massachusetts				
19	California				
20	Arizona				
21	Texas				
22	Pennsylvania				
23	California				
24	New York				
25	Connecticut				
26	California				
27	Massachusetts				

However, the researcher might still feel that too much meaningless detail appears in the simple-frequency distribution. Specifically, he might feel that telling the reader that there was one child born in South Carolina, one in Florida, and two in Alabama is not essential, and that these states are close enough to be combined. Therefore he develops the *summary-frequency distribution* presented in columns 4 and 5 of Table 6-1. Now he presents only six separate bits of data, a higher level of summarization than the simple-frequency distribution. However, now there *is* a loss of precision. The reader given only the summary-frequency distribution has no ability to know how the eight children in the category "New Jersey, New York, Pennsylvania," were distributed among the three states combined in that category. To compensate for this loss, we have saved the reader the necessity of going through the several low-frequency categories in the simple-frequency distribution.

The decision as to when and how to move from the simple to the summary-frequency distribution is the first of two decisions the researcher faces in analyzing nominal data. The rationale for the decision is the interaction of research purpose with the basic data-analysis purpose of communication. We wish to provide the data in detail sufficient to achieve the purpose for which we collected the specific piece of information, and also in appropriate detail for the reader to be able to comprehend the sense of the data. For example, in deciding upon the summary-frequency distribution in Table 6-1, the researcher has grouped New Jersey, New York, and Pennsylvania into one category and put Connecticut and Massachusetts into a different category. These all could have been grouped into a category "northeast." By not doing so, the researcher is saying that he believes the separate categories provide the more meaningful level of specificity for his research data.

The second decision the researcher faces is how to order the categories. Since there is no quantitive aspect for nominal data, there is no implicit basis for ordering the categories within the frequency distribution. The researcher has two choices for deciding how to do this. He can either use some verbal or logical or grammatical aspect of the categories, such as presenting them in alphabetical order as was done in the simple-frequency distribution in Table 6-1, or he can present them in order of frequency of occurrence, as was done in the summary-frequency distribution of Table 6-1.

Other than preparing the summary-frequency distribution, the only other descriptive procedure available for nominal data is to single out the most frequent observation or category and call this to the reader's attention. This single most frequent observation is called the *mode*. The mode can be obtained by inspection directly from either the simple or the summary-frequency distribution, although the level of precision with which the mode will be stated reflects the different levels of precision of the two types of frequency distribution. Thus the modal state is California,[2] based on the simple-frequency distribution, but the somewhat vaguer category "New Jersey, New York, Pennsylvania," based on the summary-frequency distribution.

DESCRIPTIVE PROCEDURES FOR MEASUREMENT

When measurement is the process employed, we move to an entirely different realm of description, for now we have some quantitative basis to the data. At the very least there is a basis for ordering the observations from the extremely low point or amount of the variable under study to the extremely high point or amount. Since this is so, we can begin considering the frequency distribution as an ordered series and can begin to discuss characteristics of the data like the observations at each extreme of the distribution, the location of the center of the distribution, or the tendency of the data to cluster about the center of the distribution. Which of these characteristics, and how they apply, differ somewhat for ordinal interval and ratio data, and so let us consider the ordinal data first, beginning with verbal ordinal data.

Verbal Ordinal Data

Table 6-2 presents some data on the level of adjustment of the children in three classes involved in the Phonics Study. In columns 1, 3, and 5 of the table, these data are presented in the form of the simple-frequency distribution, which is applicable to all levels of data.[3] In this instance, the researcher has decided that this is the most appropriate level of precision for these data, rather than the summary-frequency distribution, which he could have developed by combining, for example, the categories "poor" and "severely maladjusted."

The fact that these are ordinal data makes possible three advances. First, we now have a data basis for organizing the categories in the frequency distribution, and so we present them in terms of ascending levels of adjustment, from "severely maladjusted" up to "excellent." The

[2]Note that the mode is not the frequency but the *category,* that is, the mode is "California" rather than the frequency of it.

[3]This use of the simple-frequency distribution with both nominal and ordinal data illustrates the general rule that as we move up from nominal to ordinal to interval data, the procedures available cumulate. Thus *all* the procedures which can be used with nominal data can also be used with ordinal and interval data. Then the new procedures we acquire with ordinal data can also be used with interval data.

Table 6-2 Simple- and Cumulative-Frequency Distributions for Levels of Adjustment, Classes A, B, and C

Level of Adjustment	Class A		Class B		Class C	
	Simple-Frequency Distribution	Cumulative-Frequency Distribution	Simple-Frequency Distribution	Cumulative-Frequency Distribution	Simple-Frequency Distribution	Cumulative-Frequency Distribution
Excellent	5	27	5	24	10	21
Good	3	22	10	18	10	11
Average	9	19	0	8	0	1
Poor	6	10	8	8	0	1
Severely maladjusted	4	4	0	0	1	1

second advance follows from the first: Since the data are in ascending levels, we can also give the reader the *cumulative-frequency distribution.* This distribution presents, for each category, the total number of observations in that category and all lower categories. The three cumulative-frequency distributions appear in columns 2, 4, and 6 of Table 6-2.

Thus for class A, we learn from the simple-frequency distribution that four children were rated as "severely maladjusted," and six as "poor" in adjustment, and from the cumulative distribution that a total of ten were poorly adjusted or severely maladjusted.

The third advance with the verbal ordinal data is our ability to identify the extremes of each distribution, a statistic called the *range.* For example, we note that some children in class A were rated at each of the extreme categories of adjustment, but this was not true of the children in class B. None of them were rated in the category of "severely maladjusted." Stated another way, the range of ratings in class A was from "severely maladjusted" to "excellent," whereas the range of the ratings in class B was from "poorly adjusted" to "excellent."

The range, then, for verbal ordinal data is expressed as going *from* the extreme low point in the distribution *to* the extreme high point. Note that the range is concerned with these two extreme points *only* and so in class B is not affected by the absence of any children in the intermediate rating of "average." Thus class C, which only had children rated "good," "excellent," and "severely maladjusted," has the same range as class A which had children rated in each category. For this reason we shall refer to the range as a measure of *external variability,* reflecting as it does what is happening at the outsides of the distribution and unaffected by what is happening inside the distribution. Note also that the range is insensitive to numbers: Only one child, extremely different from the rest of class C, increased the range three categories. For these reasons—the insensitivity to numbers and internal variability, and the sensitivity to an extreme deviant case—the range is both a gross and potentially deceptive statistic.

We could also utilize the mode, for these verbal ordinal data, noting for the reader that the most frequent level of adjustment for class A was "average," for class B it was "good," and that class C was bimodal, that is, had modes both at "good" and "excellent."

This is all the descriptive analysis that would be appropriate for these verbal ordinal data.

Numerical Ordinal Data

When we move to the more precise level of numerical ordinal data, we acquire the ability to use additional descriptive statistics. Table 6-3

Table 6–3 Simple-, Summary-, and Cumulative-Frequency Distributions for Number of Out-of-School Interests Reported, for Class A

Simple-Frequency Distribution		Summary-Frequency Distribution		Cumulative-Frequency Distribution
Number of Interests	Number of Children	Number of Interests	Number of Children	Number of Children
23	1	21–23	2	27
22	1	18–20	2	25
21	0	15–17	5	23
20	1	12–14	6	18
19	0	9–11	4	12
18	1	6–8	5	8
17	4	3–5	2	3
16	0	0–2	1	1
15	1			
14	3			
13	1			
12	2			
11	1			
10	2			
9	1			
8	2			
7	2			
6	1			
5	1			
4	1			
3	0			
2	0			
1	1			
0	0			

presents some numerical ordinal data, the number of out-of-school interests indicated by the children in class A on the 50-item interest check list we have discussed before.[4] The table presents the simple-, summary-, and cumulative-frequency distributions.

With the numerical ordinal data, we can immediately identify the mode. From the simple-frequency distribution, the modal number of interests is 17; from the summary-frequency distribution, the most fre-

[4]Note that by considering these ordinal data we avoid assuming that each interest is equal to each other interest.

quent interval is 12–14 interests. Notice that in developing the summary-frequency distribution we change the location of the mode, as happened with the nominal data too. This may, or may not happen at any level.

We can also identify the range in interests by inspection. From the simple-frequency distribution, we note that the child who reported the most interests reported 23 interests, and the child who reported the fewest reported 1 interest. But unlike the practice for verbal ordinal data, we do not report the range as from 1 to 23 interests. Instead we subtract the lower end of the distribution from the upper end, and report the remainder, 22, as the range.[5] If we wish to use only the summary-frequency distribution to identify the range, we must make some assumption about the number of interests reported by the two students in the interval "21–23" and the one student in the interval "0–2." Arbitrarily, we use the midpoints of the interval, counting the upper limit as 22 (the midpoint of 21–23) and the lower limit as 1 (the midpoint of 0–2). The range then would be 21 interests. Notice that this is not exactly the same as the range of 22 interests we obtained from the simple-frequency distribution, but the discrepancy is not serious. As we work through the remainder of this chapter, we will note that the use of the summary-frequency distribution for computational purposes always introduces the necessity to make assumptions about the distribution of data within each interval. Therefore, there is the possibility of slight distortion in the results as compared to the results obtained from computation using the simple-frequency distribution.

In addition to these statistics inherited from weaker levels of data, the fact that the data now are both ordinal and numerical gives us the ability to use the *percentile system* for data analysis. This system perceives of an ordered numerical series in terms of the proportion of cases between the lowest point in the distribution and any other specific point. Thus in an ordered series of 80 observations, a point below which were located 20 of the observations would be perceived of as the 25th percentile, arrived at by converting 20/80 into a percent.

The applicability of the percentile system to numerical ordinal data makes available a variety of descriptive techniques. We could identify the *deciles,* or the nine points which divide the distribution into ten equal parts, that is, the 10th, 20th, 30th, and up to the 90th percentile. Or we might identify the *quartiles,* the three points which divide the distribution

[5]One interesting point to note is that this convention, accepted in all statistical practice, actually violates the basic assumption of ordinal data: We know the relative position of the observations, but the data are not additive. Treating the range in this way does imply that it is meaningful to speak of the distance between two observations, and obtaining the range by subtraction does push the researcher a long step toward treating the data as if they were additive. This reflects the general lack of compulsive attention to the relationship of statistical practice to the nature of the data.

into four equal parts, that is, the 25th, 50th, and 75th percentiles. Or, most frequently used of all, we might identify the *median*, or that point which divides the distribution into two equal parts, that is, the 50th percentile.

The popularity of the median is based on the fact that it is a measure of the *central tendency* of the data, and we are a central-tendency or average-oriented culture. In addition to reflecting this cultural tendency, the middle of a distribution is a useful reference point to give the research reader some limited insight into the nature of a set of ordinal data. Two other frequently used points of reference are those which divide the group into the lower 25 percent and upper 75 percent (the 25th percentile) or the point which delineates the lower 75 percent and upper 25 percent (the 75th percentile). Note the convention used for percentiles: The number attached refers to the proportion of the group *below* the percentile. Thus the 25th percentile is that point in the frequency distribution *below* which lies 25 percent of the group, and the 75th percentile is that point below which lies 75 percent of the group.

The 25th and 75th percentiles are widely used descriptive concepts for two reasons. First, together with the median, they break the frequency distribution into quarters or quartiles and so provide convenient reference points. Second, between the 25th and 75th percentiles lie the middle 50 percent of the group, and so this provides us with another means of describing the variability of the numerical ordinal data—in this case an estimate of *internal variability* reflected in the distance between the 25th and 75th percentiles. This, of course is a concept similar to the range just discussed, and so this statistic is called the *interquartile range* because it is based on the distance between the first and third quarters of the distribution.

Computation in the Percentile System

Let us use the data in Table 6-3 to illustrate the kind of computation involved in the percentile system. The table provides both a summary- and cumulative-frequency distribution. The cumulative distribution provides a simple basis for roughly locating the various percentile points, although it is obvious that some computation will be required to locate them with precision. For example, to locate the median for the 27 children in class A, we first need to recognize that the point which would divide any set of 27 observations in half is the location of the hypothetical observation 13.5, since the median is the 50th percentile and 50 percent of 27 is 13.5.

The cumulative-frequency distribution tells us that there are 12 children at or below the interval "9–11" interests, and the summary-frequency distribution tells us that there are 6 cases in the interval "12–14" interests. To reach the point represented by the hypothetical case 13.5, we need only 1.5 of the 6 cases in that interval. These 1.5 cases, added to the 12 below that interval, will give us case 13.5, the one we need to locate the median.

The problem is how to divide the 6 cases to provide the 1.5 cases needed. At this point we must make an assumption about how the 6 students are distributed in the interval. In this instance we act opposite to the way we did to compute the range. Now we must assume that the scores are evenly distributed throughout the interval, even if we know from the simple frequency distribution that this is not so. This assumption introduces no serious distortion and does enable us to proportionally divide up the interval of three points for our purposes. We simply take 1.5/6 of the three-point interval, or .75, and add this to the lower limit[6] of 11.5 of the interval. The resultant sum of 12.25 rounded[7] to 12.2 is the median.

Note that the median is a point, and not a case or response, and so the fact that it is reported as a whole number and fraction (a continuous concept) for these discrete data is not a distortion. Note also that whereas in class A, with an odd number of children, the median was between two students, in class B with an even number of students (24), the median would be represented by the 12th student, since 50 percent of 24 is 12.

[6]The convention with numerical data is to perceive of each interval as actually representing an area of the distribution beginning one-half unit below its overt lower limit and extending to one-half unit above its overt upper limit. Thus, in this illustration the interval with overt limits of 12 and 14 is treated, *for computational purposes,* as having the real limits of 11.5 and 14.5. This is done even with these discrete data and introduces no serious distortion.

[7]The rules for rounding decimals are verbally complex to state, but simple to follow. They can be illustrated by stating the procedure for rounding to one decimal place. First we carry out the computations to two decimal places. Then in all instances when the second decimal place is a number less than 5 (that is, 0 through 4) we drop it and leave the number in the first decimal place unchanged. Thus 12.22 becomes 12.2. Whenever the number in the second decimal place is greater than 5 (6 through 9), we drop it but increase the number in the first decimal place by 1. Thus 12.28 becomes 12.3. Whenever the number in the second decimal is exactly 5, the decision as to how to proceed depends on the number in the *first* decimal place. If it is an even number, we drop the second decimal place and leave the first unchanged. Thus in the example above, 12.25 becomes 12.2. However, if the number in the first decimal place is an odd number, we drop the second place and raise the first (in other words, 12.35 becomes 12.4). Following these rules, any distortions involved in rounding numbers will tend to balance out, and little or no overall distortion will be involved in the total set of data.

This will always be true: The median will be between two observations when there is an odd number of observations, and at an observation when there is an even number of observations.[8]

Through the same process by which we located the median, we could identify the 25th percentile and the 75th percentile for class A. These are 7.9 and 16.3 respectively, and if we subtract the 25th from the 75th percentile we have the interquartile range, or 8.4. Note that like the overall range, this is reported as a result of the subtraction, and is the remainder after the subtraction. It is not reported using the "from–to" format used with the verbal ordinal data. The convention is to divide the interquartile range in half and report the *semi-interquartile range,* or 4.2.

Overview of Percentile System

To provide a fuller understanding of the descriptive functions of the range, median, and interquartile range, Table 6-4 provides data in summary-frequency distribution form on the interest inventory for four classes, providing also the median, interquartile range, and overall range for each of the classes. Before scanning the summary data below the frequency distribution, scan the four distributions themselves and identify any immediate impressions as to the similarity or difference among the classes. Typically, this visual impression is one of difference among the four classes. However, when we scan the summary data we are fed a feeling of similarity, that is, classes A, B, and C have virtually the same median, classes A and B almost identical interquartile ranges, and classes A and C the same overall range. Furthermore, class D has nearly the same interquartile range as class B. Clear feelings of difference are communicated by class D's deviant median and class B's low overall range. Of course these are data concocted to give ambiguous impressions, but they do illustrate well realistic problems in communicating the sense of numerical ordinal data.

First let us consider the medians. This particular descriptive statistic tells nothing other than the location of the observation which divides the distribution in half. In that one respect, the distributions for classes A, B, and C are nearly identical, in that the midpoint for all three distribu-

---

[8]The student is alerted that texts on statistics differ in how the median is to be computed when you have an even number of observations. Most treat the data as is done here, identifying the median by taking 50 percent of the total N. Some suggest that you add one to the N when you have an even number of cases and take 50 percent of $N + 1$. The result of this is that the median for an even number of cases will then be a point *between* two cases, as it always is with an odd number of cases. The difference can never be numerically of any consequence, but the researcher should be consistent in the use of whichever procedure he selects.

Table 6–4 Summary-Frequency Distribution for Four Classes on Interest Check List, Together With Range, Median, and Interquartile

Number of Interests Checked	Number of Children with Indicated Number of Interests			
	Class A	Class B	Class C	Class D
27–29				5
24–26				4
21–23	2		10	3
18–20	2	4		6
15–17	5	5		2
12–14	6	4	1	
9–11	4	3		
6–8	5	8		
3–5	2			
0–2	1		10	
Number of cases	27	24	21	20
Median	12.2	12.2	13.0	22.5
Interquartile range	8.4	8.5	20.8	9.5
Semi-interquartile range	4.2	4.25	10.4	4.75
Range	21	12	21	12

tions is in the interval "12–14." The median, remember, is a statistic designed to identify only one point in a distribution. For that reason it may or may not reflect the distribution. Thus, in class B, the median of 12.2 does reflect the central tendency of the distribution reasonably well, in the sense that all of the actual observations in that class are at or near the median. The median reflects class A less well, as the observations are somewhat more diverse. It is a very weak reflection of class C, for there is only one observation near the median of 13.0. When we use the median, we should recognize what it does and does not do. It *does* identify the midpoint of the distribution; it *does* not provide any insight into the presence of or the clustering of scores about that midpoint or the overall distribution.

Some insight into clustering *is* provided by the interquartile range, although this statistic too has its limits. For example, classes A and B, with similar interquartile range, have quite different overall ranges. This is possible, of course, since the interquartile range is based only on the 25th and 75th precentiles, and neither reflects nor is affected by the observations below the 25th percentile or above the 75th percentile. The data for the several classes also provide a good insight into the different aspects of the data tested by the interquartile range and the overall range. The interquartile range provides an insight only into the extent of clustering within the middle 50 percent of the group. Thus the different interquartile ranges for classes A and B on one hand, and for class C on the other reflect the observable differences between the distributions for these classes. Classes A and B do have more clustering in the center of the distribution and, appropriately enough, have numerically smaller interquartile ranges. In contrast, class C, for which the median was such a poor reflection of the actual data, also has the largest interquartile range, reflecting the relatively large spread of scores.

In contrast, the overall range obscures most of these differences. Classes A and C, despite their overt differences in distribution, have the same overall range. The distributions for classes B and D also exemplify another critical aspect of the range: It does not reflect the location of the data within the total possible distribution. Thus classes B and D have comparable ranges, yet the data for class B begin at the interval "6–8" and are concentrated in the lower and central part of the distribution up to "18–20." In contrast, the data for class D *begin* at the interval "15–17" and are concentrated in the upper end of the distribution. Thus no one of these statistics is complete and thorough communication. The combination of the overall range, interquartile range, and median do provide good insight into the data, but the frequency distribution is still required for a complete picture of numerical ordinal data.

Interval Data

When we move on to interval data, we have advanced to data based on equal intervals or units of measurement. Therefore, while we could use nominal descriptive statistics like the frequency distribution and mode, and ordinal statistics like the cumulative-frequency distribution, range, median, and interquartile range, we would also expect to be able to perform statistical procedures which take advantage of the unique aspect of interval data, that of being additive.

Table 6-5 provides summary-frequency distributions for some interval data, the scores for the children in classes A, B, and D from the Phonics Study on a 30-item spelling test. For purposes of the example, let us assume that we are willing to consider every one of the 30 words as equally meaningful in giving us information about a child's spelling ability, but are not willing to assume that a score of zero is a true zero, that is,

Table 6-5 Summary-Frequency Distributions for Spelling Test, Classes A, B, and D

	Number of Students		
Items Right	Class A	Class B	Class D
18–20	2	5	6
15–17	3	8	
12–14	5	6	
9–11	7	4	2
6–8	5		7
3–5	3		4
0–2	2	1	1

that a child who scored zero has absolutely no spelling ability. In short, we are accepting these as interval but not ratio data.

As before, we can obtain the modes and ranges by inspection of the frequency distribution. Thus in class A, the modal interval is "9–11," while for class B it is "15–17" and for class D, "6–8." The range for all three classes is identical, 18 points, from the midpoint of the interval "0–2" to the midpoint of the interval "18–20." Note that the limitations of the range that we noted with ordinal data persist with interval data: It does not reflect the fact that no children achieved scores in the intermediate intervals in classes B and D, and it does reflect the single extremely low score in class B. This illustrates that these are limits to the range as a statistic, and not a function of the nature of the data.

As we turn to obtaining an estimate of the central tendency and internal variability of these data, we could use the percentile system, but this would not take advantage of the additive nature of these interval data.

Remember, at the interval level, we no longer speak in comparative terms like "larger–smaller," "more–less," "faster–slower," but rather in terms of precise units of measurement like "6 inches smaller," "5 years more," or "10 miles an hour faster." Because at this level we do have the ability to estimate numerically the *amount* of the variable possessed by each respondent, it makes sense to think of each subject as exercising a force in the distribution proportional to that amount. Thinking in these terms we can conceptualize a physical center to the distribution about which the forces exerted by all of the observations would be balanced. This line of thinking utilizes the *moment system* of analysis, which derives its name from the system of forces in physics in which a force exerted by a body about a point or fulcrum is seen as a function of the size or mass of the body and its distance from the fulcrum. The statistical analogy sees each piece of interval data in a distribution as having a moment or force which is a function of the magnitude of the piece of data and its distance from the physical center of the distribution. This physical center about which the distribution is balanced is the *arithmetic mean,* and is analogous to the fulcrum in physics. It is obtained by the familiar process of arithmetic averaging, that is adding up the score values of the observations and dividing by the number of observations.

Computation in the Moment System

To illustrate how computation functions in the moment system, consider Table 6-6. Here we have both the simple- and summary-frequency distribution for class A on the spelling test. The mean is readily obtainable from the simple-frequency distribution by multiplying each observation by the number of cases at the observation and adding the products. This has been done in the column headed "product" of the simple-frequency distribution of Table 6-6, with the resulting sum of scores of 277. When divided by 27, the total number of observations, this yields a mean of 10.3.[9]

To compute the mean from the summary-frequency distribution in Table 6-6, we are faced with a problem similar to that faced when we wished to compute a median from a summary-frequency distribution: What scores do we attribute to the several respondents in each interval? Interestingly enough, we solve the problem *opposite* to the way we solved it for the median. Where for the median we assumed that the respondents were evenly distributed throughout the interval, for the mean we assume that all respondents are at the midpoint of each interval. Thus to compute the mean we would assume that in class D both respondents in the interval "18–20" achieved scores of 19, the three respondents in the interval "15–17" achieved a score of 16, and so on down through the distribution. If we do this, we can proceed as we did with the simple-frequency distribution, now multiplying the *midpoint* of each interval by the number of respondents in the interval and adding the products to produce the

---

[9]Notice that to report this mean in this way, we must decide that it is meaningful to treat this discrete multiple-category variable as a continuous variable. The alternative is to round it to the nearest whole number, 10, and report the data at its own level. The decision would be made in terms of the interaction of variable and research purpose. We should do it only if it does make sense to treat the variable in this way and if it does help achieve the research purpose to report this artificial level of precision. This point is further discussed in Chapter 24.

Table 6-6 Simple- and Summary-Frequency Distribution for Spelling Test Scores, Class A

Simple-Frequency Distribution

Items Right	Number of Children	Product
20	1	20
19		
18	1	18
17	2	34
16	1	16
15		
14	3	42
13	2	26
12		
11	3	33
10	3	30
9	1	9
8	1	8
7		
6	4	24
5	2	10
4	1	4
3		
2	1	2
1	1	1
0		
Totals	27	277

Summary-Frequency Distribution

Items Right	Midpoint of Interval	Number of Children	Product
18–20	19	2	38
15–17	16	3	48
12–14	13	5	65
9–11	10	7	70
6–8	7	5	35
3–5	4	3	12
0–2	1	2	2
Totals		27	270

resultant sum of 270. When divided by 27, the number of respondents, this produces a mean of 10.0.

This difference, from the actual mean of 10.3 obtained through the simple-frequency distribution, reflects, of course, the distortion introduced by attributing the midpoint to all respondents in each interval. With reasonable intervals typically the distortion will not be serious numerically.

Since the moment system perceives the mean as the physical center of the distribution, it also provides us with a more sensitive basis for estimating the internal variability of the data. For now we can seek to estimate the extent to which the separate observations vary about the mean.

In the first two columns of Table 6-7, we have reproduced the data for class A and indicated, in the third column, how far each interval deviates from the mean of 10. Thus, the interval "18–20," with a midpoint of 19, is 9 points above the mean of 10. Similarly, the interval "0-2," with a midpoint of 1, is 9 points below the mean. Note that we indicate both the *distance* of the interval from the mean and the *direction* of that difference. If we now proceed as we did in the computation of the mean and multiply each of the deviations in column 3 by the number of respondents in the interval, we have the deviation products in column 4.

The problem now is to use these deviation products to create a statistic which will meaningfully express the internal variability of the data. The first thought, to add them algebraically (that is, considering the signs),

Table 6-7   Worksheet for Computation of Standard Deviation for Class A

Column 1	Column 2	Column 3	Column 4	Column 5	Column 6
		Distance of Midpoint			Squared
	Number	of Interval	Deviation		Deviation
	in	from Mean	Times	Squared	Times
Interval	Interval	of 10	Frequency	Deviation	Frequency
18–20	2	+9	+18	81	162
15–17	3	+6	+18	36	108
12–14	5	+3	+15	9	45
9–11	7	0	0	0	0
6–8	5	−3	−15	9	45
3–5	3	−6	−18	36	108
0–2	2	−9	−18	81	162
Algebraic sum			0		630
Absolute sum			102		

results in sums of +51 and −51 or an algebraic sum of zero, as indeed it must. These are deviations about the mean, and the mean has been conceptualized as the physical center of the distribution or the fulcrum about which the distribution is balanced. Therefore the force exerted by the observations above the mean must balance, and be balanced by, the force exerted by the observations below the mean.

There are two ways out of this dilemma. One is to ignore the fact that some of the deviations are positive and some negative. Instead, we might argue that we are seeking a measure of internal variability and that the sign is not the issue, but rather the magnitude of the variations or deviations is. This technique would utilize what we call the *absolute value* of the deviations. If we did this, we would add the column of deviations and divide the total of 102 by the 27 students to arrive at a measure of variability called the *average deviation*. For class A the average deviation is 3.78. Note that this is a statistic which works perfectly well to provide a measure of internal variability, but it has other limitations because of the mathematical unsoundness of ignoring the signs, and so is not generally used.

Therefore the second procedure has become more widely known and used: to solve the dilemma of the positive and negative deviations by squaring them and thus making them all positive. If this were done, then the six students in the interval 18 to 20 who are 9 above the mean would be considered to be 81 units of squared deviation above the mean for a total of 162 units (2 times 81) of squared deviation for that interval. In this same way, the squared deviations for the other intervals have been determined in column 5 of Table 6-7. We proceed with the squares as we did with the absolute values, that is we add them and average them among our 27 students, yielding the average of 23.33. This measure of average squared variability we call the *variance*. We then go on one step further, however, and bring our data back into the original scale of values by taking the square root of the variance to produce the measure of variation called the *standard deviation*. For class A this is the square root of 23.33 or 4.73. Note that numerically the standard deviation is not exactly the same as the average deviation but is within the same numerical region.

COMPARISON OF PERCENTILE AND MOMENT SYSTEMS

Let us now summarize this discussion of descriptive statistics to this point and compare the two quantitative systems that we have discussed: the percentile system and the moment system. The percentile system demands only ordinal data, while the moment system requires at least interval data. This means that the researcher with ordinal data has no choice but to use the percentile system, whereas the researcher with interval data can use either system.

Since the interval assumption is a difficult one to achieve, we might suspect that any sane researchers would simply use the percentile system and avoid the difficulty. The reason they do not is because the moment system is more precise and makes greater use of the data. Consider the students in class A who scored 20 on the spelling test. If we were to compute a median, we would take into account only that they achieved the highest score and pay no attention to what that score was. If on rechecking we found that they had actually scored 22 or 28, it would have no effect on the median. In fact had the 13 highest scores in class A been off by 10 points, it would have no effect on the median. In contrast any such change would affect the mean, for the mean would consider not only that these students had achieved the highest score, but that they achieved scores of 20.

As a general rule then, whenever a researcher believes that he can defend the interval assumption, he should use the moment system of description. This is consistent with the principle we enunciated earlier of always utilizing data as fully as possible. However, there are two instances in which this general rule is not followed, and the percentile system is used with interval data. These two exceptions are: (1) when the researcher has a distribution with a few atypical scores or observations; (2) when in the course of the data collection specificity has been lost.

The first exception, when we have a minority of very atypical cases within the study, produces what is called a *skewed distribution*. For example, this occurred in the data from class D in Table 6-5. In this class 14 of 20 children achieved scores between 0 and 11, but the other six children scored between 18 and 20. If we compute the mean for this class from the summary-frequency distribution of Table 6-5, the mean comes out to be 10.0, the midpoint of the highest interval other than "18–20." In fact, in this class 65 percent of the students would have scored *below* the mean, reflecting how considerably the mean was inflated by the six atypically high scores. For this skewed distribution, therefore, the mean would provide a misleading indication of the central tendency of the data. The median would avoid this, for the median would tell us that point in the distribution which divides the group in half and would not be affected by the six atypically high scores. Thus, for class D, the median of 7.6 is a better reflection of the central tendency. In general, then, whenever we have set up the frequency distribution for interval data and note that we have skewed data, it is advisable to revert to the percentile system for descriptive purposes.

The second instance in which we use the percentile system with interval data exemplifies the importance of advance planning in research, since with sufficient planning it need not happen. Let us assume that we were seeking to obtain information on the age of the parents of children in the Phonics Study. Aware that some adults are sensitive about revealing their age, we offer them a set of categories with the upper limit open, that is: 20–29, 30–39, 40–49, 50 or older.

As we have noted before, age is a variable permitting interval or ratio measurement, and so we would expect to be able to use the moment system, computing the mean as the measure of central tendency. However, as we begin to compute it, we are stopped by the open category, for how many years do we add for those parents who have checked "50 or older"? One way of handling this problem would be to compute the mean by arbitrarily assigning a value to this category saying that each parent who checked "50 or older" would be added in as 60 years old. The less arbitrary way would be to revert back to the percentile system, again take advantage of the fact that the median is unaffected by what happens at the extremes of the distribution, and so compute the median.[10]

If we were particularly anxious to obtain mean and not median ages, then, while planning the data collection we should have avoided categories which make computation of the mean subject to a high degree of arbitrariness. Therefore, if we particularly desire to be able to use the moment system, that is, compute means and standard deviations, then we must be certain not only to measure at the interval level but also be certain that we do not use open-end intervals.

Summary

We have considered the various ways of achieving the first function of descriptive statistics: communicating the characteristics of a single set of data, or of several single sets of data. We have seen how the possible descriptive techniques are set by the nature of the data. The several techniques appropriate for each level of data are summarized in Table 6-8.

The table shows that for nominal data we can achieve only three descriptive purposes, presenting either the complete or summary distribution of the data and the single most frequent observation. The table also notes that the distributions must be unordered since there is no quantitative aspect to the nominal data. It is indicated that for all other levels of

---

[10]If more than half of the parents had checked the "50 or older" category, we could not compute the median either without arbitrarily assigning an upper limit to the category. If we did not want to do this, we would have to revert back another step to the mode, noting "50 or older" was the modal age.

Table 6-8 Summary of Descriptive Statistical Techniques Available To Communicate Characteristics of Single Set of Data

Characteristic To Be Communicated	Statistic Available To Communicate Characteristic			
	With Nominal Data	With Verbal Ordinal Data	With Numerical Ordinal Data	With Interval or Ratio Data
1. Complete but *unordered* distribution of data	Simple-Frequency Distribution	N. A.[a]	N. A.	N. A.
2. Summary of *unordered* distribution of data	Summary-Frequency Distribution	N. A.	N. A.	N. A.
3. Complete, *ordered* distribution of data	N. P.[b]	Simple-Frequency Distribution	Simple-Frequency Distribution	Simple-Frequency Distribution
4. Summary of *ordered* distribution of data	N. P.	Summary-Frequency Distribution	Summary-Frequency Distribution	Summary-Frequency Distribution
5. Single most frequent observation	Mode	Mode	Mode	Mode
6. External Variability	N. P.	Range: expressed as "from-to"	Range: expressed as distance	Range: expressed as distance
7. Central Tendency	N. P.	N. P.	Median	Mean
8. Internal Variability	N. P.	N. P.	Semi-interquartile range	Standard Deviation

[a]N. A. — This characteristic is possible with this level of data but is Not Appropriate.
[b]N. P. — This characteristic is Not Possible with this level of data.

data the complete or summary presentations of the distributions of data are *ordered*.

For verbal ordinal data, we acquire one other procedure, the ability to describe the external variability of data in terms of the range, expressed as the distance *from* the lowest *to* the highest observation. With numerical ordinal data, we acquire the ability to state the range as the numerical distance between the highest and lowest point, and also the ability to describe the central tendency of the data in terms of the median and the interval variability in terms of the semi-interquartile range.

Finally, the table shows that with interval data we acquire no ability to describe additional characteristics, but rather acquire more sensitive statistics—the mean and standard deviation—to communicate central tendency and internal variability.[11]

Now let us turn to the second function of descriptive statistics: estimating population characteristics or parameters.

POPULATION CHARACTERISTICS OR PARAMETERS

If we seek to use a set of sample data to tell us something about the population, the sense of the procedure depends upon the interaction of the research problem, the methods and instruments, the sample selection and size, and what is already known about the population. For the purposes of discussion here, let us assume that all these other factors point to the fact that our sample statistics are generalizable to population characteristics. What can we then say, and how can we go about saying it?

There are two basic approaches to estimating parameters. We can estimate the parameter in a single value (that is, the population mean is estimated to be 19.6 years of age) or through an interval (that is, the population mean is between 18.2 and 21.0 years of age). Obviously, each sample statistic tells us something about the comparable population value.

[11]Two other measures of central tendency are occasionally encountered in the literature. These are the *geometric mean,* which is the mean of an exponential series, and the *harmonic mean,* which is the reciprocal of the mean of the reciprocals of scores. The geometric mean is used in an instance when the successive terms in a series increase by a constant ratio rather than an amount which is added, such as the distribution of amount of money in a bank account when no withdrawals are made and compound interest is computed. The harmonic mean is used in instances when the data are available in a form which the researcher believes bears a reciprocal relationship to a more meaningful measure. There is also a measure of internal variability, the *coefficient of variation,* which is particularly suitable for ratio data. However, none of these statistics is widely used, for even with ratio measurement the arithmetic mean and standard deviation are the accepted measures of central tendency and variability.

Equally obviously, for the sample size typically used in social research, there is little likelihood that the sample statistic is an exact estimate. Depending upon the circumstances, it may not even be a close approximation. Of course, under random sampling conditions, if we sampled successively, took the mean of each sample, and then averaged these means, the resulting mean of the means should be a precise estimate of the population mean. But the researcher is faced with one set of data, not data from successive samples.

If he must, he can use sample statistics for point estimates. Thus, both the median and mean estimate the population mean, and both the interquartile range and standard deviation estimate the population standard deviation. For a variety of mathematical reasons, the moment system statistics are preferred, and so the better estimate of the population mean and standard deviation are the sample mean and standard deviation.

However, if we have moment system data, we can move to the use of interval estimates. We shall see how this improves the precision of thinking in the estimation process. Given the moment system of measurement, it is possible to have an additional insight into the data, and that is to conjecture what distributions of interval data generally look like. This conjecture, which first was made by Francis Galton, led to the discovery that for a wide variety of interval measures the familiar bell-shaped curve in Figure 6-1 is an appropriate model of how the distribution will look under normal conditions. This curve, generally referred to as the "normal curve," suggests that for normally distributed interval data we can expect the distribution to be centered symmetrically about the mean, with a clustering of the data in the vicinity of the mean and a gradual tapering off, so that the further an observation is from the mean the less likely it is that the observation will exist. Since the tails of the curve are asymptotic,

The Normal Curve

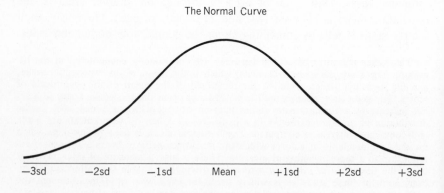

| −3sd | −2sd | −1sd | Mean | +1sd | +2sd | +3sd |

Figure 6-1   The normal curve.

that is, never reach the baseline, the normal distribution also permits for infinite variation in either direction.

The center of the distribution is of course the mean,[12] and the variation from this mean, the standard deviation, is measured along the baseline. Thus, Figure 6-1 has the mean located in the center and the standard deviation marked off in both directions, above and below the mean.

Several observations can be made from these data. Notice first that there are three standard deviations both above and below the mean, for a total of six standard deviations in the full distribution.[13] It also indicates that a majority of the distribution lies within one standard deviation of the mean, and most of the rest lies between one and two standard deviations from the mean, with very little of the distribution between two and three standard deviations away, and almost none more than three.

We can achieve a more precise level of discourse than this, for if we erect an ordinate at a point one standard deviation above the mean, we have created a four-sided figure. It then becomes a simple geometric problem to determine what proportion of the total area of the curve is occupied by that figure. This has been done for the normal curve in Figure 6-2, which has these proportions indicated for each of the three

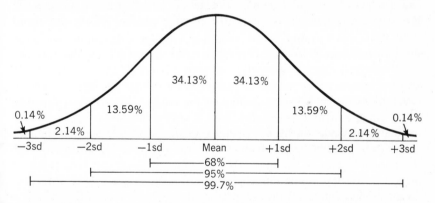

Figure 6-2 Proportion of normal curve with ordinate erected both at the mean and at each standard deviation above and below the mean.

[12]It is also the median and mode, which is one of the reasons that the mode is generally considered a measure of central tendency. It is, for the normal distribution, but not necessarily for distributions which are not normal.

[13]This is a simple convenient first test of whether or not a particular set of data can be considered normally distributed. Simply divide the range by the standard deviation. If the result is a number near six, the data can be considered normally distributed by this criterion. If more than six, this would indicate that the distribution was elongated more than is normal, and if there were fewer than six standard deviations in the range this would indicate that the distribution was more restricted than is normal.

standard deviations above and below the mean.[14] As a rule of thumb, one-third of the normal distribution lies within one standard deviation above and below the mean, and therefore two-thirds of the distribution lie within one standard deviation of the mean. It can be seen here also that 95 percent of the distribution lies within two standard deviations of the mean and 99 percent within three standard deviations.

To this point we have discussed the mean as an estimate of the central tendency of a set of interval data and the standard deviation as an estimate of the tendency of those data to vary about the mean. But we can then use these data, together with the knowledge of the number of cases in our data and the normal curve model, to take an important step forward, and that is to obtain an estimate of the stability of the mean. This statistic is called the *standard error of the mean* and is interpretable as any standard deviation, using the normal curve model we have just been·discussing. It now tells us the nature of the normal distribution of *means* to be expected if the study were repeated a large number of times. In other words, it gives us an insight into what might happen if we *did* have data from successive replications of the study.

Consider, as an example, the data from class A, which we found earlier had a mean of 10 and a standard deviation of 4.73 on the spelling test. What do these data tell us about the mean in spelling of the population from which class A was drawn? The point estimate would be 10, but as we have noted, it is unlikely that this is what the population mean is. But how likely is it that the population mean is 12? Or 8? Or 15? One insight into the amount of deviation we might expect is provided by the standard deviation of the sample data, particularly if we put this standard deviation in the context of the sample size. This is done mathematically by dividing the standard deviation by the square root of the sample size. In the case of our example, this means dividing 4.73 by 5.20, arriving at .91, which is the standard error of the mean. We can then establish the distribution of means, as on the normal curve in Figure 6-3, using the obtained mean of 10 as the midpoint, and the standard error of .91 as the unit of measurement along the base line.

The areas of the curve now tell us the proportions of samples in which different values would occur for the mean and so provide the basis for an interval estimate. For example, these data tell us that in several repetitions of the study under similar conditions we would expect one-third of the samples to have means between 10.00 and 10.91, an additional third to have means between 9.09 and 10.00, and therefore would expect two-thirds of the samples to have a mean between 9.09 and 10.91. If we

[14]These proportions have been rounded for simplicity.

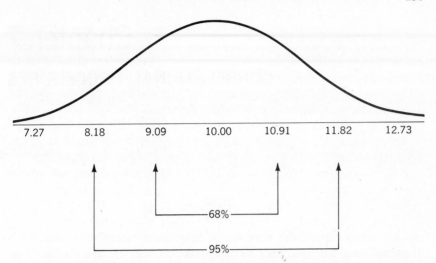

Figure 6-3 The normal curve used to delineate the standard error of the mean.

wished to turn this around we could then argue that the probability is 68 percent that the population mean is between 9.09 and 10.91. If we wished a higher level of certainty, we could go on to two standard deviations[15] above and below the mean and state that we are 95 percent certain that the population mean is between 8.18 and 11.82. In fact, we could use existing tables which give the proportion of the normal curve between the mean and fixed ordinates to state an interval estimate at any confidence level. Note the obvious: We pay a price of decreased precision as we increase the certainty with which we make the interval estimate.

This is the great contribution of the standard error as a statistic, to provide us with the basis for estimating parameters at a known level of confidence. All moment system statistics like the mean and standard deviation have standard errors, and all can be interpreted the same way as we have interpreted the standard error of the mean above to realize this second function of descriptive statistics.

[15]This value has been rounded for simplicity. The actual point involved is 1.96 standard deviations.

Chapter 7

CORRELATIONAL PROCEDURES

As we noted earlier, the third major function of descriptive statistics is possible when the researcher has available two sets of data for the same respondents. In this instance he can question whether or not there is a relationship between the two sets of data, and if so, what the direction and magnitude of that relationship is. The descriptive statistical procedures which serve this function are called measures of *association* and *correlation*. In this chapter we shall consider these measures, but first let us consider the nature of the two processes.

THE NATURE OF CORRELATION

Ideally correlational procedures are intended to answer three questions[1] about a set of data. The first question is whether or not there is a relationship between the two sets of data. If the answer to this is "no," obviously there is no point in going on to raise other questions. But if the first answer is "yes," that there *is* a relationship, we turn to the other two questions: what is the direction of the relationship? What is the magnitude of the relationship?

The Pattern of a Correlation

By relationship, in correlation, we mean any tendency in the two sets of data to vary consistently. There are two patterns of consistent variation. One is for both sets of data to fluctuate in the same way, that is, as one increases so does the other and as one decreases so does the other. We call this pattern a positive relationship, and correlations reflecting this

---

[1]This is only "ideally" true because not all procedures answer all three questions.

pattern are prefaced with a plus sign to symbolize the positive nature of the relationship.[2] The second pattern is the negative relationship or correlation in which an increase in one set of data is accompanied by a decrease in the other. These correlations are prefaced with a minus sign. There is no other meaning to the signs; they indicate nothing more than which pattern holds true for any two sets of data.

Moreover, either pattern may be logical depending again on the particular data. If, for example, we had placed a group of children, each weighing 150 pounds, on a reducing diet and wished to correlate their weight with the number of days on the diet, we would expect a negative pattern, in the sense that the more days the child had been on the diet, the lower (we would hope) the weight. Therefore as the values for one set of data (days on diet) increased, we would expect the values for the other set of data (weight) to decrease. But if, instead of correlating days on the diet with weight, we decided to correlate it with *weight loss*, we would expect a positive pattern. Now the longer on the diet, the more weight lost, and so as the values for one set of data increased we would expect the values for the other to increase as well. Thus, depending on the way in which a study is set up, and the variables chosen, the researcher may expect either positive or negative correlational patterns. For this reason the pattern itself is seldom the significant finding, except in the rare instances when it occurs opposite from what was expected. For example, if in the diet study we found a *positive* correlation between weight and days on the diet, we would begin to suspect that something was happening over which we had no control. This actually happened to a colleague who was performing a nutrition experiment with hamsters as a demonstration for second-grade children. After several days she noticed that the expected negative correlation between weight and days on the limited nutritional diet did not materialize. Investigation showed that the children could not bear to see the experimental animals go hungry and so were smuggling food to them, helping the animals, but destroying the expected correlations!

The Magnitude of a Correlation

Since the pattern of a correlation is usually predictable, the researcher is generally more interested in the magnitude of the obtained correlations. Correlational procedures have generally been developed so that no relationship whatsoever results in a correlation of zero, or, since correlations are typically reported as two-digit decimals, as .00. This correlation means

[2]In practice, the plus sign is usually omitted, so that correlations without any sign preceding them are positive correlations.

that a person's performance on one variable is unrelated to his performance on the second variable. If he is high on one, for example, he is as likely to be low as to be high on the other. At the other extreme we have the perfect relationship in which the two distributions behave identically and all respondents remain in the same relative positions on both variables. Computationally, this perfect relationship generally yields a correlation of +1.00 if the relationship is positive and of −1.00 if the relationship is negative.

But in research literature we will seldom see the perfect correlation. We will encounter the zero correlation more often but most often will encounter intermediate correlations, greater than .00 but less than 1.00, and these are reported as two-digit decimals, that is, .21 or −.53.

Illustrating Correlation

To illustrate these concepts of direction and magnitude, let us consider Table 7-1. This table presents scores in vocabulary before and after instruction and arithmetic grade equivalents for eleven children in class A of the Phonics Study. Since most correlations involve only two sets of data, let us first consider the data in the first two columns, the pre- and posttest scores in vocabulary. We notice that the children's relative performances on these two tests were similar. Freddy achieved the highest score on both tests, and Louis, Tim, and Bill were the next three highest on each test, although their relative order differed. Similarly, John, Harry, and Dick were the three lowest on each test, although their relative position, too, varied. The other four children had intermediate scores on both tests. This essentially stable ordering of the children, with the same ones doing well on both tests and the same ones doing poorly, is reflected in the fact that the correlation we computed is positive. The magnitude of the relationship, which is considerable, yet clearly not perfect, is reflected in the size of the computed correlation, .80.[3] In contrast, let us look at the second and third columns of Table 7-1, comparing the posttest scores with arithmetic grade equivalents. Here we note that Freddy, who achieved the highest score on the first measure, was now low on the second measure, and that Louis, Tim, and Bill were also high on the first but among the lowest on the second. We see the opposite kinds of reversals for Harry and John, who were last and next-to-last on the first measure

[3]Since we shall not consider computational processes in this chapter, the reader who has never actually computed a correlation coefficient may wish to refer to a statistics text to see how the computational processes operate. Otherwise this reader must accept, on faith, that the results discussed in this chapter do indeed come from the data presented in the illustrations.

but who did exceptionally well on the second measure, in fact came out one and four. These reversals are reflected in the fact that the correlation for these data is negative. The magnitude of the relationship is reflected in the size of the correlation, −.89. Comparing the two correlations not only tells us that one relationship is positive and one negative, but suggests that the second relationship is stronger and more stable than the first in that the correlation −.89 is numerically larger than the correlation of .80.[4] Note that the magnitude of the relationship is related only to the size of the correlation and not to the sign, that is, the −.89 suggests a relationship of greater magnitude than the +.80.

The data in Table 7-1 also illustrate that a correlation reflects only the ordering of separate observations and is unaffected by either the units of measurement or the magnitude of the scores. Thus, the pre- and posttest scores for vocabulary correlate .80, although the range on the pretest was from 20 to 42, while on the posttest it was from 60 to 78. This dramatic change in the scores is not reflected in the correlation: The value .80 reflects only the fact that the children remained in relatively the same order on both tests. Similarly, the second correlation is unaffected by the fact that one variable is measured in a two-digit number reflecting items correct on a test, while the other is reported in grade equivalents.

Table 7–1 Pre- and Posttest Scores on Vocabulary and Arithmetic Grade Equivalent

Child	Pretest Score in Vocabulary	Posttest Score in Vocabulary	Grade Equivalent in Arithmetic
Freddy	42	78	4.3
Louis	39	70	3.2
Tim	35	74	3.4
Bill	33	65	3.9
Peter	30	62	4.9
Steven	30	62	4.7
Abner	28	67	5.3
Frank	27	68	6.7
John	24	58	7.1
Harry	21	54	5.8
Dick	20	60	6.3

Correlation between pre- and posttests in vocabulary = .80
Correlation between spelling and arithmetic = −.89

[4] In chapter 10 we shall discuss the statistical procedures for determining if this suggestion of a difference is a statistically sound inference.

THE NATURE OF ASSOCIATION

When we are working with nominal data or verbal ordinal data expressed in a limited-category set, we cannot raise the correlational questions in the same sense that we just discussed. We saw in the preceding chapter that nominal data even lack a data basis for ordering the categories in a frequency distribution, and so we cannot speak of the relative stability of responses or respondents across two variables. Limited-category ordinal data do have a quantitative basis for ordering categories, but the categorization itself, into six or fewer gradations, is too gross to permit a meaningful application of correlational procedures.

However, this does not mean that we cannot ask questions about relationship. For example, it is perfectly sensible to inquire if preference for the Democratic or Republican candidate in an election is related to the sex of the voter. Or, we might reasonably inquire if there is a relationship between two limited-category variables like socioeconomic status and vocational aspiration. Measures of relationship appropriate in situations like these are called measures of *association*, and are applicable to nominal and limited-category ordinal data.

A measure of association reflects the tendency of the data to appear consistently within certain combinations of categories. For example, Tables 7-2 and 7-3 present two sets of data on the relationship of socioeconomic status to aspiration. Each set of data is presented in what we call a *contingency table*. These contingency tables each have cells in which the data are presented. Consider Table 7-2. Here we can see by inspection the relationship in the data. Everyone who was categorized as high socioeconomic status was also in the highest aspirational level (profession-

Table 7-2 Contingency Table Relating Socioeconomic Status to Aspirational Level

Socioeconomic Status	Aspirational Level			
	Professional	Managerial	Skilled Labor	Total
High	13	0	0	13
Middle	0	15	0	15
Low	0	0	17	17
Total	13	15	17	45

Table 7-3 Contingency Table Relating Motivational Type to Child-rearing Emphasis

Motivational Type	Parent Child-rearing Emphasis		Total
	Independent	Dependent	
Extrinsic	32	17	49
Intrinsic	28	23	51
Total	60	40	100

al), and everyone in the middle social-status level was also in the middle aspirational level. Finally, the low-status children had low aspirational levels. These data suggest a high association between the two variables.

In contrast, consider Table 7-3. In this contingency table, we obtain no visual feeling of association: Those categorized as intrinsically motivated, for example, are as likely to be categorized as having parents who stressed dependence as independence. This illustrates general lack of association. Between these extremes, of course, there are intermediate degrees of association, as we shall see when we turn to the techniques for estimating association.

At one end of the scale the measures of association behave numerically like correlations, that is, they have the numerical value of zero to indicate the absence of any association. They all also express intermediate degrees of association with two-digit decimals. However, they differ from correlational procedures in that they do not all express a perfect association through the number "one." This is because of the mathematical properties of the procedures, which we shall not go into here. As we turn now to the procedures, we shall point out for each one how to handle this problem of determining how close we are to a perfect association for a given set of data.

TECHNIQUES FOR ESTIMATING ASSOCIATION

Let us begin with the measures of association available for two variables which produce nominal data. Since nominal data have no quantitative basis, we would expect the measures of relationship available to be gross rather than precise, and we will not be surprised to find that they bear little relationship to the measures of relationship available for data with a quantitative base.

Nominal Data

There are three widely used measures of association which can be used with nominal data, two of which are used when both variables are discrete and dichotomous, and the third of which is used when both variables are discrete but one or both are limited- or multiple-category variables.

CHI SQUARE AND CONTINGENCY COEFFICIENT   Let us consider this latter case first because it covers the widest variety of cases. As an illustration, let us take data from two discrete dichotomous variables in Table 7-3: motivational type and child-rearing emphasis. In Table 7-3 we presented data for these variables in a contingency table, presenting the data on child rearing in the two columns of the table and the data on motivational type in the two rows. As before, through the contingency table we have identified visually the association between the variables, that is, the number 32 indicates that 32 of the children raised with an independent emphasis were classified as extrinsic motivational types.

The question, however, is to determine if these data indicate any association or relationship between the two variables. We can answer the question at two levels. First, we use a statistic called *chi square*[5] to tell us whether or not a relationship exists. When we compute chi square, we estimate *mathematically* what the contingency table would look like if there was *no* relationship between the two variables and then determine if the actual contingency table is or is not different from this hypothetical table indicating no relationship. If the chi square analysis tells us that the data are *not* different, then we conclude that there is *no* association and we do no more. For example, the data in Table 7-3 yield a chi square of 1.12, a value[6] which indicates that these data do not differ significantly from the hypothetical no relationship data.

But now consider the hypothetical data in Table 7-4, relating reading interest area to language group. There is a clear visual association reflected in these data. The chi square analysis corroborates it, for the chi square value of 24.19 indicates that these data significantly depart from the no relationship situation. In this instance we can move on to obtain a weak estimate of the magnitude of the relationship, but cannot raise the question about the direction of the relationship. We compute the estimate of the magnitude directly from the obtained value of chi square. The number this yields is a measure of association called the *contingency coefficient,* usually symbolized by the letter C. The contingency coefficient for the data in Table 7-4 is .57. The contingency coefficient, as a measure

[5]Chi square is fully discussed in Chapter 9 on Inferential Statistics.
[6]How to interpret the obtained value of chi square is considered in Chapter 9.

of association, functions similarly to the general correlations we discussed earlier in the sense that it has a value of zero to designate no relationship and approaches unity for extremely strong associations. However, because of the way it is computed, it can never actually be unity. Therefore, to fully understand the nature of the association reflected in any contingency coefficient, it is advisable to compute the maximum possible contingency coefficient for the particular combination of variables with which we are concerned. For example, the maximum possible contingency coefficient for the data in Table 7-4 is .816.

If we then compute the ratio of the actual contingency coefficient to this maximum possible, we obtain an estimate of association which does function like a correlation in that it goes from zero to unity. For the data in Table 7-4, this adjusted contingency coefficient is .57/.816 or .70.

The contingency coefficient is best suited for multiple-category variables, and because of the mathematics involved, only when both variables have the same number of categories can we obtain the number "one" to reflect perfect association. Moreover, it is difficult to compare contingency coefficients obtained from contingency tables of different sizes. But remember that we are working with nonquantitative data, and so cannot expect more than this approximation to a true measure of correlation.

THE PHI COEFFICIENT AND Q TEST   When the researcher has available nominal data obtained from two discrete dichotomous variables, he has available two additional[7] measures of relationship, the *phi coefficient* and *Q test*.

Both the Q test and the phi coefficient have values of zero to indicate no relationship, and the Q, like many other correlations, has a value of

Table 7-4   Second Contingency Table Relating Reading Interest Area to Language Groups

Reading Interest	Language Group			
	Vocabulary	Experiential	Structure	Total
Poetry	8	1	7	16
Fiction	4	14	2	20
Biography	3	2	10	15
Total	15	17	19	51

[7]This is "additional," since the chi square procedure could be used in this instance as well.

one to indicate a perfect one-way relationship. The phi coefficient, however, like the contingency coefficient, has varied maximum values depending on the nature of the data.

The type of data for which these two procedures are appropriate is illustrated in Table 7-5. Here we have another contingency table for two dichotomous variables: sex, and whether or not the child earned an athletic letter. Both the Q test and the phi coefficient could be computed for these data, and if this were done the values obtained would be 1.00 for Q and .41 for phi. Thus the Q test suggests a higher degree of association than the phi coefficient. This happens because of a basic difference in the nature of these two measures of association. Q reflects *one-way association*, while phi reflects *two-way association*. The difference implied here is indicated by inspection of Table 7-5. This shows that all of the children who won letters are boys, while no girls won letters. This perfect correspondence means that knowing a child won a letter definitely tells us that the child is male. This perfect correspondence is reflected in the value for Q of 1.00, indicating a perfect one-way association. However, the table also indicates that not all of the boys won letters, so that knowing that a child is a boy is *not* tantamount to knowing he won a letter. The fact that the relationship is not perfect in *both* directions is not reflected in the Q but is reflected in the value of the phi coefficient of .41, that is, much less than unity.

The range of values for Q goes from zero to unity (1.00), but the phi coefficient is one of the measures of association which does not necessarily have unity (1.00) as the value reflecting perfect two-way association. Therefore, the researcher who uses it will want to compute the maximum possible phi coefficient for his particular data. This maximum is a function of the numbers of respondents in the two categories for each variable and can be quite low (that is, .30). Therefore it is helpful to use the procedure

Table 7-5 Contingency Table Relating Sex to Winning an Athletic Letter

| | *Sex* | | |
Letter Won	Boys	Girls	*Total*
Yes	10	0	10
No	10	5	15
Total	20	5	25

$$Q = 1.00$$
$$\phi = .41$$

suggested earlier in the parallel situation we faced with the contingency coefficient—establishing the ratio of the actual phi to the maximum phi.[8]

The general rule of thumb on using these two techniques is to use the phi coefficient first because it will test the possibility of two-way association and because it is a more rigorous statistic in its derivational base. If the phi coefficient indicates little or no two-way association, then it will be worthwhile to test for the possibility of one-way association using the Q test. One point to note is that a phi of 1.00 will always yield a Q of 1.00, for if perfect two-way association has been achieved, then so has perfect one-way association.

Ordinal Data From Limited-Category Variables

If the data available are ordinal data from a limited-category variable, then we are limited to the three measures of association just discussed. Since they can be used with nominal data, they can also be appropriately used with stronger data, in other words, with ordinal data. In this instance, the researcher can add one dimension to the interpretation of the association, and that is to impute a direction to the association. Thus for these verbal ordinal data we can raise all three basic questions about a relationship. Does it exist? If so, what is its magnitude? What is its direction?

For example. Table 7-6 repeats the contingency table presented earlier for two sets of limited-category verbal ordinal data: the three-category

Table 7-6 Contingency Table Relating Social Class to Aspirational Level

| | Aspirational Level | | | |
Social Class	Professional	Managerial	Skilled Labor	Total
High	13	0	0	13
Middle	0	15	0	15
Low	0	0	17	17
Total	13	15	17	45

[8]The interpretation of this ratio is somewhat deceptive and the researcher who is using it is advised to read further on the phi coefficient. Two good references are: John H. Mueller and Karl F. Schuessler, *Statistical Reasoning in Sociology* (Boston: Houghton Mifflin Company, 1961); Helen Walker and Joseph Lev, *Statistical Inference* (New York: Holt, Rinehart and Winston, Inc., 1964).

classification of the social class of a group of children and a three-category classification of their vocational aspirational level. If the researcher were to compute the contingency coefficient for these data, it would come out to be .816. If he then were to compute the maximum possible C, it would also be .816, and the resultant ratio of 1.00 would reflect the perfect association we can see by inspection. If these were nominal data we could do no more, but since they are ordinal we can attribute a sign to the association. (We can do the same by visual inspection of the data.) We can see in the table that as social class goes higher so does aspirational level, and so we can label the association as a perfect *positive* one.

If we have more than limited-category ordinal data available, we leave the realm of association and move to correlation. Let us take this next step.

TECHNIQUES FOR ESTIMATING CORRELATION

Nowhere do the relationship of the nature of the variables, the level of measurement achieved, and the statistical procedure available interact more fully than in the discussion of correlational procedures. This discussion is made more complex by the fact that we are concerned with two variables in correlation, and of course the two variables will not necessarily be the same in nature or in level of data. Therefore, we shall consider first the simpler situation, in which the two variables we seek to correlate *are* the same in nature and in level of data, and then turn to the more complex eventuality of when they are different.

Variables Identical in Nature and Level of Data

ORDINAL DATA FROM MULTIPLE-CATEGORY VARIABLES   To estimate relationship between two sets of ordinal data from multiple-category discrete variables, we can use two procedures specifically developed for this instance: the *Spearman rank-order correlation,* symbolized by the Greek letter rho or R and *Kendall's tau.* The reason it is suggested that these procedures be used only when multiple-category discrete data have been achieved is that both of these procedures involve ranking the responses or respondents, and ranking is seldom meaningful when there are fewer than seven gradations by which to rank.[9] Essentially both the Spearman and the Kendall

[9]This is not a rigid rule. In some instances rank-order correlations can be computed with limited discrete categories of five or six gradations. This can be done if three conditions are met: (1) the distribution is a broad one; (2) there are not many more respondents than categories; and (3) the respondents are completely distributed over the set of limited categories so that no more than two are tied for any one rank.

procedures involve ranking the two sets of data and computing a correlation which will estimate the extent to which the two sets of ranks are identical.

The data in Table 7-7 indicate the circumstances under which we would use these rank correlational procedures. Let us assume that the eleven children selected from class A for the Language Study have each been ranked for potential in school and have also completed the interest inventory, providing us with two sets of ordinal data. We want to learn if there is any relationship between the numbers of interests and teacher's ranking for potential, a correlational question. The data in each instance are multiple-category discrete ordinal data, and so we decide to use a rank correlational procedure. We must use one variable as our criterion for ranking, and in Table 7-7 we have used the number of interests checked.[10] We list the children in order on this basis, noting their rank. We then rank them on the basis of potential, again noting the rank for each specific child. We are then ready to compute either rank correlation, using the two sets of ranks as the basis for this computation.

The correlation we would obtain by the Spearman procedure is +.74 and by the Kendall procedure is +.60. This indicates that while the two procedures can be used with the same data, they differ in the computational processes they apply and so are not numerically identical. Therefore, a researcher must be consistent within any one study in choos-

Table 7-7 Interests Checked and Ranks on Number of Interests and on Potential

Child	Interest Checked	Rank on Interest	Rank on Potential
D	36	1	1
A	30	2	3
H	28	3	6
I	25	4	7
C	20	5	2
B	18	6	4
K	17	7	5
G	15	8	10
F	12	9	11
E	11	10	8
L	9	11	9

[10]We could also have used the ranking for potential. It makes no difference.

ing one procedure rather than another and staying with it. Similarly, if we are doing a study in which we wish to compare our correlational data to other data, we must be procedurally consistent there as well.

Both of these correlations behave typically in that they range from zero, indicating no relationship, to unity indicating a perfect relationship (that is, the two sets of ranks are identical), and both can be both positive and negative depending upon the direction of the relationship.

ORDINAL DATE FROM INFINITE CATEGORY VARIABLES   There are no specific correlational procedures for data from infinite-category discrete variables. For correlational purposes, as indeed for most statistical purposes, these data are treated as if they were interval data from continuous variables, and so let us turn to the procedures available for those data.

INTERVAL DATA FROM CONTINUOUS VARIABLES   There are two correlational procedures specifically intended for use with interval data from continuous variables, the *Pearson product moment correlation* symbolized by the lowercase *r* and the *correlation ratio,* symbolized generally by the Greek letter eta. They are not interchangeable, and the choice between them depends upon the structure of the relationship between the two continuous variables. The Pearson product moment correlation[11] is used when the two variables are normally distributed and the relationship between them is linear, that is, a change of a certain magnitude in one variable is consistently accompanied by a corresponding change in the other, as illustrated by the data plotted in Figure 7-1. As can be seen in the Figure, every time variable *A* increases one unit, variable *B* increases about three units. This is true at all points on the scale. The second procedure, the correlation ratio, is used when the relationship between the two continuous variables is curvilinear as is illustrated in Figure 7-2. Here an increase of one unit in variable *A* sometimes results in a one and one-half unit increase on variable *B,* sometimes in a four-unit increase, sometimes in no change at all, and sometimes a decrease in *A* is accompanied by an increase in *B.* Computationally, the two procedures are similar. However, the correlation ratio does not assume a linear relationship between the variables, and since this assumption often is not feasible in the social sciences, the correlation ratio is widely applicable. Despite this it is seldom used, perhaps because it is not taught in most statistics courses!

Both the Pearson product moment correlation and the correlation ratio behave in the usual way in that they range from zero to unity and can be

---

[11]Data for which the product moment correlation would be appropriate are typified by the data previously presented in Table 7-1 on vocabulary scores and arithmetic grade equivalents.

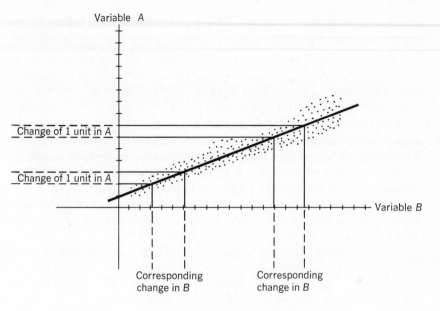

Figure 7-1 Example of two variables linearly related.

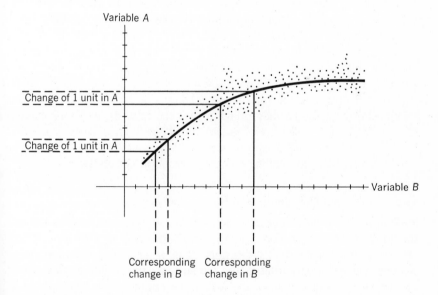

Figure 7-2 Example of two variables curvilinearly related.

positive or negative. As with all interval statistics, they belong to the moment system of analysis.

DICHOTOMOUS DATA FROM CONTINUOUS VARIABLES   In addition to developing the product moment correlation for correlating interval data from two continuous variables, Karl Pearson also developed a procedure for correlating data from two continuous variables which have been measured as dichotomies. In Chapter 5, we called this type of dichotomy a false di *omy* to imply that the variables had the potential for more precise measurement. Pearson called this procedure the *tetrachoric correlation* and developed it so that it functions as a normal correlation, in that it ranges from +1.00 to −1.00 through the zero point of no relationship.

There are two instances when the researcher will find the tetrachoric correlation appropriate. The first instance occurs because we can not obtain data any more precise than the false dichotomous data.

Often in studies involving people, we are faced with imprecise measuring techniques or insufficiently understood concepts or dynamics. In this instance, even though we are concerned with a variable which is continuous by nature, and for which interval measurement should be possible, we may be able to achieve no more than dichotomous ordinal measurement. This instance produces what we have called a false dichotomy.

The other instance occurs when the researcher is able to treat the variable as continuous and does have interval data but decides for a particular research question that there is no need to work with this level of precision. For example, the researcher in the Phonics Study has decided to consider children reading two grades below normal as "below grade" and all other children as "not below," *for the purposes of this specific study*. But he also has available the actual reading grades. However, for some relationship analyses he may prefer to use the false dichotomous classifications "at least 2 years below grade" and "not 2 years below grade." If he were to do this type of approximation with two variables, of course he would have a situation calling for the tetrachoric correlation.

Two Sets of Data Not Identical in Nature and Level of Data

WEAKENING ONE SET   Let us now turn to the eventuality when the two sets of data we wish to correlate are not of the same type or level. There are three ways out of this dilemma. The least satisfactory way is to weaken one set of data; that is, use the stronger set of data at the level of the weaker set and so equate the two. For example, if we had one set of discrete ordinal data and one set of continuous interval data, we could treat them both as discrete ordinal data and so use the rank correlation procedures. In the same way, if we had one set of dichotomous nominal data and one set of ordinal or interval data, we could treat the ordinal or interval data as if it were nominal and so use one of the associational procedures for two nominal sets of data.

CORRELATION RATIO   A second technique is to utilize existing procedures whose properties make them applicable. The one such procedure is the correlation ratio. Its basic function is to correlate two sets of interval data from continuous variables which are curvilinearly related. It can also be used to correlate two sets of interval data when one variable is continuous but the other is discrete and either multiple- or infinite-category.

BISERIAL CORRELATION   The most satisfactory way to resolve this dilemma would be to develop specific correlational procedures that would enable us to use both sets of data at the strongest level possible. To date, two such procedures have been developed, the *biserial correlation* and a *point biserial correlation*. Both of these are used when one of the variables we wish to correlate is continuous and has provided interval or ratio data and the other variable is expressed in a dichotomy. This is the only requirement for the second variable: It can be discrete or continuous, and the data can be nominal, ordinal, or interval. However, the nature of the variable which has provided the dichotomous data is the basis for deciding which of the two biserial correlations to employ. If this variable, by nature, actually is a dichotomous variable, that is, a true dichotomy, then we use the point biserial correlation. However, if the dichotomous data represent a false dichotomy, that is, come from a variable which by nature is continuous, then we use the biserial correlation. For example, let us suppose that we wished to estimate the relationship between reading grade and sex. The first variable provides us with continuous interval data, the second with dichotomous data from a truly dichotomous variable, and so we would use the point biserial correlational technique. However, if we then wished to estimate the relationship between reading grade and arithmetic grade, when arithmetic grade is measured as either "at or above grade" or "below grade," we would use the biserial correlational technique, since in this instance the dichotomous data come from a variable which is continuous by nature but which has been dichotomized during the process of data collection or analysis.

   The point biserial correlation behaves like a typical correlation in having a range of values from $+1.00$ to -1.00. The biserial correlation, however, has an unlimited range and is therefore difficult to interpret or to use as a basis for estimating the correlation in the population between the two variables under study.[12]

[12]A thorough discussion of interpreting the biserial correlation appears in Walker and Lev, *Statistical Inference*.

To this point we have spoken about estimating the magnitude of the relationship between two variables through correlational procedures. After a moment's reflection, however, we realize that this is a superficial way of considering relationships, particularly in the social sciences, for two variables do not interact in the abstract. Instead they interact in the presence of, and are affected by, many other variables. The effort to identify and describe these interrelationships is called *multi-variate analysis*, and is the fourth function of descriptive statistics. The process has only recently become widely used, because most techniques for multi-variate analysis require extensive and complex computation and were therefore impractical until programs became available for processing the data by computer. Now even the most complex of the techniques for multi-variate analysis are available to the student with access to computer facilities, and so a whole new realm of questions can be studied about the interrelationships among variables.

DESCRIPTIVE PROCEDURES FOR MULTI-VARIATE ANALYSIS

Identifying Effect of Third Variable

The first way to study the interrelationships among multiple sets of data is to identify the effect a third variable may have on the relationship we observe between two others. For example, in the Language Study, let us assume we note a high correlation between ability to read and ability to do arithmetic. But we also note that each of these abilities is related to intelligence test scores. We might then consider the extent to which the apparent relationship between reading and arithmetic is only a reflection of the fact that each was related to a more basic dynamic, intelligence. This question can be answered through a procedure called *partial correlation*.

The kind of question raised by the partial correlation procedure is indicated by the data in Table 7-8. Here we have the three possible correlations between reading and arithmetic (.70), reading and intelligence (.90), and arithmetic and intelligence (.70). This way of reporting correlations is called a *correlational matrix,* and this matrix communicates a feeling that the relationships involved are all substantial. However, if we compute the partial correlation between reading and arithmetic, we would mathematically eliminate whatever inflating effect there is from the effect of their relationship with intelligence. The resulting partial correlation between reading and arithmetic is only .24, dramatically lower than the

Table 7-8 Correlational Matrix for Reading Grade, Arithmetic Grade and IQ

Variable → ↓	IQ	Reading Grade	Arithmetic Grade
IQ	X	.90	.70
Reading Grade	—	X	.70
Arithmetic Grade	—	—	X

.70 with which we began. Thus for these data we have learned that the high relationship was deceptive.

Essentially then, partial correlation is a computational procedure for removing or partialing out the tendency a third variable has to inflate the correlation between two other variables to which it may logically be related. This is a critical aspect to note: The researcher must be able to defend the logic of selecting the variables which he subjects to this procedure. There must be an empirical or conceptual basis for the partialing procedure.

Partialing cannot be done with nominal data or dichotomous and limited-category ordinal data, for we could only compute measures of association rather than correlation. It can be done with multiple-category ordinal data *if* Kendall's tau has been used as the measure of correlation. We cannot apply the partialing procedure to Spearman's rho. This is one advantage to the Kendall procedure, and we will prefer it if we anticipate any interest in using the partialing procedure. It can also be done with interval data, based on the Pearson product moment correlation.

It is possible to continue the partial correlation procedure beyond the first level, that is to take a matrix of correlations like Table 7-8 (called *zero-order* correlations to indicate that no partialing has been done) and use this matrix to obtain a matrix of *first order partial correlations,* going on then to partial out the partial correlations to obtain the second order partials. Although technically possible this is seldom done in practice; in fact the basic procedure of partial correlation is generally neglected in research—reflecting the superficial level at which we have often been content to conduct research in the social disciplines.

A Single Value

The next aspect of describing the interrelationships among multiple sets of data is to consider procedures available to estimate, in a single value, these interrelationships in the same sense that a correlation does for two variables. We cannot do it for nominal data, for dichotomous ordinal data, or for interval data. The only procedure which does provide us with a single overall estimate of the interrelationship among several sets of data is a procedure developed by Kendall called the *coefficient of concordance*.[13] This procedure requires limited- or multiple-category ordinal data. It is applicable when a group of respondents have been ranked on several variables and we wish to obtain some estimate of the overall relationship between the ranks. One procedure would be to compute the rank-order correlation for all possible pairs of variables and then to compute the arithmetic mean of the several rank-order correlations. The coefficient of concordance is essentially a computational technique for doing just this, only doing it through one series of computational steps. In fact the coefficient of concordance itself can actually be used to obtain a numerical estimate of the average rank-order correlation. Since it is a statistic which belongs to the percentile system, it requires ordinal data only, and so it is useful in many educational, sociological, and psychological research situations when this is the level of data available.

The coefficient of concordance can assume values only from 0 to +1.00. It cannot be negative because in more than two sets of ranks, there cannot be complete disagreement. Even if sets one and two are inversely related, set three must have a positive relationship to one of them.

A frequent use for this procedure is to obtain some sense of the agreement among judges. For example, Table 7-9 presents data for three psychologists' ranking of six children in terms of potential for improvement. The coefficient of concordance for these data is .48, indicating some

Table 7-9 Three Psychologists' Ranking of Six Children in Terms of Potential for Improvement

	Child					
Psychologist	Freddy	Bill	Lew	Tom	Frank	Bob
A	1	2	3	4	5	6
B	1	4	3	6	2	5
C	5	3	4	2	1	6

[13]The reader who has heard of the procedure called *multiple correlation* may think that this is a second procedure for accomplishing this purpose. Actually this is a misleadingly named statistic and does not estimate the relationship among variables but serves a quite different purpose, in studies of prediction. It is therefore discussed later in this chapter with other statistics of prediction.

interrelationship.[14] For comparison, the three rank-order correlations it is possible to compute are .60, −.27 and −.20 between psychologists A and B, B and C, and A and C respectively. If these are added algebraically and divided by three, the resulting mean is −.36, which suggests some slight interrelationship, but also notes that the negative aspects outweigh the positive, a point the coefficient of concordance does not note.

A Correlational Matrix

Another approach to identifying and describing the interrelationships among several variables is to present all possible pairs of relationships in a correlational matrix. One advantage of the matrix approach over the single-value approach is that within any one matrix you can include different levels of ordinal and interval data and therefore different correlational procedures. Table 7-9 is such a matrix, presenting the 15 hypothetical separate correlations which could be computed by taking six variables on which information was obtained for the Phonics Study and correlating every variable with every other variable, obtaining 15 different correlations. The matrix is itself a way of presenting the interrelationships among these six variables, and does enable us to make observations about interrelationships which would not be possible without it. Thus, referring to the table, we can see that the single highest relationship (.87) is

Table 7–10 Correlational Matrix for Selected Variables in Language Study

Variable → ↓	A. Vocabulary Score	B. Social Studies	C. Reading Grade	D. Arithmetic Problems	E. Arithmetic Computation	F. Space Perception
A. Vocabulary score	X	.62	.87	.33	.27	−.19
B. Social studies	—	X	.58	.34	.18	−.21
C. Reading	—	—	X	.43	.09	.06
D. Arithmetic problems	—	—	—	X	.71	.68
E. Arithmetic computation	—	—	—	—	X	.79
F. Space perception	—	—	—	—	—	X

[14]For further discussion of this procedure see Sidney Siegel, *Nonparametric Statistics* (New York: McGraw-Hill, Inc., 1956).

between reading grade and vocabulary score. We also see that space perception is negatively correlated to vocabulary and social studies and positively correlated to arithmetic ability, but seems to have little relationship to reading. Finally, we note that reading grade and vocabulary score are not only highly correlated with each other, but that both are correlated to almost the same magnitude with the other three variables as well. For example, the correlation between reading grade and social studies is .58, while the correlation between vocabulary and social studies is .62. This suggests to us that, within the limits of the information provided by this matrix of correlations, there was little sense in including both reading grade and vocabulary score because they provided much the same information. Following this train of thinking we might then wonder how many variables are actually needed to provide us with the essential information communicated by this matrix.

Identifying the Underlying Structure

The question posed above moves us to the last aspect of describing the interrelationships among several sets of data: identifying the underlying structure of the interrelationships expressed in the correlational matrix. This involves the procedure called *factor analysis*. This procedure estimates the minimum number of separate variables or factors necessary to provide the information contained in a correlational matrix. This method of analysis of multiple interrelationships is becoming increasingly popular in research in the social disciplines in view of the increasing availability of computers to do the laborious computations involved. Factor analysis does not directly answer the question of the nature of the interrelationships among the several variables. Rather it seeks to analyze the underlying structure of the interrelationships to determine how many and which variables explain it. The procedure has had wide use in research in education. For example, in the Phonics Study, if we obtained a wide variety of measures of the children's educational and sociopsychological functioning, we could use factor analysis to identify the minimum number of factors which must be hypothesized to account for the level of school functioning of the children selected for the phonics instruction.

Factor analysis typically involves a five-step process, in which the middle two steps involve complex computation almost always done by computer, so that the researcher becomes involved only in the first, second, and fifth stages. The first stage is to identify the variables to be studied, and the second step is to develop the correlational matrix expressing the correlation between each pair of variables, like table 7-10. The third step is to put this matrix through the first computational process of factor analysis which produces what is called an *unrotated matrix* of principal components, from which the minimum number of separate factors required to account for the data can be identified. Table 7-11 is the unrotated matrix of principal components for the data in Table 7-10. It contains correlations of the original six variables (vertically) with only five principal components. Thus, in the course of this third step in factor analysis we have learned that at most five factors will be needed to account for the variability in the data. But as we look at the row in the principal component matrix labeled "percent of variance explained" we note that only component 1 (accounting for 49 percent) and component 2 (accounting for 35 percent) play a major role in producing the variability in the original data. This would suggest that ultimately we need only two factors. However, further scanning of the data produced by components 3, 4, and 5 indicates that component 3 has one relatively high loading of .52, with the social studies measure, the only loading among these other three components in excess of .40. This provides a rationale for checking into the possibility that a third factor would be useful.

And so the data are processed through the fourth step in factor analysis, a step referred to as *rotation,* producing the rotated matrix of three factors in Table 7-12. Here we see that factor III does inded have a high loading in social studies. Note that in these stages the factors are only identified with Roman numbers and not names, as the computer and the computational process can only identify how many separate factors there are. They have no ability to name or label these factors. The contents of this second matrix consist of what are called the *factor loadings.* These loading have the same characteristics as correlations, in that they are two-digit decimals in the range of +1.00 to −1.00 through a midpoint of zero. Thus, a factor can have a positive or negative loading, and the sign

Table 7-11 Five Principal Component Unrotated Matrix for Variables in Table 7-10

Variable	I	II	III	IV	V
			Component		
Vocabulary	.74	−.58	−.16	.32	−.10
Social studies	.63	−.53	.52	.17	.14
Reading	.76	−.49	−.40	.14	.13
Arithmetic problems	.83	.39	−.03	.27	−.29
Arithmetic computation	.70	.60	−.21	−.35	.04
Space perception	.46	.85	−.17	.10	.20
Percent of variance explained	49	35	8	6	2

Table 7–12   Rotated Factor Matrix for Variables in Table 7-10

Measure	Factors		
	I	II	III
Reading	.97	.11	.15
Vocabulary	.87	.05	.38
Space perception	−.06	.93	−.32
Arithmetic computation	−.02	.92	.19
Arithmetic problems	.32	.84	.18
Social studies	.40	.05	.89

tells you if the factor is operating to raise or lower the score on a particular measure. In Table 7-12, we see that factor I is operating positively on scores on the reading, vocabulary, social studies, and arithmetic problem measures, but negatively on scores on arithmetic computation and space perception. The magnitude of the loading provides the insight into the importance of the factor on each performance on each measure. Again, referring to Table 7-12, factor I would seem to be important in understanding performance on the vocabulary and reading measures, but to have little importance in arithmetic computation or space perceptions.

The fifth and final step in factor analysis is for the researcher to name or label the factor which is operating in the situation. Generally this is simply a matter of seeing the variables for which the factor has significant[15] loading and seeking to abstract a term or concept reflecting an ability which would overlap performance on all of these variables. Thus, referring to Table 7-12, we see that factor I is particularly important for reading and vocabulary. We might then label it "verbal fluency" and feel this serves to represent all measures. The name applied should serve to communicate the variables on which the factor is important, and do this as simply and directly as possible. Thus, more esoteric labels like "verbal symbolic reasoning" or "alphabetical dexterity" would not communicate as well and so would be less appropriate.

Interpreting Correlations

There are several aspects to consider in understanding and interpreting correlations. Perhaps the most basic point to understand is that the scale for correlational values, from zero representing no relationship to +1.00

[15]This concept of significance is discussed in detail in Chapter 8.

representing a perfect positive relationship and down to -1.00 representing a perfect negative relationship, is an ordinal decimal scale which has been derived from the computational processes involved and does not represent the most obvious numerical analogy, the interval decimal system which goes from zero to one in ten equal increments.

A CORRELATION AS SHARED VARIANCE   How then do we evaluate correlations? The technique is both simple and woefully ignored in the research literature. We arithmetically square the correlation, multiply it by 100, and then read it as the percent of the variance shared by the two distributions. Stated another way, the square of the correlation tells us how much knowledge of variable one will tell us about variable two. As an example, assume the correlation reported between reading grade and arithmetic grade is .65. Immediately we know from the sign (or lack of one) that there is a positive relationship between achievement in these two subjects, and we know from the magnitude of the correlation that it is less than perfect. We then square the correlation, which yields .4225, and multiply by 100. We read this as a percent, 42.25 percent. This tells us that the distribution of reading grades and arithmetic grades share 42.25 percent of their variance. We can also say that if we know a student's reading grade we know 42.25 percent of what we need to know to be able to predict his arithmetic grade. Because a correlation is reversible, we can also say that if we know a student's arithmetic grade we know 42.25 percent of what we need to know to predict his reading grade.

In this way this percent of shared variance is an estimate of the predictive efficiency of the data under consideration, in the sense that the percent of shared variation does give us some basis for knowing how efficiently we can predict one variable when we have information about the other.

We can even visualize this interpretation of the correlation as in Figure 7-3. The circle at the left represents all of the variation in reading grade, while the circle at the right represents all of the variation in arithmetic grade. Notice that in the shaded area we can see the overlap of less than half, that is, the 42.25 percent. Notice also that the square of the correlation provides an estimate of that portion of the variance which is *not* shared, that is, that portion of the variance in each variable about which we have learned nothing from our knowledge of the other. To estimate this we subtract the squared correlation from 100 percent. Doing this for this correlation of .65 tells us that 57.75 percent of the variance (100 percent $-$ 42.25 percent) was unshared.

In Table 7-13, this squaring procedure has been done for units of five, for the reader's convenience. Several points of interest are apparent in this

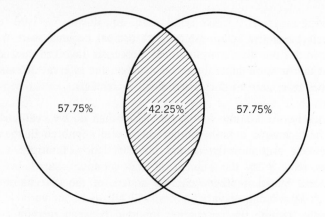

Figure 7-3 Visualization of correlation of .65 between reading grade and arithmetic grade.

table. First, since correlations are decimals or fractions, squaring them always reduces them in size. Thus we must be alert to the fact that our intuitive reaction (if correlations invoke intuitive reactions!) as to the magnitude of the correlation will be deceptively high. To most people who read research a correlation of .60 sounds reasonably high. Yet as the table

Table 7–13 Relationship of Magnitude of Specified Correlations to the Percent of the Variation Explained

Reported Correlation	Arithmetic Square	Percent of Variation Explained
.95	.9025	90
.90	.8100	81
.866	.7499	75
.85	.7225	72
.816	.6658	66
.75	.5625	56
.708	.5013	50
.70	.4900	49
.65	.4225	42
.60	.3600	36
.55	.3025	30
.50	.2500	25
.45	.2025	20
.40	.1600	16

shows, this correlation accounts for only one-third of the variation in the two distributions and leaves the other two-thirds unaccounted for. Second, notice that the correlation must reach .708 before we have accounted for half of the variation in the variables under study, and must reach .816 before we have accounted for two-thirds of it. Third, notice that correlations, which in themselves may sound substantial, like .50, actually serve little function, accounting as they do for only 25 percent of the variation. Finally and perhaps most important, the table should indicate the point made earlier, that correlations are statistical artifacts which have been developed so that they come out somewhere along the continuum from .00 to 1.00, and that the resultant number has no meaning except as reflecting relative position along that continuum.

It is important for the researcher, particularly in selecting tests for use in research, to realize that in terms of ease of interpretation of correlations the wrong statistic is generally reported in research articles and in test manuals and promotional brochures. Therefore the consumer must generally do this squaring for himself.

Correlation a Reflection of Order, Not Value

Another point to remember in interpreting and understanding a correlation is the point made earlier in this chapter: *Both* percentile and moment system correlations are measures *only* of the stability of the ordering of the two sets of data. They do not reflect the position of the scores on any absolute scale of values. Thus, if we were to administer a test to a group of children at the beginning of a unit and administer it again at the end of the unit, and find a perfect positive correlation of +1.00, this would tell us only that every child remained in the same relative position on the two administrations. It would tell us nothing about the two distributions of scores. Everyone could have changed 10 points or 100 points or different numbers of points. As long as their relative position remained unchanged, the correlation would be perfect.

Accuracy of Correlations

We have often noted how in almost all instances in which we measure psychosocial or educational characteristics there is some imprecision of measurement. In some descriptive statistical analyses, such as measures of central tendency, these errors play little role. This is because we can usually assume that the errors which remain after careful instrument development are chance errors, and chance errors tend to cancel each other out. Thus for some people the data will be an overestimate, but for others it will be an underestimate. The net effect of these errors is to cancel each other and so have no effect on central tendency, but they do increase the variability of the data. This increase on variability is called *attenuation*. Attenuation is important in correlation since it reduces the size of the correlation coefficient obtained. This has an important implication for interpreting correlations: It means that in most correlational studies the correlations obtained are *lower* than the real magnitude of the relationship involved. When the instability in the data-gathering instruments is serious and adds to attenuation, then the correlation obtained may be quite low, even if the characteristics being studied are highly related.

This means that if we are planning or interpreting a correlational study, we must be concerned with the stability of the measuring instruments as reflected in their reliability.

A second way of considering the accuracy of a correlation is available for the product moment correlation, and that is to apply the concept of the standard error discussed in Chapter 6. Thus, product moment correlations obtained from sample data can be used to make estimates of the correlation in the population, at known levels of confidence, by calculating the standard error of the correlation and applying the normal curve model as was done in Chapter 6.[16]

Effect of Distortions in Distributions

One of the problems in interpreting correlations is allowing for that proportion of a total distribution represented in the correlation. All moment system correlations are based on the assumption that the data being correlated are normally distributed. Percentile system correlations are not based on this assumption, but are still liable to the misinterpretations we shall consider now.

For most educational, psychological, and sociological variables it is a far simpler problem to identify three gross groupings—those at the extremely high point, those in the middle, and those at the extremely low point—than it is to take any one of the groupings and order the people within it. For example, consider three problems. The first is to take a group of children, talk to them for five minutes each and then divide them into three groups—the children with unusual verbal fluency, children with

---

[16]A procedure for estimating the effect on a correlation of the reliability of the measures involved is presented in Robert L. Thorndike and Elizabeth Hagen, *Measurement and Evaluation in Psychology and Education* (New York, John Wiley & Sons, Inc., 1955). The use of the standard error is presented in Helen Walker and Joseph Lev, *Elementary Statistical Methods* (New York: Holt, Rinehart and Winston, Inc., 1958).

average fluency, and the children with poor fluency. The second problem is to take only the children classified as unusually verbal, talk to them for five minutes, and place them in order from the most to the least fluent child. The third problem is to take a group consisting only of children who are either very fluent or not fluent, talk to them for five minutes, and classify each child as fluent or not.

Of the three assignments, the third is the simplest because it involves the clearest distinctions. The first assignment is next in simplicity because you are asked to make only three gross categorizations. The second assignment is very difficult, for here you are asked to make relatively fine distinctions between children who have all been placed in the same gross category.

But these three assignments represent the three different computational assignments we can give to a correlational procedure. If we seek to correlate data on two variables from a total distribution, we are posing the first problem. We are seeking to learn whether or not there has been stability in the gross ordering of people. Have the highs stayed high, the middles, middle, and the lows, low? Often in education we pose the second problem, where we have only one extreme or the other available and wish to correlate data from two variables for this subgroup only. The Phonics Study illustrates that problem, if the researcher were to take the retarded readers only and attempt to correlate reading and arithmetic scores. These children represent only one end of the continuum, and so we are asking the correlational procedure to distinguish within that one group. This situation, when data are available only from one extreme, involves a process called *curtailment*. It is a problem faced by all educational programs which only admit certain persons to a program. For example, it is extremely difficult to do correlational studies among college students because they are a select group representing only the upper end of the achievement continuum.

The third problem also exists in education, where we work with extremes only, leaving out the middle. A recent doctoral study[17] faced this problem when the researcher sought to correlate intelligence and reading ability among a group of culturally disadvantaged children. The data available came from children who were the best and poorest achievers in the fifth grades of schools in the study with the children of average achievement omitted.

Ideally a correlational procedure is based on the full distribution.

[17]Louise W. Fox, "The Effect of Variation in Measurement of Tactual-Visual Reciprocity on Its Relationship to Intelligence and Achievement Among Disadvantaged Children." Unpublished doctoral dissertation, Teachers College, Columbia University, 1967.

Distorted correlations result from *both* curtailment and the loss of the middle of the distribution, but the nature of the distortion differs. With curtailment the correlation obtained is an *underestimate* of what it would be if data from the total group were available. When the middle has been lost or eliminated, the correlation is higher than it would be if the ambiguous middle were present. In each instance, it is possible to use the correlations actually obtained to estimate what the correlations would be if data were available from the total group.[18] The important point to note is that unless we have based our correlations on the total distribution, interpretation is treacherous and should be delayed until the corrections are performed.

Evaluating Size of a Correlation

Even when the squaring procedure is completed and all other allowances made, ultimately the researcher is faced with the necessity to decide if the correlation is "high" or "low," or, stated more practically, is high enough for a particular research purpose. The size of a correlation must be evaluated in two ways, on an absolute scale and in terms of the variables being correlated.

On an absolute scale the region around zero is considered to represent no relationship beyond chance. In the next chapter we shall discuss statistical procedures for defining the term "around zero," but for each set of data there is a point at which the correlation is sufficiently far from zero to be considered evidence of a relationship beyond chance. From this point to correlations of $\pm.50$, this author would consider the absolute value as *low,* since at best 25 percent of the variance is shared. From the correlation of $\pm.50$ to the correlation of $\pm.70$, we would consider the absolute value *moderate,* that is, when 25 percent to 50 percent of the variation is shared. From $\pm.70$ to $\pm.86$ we would consider the absolute value *high,* for here between 50 percent and 75 percent of the variance is shared. Then correlations above $\pm.86$ we would consider *very high,* for here more than 75 percent of the variance is shared.

This general guide to absolute evaluation must not obscure the necessity to evaluate the correlation obtained in the context of the variables being correlated. For example, if we obtained a correlation of $\pm.60$ in the abstract this would be labeled moderate. Yet if this was a correlation expressing the relationship between scores on the reading test and vocabu-

---

[18]Corrections for both curtailment and the loss of the middle cases can be found in Robert L. Thorndike, *Personnel Selection* (New York: John Wiley and Sons, Inc., 1949).

lary test given to children in the Phonics Study, we would be concerned because this is much lower than the correlations generally reported for such tests. In contrast, if this were the correlation between two psychologists who independently studied some psychological diagnostic data we had on these children and ranked them in terms of adjustment, we would be pleased with the size of the correlation because this compares favorably with correlations reported in the literature for this kind of data. In short, to evaluate correlations in the context of the specific data, the researcher must know the literature well enough to know what levels of correlations have been reported previously. These provide a basis for knowing if we have comparable data or different relationships than those reported. If we have lower correlations, consider the possibility that our instruments did not function as reliably as those used in previous research.

Correlations as Indicators of Cause

It is critical to notice the terminology used in describing a correlation, that it expresses the direction of and estimates the magnitude of the relationship *between* the two variables. This means that once having been computed, the correlation between variables A and B expresses the relationship between A and B or between B and A. In short, a correlation is reversible and has no orientation in terms of the two variables being correlated. This is not a purely academic point because it leads to the important principle that a correlation, being reversible, can never be interpreted as reflecting a causal relationship.

This particular point has often been argued in research, and even in some books on statistics, in the sense that simple logic should be able to identify which of the variables being correlated precedes the other in time and therefore identify the direction of the relationship and attribute cause. After all, how can event B occurring three months after event A have any effect on it? A simple example in education is to consider how the possibility of a final examination in a course may affect student motivation and diligence throughout the semester, and therefore in a sense "affect" student performance on examinations given early in the semester. But even if it were not possible to defend the logic of an event affecting events preceding it in time, there would still be no basis for interpreting a correlation as reflecting cause, for as we saw when we worked with the partial correlational procedure, an apparent strong relationship between reading and arithmetic all but disappeared when we allowed for the effect of intelligence. Since it will always be true that a relationship between two variables may only be reflecting the fact that each is related to and affected by a third or fourth variable, we simply cannot attribute cause through correlational procedures. If we wish to study cause, design an experimental study, and we *will* be able to make a conclusion as to cause and effect.

Need for Rational Basis

It has long been known, and is a frequent source of amusement, that we can obtain correlations of respectable magnitude by correlating far-fetched sets of data. For example, Huff in his book *How To Lie with Statistics,*[19] cites the relatively high correlation over the years between ministers' salaries and the price of rum or the age of a woman and the angle between her feet in walking. This ability to find such relationships reflects the important point that the techniques we have discussed for estimating association and correlation are statistical procedures and have no ability to reflect whether or not the data being correlated are sensible *to* correlate. This is the researcher's problem. He must be able to defend the rationale for his correlations.

This is a problem which will become more acute in the future than it has been in the past because of the availability of computers to do the computational part of correlations. Prior to computers, when a researcher had to perform the computations himself, he made reasonably certain that if he set out to compute a correlation there was a logical reason to expect that the two variables might be related and a research reason to need to know whether or not they were. But now if a researcher has data available from several variables it is actually a simpler process to feed all of the data into the computer and have it produce one overall matrix, that is, to correlate every variable with every other variable, even when there is neither a logical nor a research basis for some of the correlations.

If enough correlations are performed some will emerge which look worth considering but which in reality are spurious. If we are to avoid this problem, we should think through the problem as if there were no computer available, identify the correlations we need for our research purpose, and which we can defend as logical, and do this *before* we look at the matrix. Then if the matrix indicates other relationships exist, we use this as motivation to rethink our logic to see if there were gaps or flaws in our original thinking. If we can find none, consider the possibility that the correlation is spurious, and do not spend hours wondering why final examination grades should have correlated with the size of hometown of the child's maternal grandmother.

[19]Darrell Huff, *How To Lie with Statistics* (New York: W. W. Norton & Company, Inc., 1954).

Now let us move on to the final function of descriptive statistics, using existing data to predict future performance.

PREDICTION OF PERFORMANCE

Let us suppose that we obtain both perceptual scores and reading grades for the children selected for the small-group remedial reading instruction, and that after one year of instruction we correlate the child's perceptual score before the program with amount of improvement during the program, and that the correlation is .68. We could then raise the question of what ability this correlation gives us to predict, for a *new* group of children, the amount of improvement a child will show as soon as we learn his perceptual score. This process, whereby we utilize the known relationship between two variables to predict one from the other, is called *simple regression*.

The process of simple regression requires that, for one group of respondents, the researcher have data available for *both* variables. Thus, in the example above, at the beginning of the Phonics Study we would have data available for the predictor: the perceptual test. But regression analysis could not be considered until the Phonics Study was completed and we also had data available for the criterion: improvement in reading grade. With data available for both criterion and predictor the computational process of regression can be begun. This is directed toward developing a *regression equation* to express the relationship between the variables. This equation is usually stated in the form: $\hat{Y} = b(X) + a$, in which $\hat{Y}$ represents the score we predict for an individual on the criterion, X represents the score we know for the individual on the predictor, and a and b are two constants to allow for variation in scale of measurement and the relative rates of change in the two variables.

This can be made clearer through an example. In columns 1 and 2 of Table 7-14, we present data on the perceptual test scores and final reading grades for nine children. If we do the computations for simple regression we learn that for this set of data, $a = 3.5$ and $b = .054$, so that the equation relating these two sets of data is $\hat{Y} = .054(X) + 3.5$. The values reflect what is apparent from scanning the numbers in columns 1 and 2, that the two tests use different scales of measurement and change at different rates. For example, the scores on the perceptual test range from 17 to 37, whereas scores on the reading grades test range from 3.7 to 6.1.

Now that we have developed the regression equation from these data, as soon as we give a beginning group of children in the remedial program the initial perceptual test, we have a basis for *predicting* the final reading grade.

Table 7-14 Actual and Predicted Scores for Perceptual Scores and Final Reading Grade

Child	Column 1 X = Predictor: Score on Perceptual Test	Column 2 Y = Criterion: Final Reading Grade	Column 3 $\breve{Y}$ = Predicted Criterion Score Using Regression	Column 4 Error of Estimate
1	37	4.4	5.5	+1.1
2	36	5.3	5.5	+0.2
3	36	6.1	5.5	−0.6
4	32	5.8	5.2	−0.6
5	27	5.0	5.0	0.0
6	25	5.2	4.9	−0.3
7	25	5.2	4.9	−0.3
8	18	4.7	4.5	−0.2
9	17	3.7	4.4	+0.7

Regression Equation—Algebraically: 0.0

$$\breve{Y} = .054(X) + 3.5$$

Regression Equation—Verbally:

Predicted Reading Grade = .054 (Perceptual Test Score) + 3.5

All we need do is take each separate perceptual test score and substitute it as the X in the regression equation, then solve the equation for $\breve{Y}$ or the predicted final reading grade.[20]

To give you some feeling for the accuracy of prediction, we have used the regression equation developed from the data in Table 7-14 to predict the final reading grades, and these predicted scores are listed in column 3, headed "predicted criterion score." Thus for child 1, who actually scored 4.4, we have predicted a score of 5.5, and so have overestimated his actual score by 1.1 grades, an *error of estimate* listed in column 4. For child 2 the error of estimate was much smaller, 0.2 grades, and so on for the nine children. Note, however, that the errors of estimate, when added algebraically, add to *zero*. This indicates that we have achieved the best possible prediction, in the sense that the overestimates have been balanced by the underestimates, and our errors have balanced out. But notice that this

[20]An extended treatment of regression appears in Walker and Lev, *Elementary Statistical Methods,* including the computational processes and techniques for estimating how effective prediction will be (from which the above data are adapted).

balancing out reflects the computational process only and does not tell the researcher anything about the accuracy of his predictions. The accuracy is reflected in the errors of estimate, and if the researcher wishes to evaluate these, or compare the errors in two comparable sets of data, he should follow the procedure used in the standard deviation, that is, to square each error of estimate and sum the squares.

Multiple Regression

In discussing correlation, we noted that correlating two variables is an artificially isolated way of looking at how human beings function. Similarly simple regression is an oversimplified approach to prediction because human behavior is not explained by one factor but by many. Thus it would be naive to attempt to predict improvement in the Phonics Program only on the basis of perceptual score. Certainly intelligence plays a part in improvement, as do reading ability before the program, interest in learning to read, and other variables as well. Equally certainly, if we took all of the relevant variables into account we should be able to generate a far superior prediction than from any one alone. The process whereby we seek to predict performance on a single-criterion variable from our knowledge of several predictor variables is called *multiple regression*.

The procedure begins exactly as simple regression does with data required for one group of respondents, for the criterion, and for all predictors. But then two problems must be resolved through the computational processes of multiple regression. First, some of the predictors may be serving essentially the same function and so all may not be necessary. For example, if we have both a reading test and a vocabulary test, we may find that these are so highly correlated that we have no better predictive ability when we use both than when we use only one of them. Therefore, the first step in multiple regression is to determine the most effective combination of predictors. What we seek is a set of predictors, each of which is related to the criterion, but which bear low relationships to each other.

The second problem is that the predictors included in this best possible combination undoubtedly differ in their predictive efficiency: Some are better than others. Therefore the computational processes are also directed toward determining a separate *regression weight* for each predictor, so that we achieve the best possible prediction.

If this sounds like a process which involves great amounts of computation, it does! Before the availability of computers, we seldom saw the procedure used in research for more than two or three predictors. Now computer programs are available for solving the problems of multiple regression for large numbers of predictors, and the technique is easily incorporated into the researcher's repertoire.

If we contemplate using this procedure in a particular study it is important that we realize that the process is limited to the moment system, but we can combine product moment correlations and point biserial correlations in a multiple regression equation. Therefore we must think through the nature of the data we will obtain and the correlational procedures which will be possible as we plan the regression analysis.

Let us now assume that we have gone through the multiple regression procedure and have determined the best combination of predictors and the weights to be used with each and so predict the amount of improvement each child will achieve during our Phonics Program. But we already know how much improvement has actually been achieved. One way to evaluate the success of our prediction would be to correlate the predicted degree of improvement with the actual degree of improvement. If we were to do this we would be computing the misleadingly named *multiple correlation coefficient*. Note that, unlike the implication in the name, it is *not* a correlation among several variables but is only a correlation between two sets of data, an actual set of scores and a predicted set of scores. The "multiple" aspect is that the predicted scores are based on multiple predictors, that is, obtained through the multiple regression procedure.

The regression procedure can be done retroactively, and has a legitimate place in research on that basis as well. For example, a school system may be interested in studying the effectiveness of already existing criteria on which children are admitted to, or excluded from, a special advanced program. One way of doing such a study would be to do a multiple regression analysis of the data available from the previous year, and a multiple correlation between the predicted performance in the program and the actual performance. However, such an analysis would run into the curtailment problem discussed earlier in this chapter, in that only part of the total distribution of children is available for this study, that is, those who did well enough on the admission criteria to be admitted to the program. Therefore, the multiple correlations actually obtained would be lower than we might expect if a wider range of students were available for study. However, techniques are available[21] for using the correlations obtained from the curtailed group to estimate what the correlations would be if this larger distribution were available.[22]

---

[21]These procedures are discussed by Harold Gulliksen, *Theory of Mental Tests* (New York: John Wiley & Sons, Inc., 1950).

[22]Of course the problem could be avoided by designing a different kind of study for a new year, admitting a sample of all students to the advanced program, whether or not they met the criteria for admission. At the end of this experimental year the multiple regression analysis could be done, and the multiple correlation obtained would not be distorted since it would have been based on the total distribution.

Predicting Group Membership

To this point in our discussion of prediction we have considered the relationships between predictors and criterion in terms of the total set of data, but often in research in education we are concerned with a different kind of prediction—into which of two groups is a child likely to enter. For example, the extensive study on predicting delinquency conducted by the Gluecks[23] essentially asked this kind of question: If we obtain certain specific sociopsychological and educational data about children early in elementary school, can we predict which children will commit sufficiently consistent and serious delinquent acts by adolescence to be considered delinquent? This question broke the criterion "delinquency" into two groups—delinquent and nondelinquent—and the prediction problem was not to predict numbers of acts of delinquency but only into which of the two groups a child would fall. Similarly, in our current concern with completing secondary school, research is under way to identify those variables that will enable us to predict whether a child is likely to be a dropout or to complete school. At the simplest level, the teacher at the beginning of a semester may be concerned with predicting who will pass and who will fail, although predicting gradations of success will also be important.

The problem of predicting into which of two groups a child is likely to fall involves a relatively little-used statistical procedure called *discriminant analysis*. The most widely used procedure for doing this is *Fisher's Linear Discriminant Function*. In computation[24] it is parallel to any other regression analysis in that it yields a regression equation with regression weights for each individual predictor. It also provides a basis for using the prediction to assign each individual to one of the two criterion groups.

A procedure has been developed by Rao[25] which enables the researcher to assign each individual to one of several groups within the criterion variable. Called the *Maximum Likelihood Discriminant Function,* it has been used infrequently in social research despite its potential for permitting us to state more subtle problems than the linear discriminant function permits. For example, instead of statistically asking only if a child will drop out or complete secondary school we could pose the more complex problem of using predictor data to decide which is most likely for an elementary school child: He will drop out in secondary school; complete secondary school but go no further; go on to college, but not complete it;

[23]New York City Youth Board Research Department, *An Experiment in the Validation of the Glueck Prediction Scale* (New York: The Board, July 1957).

[24]See C. C. Li, *Introduction to Experimental Statistics* (New York: McGraw-Hill, Inc., 1964).

[25]See C. R. Rao, *Advanced Statistical Methods in Biometric Research* (New York: John Wiley & Sons, Inc., 1952). See Chapter 8 for details of this procedure.

Table 7-15   Summary of Procedures for Association, Correlation, and Prediction

General Procedure	Specific Procedure	Requirements for Procedure as to Nature of Variables and Level of Data
I. When Research Purpose Is To Estimate the Relationship between Two Sets of Data		
Association	(a) Chi square and contingency coefficient	*None*, but particularly applicable to nominal, verbal ordinal, and limited-category numerical ordinal data
	(b) Phi coefficient	Both variables dichotomous
	(c) Q test	Both variables dichotomous
Correlation	(a) Rank order correlation	Ordinal data, best suited to multiple-category variables
	(b) Kendall's tau	Ordinal data, best suited to multiple-category variables
	(c) Product moment correlation	Interval data from two continuous variables, normally distributed with a linear relationship, also normally distributed
	(d) Correlation ratio	Interval data from either: (a) two continuous variables with a curvilinear relationship (b) one continuous and one discrete multiple-category variable
	(e) Tetrachoric correlation	Ordinal data from two false dichotomies
	(f) Biserial correlation	One set of interval data from a continuous variable and one set of data expressed as a false dichotomy
	(g) Point biserial correlation	One set of interval data from a continuous variable

II. When Research Purpose Is To Estimate the Relationships among More than Two Sets of Data

Partialing	Partial correlation	Three sets of data such that all possible pairs of correlations can be computed through either: (a) product moment procedures; (b) Kendall's tau
Estimating interrelationship in a single value	Coefficient of concordance	Ordinal data, at limited-category level or above
Estimating interrelationships in a matrix	Correlational matrix	*None*: can present different procedures in one matrix and so can utilize all kinds of variables and levels of data
Identifying underlying structure	Factor analysis	Interval data from continuous variables

III. When Research Purpose Is To Estimate the Ability To Predict Performance

Predicting a specific score for each individual	Simple regression	Interval data from two continuous variables with one designated as the predictor and one designated as criterion
	Multiple regression	Interval data from several continuous variables with one designated as criterion and all others designated as predictors
Predicting group membership only	Linear discriminant function	Ordinal data from one or more predictors and a dichotomous criterion variable
	Maximum likelihood discriminant function	Ordinal data from one or more predictors and a limited-category criterion variable
Identifying underlying structure among predictors and criteria	Canonical correlation	Ordinal data from one or more predictors and more than one criterion variable

or go on and complete college. The computational process involved in the Rao procedure essentially involves parallel discriminant function analyses. That is, we predict the likelihood of the child falling into each of the criterion groups, and then assign him to that group for which we have the greatest likelihood. This procedure has not been widely used despite its applicability and apt name.

Canonical Correlation

As data-processing capacity has increased through computers, the procedures for multi-variate prediction have also been able to move to more complex problems. One of these complex problems for which a procedure now exists is the use of multiple predictors to predict performance on more than one criterion. For example, let us say we wished to use several variables available at the beginning of the Phonics Study to predict not only improvement in reading grade, but interest in reading as well. We could do separate multiple regression analyses, but we also might want to know if there was an interrelationship among the predictors and both criteria considered simultaneously. The procedure which does this is called *canonical correlation*.[26]

Like all of the prediction statistics, canonical correlation requires one complete set of data, that is, for the predictors and the two criterion variables. These are used to develop two complete correlation matrices. Further computation can be seen as a double-factor analysis in the sense that the canonical correlation procedure tells the researcher which variable or combination of predictor variables underly the relationship between the criterion variables.

Practical Aspects of Prediction

There are two practical points to note in regard to prediction. The first is that while it is possible to develop a regression equation from any two sets of data, this does not mean that we will have any predictive ability. The clue to our predictive ability lies in the correlation between each predictor and the criterion variable. If we persist in using predictor data which do not correlate well with our criterion we will make a high proportion of errors. A recurring example of this is the inability of college admissions officers to predict who will succeed in completing college without difficulty. Over the years, fewer than 50 percent of the entering freshmen

[26]For details of this procedure see William W. Cooley and Paul R. Lohnes, *Multivariant Procedures for the Behavorial Sciences* (New York: John Wiley & Sons, Inc., 1962), pp. 35–45.

graduate with their class, despite the increasingly varied and complex set of predictors used. The basic problem is that the predictors used to date simply do not correlate highly enough with the criterion of successful completion of the undergraduate course of studies to provide a basis for better prediction.

The second point to note is that we can predict without knowing cause. Students often ask how we can discuss prediction based on correlation when at the same time we argue that correlations do not reflect a causal relationship. The answer is that while they do not show cause, correlations do reflect the strength of a relationship. Even if they are only reflecting the effect of a third and fourth variable on the relationship under study, they still show the *strength* of that relationship and so can be used to develop a prediction.

Much the same rationale explains why we can develop regression procedures based on correlations, whether or not we ultimately learn that a causal relationship existed between predictor and criterion.

At the end of Chapter 6, we summarized those procedures available within the first two functions of descriptive statistics. In this chapter we have discussed the last three functions, and Table 7-15 summarizes the procedures available for these functions. Thus Tables 6-8 and 7-15 together provide an overview of what a researcher can aspire to do with descriptive statistics.

Chapter 8

INFERENTIAL STATISTICS: THE CONCEPTS

As noted in Chapter 6, the second major area of statistical analysis is called *inferential statistics*. This area includes statistical procedures which provide the basis for consistent and objective inferences from the actual data at hand to larger situations. In Chapter 9 we shall turn to the specific techniques available for making such inferences. In this chapter we shall consider the concepts involved. To begin, let us illustrate the nature of the problem with two examples. First, assume that you are told that ten children have been selected for a nutrition experiment. The ten all weigh exactly 60 pounds when selected for the experiment and have been carefully matched for height, age, sex, and a variety of measures of food intake. They are all placed on different diets for a period of twelve weeks. At the end of the twelve-week period they are all weighed again by a carefully checked scale. The ten weights are as listed below:

Child:	A	B	C	D	E	F	G	H	K	L
Weight:	60	61	64	65	66	67	68	69	72	75

Now we ask, how many children gained weight? Without hesitating we would say that everyone but the first child gained weight. If we were then asked how many children had appreciably changed in their weight, we might hesitate a bit but almost certainly would agree that child L, who has gained 15 pounds, and child K, with a gain of 12 pounds, have changed. There would be some disagreement in making this statement about the other children. Some people would also include children G and H, arguing that gains of eight or nine pounds also reflect appreciable change. Others would say that five or more pounds reflect real change and would include children D, E, and F. Some might even argue that any change is appreciable change and so conclude all but child A have changed. Obviously in research this type of anarchy in judgments cannot be permitted, and so we need some objective way of deciding when "change" becomes "appreciable change," that is, when data reflect that our research variables have had a significant effect.

236

Let us consider the second example. Now suppose that the ten children were selected because they had all achieved a score of 60 on an objective test of social studies knowledge, and that the twelve-week period consisted not of diets but of instruction in social studies, after which they were tested again on a carefully checked alternate form of the test which has been shown to have identical difficulty. Now let the ten numbers above represent the scores on the second test. Again we are asked who changed and who gained appreciably. The second question about appreciable gain is as difficult as it was before, but the first as to who changed is also a problem where it was not in the nutrition study. Many people would question now whether child B who scored only one point higher has changed. We begin to wonder if child B might have guessed slightly better the second time and so might really not have changed at all. The same hesitation could even apply to child C. But we did not have this hesitation in the nutrition experiment, where we did not question the change in the child who gained only one pound.

The difference between the two situations, of course, is in the nature of the measure being used. In the first instance when we are measuring the children's weight, we have highly accurate and reliable ratio measurement and can therefore be reasonably certain as to whether or not change took place. In the second instance, testing for social studies knowledge, we have ordinal measurement, and moreover measurement with some element of unreliability, and so cannot be certain if small changes in score reflect change in ability or imprecision in measurement. Unhappily it is the second instance which more closely typifies the research situation in the social disciplines because we generally collect data through instruments which contain some innacuracy or unreliability. Thus we not only have the problem the physical scientist has of determining when appreciable change took place, but we also have the more basic problem of determining when change itself took place.

To help make this decision let us finally suppose that some interested party made the following data available to us. He took 100 children and gave half of them form A of our social studies test and the other half form B. As soon as they were finished with the first test, he reversed the procedure, giving the children the other form of the test. He then scored the tests and reports in Table 8-1 as to how many children achieved identical scores (the 26 children who had a change of zero) and how many changed one, two, three, or more points.[1] Scanning the table we notice that most of the children changed four or fewer points, but that a few changed more than this, up to the one child who changed eight points.

[1]For purposes of studying change, it makes no difference if the child's score was higher or lower the second time.

Table 8-1 The Percent of Times Specific Differences Occurred

Differences[a] in Points	Percent of Times Difference Occurred	Percent of Times This Difference or Larger Difference Occurred: The Significance Probability	Percent of Times Smaller Difference Occurred
0	26	100	0
1	23	74	26
2	19	51	49
3	13	32	68
4	9	19	81
5	5	10	90
6	2	5	95
7	2	3	97
8	1	1	99
9 or more	0	0	100

[a]For simplicity, we are combining all differences of the same size, no matter what sign.

But how can we explain these changes? We cannot attribute them to instruction or learning because no instruction took place and there was no opportunity for the students to learn by checking reference material between the two testing sessions. We can only attribute the differences to factors like test experience, or more likely to chance factors like guessing or mood or motivation. So Table 8-1 provides us with two things: first the basis for knowing what kinds of changes occur without instruction, primarily by chance, and second and even more important, the knowledge of how often each specific difference occurs by chance.

OBJECTIFYING THE DECISION ABOUT CHANCE

Let us see how this resolves our problem of objectively deciding when change has taken place. As we refer the ten scores to the table we note that the children who scored 69, 72, and 75 all changed more than any change reported in the table. Therefore we would be completely confident within the limits of the data in Table 8-1 in saying that they did change, and that while chance factors like guessing might have produced some of their change, they certainly did not produce all of it. But what about child G who scored a 68 on the second test for a difference of eight points? The table tells us that this large a difference might have happened by chance, since one child actually did change eight points, and child G might be another such child. However, the odds are high that he is not; in fact, based on Table 8-1, the odds are 99 to 1 that he represents real change and not chance change. Most gamblers would accept 99 to 1 odds and so do most researchers, and so we would usually say that child G also changed.

But notice that we do this knowing that there is one chance in 100 that we are wrong, that child G represents nothing more than another extreme chance difference. Stated another way we are running a 1 percent risk of error in saying that he has changed. By the same reasoning we could make a decision on child F, with his change of seven points. Changes of seven points occurred twice purely by chance according to Table 8-1, but in evaluating the change for child F it seems logical to also include the one change of eight points in the table and so state that changes of seven points *or more* happened three out of 100 times. Thus the odds that child F's change of seven points represents a real difference are 97 to 3, and so if we designate his change as real we are running a 3 percent risk of error. By this same reasoning we determine that if we call child E's change of six points real we are running a 5 percent risk of error. The risk rises to 10 percent for child D who changed five points and to 19 percent for child C who changed four points. This probability, that an observed difference or a larger difference could occur by chance, is called the *significance probability* of the result. Note that a dozen different researchers using this table would all come to the same conclusion as to the significance probability of a difference of seven points, or of any difference for that matter. So we have taken the first major step toward objectivity.

SETTING A LEVEL OF SIGNIFICANCE

But we need to take a second step before we fully achieve an objective basis for deciding which differences are so unusual that we cannot accept them as chance occurrences or so usual that we can. We take the second step by agreeing on a conventional statistical definition of "unusual," by establishing what we call the *level of significance*. How seldom must something happen before we would be willing to conclude that it was not a chance occurrence? One thing we might do is set this level so low as to make it all but impossible for our observed result to be a chance occurrence, that is, for these data, to insist on differences of nine or more. The consequence of this, however, would be that we would seldom obtain such a result in practice, and so this decision would be tantamount to agreeing to attribute nothing to research conditions. The more sensible combination of reality with research precision is to select a low but feasible level at which to draw the line between "chance" and "not chance." In the social disciplines two such levels of significance are used, one at 1 percent, the other at 5 percent. While both of these levels are used in general, research in education typically has used the 5 percent level of significance.

The level of significance can be perceived as the researcher's statement of that point at which the significance probability of a result has gotten so large that he prefers to attribute the result to chance rather than to the research conditions. Five percent may not sound "so large" to many readers, but realize that it means if a study were done only 20 times, in one of those 20 (5 percent) a spurious conclusion could be drawn. For the level of significance may also be seen as the maximum risk of error the researcher is willing to run when he concludes that a difference is *not* attributable to chance. We say risk of error because, as can be seen from Table 8-1, if we set the level of significance at 5 percent, differences of six, seven, or eight points would be attributed to the research condition even though we know from the table that they could and did happen by chance. Therefore, any specific observed difference of six, seven, or eight points might be another of these extreme chance occurrences. If our researcher were to use the 5 percent level of significance, he would designate children E, F, G, H, K, and L as having changed and all the others as not having changed. If instead, he decided that 1 percent was the maximum risk of error he was willing to run, then only children G, H, K, and L would be considered to have changed.

But note that he cannot be completely certain of his decision for he makes it in the face of his knowledge that differences as large as the one he is refusing to attribute to chance *actually did* occur by chance two times in 100, and an even larger difference occurred once. What this means is that if the observed difference of seven points in his own study is another one of these extreme chance differences, then he is making an error when he does not attribute it to chance. The table cannot help him know whether or not he is making an error; all it can do is tell the probability that he is making one or to be positive, the probability that he is avoiding one.

This is the basic function of all the inferential statistical procedures, or *tests of significance* as they are more generally called. They tell us the significance probability of our observed data, or the probability that chance alone produced the observed difference. This probability, in conjunction with the level of significance we have adopted, enables us to make decisions objectively as to whether to attribute any particular difference to chance or to the research conditions. Moreover, any researcher with our data or similar data who adopts the same level of significance will come to the same decision. In short, we have made the procedure completely objective.

SELECTING THE LEVEL OF SIGNIFICANCE BEFORE DATA COLLECTION

The last statement highlights the importance of the level of significance, and why we need conventions as to levels which are and are not acceptable within a discipline. Our example of the decision about children E or F also highlights one other aspect of the level of significance, that a researcher must state the level he will use for decision-making in advance of the data collection. Remember that for these children the significance probability of the observed result was 3 percent and 5 percent, and at the 5 percent level of significance the researcher concluded that these differences were statistically significant. But had he used the 1 percent level of significance he would have concluded that these differences were not statistically significant, exactly the opposite conclusion he drew using the 5 percent level of significance! Because this situation can and does happen, we prefer not to place researchers in the position of having to decide whether or not to make the difference a significant one. We insist that they consider the nature of their data, the application of their results, and by selecting and stating a level of significance decide, *in advance*, the maximum risk they are willing to run of making an error when they conclude that a difference was attributable to the research conditions.

Other Levels of Significance

We must not lose sight of the fact that although 1 percent and 5 percent may sound small, by the standards of other fields such as bridge building they are grotesquely large. If we were building a bridge by having two teams of builders each start from one side of the river, we would be stunned to discover that our calculations were 5 percent off. Our level of significance or tolerance for error would be of the order of .0001 or one-hundredth of 1 percent. This point is stressed because as this book is written a tendency this author considers unfortunate is obvious in the research literature in education: a willingness to accept the less stringent level of significance of 10 percent. Coming under a variety of labels, such as "tendency toward significance" or "trend in the direction of significance," the net effect is the same: to increase the risk of error when a difference is attributed to the research conditions, doubling it in comparison to the 5 percent level of significance, and increasing it ten-fold in comparison to the 1 percent level.

This seems to have come about from an increased recognition of the weaknesses in our ability to measure the research variables in the social sciences. Because our ability to measure is weak, it is argued that it is more difficult to obtain statistically significant differences when in fact they do exist. Therefore, instead of losing all these differences, the movement has been to adopt this less stringent level of significance, and so label more differences as statistically significant. There are two problems with this line of reasoning. First, weaknesses in measurement are as likely to lead to spuriously large differences as to spuriously small differences, and so the basic premise is unsound. Second, even if weaknesses in measurement did more often lead to spuriously small differences, it would make more sense to improve the measuring devices and techniques than to use a less stringent level of significance. This would seem to be particularly true in education where the consequences of error are serious and where to conclude that a difference is not chance will usually mean change of some sort in the sense of a new method or procedure or program.

There is a second aspect worth examining in the way the research literature treats the concepts of significance. That is the frequency with which researchers, after a finding has been shown *not* to be statistically significant, refer to it with phrases like "almost significant," "nearly significant," "tending toward significance," and similar wistful expressions of regret. On a quick reaction it would seem perfectly sensible, if you were using the 5 percent level of significance and your significance probability came out to be 6 percent, for you to note that while the result was not statistically significant, it just missed, that is, was nearly significant. But think back to the reason why the entire inferential statistical process was developed: to make possible objective and consistent evaluations of results and decisions on the basis of results. For this reason we established a procedure by which a researcher states in advance his standard by selecting the level of significance, does his study, by appropriate computations arrives at the significance probability of his observed result, and so decides whether or not to attribute his result to chance or to the research condition. By doing this we avoided the alternative situation in which every researcher would decide for himself which differences were "so large" that they must be attributed to the research condition or "so small' that they were better attributed to chance.

But having established this elaborate procedure to avoid individual subjective judgment, why then tack onto the procedure the individual subjective judgment as to which nonsignificant differences are so close to significance that they are "nearly" or "almost" or "just short of significance?" This movement, in the author's opinion, defeats and negates the whole purpose of the inferential procedures. Of course it may ultimately lead to the absurd but logical end product, the "just short" test, a new procedure to test nonsignificant differences to find out which can be properly called "just short" of significance!

What is particularly interesting in this regard is that the same researcher who notes a difference which "just missed" being significant often within the same study will not feel the same compulsion to note that a difference with a significance probability of 4 percent "just made" significance or was "just short of nonsignificance."

But since the "just short" test has yet to be developed, let us move on to consider how inferential procedures are developed.

To take inferential action we need tables like Table 8-1. A basic question is how we develop such tables. What we do is identify the mathematical structure of our research hypotheses and research data and seek a mathematical function which can serve as a *model* for our research situation. This is a subtle and complex problem, but it can be illustrated with some simple data.

SELECTING A MODEL FOR DATA

Let us assume that in one of the schools participating in the Phonics Study, a previous study has shown that only 40 percent of the children aspired to complete high school. Therefore, one aim of the study is to increase the level of aspiration of students, so that after the period of instruction greater proportions of students than heretofore will aspire to complete their secondary-school education. This expectation, stated as an hypothesis, could be phrased this way: "Significantly more than 40 percent of students exposed to small-group instruction in phonics will aspire to complete their secondary-school education." Then let us, for purposes of this illustration, assume that the researcher selects the 5 percent level of significance, and further assume that on one particular day, after instruction, the researcher has an opportunity to question two children, both of whom say they wish to complete high school. Forget for the moment the fact that two children hardly constitute a sample, and consider the inferential problem: What is the probability that this finding (of 100 percent) came about by chance, that is, what is the significance probability? What action should the researcher take on the hypothesis?

The first step is to identify the mathematical structure of the data. We could say that this inferential problem could be mathematically identified as having the following four characteristics: (1) we have a two-choice situation (aspire to complete high school or not aspire to complete high school); (2) we have a basis for dividing the population on these choices (we know from previous data that 40 percent did aspire and 60 percent did not aspire to complete high school); (3) the two options are inclusive (40 percent and 60 percent add to 100 percent); and finally (4) we have two repetitions of the question and therefore three possible outcomes (both children could aspire to complete high school, both could not, or one could and one could not).

The second step is to find some mathematical function which could serve as a model for this research situation. One which could is a mathematical function most people study in high school and forget soon after, the *binomial expansion* $(X + Y)^n$. This is a mathematical expansion which has four characteristics: (1) there are two terms (or outcomes) X and Y; (2) each term has a specific probability of occurrence; (3) X and Y are inclusive outcomes so that the probability of X plus the probability of Y add to 1.00; and (4) the universe of X and Y is sampled n times. Because we have sampled twice, for our data $n = 2$ and so we are interested in the expansion[2] of $(X + Y)^2$ or $X^2 + 2(X^1Y^1) + Y^2$.

If we apply this model to our data we would say that X represents the child who does aspire to complete high school and Y represents the child who does not. The binomial expansion $X^2 + 2(X^1Y^1) + Y^2$ is then an interesting analogy to our three possible outcomes. We could see the first term X^2 as representing a sample of two X's, that is two children who *do* aspire to complete high school. Similarly the term Y^2 would represent the outcome of two Y's, that is two children who do *not* aspire to complete high school. Finally the intermediate term involving X^1 and Y^1 would be seen as the outcome with one X and one Y, that is, one child who does, and one who does not, aspire to complete high school.[3] But because the model has the same characteristics as the data, we can use is to determine the significance probability of our actual result. What we wish to test is whether our observed frequency for X of 100 percent

---

[2] For those who have not had algebra, or do not remember it, $(X + Y)^2$ means $(X + Y)$ multiplied by itself, that is,

$$
\begin{array}{r}
X + Y \\
X + Y \\
\hline
XY + Y^2 \\
X^2 + XY \\
\hline
X^2 + 2XY + Y^2
\end{array}
$$

[3] When an exponent is 1 it is not usually written out, so that the term $2X^1Y^1$ would appear as $2XY$. The exponents are included here to make the illustration clearer.

Table 8–2 Probability Distribution Using Binomial Expansion

Research Outcome	Term in Model	Probability
Two who aspire	X^2	$(.4)^2 = $ .16 or 16%
One who aspires, One who does not	$2X^1Y^1$	$2(.4)(.6) = $ .48 or 48%
Two who do not aspire	Y^2	$(.6)^2 = $ .36 or 36%
		1.00 or 100%

is significantly different from the original probability of .40. If we then substitute .40 for each X and .60 for each Y we have what we call a *probability distribution,* as seen in Table 8-2.

The researcher now knows that if the probability of aspiring to high school was *still* .40, there is a 16 percent probability that he would obtain his actual data, that is, would find two X's (two children who do aspire to complete) in a sample of two. At the 5 percent level of significance he would therefore be forced to reject his hypothesis that there had been change.

Developing a Table for the Model

Note two points. First, we could sit down and for the n of 2 develop probability distributions for all possible combinations of probabilities of X and Y (that is, .01 and .99; .02 and .98; and so on). Then we could do the same thing for the n of 3, 4, and so on. Having done this we would have a "Table of Binomial Probabilities" which any future researcher could use to save himself the trouble of computing his own significance probabilities when he felt that the binomial expansion was an appropriate model for his hypothesis and data. This of course has been done for the binomial expansion and for many other applicable mathematical functions.

The second point to note is that if the researcher had consulted the table for the binomial expansion, he would easily see that with a sample of two and using the 5 percent level of significance, it would never be possible to accept the research hypothesis that change had taken place. He would have recognized that a larger sample was necessary. This suggests that some models also provide a basis for determining the minimum sample size needed to achieve a given level of precision, and in the chapter on sampling we shall see how this can be done.

Once the model is selected it becomes a simple matter of applying the model through the appropriate computational process to obtain the significance probability and thereby make a decision about the hypothesis. In an age when most college, university, and educational and industrial research facilities have computer facilities in which the computational aspects can be handled electronically, it is particularly crucial that the researcher have the ability to understand the relationship between characteristics of data and the available mathematical models, because once he selects a model someone else usually performs the actual computations.

The key skills needed to select a model are the abilities to identify the characteristics of your data, know the available models, particularly the assumptions underlying each model, and then match up data with model. In Chapters 5, 6, and 7, we have discussed characteristics of data, and in the next chapters we shall consider the available models and how models and data best interact.

In selecting a model we must be certain to move our thinking past the obvious or superficial level, for the superficially appropriate model may have assumptions our data do not meet. For example, let us say that we are asked to wager whether or not a coin to be flipped will come up heads or tails. We decide that if the coin is fair then heads will come up 50 percent of the time and so will tails. So we have developed a model for this two-choice situation in which each possible outcome has a 50 percent probability of occurrence. But does this model hold beyond coin flipping to the general problem of probabilities in two-choice situations? Is it sensible to apply the 50 percent–50 percent model to other such situations? We might decide to use this model in predicting the sex of unborn babies. If we tested this model by predictions over several months we would find that it works fairly well but not perfectly, since the proportion of males born is slightly higher than the proportion of females. We might then go on to say that a student taking a college course is faced with two alternatives, he might pass or he might fail, and so we proceed to apply our 50 percent–50 percent model to this situation. Now if we tested the model with data, we would find that it does not work well at all. The actual proportions are far from 50 percent–50 percent and more like 95 percent–5 percent.

Note that the test of a model is whether or not it fits a given set of data rather than the logic of the model. As we rethink the problem we realize that the reason our model didn't fit the college situation is that we had not recognized a critical assumption underlying the model, that the probability of occurrence of each of the two alternatives was dictated only by chance and so each outcome was equally likely. Since factors other than chance dictated the pass–fail outcome in the college courses, the two outcomes were not equally likely, and so these data did not meet the underlying assumption of the model. The model therefore was inappropriate, that is, did not fit the data.

This indicates the critical element in selecting a model as the basis for any inferences to be made from data: We must understand both the nature of our data and the assumptions of the model we are intending to use if our decisions and generalizations are to make sense.

As an example of how models can differ and yet be logically correct, consider the problem of predicting the probability that there are two boys in a specific two-child family. One model we might construct could be based on the argument that there are *three* kinds of two-child families, a family with no boys, one boy, or two boys. We might then assume that each of these possibilities is equally likely, and that therefore the chances are one in three or 33 percent that the family has two boys. However, a different model could be constructed on the argument that there are four kinds of two-child families: two boys, two girls, girl-boy, and boy-girl. Under this model, if we assume each possibility to be equally likely, the probability is one in four or 25 percent that the family has two boys.

Both models can not be correct, and if tested with data on large numbers of two-child families, we find that the second model fits the data better. But at the model-building stage both are appropriate and both are specific enough to test and so be accepted or rejected. Note again the critical interrelationship between the model and the data to which it is to be applied, because if the model is inappropriate then erroneous conclusions will be drawn.

SOURCES FOR MODELS

In the social disciplines, we develop models in two ways: (1) by making assumptions about the nature of the population from which the sample was drawn, and particularly about the characteristics or parameters of the population; and (2) by using analogies between sets of data and existing mathematical statements, like the binomial expansion or the laws of probability.

Parametric Inferential Procedures

Since the procedures which stem from the first process are built on assumptions about parameters they are called *parametric inferential procedures*. The three most frequent assumptions they make are, first, that the characteristic under study exists in the population; second, that it is normally distributed there; and third, that the sample statistic provides an estimate of the parameter. Thus if we are considering the mean reading ability of the children in our sample, to consider a parametric model, we must argue that the characteristic "reading ability" exists in the population as well as in the sample, is normally distributed in that population, and that the sample mean is an estimate of the population mean. The second of these assumptions, about the normal distribution, limits parametric procedures to instances when interval measurement has been achieved, since we noted in Chapter 6 that discussions based on the normal curve require interval data. They also require continuous variables, but this is often ignored, and the parametric procedures used with infinite- and even multiple-category discrete variables. Because of these demands, however, the parametric procedures are limited to testing hypotheses involving moment system statistics like means, variances, and product moment correlations.

A typical illustration of a problem for which we would seek a parametric procedure is to determine if the mean reading grade of the children taught by the phonics method differed from the mean reading grade of the children taught by the look-say method. This is a parametric problem because we are concerned with a continuous variable (reading ability), have achieved interval measurement, can assume the variable is normally distributed in the population, and are testing a statistic (the sample mean) which has a parallel parameter (the population mean).

Thinking about this problem we could gain some insight into the type of model we would want. For example, if the two methods were identical in effectiveness and if all other conditions were equal, we would expect no difference between the groups in test performance. However, we would not be surprised if they differed slightly, but as the difference grew larger the likelihood that this was a chance occurrence would drop. Moreover the model should allow for either of the two groups to do better by chance. Since the likelihood of the phonics group exceeding the look-say group by one point or five points (or any amount) purely by chance is exactly the same as the likelihood that the look-say group will exceed the phonics group by one, five, or any number of points, the model should be symmetrical about the midpoint of zero or no difference. Finally, since we have no basis for knowing what the largest possible difference would be, the model should allow for a difference of any size.

In Chapter 6 we discussed a model for data, the normal curve, which possessed the characteristics that we have listed above. It has a midpoint which could be conceptualized as representing no difference, and it is symmetrical about this midpoint. The right-hand half of the curve would represent the instances in which the phonics group exceeded the look-say group, while the left-hand half of the curve could represent the instances in which the look-say group exceeded the phonics group. Since the normal curve has its mode at the midpoint, this would provide us with the most likely single value of zero, and since it tapers off from this midpoint rather sharply, it also has the greatest proportion of its area near the midpoint, with the probability of extreme values lessening considerably as the value gets further and further from the midpoint.

To use the normal curve as a model for inferences about differences between two means, we use the standard error of the mean. This is the same unit of measurement we discussed in Chapter 6, as a basis for estimating the stability of any one mean. However, in the inferential problem we are now considering, there are two means involved, each of which has a standard error. But our interest is not in either mean per se, but rather in the difference between them.

We said in Chapter 6, in the discussion of standard error, that every moment system statistic has a standard error, and so the difference between the two means must have one also. If we were able to estimate the standard error of the difference between the means, we could then use this as the basis for our inference. If we now combine two pieces of information, we have the basis for a decision: (1) that 95 percent of the normal curve lies within approximately two standard deviations[4] of the mean; and (2) that the 5 percent level of significance is the conventional criterion for decision making. Thus any time the observed difference between the means of our two groups is at least twice as large as its standard error, the difference could occur by chance less than 5 percent of the time. Therefore, if we had a difference between the groups of 10 points on the test (that is, one mean was 83 and the other 73) and a standard of error of the difference was found to be eight points, the difference is only 1.25 times larger than its standard error (10 divided by 8 = 1.25). Differences this large could happen by chance more than 5 percent of the time, and so at the 5 percent level, this ten-point difference would not be statistically significant. Had the difference been eighteen points, with the same standard error of eight, the resulting quotient of 2.25 (18 divided by 8) could occur by chance less than 5 percent of the time and so would be statistically significant.

Nonparametric Inferential Procedures

The second set of inferential procedures makes no assumptions about populations and does not perceive the sample statistics as representing

[4]The precise value is 1.96 standard deviations.

parameters, and so these procedures are called nonparametric inferential procedures. They do not place similar demands upon the data and so are appropriate for ordinal data, and some for nominal data as well. Thus nonparametric procedures are used for testing hypotheses involving frequency distributions, or ordinal statistics like medians. The illustration earlier of the binomial expansion typifies the use of nonparametric models. In that illustration, we made no assumptions about any distribution of the number of children interested in completing secondary school, or about a parameter corresponding to the proportion of children in the sample who are so interested.

One practical advantage of the nonparametric procedures is that they are applicable to small samples, for they make no assumptions about the normality of distributions.

RELATIVE POWER OF PARAMETRIC
AND NONPARAMETRIC PROCEDURES

In view of these easier demands of the nonparametric procedures, we may wonder why every researcher does not use the nonparametric procedures and so avoid assumptions about parameters and about the nature of the distribution of the statistic. The answer is because of a characteristic called *power*, which inferential procedures possess to varying degrees. *Power* is defined as the ability of the inferential procedure to reject a null hypothesis when it should be rejected. For comparable situations, any one nonparametric procedure is less powerful than the parallel parametric procedure, and so the researcher would pay a price in loss of power if he routinely used the nonparametric procedure. The reason for this can be understood if we consider some interval data with which we *could* perform a parametric procedure. As always, we could also work with the data at a weaker level, that is, treat these interval data as if they were ordinal and so use one of the nonparametric procedures. Simply stating this process illustrates that the nonparametric procedure would be using less of the information in the data than the parametric procedure would, for the nonparametric procedure would consider only the order of the observations and not how far apart they were. Because they use less of the information available, for comparable data, the nonparametric procedures are less powerful. In practical terms this means that while for most data both procedures would lead to the same conclusion, there would be *some* data for which the parametric procedure would lead us to reject the null hypothesis and the comparable nonparametric procedure would lead us to accept it.

This discussion of power also illustrates the basic research application of inferential procedures: hypothesis testing. Let us turn to that aspect now.

HYPOTHESIS TESTING THROUGH INFERENTIAL PROCEDURES

The direct application of inferential procedures in research is the objective basis they provide for making decisions about the research hypotheses. Typically most survey and experimental studies are begun with a belief that certain specific outcomes will eventuate. For example, a researcher may believe that students in one type of school surveyed will have higher achievement levels than another, or he may believe that children exposed to the experimental phonics program will show significantly greater improvement than children of comparable retardation who have not been exposed to this program.

The area involving the relationship of the hypothesis and the statistics is one which often causes deep confusion for beginning researchers. This stems primarily from the failure to distinguish sharply enough between *research hypotheses* and *statistical hypotheses*. As we have noted in earlier chapters, a research hypothesis is the researcher's prediction of a specific outcome. In some instances a research hypothesis may state that *no difference* is expected. This occurs when the researcher expects no differences beyond those produced by chance, and so states his hypothesis in the null form. For example, in the Language Study, because the content of the lessons was identical, we expected no differences between vocabulary and structure students in their knowledge of community activities and workers, the subject of one series of units in the fourth grade. Stated as an hypothesis, this would be: "There will be no significant difference in knowledge of community activities and workers between students taught by the structure and by vocabulary method."

In other instances, however, the researcher expects a difference and so in the research hypothesis states an expectation of *difference*. Thus in the Phonics Study, the researcher obviously expects the children taught by the experimental phonics program to improve more than children taught by the look-say method. This expectation would lead him to state an hypothesis of difference: "Retarded readers given small-group instruction in phonics will improve significantly more in reading ability than a comparable group taught by the look-say method."

But where we have this choice of stating research hypotheses either in terms of no difference or of difference, every inferential statistic we have can only test hypotheses of *no difference*. In other words, no matter what inferential procedure we select, we can only test a *statistical* hypothesis of no difference. Thus in the Phonics Study, despite his expectation of differences, the researcher would have to state a statistical hypothesis that there was no difference in improvement between the children taught by the phonics and the look-say method. The statistical hypothesis is not formally stated in the same way that the research hypothesis actually appears in the proposal and report of a study. It is sufficient that the researcher simply recognize and understand that this is the hypothesis he is testing with the inferential procedure. If it is not understood some serious problems of interpretation can occur.

There is no problem of interpretation when the research hypothesis is one of no difference. Then it is consistent with the statistical hypothesis being tested, and whatever action we take on the statistical hypothesis, we also take on the research hypothesis. In the Language Study example above, if the results of the inferential procedure were such that we concluded that there was no statistically significant difference between the vocabulary and structure students, we would accept the statistical hypothesis of no difference and also accept the research hypothesis of no difference. However, if in the Phonics Study, where we hypothesized a difference, the data were to come out not significantly different, we would *accept* the statistical hypothesis of no difference but *reject* the research hypothesis of difference.

The variety of possibilities and interactions is summarized in Table 8-3, as a guide to decision in this verbal confusion. The table indicates simply that when the researcher has hypothesized no difference, the action he takes on his statistical and research hypotheses is identical. However, when he has hypothesized a difference, then the action he takes on the statistical hypothesis is opposite to the action he takes on the research hypothesis.

Table 8–3   Interaction of Research Hypothesis Inferential Result and Action on Statistical and Research Hypothesis

Research Hypothesis	Inferential Result	Action on Statistical Hypothesis	Action on Research Hypothesis
No difference	No difference	Accept	Accept
	Difference	Reject	Reject
Difference	No difference	Accept	Reject
	Difference	Reject	Accept

No Difference Does Not Equal Sameness

In addition to this confusion about what action to take, the fact that all inferential procedures only test hypotheses of no difference also limits what the researcher can say when this hypothesis is supported. He can talk about the lack of a difference, but he *cannot* talk about similarity or sameness. In short, the inferential procedure makes possible posing a question which can be paraphrased as: "Is the difference we observe large enough for us to dismiss the possibility that it was produced by chance?" If the statistical answer is "no," we conclude no difference. But notice, at no time have we posed a question "Are our observed data the same as they were originally?" For example, let us consider the child in our nutrition study who started out at 60 pounds and weighed 65 pounds at the conclusion of the study. Table 8-1 told us that the significance probability of this result was 10 percent and using the 5 percent level we concluded that the weight of 65 pounds was not significantly different than the original weight of 60 pounds. But we did not and cannot say that the weight of 65 pounds is the *same* as the original weight of 60. Obviously 65 is not the same as 60, and no statistical test pretends that it is. However, it may not be far enough from 60 for us to get excited about the difference, and that is what the inferential procedure is designed to determine.

ONE- AND TWO-TAILED TESTS

There is one additional distinction between research hypotheses of difference and of no difference.

To illustrate this, recall how earlier in this chapter we used as an illustration of a situation in which the researcher expected no difference, the hypothesis: "There will be no significant difference between vocabulary and structure children in knowledge of community activities and workers." Now let us consider the experiential children who as part of their language-learning experiences went on several trips through the community. We might reasonably expect these firsthand experiences to provide them with greater knowledge of community activities and workers than either of the other two groups. Therefore in comparing them to the vocabulary children, we would hypothesize: "Experiential children will have significantly greater knowledge of community activities and workers than vocabulary children."

Now assume that the researcher is willing to accept his test of knowledge of community activities and workers as providing interval data and

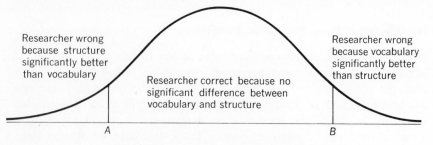

Figure 8-1 Visualization of two-tailed test.

so believes the normal curve to be an appropriate model for testing these hypotheses. In using this model he must consider the three possibilities pictured in Figure 8-1.

Let us consider first the comparison of vocabulary and structure children where the researcher expected no difference. In this instance, Figure 8-1 indicates that he would be correct if the data supported the expectation of no difference. But the figure also indicates that there are *two* ways in which there could be a difference: The structure children could do better or the vocabulary children could do better. In either case the data would lead him to reject the hypothesis of no difference, and conclude his expectation was wrong. But because of these two possible ways for there to be a difference, in selecting the critical values on the normal distribution at which to establish his level of significance, the researcher must select a critical value in each tail of the normal curve, that is, at points *A* and *B* of Figure 8-1, so that he would be able to determine the significance of either of the two possible differences. Recognize that either group doing better would represent difference opposite to what was hypothesized, and so the researcher would want to have the ability to label either difference as statistically significant or not. If he were to use the 5 percent level of significance he must divide his 5 percent so that some of it is in either tail of the normal curve, and therefore he will have what we call a *two-tailed test* of significance. The typical procedure is to divide it symmetrically, that is, identifying the extreme 2½ percent of the curve at either end. There is no statistical need to do this at all, as the researcher could if he wished draw one line at the extreme 1 percent of the lower tail and the other line at the extreme 4 percent of the upper tail, but this is seldom done.

In contrast, the researcher testing the second hypothesis, that experiential children will do better than vocabulary children, does not need to be concerned about both tails of the curve. His visualization is in Figure 8-2.

Now to test the hypothesis he need only be concerned with two out-

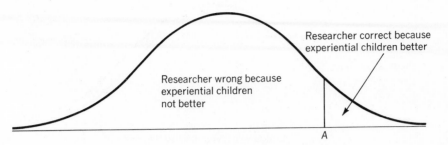

Figure 8-2 Visualization of one-tailed test.

comes, for either the experiential children will do better than the vocabulary children or they will not. Note that to act on the hypothesis that experiential children will do better, there is no need to distinguish beween the finding of no difference and the finding that *vocabulary* children did better. In both instances, the experiential children did *not* do better, and that is all that needs to be tested for the hypothesis to be accepted or rejected. The researcher could then place the entire 5 percent region of significance in the critical upper tail of the distribution, selecting one critical value at point *A* in Figure 8-2. This approach is called a *one-tailed test of significance.*

Comparison of One- and Two-Tailed Tests

The generalization is that when the research hypothesis specifies the nature of the change or difference that is expected, a one-tailed test will be sufficient to test the hypothesis. When the research hypothesis does not specify the direction of the difference or change to be expected, then a two-tailed test is required to fully test the hypothesis. You should also realize the practical issue, that it is always simpler to achieve statistically significant results using the one-tailed rather than a two-tailed test. Figure 8-3, which is a normal curve, illustrates this point directly.

The two solid lines in either tail represent the critical values for a two-tailed test of significance at the 5 percent level. The dotted line in the upper tail represents the comparable critical value for a one-tailed test of significance. The shaded area represents the basis for the claim of "simplicity" above. For all the research results which fall into the shaded area would be statistically significant by the one-tailed test but would not be statistically significant by the two-tailed test.

This difference has led to a considerable body of criticism of the one-tailed procedure. The critics argue that in almost every research situation one direction for the differences is far more logical than the

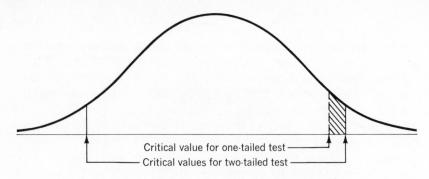

Figure 8-3 Illustration of one- and two-tailed tests.

other. Therefore almost any researcher can state hypotheses with a directional base and so justify the use of the one-tailed test, with its greater ease of obtaining the statistically significant result. The critics also point out that the use of the one-tailed test also destroys the researcher's defense against the possibility that he was wrong in his perception of direction, and that a statistically significant change did occur, but in the *opposite* direction.

TYPE I AND TYPE II ERRORS

The type of error involved in accepting an hypothesis of no change when in fact there has been change is called a "Type II" error or "Type B" error in contrast to the error discussed earlier involving the level of significance. When a researcher sets out to test an hypothesis and establishes a level of significance, say 5 percent, he is saying that he will consider statistically significant any difference which could occur by chance 5 percent of the time, or less often. But as we noted, when he actually makes this judgment and labels a difference "real,' he does this in the face of the fact that there is a 5 percent probability that it was a chance occurrence, and therefore he is running a 5 percent probability of making an error. This particular error—labeling a difference real when in fact it was chance—has been called the "Type I" or "Type A" error, and its probability is the same as the level of significance.

But what of the other possible error, labeling something "chance" when in fact it was real? This is a more subtle problem and involves a risk which is more difficult to estimate. Here we shall consider the nature of this error, and point up when you should be concerned with it in a study. Let us work through the thinking in an example to illustrate the two errors and how they interact. Let us assume that one group of students has averaged a reading grade of 3.5 before the Phonics Study. We institute the experimental program and are so convinced that the new program is better than we hypothesize that "students taught by the Phonics Program will have significantly higher reading grades than at the beginning of the program." This hypothesis calls for a one-tailed test against the statistical null hypothesis that the mean is not different than 3.5, with the entire critical region in the upper tail of the curve. This curve is the upper-most curve in Figure 8-4, centered about the mean of 3.5. The critical region in the upper tail of the curve represents the probability of a "Type I" error, that is, the probability that even though nothing significant has happened, there will be such a large chance deviation that we will be deluded into

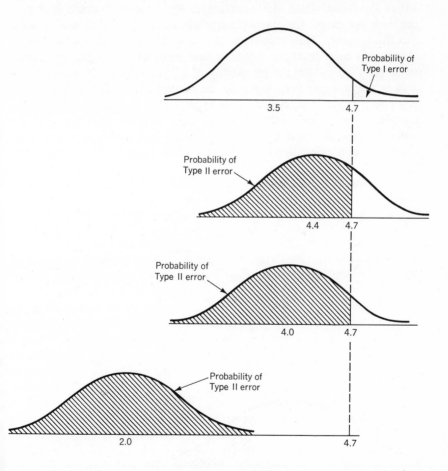

Figure 8-4 Illustration of Type I and Type II error with one-tailed test.

thinking a real change has been effected. In terms of the standard error of this test, the critical region is at 4.7. Thus if the students average a reading grade of 4.7 or higher we will conclude that they *have* changed significantly. If they average less than 4.7 we will conclude that no change has taken place.

Now let us assume that in fact change has taken place but only to a mean reading grade of 4.4. By the procedure we have established we must conclude that no change has taken place, because the students average less than 4.7. We have now made a "Type II" error, drawing a conclusion of no difference, when there has been change. The second curve centered around 4.5 illustrates that error. The shaded area to the left of the critical value, 4.7, contains all the values that would lead us to conclude no change has taken place when, in fact, it has. However, notice the third curve. This represents the data for the situation where the change has been from the 3.5 to a new mean of 4.0. Again the critical value of 4.7 delineates the probability of a Type II error. Now the shaded area is much larger than it was in the second curve. This illustrates two key points: (1) the probability of a Type II error is determined in part by the alternative hypothesis being tested, and therefore there are as many different Type II errors as there are alternative hypotheses; and (2) the closer the alternative hypothesis is to the null hypothesis, the greater the probability of a Type II error.

Now look at the lowest curve in Figure 8-4. This curve represents the eventuality the researcher did not expect: student achievement declined. In fact, the decline was a large one to a mean reading grade of 2.0. Note

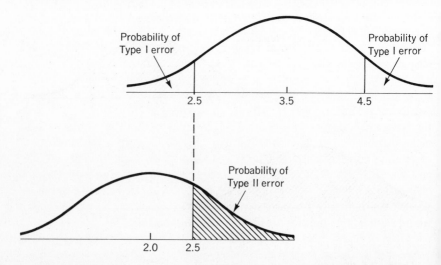

Figure 8-5   Illustration of Type I and Type II error with two-tailed test.

that this decline of 1.5 grades is further *below* the initial mean of 3.5 than the critical value of 4.7 is above that mean. Nevertheless, with the one-tailed test, the researcher has no choice but to accept the null hypothesis, that the mean has not changed significantly from 3.5. In short with the one-tailed procedure the researcher is defenseless against a Type II error whenever change has occurred opposite to that hypothesized.

Figure 8-5 illustrates how a two-tailed test would alleviate this situation. Here again the original null curve is graphed as the curve with the mean of 3.5. In this instance, however, a symmetrical two-tailed test was established, so that there was a critical region in the upper tail beyond 4.5 and in the lower tail below 2.5. The curve with the mean at 2.0 still has a portion of its area within the acceptance region and so there is still some probability of a Type II error, but the great majority of the curve is in the critical or rejection region. Now the researcher would be aware that a statistically significant drop in achievement has occurred.

Importance

You seldom see any reference in a research report to the Type II error. Why then discuss it here? For two reasons. First, whenever we use a one-tailed test and the actual data come out in the direction *opposite* to the hypothesis, we must be aware that we have no ability to determine if this change or difference was statistically significant. The second reason is that until we begin asking about the probability of Type II errors, we will remain at an imprecise level of research in which we permit researchers to avoid stating the alternative hypothesis or hypotheses with which they are concerned. It is a relatively gross level of research for a researcher to state "I wish to learn if the mean level of reading achievement has changed from a mean reading grade of 3.5, using the 5 percent level of significance." The level of significance specifies the maximum risk of a Type I error the researcher is willing to run. If we also insisted that he specify the maximum risk of a Type II error he was willing to run, this would force the researcher to state an alternative hypothesis so that he would have to make the much more precise statement: "I wish to learn if the mean level of reading achievement has changed from a mean reading grade of 3.5, and I wish to be able to do this in such a way as to be able to detect *a change to a mean of 4.1 or more.*" All of the italicized phrase would be needed for him to estimate the probability of the Type II error, and it would push us to a far more meaningful level of research.[5]

[5]We shall see in the chapter on sampling that it would also make it possible for researchers to know exactly how large a sample they needed to achieve this level of precision.

Establishing Desirable Levels

Let us assume that the researcher has reached this desirable level of precision: He is willing to state both a null hypothesis and an alternate hypothesis. How then can he control the levels? There are two ways available: by manipulating the level of significance, and by varying the number of cases in the study sample. Manipulating the level of significance is not usually an effective technique because, for any given set of data, manipulating the level of significance has opposite effects on the two types of error. This is indicated by the three pairs of curves in Figure 8-6. In the first pair of curves labeled Set I, the data of Figure 8-4 are repeated. In this set, the 5 percent level of significance has been set and the critical value for that level of significance, a reading grade of 4.7, is shown at point A on the null curve. Using this critical value, the researcher identifies the risk of a Type II error on the curve for his alternative hypothesis: The reading grade is 4.5. Considering these, he decides that he is unhappy that the risk of a Type I error is too high, and so he decides to reduce this by working at a higher level of significance, that is, moving from the 5 percent level to the 1 percent level. Therefore, his critical value, A, is moved further out in the tail of the null distribution to a mean of 5.2, as indicated in Set II. As the curve indicates, he has reduced the risk of a Type I error, but notice that in the curve of the alternative hypothesis, he has *increased* the risk of a Type II error.

Be alert to the fact that these are not arithmetically the same changes, because different portions of the null and the alternative curves are involved and, therefore, different portions of the areas affected. Thus we cannot state any mathematical rule that a decrease of 1 percent in the risk of a Type I error will result in any specific percent increase in the risk of a Type II error. This will depend on the alternative hypothesis being tested. We can state the general rule that simply decreasing the risk of a Type I error by moving to a higher level of significance will result in an increase in the risk of a Type II error.

Set III indicates the more typical side of the problem: trying to reduce the risk of a Type II error by raising the level of significance. It has been raised to 8 percent, lowering the critical value to 4.5. As is obvious in the curves of Set III, this has the immediate effect of increasing, often seriously, the risk of a Type I error.

It is because these two risks interact that the preferable procedure is to manipulate them through the number of cases in the sample. For example, in Chapter 6 we noted that for all moment system statistics, the standard error is inversely related to the number of cases. This is true because we estimate the standard error by dividing the standard deviation by the square root of the number of cases. Thus as the sample increases in

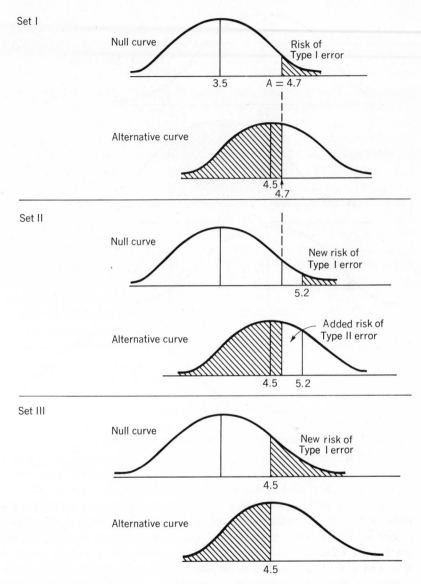

Figure 8-6 Illustration of interaction of risk of Type I and Type II errors.

size, standard errors decrease in size. But it is the standard error which is the basic unit of measurement in many of the inferential models, like the normal curves in Figure 8-6. Thus, if we reduce the standard error by increasing sample size, this has the effect of pulling the null and alternative curves further apart. This is illustrated in Figure 8-7. Here Set I consists of the same null and alternative curves in Figure 8-6, with the

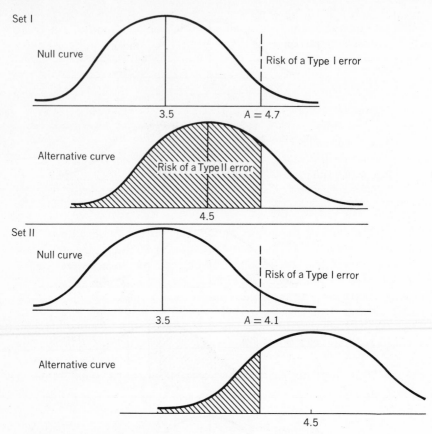

Figure 8-7 Illustration of effect of increasing sample size on interaction of Type I and Type II errors.

same critical value at A of 4.7 and the same risks of the Type I and Type II errors. But Set II now consists of the null and alternative curves for the same data, with a sample four times larger. The standard error then would be halved, and so the critical value (as always, for the 5 percent level, 1.96 standard errors from the mean) is now at a reading grade of 4.1. The net effect is to move the alternative curve sharply to the right, cutting the risk of a Type II error appreciably, without any increase in the on the risks of a Type I and II error.

This illustrates once again how the various stages of research interact, and why it is critical to consider the inferential aspects of the data analysis early in the research process. If the researcher can establish a meaningful alternative hypothesis, he can test out the effect of tentative sample sizes on the risks of a Type I and II error.

Table 8-4 Interaction of True Situation and Action on Hypothesis in Terms
of Errors

Researcher's Action	True Situation	
	No Difference	Difference
Accepts null and con- cludes no difference	Correct Action	Type II error
Rejects null and con- cludes a difference	Type I error	Correct Action

Notice that both of these risks must be considered in advance of data collection. However, once the data are collected, analyzed, the inferential procedures completed, and action taken on the hypothesis, the researcher is faced with the possibility of making one error *or* the other. If he actually rejects his statistical null hypothesis, the only error he need be concerned with is that he has *falsely* rejected it, that is, made a Type I error. On the contrary, if he actually accepts his null hypothesis, he need be concerned only with the possibility that he has *falsely* accepted it, that is, made a Type II error. This interaction of the action on the hypothesis and the "true" situation in terms of possible errors is summarized in Table 8-4.

PRACTICAL SIGNIFICANCE

This discussion of the concept of statistical significance and techniques for determining it has, it is hoped, convinced the reader that it is impossible to evaluate the importance to be attached to a set of research data without a test of significance, and that only those results which can be shown to have a chance probability of less than 5 percent can be considered seriously. Let us conclude the discussion with a qualification to this concept of statistical significance: Not all results that are statistically significant have practical significance, or, in other words, have any meaning to the practitioner.

The concept of practical significance cannot be presented in any definitive way, for there are no procedures to discuss and no levels to be identified. Instead, this is a judgment which can only be made by the person involved in each specific situation in which the research finding is or is not to be applied. It is the researcher's responsibility to analyze the data in such a way as to determine whether or not the observed differences, no matter what the research problem, are more sensibly attributed to chance or to the research variables. He does this with the test of significance appropriate for his data. If the answer at this point is that the results are more sensibly attributed to chance, then the practitioner knows that any observed differences are not likely to reflect consistent differences between the phenomena under study. He must still decide whether or not to implement the research variables, but this cannot be supported by the data; it is purely a professional decision.

However, if the researcher reports that the observed differences are statistically significant, then the conclusion is they are not sensibly attributed to chance but rather to the research variable. At this point the researcher has done all he can to assist the practitioner, who is faced now, *just as when the results were not statistically significant,* with the decision as to whether or not to implement the research findings. Now he must decide if this statistically significant difference has enough practical implications, if it suggests a dramatic enough change or improvement to justify whatever implementation of the research results entails. Let us take a specific illustration in which a school director implements a new teaching program under which she increases the number of staff appreciably, so that student-staff ratio is considerably reduced and the students more thoroughly supervised. She decides to evaluate the benefits of this procedure in several ways, such as student ratings of satisfaction, faculty ratings, efficiency reports, and others. After a six-month trial period, she finds statistically significant differences on several measures, all indicating that the new program results in greater efficiency, learning, and satisfaction. Now she is faced with the professional decision as to whether these statistically significant and therefore real changes are important enough to merit the additional expense and time that the new program required. No statistic can answer that question, for it is a judgment which only the decision-maker in the situation can make.

However, even though no statistic can answer the question, statistics can provide help in varying degrees. This is one of the most important areas where procedures like the use of the standard error, referred to in Chapter 6, make a contribution because they provide the practitioner not only with the knowledge that there was a statistically significant difference, but also with some estimate of the magnitude of that difference. Given this estimate of the magnitude, it becomes more feasible to decide whether or not the change is worth implementing.

The readers of educational research should recognize that research articles and reports in education, as in all of the other social disciplines, pay little attention to this issue of practical significance. The researcher is generally concerned with statistical significance exclusively, for this is the relevant *research* criterion. Once results are achieved, researchers discuss the implications based on the statistical significance only. This is generally understandable, particularly in a field like education where so many researchers are not practitioners and often are not even trained in the practice of teaching. It would be pointless, and some feel even presumptuous, for these researchers to make the practical significance judgment. So they avoid this issue entirely. This places the burden completely on the consumer, who must interpret the data and decide whether or not they have professional implications.

This point may be a critical one in understanding why so little of the research in the social disciplines is implemented with any speed. The researcher sees his criterion as statistical significance and his responsibility to determine whether or not it has been achieved. The practitioner cannot accept this as the ultimate criterion, and often reads in research reports about the statistical significance or what to the practitioner are transparently small differences with little practical implication, or sees the researcher dismissing as "not statistically significant" what seem like obvious changes or differences. Hopefully, at some point in the near future there will be greater communication between researchers and practitioners so that some middle ground is achieved in which the researchers pay somewhat greater attention to practical significance and the practitioner to statistical significance.

Chapter 9

INFERENTIAL STATISTICS:
NONPARAMETRIC MODELS,
THEIR APPLICATIONS, AND PROCEDURES

As we move now to the application of the inferential process, we shall distinguish five separate aspects: (1) the model, (2) the research application, (3) the inferential procedure, (4) the level of data, and (5) the descriptive statistic involved. If this seems unnecessarily complex, it is required because many procedures use the same model. The question of knowing when a model is appropriate for a particular research application must be considered apart from the question of knowing when a particular procedure is appropriate within that model. Similarly, there are instances when several procedures are available for a particular descriptive statistic, and so the level of data must be considered in making *this* decision. In this chapter we shall consider three nonparametric bases for developing a model probability distribution on which to base an inferential conclusion: (1) probability theory, (2) the binomial expansion, and (3) the chi square distribution. In Chapter 10 we shall consider three parametric bases for developing the model distribution: (1) the normal curve, (2) the *t* or student's distribution, and (3) the *F* distribution. The three nonparametric models are applicable to nominal and ordinal data; the three parametric models to interval data.

PROBABILITY THEORY

When our samples are small and we wish to obtain the significance probability distribution of a particular result, one immediately available source is to utilize probability theory, or mathematical statements as to the ways in which things occur by chance. For example, assume that in the Language Study we had three experts visit one of the elementary schools in the study and observe the teachers teaching the vocabulary, experiential, and structure classes. In assigning these teachers to a method, let us also assume that we felt they were of comparable ability. In discussing

their observations with each expert, each spontaneously and independently offers his evaluation that the vocabulary teacher was the best teacher of
the three. We wonder if this is a chance phenomenon or indicates that our
original assumption of comparability is suspect.

We could obtain some basis for evaluating this by considering all the
different patterns possible by chance when each of three judges selects one
of three people as "best." One of these patterns would be our observed
result of all three judges agreeing on the vocabulary teacher as best.
Another result would be for two to believe the vocabulary teacher was
best while the third thought the structure teacher was. After we listed all
possible results, we could then use probability theory to estimate the
probability of each outcome occurring by chance, and so have a basis for
assigning a significance probability to our observed piece of data. We
begin by considering the result which we obtained: All three judges agree.
That result could happen in three different ways. All three could select
the vocabulary teacher as they did, or all three could have selected either
the experiential or structure teachers. A second possible pattern would be
for two judges to have selected one teacher while the third judge selected
another teacher. This pattern could occur in six ways:

1. two vocabulary—one experiential
2. two vocabulary—one structure
3. two structure—one experiential
4. two structure—one vocabulary
5. two experiential—one structure
6. two experiential—one vocabulary

Finally, each of the judges could have selected a different teacher, and
this could happen only one way, that is, one vocabulary, one structure,
and one experiential. Thus, we have enumerated ten different outcomes.[1]
If nothing but chance is operating, we would be willing to assume that
each of the ten outcomes is equally likely,[2] and each therefore has a
probability of one-tenth. If we summarized these into a probability distribution, we would have the distribution as shown in Table 9-1.

It is obvious from the distribution that the observed result does not cast
serious doubt on the assumption that the teachers were comparable, for

[1]This way of spelling out the possible patterns of response does not consider the
order in which the judges made their selection. If we were to consider this as well,
we would have a different set of events to evaluate. For example, if we were to consider order we would note that the pattern "two vocabulary, one structure" could
come about in three ways: VVS, VSV, and SVV. This view of the problem would
conclude with twenty-seven different events, three in which all judges agree, eighteen
in which two agree, and six in which none agree.

[2]The consideration of each outcome as equally likely is a basic computational assumption in the use of probability theory.

Table 9–1   Probability Distribution for Three-Judge Problem

Result	Number of Ways Result Could Occur	Probability of Result
All three judges agree	3	30%
Two agree; one differs	6	60%
All three different	1	10%

there is a 30 percent probability of all three judges agreeing by chance on any one teacher being "best." Note also how intuitive reactions are deceptive in probability situations. Most people respond to this three-judge situation with a feeling that all three judges *agreeing* is more unusual than all three completely *disagreeing*. Yet Table 9-1 shows that the most unusual result, by chance, would be if each judge had selected a different teacher!

Developing Models from Probability Theory

Notice that in this example we have worked with an extremely small sample of three judges, have made no assumptions about the nature of the variables or the level of measurement, and have been unconcerned as to whether or not the observed data can be perceived as a sample from a population with specific characteristics. In other words we have been thinking nonparametrically, which will always be true when the laws of probability are used as the basis for an inferential procedure. Without going into elaborate detail which would be inappropriate, let us consider briefly the two most frequent kinds of situations for which probability theory is used as the basis for deriving a model probability distribution: (1) delineating the different patterns or outcomes and the probability associated with each pattern, as in the example we just discussed of the three judges; (2) delineating the possible combinations of ranks when subsets of ordinal data are ranked together.

Utilizing Patterns and Outcome

Perhaps the simplest approach to statistical inference is in the utilization of patterns and outcomes. This approach can be utilized with any level of data, but is particularly appropriate for nominal data. This is true since the approach makes no quantitative demands and no assumptions about the nature of the data. This makes for an ideal match, for to analyze nominal data inferentially we must have an approach which makes no such demands, since nominal data could not meet any such demands.

In the example we used earlier of the three judges selecting the best of three teachers, we spelled out all of the patterns. Obviously, in more complex research situations no researcher will want to take time to sit down and spell out all the possibilities. Moreover, the researcher really does not need to know *all* of the separate possibilities to estimate the significance probability of his observed result. All he needs to know is the total number of possible outcomes and the number of outcomes as extremely different as his own from the most likely outcome. Knowing these two numbers he can set up a basic ratio for determining the significance probability of his observed data. This ratio is:

$$\text{significance probability} = \frac{\text{the number of outcomes as extreme or more extreme than the observed result}}{\text{total number of possible outcomes}}$$

While it would be impossible here to discuss all of the techniques for estimating outcomes,[3] we can consider the two most useful techniques: the concepts of *factorial* and of *combinations*. Mathematically the process of factorial, symbolized by an exclamation point (!), involves multiplying a series of consecutive numbers inversely down to the number 1. Thus 5 factorial (written 5!) means multiply $5 \times 4 \times 3 \times 2 \times 1$ for a total of 120. Its use in inference is that it tells us the total number of different *patterns* we can have for a set of any specific number of elements. This can be used to answer a pattern question like "How many different patterns are there for N things?" Thus if we wished to know how many different patterns we could make from the letters *A, B,* and *C,* the factorial answer would be 3!, for there are three letters. This comes out to be $3 \times 2 \times 1$ or 6. We can verify this by spelling out all possible patterns: *ABC, ACB, BAC, BCA, CAB,* and *CBA.*

The factorial technique is useful if we are seeking to estimate the different patterns possible for a total set of N things. The combination technique is used when we are concerned with knowing how many different subsets of s things we can make from the total set of N things, which is symbolically listed as $\binom{N}{s}$. Thus, a combinational question might be how many different sets of two letters each can we make from *A, B, C, D,* and *E.* In this instance, $N = 5$ and s (the subset) $= 2$, so the mathematical question we are posing is how many combinations of two elements can we

---

[3]A complete discussion of probability theory and techniques for estimating outcomes appears in J. L. Hodges, Jr. and E. L. Lehman, *Basic Concepts of Probability and Statistics* (San Francisco: Holden-Day, 1964).

make from a total set of five elements. The computational process for combination is slightly more complex:

$$\text{number of combinations of } N \text{ things } s \text{ at a time} = \binom{N}{s} = \frac{N!}{s! \, (N - s)!}$$

For our example this is

$$\binom{5}{2} = \frac{5!}{2! \, (5 - 2)!} \text{ or } \frac{5!}{2! \, 3!}$$

which comes out to

$$\frac{5 \cdot 4 \cdot 3 \cdot 2 \cdot 1}{(2 \cdot 1)(3 \cdot 2 \cdot 1)} = \frac{120}{12} = 10$$

Again we can verify this by spelling out the combinations:

$$
\begin{array}{llll}
AB & & & \\
AC & BC & & \\
AD & BD & CD & \\
AE & BE & CE & DE
\end{array}
$$

In combinations we are not concerned with order, so that the letters A and B represent one combination whether we write them AB or BA. If we were concerned with order as well as the combinations, we would be raising simultaneously the combinational and pattern questions and so would combine both computational procedures by simply multiplying the number of combinations by the factorial of the size of the subset, that is, by $s!$ For this example this would be achieved by multiplying 10 (the number of combinations) by 2! (since $s = 2$). Since 2! is 2×1 or 2, and $10 \times 2 = 20$, we have learned that we have the possibility of 20 ordered combinations.

RESEARCH APPLICATIONS OF PATTERNS AND COMBINATIONS

There are two major applications of patterns and combinations in research. The first is the direct use of the procedures in problems like our example of the three judges. Here the researcher is concerned with estimating the significance probability of the specific observed pattern in his data.

The second research application of patterns and combinations is to determine the probabilities associated with the particular patterns of results in 2×2 contingency tables. This has particularly frequent research applications, for often we design studies involving the comparison of two groups or treatments (one of the 2's in the contingency table), and the data are obtained at the dichotomous level (the other "2" in the 2×2 table).

These applications of probability make no quantitative demands upon the data and so can be used with nominal data.

In terms of procedures, most of the uses of patterns and combinations have no specific name attached. However, two specific uses have been developed and reported in the literature by individuals and so their names have become associated with this application. These are: (1) the *Fisher Exact Probability Test,* used to estimate the significance probability in a 2 × 2 contingency table, (2) the *Kolmagorov-Smirnov Test,* used to test whether a cumulative frequency distribution differs significantly from chance. This procedure requires ordinal data because it is based upon the order of the pattern.

Utilizing Rank Ordering

The second way of using probability theory in statistical inference is to rank sets of ordinal data together and estimate the probability of the ranks which might be assigned each subset. For example, let us assume that within one of the groups in the Phonics Study, the researcher notes his impression that the six girls in the group are doing better than the seven boys. Since he is aware of the treachery involved in intuitive and observational judgment, he decides to explore it more rigorously and so goes to his most recent test scores and ranks the 13 children as one group. He now notes that the six girls have been assigned ranks of 1, 2, 4, 5, 7, and 9. To evaluate this piece of observed data he would need to know what are the possible outcomes if chance only were operating to order the boys and girls. To utilize probability theory for this we could work either with the pattern of ranks or with the sum of the ranks assigned one of the subsets. If we decide to use the sum of the ranks assigned a subset, we would use the girls, for there are fewer girls than boys and therefore the possibilities involved are fewer. The ranks assigned the six girls add up to 28. The smallest possible sum of the ranks for the girls would happen if they had received ranks of 1, 2, 3, 4, 5, and 6 for a sum of ranks of 21. The second smallest sum would be if they had received the ranks of 1, 2, 3, 4, 5, and 7 for a sum of 22. The next sum of ranks, 23, could happen in more than one way: 1, 2, 3, 4, 5, and 8 or 1, 2, 3, 4, 6, and 7. We could proceed on, delineating all the possible sums of ranks up to the largest possible sum of 63, arrived at if the girls had ranks of 8, 9, 10, 11, 12, 13.

It is possible to compute mathematically the separate ways in which the different sums could be reached, which is fortunate because there are many more than we would suspect. For example, in this illustration involving two subsets of six and seven, there are 1716 different outcomes possible![4] Once we have estimated the total number of outcomes and the number as or more extreme than our observed sum, we proceed as we did with patterns, by establishing the same ratio:

$$\text{significance probability} = \frac{\text{number of outcomes as extreme or more extreme than the observed result}}{\text{total number of outcomes}}$$

For the data in this illustration, there are 44 outcomes as or more extreme than the observed finding of a sum of 28. Dividing this by the total number of outcomes of 1716 yields a significance probability of .025. If we were using the 5 percent level of significance, the researcher would then conclude that his intuitive judgment that the girls were doing better is supported by the data.

To work with the pattern instead of the sum we would consider the fact that if the results were *perfectly* random, we would expect a boy and a girl to alternate in order, with no clustering of either sex. For subsets of seven and six then, we would expect the pattern BGBGBGBGBGBGB. In that case, the maximum *successive* number of boys or girls would be one, and we would have 13 such runs of one. The opposite extreme would be to have each sex completely clustered, that is, BBBBBBBGGGGGG, all of the boys followed by all of the girls. In this case we would have only two runs, one of seven for the boys and one of six for the girls.[5] In the example we are considering with the girls ranked 1, 2, 4, 5, 7, and 9 we have this ordering:

Rank: 1 2 3 4 5 6 7 8 9 10 11 12 13
Sex: G G B G G B G B G B B B B

and the eight runs are underlined, beginning with the run of two girls, the single run of the boy who ranked third and so on.

Just as it was possible to determine all the sums of ranks and the probability associated with each sum, so is it possible to determine all possible patterns of runs and the probability associated with each.[6] Using this as a criterion, the researcher can determine the significance probability of any observed pattern of runs. For this example, if we tested the data we would find that there was *no* statistically significant difference between

[4]This total is simply the number of combinations of N things s at a time, when N is the total of the two subsets and s is the subset whose sum is being evaluated. In this case it is $\binom{13}{6}$ or $\frac{13!}{6!\,7!}$ which equals 1716.

[5]This would also be true if the cluster of girls came first followed by the cluster of boys.

[6]Tables for computing these appear in Sidney Siegel, *Non-Parametric Statistics* (New York: McGraw-Hill, Inc., 1956).

the boys and girls, which is opposite to the conclusion we came to using the sum of the ranks.

This illustrates the concept of power we discussed in Chapter 8. In this instance, the procedure using the sum of the ranks is more powerful than the procedure based on the runs. This is quite logical, since working with the sum of the ranks does use more of the information available than does working with the runs only. In other words, the sum of the ranks procedure considers the fact that the girls who ranked first and second were as high in rank as possible, the runs procedure considers only that they were two consecutive girls.

Research Application

There are several uses for this particular probability concept, for it enables us to make inferential judgments about two sets of ordinal data without demanding more than the ordinal data can meet. For example, if we wish to compare 16 phonics and 13 look-say children on their interest in school, it would be difficult to obtain any measure of interest in school which would permit us to consider the data interval data for which we could compute means and standard deviations and use parametric inferential procedures. However, it would be perfectly feasible to ask the teachers to rank the children from 1 to 29 and then evaluate the subset of ranks assigned to the look-say children. Thus, the basic application is when we have verbal or numerical ordinal data for two or more groups, which enable us to rank the several groups on *one* overall ranking.

The procedures available serve three purposes within this general comparative purpose. The first purpose is to test hypotheses for one variable about whether two independent groups come from the same population. This can be done with the *Mann-Whitney Test*, the *Wilcoxon Test*, or the *Wald-Wolfowitz Runs Test*. These are listed in descending order of power, so that when all three are applicable the Mann-Whitney would be preferred because it is the most powerful. The second purpose is to test hypotheses about differences between more than two groups, that is, whether the several groups come from the same population. Two procedures are available for this purpose, the *Friedman Test*, which requires that the several groups be matched samples, and the *Kruskal-Wallis Test*, which does not. The third purpose is to test hypotheses about differences between two groups in range. These hypotheses can be tested with the *Moses Test of Extreme Reactions*.[7]

[7]Extended discussions and computational techniques for all these procedures are available in Sidney Siegel, *Non-Parametric Statistics*.

THE BINOMIAL EXPANSION

We saw in Chapter 8 how the binomial expansion provides a useful model for a specific research situation which has three specific characteristics: (1) only two possible outcomes; (2) a specific probability attached to each outcome; and (3) a finite and relatively small sample. There is nothing in the computational process of the binomial expansion which places a limit on sample size. Rather the limit is based on the practical fact that available tables for use with the binomial model typically stop at sample sizes of 25. To go beyond this then involves considerable computation. Since we illustrated the thinking behind the binomial model in Chapter 8 we shall not repeat it here. Instead let us consider the research applications.

Research Applications and Procedures

The basic research application of the binomial expansion is to determine the significance probability of a specific outcome when nominal data are available from a dichotomous variable. But the binomial model can also be used to determine the significance of differences in two sets of ordinal data when only a minimal ordinal judgment can be made. The procedure involved is called the *Sign Test*. It is applicable to two types of situations: when we wish to compare a sample of matched pairs to test the hypothesis that they came from the same population or when we wish to test the hypothesis that one set of individuals has not significantly changed over time. In either case, to use the Sign Test we must have ordinal data, and it must be possible for each individual to improve, decline, or stay the same on the measure being employed. But this is all the judgment required, so that we need no estimate of rating of where each individual stood at the beginning or end, only a judgment as to whether he has *changed* and if so in which direction. This procedure has far wider applicability to social research than its infrequent use would indicate, for it has two very considerable virtues as an inferential procedure: It is applicable to small samples, and it functions at the grossest level of ordinal measurement.

For example, column 2 of Table 9-2 presents for 12 children a teacher's judgment as to whether or not she has observed any difference in their general interest in and/or liking for school during the Language Study. Notice that we have no initial rating of that interest or liking, and no final rating. We have only the judgment of change or not, and if there was change, the direction of that change. In column 3, we have put a zero

Table 9–2 Teacher's Judgment as to Change in Interest in School, for 12 Children

Child	Teacher's Judgment	Sign
1	Increase	+
2	Increase	+
3	No Change	0
4	Decrease	−
5	Increase	+
6	No Change	0
7	Increase	+
8	Decrease	−
9	Increase	+
10	No Change	0
11	Increase	+
12	Decrease	−

next to the children for whom no change was observed, a plus sign next to those for whom improvement was noted, and a minus sign next to those for whom a decline was noted. It is from this use of signs that the procedure was named. We now consider the no-difference situation as always, and ask what we would expect if the Language Study had no effect on interest in school. We would expect that many children would show no change in interest, but because of chance factors at any one time, some children would show declines and others improvements. If this is a chance phenomena, however, as many should improve as decline—another way of saying the probability of improvement or of decline is .50.

But if we ignore the three children who did not change and consider only the nine who did, we can now use the binomial expansion as our model, setting the probability of improvement at .50, considering n to be nine, the number who changed in one direction or the other (that is, those with a plus or minus sign) and then proceed to test whether the six improvements (the six plus signs) differ significantly from the chance probability of .50.

Note that like the earlier discussion of the assumption of equally likely alternatives in the use of chi square, here too we are assuming that improvement and decline are equally likely, i.e., no systematic factor is operating to produce change. There is nothing in the procedure, however, which limits it to this situation. We can use the Sign Test for any probability of improvement.

THE CHI SQUARE DISTRIBUTION

The most widely used model for inferential purposes is the mathematical function called chi square. We discussed the procedure in Chapter 7, considering its use as a measure of association. In that instance, it was used to determine if there was reason to believe that two frequency distributions were associated. Turning that use around, we could say it was used to test the hypothesis that the two distributions came from the same population. Questions about distributions are so frequent in research that chi square has wide applicability.

One particularly common problem in research is to determine whether or not an observed frequency distribution differs significantly from the distribution we would expect by chance. To illustrate this problem, and to provide some data on the basis of which we can seek a model, let us suppose that as part of the Phonics Study we decide to provide each child with the opportunity to discuss any school or personal problems with a teacher-counselor. We also provide the children with a free choice of counselor from among the three teacher-counselors available. After this plan has been put into operation, Mr. Brown comes to the director of the project and says that he feels he is receiving a disproportionately large share of the children, and that while this is flattering it is giving him an unduly heavy caseload. He further states that some consistent factor must be biasing the selection. Thus Mr. Brown is hypothesizing that the distribution differs significantly from a chance distribution. The director then agrees to study this problem and so goes back to the 60 children involved and records which teacher each selected. These are the data presented in Table 9-3.

On inspection, it would seem that Mr. Brown is correct, he *is* receiving more children than either of his colleagues. What of his contention that some factor is consistently biasing the selection? After all, the director might think, this may be just a chance variation, a quirk of the data.

Table 9-3   Number of Children Who Chose Each Teacher

Teacher	Number of Children Selecting This Teacher
Mr. Brown	23
Miss Smith	18
Miss Thompson	19
	60

This, of course, is the situation for which we need an inferential procedure to estimate for us the likelihood or probability that our observed frequency distribution occurred by chance. The director decides that he will use the 5 percent level of significance and now must estimate the significance probability.

The first thing he needs is some basis for deciding what he should have expected to happen if nothing but chance had been operating. In this case it is fairly simple. He decides that under pure chance conditions he would have expected each of the three teachers to be selected by one-third of the children. Since there were 60 children, he would have expected each teacher to be selected by 20 children. In Table 9-4, we have set up in the first column the observed data copied from Table 9-3. In the second column we have put down the expected frequencies of 20. These two columns of data provide us with an obvious and simple basis for evaluating this particular difference; we simply subtract the expected frequency from the observed frequency. This has been done in column three.

To obtain an overall evaluation of the difference we would intuitively expect to add up these differences, except that we face a problem similar to the one we faced with the standard deviation: The differences add to zero. We solve the problem in the same way that we did with the standard deviation. We square the differences. This has been done in column four. But we do not add at this point either, because we must consider one other problem: A squared difference (of 9, for example) is not interpretable in the abstract. We obtained this one by squaring the remainder after subtracting 20 from 23. But we could have achieved this same squared difference of 9 had our observed frequency been 1,575,625 when our expected frequency was 1,575,622. Yet these two differences of 3 or squared differences of 9 reflect quite different discrepancies. In our illustration the difference consists of about one-seventh of the expected fre-

Table 9-4 Computational Table for Teacher Study

Teacher	Column 1 Observed Frequency of Choice	Column 2 Frequency Expected by Chance	Column 3 Observed Minus Expected	Column 4 $(O - E)^2$	Column 5 $\dfrac{(O - E)^2}{E}$
Mr. Brown	23	20	+3	9	.45
Miss Smith	18	20	−2	4	.20
Miss Thompson	19	20	−1	1	.05
	60	60	0		$.70 = \chi^2$

quency, while in the second it is 1/525,000 of the expected frequency. Therefore, to bring the squared difference into the context of the actual data, in column five we have divided each one by the expected frequency and then added these results to obtain a sum of .70.

To make any use of the .70 to accept or reject the hypothesis that the observed distribution did not differ significantly from the distribution expected by chance, we need some model for these data. As before, let us, as a first step, think about the characteristics of the data. We have taken two frequency distributions, subtracted the observed from the expected frequency in each category, squared these deviations, divided by the expected frequency, and added the quotients. What would such data look like if *nothing* was happening but chance? First, what would happen if there were no differences in any category? In that case observed and expected frequencies would be identical, the differences all zero, and the sum zero. This would be the smallest possible sum, for we square the differences and we could never obtain a negative sum. Therefore, we need a model which begins at zero and is always positive. Then we could consider that even with nothing happening but chance, we would not be surprised at small differences. Because these are being divided by the expected frequency the sums in these instances would also be small, so the second characteristic we seek in the model is that it have most of its values close to zero. We might obtain some extreme chance deviations and so would also like the model to allow for extreme variation, although this would be unlikely.

The mathematical function called chi square has these properties. A typical chi square curve is graphed in Figure 9-1, and as can be seen there is a steeply peaked curve, beginning at zero, with most of its area concentrated at the lower end of the curve. It does have larger values, although these are less probable, and because it is asymptotic (that is, never touches the baseline) it permits of infinite variation. Thus chi square could serve as a model for these data, and in fact the sum of .70 has been derived by the chi square procedure and is the value of chi square for these data.

The mathematical distribution of chi square has been determined, and is expressed in summary tables. A portion of such a table is reproduced in Table 9-5. This table tells us how often, *purely by chance,* we would obtain specific values of chi square. But Table 9-5, like the full chi square table, has several columns. Therefore, to use the table to evaluate the chi square of .70, we must take one additional factor into account. Since χ^2 is obtained by adding up a series of terms we must utilize the fact that this particular χ^2 was achieved by adding up *three* terms. We would have had an entirely different opinion of a χ^2 of .70 obtained by adding two terms

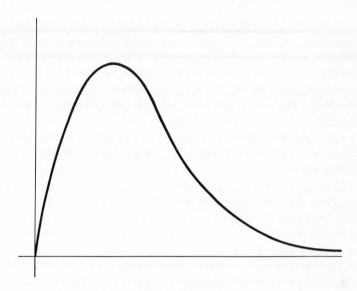

Figure 9-1 Typical chi square curve.

or twenty-one terms. In statistical terms this aspect of a statistic is called the number of *degrees of freedom* possessed by the statistic and is almost universally symbolized by the letters *df*. The degrees of freedom possessed by a statistic can be considered to represent the number of free observations which have produced the statistic.

This concept of free observations can be illustrated through a simple example. If we were told that a group of six mothers had a total of twelve

Table 9-5 Excerpt from Chi Square Table

Percent of Times This Chi Square or Larger Occurs	Degrees of Freedom		
	2	3	20
99	.02	.11	8.26
90	.21	.58	12.44
75	.58	1.21	15.55
50	1.39	2.37	19.34
20	3.22	4.64	25.04
10	4.60	6.25	28.41
5	5.99	7.82	31.41
2	7.82	9.84	35.02
1	9.21	11.34	37.57

children and were told that the first woman had one child, the second had three, the third two, the fourth one, and the fifth two, for a total for the first five women of nine children, then the sixth woman must have the remaining three children needed to make the total of twelve. In other words, by telling us that the total was twelve we placed one restriction on the data: The six numbers must add up to twelve. Placing this one restriction on the data meant that one of the six numbers lost the freedom to vary, and that as soon as we knew any five of the numbers we knew the sixth as well, since it was whatever was needed to arrive at the known total of twelve.

In the χ^2 example we have been using, we placed one restriction on the data, that the total number of teachers with whom we were concerned was three and thus, in our example, we have one fewer or two degrees of freedom connected with this chi square. The question we really put to the chi square table then is not "How often would a chi square of .70 occur by chance" but rather, "How often would a chi square of .70 occur by chance *when there are two degrees of freedom?*" Hence, this means that for research purposes we need several chi square curves rather than one, and in reality chi square is really a family of curves, one for each specific number of degrees of freedom.

Thus, we use Table 9-5 by reading down the column for two degrees of freedom. The value of .70 which we obtained lies between two values in the table, .58 with a significance probability of 75 percent and 1.39 with a significance probability of 50 percent. We have no need for any greater precision because both of these values are far in excess of the 5 percent level of significance the director of the project has selected.

Therefore, the director would conclude that the observed variation in the frequency distribution from the distribution expected by chance was not statistically significant, and thus accept the statistical hypothesis of no difference. This means that he will decide to attribute these variations to chance factors and not to any systematic selection factor.[8]

The effect of the degrees of freedom upon the interpretation of the statistical significance of any obtained chi square is illustrated by the three columns of Table 9-5. The chi square required to achieve any one significance probability gets larger as the number of degrees of freedom gets larger. Thus, for significance at the 5 percent level, we would need to obtain a chi square value of 5.99 if we had two degrees of freedom. This

[8]This is a good illustration of the practical significance issue discussed in Chapter 8. Imagine the practical issue of convincing Mr. Brown that a pupil load of 23 is not "significantly different" from a pupil load of 18 or 19! All he knows is that he has to see 23 children, and Miss Smith only has to see 18 and Miss Thompson 19. Would the knowledge that this is not significantly different from a chance distribution make him feel any less overworked? This author doubts it.

increases to 7.82 for three degrees of freedom and to 31.41 for 20 degrees of freedom. This illustrates dramatically the need to place the obtained chi square in the context of the degrees of freedom to interpret its statistical significance. It also illustrates a handy rule of thumb about chi square: An obtained chi square smaller than the number of degrees of freedom is never statistically significant.

Estimating the Chance Distribution

The one difficulty in using chi square as a measure of the variation of a frequency distribution from a chance distribution is developing a rationale for what the chance frequencies should be. In social research we have generally used the simple level of thinking exemplified by what we did in the illustration here: Divide the total evenly among the categories. Thus, we decided that by chance 60 children would be distributed 20–20–20 among three teachers. However, suppose that when the children were offered their choice of counselor this was done by giving them an alphabetical list of the three teachers, with Mr. Brown listed first, followed by Miss Smith and Miss Thompson. Let us assume that in the absence of any basis for selection, children tend to select the first name on the list. Let us assume further that we know that by chance, 50 percent of the children choose the first name, 40 percent the second name and only 10 percent the third name. If this were so, we would have an entirely different perception of a chance distribution, and the data would appear as they do in Table 9-6. If we compute chi square for *these* data, we obtain a chi square value of 31.29, which *is* statistically significant (by reference to Table 9-5) at the 5 percent level.

Even more intriguing, by these chance data, Mr. Brown now seems to be a teacher the children were *avoiding*, while they were attracted by Miss Thompson!

Table 9-6 Chi Square Table for Alternate Chance Distribution

Teacher	Observed	Expected by Chance	$O - E$	$(O - E)^2$	$\dfrac{(O - E)^2}{E}$
Mr. Brown	23	30	−7	49	1.63
Miss Smith	18	24	−6	36	1.50
Miss Thompson	19	6	+13	169	28.16
	60	60	0		$31.29 = \chi^2$

Which of these two chance distributions is correct, or whether a third is actually correct, cannot be determined in the absence of data. What is suggested here is that we not blithely assume that every chance distribution is a simple symmetric one in which the total available observations are evenly divided among the categories. We may be able to use data available in the literature to provide some empirical basis for estimating the chance distribution for chi square purposes, or if not, we may have to collect separate data for this purpose alone. Thus, in our example, we could go to larger numbers of children, offer them a list of three fictitious teachers' names, and ask them to select the teacher they would prefer. If we randomly rotate the names on the list we could use these data to determine what proportion of children choose the first name, the second name, and the third name and thus have an empirical basis for the frequencies to use in the chance distribution.

Interpreting Chi Square

We have often said that inferential procedures are specific in that they test specific hypotheses. The chi square procedure and model tests hypotheses about frequency distributions as a *total entity* only. In other words, the significant chi square for the data in Table 9-6 tells us that this distribution of 23, 18, and 19 differs significantly from the chance distribution of 30, 24, and 6. That is all it tells us. But what about a question like: "Is the proportion of children who selected Mr. Brown significantly different from the proportion expected by chance?" Or, "Did Miss Thompson attract significantly more children than we would have expected by chance?" Chi square does *not* provide a basis for answering these questions, for they are not questions about the total distribution but rather about the differences between two proportions; that is, is 38 percent significantly different from 50 percent when there are 60 cases in the sample?

In Chapter 10 we shall discuss the procedures available for testing the significance of the difference between two proportions. Here let us recognize that whenever a chi square test has been performed for limited-, multiple-, or infinite-category frequency distributions,[9] and results in a statistically significant difference, it provides a basis only for concluding that the distributions being tested are different. If there are additional hypotheses about the possibility of differences in proportions in specific categories, the chi square procedure must be followed by supplementary tests appropriate for testing those hypotheses about proportions. An im-

[9] For dichotomous distributions, of course, a significant chi square can be interpreted specifically.

portant second aspect of this interpretation is that if the chi square procedure produces no statistically significant differences between the distributions, no further tests should be done. We now conclude that the distributions did not differ and so do not look for specific differences within the distribution. It is possible if we did the specific tests that some might result in significant differences between proportions, but these would be spurious in the context of the overall conclusion that the distributions did not differ. To avoid this possible confusion, we will do no further analysis within distributions which have been shown not to differ by the chi square procedure.

Research Applications

This illustration typifies the use of chi square to determine if any one observed frequency distribution differs from a chance distribution. It can be used with any level of data (nominal or better) expressed as a dichotomy, in limited categories or in multiple categories. However, it can only be used with mutually exclusive categories. This is because an implicit assumption in the computational process of chi square is that the observations in each cell are independent. In simple terms this means that each response or respondent can be classified only once, and this holds only when the categories are mutually exclusive.

There is one additional limitation researchers often face in the use of chi square, which stems from the computational process involved. Remember that in an effort to bring the squared differences obtained into relationship with the data which produced them, we divided each squared difference by its corresponding expected value. This practice contains the possibility of serious distortion: When the expected value is zero or close to zero the result of this division will be spuriously high. This has led to two rules about χ^2; first, that it can never be done in such a way that the *expected* frequency in any cell is less than one, and second, that it should never be done in such a way that the expected frequencies fall between one and five in more than 20 percent of the cells.

But what is a researcher to do if he is faced with such data, that is, if in his study the data violate one or both of these rules? The accepted solution is that he is to combine logically related categories until the data meet these two conditions. For example, in Table 9-7, columns 1 and 2 present such data. In column 1, ten countries are listed which include the birthplace of all 60 children in two classes. Assume that the researcher analyzes the school records and discovers what proportion of children were born over the past ten years in each of these countries, and uses these proportions to develop the expected frequencies in column 3. But notice that one of the expected frequencies is less than one and four others less than five, more than the 20 percent limit. The researcher's problem now is to see if he can meaningfully and logically combine categories to raise the expected frequencies to meet this condition. Note that if he could not combine the categories meaningfully and logically, he could *not* proceed with the chi square analysis, and so could not perform any test of significance for these two distributions. However, in this instance the researcher feels that he can sensibly combine the ten countries to form the five-category summary-frequency distribution which appears in columns 4, 5, and 6 of Table 9-7. Now none of the categories has an expected frequency of less than one, and only one an expected frequency between one and five, within the 20 percent limit. Now chi square can be performed.

The technique we have just illustrated is called *collapsing* a frequency distribution for purposes of chi square analysis. It is a perfectly legitimate procedure, so long as the collapsing is based on rational considerations, and only logically related categories are combined.

Table 9–7 Observed and Expected Frequencies for Simple and Collapsed Frequency Distributions for Birthplace

Column 1 Country	*Column 2* Observed Frequency	*Column 3* Expected Frequency	*Column 4* Country	*Column 5* Observed Frequency	*Column 6* Expected Frequency
United States	15	20	United States	15	20
England	12	11	England	12	11
Germany	9	14	France, Italy, Germany	17	19
Cuba	9	8	Cuba, Puerto Rico, Brazil	17	14
Puerto Rico	7	5.5	Japan, China	6	3
Italy	6	4			
Japan	4	2			
China	2	1			
France	2	1			
Brazil	1	.5			
Total	67	67		67	67

Testing Significance of Dichotomous
Frequency Distributions against Chance

If a researcher desires to test a dichotomous variable against chance, he has available special and somewhat simplified computational formulas[10] and the availability of a correction procedure if the frequencies are too low. Otherwise this chi square proceeds just as before.

Testing Whether One Frequency Distribution Is Different
from Norm and Expectation Other than Chance

The second inferential problem which can arise involving frequency distribution is presented when the researcher wishes to know if his observed distribution is different from some expectation other than chance. Procedurally, this too is a chi square problem, somewhat simplified now since there is a specific basis for estimating the expected frequencies.

One application of this chi square is possible when data are available from other research or records, as in the illustrative data in Table 9-7. A particularly important application is to help a researcher know if a set of interval data is normally distributed. We discussed in Chapter 6 how the Table for the Normal Curve provides the proportion of the curve between the mean and several points at fixed distances from the mean. These points are expressed in terms of standard deviations. We know, for example, that 34 percent of the normal distribution should lie within the mean and one standard deviation above the mean, and another 34 percent between the mean and one standard deviation below the mean. From the Table for the Normal Curve, however, we can learn more precise information than this, such as that 19 percent of the normal distribution lies between the mean and one-half of a standard deviation above or below, or that 9 percent lies between one and one and one-half standard deviations away from the mean. But we can then apply these proportions to our sample, and so determine how *many* of the elements in the sample would be within specified parts of a standard deviation from the mean if the distribution were normal. Once this is done, we could use these as the expected normal distribution. Thus in a sample of 150 persons, 34 percent or 51 persons should have scores between the mean and one standard deviation above, and another 51 between the mean and one standard deviation below; 9 percent or 14 should be between one and one and one-half standard deviations, and so on through the distribution. The

---

[10]These are fully discussed in Sidney Siegel, *Non-Parametric Statistics*.

observed distribution can be obtained simply by counting how many cases actually do lie between the mean and certain standard deviation points. Chi square can then be used to test whether the two distributions are significantly different. If they are not, we have demonstrated that the observed distribution does not differ significantly from the normal distribution, and for all subsequent purposes the data can be assumed to be normally distributed. If they do differ significantly, then the distribution cannot be considered normal, and this difference would suggest nonparametric rather than parametric inferential procedures be used thereafter.

Testing Difference of Two or More Frequency Distributions

When the researcher has stated hypotheses involving more than one frequency distribution, he can test these with chi square as well. The most limited case for this use of chi square, when there are only two frequency distributions to be considered, has already been discussed in Chapter 7, as a measure of association. In this instance, the use of chi square as a measure of association and as the basis for an inference as to whether or not two frequency distributions differ, coincide. If the chi square we obtain is not statistically significant, we conclude that the distributions do not differ, which can be turned around to the conclusion that there is some association between the variables. If the chi square is statistically significant, we conclude that the distributions do differ or that there is no association between them.

This use of chi square to test for differences between distributions can be extended to more than two distributions, to test for differences, although it ceases to be meaningful as a measure of association. Whether used to test for two or more than two distributions, the main point to note in this application of chi square is that the researcher can use the observed data themselves to generate the expected frequencies. Table 9-8 provides some data to illustrate this use of chi square in testing whether three classes differ in the distribution on adjustment as rated by the school psychologist. Table 9-8 presents the data for the 80 children in the three classes. In this instance we have three sets of observed data and wish to test the hypothesis that they do not differ from each other.

As always, the only problem in chi square is to develop the expected frequencies. In this instance we use the observed data themselves. The data have been collapsed so that the expected frequencies meet the demands of chi square, and so the data in Table 9-8 are ready to be used to compute chi square. Let us consider the first category, "excellent adjustment," in which we have a total of 24 children in all three classes.

Table 9–8 Observed and Expected Frequency Distributions for Levels of Adjustment

| Level of Adjustment | *Observed Distributions* | | | | | *Expected Distributions* | | | |
	Class A	Class B	Class C	Total		Class A	Class B	Class C	Total
Excellent	5	2	17	24	$\dfrac{30}{80} \times 24 = 9$		6	9	24
Good—fair	15	6	11	32		12	8	12	32
Poor or severely maladjusted	10	12	2	24		9	6	9	24
Total	30	20	30	80		30	20	30	80

We argue that if this were a chance situation, and the three classes *did not* differ, then the 24 excellently adjusted children should be distributed among the three classes in direct proportion to class size. Thus, class A which has three-eighths of all the children (30/80) should have three-eighths of the excellently adjusted children as well. Therefore, we have listed three-eighths of 24, or 9, as the *expected* frequency for class A in the "excellent" category. By this same thinking, class A should have three-eighths of the children in each category of adjustment, class B, two-eighths, and class C the other three-eighths, and so we can generate all of the expected frequencies.

Chi square then proceeds as usual, except that we now have nine separate terms, in each of which we must subtract observed and expected, square the deviation, and divide by the expected. These nine terms are presented in Table 9-9, which also indicates that the sum or chi square is 26.0.

To determine whether or not this chi square is statistically significant, we need to determine the degrees of freedom associated with it. In any contingency table like Table 9-8 we have placed as many restrictions on the data as there are column or row totals, minus one for the overlapping effect of the corner cell. We have three columns and three rows in Table 9-8 for a total of six restrictions minus one, or five. Subtracting the five from the nine cells leaves us with four degrees of freedom. You can easily verify this with Table 9-10 which has only the column and row totals. Write in any number less than the totals, and once you have filled in any

Table 9-9 Computational Illustration for Chi Square for Data of Table 9-8

Level of Adjustment	Class A		Class B		Class C
Excellent	$\dfrac{(5-9)^2}{9}$	$+$	$\dfrac{(2-6)^2}{6}$	$+$	$\dfrac{(17-9)^2}{9}$
Good—fair	$\dfrac{(15-12)^2}{12}$	$+$	$\dfrac{(6-8)^2}{8}$	$+$	$\dfrac{(11-12)^2}{12}$
Poor or severely maladjusted	$\dfrac{(10-9)^2}{9}$	$+$	$\dfrac{(12-6)^2}{6}$	$+$	$\dfrac{(2-9)^2}{9}$

$$\chi^2 = 26.0$$

Table 9-10 Illustrative Table for Degrees of Freedom for Data of Table 9-8

Level of Adjustment	Class A	Class B	Class C	Total
Excellent				24
Good—fair				32
Poor or severely maladjusted				24
Total	30	20	30	80

four of the cells, you can obtain the other five numbers by subtraction. Thus only four of the numbers are free to vary, and so the chi square of 26.0 has four degrees of freedom. Reference to the chi square table tells us that this is statistically significant at the 5 percent level, and so we reject the hypothesis of no difference and conclude that the distributions *are* different.

PROCEDURES

Several different procedures use the chi square model other than the chi square procedure itself. These other procedures begin differently but ultimately conclude with data for which chi square is an appropriate model. The most widely used of these is the *Median Test*, because it permits the researcher to test hypotheses about differences between sets of ordinal data, as expressed in the medians. The median test is quite simple. We combine the data from all of the separate groups and compute the median for this one total distribution. Then for each group separately, we count how many respondents have scores either "at or above the median" or "below" the median, establishing a contingency table with these two rows, with as many columns as there are groups. The hypothesis is then tested with the chi square procedure and model.

In terms of data, the median test requires numerical ordinal data for the computation of the median and samples large enough to meet the demands of chi square. If the samples are not large enough, and there are only two groups, the *Wilcoxon sum of ranks* procedure can be considered an alternate to the median test.

Another useful procedure which uses the chi square model is the *McNemar Test for Change.* The procedure is applicable to pre- and post-data from one group which we wish to use to test hypotheses about change.

The McNemar procedure can only be used if the variable under study is a dichotomy, but it is applicable to both nominal and ordinal data. All that is involved is to establish a 2×2 contingency table identifying those who stayed the same and those who changed in each direction. Notice that these are the same students, classified at two points in time, and so these data *do not* meet the critical assumption of the normal chi square that the categories be mutually exclusive and the data in the cells be independent observations. There is an analogous procedure to the McNemar Test, Cochran's Q Test, which can be used with more than two sets of dichotomous data. It, too, uses the chi square model for determining the significance probability of the observed data.[11]

[11]Both the McNemar and Cochran procedure are fully discussed in Sidney Siegel, *Non-Parametric Statistics.*

Chapter 10

INFERENTIAL STATISTICS: PARAMETRIC MODELS, THEIR APPLICATIONS, AND PROCEDURES

When interval data are available, the researcher can move to the realm of the parametric models for statistical inference. Let us turn to these models now.

THE NORMAL CURVE

Probably the most familiar model available for inferential purposes is the bell-shaped curve or normal curve. We discussed it in Chapter 6 as an appropriate model for the distribution of many physical, social, psychological, and educational characteristics. Its inferential use is in situations when we are concerned with evaluating the significance of differences between two moment system statistics. For example, assume that two of the experimental groups in the Phonics Study began at the same reading grade, and we hypothesized that the phonics group would be better at the end of the study. When we reach the end of the study, let us assume that the look-say group has a mean of 5.6 and the phonics group a mean of 6.2, and we wish to determine if this observed difference between the means is statistically significant or not. Or consider the possible hypothesis in the Language Study that the relationship between the abilities to speak and write English would be higher for children taught by the structure method than for the experiential childen. Again assume that after the Language Study we compute the product moment correlation between ability to speak English and ability to write English and find it is .65 for the structure children and .49 for the experiential children. Now we would wish to know if this observed difference between the correlations is statistically significant.

To utilize the normal curve as a model for hypothesis testing in these situations we need only one piece of information besides the observed difference. That piece of information is the standard error of the difference. We noted in Chapter 6 that all moment system statistics had a standard error, and logically, the difference between two moment system statistics also has a standard error. Thus a difference between two means, or between two correlations, or between two proportions would each have a standard error. If the standard error is known, then the normal curve can be used as an inferential model. The computational entry to the model is simply to divide the observed difference by the standard error of the difference, using this basic ratio:

$$\frac{\text{the observed difference}}{\text{the standard error of}}$$
$$\text{the difference}$$

For example, suppose that in the illustration above where the look-say mean is 5.6 and the phonics mean is 6.2, we compute (through processes to be discussed later) the standard error of the difference to be .25 of a grade. In this instance, the observed difference of .6 when divided by this standard error yields a quotient of 2.4. This quotient can be considered a measure of distance along the baseline of the curve from its midpoint. Thus, in our example, we are at a point 2.4 standard errors away from the midpoint, as illustrated in Figure 10-1.

To convert this to a significance probability we need to know what proportion of the area of the curve lies to the right[1] of 2.4. It is this portion of the curve which represents the values more extreme than our obtained value, and as in all tests of significance, it is this proportion which represents the significance probability. To learn the proportion, we refer the ratio of 2.4 directly to the tables of the normal curve. An excerpt from a normal curve table appears in Table 10-1. Some of the values should be familiar; for example, we have previously noted that for a

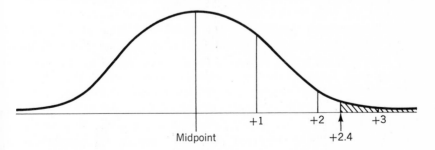

Figure 10-1   Illustration of application of data to normal curve.

[1]If we were conducting a two-tail test we would also be concerned with the proportion of the area below −2.4.

one-tail test, only 5 percent of the area of the curve lies beyond 1.645 standard deviations (or standard errors), and that for a two-tail test this value is 1.96 standard deviations (noted on the table at 2.5 percent). Considering these values, we can, by reference to this table, see that the significance probability of a ratio of 2.4 is less than 1 percent. We would therefore conclude that the difference of .6 was statistically significant and attribute it to the experimental variable rather than chance.

What the excerpt from the table of the normal curve shows us is that for a one-tailed test, unless an observed difference is 1.645 times larger than its standard error, it is not statistically significant at the 5 percent level, with 2.33 the corresponding 1 percent level value, and the 1.96 and 2.58 the values for the two-tailed test.

The applicability of the normal curve as a model in this situation is based on the fact that when we divide differences by their standard errors, the possible outcomes parallel the characteristics of the curve, as we noted

Table 10–1 Excerpt from Table of Normal Curve

Ratio of Difference to Its Standard Error	Significance Probability of This Ratio in Percent	
	For One-tail Test	For Two-tail Test
1.5	6.7	13.4
1.6	5.5	11.0
1.645	5.0	10.0
1.7	4.4	8.8
1.8	3.6	7.2
1.9	2.9	5.8
1.96	2.5	5.0
2.0	2.3	4.6
2.1	1.8	3.6
2.2	1.3	2.6
2.3	1.1	2.2
2.33	1.0	2.0
2.4	.7	1.4
2.5	.6	1.2
2.58	.5	1.0
2.6	.47	.94
2.7	.35	.70
2.8	.26	.52
2.9	.19	.38
3.0	.13	.26

in Chapter 8. The most likely outcome in a chance situation is that there will be no difference, but slight differences in either direction would not surprise us. The normal curve has its modal point in the center and most of its area near the center. If we set that center to represent no difference, then most of the area is near this point of no difference and would therefore represent only slight differences. Moreover, the symmetry of the curve makes differences in either direction equally probable, which also parallels the data, since to use this reading illustration, in a pure chance situation there is as great a likelihood that the look-say children would be the ones who did better as there is that the phonics children would do better. The symmetry of the normal curve around its midpoint allows for this. Finally, the fact that the curve never touches its base line allows for infinite extreme differences, which theoretically would be possible.

Difficulties in Using Normal Curve

The researcher's problem in the use of the normal curve is to estimate the standard error of the difference with which he is concerned. In this example of the difference between the means, the researcher is seeking to estimate the standard deviation he would obtain if he took several pairs of samples from the same population, computed the difference between the means for each pair, and then computed the standard deviation of the several differences. This concept is illustrated in Figure 10-2.

This was referred to as the researcher's problem since obviously no researcher will draw several pairs of samples so as to be able to compute the standard error of the difference. He therefore must estimate it. One basis for estimating it would be the standard deviation of the population or populations. For example, the standard error of a difference between two means would be estimated from the population standard deviations by use of the formula:

$$\begin{matrix} \text{standard error of the} \\ \text{difference between} \\ \text{the means} \end{matrix} = \sqrt{\dfrac{\text{variance of population 1}}{\text{size of sample 1}} + \dfrac{\text{variance of population 2}}{\text{size of sample 2}}}$$

In this instance, with population data available, the normal curve is an appropriate model. But a major limitation in the use of this model is that the researcher seldom knows the population standard deviation. The other limitation in the normal curve as a model for this type of research situation is that even if the population standard deviation is known, we need samples large enough for us to assume that the difference between the means is normally distributed. If we cannot make that assumption and nevertheless use the normal curve as a model, we run the risk of making a

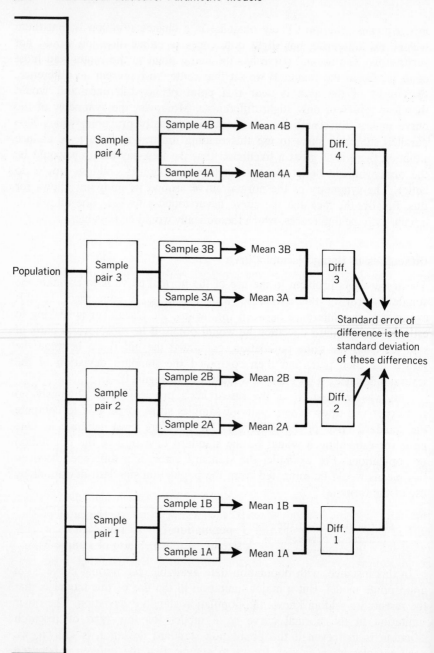

Figure 10-2 Visualization of the standard error of the difference between two means.

spurious generalization of statistical significance. The reason for this is simple: The stability of the mean as a reflection of the central tendency of a set of data is a direct reflection of the size of the sample on which it is based.

THE *t* DISTRIBUTION

If we do not know the population data, we can use the sample data to estimate the appropriate standard error of the difference. But the normal curve is no longer the appropriate model. Similarly when our samples are small[2] we cannot use the normal curve, for we have not met its assumptions. The model that is used was developed by William Gosset. He was an employee of the Guinness Brewery in England at the time, and company rules forbade employees to publish articles under their own name. Therefore he published the article developing this model under the pseudonym "Student," and so the model has come to be known as "Student's Distribution." It is probably more familiarly known as the *t* distribution, for the lower case *t* is used as the symbol for the model. The *t* distribution looks like the normal curve in that it is symmetrical about a midpoint which is its mode, and so can be used to represent either the instance of *A* greater than *B* or *B* greater than *A*. In general it is shaped like the normal curve except that it is lower and flatter, and therefore more of its area is in the tails of the distribution. Put into the terms we have been using, this means that extreme values are less unusual in the *t* distribution than in the normal curve, as can be seen in Figure 10-3 where the two curves are superimposed and the same data are tested using both the normal and the *t* distributions.

Under the normal distribution, the particular difference which we are seeking to evaluate is marked at point *Z*. Under the normal distribution this is at a point beyond which lies only 3 percent of the area of the normal curve. Therefore at the 5 percent level of significance we would reject the null hypothesis of no difference, and conclude that chance alone could not satisfactorily explain this difference. But had we used the appropriate *t* distribution for these data, the same difference is at a point on the *t* curve beyond which lies 9 percent of the area of the curve. Therefore at the 5 percent level of significance we would accept the null hypothesis and attribute this difference to chance, exactly the opposite conclusion from the one we reached using the normal model. Of course, for many sets of data, in fact for most, both curves yield the same

[2]Statistically, a small sample is defined as one with fewer than 30 cases.

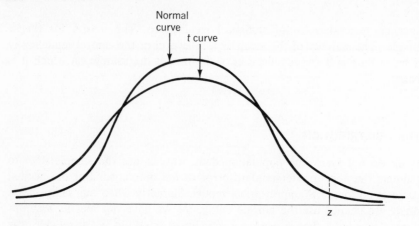

Figure 10-3 Application of the normal curve and *t* distribution to one set of data.

conclusion. There will be instances when they do not, and it is in these instances that the use of the normal curve would lead to a spurious conclusion of statistical significance.

Interpreting the *t* Distribution

Since the *t* distribution is tied to the size of the sample involved in the data, then there must be a family of *t* curves rather than the one normal curve. This use of sample size is analogous to the degrees of freedom used for the different chi square curves. For the *t* distribution, every specific sample size has a corresponding *t* curve. For any one curve, the interpretation is exactly like that of the normal curve: The ratio of the difference to the standard error is considered the distance along the base line of the curve from the midpoint. The significance probability is then the proportion of the area of the curve beyond that. Because it is a family of curves rather than a single curve, the table of the *t* distribution is typically presented with data for specific degrees of freedom. Table 10-2 is an excerpt from such a table. This excerpt indicates that to use the table, the researcher needs to determine the degrees of freedom. For testing inferences about means, this is determined by simply subtracting one from each sample and adding the two results. For correlations, it is the sample size less two. Once the degrees of freedom are determined, this tells the researcher the *row* of the *t* table to use. His level of significance, and the fact of his using a one- or two-tailed test will tell him the *column* to use. The intersection of row and column will provide the actual critical value of *t* for that combination of degrees of freedom and level of significance. To see how this works, using the excerpt of the *t* distribution which

Table 10–2   Excerpt from *t* Table

| | *Critical Value of t Required for Significance* | | | |
| | at 5% Level | | at 1% Level | |
Degrees of Freedom	One-tail Test	Two-tail Test	One-tail Test	Two-tail Test
1	6.31	12.71	31.82	63.66
2	2.92	4.30	6.96	9.92
3	2.35	3.18	4.54	5.84
5	2.02	2.57	3.36	4.03
10	1.81	2.23	2.76	3.17
15	1.75	2.13	2.60	2.95
19	1.73	2.09	2.54	2.86
20	1.72	2.09	2.53	2.85
25	1.71	2.06	2.48	2.79
30	1.70	2.04	2.46	2.75
60	1.67	2.00	2.39	2.66
Infinite	1.645	1.96	2.33	2.58

appears in Table 10-2, consider that the means referred to earlier of 6.2 and 5.6 came from groups of 12 and 9 children respectively. This would add to 19 degrees of freedom (11 plus 8), and if the level of significance was 5 percent and a two-tailed test was employed, the intersection of the row for 19 degrees of freedom with the 5 percent level of significance for a two-tailed test yields a critical value for *t* of 2.09. The interpretation proceeds as usual from here on in the sense that our obtained value of *t* must be as large or larger than the critical value for us to conclude that we have a statistically significant difference.

As the number of degrees of freedom increases the *t* distribution changes and begins to more nearly approach the shape of the normal distribution. It is sufficiently close when the degrees of freedom equal 30 in each sample. We have adopted this as the statistical definition of a small sample: A small sample is one smaller than 30.

Thus, whenever we have a research problem in which the inference to be made is one involving the difference between two moment system statistics, we have two models available, the *t* distribution for small sample research and the normal curve for large sample research when the population standard deviation is known.[3]

---

[3]Walker and Lev's *Statistical Inference* is a good source for the computational techniques involved in the use of both these distributions.

Research Applications of Normal and *t* Distributions

The basic concept of the ratio of the difference between two moment system statistics to the standard error of that difference has many research applications.[4] All of these applications involve three major areas: hypotheses involving means, correlations, and proportions or percentages. In the first area, involving means, we have discussed one use—to test the significance of a difference between two sample means. It can also be used to test for statistical significance of the difference between a population mean and one sample mean, or the difference between some standard or expectation and a sample mean. For correlations, the models apply to test the difference between two sample correlations, the difference between one obtained sample correlation and one population correlation, the difference between one sample correlation and a correlation of zero, and the difference between an obtained correlation and some norm or expectation other than zero.

In the area of proportions, the same pattern holds: The normal or *t* models can be used to test hypotheses about the difference between the proportion in the sample with a specific characteristic and the proportion in the population, the difference between two sample proportions, and the difference between a sample proportion and some norm or expectation.

In addition to these applications for which the normal curve and *t* distribution can both be used as a model, depending upon the basis of estimating the standard error of the difference, there is one instance in which the *t* distribution is uniquely applicable: when the hypothesis being tested involves change or difference in two sets of data from the *same* people. In this instance, the data are dependent in that the second set of observations is related to the first. For data like those, a special version of the *t* procedure is used, generally called a *t* test for correlated means.

Assumptions and Limitations of Normal and *t* Distributions

Both the normal and *t* distributions assume that the data are interval data, and this assumption must be met to use the procedure sensibly. They both also assume that the populations sampled are normally distributed on the variable under study, but the most recent books on statistics[5] suggest that moderate departure from normality is not serious. Unhappily these books typically do not define moderate. If sampling has been by random

---

[4]In fact this ratio is used as the inferential criterion in so many research situations it is referred to as the *critical ratio,* sometimes abbreviated as CR.

[5]For example, see William L. Hays, *Statistics for Psychologists* (New York: Holt, Rinehart and Winston, Inc., 1965).

procedures and sample size is more than ten, the researcher can usually be confident that this assumption has been met. If smaller samples, or nonrandom sampling methods are contemplated, the researcher should consider reverting back to parallel nonparametric inferential procedures like the Mann-Whitney test.[6]

The *t* distribution makes a second assumption, when means are being tested, that the populations involved are homogeneous in variability. In the next section of this chapter we shall discuss the *F* test, an inferential procedure to test whether or not two variances are significantly different. Performing the *F* test prior to a *t* test is the most thorough way to determine if the sample variances differ. If they do not, it is sensible to assume that the population variances do not differ. In this instance, there are computational procedures[7] which pool the separate sample variances to provide the estimate of the standard error of the difference between the means.

If the sample variances do differ significantly, this, of course, suggests that the assumption about invariate population variances is unsound. In that case, the researcher is advised to avoid the pooled estimate procedure and instead use computational procedures, which treat the sample variances separately in the computation of the standard error of the difference. In addition, the researcher should use the special formulas available[8] to estimate the degrees of freedom in this instance. These formulas reduce the degrees of freedom, making it more difficult to achieve statistical significance, thus countering the effect of the difference in the variances.

There is an often unrecognized limitation in the use of the normal curve and *t* procedures, and that is their sensitivity to sample size. As we saw earlier in this discussion, both procedures use computational techniques which place the sample sizes in the denominator of the critical ratio. Thus both are susceptible to distortion in the event that sample sizes are large, that is, close to or in the hundreds or thousands. In this instance even small differences of no practical significance do achieve statistical significance. For example, in a survey of pupil achievement connected with the Language Study, pupils were surveyed before and after a period of instruction. A change of .1 of a reading grade over a four-month period was statistically significant, primarily because there were hundreds of children in the samples tested. Not only would no one get excited about the practical significance of a change in reading grade from 4.3 to 4.4, but the improvement, of course, was far less than would be expected in a four-month period.

[6]Discussed on page 273.
[7]These are given in Walker and Lev's *Statistical Inference.*
[8]From Walker and Lev's *Statistical Inference.*

The whole branch of nonparametric statistics developed in part[9] because of the desire to enable the researcher to function with the small samples typically available in the social disciplines. But in recent years our ability to process masses of data has improved immeasurably, and organizations to assist in the collection of mass data have also been established.[10] This has created the need for large sample statistics to parallel the small sample, nonparametric statistics. As yet these have not been developed. Therefore we can do only two things: First, recognize that the normal curve and t procedure yield statistically significant results even with small differences, when the sample size exceeds 100; and, even more important, begin to develop the precision of thinking which will make it possible to compute appropriate sample sizes. These techniques will be discussed in the chapter on sampling which follows. However, here let us note that if a researcher can specify the precision with which he wishes to function and state the maximum risks of a Type I and Type II error he is willing to run, he can mathematically determine the sample size which will achieve these goals. This computed sample size can be seen as a minimum needed to achieve his goals, but it can also be seen as a relevant maximum beyond which he may be unduly exposed to the large sample fallacy.

THE *F* DISTRIBUTION

To this point we have considered models which are appropriate for hypotheses about frequency distributions and measures of central tendency. The last major aspect of descriptive statistics to consider is variability.

The model that is used to test hypotheses about differences in variability between two groups is called the F distribution, named after its discoverer, R. A. Fisher, and after the letter used to symbolize the distribution. It utilizes the variances as the estimate of variability and computationally is the simplest of all tests of significance. All that is required to utilize the F distribution is to divide one variance by the other variance:

$$F = \frac{\text{variance } 1}{\text{variance } 2}$$

You then refer the quotient to the appropriate entry in the table of the F distribution to decide whether the likelihood of the result occurring by chance was or was not greater than the level of significance.

Remember a point made earlier in the chapter on descriptive statistics,

[9]A second motivation, equally important, was the need to develop inferential procedures which demand no more than ordinal measurement.

[10]Such as the National Opinion Research Bureau at the University of Chicago.

which applies here as well, that the mean as a measure of central tendency and the variance or standard deviation as measures of variability are independent of each other. Specifically, this means that significant differences or lack of them in one of these characteristics does not tell you whether or not there are significant differences in the other characteristic. This can be illustrated visually as in Figure 10-4.

The first set of dots represents one set of data with the horizontal line representing the central tendency of these data. The second set of dots represents a second set of data, with the same central tendency but, as the spread of scores indicates, considerably greater variability. The third set of dots represents a third set of data with the same variability as the second but with a different central tendency. Remember, then, as you analyze research data that these are separate measures, reflect separate aspects of a set of data, and therefore require separate tests of significance. This is emphasized here because the *F* test is largely omitted in the research literature as a test of significance of the differences between the variability of two distributions.[11]

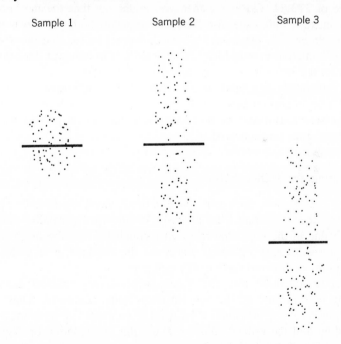

Sample 1   Sample 2   Sample 3

Figure 10-4   Illustration of samples differing in central tendency and variability.

[11]We shall see later in this chapter that the *F* test has a second use in a procedure called the analysis of variance, which *is* frequently encountered in the research literature.

The infrequency of its use reflects the fact that researchers have tended to be preoccupied with central tendency, as indeed the culture is, and so have overlooked what is at times an equally critical aspect of a set of data, variability. This neglect is even true in using the F test prior to the t test to verify that the basic assumption of the t test of comparable variability has been met. More often than not, this is ignored in research studies, and the most recent books on statistics suggest that this is not too serious an omission, as moderate differences in variability do not introduce serious distortion.

Whether or not they distort the results of the t test, differences in variability *can* be the critical aspect of a set of data. As an example, let us suppose that after the new instructional program in phonics, the mean vocabulary score for 28 students exposed to the new program was 86 items correct on a 100-item test, with a standard deviation of 6.62 and a variance of 43.82. As a comparison, these data were compared to the data obtained the previous year from 41 students exposed to the previous program who had a mean of 87, a standard deviation of 16.53, and a variance of 273.24. On first glance you might say that the new program did not make a difference, for the mean score in both years was almost identical, 86 and 87. On second glance, however, we see that there was an observed reduction in variability as reflected in the standard deviations. In fact, when the two variances are tested by the F test, the obtained F[12] of 6.24 *is* statistically significant at the .05 level. This difference in variability highlights an important aspect of the new program, to reduce the variability of the scores. But had we not done the F test, this aspect of the study would have gone undiscovered.

Interpreting the F Distribution

In the F distribution, the usual rule for determining significance applies: Whenever the F obtained in a study is numerically smaller than the critical value in the table, the researcher concludes that the two variances were not significantly different; whenever the obtained F is greater, the variances are considered significantly different.

Unlike χ^2 or the t test, the F test involves two different degrees of freedom, one for each of the two variances being compared. That is why in the table of the F distribution we need to consider two different degrees of freedom and the critical value of F for this combination of degrees of freedom. The degrees of freedom associated with a variance are determined by subtracting one from the number of cases in the sample which

[12]The usual practice in an F test is to divide the larger variance by the smaller.

Table 10-3 Excerpt from Table of *F* Distribution: Critical Value of *F* for 5% Level of Significance

Number of Degrees of Freedom Associated with Variance Placed in Denominator of F Ratio	Number of Degrees of Freedom Associated with Variance Placed in Numerator of F Ratio					
	1	5	10	20	30	40
1	161.0	230.0	242.0	248.0	250.0	251.0
2	18.51	19.30	19.39	19.44	19.46	19.47
3	10.13	9.01	8.78	8.66	8.62	8.60
5	6.61	5.05	4.74	4.56	4.50	4.46
10	4.96	3.33	2.97	2.77	2.70	2.67
20	4.35	2.71	2.35	2.12	2.04	1.99
25	4.24	2.60	2.24	2.00	1.92	1.87
27	4.21	2.57	2.20	1.97	1.88	(1.84)

produced the variance. Thus, in the example above, where one sample of 28 students had a variance of 43.82 and the second sample of 41 students a variance of 273.24, the degrees of freedom would be 27 and 40 respectively. Table 10-3 is an excerpt from a table of the *F* distribution, for the 5 percent level of significance. We use the table by finding the column appropriate for the degrees of freedom associated with the variance in the numerator of the *F* ratio, and the row appropriate for the degrees of freedom associated with the denominator. The cell in which this row and column intersect provides the critical value of *F*. In this example, the column for 40 degrees of freedom and the row for 27 intersect in the circled cell, which tells us that the critical value of *F* for this combination of degrees of freedom is 1.84.

The *F* ratio is one of the inferential procedures which *can* be specifically interpreted. A statistically significant *F* means one variance is larger and the other smaller.

Assumptions of the F Distribution

There are two basic assumptions involved in the *F* distribution. First, since the distribution is used for the ratio of variances, it is captive to the basic assumption of the moment system of statistics—that the data are at the interval level. This is true, of course, for both of the variables involved. The second assumption, also true of both variables is that the population distribution is normal. If either of these assumptions is violated the researcher is better off with the nonparametric procedure, which is a generalized test of characteristics of ordinal data, including the variability.

Research Applications

As we have noted, the direct research application of the F distribution is to test for the significance of the difference in variability between two variables. This enables the researcher to determine for any specific characteristics if two groups differ in variability. This direct application has been extended to a wide variety of research problems under the general heading of a procedure called *analysis of variance*. Through the analysis of variance, the researcher is able to test hypotheses involving comparisons of two or more groups on a single variable or involving the interaction of two or more variables.

The logic of analysis of variance is relatively simple, and once understood, the ramifications and uses of the technique become clear, Let us use the Language Study as an illustration. Consider two groups of ten language learners, all of whom were comparable in intelligence, language learning ability, and any and all other variables. We then expose these two classes to different methods of instruction, one to the vocabulary emphasis and the other to the structure emphasis. After ten weeks of instruction we test them on a 25-item test of ability to understand spoken English. The two sets of ten scores are listed in Table 10-4.

First let us consider the ten children exposed to the vocabulary emphasis. Had they been completely comparable at the beginning and had they been exposed to identical teaching and learning conditions, we would

Table 10-4 Scores on Test of Ability To Understand English, by Emphasis

Child	Vocabulary Emphasis Class	Structure Emphasis Class
1	23	16
2	15	18
3	17	21
4	14	23
5	20	22
6	12	22
7	14	17
8	9	15
9	13	24
10	16	20

expect their scores to be identical after the period of instruction. Obviously, they are not. There are three ways of accounting for this variation within the vocabulary group. First, it may be that the assumption of comparability was sound but that chance errors caused by factors like guessing, children's energy level, mood, or understanding of instructions, caused some or all of the variation. A second possibility is that errors of measurement produced the variation. In other words, we have measured somewhat incorrectly, and that is why all ten students in the class did not have the same score. The other possibility is that the assumption of comparability was not sound, and that the individual students in the class did differ from each other, either in the initial measures or in their response to the instruction or both.

Now let us also consider the ten children exposed to the structure emphasis. Here we see the same type of variation within the group that we saw for the vocabulary group. We also see, by considering both groups, that the scale of scores for the structure group seems somewhat higher than for the vocabulary group. In other words, in addition to the variation within each group, it seems that there is also variation between the groups. What would account for this variation? We have already allowed for chance, individual variation, and errors of measurement, so the fact that the groups were exposed to different methods would account for this additional variation.

Forgetting numbers for the moment, we could argue that if we could determine how much of the variation in the data was attributable to method on the one hand, and how much to chance error and individual variability on the other, we would have a basis for making an inferential judgment as to whether or not the methods differed. We have already discussed the *F* test, a model which is appropriate for comparing two estimates of variability. If we could compute these two estimates in this problem we could compare them via the *F* test. In this instance, we would argue that if the variation *between* the groups was significantly greater than the variation *within* the groups, we would consider the groups different. Stated in other terms, this is equivalent to saying that if the variation attributable to method was significantly greater than the variation attributable to chance error or individual variation, then we would consider the methods to have had different effects.

ANALYSIS OF VARIANCE

Procedurally, the analysis of variance is exactly what the name implies: The researcher identifies all of the variation in a set of data and proceeds to "analyze" it. This analysis consists of determining mathematically how much of the variation is attributable to the variation within each of the separate groups and how much is attributable to the variation from group to group. This process can be best understood by working through a simple set of data. Section A of Table 10-5 presents hypothetical scores on a vocabulary test for three children assigned to each of the three methods in the Language Study. While in reality we would not perform an analysis of variance with this small number of cases, these data will serve to illustrate the processes involved better than masses of numbers would.

The first concept in the analysis of variance is to estimate the total variation in these data. We base this estimate of variation, as we do all estimates of variation, on the variation of the separate observations around a mean. Because we are concerned with total variation, we use the mean of all the nine observations in the three groups. In our example, we would obtain the variation around the mean of the nine scores, which is the mean of 8 indicated at the bottom of section A in Table 10-5. This variation, referred to as the *total sum of squares*, can be obtained by actually subtracting each observation from this overall mean, squaring each deviation, and adding the squared deviations. This has been done in section B of Figure 10-5.[13] The sum of 114 is the total sum of squares for these data, that is, it represents all of the variation in the nine scores around the overall mean of 8.

As we scan the data we can see that this variation came into being from two sources. First, within each of the groups the children varied. If all three children in the vocabulary group had been identical at the beginning of the study and had reacted identically to the instruction under the vocabulary emphasis, they would all have gained the same amount. But they did not, nor did the children in the other two groups. We can also use the direct method to determine the variation within each group, and by adding these across the three groups we have the *within sum of squares*, that is, that portion of the total variation contributed by the variation within the three groups of children. This variation is derived in section C. Thus, we can see that 14 units of variation come from the variability within the experiential group, 8 units from the variability within the structure group, and 14 units by the variability within the vocabulary group, so that the within sum of squares is 14 + 8 + 14 or 36.

However, the total of these three within group variations does not equal the total variation of 114 we have previously computed. This is because of the second source of variation: the variation from group to group, based on the fact that the children in the different groups might have been affected differentially by the period of instruction. We can also estimate

[13]Obviously, there are computational shortcuts far simpler than this direct method. The direct method is used here for illustrative purposes only.

Table 10-5 Data Illustrating the Computational Process of Analysis of Variance

Method Group	Section A Data	Section B: Obtaining Total Sum of Squares		Section C: Obtaining within Sum of Squares			Section D: Obtaining between Sum of Squares		
	Child's Gain	Deviation from Overall Mean of 8	Squared Deviation from Overall Mean	Group Mean	Deviation from Group Mean	Squared Deviation from Group Mean	Representing Each Child by Group Mean	Deviation	Squared Deviation
Experiential	8	0	0	5	+3	9	5	-3	9
	4	-4	16		-1	1	5	-3	9
	3	-5	25		-2	4	5	-3	9
Group total	15				0	14			
Structure	7	-1	1	7	0	0	7	-1	1
	9	+1	1		+2	4	7	-1	1
	5	-3	9		-2	4	7	-1	1
Group total	21				0	8			
Vocabulary	10	+2	4	12	-2	4	12	+4	16
	15	+7	49		+3	9	12	+4	16
	11	+3	9		-1	1	12	+4	16
Group total	36				0	14			
Total for all children	72	0	114			36			78
Overall mean	8								

Table 10-6   Summary of Analysis of Variance for Illustrative Example

Source of Variation	Sum of Squares	Degrees of Freedom	Variance Estimate	F Ratio
Between groups	78	2	39	6.50
Within groups	36	6	6	
Total	114	8	x	

this variation in a direct way. We represent each of the three children in each group by the mean for the group rather than their actual score, as is done in section D, then we compute the sum of squares around the overall mean. In Table 10-5, this yields a *between sum of squares* of 78. Since the between sum of squares of 78 and the within sum of squares of 36 add to the total sum of squares of 114, we have accounted for all of the variation in the data.

We report these findings in a summary table like Table 10-6. The table lists the source and the variation (represented in the column headed "sum of squares"). Note that the separate sums of squares arithmetically add to the sum of squares for the total line. Table 10-6 goes two steps further; it also lists the degrees of freedom attached to each of the sums of squares. For the between group variation the degrees of freedom are one less than the number of groups. Thus, in our example with three groups, there are two degrees of freedom for the between group sum of squares. The degrees of freedom for the within group sum of squares is based on the total number of subjects in each group, with the loss of one per group. Thus, the three subjects in each of three groups produce the total of six $(3[3 - 1])$ degrees of freedom. The separate degrees of freedom, too, add arithmetically to the degrees of freedom for the total line, because the degrees of freedom for the total are one less than the total number of respondents.

As in all other inferential procedures, we do not base our statistical test on the gross amounts of the statistical computation (which is what the sum of squares is), but rather relate that gross amount to the degrees of freedom on which it is based. This is done in the analysis of variance procedure by dividing each sum of squares by the corresponding degrees of freedom. This has been done with the data of Table 10-6 with the quotients reported in the column headed "variance estimate."[14]

[14]This is also referred to as the *mean square*.

It is these variance estimates which we now use for the actual test of the hypothesis about differential gain. We argue that unless the variation between groups is significantly greater than the variation within the several groups, there is no basis for concluding that the groups differed. This is equivalent to saying that if the children assigned to the vocabulary emphasis groups differ from each other in achievement as much as they do from the children assigned to the structure groups, there is little evidence that the methods, in and of themselves, had a significant effect.

How do we decide if the variation is significantly greater? It is at this point that the F test provides the model for the statistical inference, for as we have seen earlier, it *is* an appropriate model for testing if there is a significant difference between two variance estimates. In this example, dividing the variation attributable to between group differences by that attributable to within groups differences produces an F value of 6.50. We evaluate this F as we do any other F, by reference to the F table using the degree of freedom previously determined. With two and six degrees of freedom, at the .05 level, the critical value of F is 8.65. Since the F value obtained from the data, 6.50, is smaller than the F of 8.65 required for statistical significance at the .05 level, we conclude that despite the observed differences, there are no statistically significant differences between the method groups.

This procedure can be applied when a researcher has data on a single variable, from two[15] or more groups and is generally referred to as a *one-way analysis of variance*. In the instance when, as in our illustration, we conclude that the data indicate no statistically significant differences, there is no further analysis to be completed. However, the analysis of variance is similar to chi square as a test of significance, in that it is an overall test of differences in a total set of data. Therefore, like chi square, if it yields the conclusion that there *are* statistically significant differences within the total set of data, additional analytic steps are required.

For example, let us consider Table 10-7, summary table for an analysis of variance of a different set of data from three groups of three children each. Here we can see that the obtained F of 9.14 *is* statistically significant at the .05 level.[16] This tells us that there are statistically significant differences among the three groups. Which of the three possible specific differences are statistically significant? Did the vocabulary children do better than the structure children? Better than the experiential children? Did the structure and experiential children differ? The analysis of vari-

---

[15]Generally, with only two groups, researchers use the t test rather than analysis of variance to test for statistical significance.
[16]The critical value of F is the same 8.65 as in the previous example, since the degrees of freedom are identical in both examples.

Table 10-7 Summary of Analysis of Variance with Statistically Significant *F* Ratio

Source of Variation	Sum of Squares	Degrees of Freedom	Variance Estimate	F Ratio
Between groups	115.2	2	57.6	9.14
Within groups	37.8	6	6.3	
Total	153.0	8		

ance procedure does *not*, and is not intended to, tell us the answers to these questions about specific differences. It serves only to answer the general question, "Are there any differences in the total set of data which would merit our searching farther?" If the answer is "Yes, there are such differences," then we need additional procedures to identify these specific differences.

Procedures for Testing Specific Differences

Traditionally, researchers handled the problem of testing specific differences by performing *t* tests between each pair of means which had to be compared to test the specific hypotheses of the study. However, in the 1940s, and particularly in the 1950s, a variety of new techniques began to appear in the literature which had conceptual and computational advantages over the *t* test. These techniques have continued to appear with such frequency that we shall only consider the ones of greatest use and applicability to educational research problems and designs.[17]

Before considering the specific procedures, let us note some of the criteria which the researcher should consider in selecting a procedure. There is the practical criterion of the computational complexity of the procedure, particularly in this area, for computer programs are not available for many of the newer techniques for testing specific differences. A second criterion involves the number of specific tests required, that is, whether every difference needs to be tested or whether a cutoff can be established below which none of the differences are statistically significant and above which all are. Then there is the more subtle question of the

[17]A thorough treatment of these techniques appears in Walter T. Federer, *Experimental Design* (New York: Crowell-Collier and Macmillan, Inc., 1963). Also, in Allen Edwards, *Experimental Design in Psychological Research* (New York: Holt, Rinehart and Winston, Inc., 1963).

confidence level with which the procedures are done, that is, if several specific tests are performed are all of the conclusions made at the same level of confidence? The question of sample size enters as well, in terms of whether or not the procedure demands groups of the same size. Then there is the question as to whether or not the comparisons to be tested need to be specified in advance of the analysis of variance. The sensitivity of the procedure to the normality of the distributions or to the homogeneity of the separate variances involved is also an important criterion. Finally, when the difference between a pair of means *is* shown to be statistically significant, the researcher would prefer a procedure which also provides some estimate of the magnitude of that significant difference.

In terms of these criteria, the procedure developed by Scheffé[18] is generally considered the best method of making the specific comparisons. It is relatively simple in terms of computational demands, functions at a standard level of confidence in all comparisons, is relatively insensitive to departures from either normality or from homogeneity of variances, and can be used with unequal samples. The comparisons made do not need to be specified in advance of the analysis of variance, and computations can be done in such a way so as to yield an interval estimate of the size of each statistically significant difference. The only criterion it does not meet is the ability to establish a cutoff point and so limit the tests that need to be performed.

A procedure developed by Duncan does meet the cutoff criterion, and if appropriate tables[19] are available it is computationally simpler than the Scheffé procedure. However, Duncan's "multiple range test" does not provide an estimate of the magnitude of the statistically significant differences, an important aid to decision making based upon research data. Thus, if the researcher needs nothing more than the information as to whether differences are or are not statistically significant, the computational simplicity and limited number of tests to be performed make the Duncan procedure preferable. However, if the researcher or someone else must go beyond this and make decisions on the basis of the data, then the estimate of the difference provided by the Scheffé procedure makes it preferable. For example, if an administrator must decide about implementing the phonics program, we give him only minimal help when we tell him the children in the phonics group gained "significantly more" in reading than the children in the look-say group. We give him much more help when we tell him that we are 90 percent confident that they gained

[18]The computational process for the Scheffé procedure is presented in Hays, *Statistics for Psychologists.*
[19]These tables are available in Edwards, *Experimental Design in Psychological Research.*

between .6 and 1.4 years in reading. Given this estimate of the magnitude of the difference, he can sensibly evaluate the cost in personnel and supplies, the administrative difficulties and other factors, and so determine if the gain is "worth it."

Another of the new procedures of specific interest to the researcher in education is the procedure developed by Dunnett.[20] Its applicability lies in the fact that it is specifically designed to compare each of a series of experimental groups to a common control group, a popular educational research design. It also has the procedural advantage of providing a single critical value of the minimum difference needed for statistical significance and so eliminates the necessity for multiple computations.

Testing for the Homogeneity of Variances

In the explanation of the analysis of variance, we noted that the basic conceptualization involves considering all of the variation represented in the separate observations. To obtain this estimate we combine observations across our different method groups, in order, ultimately, to compare means. For this procedure to make sense, the separate experimental groups involved should not differ significantly in variability. If they did when we obtain the total variability we would be adding "unlikes." Therefore, the first computational step in analysis of variance is usually noted in statistics texts as testing the separate variances involved to determine if they can be considered homogeneous.

This advice, however, has been more consistently violated than followed—as any review of the educational research literature will verify. Most often the analysis of variance is reported without any reference to a preceding test for the homogeneity of the variances. Recently, some books on statistics have supported this practice of ignoring any test for homogeneity. For example, Hays, in *Statistics for Psychologists,* notes that these tests for homogeneity are highly sensitive to nonnormality in the populations even though this nonnormality would not rule out testing for differences among *means.* Given such data, however, the researcher who tested for the homogeneity of the variances would never get to testing the means, for his analysis of variance would be eliminated by the indicated heterogeneity of the variances. Therefore Hays concludes:

> Consequently, a test for homogeneity of variance before the analysis of variance has rather limited practical utility, and modern opinion holds that the analysis of variance can and should be carried on without a preliminary test of variances, especially in situations where the number of cases in the various samples can be made equal (p. 381).

[20]The computational procedure appears in Edwards, *Experimental Design in Psychological Research.*

For the old-fashioned student interested in testing the variances, Bartlett's test for homogeneity of variance is the procedure which has tradiionally been employed. It is presented in Walker and Lev's *Statistical nference,* where a computationally briefer technique developed by Hartey is also presented. The Hartley procedure involves determining the maximum F ratio within the data by dividing the largest of the separate variances by the smallest and using special tables (presented in Walker and Lev) to test this maximum F for significance. Obviously if this largest F ratio is not statistically significant, no other will be, provided the samples are the same size.

THE STUDY OF INTERACTION

We have noted at several places in the book that one of the major advances n social research has been the developing ability both to conceptualize research problems involving a multiplicity of variables and to study statistically the interrelationships and interactions of these variables. Thus, the multiple regression procedure represents a great advance beyond simple regression. In this same way the use of analysis of variance with more than one variable permits us to move far beyond the t test, or simple analysis of variance, in evaluating the effect of experimental variables on obtained data.

Consider the data in Table 10-8 from the two experimental groups in he Phonics Study, Here we are considering separately the data for boys and for girls. Data are presented in two dimensions, the two rows representing the two reading emphases and the two columns representing the two

Table 10-8   Gains for Children in Phonics Study, by Method and Sex

Method Oroup	Sex	
	Girls	Boys
Phonics	Cell 1	Cell 3
	10	3
	14	5
	15	7
Look-say	Cell 2	Cell 4
	2	13
	1	15
	3	8

sexes. Each of the four cells in this table now represents the data produced by the interaction of the two variables in the way unique to that cell. Thus, cell 1 in the first row and first column represents the scores of the three girls assigned to the phonics group. In contrast, cell 3, to the right of cell 1, represents the scores of the three boys assigned to the phonics group. Notice that in describing the cells we must take into account both variables, and so we consider the data in the cells as representing the interaction of the variables.

We now have a variety of ways of conceptualizing these data. At the grossest level we can consider the data as a total set of twelve observations, or, as before, we can ignore sex and consider the data as two rows of six observations each, with each row representing a different reading emphasis. Or we can ignore emphasis, and consider the data as two columns of six observations each, with each column representing one sex. We can consider the data in terms of the four cells, with three observations each, with each cell representing one of the possible interactions of the two variables.

When we turn to analysis of variance, the total sum of squares is still the sum of the squared deviations of the twelve separate scores about the overall mean of eight. For the data in Table 10-8, this total sum of squares is 308. However, we must now allow for a more complex set of factors in the effort to account for the total amount of variation in the data. Our basic unit now is the cell, where it had been the group, and when we consider what we have called the "within" variation, it is now the variation within the four cells. The variation "between" groups is also different, for we now have two kinds of groups, the one based on method and the one based on sex. Finally, we have a new source of variation, that from cell to cell. This we can attribute to interaction.

Computationally, we can implement this perception of the data by carrying through the basic procedure for estimating variability with the appropriate means and observations. For example, to estimate the contribution to the total variability of sex, we could take the mean for the boys and assign this to each boy, and the mean for the girls and assign this to each girl, and obtain the sum of the squared deviation about the overall mean, which for these data comes out to be 3.00. In the same way we could take the means for each method group, assign that mean to the children in the group, and obtain the sum of the squared deviations about the overall mean. For these data the method sum of squares is 12.00. Finally, we could take the mean for each of the cells, assign that to each child in the cell, and obtain the sum of squares representing cell variability about the overall mean. When this is done, the sum of squares is 258, but it contains within it the sum of squares for sex (3) and method (12).

When these are subtracted we obtain the interaction sum of squares of 243. The summary table which appears as Table 10-9 presents these data.

In the summary table for this two-way analysis of variance we express the variability attributed to each source in the sum of squares column and obtain the variance estimate by dividing this by number of degrees of freedom attributable to each source. In the one-way analysis of variance the final step was to test for significance by computing the one possible F ratio, that is, that between the variance estimates between groups and with groups. However, in the two-way analysis of variance example in Table 10-9, there are four variance estimates rather than two, and so the possibility exists for six rather than one F test. We might compare any two of the mean squares, for the F model serves to test for the significance of any two variance estimates.

Generally the between and interaction variance estimates are first compared to the within variance estimate. This is consistent with the basic rationale of the analysis of variance outlined earlier, in which we argued that unless the variation between groups was significantly larger than the variation within groups, the difference was not worth further consideration. Now we extend the argument to the general rule that unless the variance estimate being evaluated (whether based on variation between groups or on the interaction of cells) is larger than the basic within variance estimate, the difference is not worth further consideration.

For the data in Table 10-9, this means a basic set of three F tests needs to be performed—comparing the within variance estimate to the variance estimate for: (1) sex; (2) method; and (3) interaction. These three F tests yield F ratios of .48, 1.92, and 38.88 respectively, and when compared to the appropriate critical value of F indicate that neither the

Table 10-9 Summary of Analysis of Variance for Illustrative Example on Interaction

Source of Variation	Sum of Squares	Degrees of Freedom	Variance Estimate
Between:			
Sexes	3	1	3.00
Methods	12	1	12.00
Interaction	243	1	243.00
Within group	50	8	6.25
Total	308	11	

variability attributable to method nor to sex can be considered statistically significant, but the variability attributable to the interaction of the two variables can be considered statistically significant.

Dimensions Possible with Complex Analysis of Variance

The logic just discussed involving the concept of interaction in analysis of variance with two research variables can be extended to more than two variables. Theoretically, in fact, the same logic would apply to a multiplicity of variables in the sense that the analysis of variance procedure would permit the researcher to parcel out the total amount of variation in the data to all possible sources of variation. However, with many more than three variables the number of possible sources of variation become so numerous that the analytic process becomes extremely complex. For example, listed below are 32 possible sources of variation which would have to be considered if we wished to analyze the data we have been considering, taking into account not only method and sex, but three additional variables: age, sibling position, and intactness of family. In such a five-way analysis we must first consider the variation attributable to each of the five variables operating singly, then consider all ten possible interactions of two variables, all ten possible interactions of sets of three of the five, all five possible interactions of sets of four of the five, the single interaction of the five variables, and the residual variation within the cells attributable to chance. Despite this complexity, this analysis of variance is not only computationally possible, but computer programs for these analyses exist.

Single Variables
1. Method
2. Sex
3. Age
4. Sibling position
5. Family intactness

Interactions of Pairs of Variables
6. Method and sex
7. Method and age
8. Method and sibling position
9. Method and family intactness
10. Sex and age
11. Sex and sibling position
12. Sex and family intactness
13. Age and sibling position
14. Age and family intactness
15. Sibling position and family intactness

Interactions of Sets of Three Variables
16. Method, sex, age
17. Method, sex, sibling position
18. Method, sex, family intactness
19. Method, age, sibling position
20. Method, age, family intactness
21. Method, sibling position, family intactness
22. Sex, age, sibling position
23. Sex, age, family intactness
24. Sex, sibling position, family intactness
25. Age, sibling position, family intactness

Interactions of Sets of Four Variables
26. Method, sex, age, sibling position
27. Method, sex, age, family intactness
28. Method, age, sibling position, family intactness
29. Method, sex, sibling position, family intactness
30. Sex, age, sibling position, family intactness

Interaction of Set of Five Variables
31. Method, sex, age, sibling position, family intactness

Chance Variation
32. Within cells, residual variation

Interpretation, of course, becomes increasingly complex in such an analysis as do the problems of considering the several sources of variation as functionally independent of each other. Procedurally and computationally they are analyzed separately, but the researcher may have difficulty communicating to his readers how the combination of sex, age, and sibling position represents a research entity separate from the combination of sex, age, sibling position, *and* family intactness. This is particularly true in educational research where so much of recent effort in teacher education has been devoted to the idea of seeing a child as a totality, rather than in segmented psychological, sociological, and educational units.

Nevertheless, the concept of interaction, and the ability to isolate it statistically, is a tremendous step forward in our ability to conceptualize research problems at a level of complexity appropriate to the complexity of the human being. It is an area where our ability to analyze data has now gone far beyond our ability to identify the meaningful dimensions of the human being which should be studied, and our ability to measure those dimensions once they are identified. The very difficulty in reporting and communicating the results of complex analyses of variance like the five-way analysis discussed above makes it critical that the researcher be able to defend the necessity to use all five variables (or dimensions). Moreover, the precision in the procedure whereby the total amount of variation in the data is precisely assigned to many different sources of variation, like the 32 sources listed, is exactly what has been stated: It is precision *in a procedure*. Unless the measures employed and the data fed into the analysis are reasonably sound, valid, and precise, this procedural precision is spurious, and false conclusions can be derived.

In summary, analysis of variance does provide a procedural model more appropriate to the study of differences with complex human subjects than other procedures we have discussed. However, like all these other procedures, it is no better than the data upon which it is based.

ANALYSIS OF COVARIANCE

Often in educational research the researcher has no ability to control the composition of groups with which he must work. For example, a principal might be willing to make available classes 5-1 and 5-4 for a study provided that the classes remain intact as the school has organized them. But what if these classes differ on an important variable or variables? Does that rule out their use in any research related to these variables on which they differ? It does not, for the procedure known as *analysis of covariance* makes it possible to compare these groups on final research measures, statistically allowing for the differences known to exist.

Procedurally[21] the analysis of covariance integrates regression and analysis of variance to accomplish this after-the-fact statistical equating of the groups. If the groups differ on a single variable, then simple regression is used, whereas if the groups differ on more than one variable, multiple regression is used. What the process does is to utilize the regression procedure to predict the final status of the groups on the research variables on the basis of their initial differences. The procedure then identifies the gains or changes or differences beyond those attributable to the initial differences, and the analysis of variance procedure is used to test whether these increments differ significantly.

[21]Computational guides for the analysis of covariance are available in Hays, *Statistics for Psychologists*, and Edwards, *Experimental Design in Psychological Research*.

Chapter 11

SAMPLING AND TECHNIQUES
FOR SAMPLE SELECTION

In most research instances in the social sciences, it is not possible to collect data from every respondent relevant to our study but only from some fractional part of all the respondents. The process of selecting the fractional part is called *sampling*. While the basic motivation for sampling is the simple impossibility of studying every respondent, the process is sensible because in practice it is not necessary to obtain data from all possible respondents to accurately understand the nature of the phenomena under study. Typically, we can achieve this understanding with some portion of the respondents. Since this is so, we can enjoy the advantages of sampling, that it cuts the cost of research in terms both of time and money. However, it is important to note that this advantage is contingent upon the truth of the first point. Saving time or money through sampling is sensible only in instances when you can defend the fact that the data obtained from the sample will provide a sound basis for accurately understanding the phenomena under study. It would be absurd to save time and money through sampling if the data to be obtained would be spurious!

Despite these two advantages of sampling, some research does not sample. The outstanding example is the United States census, which every ten years seeks to obtain data from all of the people living in the country at that point in time.[1]

THE STAGES OF SAMPLING

In discussing sampling we shall be differentiating between five stages, or elements in the sampling process: (1) the universe; (2) the population; (3) the invited sample; (4) the accepting sample; and (5) the data-producing sample.

[1] In 1960 even the Census Bureau began to sample in some of its substudies, and the Bureau has announced plans to sample more widely in 1970.

By the *universe*, we mean all possible respondents or measures of a certain kind. Thus in our study of language teaching, one universe was all fourth-grade non–English-speaking Puerto Rican children in continental United States schools. A second universe was all possible seventh-grade non–English-speaking Puerto Rican children in continental United States schools, and the third universe was the tenth-grade non–English-speaking Puerto Rican pupils. As is usual in research we did not have access to these universes, but rather had access only to a portion of each: those non–English-speaking Puerto Rican children attending the fourth, seventh, or tenth grade in the New York City public schools. The portion of the universe to which a researcher has access is called the *population*.[2] In most research it is the population and/or universe which is the focus of interest. As we shall see later in this chapter, we actually collect data only from the sample, but we intend to use these sample data to make inferences about the population. Thus, at the other end of the sampling process is the sample. However, we divide the general concept "sample" into three parts: the invited sample, the accepting sample, and the data-producing sample. In considering the definitions of these three parts we shall see the distinctions being made. The *invited sample* is defined as all elements of the population to which an invitation to participate in the research is extended. The *accepting sample* is that portion of the invited sample that accepts the invitation and agrees to participate. The *data-producing sample* is that portion of the accepting sample that actually produces data.

To continue with the illustration of the Language Study, we decided we wished the children in four elementary schools to participate in the experiment in the fourth grade. Three of the first four principals invited accepted, but one declined. We then invited the first school on our list of alternates, and the principal accepted. Thus we had an invited sample of five schools, but an accepting sample of four (the number we set out to obtain), and it was the fourth-grade non–English-speaking Puerto Rican children in these schools from whom we sought to collect data. However, not all these children actually produced data. We discussed in Chapter 1 how some children who were in the selected sample transferred to other schools or were absent on days of testing and so did not actually produce data for the research. Therefore, our data-producing sample of children was smaller than the accepting sample of children.

[2]In some other books the population is defined as all possible measures or people of a certain kind. This conceptualization seems unrelated to the realities of research since researchers seldom, if ever, have access to all possible measures or people. Therefore I have used the term *universe* to describe this all-inclusive entity, and define the population, then, as that portion of the universe from which the sample is selected and to which we want our generalizations to apply.

THE SAMPLING CYCLE

Thus, a five-stage sampling cycle is proposed here, sketched out in Figure 11-1 below. In this cycle, the researcher identifies the universe that is relevant for his research problem and purpose, and then identifies his population, that is, that portion of the universe to which he has access. Then by applying the techniques for sample selection which we shall discuss later in this chapter, he decides how large a sample he needs, selects, and invites that number to participate. To this point, the researcher has complete control over the process, but at this point the respondents assume most of the control. For now, some do and others do not accept the invitation, and so typically more invitations are extended until sufficient numbers accept so that the sample is the desired size. Those who do accept form the accepting sample. Then the researcher applies his data-gathering techniques to the accepting sample. Depending upon factors like the data-gathering design, method, and techniques, all or only some of

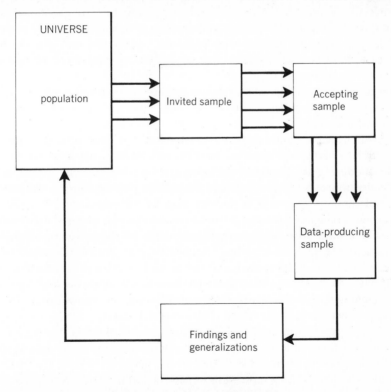

Figure 11-1   The sampling cycle.

the accepting sample actually produce data. Those who do form the data-producing sample. It is from these data that the researcher obtains his findings and makes his conclusions.

As we noted in the beginning, the data-producing sample is seldom the focus of the researcher's interest. Rather he is interested in learning about the population and sometimes the universe. And so the sampling cycle is completed as the researcher seeks to use the findings to make estimates of population characteristics and to make generalizations from the sample data which will apply to the populations.

Representativeness

Completing the sampling cycle by applying findings and generalizations to the population and universe makes sense in one set of circumstances only: when the various samples can be considered representative of the population and universe. But as the sampling cycle is intended to illustrate and emphasize, representativeness is a recurring concern throughout the sampling process. When we identify the universe of relevance for our respondents and research problem and select the population, we face the first "representative" question. Can the population be considered representative of the universe? If it can, we move on to identify and select the invited sample, and from this derive the accepting sample. At this stage there is a second concern with representativeness of the accepting sample to the population.

Then when the data-gathering instruments are administered and the researcher learns what kind of attrition has taken place in terms of the data-producing sample which has emerged, he must face the critical issue of determining if he can consider the data-producing sample representative of the accepting sample and therefore of the population. But we are using an ambiguous concept at the heart of this discussion: "representative." We want every stage to be representative of the preceding stage, but representative in terms of what? Age? Sex? Shoe size? Intelligence? Voting record? We could extend a list of possible human characteristics and attributes endlessly, but the answer to the question limits the list. We want representativeness in terms of those variables that are known to be related to the phenomena under study. Thus in our Language Study, we sought representativeness in terms of characteristics of children known to be related to ability to learn a second language. If we were studying a sample with a view to predicting the winner of the next presidential election, we would seek to achieve representativeness in terms of characteristics that are known to be related to voting behavior.

ACHIEVING REPRESENTATIVENESS   The last sentences contain a phrase which introduces the first of three problems in achieving representativeness, the phrase "known to be related." This implies that to discuss representativeness intelligently and to achieve it, we must know the characteristics which are related to the phenomena and/or behavior that we are about to study. There are two sources for this knowledge: previous research and theory. Of the two, previous research is far superior since this provides us with empirically demonstrated relationships, whereas theory simply suggests that a relationship should exist. In many research problems in education, there is at least some previous research which we can use as the basis for identifying the factors or characteristics on which we would want to achieve representativeness. For example, in the Language Study we knew from previous research that boys and girls progressed at different rates in language learning, and that girls consistently scored higher than boys on tests of verbal fluency. This suggested that sex was an important characteristic on which to achieve representativeness. Available previous research also demonstrated the relationship between language learning and intelligence, identifying intelligence as a second characteristic. There was also research to demonstrate that success in any learning task was based on prior learning. This suggested that the amount of English already known was a third critical characteristic.

Experts in the field of learning in general and language learning in particular provided a much longer list of characteristics which, on the basis of their theories, they believed were related to language learning. This list included characteristics like language spoken at home or in the neighborhood, the status of English among peers, verbal memory, motivation, interest, attitude toward school, and the learning climate of the child's home. These were just hunches, and while in the future some will undoubtedly be empirically verified, undoubtedly others will not. In the Language Study we had no basis for knowing which were which, and this is generally true. Therefore, these hunches generally provide little practical help for the researcher in identifying the characteristics on which he shall seek representativeness.

Unfortunately, the relative size of the lists we faced, with the "hunch" list far longer than the empirical list, is typical of almost all research in education in particular and the social disciplines in general. At present, we simply do not have a broad base of studies relating sociopsychological and educational characteristics to each other, and, until we do, the empirical basis for selecting characteristics on which to seek representativeness in sampling will remain as limited as it now is. What we need is a massive series of studies whose primary function is to learn the nature and extent of the relationship between matrices of educational characteristics on the one hand and psychosocial characteristics on the other. If such studies were conducted, the researcher on any particular educational problem would then be able to know what characteristics were critical for him as he prepared to establish a sampling plan.

Knowing the critical characteristics solves only the first of the three problems we referred to earlier. In the Language Study, empirical studies *had* identified sex and intelligence as two critical characteristics in language learning, and so these were two variables on which we sought representativeness. We therefore decided to hold the balance of boys and girls in the experimental classes typical of the balance in the population. But what of intelligence? Here we were faced with the difficulty of measuring this characteristic for non–English-speaking Puerto Rican children,[3] and so even though we had an empirical basis for knowing this characteristic *was* related to language learning, our inability to measure it meant we could not deliberately set out to make our samples representative on intelligence.

This inability to measure is the second of the three problems and also typifies research in education. It is true particularly of those characteristics suggested by theorists. For whole areas of characteristics such as those involving attitudes, interests, and motivations, deliberate attempts to achieve representativeness are impossible because of the lack in our ability to measure. This is a second area where, until we begin and complete programs directed toward filling in gaps in our measurement techniques, no major improvement in our ability to sample these characteristics will be possible.

In some instances, a characteristic is so critical to a research plan that when no measures exist for the characteristic the researcher himself must go off on an instrument-development tangent. This was true in the Language Study, where we could not dismiss the characteristic "previous knowledge of English" by saying no measure existed of the English language knowledge of the non–English-speaking Puerto Ricans. We *had* to know that our separate experimental groups were comparable on this characteristic. Therefore we devoted time to develop a set of measures of previous knowledge of English, including a test of the child's ability to understand spoken English. But this instrument-development tangent did *not* help us deliberately achieve representativeness on this characteristic, for now we faced the third problem, the unavailability of population data. We developed these measures, and yet if we tried to use them as the basis

---

[3] At the time the study was conducted the Puerto Rican school system did not test for intelligence, and there was no test widely accepted as a valid measure for non–English-speaking children.

for achieving representativeness, we were faced with the fact that we had no data about the population that we could use. The measures were new and obviously had never been given to the population, that is, all of the non–English-speaking Puerto Rican children in the fourth grade in the New York City public schools. Without these data on the population we had no way of knowing whether or not any particular sample was representative in terms of ability to speak or to understand spoken English.

The preceding discussion illustrates the three conditions necessary to achieve representativeness: (1) we must know which characteristics are related to the phenomena under study; (2) we must have the ability to measure each such characteristic; and (3) we must have population data on the characteristic to use as the basis for comparison. If for any one characteristic we lack any one of these three conditions, we lose the ability to deliberately seek representativeness for that characteristic.

Thus we shall discuss two sets of techniques in this chapter: (1) techniques to guarantee representativeness on a characteristic or characteristics when we *do* have the ability to seek it; and (2) techniques to use when we lack the ability or decide not to seek representativeness directly.

IDENTIFYING A REPRESENTATIVE POPULATION   The representative issue comes to the fore first in the identification of the population within the universe. For every research problem there is one completely relevant universe, but any number of populations. For example, for a study concerned with the relative teaching ability of liberal arts graduates and school of education graduates, the obvious universe of relevance is all liberal arts and education graduates functioning as teachers who graduated two years prior to the date at which the study will collect its data. But clearly no researcher will have access to this universe. Let us say researcher A describes for us a population consisting of the teachers in ten schools in a large Northeast city. The immediate response should be to question whether *in terms of the research problem* this is a sensible population. As we thought of the large variety of college programs, and the equally large variety of teaching programs and staffs and school policies, we would probably conclude that this seems like a population so limited in scope as to be difficult, if not impossible, to accept as representative of the universe. The implication of this is that we would refuse to generalize to the universe, but would consider that the researcher's findings apply to his limited population, and not beyond. Notice the immediate waste of the research in two senses: first, in the sense that we have not learned about the universe of interest; and second, that we have probably learned something about some entity larger than the teachers in these ten schools, but we have no way of knowing what that entity is. So we have the frustrating circumstance of having a set of data with applicability, although we do not know to whom.

In contrast let us take researcher B, who has studied the same research problem and therefore has the same universe. However, his population consists of teachers in the schools in all cities larger than 25,000 in 12 different states east of the Mississippi River. As we consider the representativeness of his population of the universe, we might think of the large proportion of liberal arts and education programs in the West and Far West and wonder if these might not be different in significant respects, and so hesitate to accept even this population as representative of the universe. But if we were to conclude this, and so limit his findings to the population, then we still have extensive applicability of the findings. Moreover, we might also conclude that even the population east of the Mississippi can be considered representative of the universe in terms of characteristics like variety of programs, facilities, staff, and so on. In this event we would accept the population as representative of the universe and consider the findings as applicable to the universe.

Then, of course, we might come upon the project of researcher C who has, for this same research problem and universe, identified as a population schools located in the several geographic regions of the United States. Here we would have no qualms about accepting the findings as applicable to the universe.

Notice that in this discussion of the researcher's ability to generalize from population to universe our concern has not been with numbers. The issue is not how large the population is, nor how large a proportion of the universe is represented in the population. Rather we have been concerned with whether or not, in terms of factors critical for the research problem, we can consider the population representative of the universe.

The next step in the sampling cycle is the identification of the invited sample. At this stage we can seek to guarantee that the invited sample is representative of the population on selected characteristics. In doing so we must consider two different aspects of representativeness: (1) assuring that all significant aspects of a characteristic are represented in the sample; and (2) assuring that each aspect is the same proportion of the sample as it is of the population.

Identifying a Representative Sample: Stratification

Assuring that all significant aspects of a characteristic are represented in the sample is achieved through a process called *stratification*. This involves dividing the population into subgroups or strata on the basis of the characteristic for which we seek representativeness and creating our sample by separate selections from each stratum.

For example, in the Language Study, we used the concept of stratification in selecting schools, when, after analyzing the variation in the population for the characteristic "percent of enrollment which was Puerto Rican," we decided there were four educationally meaningful strata: (1) less than 20 percent Puerto Rican children; (2) 20 percent to 50 percent; (3) 51 percent to 75 percent; and (4) more than 75 percent Puerto Rican children. We then selected one school from each stratum, assuring us that each type of school would be represented in the sample. This process, in which a constant number is selected from each stratum, is called *stratified constant sampling*.

In our sample all four strata were equally represented: Each was 25 percent of the sample. However, in the population they were not equal. For example, only 5 percent of the schools had more than 75 percent Puerto Rican enrollment. We ignored this because we viewed each school as a separate entity or replication of the Language Study, and the reason for stratifying was to make certain that the study was carried out in all four types of schools.

Let us assume that instead of a language study we were conducting a survey of Puerto Rican children's attitudes toward school, and instead of viewing each school as a replication, we intended to pool all of the data obtained to form one group of Puerto Rican children. Then we might feel that it would be erroneous to have 25 percent of the sample from a stratum which contained only 5 percent of the population, since the attitudes of Puerto Rican children toward school might be related to the proportion of Puerto Ricans in the school. For this study of attitude, we would prefer that the proportions in the sample represent the proportions in the population, and so would use *stratified proportional sampling*. As the name implies, the number we select from each stratum is in proportion to the size of that stratum in the total population. In essence we create the population in miniature. For example, if considering the four strata above on percent of Puerto Rican enrollment in the school system we learned that 40 percent of the schools were in stratum "a," and 20 percent in each of the other three strata, we could have selected one school each from the three strata with 20 percent of the population and two schools from the stratum with 40 percent. This would have given us a sample exactly like the population: 20 percent (one of five) of the schools in strata "b," "c," and "d" and 40 percent in stratum "a." Compared to constant sampling we increased the sample to five rather than four schools. This increase in sample size is a usual consequence of proportional selection.

This problem of increase in sample size becomes a particularly critical problem when one stratum is small, that is, contains 10 percent or less of the population. In that instance, to have all strata represented and still maintain the proportions, the researcher might have to accept a great increase in sample size. For example, rather than the hypothetical 40 percent–20 percent–20 percent–20 percent break discussed above, let us consider the actual proportions of the four strata in the population, which were as follows: 40 percent, 20 percent, 35 percent, 5 percent. With this break, if we selected one school to represent the 5 percent stratum, we would have to select eight schools from the 40 percent stratum, four from the 20 percent stratum, and seven from the 35 percent stratum for a total of twenty schools.

If faced with this situation there are three alternatives available to the researcher. The first is to use the technique fully and use the large sample. The second alternative, particularly when there is only one small stratum and it is considerably smaller than the next smallest as in the example above, is to drop that one stratum from consideration and select the sample so that it is proportional in all other strata. The third technique available is like the second in that we ignore the small stratum in deciding our proportions, basing them only on the other strata. However, in the third technique we arbitrarily add one element to the sample selected from the small stratum, even though this will inevitably over-represent it.

The choice between the three must be made in terms of the interaction of research problem and the characteristic being used for stratification. The first procedure is least widely used, since typically it involves far larger samples than the researcher feels are needed to study the problem. It would be used only in instances when every stratum was extremely critical and when the researcher had no way of distinguishing responses, such as in an anonymous mail questionnaire study. In such a study, once the questionnaires were mailed out, there is no way of knowing from which stratum they come. If each stratum is critical, then we have no choice but to work with this procedure. When would it be this critical?

The only time when this level of completeness is critical is when the small stratum is believed to be unique or extreme in such a way as to distort data, particularly descriptive statistics for the total group. A simple example of such a situation would be a research study on the extent of charitable contributions where income level was used as the basis of stratification. Only a small proportion of the population would be in the stratum "income of more than $1,000,000." We could not ignore this stratum, however, because these people represent a unique level of charitable contribution, and so we could not employ the second procedure. But we also could not permit this stratum to be over-represented in the sample, for it might seriously distort the data. Therefore we could not use the third procedure, but would have to develop a proportional sampling plan based on this smallest stratum.

In instances where we do know the identity of specific respondents, or at least know the stratum from which they were drawn, the third alternative, where we arbitrarily select at least one from the small stratum, is usually a sound alternative. This provides us with insight into the response pattern from this stratum and yet enables us to avoid any distortion in the computation of descriptive statistics for the total group. The second alternative, omitting the small stratum, is sound provided we can defend the assumption that this stratum is not only small in size but also small in significance to the research.

To illustrate the process of stratification, let us consider a hypothetical population of 200 fourth-grade pupils, 120 boys and 80 girls. Let us also assume that of the 120 boys, 36 or 18 percent are nine years old, 58 are ten years old, and 26 are eleven years old. Of the 80 girls, four are nine years old, 32 are ten, and 44 are eleven. Then let us further assume that a researcher wished to select a sample of 20 children from this population which he could be certain was representative of the population in terms of both age and sex. Because he wishes to be certain of representativeness, he decides to use stratified proportional sampling. Table 11-1 presents the conceptualization he would use for this plan.

In the upper part of the table, the population is sketched out. The first variable, sex, is a dichotomous variable and the second, age, while continuous by nature, for sampling purposes has been treated as a three-gradation limited-category variable. These two interact to form six strata: (1) nine-year-old boys; (2) ten-year-old boys; (3) eleven-year-old boys; (4) nine-year-old girls; (5) ten-year-old girls; and (6) eleven-year-old girls. These strata and the number in each are spelled out in the table. Since the researcher has decided that he wishes a sample of 20, he then computes six numbers, each representing the proportion of 20 corresponding to the size of one of the strata. Thus since stratum 1 comprises 18 percent of the population, it should comprise 18 percent of the sample. However, 18 percent of 20 equals 3.6, and he is dealing with the discrete variable "number of children," so he rounds this to 4. In this same way he determines how many children should be selected from each of the other five strata, and in each case he rounds by the rule developed in Chapter 6, except for the stratum "nine-year-old girls." This stratum is only 2 percent of the population, which comes out to be .4 of a student, which would round to zero rather than one. However, the researcher decides that he wants this stratum represented and so "rounds" it to one child. With the rounding, the final sample consists of 21 students, reasonably close to the 20 he desired.

To evaluate how well the process has worked, Table 11-2 summarizes the relative size of the strata in the population and in the sample. Notice that the process has worked quite well to provide a sample in which the six strata are reasonably well represented in proportion to their size in the population. The largest deviation occurs for the nine- and eleven-year-old girls, and even this deviation is only 3 percent. It occurs, of course, because we rounded the .4 of a child technically needed to represent one stratum to one child. The table also shows that the basic stratifying

Table 11-1 Illustration of Stratification and Proportional Sampling

Population		
Stratifying Variable One: Sex		*Stratifying Variable Two: Age*
Boys $N = 60\%$	Girls $N = 40\%$	
Stratum 1: $N = 36$ or 18%	Stratum 4: $N = 4$ or 2%	nine years
Stratum 2: $N = 58$ or 29%	Stratum 5: $N = 32$ or 16%	ten years
Stratum 3: $N = 26$ or 13%	Stratum 6: $N = 44$ or 22%	eleven years
Total boys $= 120 = 60\%$	Total girls $= 80 = 40\%$	
Sample		
$n_1 = 3.6$ or $4 = 19\%$	$n_4 = .4$ or $1 = 5\%$	eleven years
$n_2 = 5.8$ or $6 = 29\%$	$n_5 = 3.2$ or $3 = 14\%$	ten years
$n_3 = 2.6$ or $3 = 14\%$	$n_6 = 4.4$ or $4 = 19\%$	nine years
Total boys: $13 = 62\%$	Total girls: $8 = 38\%$	

Table 11-2 Summary of Results of Stratified Proportional Sample

Stratum	Percentage in Population	Percentage in Sample
Boys		
nine years old	18	19
ten years old	29	29
eleven years old	13	14
Girls		
nine years old	2	5
ten years old	16	14
eleven years old	22	19
Total boys	60	62
Total girls	40	38
Total nine-year-olds	20	24
Total ten-years-olds	45	43
Total eleven-year-olds	35	33

variables, sex and age, are, of course, also represented in proportion to their size.

Stratification then is the technique available for assuring representativeness on the dimensions of a characteristic, and proportional selection is the technique for assuring representativeness on the relative size of the different strata.

Since stratified proportional sampling insures representativeness on a characteristic, the obvious question is why every researcher does not use the technique for as many characteristics as possible. The answer is that the number of strata increases geometrically, and soon gets out of hand. For example, let us stay with the characteristics, age, with three gradations and sex, with two. We saw how these combined into six strata. Say we wished to stratify on birthplace by geographic region as well, and so divided the United States into nine regions. Within each of the nine regions we will need the six strata for age and sex, and so we now have nine times six or fifty-four strata. If we then added a fourth variable, intact family or not with two gradations (yes or no) we would have two times fifty-four or one hundred and eight strata. Attempting proportional sampling from one hundred and eight strata or even fifty-four strata would be beyond the means of most research projects which have been done to date in the social sciences. Therefore, when we see stratification employed it will generally be for but one or two characteristics.

Alternative to Stratification

The alternative to stratification is to sample the total population as an entity. There are several instances when this is done. First, if the population is homogeneous in all characteristics relevant to the research problem, there is no virtue to stratification. A second instance is when for any of the three reasons discussed earlier, we lose the ability to stratify on the important characteristics. A third instance when we do not stratify is when we intend to select a sample large enough for us to trust the laws of probability to achieve representatives for the significant variables. This is sensible only when the population is large enough to be considered infinite for statistical purposes (at least 1000) and the sample to be selected will be at least 10 percent.

SELECTION OF SPECIFIC POPULATION ELEMENTS

Whether we decide to sample using the entire population as a single entity or decide to stratify and/or to use proportional sampling, ultimately we reach the point of having to select from the population some, but not all, of its constituent elements. For example, referring to Table 11-1, we have thirty-six boys who are nine years old and only four of them are needed for the stratum "male, age nine," to be proportionately represented in the sample. Therefore we need selection procedures for determining which four males to use. We shall consider four selection procedures: (1) random; (2) systematic; (3) deliberate; and (4) cluster.

Random Selection

The most widely known procedure, and undoubtedly one of the most misunderstood research concepts, is *random selection*. The definition is simple: A random-selection procedure is one in which every element in the population has an equal chance to be selected for the sample, and therefore every possible sample of a certain size is equally probable. Because this is so, this is a selection process which is bias-free. There is no way in which any factor or tendency can affect who is chosen, for random procedures leave this to chance alone.

One random-selection procedure widely known to the lay public is the "fishbowl technique" in which slips of paper representing each element in the population are placed in a fishbowl and a sample selected by reaching in and selecting a slip. This technique became famous in 1939 when it was used to determine the first numbers to be called up by selective service.

Let us imagine that we wish to use the fishbowl technique to select four children from the thirty-six in the stratum "male, age nine." We number each child, write the numbers from 1 to 36 on slips, place the thirty-six slips in the fishbowl, shake them up, and select one. The number had one chance in thirty-six of being selected. We then record this number and *return* it to the bowl, shake the slips again, and select our second number, recording it and returning it. This process, called *sampling with replacement*, assures that each slip pulled out of the bowl has the same probability, one chance in thirty-six, of being selected. Had we not replaced the first slip, the second one selected would have had a probability of one chance in thirty-five of being selected, and this would not have met the criterion definition of a random-selection process.

We would continue the process until we have four different numbers selected. If a number previously picked comes up again, we would ignore it and replace it. To many students this seems to make the whole replacement procedure a waste of time, and yet it is not. Let us take the simple example where number 5 is picked on the first selection number and then is picked again on the second selection. The typical question asked is, since we are not going to use child number 5 twice, why bother to put his number back in the first place? We put it back so that all selections occur with the same probability, one in thirty-six. Had we not replaced 5, some other number, say 22, *would* have occurred on the second selection. Phrased in probability terms, with the probability kept at one in thirty-six, child number 22 was not selected. Had we been willing to increase the probability to one in thirty-five, child 22 would have been selected. So even though we do not usually[4] count any one case more than once, replacing each case to hold the probability constant does serve the function of stopping some other case from being selected on that pick.

The sophisticated version of the fishbowl technique is to use a table of random numbers as the basis for selection. An excerpt from such a table is reproduced in Table 11-3. Like the table, this excerpt consists of columns of digits in random order. To use the table we need only number the elements of the population in some way and then refer to the appropriate numbers of columns in the table and read the numbers to be selected. For example, let us imagine that for a study we wish to select a sample of 13 out of the 92 public and parochial schools in a city. We take a list of the schools available to us and number the schools from 1 to 92. It makes no difference how the list was made up. It could be alphabetical, it could be

[4]We will note later in this chapter certain circumstances when a case is used as often as it is selected.

Table 11-3   Excerpt from Table of Random Numbers

							Column Number								
1	2	3	4	5	6	7	8	9	10	11	12	13	14	15	16
6	5	9	2	9	5	5	3	4	4	1	1	4	7	0	8
0	5	8	4	7	6	9	8	2	6	1	2	1	9	9	6
0	4	6	7	6	6	0	4	9	3	6	1	0	0	6	5
0	3	4	6	2	1	7	7	2	2	7	3	8	5	7	2
8	4	9	9	4	4	2	5	2	3	3	4	7	2	2	6
4	6	0	5	8	4	5	3	6	9	4	4	8	2	0	2
7	9	3	6	9	4	9	5	2	5	7	5	4	4	2	6
4	7	6	1	9	6	4	0	3	2	7	2	1	6	0	6

in order of ascending size, or it could be a list made up as we recalled the names of the schools.

The list simply serves as the basis for assigning a number to each element of the population. We have 92 schools, and 92 is a two-digit number, therefore we need two columns in the table. For simplicity in reading the table we usually use two adjacent columns. To decide which two of the sixteen columns in the table, we can use the first number less than 16, picked at random, and use that column and the one to the right (or left), or we can ask someone to pick a number from 1 to 16 or we can stick a pin in the table. Again, procedure makes no difference. Let us assume we use columns 7 and 8. The first number in column 7 is 5 and the first number in column 8 is 3, making up the two-digit number 53. Therefore school 53 is the first one to be selected. As we read down the columns, the second two-digit number made is 98. However, we have no such school, and so we go on to the third number which is 04, telling us to select school number 4. In this way we go on to select school 77 and school 25, but then we come to 53 again.[5] We have already selected school 53 so we continue on, past 95, until we reach 40. In this way we have selected five different two-digit numbers of 92 or less.

We would continue on through the table (moving to columns 9 and 10 if necessary) until we had our 13 schools. In this way, just as through the fishbowl technique, and far more efficiently (and elegantly) we would have selected the sample by random procedures, and so could be confident that bias had played no part in the selection process.

It is critical that we recognize that in this discussion of random-selection

[5]Notice that the fact that 53 was and could be repeated makes this procedure analogous to sampling with replacement in the fishbowl technique.

procedures we have used the words "random" and "bias-free" to describe the selection process and not the sample. It is not correct to speak of a "random sample," rather we should refer to a "randomly *selected* sample." Nor is it correct to assume that a randomly selected sample is necessarily unbiased, that is, is necessarily representative of a population. In fact, whenever we are working with samples of 30 or fewer we cannot assume that a bias-free selection procedure will necessarily produce an unbiased or representative sample. This apparently contradictory statement is well illustrated by the sampling problem which occurred on a research project directed by the author. The project was intended to identify the satisfying and stressful experiences of students in three different educational settings—colleges for women and two types of nursing programs (hospital-run programs yielding a diploma, and collegiate programs yielding a baccalaureate degree). We decided to sample each of the three types of programs separately, and within the geographic area we decided to study there were sixteen baccalaureate degree programs in nursing. We had decided to select a 15 percent sample, so we sought to select three of the sixteen. We had no basis for knowing which characteristics were critical, hence we decided on sampling from the total population as an entity, using random-selection processes. We therefore numbered each school and used a table of random numbers to identify the three schools in the invited sample. The first program selected was Catholic University, in Washington, D. C., the second program was Georgetown University, another Catholic institution in Washington, D. C., and the third program was Simmons College in Boston, Massachusetts. So we had a sample, two-thirds of which consisted of Catholic universities located in Washington, D. C., a proportion far greater than the population in terms of Catholic universities or of schools located in Washington, D. C. This was hardly an unbiased or representative sample on these two characteristics, yet it was a sample selected by a bias-free method.

What does a researcher do in this instance? He cannot throw this sample away and continue on to select another sample until he achieves one that he likes, for this violates the whole premise of random sampling. There are only two choices open, to proceed with the study using the unrepresentative sample, or to continue to select additional elements from the population even though the study will have a larger sample than originally intended. Hopefully the additional elements selected will lessen the bias in the sample. We chose the second alternative, adding three additional schools, so that the final sample of baccalaureate degree programs consisted of six programs, three of which were at Catholic universities—still disproportionately high but somewhat better than the proportion in our original randomly selected sample.

ADVANTAGES   Random-selection procedures are always bias-free and so if bias is a concern in a particular research study, random selection is advisable. There are two aspects to the use of bias in connection with sampling, a statistical aspect and a logical aspect. The statistical aspect is that when random-selection procedures have been used this is usually accepted as sufficient evidence that the basic underlying assumptions of the parametric statistical procedures have been met. Thus if the data themselves meet the demands of the procedure (that is, are interval data) the researcher can proceed to use these statistical procedures. When logical or deliberate selection procedures have been used, these being nonrandom, the researcher faces the problem of defending the underlying distribution as normal and unbiased so that he can use the parametric procedures. Because this is often extremely difficult to do, and because in some instances the data are not available to do it, the bias-free aspect of random-selection procedures is a great advantage in statistical analysis.

The logical aspect of bias that is involved concerns the bias that would be implied if after a particular study was completed someone were to criticize it by saying, "Of course you achieved those results; you selected the sample so that you would achieve them." The best answer to this type of accusation is to be able to say that the sample was selected through random procedures, that is, that every element in the population had an equal probability of being selected. This issue has often come up in discussions of the nursing Stress–Satisfaction Project noted before. People always want to know how the schools were selected. They wonder, and rightly so, if some of our findings, particularly the ones that were critical of practices then current, might not have been a function of our deliberately selecting schools in which we knew these practices to exist. The possibility of such bias was certainly present as we began the study, but we used random-selection procedures, and so have the perfect response. We can tell those who inquire that the schools were selected by random procedures, and so we had no control over which schools were selected and asked to participate.

Therefore as we plan our sample selection procedure, we must make the professional judgment of whether or not, in view of the nature of the research problem, bias-free selection is important. In view of the statistical and public relations advantages of random selection, we should use random-selection methods whenever possible. If we use any other procedure we should include an explanation of our rationale for this in the section of the report describing our research procedures.

DIFFERENCE BETWEEN INVITED AND ACCEPTING SAMPLE   When we select a sample by random procedures this tells us something about the selection process: that it was bias-free. It also tells us that the specific elements of the population invited to be in the sample were determined by chance. However, a consideration often ignored is what we can say about the final sample who accepted the invitation to participate. Was it determined by chance? If the invited and accepting samples are the same, or there were only one or two declinations, we can say with complete confidence that the accepting sample was determined by chance. However, if there were several declinations, then the best we can say is that the original selection was by chance but the final sample was determined "largely" by chance.

There is a qualifying phrase in the paragraph above which is important to note, that even under random procedures, when there have been declinations we can only consider that the elements in the population which appear in the sample were dictated "largely" by chance. This caution reflects the heart of the distinction between invited and accepting samples, that is, that not all elements of the population who are invited to participate in a study accept the invitation to be part of the sample. It is one thing to argue that because the selected sample is selected by random procedures and the list of alternates is similarly selected by random procedures, the sample which eventuates has been selected by random procedures without any deliberate biasing factors entering. This perception loses sight of the fact that some elements of the population invited to participate decline the invitation. It may well be that a selective factor enters at this level, in terms of the issues that make some of those invited to participate accept and others decline.

It is unrealistic to expect researchers to provide detailed information on those elements of the population who have declined to participate in a study. It *is* perfectly realistic to expect the researcher to provide the numbers involved, that is, how many had to be invited to provide the final selected sample. Based on this information a reader can make his own judgment as to the possibility of any selective factor entering the sample picture at this point. For example, in the Stress–Satisfaction Project, in obtaining our sample of hospital diploma programs we had two declinations, so that we had to invite 25 programs to obtain our accepting sample of 23. In terms of these numbers there is relatively little likelihood that any significant selective factor could operate even if both schools had declined for the same reason, whatever that may have been. However, for the undergraduate collegiate programs for women we had to invite 30 programs to obtain the accepting sample of 15, and so there is the real possibility that some consistent factor determined which schools accepted and which rejected our invitations.

Generally this problem is ignored in research. It need not be, however, for there are two things a researcher can do to inform himself and his readers about any differences between invited and accepting samples. First, in his letter of invitation he can ask for a reason if the invitation is being rejected. This gives him some understanding of the overt reasons for saying no. Even allowing for the pressures which may make these answers less than completely frank, they do provide some insight into what motivated refusals from the invited sample.

The second thing he can do is to compare those elements of the population who were selected and accepted to those who were selected but refused. The comparison would be in terms of the key characteristics previously identified for the study. This is done from time to time, but is something which should become a more general practice.

Now let us consider the other selection procedures available.

Systematic Selection

A second procedure for selecting elements from the population to be invited to participate as the sample is *systematic selection*. This is defined as a selection process whereby population elements are selected by the researcher by setting up a rationale for routinized selection. Perhaps the most widely known procedure for systematic selection is to alphabetize the population and select every Xth (for example, every fifth or tenth) element. Another popular use of systematic selection is in a situation when the researcher does not have easy access to the population as a total entity, but instead has access to successive portions of the population. For example, in marketing research, when public opinion is desired, rather than seeking to identify a population and randomly select a sample, it is often simpler to station the data-collecting team at a busy intersection and tell them to stop and question every twelfth person who passes. Similarly, in house-to-house canvassing, it is far simpler to instruct the interviewer to ring every fifth doorbell than it would be to canvas the entire area to obtain a complete list of all households and randomly select a sample to be interviewed.

However, as always in the research process, we pay a price for ease and simplicity: In this case the price is the loss of the random character of the selection process and therefore the loss of the bias-free aspect of the selection process. We can illustrate both of these points using the same illustration we used for random procedures, the problem of selecting a sample of 13 schools from a population of 92 schools.

To select the 13 schools we alphabetize the population and since 13/92 is about 1/7, we decide to select every seventh school. To help make the procedure random, we ask a colleague to close his eyes and stick a pin into the list so that we can know where within the list to begin selecting schools. After he has so selected the first school, we proceed down the list, selecting every seventh school. After counting to the bottom of the list we go back to the beginning and continue counting schools. This may sound bias-free and even random. After all, we had no control over where he would stick the pin. But not only does it not meet the definition of random selection, it also introduces a definite bias against the selection of parochial schools!

First let us see why it is not a random procedure. As the pin is stuck into the list, it lands on school 53, the same school we selected using the table. Moreover, since there were 92 schools in the list, this school had 1 chance in 92 of being chosen, exactly the same probability it had in our selection from the table of random numbers. But what about school 54, 55, or 52 on the second selection? Using the table of random numbers they had 1 chance in 92 of being selected. But now we are to select every seventh school, and so on the second selection they have *no* chance (a probability of zero) of being selected. By this same reasoning, school 60 is certain of being chosen. In other words, it has a probability of selection of 1.00. So in this process there are three different probabilities of a school being selected, the probability of 1/92 which only holds for the first school, the probability of 1.00 which holds for the 12 schools at the correct distance from the first school selected, and the probability of zero which holds for all other schools. The first definition of random-sampling procedures, that every element in the population has an equal probability of being selected, is clearly violated.

It also introduces a subtle bias, in this case, against the selection of parochial schools. A large proportion of these schools are named after saints and so the school name begins with the word "Saint." Therefore all of these schools are grouped together in one section of an alphabetical list. Using a table of random numbers, we might, as likely as not, select adjacent schools. However, by the systematic procedure of alphabetical selection it is impossible. We will go through this section of the list as quickly as possible, and thus minimize the possibility of selecting from among these schools.

We are talking about *possibilities* only. It may well be that in a particular research project, if these two methods were actually used, fewer parochial schools would be selected by random than by systematic procedures and that the systematically selected sample was representative while the randomly selected sample was not. This would not obviate our describing the random procedure as bias-free and the systematic procedure as not bias-free. This highlights the distinction made earlier: The terms "random" and "bias-free" refer only to the selection process, not to the resulting sample.

Combining Random and Systematic Selection

The most important advantage of systematic selection is that it frees the researcher from the necessity of identifying and numbering all of the elements in the population prior to sample selection. This advantage can be retained and combined with random selection, if the researcher has some estimate of population size. Let us say we wished to obtain some estimate of community interest in new bond issue for school construction. We know there are about 1200 households in the community we wish to survey. We decide that a relatively small 10 percent sample or 120 households would be reasonable, since there are only three possible positions (favorable, neutral, or unfavorable) a person could take on the issue. A completely random procedure would be to number the 1200 households and use a table of random numbers to select 120 households. A completely systematic procedure would be to send interviewers into the neighborhood and tell them to interview in every tenth household. The combinational approach would be to use the table of random numbers to make up a list of 120 numbers between 1 and 1200, and tell the interviewers to begin at one end of the community and count households, using this list to determine which households to interview.

The second frequent use of systematic selection, when the researcher wishes to sample a functionally infinite population, can also be combined with random selection. In this instance, the researcher must arbitrarily select some finite number to limit the sample selection. Thus the market researcher referred to earlier might decide that he wishes to sample 10 percent of the first 1000 persons to pass the street corner. As before, he can use the table of random numbers to select the list of 100 persons to interview. But again, the process is not completely random, first of all because only the arbitrarily limited subpopulation was used for sampling, but also because factors like the day of the week, time of the day, and location of the intersection will determine which 1000 persons pass.

Deliberate Selection

As the name implies, deliberate selection is a process whereby the researcher directly and deliberately selects specific elements of the population as his invited sample.

Deliberate sample selection is often sensible and simple to justify. If within a population there are some elements which we believe are particularly crucial to study, then the only way to assure this is to deliberately select them. It may be that these elements are schools whose programs are new and intriguing, or it may be that they are persons whose backgrounds or experiences we wish to include in a survey. In any event, the only way to be certain they will be invited is to directly select them.

Obviously, deliberate selection is not a random-selection procedure and leaves the researcher open to attack about biased samples. The openness to attack in and of itself is not serious. What is serious is that there is no defense against this attack. Deliberate selection *inevitably* results in a sample which is biased in terms of whatever criteria the researcher used to select deliberately. Therefore, we should think and rethink a sampling situation before committing ourselves to a deliberate selection procedure. We should use it only if the research advantages of having certain elements of the population in our study clearly outweigh the loss of both the statistical and public relations aspects of bias-free selection.

In developing the sampling plan for the Stress–Satisfaction Project, we considered deliberate sampling before settling on random selection. We considered it because there were innovations in nursing programs which we were anxious to study to learn if the innovations had had any effect on student stress and satisfaction. Since we planned no moment system statistical analysis, the loss of the statistical aspect of bias-free selection did not trouble us at all. However, we concluded that the public relations aspect of bias-free random selection was too essential for us to use any other method of sample selection. As it happened none of the schools which intrigued us were selected by the random method we used, but of course that is the risk of random sampling and the virtue of deliberate sampling.

Cluster Selection

A fourth selection procedure, *cluster selection*, must be used in conjunction with one of the first three procedures we have discussed. Cluster selection involves the selection of a sample of one kind of element by actually selecting some larger unit which contains several of the elements. Thus, in the Language Study, we wished to study *children* but actually selected a sample of *classes,* and included in our sample all of the children (the cluster) in each class we selected. Because cluster selection always involves the prior selection of the parent or larger unit, it must be combined with another procedure through which the larger units are selected. Thus a researcher might randomly select 12 schools from the 46 schools in a city and then consider the faculty of each of the 12 a cluster for a study of teacher attitude. Or he might randomly select 20 school systems in the Midwestern states and use all school buildings in each system as a cluster for a study of school building practices.

The important point to note in the combination of random and cluster selection is that the basis-free virtue of random selection applies to the sample of larger units and *not* to the clusters. Thus in the example above, the researcher has a randomly selected sample of *schools*, not of teachers, or of school *systems*, not of buildings. This combination of random and cluster selection has great applicability and appeal in educational research, because the basic units of research interest like pupils, teachers, or parents are extremely difficult to sample directly but relatively simple to sample as clusters, using the larger unit of class or school. In the literature we often see references to such samples when in reality the researcher did not select a sample of children from a population of children but rather selected a sample of schools from a population of schools and used every child in the school. When this is done, the resultant sample cannot be considered randomly selected, no matter how the larger units were selected.

Thus, just as with deliberate selection, the researcher contemplating cluster sampling must weigh the practical advantages against the loss of the bias-free state. Often it is not a difficult decision because there is no practical alternative to the use of cluster selection. When this is so, then the best combination is random selection of the larger unit followed by cluster selection of the basic sampling unit.

INTERACTION OF SAMPLING STAGES

To this point we have discussed three stages of sampling: (1) the decision as to whether to stratify or to sample from the total population as one entity; (2) the decision as to whether to use constant or proportional selection; (3) the choice among random, systematic, deliberate, and cluster selection techniques. We have seen how the first two stages can interact, but it should also be recognized that any of these interactions can be combined with any of the selection processes. Thus a researcher could use stratified, proportional random-sample selection or stratified, constant, deliberate sample selection. This highlights the importance for the researcher of keeping clear just what each of these stages implies. Stratification tells us the researcher has broken the population into strata on the basis of one or more characteristics and sampled separately from each stratum. If he has done this in proportion to the importance of each stratum, then he has achieved representativeness on that characteristic. If he has selected the specific elements by random procedures, then he has achieved bias-free selection.

Testing for Representativeness

We have considered the various aspects of the sampling process and noted that we must determine the representativeness of three separate elements: (1) the invited sample; (2) the accepting sample; and (3) the data-producing sample. Let us consider now the issue of how the researcher can test for representativeness at these three points. The approach for the first two points hinges on whether or not population data are available.

When population data are available, the researcher is able to compare the invited and accepting samples to the population. He should test for differences on those characteristics which he has already identified as critical for his research problem, omitting, of course, any which he has used as the basis of a stratification plan. In these comparisons, the researcher can use one of the appropriate tests of significance to determine whether or not these samples are representative of the population. The researcher is hoping that there will be *no* significant differences. We did such tests for the sample on the Stress–Satisfaction Project, and reported the results as follows:

> The samples of participating diploma programs, degree programs and women's colleges were compared to their respective populations, i.e., the populations of such programs located within 1,000 miles of New York City, on length of program, student enrollment, type of control, and religious affiliation. There were no statistically significant differences (at the .05 level of significance), on the basis of chi square tests between each sample and its population, and so for the characteristics studied the samples of participating schools can be considered representative of the populations from which they were drawn.

Chi square was used in these tests because type of control and religious affiliation were nominal data. Although length of program and student enrollment provided interval data, we also used chi square because we wished to test the frequency distributions for these variables. We could also have used the *t* tests for testing the mean of the sample on these characteristics against the mean of the population, and the *F* test to compare the variation in our sample on them to the variation in the population. This would have provided a more thorough test for representativeness.

If the tests show no differences between these samples and the population, the researcher can conclude that, for the variables tested, he has achieved representativeness. Of course he has learned nothing about the representativeness of the samples on any other variables. However, if these tests show that for any variable or variables he has not achieved representativeness, he has only the two choices we noted earlier open to him: to live with the unrepresentative sample or to select more elements from the population in the hope that the larger sample will be representative. If he chooses to live with the unrepresentative sample, this will be a limitation to the study and a qualification to all analyses of data on which the unrepresentative variable might have had an effect.

When population data are *not* available, obviously the researcher cannot test the representativeness of either the invited or the accepting sample against the population. In this instance, the researcher would be wise to consider using a combination of random selection and larger samples than he might have used if it were possible to test for representativeness. He also would be wise to attempt to obtain data from all members of the invited sample on these characteristics for which he ordinarily would wish to test representativeness. If he does this successfully he can then test for the representativeness of accepting and invited samples. For example, let us say that in the Stress–Satisfaction Project we were anxious to have a sample representative on faculty-student ratio and on laboratory facilities, but no population data were available to us. In the letter of invitation we might have included a simple postcard questionnaire asking for this information, *whether or not* the school was willing to participate in the project. If they provided this, we would at least have some basis for knowing if these factors distinguished the invited and accepting samples.

Whether or not population data were available, when it comes to considering the representativeness of the data-producing sample, the researcher generally has data available, for the referent now is not the population but the accepting sample. Therefore it is reasonable for us to ask a researcher to inform the reader who it was who declined to provide data and the extent to which this introduced a new possibility of bias late in the sampling process

It is here that it is critical to distinguish between those who are selected from the population, invited to participate, and decline, and those who are invited, accept, and then *refuse* to provide data. When a member of the invited sample refuses to participate, he is refusing on the basis of the limited initial contact between researcher and respondent. He may refuse for a wide range of reasons, some of which have nothing to do either with the specific research project or the particular data-collection instrument. He may dislike research participation in general or be too busy to consider responding, reasons which have no specific *project* orientation. Other reasons for declining are project-oriented, such as disinterest in the research, feeling the material requested would take too long to prepare or that it is too personal. However, the respondent who accepts an invitation to participate and then refuses to provide data will almost always be reacting for a project or instrument-oriented reason, and so is a more serious loss.

In either instance, the researcher should test the effect of the loss of some of the accepting sample. The most effective way to do this is to use one or more of the appropriate inferential procedures to test whether or not the accepting sample and the data-producing sample differ significantly in any of the basic characteristics selected for the evaluation of the sampling process. Thus if years of teaching experience was selected, the researcher can use the *t* test to determine if there was a significant difference in the mean years of experience between those in the accepting sample who did and did not produce data. If they did not differ, then the reader knows that this factor was not the basis of the participation decision. If they did, then the reader, knowing this, can make a sounder professional evaluation of the results of the study, for he can take into account in this evaluation the fact that those teachers with longer experience did (or did not) decline to produce data for the study. This in itself becomes a research finding, although usually a more provocative than definitive one.

Of course this testing of the means is simply one illustration of how tests of significance can be used to provide some solid information on the relationship of accepting and data-producing samples. All of the various tests of significance have relevance, whether it be chi square to test distributions on nominal or ordinal data or the *F* test to test the significance of the differences between the variances. What is important is not how it is done, but that the researcher *does* determine the extent to which his data-producing sample is representative of the accepting sample, and informs the reader of the results.

It is not possible to provide any rules as to when the attrition from accepting to data-producing sample has been serious. However, when attrition reaches 25 percent or higher, even assuming that there are no statistically significant differences between accepting and data-producing samples, the researcher and reader must be concerned with the phenomena of nonparticipation. There is extensive evidence in the literature that whether comparable on selection characteristics or not, nonresponders generally hold different opinions than responders. There are studies in which considerable effort and funds have been expended to obtain a response from those who initially declined to answer. These studies generally reveal that those who answer initially hold different opinions from those who do not. As we analyze data for any one study this means that we must continually evaluate the data, particularly any data of particular significance, to determine if the nonresponders could have affected the response pattern. For example, assume we find that 70 percent of the selected sample of 100 actually produced data. In studying data for a particular question, we find that of the 70 respondents, 52 answered "yes" and 18 answered "no." We can have good confidence in these data, for even if the 30 nonrespondents had the same opinion, and it was "no," the majority would still be on the "yes" opinion. However, if the 70 respondents split 39 to 31 on another question, we could have little confidence in these data, for if a majority of the nonrespondents held to either point of view they could alter the result.

This also means that any study in which the data-producing sample falls below 50 percent of the selected sample should be written (and read) with caution. This is another area in which we have been lax far too long in research in the social sciences. We have too readily followed the philosophy that once a study is planned and under way, the data are worth reporting no matter how small a proportion the data-producing sample is of the selected sample. In the author's opinion, when the proportion falls below 60 percent the data are fragile, and when it falls below 40 percent they should not be reported or considered as substantive findings. They are useful as pilot data, but cannot be accepted without replication by a more substantial study.

DETERMINING SAMPLE SIZE

Notice that throughout this discussion of sampling, we have been concerned with representativeness and not with numbers per se. This is deliberate, for the author believes that sample size is far less important than sample representativeness. A study with a representative sample of 39 is preferable to one with an unrepresentative sample of 380. The question of how large a sample should be is basically unanswerable, other than to say that it should be large enough to achieve representativeness. How large this is will vary, of course, from study to study. The one instance in which the question can be answered with a specific number is when the researcher knows five things: (1) a reasonable approximation of the value he is seeking to estimate; (2) the precision with which he wishes to estimate it; (3) the risk of a Type I error he is willing to run; (4) the alternative hypothesis he wishes to be protected against; and (5) the risk of a Type II error he is willing to run against falsely accepting the null hypothesis when this alternative hypothesis is true. If a researcher were able to say, "I believe about 50 percent of disadvantaged children aspire to complete high school, but I wish to estimate the actual proportion within 5 percent, with a risk of a Type I error of 2 percent and with a risk of a Type II error of 12 percent if the proportion is 60 percent," he could statistically determine how large a sample would be needed to achieve this precision.[7]

But of course, this kind of statement is seldom possible in research in the social sciences. Of the five pieces of information only the third, the risk of a Type I error, is always known, for it is the same as the level of significance. The approximate value of the statistic may or may not be known. The alternative hypothesis and risk of a Type II error are almost never stated, and the level of precision is also seldom stated, so that this procedure is almost never employed, and sample size is determined by arbitrarily selecting a number or proportion like 10 percent or 20 percent of a population.

More important than wondering if a 10 percent sample will be more useful than a 20 percent sample is to think ahead to the nature of the data analyses we contemplate. In the earlier discussions of inferential procedures, we noted several points which can guide the researcher in considering sample size. One such point is the fact that the statistical dividing line between large and small samples is a sample size of 30. This is because with two such samples, the curve of the t distribution and of the normal curve are so close as to be the same for purposes of hypothesis testing. Therefore, if we wish to have what will *statistically* be considered large samples, we will want to have at least 30 in each of two samples, or 60 in one sample.

A second statistical consideration in sample size is the demand of some correlational procedures for multiple-category data. For example, if we are planning a study in which we hope to use the Spearman rank order procedure, samples of more than 10 are desirable, and the more we go above it the better. Another statistic which interacts with sample size is chi square. We noted in the discussion of the inferential use of chi square that it cannot properly be used when the expected frequencies drop below 5 in more than 20 percent of the cells. The researcher planning to use chi square must think ahead to the nature of the variables for which he

[7]There is no single computational formula for determining this sample size, since the computational process used will depend upon the inferential model. The basic process in all the formulas is to express the null and alternative distributions in separate statements, each of which will involve an unknown critical value and the number of cases (that is, as the denominator in the standard error). However, the unknown critical value in each statement is the *same* critical value as we saw in Chapter 8. Since each statement can be expressed as equal to the same critical value, they can be set equal to each other. This leaves one equation with one unknown, *n,* or the sample size, which can be solved algebraically.

intends to use it and consider the number of cells for each variable and the probable distribution of his respondents among these cells so that he has more than enough in the sample to make chi square appropriate.

A final consideration is to take into account not only the statistical analyses contemplated, but also the data-gathering processes which will be employed and the possible effect on these in terms of attrition in the accepting sample. For example, if data are to be collected from captive groups of students, the researcher is reasonably certain that his accepting and data-producing samples will be close together in size. However, if he plans to use data-gathering instruments which will be mailed to the accepting sample, then he will find that serious attrition is a very real threat, for returns of 30 percent are common, and even lower returns occur with disheartening frequency. In the chapter on Data Gathering we discuss techniques for maximizing returns, like promising a copy of the results. Here let us note that the researcher, in his decision on sample size, should allow for the worst attrition he has reason to fear. This is particularly true if he will have difficulty in obtaining additional data, or if, as often happens with students, he cannot afford the time for additional data collection. He should then select a sufficiently large and diverse sample so that even if serious attrition occurs, he still has a sufficiently large data-producing sample to have the basis for a reasonable study. In practice this means that we do not select a sample of the size we would like to conclude with, but select a sample one or more times larger.

In this way, by taking into account the variables, data-gathering process, the statistical analyses planned, and any public relations aspects of the desirable sample size, and adding these to the sampling considerations we have discussed in this chapter, the researcher can develop a rational basis for determining an approximate sample size.

Sequential Sampling

If because of inability to specify a minimum difference or the relevant alternative hypothesis, the researcher cannot use formulas to determine appropriate sample size, he has one other direct technique available—*sequential sampling*. In sequential sampling we take not one large complete sample, but successive smaller samples. After the second sampling we analyze the data to determine if the last sampling has altered the data in any significant detail. If so, this suggests the need for further samples; if not, this suggests that we have reached the point of diminishing returns, where additional data will provide no new insights into the phenomena under study.

For example, let us suppose that we wish to learn about teachers' attitudes to phonics instruction and have no idea how many we need to sample to learn about all significant dimensions of attitude in their relative proportion. We decide, arbitrarily, to select a sample of 20 cases. Since we have no opportunity to stratify, we decide to select the samples by random procedures. To begin the process of sequential sampling, we need three samples, selected in order. Thus we would select three separate samples of 20 cases and analyze the data from each sample separately. We would then create two sets of combined data, one based on the combination of samples 1 and 2, the second set based on the combination of all three sets of data. We can then prepare a summary table like Table 11-4, in which the first three columns of data refer respectively to the three separate samples of 20, and the next three columns present the distribution in percent of the first sample of 20 alone, the first two samples combined, and all three samples combined.

Referring to Table 11-4 we notice that the combination of the first two samples is a different set of data than the first sample alone in two important aspects. First the combined sample has people in the category "strongly negative," which was not represented in the first sample of 20. Second, the relative proportions in some categories are considerably[8] different when we compare the first and the combined sample. For example, 25 percent of the combined sample reported "neutral" feelings compared to 15 percent in the first sample. However, we see that adding the

Table 11-4 Illustration for Sequential Sampling

| | Individual Samples | | | Sequential Comparisons in Percent | | |
| | | | | | | |
Category	1	2	3	Sample 1	Samples 1 and 2 Combined	Samples 1, 2, and 3 Combined
Strongly positive	8	4	6	40	30	30
Mildly positive	6	3	3	30	22.5	20
Neutral	3	7	6	15	25	26.7
Mildly negative	2	3	2	10	12.5	11.7
Strongly negative	0	3	2	0	7.5	8.3
No opinion	1	0	1	5	2.5	3.3

[8]Generally in sequential sampling, simple observation is sufficient to decide if additional sampling is required. If a more precise estimate is needed, the researcher can test the separate sets of data for statistical significance.

third sample of 20 cases has neither added a new category nor appreciably altered the proportions in the separate categories. It is generally a sound idea to go one sample beyond the first point of no difference. Thus, in this example, we would select a fourth sample of 20 cases, and if the newly combined distribution still added no new dimension to the data picture, we would feel reasonably confident that we had a sufficiently large sample to learn all there is to learn about the attitudes and the proportion of people who hold each attitude.

Sampling in Data Analysis

One additional technique to remember in considering sample size is to recognize that sampling can be done in data *analysis* as well as during collection. This is particularly useful to remember when it is difficult to sample but relatively easy to obtain masses of data. For example, in the Phonics Study we may wish to obtain data from a sample of children in the fourth and fifth grades of several schools to provide some comparative data for the study. To obtain coverage for a variety of classes, the researcher decides he wants data from only ten children in each class in the grade. Administratively it may be far simpler to go into a class, test all of the children, and sample at the data-analysis stage. Thus, the researcher could randomly select one-third of the test papers in each class to be scored and analyzed.[9] Sequential sampling, particularly, can be implemented at the data-analysis stage to guide the researcher in deciding how large a proportion of his data need be analyzed.

CONCLUSION

Throughout this chapter we have emphasized the importance of representativeness rather than sample size as the critical aspect of sampling. We have done this because students and the general public are often overly concerned with and impressed by sheer size. In addition, as noted in the previous chapter, the sample size can actually get too large in the sense of communicating statistical significance for small differences of little practical significance. Therefore, the proper sample size is the size needed to achieve the precision the researcher wishes and to hold the risks of Type I and Type II errors to the limits he wishes.

[9]In the discussion of random-selection procedures earlier in this chapter, we mentioned that in some instances if a case were selected more than once through a random procedure, it could be used more than once. Sampling in data analysis is such an instance: The researcher can, if he wishes, use the data for any one case as often as it is selected.

The general impression of the research consumer that large numbers are needed and build up the strength of a sample is contradicted by many studies. Perhaps the most striking and well-known illustration of this is the accuracy with which computers were able to predict the results of the 1964 presidential election with less than 5 percent of the vote cast. This was possible because of careful stratification of the voting population on several variables previously shown to be related to voting behavior, followed by proportional random selection.

Equally dramatic evidence that representativeness, not sample size, is the critical concern is provided by the instances in which researchers erred in public by not realizing this. Specifically, the best known of these errors concerned the presidential elections of 1936 and 1948. In 1936, the *Literary Digest* received ballots from more than two million people with a clear majority expressing a preference for Landon. The magazine therefore predicted the election of the Republican candidate. When Roosevelt won 46 of the 48 states, the public loss of confidence in the magazine was so great that it went out of business. Its error was simple to see in retrospect. The universe of voters was sampled by sending ballots to names obtained from automobile registration lists and telephone books. These are now easily recognized as biased sources for a sample of voters in the depression year of 1936. The millions polled did not save the research from the error introduced by this bias, for the sample was simply not representative of the voting universe.

In 1948 a different type of bias was involved. Researchers had profited from the 1936 mistake and so in 1948 carefully stratified the universe by income level, ethnic background, sex, occupation, and the many other variables known to be related to voting behavior. However, they found such a clear preference for Dewey over Truman that they stopped polling early in October. Truman's subsequent victory added a new adage to the pollster's rule book: Samples in October are not representative of the voting universe in November!

We could move from this to a general adage for research: No data are sounder than the representativeness of the sample from which they were obtained, no matter how large the sample.

Chapter 12

DESIRABLE ATTRIBUTES
OF RESEARCH TECHNIQUES

The quality of research can be no better than the quality of the procedures used to collect and analyze the data. If these procedures lack some of the basic attributes of good procedures then the research data will also lack these, and misleading and inaccurate interpretations and conclusions become probable. If the procedures used possess all of the necessary and desirable attributes then the potential for sound research is present.

Obviously, one of the most important foundational skills needed by the researcher is the ability to appraise the procedures he intends to use both for the collection *and* analysis of data. Note that data-analysis procedures are included here as well. All too often researchers who pay reasonable attention to the characteristics of their procedures for data collection pay little or no attention to the characteristics of their procedures of data analysis. But these, too, determine the quality of research data, and so must be considered. In this chapter we shall consider seven basic characteristics. Five of these are characteristics research procedures must possess for data to have any interpretability. They are: (1) reliability; (2) validity; (3) sensitivity; (4) appropriateness; and (5) objectivity. Then we shall discuss a sixth, feasibility, which does not affect interpretability but which, nevertheless, is obviously a desirable attribute. Finally, we shall discuss a seventh attribute which does not affect interpretability either but which is, in the author's opinion, equally critical for the researcher in the social disciplines, and that is the extent to which the demands of the data-collection techniques and procedures are ethical.

RELIABILITY

We shall consider reliability first because it is the basic attribute which every procedure must possess. Only if it is reliable do we worry about

352

whether it has the other characteristics. By reliability we mean the accuracy of the data in the sense of their stability, repeatability, or precision. A perfectly reliable data-collection instrument is one which, if administered twice under the same circumstances, would provide identical data. The techniques for estimating reliability have been developed to provide two sets of data collected under the "same circumstances" so that the results can be compared. If they are identical, the instrument can be considered to have perfect reliability. If they have no relationship to each other, the instrument can be considered to have no reliability. If they have some, but not a perfect, relationship to each other the instrument can be considered to have some, but less than perfect, reliability.

The preceding sentence should sound familiar to you, because it parallels the description of the different size correlation coefficients discussed in Chapter 7. Because the parallel holds so well, the correlation is the basic statistic used to estimate reliability. Correlations of $+1.00$[1] would indicate perfect reliability; correlations at or close to 0.00 would indicate no reliability, and correlations at intermediate points between 0.00 and $+1.00$ would indicate intermediate levels of reliability. Of course perfect reliability is seldom achieved, and it is the intermediate correlations which are found in practice. To evaluate them we can use exactly the same technique (squaring and converting to a percent) used to evaluate any correlation. Thus an instrument with a reliability of .80 which comes to 64 percent by the squaring technique, tells us, on one administration, 64 percent of what we need to know to predict the data we would obtain on the second administration of the same instrument to the same people.

We shall consider four techniques for estimating reliability: test-retest reliability, alternate-form reliability, split-half or odd-even reliability, and Kuder-Richardson reliability. The goal in each is to produce two sets of data which can be correlated to provide an estimate of reliability.

Test-Retest Reliability

Test-retest reliability is exactly what the name implies; we produce the first of the two sets of data by administering the instrument (the "test"), then after some period of time long enough for forgetting to take place but not so long that change would be expected, we produce the second set of data by administering the instrument to the same people a second time (the "retest"). Thus this technique involves administering the same instru-

[1] A correlation of -1.00 also reflects a perfect relationship but for purposes of reliability this complete inversion of the data would cast almost perfect doubt on its reliability.

ment to the same people on two separate occasions. We then correlate the two sets of data, and the correlation estimates the reliability of the instrument.

The major problem in test-retest reliability involves the time interval. How long is "long enough for forgetting but not so long" for change? In some research studies it has been defined as briefly as the amount of time it takes to collect a set of papers, for some researchers have administered an instrument, collected the papers, and administered the instrument again as the basis for test-retest reliability. It has also been defined as long as one year, for in a study with which the researcher was associated the test-retest reliability of an instrument was estimated with that long an interval between the original test and the retest. How long a time is appropriate can only be answered by the phrase used so often in research, "it depends." In this case it depends on the research data being collected or analyzed.

Let us assume we wished to estimate the reliability of a 75-item test designed to measure students' ability to handle fractional computations. To use the test-retest procedure to estimate the reliability of the instrument, we might decide on immediate readministration. In this instance we could argue that since the test has 75 problems, if we give them in scrambled order the second time, there is little likelihood that anyone will remember many of the answers he gave the first time and so no time interval is necessary. In contrast, if we were developing an instrument to measure the attitudes of teachers toward administrators we might argue that once a person has answered the questions on the instrument, to give it again would be pointless for he would remember some of his answers, no matter how many questions or how scrambled the order. If he did, we would undoubtedly obtain a very encouraging estimate of the reliability of the instrument, but it would be spuriously high, reflecting not reliability but memory. So we decide to wait two weeks before the second administration, but we would be troubled by the fact that specific incidents might happen to one or more teachers which would change their attitude. If this happened to many teachers, when we readministered the instrument we would obtain a spuriously low estimate of the reliability, reflecting not the instability of the instrument but the fact that change took place and the instrument was reflecting that change.

For this reason, the test-retest procedure is most effectively used to estimate reliability in instances when the procedure being evaluated is seeking to elicit stable information or measure some skill which is slow to change or develop or else is one the respondents are not in the process of developing, such as the spelling ability of adults. The test-retest procedure is particularly appropriate to estimate the reliability of data-analysis procedures. Here no change is able to occur and analyses of the same data at two different points in time should produce identical results. But for collecting data in conceptual areas like attitudes, interests, or current skills, the usefulness of the test-retest procedure is limited by the difficulty of deciding how long the time interval should be. In all areas it is further limited by the practical difficulty of reassembling the same group of respondents for the retest procedure. Outside of school settings, this is often so difficult as to rule this procedure out entirely.

One additional danger in the test-retest procedure as a measure of reliability is that responses are being correlated to two exposures to the same content. Thus whatever bias exists in the content of the instrument will, of course, be a consistent bias on each exposure to the instrument. Thus, if the instrument on teachers' attitudes tended to produce favorable scores for those who think well of their principal's ability to organize the grades each June, this would be true each time they responded to this instrument. Because of this, some researchers seek to make a subtle distinction between stability and reliability, arguing that the test-retest procedure will provide evidence of the stability of the data to be produced by the instrument, but not its reliability if reliability is taken to mean accuracy or precision.

Alternate-Form Reliability

To estimate reliability through the alternate-form procedure, the researcher must develop two parallel or equivalent forms of his instrument, administer both to the same people, and correlate the two sets of data obtained. The administration of the two forms can be with an intervening time interval or can be at one sitting, with the forms administered consecutively. In either instance it is preferable to alternate the order of the forms, that is, give half of the respondents form A followed by form B, and the other half form B followed by form A. This alternation eliminates any consistent practice effect, or the effects of factors like fatigue and boredom on the instrument administered second.

The practical difficulty of this procedure must be discussed first, because it is this which has limited the frequency with which alternate-form reliability has been used. In most instances researchers find it difficult enough to develop one form of an instrument, let alone two. Moreover, with instruments like questionnaires seeking information, or studies of reactions to specific situations there is no sensible way of asking the same or similar questions twice.

Where the procedure does work well is in areas of skill, ability, or knowledge. In these areas, whether or not the respondent has the skill or ability or individual bit of knowledge can be tested in more than one way. Therefore, alternate forms of instruments are perfectly feasible to develop. Moreover, in these areas, there is often a genuine need for more than one form for purposes other than reliability testing. If we wish to test before and after a course of study, for example, we would want to have more than one form of the basic testing instrument. Therefore, in these instances we might reasonably expect a researcher to use the alternate form procedure.

If we use the alternate-form procedure we do lessen the problem noted above of a consistent bias in content. Now we have two different samples of content, and it is unlikely that both forms will have the same content bias. If we make them meticulously equivalent, of course, they might. This possibility leads us to a problem raised by some who agree that the alternate-form procedure does produce an estimate of the extent to which the forms are equivalent, but argue that equivalence is not accuracy and precision any more than stability is. For example, assume form A tends to attribute spuriously negative attitudes toward supervisors to teachers of the early childhood grades because they have to reply "don't know" to many of the organizational questions. Assume form B is constructed along the same outline. It, too, will attribute spurious negative attitudes to these teachers, and the reliability estimates may be high. The critics of the procedure would say that the spurious reliability estimate is in reality only an estimate of the equivalence of the two forms, and that is what is high. They would argue that through estimating equivalence, we cannot estimate the accuracy of a measure.

If the alternate-form procedure is used with a time interval intervening between forms, then it raises, for the researcher, the same practical problem of reassembling the groups that the test-retest procedure did. Administering forms consecutively brings two lesser practical problems: securing the double testing time required for the two administrations and maintaining sufficient interest in the respondents as they work through essentially the same material for the second time. For these reasons, the procedure is seldom used in research beyond the area of testing.

Split-Half or Odd-Even Reliability

A third procedure, called split-half reliability or odd-even reliability, solves each of the practical difficulties mentioned so far. Unlike the test-retest procedure, it involves only one administration of the instrument. Unlike the alternate-form procedure, it involves only one form of the instrument. What is done is simple: The total instrument is administered once to one group of respondents. However, it is then scored or analyzed in such a way as to yield two separate scores for each respondent. These two sets of scores are then correlated. Thus, if the teacher attitude survey instrument had 100 items, to estimate odd-even reliability we would obtain a score or estimate of the attitude of each respondent based on the 50 odd-numbered items (that is, items 1, 3, 5, 7, on up to item 99) and then obtain a separate score for each respondent based on the 50 even-numbered items (that is, items 2, 4, 6, on up to item 100).

It is possible, but not preferable, to use the split-half procedure, that is, to obtain one score for the respondent based on items 1 through 50 and a second score based on items 51 through 100. The odd-even version is preferred to the split half for two reasons. The first reason is that in research instruments, different content areas are covered in different sections. Thus, questions 1 through 26 may refer to the teacher's opinion of the principal's interest and concern in teacher welfare, items 27 through 41 to his appraisal of the principal's efficiency and ability, items 42 through 72 to his reaction to the principal's appearance and personality, and items 73 to 100 to interpersonal relationships and ethics. If we split at item 50, the first half would include all of the items on interest and concern and on efficiency and ability and 9 of the 30 items on appearance and personality. The second half would have the other items on appearance and personality and all of the items on interpersonal relationships and ethics. In short, we would have created two dissimilar halves. Had we used the odd-even basis, however, we would have half of the items from each content area in each of the two halves for the reliability estimate. In a sense, then, we seek equivalent halves just as in the alternate-form procedure we try to create equivalent forms.

The second advantage of the odd-even procedure is hardly needed because the one above is so critical, but this procedure also eliminates the possible biasing effects of factors like fatigue or loss of interest causing a respondent to omit the last several items or questions or answer them with less care than he answered the items on the earlier part of the instrument.

But no matter which procedure is used, estimating reliability from halves of an instrument is not without its problem, principally based on the fact that reliability is related to the number of items in an instrument. Generally, the longer the instrument, the more reliable it is. The logic of this is that more items provide us with a broader base for making a statement about a person, that is, they enable us to obtain a more stable sample of his attitudes, skills, knowledge, or whatever it is that we are studying. If reliability is related to length, then either the split-half or odd-even procedure would tend to produce a deflated estimate of the reliability, for they are based on only half the number of items in the full instrument, that is, the 50 even, or 50 odd, items, rather than the 100 in the total instrument.

Therefore, a procedure has been developed to use following the split-half procedures to estimate what the reliability would be of the full instrument. Named after the two men who independently developed it, the procedure is called the Spearman-Brown Prophecy Formula. It uses the actual reliability obtained by correlating scores on the two halves of the test to prophesy what the reliability would be of the total instrument, through the simple formula below.

$$
\begin{array}{l}\text{estimated Spearman-Brown}\\\text{reliability of}\\\text{total instrument}\end{array} = \frac{2 \times \left[\begin{array}{l}\text{actual correlation}\\\text{between halves}\\\text{of instrument}\end{array}\right]}{1 + \left[\begin{array}{l}\text{actual correlation}\\\text{between halves}\\\text{of instrument}\end{array}\right]}
$$

Thus, if the actual correlation between the two halves of the test was .60, we would substitute .60 for each of the brackets in the formula so the numerator would be 2(.60) or 1.20 and the denominator 1 + .60 or 1.60, yielding a quotient of .75, which would be the estimated reliability of the total test as prophesied by the Spearman-Brown procedure.

The "prophecy" aspect is stressed here for two reasons: First, what the formula yields is only a prediction, or estimate of the reliability the researcher could aspire to for the total instrument based on the reliability obtained for half of it. In this sense it is a way of estimating the maximum reliability that can be attributed to, or expected from, the total instrument. The second reason for the emphasis on prophecy is that in the research and measurement literature the procedure is typically referred to as a "correction formula," as if some error were being undone.

It is important that the educator as researcher, and as consumer of research and measurement reports and tests, understands the computational properties of the Spearman-Brown Prophecy Formula because the single most frequently used reliability procedure is the odd-even method followed by the Spearman-Brown formula. This is perfectly legitimate if the actual split-half reliability is reported as well as the Spearman-Brown prophecy. But unfortunately, the practice has grown of reporting only the final Spearman-Brown estimate. It is not hard to know why researchers and test constructors prefer to do this, because the Spearman-Brown reliability is always higher.

The reason that caution is required in assuming that the Spearman-Brown estimate is necessarily the reliability of the total instrument is that it would be the actual reliability only if the total instrument could be considered twice as thorough a sample of the respondent's behavior or knowledge as each half of the instrument is. But instruments typically have some redundancy. In the example above, the attitude instrument has 26 items on the principal's interest in, and concern for, teacher welfare. Obviously the researcher believes that each of these is telling him something unique about the principal, but if they are not, then we may learn little more about his concern and interest in teacher welfare from the 26 items in the total instrument than we learn from the 13 items in each of the halves of the instrument. And if this were so in each area covered, then the reliability of the total instrument would not be substantially higher than the actual reliability obtained from the split-half procedure. An example of this is given by Thorndike and Hagen in their book on measurement and evaluation. They present both the split-half and alternate-form reliability for seven tests of intelligence and achievement. In every instance the alternate-form reliability for the total instrument is lower than the estimate of the reliability of the total instrument based on the split-half procedure, with the differences in reliability ranging from .04 to .14.[2]

The major advantage of using the correlation between halves as an estimate of the reliability of the total test is the obvious practical one: we need only one test and one testing session with our respondents. Its disadvantages are included in the same statement. Since we have only one test, our reliability estimate is based on this one set of content, unlike the alternate-form procedure which involves two sets of content. With only one testing session, our reliability estimate is based on only one contact with the respondents, unlike the test-retest procedure where we have two contacts. Thus, any short-term, temporary conditions affecting the respondents will be reflected in this one contact. However, if use is considered some estimate of the evaluation of the procedure by researchers, then the evaluation is that the practical advantages outweigh the conceptual disadvantages, for, as noted earlier, this is the most widely used procedure for estimating reliability.

Reliability Estimated from the Item Response Pattern

A technique for estimating reliability which has achieved some use in the field of objective testing is a procedure developed by Kuder and Richardson and named after them. Their procedure is quite different from any we have discussed because it uses the individual item response patterns to

[2]Robert L. Thorndike and Elizabeth Hagen, *Measurement and Evaluation in Psychology and Education* (New York: John Wiley & Sons, Inc., 1955), p. 138.

provide one of the two sets of data needed to estimate reliability, with performance on the total instrument used to provide the other set of data. It is applicable to those instances in which the response to an item can be graded as right or wrong, because the most widely used computational formulas for applying the Kuder-Richardson procedure involve the proportion of respondents who get each item right and the proportion who get it wrong. For research purposes, then, it is limited to those studies using objective testing as a data-gathering technique.

In a sense the Kuder-Richardson procedure can be seen as the ultimate extension of the split-half or odd-even thinking. Thus, where the split-half thinking perceives a 100-item test as consisting of two 50-item subtests, the Kuder-Richardson procedure perceives it as consisting of 100 one-item subtests. For most research purposes it does not accomplish anything more of significance than the odd-even procedure, and has both the same procedural advantage (it requires one administration of the single test to one group of respondents) and the same disadvantages (the reliability estimate is thus based on one contact with the respondent and on his reaction to one set of content). If the researcher has analyzed the data in a typical item analysis process through which he routinely has obtained the proportion who passed and failed each item, then the Kuder-Richardson procedure might have some slight computational advantages.[3]

Evaluating Reliability

The basis for evaluating the estimated reliability of an instrument comes from the recognition of the factors that cause an instrument to have less than perfect reliability. Why should a questionnaire not produce perfectly accurate responses, or a test a perfectly accurate picture of what an individual knows? There are five major factors to consider: (1) the certainty of the information which is sought; (2) the stability of the dynamic over time, within the individual; (3) the researcher's understanding of the dynamic being studied; (4) current ability to translate that dynamic into instrument form; and (5) chance factors.

First, consider the question of certainty of the information sought. Some variables which are studied in research, like birthplace, are fixed and

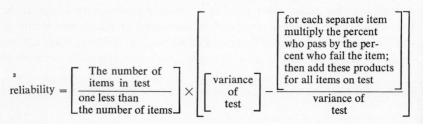

unchanging, and respondents know this information with utmost clarity. Other variables are equally fixed, like the size of town in which the respondent was born, but the respondent may be less certain of this information. Similarly, in the study of interests, if we ask the respondent about his interest in a sport he has followed for years, we would assume that his interest is well defined and known to him. If, in contrast, we question him about his interest in an activity in which he has never participated and about which he has thought little, his response is much less certain. Obviously, the more certain the nature of the information sought and the better the respondent knows it, the more reliable the instrument should be.

Allied to this factor of certainty is the factor of stability of the information sought. Many aspects of people change over time, particularly in the areas of attitudes, interests, or opinions. Other aspects, like skills and knowledge, are more stable. If the procedure for estimating reliability is sensitive to these changes, then the estimate may be low, not solely because of unreliability in the instrument.

The third and fourth factors reflect an important aspect of evaluating reliability—the current state of our knowledge in the social disciplines. Assume that in the Language Study we wished to develop an instrument to estimate children's liking for school. The first problem would stem from the limited understanding we now have of this dynamic. What are the intellectual, psychological, and sociological components of liking for school? There are hypotheses about what should be studied through such an instrument, but no consistent agreement. This insufficiently clear understanding of the dynamics involved could mean that the instrument is studying the wrong things and so provides an unreliable estimate of the children's attitudes. The fourth factor, the ability to translate the dynamic into instrument form, raises the next question in the sequence. Assume that all educators and psychologists we consult agree that one of the components of attitude toward school is the child's perception of the impact education will have on his success in adult life. We then face the problem of how to obtain some estimate of this component through the instrument we develop. Here we know the component to measure but face the difficulty of transforming it into an instrument or part of an instrument.

Finally, a cluster of chance factors like fatigue and boredom, external distractions like noise, other people, or other activities, and internal distractions like tension or anxiety can all operate to reduce the stability of an individual's response at any one point in time.

To achieve high reliability we must have a set of conditions something like these: The researcher is seeking relatively certain information which the respondents have in their repertoire of responses, which is stable over time, and which involves dynamics whose components the researcher not only knows but can translate into instrument form. Moreover, the conditions under which the instrument will be tested are suitable for data collection, being peacefully quiet and distraction-free, with the respondents rested and relaxed.

This description of the utopia for reliability has two implications for the researcher seeking to establish and evaluate the reliability of a new instrument. First, in estimating reliability we must make the maximum efforts to establish conditions that minimize the effects of the chance factors. Distraction should be eliminated. Fatigue should be anticipated, that is, work with school children in the morning rather than the afternoon, and in early morning rather than just before lunch. Through thorough explanations of the nature of the task, many of the internal distractions which accompany anxiety about research and testing should also be eliminated. While all of these instructions are sound for any data-collection session, they are particularly critical for a session that will produce data on the basis of which reliability will be estimated.

The second implication is that the expectations for the reliability of an instrument will differ depending on the nature of the information sought. If we are seeking fixed, demographic, census-type information about birthplace, schooling, and job experience we would expect high reliability from the instrument. In correlational terms this means reliability at or above .90. Any differences here are due to chance factors or to the instability that comes from faulty memory by the respondent or his efforts to conceal the truth. If we seek to estimate knowledge and ability, these two are relatively fixed characteristics, and so we have high reliability aspirations here as well, generally above .85, but with .80 usually a useful minimum, for at this level two administrations of the instrument would have a shared variance of 64 percent, or about two-thirds. If we move to the area of attitudes and interests we know the data are more flexible and changeable, and so expectations for reliability must be adjusted down typically to where correlations in the .70's are accepted. Finally, when we move to projective instruments used in clinical research, where the information sought is stable but the dynamics insufficiently understood or in which we do not yet know how to translate newly developing concepts and theories into instrument form, we find that the reliability of such analysis typically falls below .70 and in some studies below .60 as well. Of course, when reliability drops this low, the data can only be interpreted with the greatest caution and not taken seriously until repeated studies are completed.

Improving Reliability Which Is below Expectations

What happens when the reliability estimates for a particular instrument are lower than the appropriate standards for the information sought by the instrument? In part this depends upon when these estimates are obtained. If they are obtained when they should be, that is during the planning stages of research and prior to the use of the instruments in the actual data collection, then obviously the instrument must be revised until the reliability is improved. If instead, the reliability is estimated during the course of the data collection, then the researcher either junks the data, improves the instrument, and begins again, or he attempts to take the low reliability into account in discussing and interpreting his data by qualifying almost any statement he makes.

During the data-collection phase, improving reliability must be based upon analysis of the factors just discussed which affect it. That is, the researcher must rethink the nature of the dynamic he is studying to see if the low reliability might reflect insufficient understanding of the dynamic. He should examine the items in the instrument to be certain they are clear and unambiguous statements of what he seeks to obtain. He might also return to the literature to see if there are other ways of translating the dynamic into instrument form. He should re-examine the nature of the situation under which the reliability data were obtained to see if anything in that situation might explain the low estimates.

Finally, he might consider how altering the length of the instrument would affect the reliability. In doing this he can use a general form of the Spearman-Brown procedure, which provides an estimate of the maximum reliability to be expected if an existing instrument is lengthened. The formula used is that below:

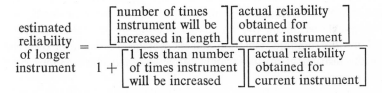

$$\begin{array}{l} \text{estimated} \\ \text{reliability} \\ \text{of longer} \\ \text{instrument} \end{array} = \dfrac{\left[\begin{array}{l}\text{number of times}\\ \text{instrument will be}\\ \text{increased in length}\end{array}\right]\left[\begin{array}{l}\text{actual reliability}\\ \text{obtained for}\\ \text{current instrument}\end{array}\right]}{1 + \left[\begin{array}{l}\text{1 less than number}\\ \text{of times instrument}\\ \text{will be increased}\end{array}\right]\left[\begin{array}{l}\text{actual reliability}\\ \text{obtained for}\\ \text{current instrument}\end{array}\right]}$$

Thus, if the reliability estimate obtained for a 30-item instrument was .60 and the researcher wonders what would happen if he tripled the length of the instrument to make it 90 items, he would substitute in the formula so that his numerator would be $(3 \times .60)$ or 1.80 and his denominator would be $1 + [(2) \times (.60)]$ or $1 + 1.20$ or 2.20. Dividing the 1.80 by the 2.20 yields an estimate of the maximum reliability of the 90-item instrument of .82, considerably higher than the actual .60. There are three critical assumptions in this procedure: (1) that the items to be added are comparable in function and quality to the 30 items already in the instrument; (2) that they supplement these 30 in content and so tell us something new about the respondent and the dynamic being studied; and (3) that the additional items will not introduce new factors of fatigue and boredom which will operate against the improvement to be expected from the greater length. There is also the practical problem of obtaining the time required to administer the longer instrument.

The researcher considering this route for improving reliability should calculate the improvement which might be achieved for different increases in length. For example, with the illustration considered here, increasing the instrument one and one-half times to 45 items would make possible a reliability of .69, and doubling it to 60 items, a reliability of .75. As we learned above, tripling it to 90 items would raise the possible reliability to .82. Considering these data, the researcher may decide to try the 60-item instrument as a good compromise, feeling that the additional gain in reliability to be expected from the increase from 60 to 90 items is not worth the additional administration time required, with the attendant risk of fatigue.

Once this decision is made, then the new instrument must be developed and its actual reliability estimated. Assuming sound instrument development, this estimate will not be significantly far from the expectation obtained from the shorter instrument. If it is much below, the researcher knows he has not met the three assumptions of the procedure and so must reanalyze what he has done to identify which one or ones he failed to meet.

Estimating the Effects of Unreliability upon Data

There are two instances in which the researcher can numerically estimate the impact of less than perfect reliability upon his data. The first instance occurs when he has numerical data at the interval or ratio level, and so has been able to obtain the standard deviation of the data. He can then substitute this standard deviation and the obtained estimate of the reliability of the instrument in the formula below to obtain the *standard error of measurement*.

$$\text{standard error of measurement} = \left(\text{standard deviation}\right) \times \left(\sqrt{1 - \text{reliability}}\right)$$

For example, if the reliability estimate of a test of children's ability to understand English was .84 and the standard deviation of this test when administered to the children in the structure group of the Language Study was 8.4 points, the standard error of measurement would be $(8.4)\sqrt{(1 - .84)}$ or $(8.4)\sqrt{(.16)}$ which simplifies to $(8.4)(.4)$ or 3.4 points. This measure is the standard deviation we would expect in an individual child's scores if we administered this test to a child several times. In other words the standard error of measurement is interpreted like the other standard errors discussed in Chapter 6. Applying the normal curve model to these data, we could then say that the probability is 68 percent that the score we obtain for any child is within 3.4 points of what his hypothetical true score is, and 95 percent that it is within two standard errors, or 6.8 points.

The second possibility for estimating the impact of reliability on data involves its effect on the correlation between two variables. Logically we would assume that correlating data obtained from two less than perfectly reliable instruments provides us with an underestimate of the true correlation between the variables the instruments are intended to measure. This occurs because the "unreliable" aspects of each instrument have only a chance relationship to each other, and so diminish the relationship actually being measured. Thorndike and Hagen[4] report a simple procedure for resolving this by estimating the true correlation between two variables using the correlation actually obtained between two instruments and taking into account the reliability of each instrument. This procedure involves substituting the correlation and reliabilities in the formula below:

$$\text{estimated correlation between the variables} = \frac{\text{actual correlation between instruments}}{\sqrt{\left(\begin{array}{c}\text{reliability of}\\\text{instrument 1}\end{array}\right) \times \left(\begin{array}{c}\text{reliability of}\\\text{instrument 2}\end{array}\right)}}$$

Thus, assume we obtained a .62 correlation between children's ability to understand English (using the test discussed above with a reliability of .84) and their ability to understand Spanish, using a test with a reliability of .74. To estimate the "true" correlation between the variables "ability to understand English" and "ability to understand Spanish," we would substitute the correlation obtained of .62 in the numerator. The denominator would be the square root of the product of the two reliabilities, that is, $\sqrt{.84 \times .74}$, or $\sqrt{.6216}$ or .79. The quotient obtained by dividing .62 by .79 is .78, and this is the estimate of the correlation between the two variables freed of the unreliability of the instruments.

Reliability in Data Analysis

The concept of reliability occurs at a second point in the research process, in the analysis of the data. At this stage it has the same meaning as in data collection, that is accuracy, stability, or precision. Procedurally, however, it is generally far simpler for the researcher to estimate because of the greater control he has over the materials and people involved in data analysis than in data collection.

Typically there are three different aspects of data analysis in which reliability should be estimated: (1) the tallying or transcribing of specific

[4]Thorndike and Hagen, *Measurement and Evaluation in Psychology and Education,* p. 141.

data; (2) the analysis of data involving coding; (3) the analysis of data involving judgment.

In the first of these, the tallying or transcribing of specific data, the researcher should estimate the reliability with which the data-analysis process he has established can be reliably performed. To do this he simply has two different persons tally or transcribe the same set of data, and he then computes the percent of times they tally units of data identically. The computation in this percent agreement method is made by applying the formula below:

$$\text{percent agreement} = \frac{\text{number of units of data tallied identically}}{\text{total number of units of data in reliability sample}}$$

For even the most complex hand-tally operations, 95 percent agreement is a reasonable standard to expect and to achieve. This sets a 5 percent error as the maximum level for sound research. For most tallying operations, a sample of 100 units of data is sufficient to test reliability in this way.

To estimate the reliability of the work of any one staff member, the same process can be adapted. Here the researcher should develop carefully checked sets of 100 units of perfectly analyzed data to use as standard sets against which to estimate the reliability of any one worker. With this standard set available, the process for estimating it is the same as above: The new worker tallies the standard set of data, and the percent of times he is correct is computed. Here the same standard of 95 percent accuracy is sound and reasonable.

The second aspect of data analysis in which reliability should be estimated involves the analysis of specific data in which coding is involved. This occurs, for example, when the data analysis involves transforming nominal data like place of birth or type of college program into a numerical code for purposes of machine tabulation. Thus, Alabama may be coded 01, Alaska, 02, and so on up to Wyoming which is coded 50. Here again, a sample of 100 coding units should periodically be recoded by a different coder to make certain that the 95 percent level of accuracy is maintained.

A third aspect of data analysis in which reliability should be estimated is when data analysis involves some judgment on the part of the analyst. For example, let us suppose that for the Language Study we wish to establish the socioeconomic status of each child's family. One standard method is to use the father's occupation and some scale such as the one developed by Warner.[5] The Warner scale specifies clearly the socio-economic status of most occupations, but obviously does not spell out the

[5]Lloyd Warner and others, *Social Class in America: A Manual for Procedure for the Measurement of Social Status* (Chicago: Science Research Associates, Inc., 1949).

correct placement of every single occupation. Therefore, whoever is responsible for the analysis of these data will have to exercise some degree of judgment if he is to classify every child. It is the reliability of the judgmental process which should be estimated, using the percent agreement method, and the same 95 percent standard for deciding if the reliability is satisfactory.

VALIDITY

While reliability is the basic prerequisite for any research procedure, validity is the most important characteristic for the procedure to possess. This is because validity deals with the relationship of the data obtained to the purpose for which it was collected. Thus validity is defined as the extent to which the procedure actually accomplishes what it seeks to accomplish or measures what it seeks to measure.

There is a one-way relationship between reliability and validity. Reliability for a procedure is essential before its validity can be considered, and the actual reliability sets the ceiling for the maximum validity the instrument can possess. Thus a procedure with a reliability of .00 cannot possibly have any validity, for the data obtained from it are based on nothing but random chance factors. At the opposite extreme, a procedure with a perfect reliability of 1.00 can *possibly* be perfectly valid. For the more usual intermediate degrees of reliability the maximum validity can be estimated from the square root of the reliability coefficient. Thus if, for the test of ability to understand English, we obtained a reliability estimate of .60, we would know that the maximum correlation we could expect between this instrument and some criterion measure of the children's ability to understand English would be the square root of .60 or .77.

However, the direction is only one way. It may well be that this instrument with its reliability of .60 has much lower validity than .77 and indeed may have no validity at all. In fact, even the procedure with perfect reliability, and therefore possibly perfect validity, may have no validity in practice. This is because while reliability sets the limit on validity, it is absolutely no guarantee of it. This can be most simply understood through an example.

Consider the researcher who decides to estimate the IQ of a group of Puerto Rican fourth graders by measuring the child's height in inches in stocking feet. This measure has many attributes we seek in measures of intelligence for children who have lived in two cultures. It is nonverbal, requiring neither fluency in English by the child nor in Spanish by the examiner, for example. Knowing the mean height of fourth graders to be

48 inches and the mean IQ 100, the researcher decides he will obtain the height in inches and add a constant of 52.

Now the variable being measured, height, is stable, changes extremely slowly over time, and is not subject to chance factors at all. What then would we expect about the reliability of such an estimate of IQ? It should be nearly perfect, for if we measured the students on Monday of the first week and then again on Thursday (the test-retest procedure), we should obtain identical readings for everyone, except for errors in measurement, and therefore would produce near perfect reliability. But what about the validity? From the nearly perfect reliability we know validity too might be nearly perfect. But data available indicate no relationship between height and IQ, so that this perfectly reliable instrument with possibly perfect validity in theory would, in practice, have no validity whatsoever.

We conclude that reliability is a prerequisite, for an instrument must measure something accurately before we can worry about what it *is* measuring. We also conclude that the mere fact that an instrument is measuring *something* accurately does not mean it is necessarily measuring what we believe it to be measuring. Validity, then, must be estimated separately, once the reliability of the procedure or instrument has been established satisfactorily. In this section we shall consider six procedures for estimating validity. Unfortunately, no one of them provides both a theoretically sound and practically satisfactory basis for estimating validity for research purposes. Whereas all of the techniques for estimating reliability were based on data and yielded correlations, two of the procedures for estimating validity are not data-based and do not yield a statistical estimate of the validity through a correlation. A third provides only a gross statistical estimate. In this section we shall discuss the six validity procedures in increasing order of strength, considering first the data-free procedures.

Face Validity

The weakest procedure is called *face validity*. This claim for the validity of an instrument is based upon a superficial examination of the nature of the instrument, that is, the face of the instrument. Thus, referring again to the 100-item survey of teacher attitude toward administrators, if we wished to defend the face validity of this instrument we would argue that all 100 items, as we read them, refer to different aspects of teacher-principal relationships and interactions. Therefore, on the surface at least, it seems sensible to believe that this instrument measures teacher attitude toward principals.

This should strike the reader as a weak argument presenting little evidence for the validity of the instrument. It *is* both weak and little evidence. The instrument might also measure the positiveness or negativeness of the most recent hour in school. The teacher who in that hour had a difficult class, a visit from an angry parent, and a disappointment when a film she expected did not arrive may express this negative feeling through the instrument even though she may have a generally positive appraisal of principals at other times. The opposite might also be true. A teacher who had an exciting class, and heard some good news from an associate with whom she owns stock may carry this over as she completes the instrument, despite a generally unfavorable impression of principals. Lacking data, the face validity argument can never answer this objection or any objection. It rests solely on the defense that the instrument measures what it looks like it should measure.

Another serious objection to the face validity approach is that it tries to defend the fact that the instrument is valid in an either-or sense, which is in itself a distortion since validity is a characteristic which an instrument possesses to some degree or other, and does not either have or have not. This is a limitation of the next two techniques we shall discuss as well, but it is seen in its most severe form with face validity. Researchers can offer us no estimate of the extent to which an instrument has face validity corresponding to what the correlation squared tells us about the reliability. All they can say is that "on the face of it, the instrument looks like it is measuring what it is supposed to measure."

Of course there are instances in which the face validity argument holds better than others. These instances are similar to the circumstances under which test-retest reliability is appropriate: when the data being sought are relatively fixed and finite. Thus if we were developing the test referred to earlier, of ability to handle fractional computations, the fact that all of the items involved fractional computations would be the substance of the face validity argument and would have considerable weight. It seems logical to believe that this test measures ability to handle fractional computations, and it is probable that, if it measures anything, that is what it measures.

Which brings us to the final caution about face validity: It does not deal directly with the critical question of whether or not the instrument measures *anything*. Because this technique produces no data the researcher is unable to provide us with any evidence that the instrument actually does function, much less evidence that it functions in the desired way.

Content Validity

Next in strength is the procedure called *content validity*. There are important distinctions possible between face and content validity, and the careful researcher should be alert to them. For many data-gathering procedures, such as questionnaires and interview guides, content validity is the strongest technique available to the researcher. Fortunately, then, content validity is stronger than face validity, although it too is data-free and relies on an either-or judgment. True content validity argues that the instrument measures what it seeks or purports to measure because there was a rational, and ideally an empirical, basis to the selection of the actual content.

Another way of conceptualizing content validity is to consider it an estimate of the representativeness of the content of the instrument as a sample of all possible content. No questionnaire has every possible question but only a sample of questions. Similarly, no test contains every possible question, no checklist every possible option. Considering content validity this way raises the question of how representative the sample of content which the instrument includes is of the total population, and even possibly of the total universe. This is a two-fold problem, the issue being not only what *is* asked but what *is not*. In other words, what areas of information does the research instrument include and what does it omit?

The minimal consideration a researcher should pay to this characteristic is to demonstrate, through his knowledge of the literature, and/or the breadth of his own experience, that he does know the universe or population of content, and that the instrument has been selected to represent either the population or universe. This means in his description of the instrument the researcher should indicate the major areas of this problem, describe how closely he has covered all the major areas, how many items he has devoted to each area, and why the proportion of items devoted to each area seems sensible in terms of the relative importance of the area.

For example, a defense of the content validity of the teacher attitude survey might be as follows. After reading the literature on teacher attitudes toward principals and particularly after looking at previous research studies we have identified five different general areas of concern in the literature: (1) the principal's interest in and concern for teacher welfare; (2) the principal's efficiency and ability; (3) his interpersonal relationships; (4) his ethics; and (5) his personal appearance and personality. Therefore the attitude survey has been developed to include these five areas. Moreover, since the previous research studies indicated that efficiency and ability, and concern for welfare were the two most important areas, more items on the new instrument are devoted to these areas than to any other. Finally, we would like to be able to refer to some studies which collected free-response data from teachers as to the specific nature of satisfactions and dissatisfactions in each of the five areas, so that we could defend the inclusion of the specific items. This step is so critical to the content validity argument that if we want to use this argument we should collect these free-response data in a pilot study if they are not available from the literature.

Notice that we could then present the rationale for the areas covered in the instrument, the proportion of items devoted to each area, and the nature of the specific items. This would be a strong case for the content validity of the instrument and far stronger than the face validity argument. Nevertheless, it would still be open to the same qualms expressed earlier. For despite this elaborate effort to know what should go into the instrument, it still may be that it really does not measure attitude toward principals at all but instead measures the positiveness or negativeness of the teacher's immediately preceding hour in school.

Validity Estimates Based upon Data: The Need for a Criterion

There are four procedures which actually do produce an empirical basis for estimating the validity of the instrument: construct validity, concurrent validity, congruent validity, and predictive validity. Of the four, construct validity provides the weakest statistical data, for it is a statistical extension of the either-or argument of content validity. The statistics used are the statistics of difference, like the t test, and so do not provide the estimate we would prefer of the *extent* to which the instrument is valid. In contrast concurrent, congruent, and predictive validity express validity in a correlation, and so provide an estimate of extent.

All of these procedures to produce the statistical estimate of validity require the researcher to have available some other measure for the variable under study. In this way he can relate the judgments he obtains on the new instrument to the judgments obtained on the other measure, or criterion. Thus, if we wished to obtain some statistical estimate of the validity of the 100-item survey of teacher attitudes toward principals we would need some other measure of teacher attitude or some different criterion to decide which teachers had positive attitudes and which had negative attitudes. This necessity to have an already existing criterion or alternative measure available before validity can be estimated statistically is the reason we see the statistical estimates of validity in the literature relatively seldom. The simple and unhappy truth is that in the social disciplines we do not have very many existing measures or criteria of sufficient relevance, reliability, and validity in their own right for researchers to be willing to use them as the basis for estimating the validity of a new instrument. For unless a criterion is available which in itself is a reliable and valid measure of the characteristics under study, then the effort to obtain a statistical estimate of the validity of a new instrument is only an academic exercise and provides no meaningful evidence of validity.

This is particularly true in doctoral dissertations in the social disciplines. University doctoral committees have traditionally encouraged students to present some statistical evidence of validity of instruments developed for their studies. Where no meaningful criterion measures exist the student is in the position of having first to concoct a criterion measure, then show that the measure he desires to use is related to this concocted criterion. That is not the criterion we are talking about here when we speak of statistical estimates of validity; we mean estimates based on an already existing measure of demonstrated validity. If there are no such measures, then content or face validity are preferable to concocted criteria.

There is one last general point to note before we consider these statistical approaches separately. When a researcher offers some statistical estimate of the validity of his instrument, by showing how it is related to a criterion, it is relevant to ask why he used the new measure and not the pre-existing criterion. It may be that the new instrument is of a different kind (that is, a paper-and-pencil group instrument instead of an individual test), or it may be that although it is the same kind of measure as the pre-existing instrument, the new one has advantages like speed of administration. Whatever the reason, we should expect to make clear to the reader why we chose to develop a new instrument when we felt a measure was already available of sufficient stature to use as a criterion against which to evaluate the new instrument. Now let us consider the procedures.

CONSTRUCT VALIDITY   Construct validity is a statistical extension of content validity and in some texts is discussed with it. However, it can be developed to yield some statistical estimate of the measure under study, and so here is considered separately. It is defined as the ability of the instrument to distinguish between groups known to behave differently on the variable or construct under study. Procedurally, determining construct validity has two stages. The first stage is to use the criterion to identify two groups who differ on the construct our new instrument seeks to measure. The second stage is to administer the instrument to these two groups and determine if they differ significantly on the new instrument as well. If they do, then we have some data on which to defend the validity of the new instrument. There are two sources for the construct or criterion on which the groups can be said to differ. One source is overtly relevant behavior. Let us assume we formed two groups of teachers, one which had been complaining to the superintendent about the administration and seeking to obtain a new principal, the other which had praised the principal and wanted him to remain. Overtly these groups can sensibly be considered to be different in behaviors directly related to attitudes to the principal. Therefore they would be expected to differ on the instrument for the attitude survey, with the laudatory teachers significantly more positive than the critical teachers. If after administration of the instrument to the two groups we actually found such differences, we would advance this as evidence of the construct validity of the instrument.

A frequent parallel to this behavioral basis for construct validity is the development of the groups to be tested on the basis of indirectly related behavior. In the teacher attitude example let us assume we had no way of knowing how teachers felt about the principal, but did know which teachers had asked to transfer to another school for the coming school year and which had elected to remain. We might argue that here was a behavioral criterion on which we could develop two different groups for validating the survey of attitude toward principals, expecting that the group wanting to transfer would have attitudes more negative toward the principal than the teachers who had elected to remain with him. But before using an indirect behavioral criterion the researcher should be certain that the construct for which he is using it is the most relevant explanation of the behavior. In this example the researcher would have to rule out that the teachers seeking transfer had not themselves moved so that the school was no longer convenient, or that they were not transferring to a school with more elaborate facilities and equipment in their content fields, or to teach a grade they preferred to teach. The reason this must be done in advance of using the criterion is that once he uses it the researcher cannot reject the data if they come out unfavorable to the validity. In other words he cannot reject an unfavorable estimate of construct validity by noting that the criterion was probably wrong! If he uses it, he is committed to accepting the data, and so the time to think through these indirect criteria is *before* committing the validity of the instrument into their hands.

There is a final point to which we should be alert concerning construct validity data as evidence that an instrument does measure what it is intended to measure. The data themselves, as the data in the illustrations above would, always show a difference between two groups, and moreover, often two deliberately extreme groups. Thus, construct validity is at best evidence that at a gross level the instrument measures what it seeks to measure. We should ask ourselves if this gross level of distinguishing relatively extreme groups is appropriate for the use to be made of the instrument or if it is to function (that is, be valid) at a finer level of measurement. If it is to be used at this gross level, then the construct validity argument is relevant. If it is to be used at the finer level, then it is not a fully satisfactory method of estimating validity.

CONCURRENT AND CONGRUENT VALIDITY   The next approaches to measuring validity we shall consider are *concurrent and congruent validity*, which are essentially the same. Procedurally these are the only ones of all of the approaches to validity that parallel the approaches to reliability. The researcher who offers concurrent or congruent validity presents correlational data to show that performance on his new instrument correlates with performance on some already existing and accepted measure of the characteristic under study. If the criterion being employed is of the same family as the new instrument (for example, validating the new attitude survey by correlating scores on it with scores on some existing survey of attitude to administration), this is considered congruent validity. If, instead, the criterion is a quite different kind of measure (for example, correlating scores on the new survey with the number of times the teacher has complained about the administration to the school representative of the teachers association), it is an example of concurrent validity.

The heart of the argument for congruent and concurrent validity is the relevance and validity of the criterion. There can be no compromising standards on this point: The criterion *must* be valid. This amounts to saying that we have little opportunity in the social disciplines for using concurrent or congruent validity because we have few instruments or criterion measures of demonstrated validity.

The one area in educational research where reasonably reliable, relevant, and valid criterion measures are available is the area of achievement testing. Here we run into the question noted earlier. If these measures exist, why develop a new one? Unless there is a sensible answer to this question, the researcher should consider using the existing measure. This question sometimes gives an odd aspect to congruent and concurrent validity in that test developers using it sometimes do not aspire to extremely high correlations, for these would raise the question of whether the new instrument measures anything the old and proven one does not. Therefore, they hope to obtain a correlation high enough to support the argument that the new instrument is measuring the same characteristic as the old one, but not so high as to rule out the possibility that it is providing anything more than the criterion instrument! In practice, researchers are seldom faced with this particular problem, and when they are they can usually defend the new instrument as simpler to administer, easier to score, or possessing some other similar practical advantage over the old one.

PREDICTIVE VALIDITY The last approach to validity, and, in a sense, the most powerful evidence for it, is *predictive validity*. This is also the least often seen in the research literature in the social disciplines, and in that respect education is no different. However, education is different in having a uniquely applicable set of conditions for predictive validity and for acquiring the data needed to estimate the extent to which an instrument has it.

The researcher offering predictive validity is arguing that he has used data obtained from his instrument to make predictions about the respondents, generally predictions about their future behavior in the area under study. He has then waited until sufficient time has elapsed for him to know whether or not those predictions came true and evaluated the extent to which he was correct. These data may be presented in a variety of ways, such as the correlation between actual and predicted scores, or the percentage of correct predictions, or the differences on the instrument between those who did and did not succeed in a particular situation. Thus, predictive validity can be offered as a correlation like concurrent validity, or in terms of differences like construct validity. But in this particular instance, when predictive validity is analogous to construct validity, the time-line is reversed. In construct validity the groups are formed on the basis of an already existing construct and then tested to see if they differ on the instrument. In this form of predictive validity, the groups are formed on the basis of the instrument and then watched to see if they behave differently at some future point in time.

To see how predictive validity works, let us assume that a researcher has completed a study of the relationship of selected psycho-social characteristics to success in college as measured by Graduate Record Examinations. As an outcome of this study he has developed a School Success Index, which he claims is a valid measure of probable success on Graduate Record Examinations. To obtain predictive validity he could administer this instrument to large numbers of entering freshmen and predict how well each will do on the Graduate Record Examination. He would then wait until these students take the examination and correlate his Success Index and Examination Scores.

Predictive validity is considered the ultimate test of the validity of an instrument when it provides a correlation with the direct behavioral criterion. Either the instrument does predict the behavior it is seeking to measure or it does not: This is the simple direct argument of predictive validity. But unlike the other measures of validity, this is a time-consuming enterprise, involving as it does the passage of time for the acquisition of the criterion behavioral data. These are the validity data to take most seriously, for they provide the most convincing evidence available of the validity of an instrument, provided of course they are positive data!

Education is a particularly fruitful field for predictive validity because of the frequency with which behavioral cycles occur and the availability of multiple respondents. For example, predictive validity for measures of pupil progress in academic achievement is relatively simple to acquire, and once data are collected and predictions made, the time periods for testing the predictions are relatively brief. Thus, annual measures are available for pupil progress and achievement. Moreover, if the predictive validity is not sufficiently high and the instrument needs revision, another group of children beginning the same instructional cycle is soon available for re-estimating the validity of the revised instrument. Thus, the educational researcher should consider the possibilities for obtaining predictive validity data for instruments as research into the quality of education and teaching develops in the next several years.

The Generalizability of Reliability and Validity

Until recently, texts in research and measurement discussed reliability and validity as if they were implicit characteristics of instruments, possessed by the instrument under any and all conditions appropriate to its use. This has led to the development of what are called *standardized* instruments for research and evaluation. These are instruments for which reliability and validity data have been collected and reported by the developers. Traditionally researchers wishing to use these instruments have reported the *original* reliability and validity data in their defense of the instruments and have not felt any personal or professional pressure to acquire their own reliability and validity data.

Recently, a contrary movement has begun which questions the generalizability of these characteristics and which raises questions at the following level: "If reliability data were collected in 1962 on this questionnaire from 743 students in eight colleges in three Midwestern states, do these data reflect the reliability of the questionnaire when you wish to use it for students in five schools in a Northeastern state? Or a Southwestern state? Or in 1969, on students in the original eight schools?"

Studies which have begun to test the generalizability of the characteristics have begun to find, unfortunately, that they are not generalizable. Studies have begun to appear which obtain new reliability data for previously accepted instruments. The new data are often significantly different from the original data. The implication of these studies is obvious. We should speak of the reliability of an instrument for a specific group of respondents, and demand that each researcher establish (or re-establish) the reliability and validity of any instrument he plans to use on groups like those for whom he intends to use it.

As this is discussed in the literature at present, there is agreement that validity is not a generalizable phenomenon and might vary from group to group. Therefore, it would need verification in each new study, and certainly in each study which uses as respondents a group different in some significant respect from the group for which the instrument was developed. There is less agreement on reliability, with some saying that it is still feasible to consider reliability a generalizable characteristic and others insisting that it, too, is a characteristic which is sensitive to the group on which the instrument is to be used. This author's feeling is that reliability is sensitive to changes in respondent group just as validity is. The only fully convincing defense for using "old" data on reliability or validity would be that the respondents of the current study do not differ in any significant respect from the respondents of the original study, and so it is sensible to consider the reliability and validity data as applicable.

It is hardly necessary to point out why researchers have been reluctant to accept this limitation on generalizability—it means a tremendous extra effort and a serious delay in time to stop and obtain their own data on these characteristics. It also means that the researcher opens himself to the danger that, once obtained, the data will not be sufficiently high, and so he will have still further delays in time as the instrument is revised and the characteristics re-estimated. If he simply accepts the reliability or validity data of some previous research, none of these problems arise. This problem is stressed here because it seems unrealistic to expect students to change practice in this area with any speed unless there is increased demand from the academic community to reinforce the pressure for change that is slowly growing in the research professions.

SENSITIVITY

The third characteristic we shall consider is sensitivity, defined as the ability of an instrument to make the discriminations required for the research problem. It is hoped that discussing this characteristic will alert researchers and educators to its existence, for it has been largely ignored in the social disciplines. It is a pity that it has been ignored since it is both critical and testable. It is critical in the sense that any study that seeks to test for change or difference must evaluate whether or not the hypothesized change or difference occurred. Inevitably this involves measurement. If change is detected, then there is no problem of sensitivity, for clearly the instruments were able to measure the change. However, if significant changes were not detected, then the sensitivity of the instrument comes to the fore, as the researcher and reader must consider which of two alternative explanations best accounts for the lack of difference: (1) that there really was none and the finding is correct; or (2) that there really was change but the instrument was too insensitive to detect it.

In some fields, such as astronomy or physics, the entire structure and theoretical systems have periodically been challenged as the sensitivity of measuring instruments improved. Similarly in psychiatry, the question of whether or not there are physiological concomitants of schizophrenia is being answered differently in 1969 than it was a few years earlier. The difference is due to recent studies of blood chemistry which have found differences between schizophrenics and nonschizophrenics even though the same studies done a few years earlier found and reported no differences. The difference in the studies? Improved and more sensitive measures.

The need for improved sensitivity has been recognized beyond the research field, as the editorial below from the *New York Times* illustrates.

> One of the most precise experiments in the history of science is to take place soon in an elaborately sheltered laboratory at the University of Maryland. It will attempt to verify a prediction implicit in equations the late Albert Einstein published nearly 50 years ago—namely, that in addition to the usual forces of gravity so familiar to us all, the universe is also permeated by gravitational waves obeying a different law of attraction and repulsion. If such gravitational waves exist, the influence they exert on objects on this planet is extremely minute. As a result, the experimenters seeking to detect these waves must use equipment capable of detecting motion over a distance less than 100th of the diameter of an atomic nucleus. Yet even this fantastic sensitivity may prove inadequate.
>
> All this points up the enormous dependence of modern science upon the ingenuity of instrument makers in pushing forward the limits or precision in measurement and detection. The electron microscope, for example, has already made routinely available to the biologist pictures of incredibly small viruses. Today astronomers can detect and analyze light and radio waves originating in stars billions of light-years away. Physicists and engineers can

measure and study phenomena taking place in a nanosecond—that is, a billionth of a second.

And yet, as the doubts about the outcome of the Maryland experiment indicate, even today's incredible precision is not enough to meet all needs. The pressure for greater sensitivity of measurement will continue with all the insistence of man's effort to learn more about the origins and potentialities of the universe.[6]

When it is said that the characteristic is testable, what is meant is that a researcher can go into a situation where there are known differences and test whether or not his instrument can detect these. In developing instruments, he should begin with gross differences, and if the instrument functions, proceed to work with increasingly smaller differences until the instrument no longer is able to make the discriminations. In this way he obtains some estimate of the minimum difference the instrument can detect.

The researcher who has not estimated the sensitivity of his data-collecting instruments should keep this characteristic in mind and not shut the door completely to the possibility that change took place and differences existed in studies where he found neither change nor difference. This is particularly true if the instruments involved were new, and of relatively low reliability and validity. This is the combination which breeds low sensitivity as well, and so if this combination produces a null finding, in the discussion consider the fact that sometime in the future some other researcher with a more sensitive instrument may very well find a significant change or difference.

Generalizability of Sensitivity

The movement to consider characteristics like reliability and validity as characteristics which must be considered in terms of the respondent groups also applies to sensitivity, although this has not been discussed in the literature, for few authors have considered it at all. But the same rules would hold for this characteristic, except that the issue does not involve the respondents as much as it does the program or method or treatment or whatever it is that is being measured. An instrument sensitive enough to detect change in program X is not necessarily sensitive enough to detect change in program Y.

[6]"Science and Measurement" (Editorial), *The New York Times,* September 30, 1963. © 1963 by The New York Times Company. Reprinted by permission.

APPROPRIATENESS

The consideration of reliability, validity, and sensitivity as characteristics which must be seen in terms of the relationship of instrument to respondent groups leads us to the next characteristic to consider, appropriateness, defined as the extent to which the respondent group can meet the demands imposed by the instrument.

Every research instrument makes demands upon the respondent varying from demanding an ability to read, to follow directions, to understand English, or to think symbolically (that is, by recognizing that an arrow means turn the page). These are not always appropriate demands, and researchers must recognize this as they select or develop a particular instrument for use in a particular study. Here is an area in which the professional practitioner may be as qualified or more qualified than the researcher in deciding whether or not the demands of a particular instrument are appropriate for a particular group of respondents. If they are not, then the findings are suspect, as they may reflect other aspects of behavior, like poor reading ability, and not the one studied.

Appropriateness is of particular concern in view of its relationship to and affect on the generalizability of validity data. It may be arguable whether validity data are ever generalizable, but if they are it is only when the instrument is as appropriate for the new respondents as it was for those from whom the validity data were obtained originally.

OBJECTIVITY

The next characteristic which we shall consider is objectivity. This is defined as the extent to which the data obtained are a function of what is being measured. Ideally, of course, instruments are completely objective. However, a wide variety of factors impede the realization of this ideal. For example, the interpersonal relationships in the research situation often affect objectivity. A researcher who stands before a group of potential respondents and explains how they are to complete an instrument affects them in certain ways. If the instrument permits this to be reflected in the data, there is a loss of objectivity.

Some techniques are particularly sensitive to the loss of objectivity. The face-to-face technique of questioning used in most interviewing is probably the most sensitive. There is ample research to indicate that variables like age, sex, race, and manner of dress of the interviewer all can affect the data obtained through face-to-face interviewing. In this sense, then, the objectivity of the data from this technique is always suspect, and researchers offering such data must be prepared to spell out the steps they took to maximize objectivity.

Another factor which affects objectivity is the extent to which the researcher plays an active role in the determination of the nature of the data. An observation guide is an instrument which illustrates this problem well. If the researcher must make judgments as to the nature of the behavior being observed as he fills out the guide, again objectivity is at issue. And again, the researcher should expect to spell out the steps he took to safeguard the objectivity of the data.

A third factor which can affect objectivity adversely, and in a particularly subtle way, is the nature of the instructions printed as part of paper-and-pencil instruments. Instructions should provide the necessary information needed to know how to complete the instrument, but should not suggest the content of the response in any way. In preparing instructions, we should be particularly careful in the use of examples of the kinds of responses expected. This is a perfectly acceptable research technique, particularly when the impersonal contact is used and the researcher tries to be as clear as possible in his directions. However, research done by the author, and that done by many others, has shown that we obtain a disproportionate share of responses similar to the examples given. The simplest way out of this dilemma is to give the examples in the directions from a content area other than the one in which the respondent is expected to answer. In this way he sees an illustration of the kind of response we want, but does not obtain a model answer which he can imitate or paraphrase.

Unlike reliability or validity, there is no formal or statistical technique for estimating objectivity. Like appropriateness, it is a judgment which the researcher must make as he evaluates the research situation, the directions, and the nature of the instrument.

FEASIBILITY

Another important characteristic of instruments, particularly for students, is feasibility. As a criterion, feasibility includes three aspects of instrumentation: skills, cost, and time. Skills refer to the skills required to develop and use the instrument and analyze the data obtained; cost refers to the financial outlay involved; and time refers to how long would be required to administer the instrument and analyze the data.

The reader should recognize that there is some distortion involved in talking about this feasibility criterion in the context of instruments, for it is not instruments which differ in feasibility, but rather the data-gathering methods and techniques which they exemplify. However, students and professional researchers alike typically think about feasibility in terms of instrumentation, and so this question will be considered briefly here, and considered again in the chapters on method and technique. The distinction in the two discussions will be that here we shall consider the feasibility of using the various instruments in the sense of collecting and analyzing the data obtained. The concern with developing instruments and analyzing data will be delayed for the chapters involving method and technique.

Instruments differ dramatically in the skill required to use them. At one extreme are the available standardized instruments, such as group achievement tests in content areas like reading, arithmetic, and science. Here the instrument is fully developed and comes equipped with standardized instructions for administration. The skills required are the ability to read these instructions effectively while maintaining reasonable standards of control and quiet for the children taking the test. These are important skills, but also skills which graduate students can acquire with a little practice. Closely allied to this end of the continuum of skill demands are the nonstandard group paper-and-pencil instruments like the questionnaire, check list, or critical incident blank. Here the directions need to be developed, but this, too, is not a complex task. Once it is accomplished, the skills of administration are the same as for testing: reading effectively and controlling the group.

More difficult are the instruments which require the administrator to pace the group through the instrument. Many of the group instruments for children in the lower elementary grades involve this. Under these conditions, the test administration skills become more complex, for now the administrator must pace without providing cues, keep the entire group working, and provide all children with an opportunity to respond without violating the time limits for the test. Difficulties increase as we move on to instruments such as interview guides or individual tests where the interaction between respondent and research data gatherer is in a one-to-one relationship. Note that the research data gatherer's role has not changed. It is still to transmit questions and obtain responses without providing cues as to the appropriate response. But the nature of the interaction makes this passive transmittal role far more difficult to achieve, and thus requires a higher level of skill to achieve.

An entirely different kind of skill is required for those instruments in which the data gatherer has a more responsible role than the passive transmittal of instructions and questions. Using observation guides, for example, requires knowledge of the dynamics to be observed as well as knowledge of how these appear in behavior. If our task is to observe the frequency of overt aggression in a group of nursery school children, we need to know how overt aggression is manifested in nursery school children. Use of observation guides also requires the ability to record what is seen objectively, without our own value judgments intruding. Thus, while we can be assured that we can readily acquire the skills needed to administer objective tests of achievement, it is not possible to know how long it will take to become a reliable and valid observer of behavior.

Cost is a real concern to the student who is financing a research project out of his own pocket. In the social disciplines, it is less critical than it was as late as 1960, for increasing amounts of money became available in the 1960s to support student research, particularly at the doctoral level. While these funds do not approach the sums available in the physical sciences, they are still significantly higher than the negligible amounts available earlier. So the first point to consider in looking at the cost criterion is the possibility that some support can be obtained for the proposed project. In estimating costs we should consider the nature of the instrument, the process of reproduction desired, and the way in which it will reach the respondents and be returned to us. The easiest estimates to make are those for purchasing standardized instruments. Here we have a price list and can precisely estimate what it will cost. More difficult to estimate are the costs involved in reproducing our own instruments, that is, a questionnaire or interview guide. If the instrument is one we or our assistants will fill out, and which the respondent will not see, then it is perfectly sensible to use inexpensive methods for reproduction like mimeographing. However, if the instrument is one which the respondent is to be asked to complete, then we should consider the merits of more formal methods of reproduction like photo-offset printing. This is particularly true if the instrument is to be sent to a professional group. Here the initial visual impact may be critical in determining if the instrument is immediately cast aside as another in the endless string of appeals for data, or if it will be examined seriously. Printing an instrument suggests to the recipient that we were sufficiently involved in the project to go to this expense. This often has a subtle influence on whether or not he will complete it. Another element of cost which we must absorb is the expense involved in returning a mailed instrument. A stamped, self-addressed envelope must be included with any instrument given to respondents with instructions to return it by mail.

This use of printing and providing return envelopes illustrates the most difficult aspect of the cost criterion in studies in which the respondents must voluntarily return the data-gathering instrument: Every step we take to maximize the rate of return will increase costs, often dramatically increase them. For example, one effective technique for increasing returns is to provide a second copy of the instrument so that the respondent can make a carbon copy for his own record and use as he completes the original instrument for us. This increases our printing costs, and mailing costs as well, if the instrument reaches the respondent through the mail. Similarly, offering respondents a summary of the results of the study, if they participate, is a good device to increase participation. But again this increases costs. As a matter of professional practice, the author believes that unless a study is done properly it should not be done. This means that we should design a study within our limits of feasible costs, so that we can do it thoroughly and properly. It is better to plan a limited study and do it properly than to plan a more extensive study and cut several elements out to bring it within a budget.

The final aspect of feasibility is the question of time required to administer the instrument. This involves the respondent as well as the researcher, for in most research we do not have unlimited access to the respondents. Thus, in evaluating the instrument in its developmental stages we should obtain some estimate of how long it takes to complete, and how much of the respondent's time we will have available. An instrument can meet all the other criteria we have discussed, but if it requires two hours to complete when we have only one hour available to us, it will serve no function. In this context remember that estimates of reliability and validity obtained for a total instrument do not apply to some arbitrarily reduced version to meet a time demand. Thus, it is important to consider this aspect of feasibility early in the thinking about instruments.

ETHICAL STANDARDS

The last characteristic we shall consider is difficult to label, but it concerns the extent to which the instrument and its accompanying data-collection process meet acceptable ethical standards. This characteristic raises the issue of the rights of respondents as human beings, the responsibility of the researcher to treat respondents as human beings, and when they are in his own field, to respond to their needs as fellow professionals.

This means that an ethical instrument meets the following six conditions.

1. The respondent is told the purpose of the research and the use to be made of the data he is being asked to furnish. He is equally entitled to

decide for himself whether or not he wishes to provide data for this purpose and use. There are no exceptions to this basic first requirement of ethical research. Captive audiences should play no role in research in the social disciplines. Instances in recent years in which hospitalized patients were participants in research projects without ever having been informed of this have created considerable stir in the public press, and well they should. And finally, in the mid-1960s a comparable stir in professional circles has been aroused by the frequent use of captive audiences of students to furnish data in education and psychology. For this, too, violates this basic principle, that ethical research is conducted with respondents who have willingly agreed to participate with full knowledge of what use is to be made of the data.

This point also means that an ethical conflict results when instruments or data-gathering procedures are used where the respondent is unaware that data are being collected. This is an issue with many sides, and the very real argument can be advanced that if only informed respondents are to be used, certain types of data cannot be collected. This author is perfectly willing to pay that price. That others are not is reflected in a book published in 1966[7] in which a variety of techniques for collecting data without this awareness are detailed. In the preface the authors recognize but choose to ignore the ethical issue, saying, "In presenting these novel methods, we have purposely avoided consideration of the ethical issues which they raise. We have done so because we feel this is a matter for separate consideration."[8] In the view of the author of this book, it is impossible to divorce the ethical aspects of instrumentation from the instrument, which is why this discussion has been placed in this chapter.

2. Allied to this is the second condition, that respondents know the nature of the instrument and the research conditions, to as great an extent as possible, *prior* to the data collection. Here it is recognized that there are legitimate instances in which the researcher cannot be fully candid without destroying the validity or objectivity of the instrument. Where this knowledge would affect validity or objectivity of the data, then it is provided as soon as possible after the data collection. But under this circumstance the researcher does not lie to the respondents by giving them spurious information, but instead tells them he cannot let them know the nature of research, as it might affect the data. This author knows of no evidence to justify lying to respondents about the nature of research. Personal experience, and that of several colleagues, has been that people

[7]Eugene J. Webb, Donald T. Campbell, Richard D. Schwartz, and Lee Sechrest, *Unobtrusive Measures: Nonreactive Research in the Social Sciences* (Skokie, Ill.: Rand McNally & Company, 1966).
[8]Webb and others, *Unobtrusive Measures:* . . . .

understand our inability to inform them fully about the nature of a project or of an instrument if we frankly tell why we cannot so inform them.

3. The fact of participation does not have any unpleasant effects on the respondents or their setting. Researchers often seem to ignore the fact that active participation in a research project, even on the purely verbal level, may arouse feelings, stir memories, or force perceptions which otherwise would not have occurred. When there is some risk of this the researcher should be willing to establish whatever conditions are needed to remedy the situation. This is why explanation of the nature of the research is critical, so that respondents can determine if participation will involve them in situations they would prefer to avoid. But it is not just the actual respondent who is involved in this, the entire setting must also be considered. For example, a researcher entering a school to do the study of teacher satisfaction and dissatisfaction with the principal may find that the teachers are perfectly willing to respond, and so feel that he has no unpleasant after-effects about which to be concerned. But what about the possibility that after being asked to recall unpleasant situations involving the principal, the teachers are left with a more hostile perception of him than they had before completing the instrument? It may then be that the principal walks into hostile interpersonal situations which he is at a loss to understand. The ethical researcher would anticipate this, and alert the principal to this possible after-effect. If he is, nevertheless, willing to participate, the researcher should discuss with him possible actions to counter it.

One specific application of this general point occurs when the research design calls for engendering unpleasant psychological states such as anxiety, fear, or guilt. Here the researcher faces a more complex ethical issue, for there is no assurance that such states, once engendered experimentally, can be alleviated by simply informing the respondents that it was all false and done purely for research purposes. Instead the researcher must first face the question of whether he has any right to engender such states at all, for any purpose, and whether this type of experimental manipulation of human beings violates basic human rights. Minimally, the researcher must meet the responsibility imposed by the first condition, that the respondents be fully informed that the study in which they are being asked to participate involves manipulating of psychological climate, and informed sufficiently fully so that if they consent, this can be considered an informed consent. This becomes difficult with children, who cannot legally be considered able to consent, and so here parental permission comes into the picture.

It is astonishing how long researchers in education and psychology were able to abuse this particular ethical consideration. It was not until 1966 that the Congress became sufficiently concerned to insist that the United

States Public Health Service institute regulations which made it possible to supervise the care with which researchers were considering the rights of human subjects. It is a profound criticism of researchers in both education and psychology that the intra-disciplinary voices objecting to some of the abuses and indignities to which people were subjected in the name of research were so few and so ineffectual that it required legislative action for the nature of the problem to be recognized. Now that it has been recognized, as this book is written a bandwagon effect is already noticeable. Many organizations are expressing appropriate horror at some of the excesses, even though in some instances, in earlier years, these same organizations published articles in their journals reporting these same studies with little criticism or comment!

It also seems clear as this is written that the typical pendulum effect will take place, in which restriction will be piled upon restriction until perfectly ethical and potentially significant research will be hindered or stopped along with the unethical research which should have been stopped years ago. However, if this is the price which social research must pay to restore its adherence to simple standards of respect for human dignity and the right of a person to decide for himself if he wishes to be exposed to what the researcher has in mind for him, then this author feels that the price is well worth paying.

4. Respondents are entitled to have their confidence respected. They should be fully informed as to the nature of the identification of individuals and institutions which will be possible as well as the extent to which individuals and institutions will be identified in reports of the research. This information should be provided prior to the respondent's decision about participation, so that he can use this in making that decision. Whatever is told the respondent about identification should be rigidly adhered to.

This may seem like an unnecessary condition, and yet it is one which is frequently violated, specifically when respondents are told that they are answering anonymously in situations when the researcher actually does know who each individual respondent is. It would seem a basic expectation for a researcher to tell the truth to his respondents. Yet we find a variety of studies reported in the literature in which instruments were precoded in subtle and ingenious ways to enable the researcher to know specifically which respondent completed each instrument although respondents were told they would be anonymous. One study known to the author sent out a questionnaire by mail including a stamped, self-addressed envelope for "the convenience" of the respondent in returning the questionnaire. By using a wide variety of commemorative stamps and placing them at different distances from the top and right-hand side of the return envelope, the researcher was able to identify, by name, every respondent!

Why do researchers lie about anonymity? Generally for a combination of three reasons: First, they fear that people will be less likely to respond at all if they believe that they are known by name to the researcher; sceond, they feel that those who do respond will be less frank and honest than if they were anonymous; third, the researcher often wishes to do additional analyses of the data using information he already has about the respondents, but which he could not do if they were not identifiable by name. Therefore he decides that he can have all advantages by telling the respondent that he will be anonymous while at the same time using some of the precoding devices to enable him to know who each respondent is and so do the analyses he wishes to do. There has been no particular outcry against this practice by the professions. In fact, devices are offered more and more widely which will expedite the process.

This author objects to the procedure on ethical grounds, for to him it is simple lying to tell a respondent that we will not know who is who when in fact we will. The author recognizes that following this procedure rigidly means that some types of data analysis are lost to research. For example, a few years ago the author directed a study designed to identify satisfying and stressful experiences reported by nursing students as they progressed through school. Had we known which response was related by each student, we could have done a wide variety of substudies, such as comparing the types of satisfactions and stresses reported by students who ultimately dropped out of school to those reported by students who remained in school. We might have answered such questions as whether or not students who dropped out had some unique perceptions of the satisfaction and stress in the first months in nursing school to which guidance counselors or instructors might be alerted. Thus, they could possibly recognize early a girl who was a potential drop-out, and take appropriate action.

Yet to do this we would have had to be able to know which responses were written by which students. We feared that if the students did not believe they were anonymous, they might not describe situations frankly and fully and might also be more selective in choosing situations to describe. We were faced then with three choices: (1) to let the students remain anonymous and lose the possibility of any analyses based on the records of specific individuals; (2) to tell the students they were anonymous but precode the material in some way so that we would know who was who; or (3) to use some coding device selected by students which would lose the personal identification but give us the ability to place all of the material written by any one student together, so that we could follow her experiences through the year.

We told the students they were anonymous and we meant it, so we sacrificed all possibility of analysis based on personal identification. We tried to save some analyses by the self-selected coding device, but too large a proportion of students forgot these code numbers from one data collection to another, and even these analyses were lost. Loss of data and possible analyses is a most unpleasant choice for a researcher to have to make, but maintaining the conditions necessary to obtain the critical research data and also maintaining ethical standards are more important. In short, if the choice comes to giving up data or lying, researchers should give up the data.

This means that some studies as well as some analyses will not be done, but this price is worth paying in preferences to seeing researchers, who should be committed to truth, lying to respondents.

5. The instrument and the research situation do not require that the respondent behave in an unprofessional way. By this is meant that the instrument does not request information which the respondent would not be expected to furnish under ordinary circumstances, or that the research situation does not demand behavior which ordinarily the respondent would not be expected or even permitted to display. In its simplest terms it means that a professional is expected to function under professional standards and do his best at all times. Research is no excuse to deviate from these standards.

6. The research situation permits the respondent to profit maximally from the fact of participation. The respondent should learn whatever there is to learn from the research, and the researcher should recognize his obligation to the respondent in this regard. For example, if the data themselves are of value to the respondent, he is entitled to a copy of the data. As noted earlier in the discussion on feasibility, a simple way to achieve this in paper-and-pencil instruments is to include a copy for the respondent to retain. Another simple expectation for the research respondent is to be furnished a summary of the data after they are analyzed. This need not involve any violation of anonymity. All that is required is for the researcher to include a separate postcard which the respondent returns with his name and address if he wishes a summary of results. In this way, instead of research participation being a one-way street going from respondent to researcher only, it becomes a two-way street with a return flow from researcher to respondent.

AN OVERVIEW OF INSTRUMENT DEVELOPMENT

To conclude this discussion of the characteristics of instruments, let us outline the entire process of instrument development briefly and indicate where each characteristic belongs. The process begins with previous research or the analysis of the research situation which forms the foundation of the new instrument and from which its content is derived. If there is no relevant previous research or situational analysis, then the researcher himself is obligated to conduct sufficient pilot studies so that the combination of the pilot data and his and others' experience forms a sensible foundation for the content of the instrument. It is at this point that the characteristics of content and face validity are considered. For content validity particularly, data are needed on which to base the judgment of the representativeness of the sample of content within the instrument.

With a prototype of the instrument available, it becomes possible to try it out on sample respondents similar to those who will ultimately be the respondents of the research. At this point it is possible to estimate the appropriateness of the instrument and its objectivity, and in some instances the sensitivity as well. This is also the point at which the researcher obtains a first estimate of the reliability, typically through the odd-even procedure. Unless success has been remarkable, this first trial is followed by revisions and refinement, and the revised instrument is tried out again. This is the point at which the researcher hopefully obtains his final reliability and validity data. Any of the reliability techniques can be used at this point, as can construct, congruent, or concurrent validity.

Should all of the feedback from these efforts be positive, the researcher is then ready to use the instrument by establishing an ethical set of circumstances for the data collection. It would also be at this point that he would use the instrument to make some predictions about the respondents, to serve ultimately as the basis of an estimate of its predictive validity.

PART III

The Process
of Data Collection

Chapter 13

LEVELS OF RESEARCH

The next foundational aspect of research which we shall consider before turning to the more formal methodological aspects is what we shall call the *levels of research*. This concept of level of research integrates the nature of the information the researcher is seeking with the way in which he seeks it, to delineate the different levels at which research can be done. As will be discussed in this chapter, the level of research has implications for data-collection method and technique as well as for data analysis and research reporting. Therefore the discussion of levels is placed here as the first of the methodological concepts.

For purposes of this discussion we have identified four different levels at which research can be conducted in the social disciplines. Three of the four levels will be considered *conscious levels,* the fourth, a *nonconscious level.* By conscious, we mean that we are seeking information of which the respondent is aware, that is, psychologically it is in his conscious. This is information he is capable of providing us if he wishes to. In contrast, we may seek data related to motivations, attitudes, or expectancies about which our respondent is unaware, that is, data not in his conscious. Thus, our respondent cannot provide these data directly even if he were willing, for he is not consciously aware of what they are. This aspect of research, then, would be the fourth, or nonconscious level.

CONSCIOUS LEVELS

Let us consider the three conscious levels first. They can be ranged along a continuum based on the depth of the research: (1) the *conscious-surface* level; (2) the *conscious-subsurface* level; and (3) the *conscious-depth* level. The three points along this continuum differ in the nature of the data they seek, in the types of questions they ask, in the relationship of question and answer, in the kinds of data they return, in the kinds of analyses they permit, in the kinds of generalizations they permit, and most basically in the nature of the conceptualization of the interaction of researcher and respondent.

Conscious-Surface

The simplest level at which to do research is the *conscious-surface* level. This level is one in which the information we seek is fixed, unchanging and highly specific, and close to the surface of an individual's thinking. It is information for which there is a one-to-one relationship between question and answer, that is, when each specific question is asked each respondent there is only one answer true for him. This means that at this level we can usually provide our respondent with predetermined categories of answers from which to select. For example, when we seek to find out how many years of experience a person has had on a job, this is so structured a variable that after asking the question we can also provide alternative answers like

1. fewer than three years
2. between three and five years
3. between six and ten years
4. between eleven and twenty years
5. more than twenty years

and have our respondents check the one that applies.

The questions we ask at the conscious-surface level generally seek unthreatening, unchallenging information which has little overtone of personal involvement. Typical of information at this level are questions like address, age, years of experience, schools attended, degrees received, and work experience. While there are specific situations in which any of these pieces of information might be threatening (like asking "age" to some women), in the vast majority of research instances, they are not. Consequently people can and do respond to them quickly and without hesitation. This brings us to the second characteristic that distinguishes this level of research and makes it conscious-surface: The respondent has the information that we seek readily available at the "tip of his tongue," and is generally readily willing to impart it.

If we were to try to schematize this level of research, we could borrow a model from psychology and use the stimulus response paradigm. In this application, however, the stimulus is the researcher's question (Q) and the response is the respondent's answer (A). Thus, as illustrated in Figure 13-1, at the conscious-surface level of research, as the question (Q) is asked, the true answer (A_t) comes to the respondent's mind immediately and is stated (S_{A_t}) without any intervening hesitation.

	Respondent's Actions		
Researcher's action	Initial mental response	Second mental response	Actual response
Asks question	True answer comes to mind	None	States true answer

$Q \longrightarrow A_t \longrightarrow S_{A_t}$

Figure 13-1   Conceptualization of conscious-surface level of research.

Because the answer that comes to mind immediately becomes the stated answer, we can safely make the critical assumption in research in the social disciplines that the responses we obtain are honest and that the respondent has answered without any effort to distort.

While the nature of the conscious-surface level makes it sensible for the researcher to assume that the responses he receives are honest, it is more complex a matter to evaluate their accuracy. All that the model for this level assures is that the response is the association which the respondent has to the stimulus that is offered. It is perfectly possible, particularly when memory is involved in producing that association, for that first association to be wrong in some objective sense. Thus, the researcher must separately evaluate the likelihood that the data will be accurate at this first level by considering the extent to which the response is based on memory. The greater the extent to which memory is involved in producing the response (that is, the greater the length of time over which the respondent must travel to identify the response), the greater the possibility for error. But at the conscious-surface level this must be considered honest error, in the sense that this is how the respondent remembers the event or information.

The combination of specific questions and answers obtained quickly without hesitation, means that at the conscious-surface level a wide variety of material can be covered in a relatively brief period of time. Furthermore, the one-to-one correspondence between question and response is repeated in a one-to-one correspondence between the response and the data-analysis plan. In other words the response is analyzed directly for what it is—a "Yes" answer counted as one "Yes," age of 48 counted as one age 48 or one between 45 and 50. This specificity means that simple techniques of both data collection and of data analysis are possible, and data we obtain at the conscious-surface level are readily processable by electronic computing equipment. Therefore, this level of research is most appropriate when we are concerned with broad coverage of an area, and/or with obtaining data about populations. But it is not necessary to study populations, for a final virtue of the conscious-surface level is that it is one at which samples, even small samples, can provide useful and meaningful data. This is true because the data we seek are finite and fixed and generally with a clearly defined range. Therefore with proper sampling techniques we generally can identify the range of responses and their relative frequencies for the variables under study, with relatively small samples.[1]

The major problems of research at the conscious-surface level involve respondent participation and the use to which the data can be put. Because it is conducted at such a superficial level, the respondent seldom is involved either in the task or in the information provided. Therefore, we have to beware of boredom or complete lack of concern mitigating against completion of the task. Once surface data are obtained the most the researcher can do with those data is use them to describe the characteristics of groups studied. They are not useful for predicting group behavior. Nor do they tell us anything particularly significant about the individuals in the groups, and certainly provide no basis for predictions of individual behavior.

If group description will be sufficient for a research problem or question, the ease of the assumption of honesty and the high specificity of data collection and analysis make the conscious-surface level an ideal level of research for the beginner. The simpler data-gathering techniques such as questionnaires and check lists can be used at this level, and relatively little research experience or sophistication is needed to collect or analyze the data.

Conscious-Subsurface

The second conscious level of research is the *conscious-subsurface* level. This level is still "conscious" in the sense that the respondents have the

---

[1] As we noted in Chapter 11, the United States census then becomes a classic case of research unnecessarily huge in scope. Although seeking information essentially at the conscious-surface level, until 1950 the Census Bureau studied the entire population rather than sample.

information requested, are aware of it, and are able to produce it should they wish. It is subsurface rather than surface because the information requested is a bit more personal and involves the respondent more. Many questions at this level are as specific as those at the surface level, but the one-to-one relationship of question to answer no longer exists. At the subsurface level questions do not seek the fixed, unchanging kinds of information sought at the surface level but seek information that involves opinions, judgments, and commitments that are more than superficial, although not yet commitments in depth. This is the level at which opinion polls function, as do attitude and interest surveys. This type of information is not fixed and may drastically change for each respondent, often in the course of a brief period of time. This is one of the major problems public opinion polls have at election time—the changing nature of information they gather at the conscious-subsurface level.

If we were to apply the same model used above to the conscious-subsurface level it would appear as in Figure 13-2. Again as we ask the question (Q) the true answer (A_t) comes to the respondent's mind. However, the increased involvement this level implies for the respondent means that he is less likely to respond freely than he was at the surface level and may be reluctant to give some of the information requested.

Researcher's action	Respondent's Actions		
	Initial mental response	Second mental response	Actual response
Asks question	True answer comes to mind	Hesitates as alternatives are considered	Depends on circumstances

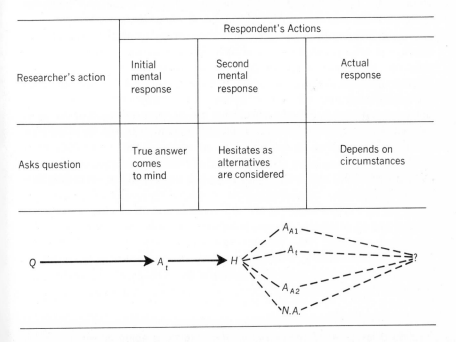

Figure 13-2 Conceptualization of conscious-subsurface level of research.

Therefore, once the answer comes to mind, what follows is hesitation (H) as the respondent decides whether to state that true answer (A_t) or state some alternative answer (A_A) or refuse to answer $(N.A.)$. Thus, having moved below the surface we have raised questions in the mind of the respondent as to whether or not he should utter the true answer. These doubts can vary along a continuum from slight to serious and obviously there is an inverse relationship between the seriousness of the doubt and the probability of obtaining the true answer.

The respondent's increased involvement at the subsurface compared to the surface level is a virtue in that it lessens the threat of boredom diminishing our yield of data, but is a problem in that it also weakens the confidence with which we can assume complete honesty in our respondents and complete accuracy in our responses.

The model above also points up the importance at this level of data-gathering techniques that maximize the probability of obtaining the true answer and of assuring the respondent that he can respond frankly. The model also cautions every researcher working at this level never to forget that the data obtained may be false. In view of this there is a corresponding increase both in the complexity of the techniques used and in the amount of experience and sophistication required by the researcher to work well. This is particularly true in terms of experience with the techniques for maximizing the likelihood of obtaining a truthful response and for estimating the extent to which the respondents have been truthful. Thus, instruments at this level require internal checks within an instrument in which the same information is sought by different questions. Finally, the subsurface level demands more attention to sampling, as the introduction of the alternative answer and equally important, the no answer, requires a large enough sample for the proportions of these to be estimated and for some idea of probable distribution of the no answers to be determined. Thus, at election time as we read the interpretations of political polls we notice that a great deal of concern is expressed about the "undecided" vote, and a variety of bases are developed for estimating how it will finally vote.

At the subsurface level we are still concerned with groups of people as groups and in describing group characteristics. Now we wish to be able to predict group behavior. We are still not able to predict or even to understand individuals, although we may be concerned with describing one or more subgroups within the main group.

Conscious-Depth

The third level, called the *conscious-depth* level, is again conscious in that the respondent knows the response desired and is capable of responding.

It gets down to depth in that the information sought is of a deeply personal nature, requires great personal involvement, and does not spring to the respondent's mind as the question is asked but must be thought through. This is the level of research where we seek evaluation and reaction and emotional response. It is the level where we try to learn information as profound as the respondent is capable of consciously communicating.

The complex and deeply personal nature of the information sought at the depth level means that it is not "on the tip of the tongue." The respondent must think about the question before he can determine the answer. But of course, he then might or might not want to provide that answer, just as in the subsurface level. Scanning the model of the depth level in Figure 13-3 we notice, therefore, that the question does not elicit an immediate answer, but instead triggers a period of hesitation and thought (HT) while the respondent thinks through several possible answers (A_{1-3}) to the true answer (A_t). When the true answer is reached, however, it is followed by a second period of hesitation. Now, as in the subsurface level, the respondent decides whether to give the true or an alternate answer or not to answer at all. It is the first hesitation, then, which distinguishes the depth level. Here for the first time we ask a

	Respondent's Actions		
Researcher's action	Initial mental response	Second mental response	Actual response
Asks question	Thinks through to answer	Hesitates as alternatives are considered	Depends on circumstances

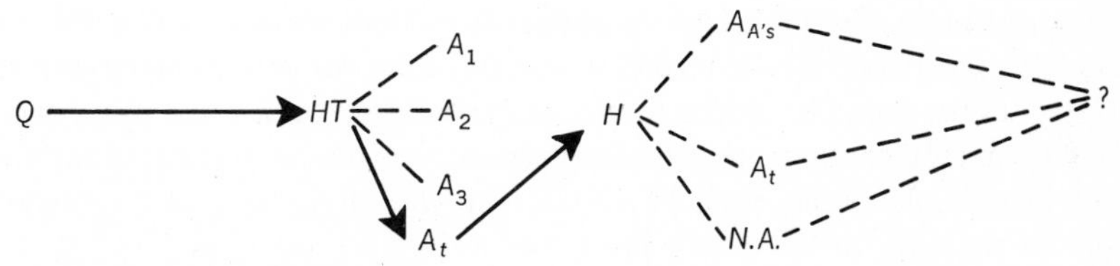

Figure 13-3 Conceptualization of depth level of research.

question to which no immediate answer comes to mind. Note that the respondent will be able to think through to the true answer because this is still a conscious level, and so by definition, the respondent *does* know the answer we seek.

To function at the depth level involves extremely complex problems of instrument development, data gathering, and data analysis. At this level we have left the realm of structured questions with neatly prestated categories of response. Instead we have moved to the semistructured question or stimulus which does little more than indicate to the respondent the area about which we want him to think and respond. "Why did you want to teach?" or "What satisfactions do you obtain from teaching?" typify the kinds of questions intended to elicit information at the depth level. The semistructured nature of the questions means that the data resulting are also semistructured, and so typically must be analyzed through the content analysis procedure.

In view of these complexities, the depth level is one which calls for sophisticated use of research techniques. It is not a level of questioning to which the beginner should aspire. Perhaps the best example of the kinds of problems involved in this level is the problem the researcher faces in trying to make certain that the respondent accepts a depth question at the depth level. People typically do not like being questioned at this level for research purposes. Thus, it is quite possible for the researcher to ask what is intended to be a profound deeply complex question and for the respondent to react to it at the surface or subsurface level, responding with a glib and immediate association rather than with the thoughtful consideration of alternative answers until the true answer is ultimately recognized. Thus, the researcher must creatively develop his questions and his ways of asking them to maximize the likelihood that the respondent will not or cannot take the surface or subsurface way out. To do this involves knowing our respondents well enough to anticipate the ways they might employ to avoid grappling with the intellectual and personal challenges of the depth level. For example, a colleague studying the motivations of teachers of mentally retarded children knew that if he asked the direct question, "Why did you become a teacher of mentally retarded children?" he would obtain the immediate response "to help children." He knew also from the speed with which response was obtained that it characterized the surface rather than the depth level. There was no initial hesitation while the respondent thought about alternatives nor the secondary hesitation while he thought about what he should say. To alter this and get respondents to function at the depth level, the researcher continued to ask this question but as soon as he obtained the answer, "to help children," he followed this up with "But why did you want to help *retarded* children?

After all, all teachers help children." He found that he seldom obtained an immediate answer to this second question. Instead the respondent's behavior characterized the depth level: There was the initial hesitation and thought as the answer was sought and the second hesitation as the response was evaluated.[2]

This kind of interaction between researcher and respondent is often necessary to assure that the depth level is achieved. It means that the techniques of individual interaction like interviewing are often required, and so sample sizes are often small in studies at this level. In fact, this is the level at which case studies are appropriately done, in which the sample is built up with units of single respondents studied in depth. This focus on the individual is carried over into the use made of depth data, for it is used to learn about the individual and to provide a basis for predicting individual behavior. Some researchers point to the difficulty we have in predicting individual behavior as evidence of the impossibility of conducting research in depth at this time. There is little doubt that it is difficult to do successfully. Moreover, as has been noted so often in this book, the weaknesses in instrumentation also add to the difficulty of successful functioning in depth. Despite these difficulties, this author believes that experienced and sophisticated researchers content to work with small samples of respondents do have the ability to conduct research at the depth level.

NONCONSCIOUS LEVEL

The fourth level of research is clearly distinguishable from the three discussed above in that it is asking questions at the conscious level but seeking information available only at the nonconscious level. This means that whatever the questions, the researcher's concern is with uncovering information about the motivations, feelings, or behaviors of which the respondent is not consciously aware. It is a level of question-asking which is necessarily indirect, for the specific response elicited is not the specific information we seek, rather it is used to provide us with the basis for an inference about the nonconscious level, which *is* what we seek. This, then, is the second major difference between conscious and nonconscious levels in research; that at the three conscious levels we are analyzing the direct response we obtain through our data gathering, while at the nonconscious level we are using the latent meaning of this response as the basis for an inference.

[2]The author is grateful to Dr. Stuart Wright for the illustration upon which this example is based.

To schematize the nonconscious level we need a more complex model than any to date. Figure 13-4 contains that model. First we conceptualize the researcher's interest in some dynamic aspect of the respondent's functioning (D), such as his motivations to become a teacher. Then to oversimplify the situation considerably, let us say we construct a stimulus (S) so that his response will provide us with the basis for inferring something about the dynamic.[3] The stimulus may bear some overt relationship to the dynamic, as would a question about the values in life he treasures most. Or it may bear no overt relationship at all, that is, be an ink blot. Most often it does not, for when it does not, then the respondent is less likely and less able to give us an alternate rather than the true response.

Notice that at the nonconscious level we assume, as we did at the conscious-surface and subsurface levels, that the stimulus does elicit an immediate true answer (A_t) (or association) in the respondent's mind. After this the respondent may hesitate (H) as he considers whether or not to state the true answer, state some alternative (A_A), or refuse to answer $(N.A.)$. To this point the model parallels the subsurface level, but at the nonconscious level we need move further. Remember, it is not the answer itself we seek but rather the inference about the dynamic that we can make on the basis of the answer. As the model indicates, however, a variety of possible inferences exists. Having obtained a true answer, we can make a correct inference (I_c) or incorrect inference (I_I). These same two possibilities exist when the respondent states an alternative answer which is not true. In short, the true answer may be the basis for a wrong inference, just as the false answer may be the basis for a correct inference. Hopefully of course, we believe that the highest probability is of making a correct inference after we have obtained a true answer!

The refusal to answer also provides the basis for either a correct or an incorrect inference about the respondent, or may lead to an alternative inference (I_A), particularly if it is accompanied by a refusal to answer other questions. The alternative inference would be about the respondent's hostility or concern or disinterest, but generally this refusal does not provide us with the basis for an inference about the dynamic under study.

Almost any unstructured data-gathering technique available in research can be used at this level. There are techniques using verbal stimuli, such as incomplete sentence blanks, and techniques using pictorial stimuli, such as the Thematic Apperception Test which uses ambiguous pictures, or the Rorschach Test which uses ink blots. Since the variety of possible stimuli is so vast, in this sense the nonconscious level may seem like the simplest

[3]The oversimplification is that we never seek to make this inference on the basis of any single piece of information but rather on the basis of a wide variety of information.

		Respondent's Actions			
Researcher's initial action	Researcher's second action	Initial mental response	Second mental response	Actual response	Researcher's final action
Identify dynamic of interest	Translates dynamic through theory into stimulus	Associates response or true answer to stimulus	Hesitates as alternatives are considered	Depends on circumstances	Makes inference back to dynamic

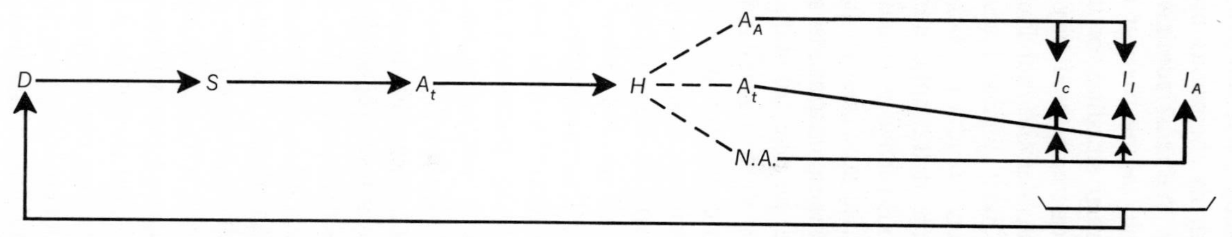

Figure 13-4 Conceptualization of nonconscious level of research.

level for data-gathering techniques. However, the chief requirement for technique at the nonconscious level is not that the technique be unstructured but that it elicit data which can be reliably used as the basis for inferences about the dynamic under study. The only way to learn this is through the laborious process of try-out, prediction, and testing against reality. We must administer the instrument, make an inference about the dynamic on the basis of the obtained data, and test this inference against the actual situation, or behavior of the individual. The demand that the technique have predictive validity and be able to provide data upon which inferences about individuals and individual behavior can be made makes it the most difficult level at which to function. Moreover, it requires the broadest breadth of background and experience in the researcher. For to function at the nonconscious level, he must not only know research but must also have a sound theoretical foundation in the discipline whose dynamics he wishes to study and be technically trained in the administration of these instruments and analysis of the data derived.

The purpose of data gathering at the nonconscious level is almost exclusively to understand and eventually to be able to predict individual behavior. The problems at this level are many and complex. The degree to which we can assume accuracy or honesty now depends on two factors— as always, on the degree to which the respondent has responded with his true feelings, and second, the degree to which the inferences we make are sound. This means that we have two points of uncertainty at the nonconscious level. The first uncertainty comes at the point where the respondent gives his response and the second at the point where we decide what he meant by that response. For example, if Johnny completes a sentence stem, "My teacher . . . ," by adding the words ". . . is pretty," we may ask one set of questions about how accurate and honest an expression of Johnny's true feelings about his teacher these few words are, or whether he feels this is the safe, tactful thing to say. If the researcher is willing to assume Johnny's response is accurate and so counts Johnny, on the strength of this response, in a category called "thinks teacher is a good teacher," we may also ask a set of questions about the accuracy of the inference by which Johnny's response is placed in that specific category. Because all data gathering at the nonconscious level is based on unstructured situations, it all falls prey to this second set of questions about the validity and reliability of the inferences and of the schema by which they were made.

This puts the greatest premium on our having a sound theoretical basis for the system under which we make the inferences. It means that one does not approach this level of research without such a theoretical basis. It should be recognized that it is always possible to create an unstructured stimulus, obtain responses, and make inferences, and thus claim correctly to be functioning at the nonconscious level. But there is sound nonconscious research and unsound nonconscious research, and what distinguishes the two is the soundness of the theoretical rationale by which the inferences are made.

In all three conscious levels we could do our data analysis without making inferences. In other words, we can say that 10 percent of our respondents were between twelve and fourteen years old, or that 45 percent say that they intend to vote for Candidate X, or even that 56 percent dislike their jobs because they think that the salaries are too low. While similarly descriptive statements can be made of data from projective type studies conducted at the nonconscious level, they have less meaning. To say that 10 percent of our pupils finished a cartoon showing a teacher talking to a pupil by having the teacher say, "Why didn't you hand in your homework?" is perfectly feasible but is not functioning at the nonconscious level. Nor does it utilize the unique characteristics of this level. If we gather our data at the nonconscious level, we do it to be able to say things like "43 percent of the students like school well enough to continue in school next year," that is, to make inferences about behavior on the basis of the data. If there is no necessity in the research for this type of inference, then the other levels are more appropriate ways of gathering descriptive data than the nonconscious level.

LEVELS FOR SPECIFIC RESEARCH PROJECT

Although the four levels of research have been discussed here separately, they can easily be combined within a single research study and even within a single data-gathering instrument. Thus it is perfectly possible to construct a questionnaire which includes questions at the surface and subsurface levels, and even to include questions seeking to reach the depth level. It is more difficult to combine the nonconscious level with the conscious levels, since the entire orientations are so different. In developing his plan for data gathering, the researcher should first consider the level at which the different pieces of information need to be collected. He must candidly appraise his own ability to achieve that level both in collecting the data and in analyzing the data. Then if he is considering working at the nonconscious level, he must also appraise the developmental state of the theories required for his inferences.

The result of all these appraisals is an awareness of the levels at which it will be possible for the individual researcher to function for a specific project. Given these insights, it is then possible to decide if a sufficiently appropriate level can be achieved for the research to be successfully completed.

Chapter 14
THE HISTORICAL APPROACH

The historical approach, as has been noted before, is past-oriented research which seeks to illuminate a question of current interest by an intensive study of material that already exists. The better known and more dramatic approach to historical research is that phase of it which seeks to discover material whose existence had not previously been known to recent generations. Thus, the discovery of the Dead Sea Scrolls made headlines far beyond the professions and disciplines involved. But while this and similar findings are undoubtedly exciting examples of historical research, the less exciting aspect is the more frequent and important: the reinterpretation of events in the light of the increased amount of information available. This is critical to realize in planning research using this approach, for good historical research is not simply a massive searching party, but rather a thorough study of all available material by an expert in the discipline, leading to new insights and conclusions.

The good historical researcher must be that rare person, expert enough to be able to encompass all of the known information and interrelate it and yet flexible enough to break the set of pre-existing notions so that he can see a *new* relationship or explanation or finding, if it exists in the data. This makes the historical approach a particularly difficult one to do well, for in most fields there is a negative correlation between experience and expertness on the one hand and flexibility and set-breaking ability on the other. Generally, the longer we work in an area the more committed (at a mental and psychological level) we become to the beliefs and presumed facts of the field. Therefore when some new discovery of importance is made we tend to attempt to incorporate this into our existing framework or belief system, even if it involves bending the walls considerably. It is the rare person who, after years of experience within a field and years of advocating and believing a particular point of view, can break with that point of view in the light of new material unearthed by historical research.

This is not to say that every discovery means a rewriting of the basic beliefs in every field. Many new discoveries expand and reinforce what is known and believed. It is to say that every major new historical discovery should stimulate a rethinking and reconsideration of what we think we know, and this willingness to rethink and reconsider characterizes the able historical researcher.

DEVELOPING DATA

Like the other research approaches, the historical approach is based on data. For the historical researcher, however, the problems involved in the use of data are unique. Because his data already exist and he has no ability to generate new data, he can only find them. Similarly, he has no ability to alter the form in which the data appear but can only accept them in the form in which he finds them. Thus the historical researcher in essence cannot control his data in the same sense the survey and experimental researcher can.

Not only does the historical researcher have no ability to create data, the fact that he must analyze what he finds without the ability to ask clarifying questions means he also has the problem of interpreting those data he has available. Later in this chapter we shall consider the different kinds of historical data and the techniques for evaluating them. Here let us note only that no piece of historical data interprets itself, and even thorough verbal statements need supplementary interpretation. Consider, for example, the apparent paradox of a group of slaveholders sitting down to write and sign a document like the Declaration of Independence, which declares among other "self-evident truths" that "all men are created equal." The historian today cannot interpret this statement in terms of the absolute meanings of the words or what they would mean today but must interpret them in the context of the time, trying to understand what they meant then. In other words he must interpret what was said in an effort to learn what was meant.

Thus interpretation is as basic a part of the process of historical data gathering as is the collection of the data itself. In fact, historical information does not become data until the researcher places it into some context relevant to the problem. Thus the historical researcher is faced with a double problem in his development of data. He lacks the basic elements of control necessary to produce data of a kind he wishes and in the form he wishes, and then must apply some frame of reference to the data he has if they are to be meaningful.

THE SAMPLING PROCESS

Perhaps the major problem in historical research is the lack of control that the researcher has over his data. Moreover a second severe problem, the possible nonrepresentativeness of the sample of data, is implied by the fact that the historical researcher can only work with data which already exist and either are known or which he discovers. These data almost certainly represent a twice selected sample, as illustrated in Figure 14-1 below. Experience in all fields has shown that at any one point in time the data which are known are only a sample of the data which actually exist. But these are only a portion of the total amount of relevant data, for in most instances more data once existed than have survived to the present. As noted in the figure, these stages are analogous to the stages of sampling with a universe, population, and sample. The historical researcher, like all researchers who utilize samples, must be concerned about the homogeneity of the conclusions he draws based on the data available to him (his sample) and the potential conclusions he would draw based upon all those data which exist (his population). But the historical researcher must also be concerned with the hypothetical conclusions based upon all the data which have ever existed (his universe).

This means that the good historical researcher will not only deal with and interpret what exists but will also take into account what factors

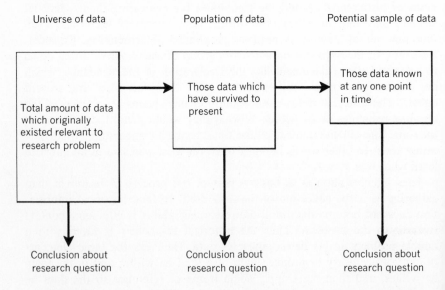

Figure 14-1   Conceptualization of sampling process in historical research.

might have determined which of the surviving data are known and which are unknown, or which data survived and which data did not. Putting this into sampling terms like those we discussed earlier, the historical researcher is concerned whether the data he has available with which to work can be considered a randomly selected sample of those data which exist or if they must be considered a biased sample. For example, the private papers of historical figures are often supressed by their own directive until some years after their death. Several American presidents have so limited access to their personal papers. When this happened, obviously the data available during the years that these data are suppressed cannot be considered a random selection of existing data.

Even more difficult is the researcher's problem of determining the character of the sample he has of all the data which once existed. Moreover, the further back in time the research goes, the more difficult this particular problem becomes. Deliberate destruction of historical data has occurred often enough in the recorded past in full public view for us to accept the fact that it undoubtedly has occurred innumerable times without public knowledge. And the laws of probability tell us that as we go further and further back in time, it becomes more and more likely that at some point, some individual or groups deliberately destroyed objects and records they found distasteful or inadvertently destroyed material they considered useless or were unable to store.[1]

There is one other aspect of the sampling process which is also critical in understanding historical research, and that is that the universe itself is unstable and may shift as the generations alter their perception of what data are relevant for any particular problem. For example, for many years historians operated without considering economic influences on historical events. When it was realized that this was an important omission, this expanded the entire perception of the "universe" of data relevant to understanding any specific historical problem, and brought a whole new set of questions as to the nature of the population and sample of economic data and the processes which brought *this* population and sample into being.

In education too, it is a relatively recent development to place educational developments and changes into their social, economic, and historical contexts. The psychological and sociological aspects of educational change were not considered part of the universe of fact and data of educational history as recently as the 1950s. As this book is written in the late 1960s, politics is just beginning to be included in the universe of

[1]Well-known examples of this destruction of data are the destruction of the library at Alexandria by Theodosius I in A.D. 391 and the destruction of ancient manuscripts during the Middle Ages.

information needed to understand educational events, and economics still is not. Yet both of the fields must be understood by the educational historian who in 2060 attempts to write the history of the first ten years of the Elementary and Secondary Education Act.

The problem of a shifting universe has another and more complex aspect. Even if the universe or elements of it, in an abstract sense, remain constant or static, over a period of generations the terms used to define that universe may have changed dramatically. The Language Study furnishes one obvious example, in the sense that "non–English-speaking" as a definitional concept would have no stability across different historical periods in education. But even more commonly used terms, which would seem stable on first glance, are similarly unstable: terms like "farm," "rural," "secondary school," or "immigration." All of these have been defined differently at different historical periods and in addition have had wide varieties of popular uses.

Thus the historical researcher has a more complex task than to find the historical references he seeks. He must almost translate these into some common set of concepts by knowing how each historical period defined and used the term. In short, he must become sufficiently well versed in the relevant definitions and standards of each historical period involved so that he can read the material of each period in its own terms. For example, the student developing a history of the American rural school must read and study with a constantly shifting definition of rural. He must not only know when and how the United States Census Bureau altered its numerical definition of rural, he must also know the historical periods sufficiently well to know when "rural" meant isolated from other human society with extremely limited communication, when it meant living in isolation but with telephone, regular mail, and the Sears catalogue, and when it meant living in communities with fewer than 5000 people but with television and within a 20-minute automobile ride of a huge shopping center with motion pictures and all of the latest products available. The "rural" school is a quite different school in each of these instances.

REINTERPRETATION

If we combine all of these elements—the unstable universe, the unknown nature of the process by which the population came into being or survived, and the often unknown extent to which the sample represents the population—we understand why history is constantly being reinterpreted. Any major restructuring of the universe, or new perception of the population, or new insight into existing data can demand reinterpretation of an event or series of events.

Because of this, historical research of the most intellectually challenging sort is available to the graduate student who may not have the time, resources, or freedom of movement to mount an historical research project which involves the search for previously unknown elements in the population. What he can do is take a fresh look at the validity of current interpretations of the history with which he is concerned to see if his fresh look will yield any new insights, interpretations, or hypotheses. For example, in 1966, the historian Seabury Colum Gilfallan, using only data and facts already available to the historical community, put forth an entirely new explanation of the decline of Rome.[2] This new hypothesis (simplified considerably) was based on long-known facts. One basic fact was that preceding the decline of Rome there occurred a selective decline in the birthrate, selective in that it occurred only among the aristocracy, who in essence did not reproduce themselves. Dr. Gillfallan, unlike previous historians, explained this selective decline in birthrate by another long-known fact: The Roman aristocracy had developed as one of its status symbols the use of expensive utensils for eating and drinking made of lead, in contrast to the earthenware utensils used by the poorer masses. Then adding one other well-known fact from the physical sciences, that minute quantities of lead when absorbed into the human system can cause sterility and death, he concluded that the Roman aristocracy simply destroyed itself by destroying the potency of its males through lead poisoning.

Whether right or wrong, and of course we never will know if Gilfallan or Gibbon or any other historian was "right" or "wrong" as to the causes of the decline of Rome, we nevertheless must concede that Dr. Gillfallan has developed an ingenious and creative reinterpretation combining known historical and scientific truth. Notice in considering this illustration that no new facts were discovered. Dr. Gillfallan found no new material or primary data and need not have ever set foot in Italy. Instead he simply studied all that was known of the conditions and practices of the populace at the time that Rome declined and added to this a new insight, a new sensitivity to one particular dimension of the historical picture. Out of this came a new interpretation of history.

This also illustrates another key aspect of the function of historical research, that is, it searches for causes and explanations and interpretations as much as for facts or data. All too often the student contemplating or undertaking an historical research project limits his aspirations to the acquisition of fact and figure, not realizing that this is relatively cold and sterile history until some meaning is attached to the data. Certainly the intellectually challenging aspect of history is interpretation, conjecture, explanation, or hypothesis development.

[2] Speech before Third International Congress of Human Genetics, as reported in *Time*, 88, September 23, 1966, p. 79.

SOURCES OF HISTORICAL DATA

The problems involved in the nature of historical data mean that the historical researcher is vitally concerned not only with evaluating the data in the context of sampling, but also in evaluating the source of the data. The most important bases for evaluating the source are: (1) to consider whether the recording of the data was deliberate or inadvertent; and (2) to consider whether or not the source can be considered primary or secondary.

Deliberate and Inadvertent Sources

Deliberate sources of data are those in which there has been a conscious effort to record some event or preserve information. These range from the brief chronological notes on tombstones to paintings or to the extended diaries and autobiographies which have always characterized public figures, and do so today more than ever. While deliberate sources are most often written down, they also include material like myths and folk songs which are deliberately passed down from generation to generation by word-of-mouth to keep the materials alive.

In contrast are inadvertent sources of data, which provide information for the historical researcher even though that was not the original intent of the source. Archeologists who develop descriptions of cultures based on artifacts they unearth are using inadvertent sources. A rich variety of inadvertent sources can be seen in any museum, for almost all cultural artifacts which are presented for their historical interest were not original-ly created as a way of communicating the culture across generations. After all a clay pot was created to carry water and decorated to make it look pretty, not to make it possible for later generations to date a culture through carbon-14 tests or to show how perspective developed in line drawings.

Each of these two kinds of sources has its advantages and disadvantages for the historical researcher. The deliberate source, of course, un-doubtedly is presenting a subjective view of events. Thus, if there are only a few such sources for a particular period, it may be difficult to obtain a well-rounded view of events. On the other hand, the deliberate source is concerned directly with the event at hand and, however subjective, is preserving an individual impression of that event. In contrast, the inadver-tent source is being used for something other than it was intended, and so inference must play a large part in any understanding or interpretation of it. And inference can be right or wrong. However, one could argue that since it is being used for some purpose other than that for which it was created, the inadvertent source must be an objective piece of evidence or data. And so, as often happens in research, the researcher must balance virtue against handicap. In this case he must balance the potential for bias in deliberate sources against the directness of these sources with no need for inference. Then for the inadvertent source he must balance the ambiguity and need for inference with all of its possibilities for error against the accompanying objectivity. Of course in much historical research, particularly if it is concerned with a period more than a century ago, the total amount of data available is so limited that the researcher would be pleased with either type, should it be available.

Primary and Secondary Sources

The other distinction, between primary and secondary sources of historical data, involves the familiar distinction between firsthand and secondhand material. A primary source is firsthand, and always involves the direct reporting or recording of an experience. It can be an animate primary source, that is, a person reporting an experience which happened to him or in which he participated. Or it can be an inanimate source, such as the physical artifacts one finds in museums; or mechanically reproduced direct records of events or a set of proceedings such as films or records; or it can be verbal material like the official transcripts or minutes of a meeting or convention. What characterizes both animate and inanimate primary sources is the immediacy of experience of the source and the minimization of intervening persons between the experience and the recording of it. Thus while minutes of a meeting do not spring into being as soon as the meeting is adjourned but instead are written by a person or persons, those persons doing the recording also experienced the event and typically will have their version of the record checked by others who also experienced the event. This is why the first action at a meeting of an official organization is to consider whether or not the minutes of the preceding meeting are accurate as recorded.

This does *not* mean that the primary source necessarily is true and accurate in an absolute sense. If a man from Mars were watching a meeting and had the ability to note everything which went on, he might feel that the official minutes omitted some of the events, presented others exactly as they happened, and presented the rest of the events in varying degrees of distortion. Similarly, anyone who sets down an entry in a diary does not record an impartial, impersonal version of what happened but instead records a personal version with all of the possibilities for selective perception, selective recall, and conscious and unconscious distortion psychological research has demonstrated. Nevertheless both the incomplete and partially distorted minutes and the highly personal diary entry would be primary sources. In short, the "primary" refers only to the fact that the source is the minimum one step removed from the event itself; it does *not* refer to the accuracy or truth of the source.

Secondary sources are all the other sources of information and are always at least two steps removed from the event. Therefore they are not tied directly to the event either as official records or as the memoirs of a participant. Secondary sources can range in immediacy from those which are close to the primary source, such as a newspaper story reporting an interview with a participant in an event, to those which are a considerable distance from the primary source such as the historical researcher himself, writing years or even generations after an event.

There are two essential differences between primary and secondary sources. First is the difference already noted in immediacy: The primary source is tied directly to the event; the secondary source is not. The second difference is that the secondary source introduces at least one other individual into the production of the data, and with this one other individual comes a second set of possibilities for selective perception, selective recall, and conscious and unconscious distortion. Note that the list of differences does not include the necessary superiority of primary sources. While the discovery of a previously unknown primary source relevant to an important event or period is an exciting event, the discovery of secondary sources can be equally important. For example, the discovery in the 1960s of parts of the diaries of John Adams was an exciting event, particularly to students of the early history of the United States. It would also be exciting to these students if we discovered the journals and records of a newspaperman of the period, who, while not himself present at any of the meetings and conventions which led up to independence, had spoken to most of the participants. If his record reported and discussed the reactions and perceptions of these several participants, while clearly secondary and subject to the additional possibility of distortion implicit in the secondary source, nevertheless it would be as valuable or more valuable than the journals of any one of the participants.

EVALUATING HISTORICAL DATA

One of the most complex aspects of the historical research process comes after data collection has begun and the researcher must evaluate his data. Evaluate is used here to mean the decision as to which data can be considered sufficiently well established to be reported as fact, which can be considered probable, which possible, and which can only be considered as unsubstantiated and/or one-sided. Any reader of this book who viewed some of the proceedings of the United Nations Security Council during the middle eastern war in 1967 will know how difficult it was to establish what was happening on the Syrian border at the very moment it was happening. Think, then, of the problems which the historian will face in 1997 when he writes the history of this period.

All historians face this type of problem, even if their research does not involve problems of international import. All of their data, by definition, are based on a period in the past, and so all involve the two-fold aspect of first identifying the data and then deciding which are to be believed and which doubted.

In deciding what data to believe and what to doubt, the researcher first evaluates the source of the information, seeking to establish how reputable the source is and how expert in the field under study. He also evaluates the information, independent of the source, seeking to establish how consistent it is internally and externally.

In evaluating a source the researcher first should establish the contemporary reputation of the source. He is seeking here not only to learn what his (the source's) peers thought of him in general, but also what they thought of his integrity, ability, and the quality of his opinions in the area under study. Ideally, something is also learned of his reputation for veracity, but this is rarely available. Then the reputation of the source over the years should be evaluated, if previous researchers have evaluated or referred to him and his work.

With the source evaluated, the researcher next seeks to evaluate the information as information. The techniques for this are relatively simple. First, the researcher looks at the internal consistency of the information, arguing that the more internally consistent a set of data, the more likely it is to be accurate. Second, the researcher estimates the external consistency of the information, that is, the extent to which it is consistent with other information about the same event. In this stage of the evaluation of information the distinction between primary and secondary sources becomes important. If two independent primary sources which have stood up to evaluation as reputable sources agree on the same point of information, and if there are no primary or secondary sources who disagree, then we have as solid an historical fact as we are likely to identify. Since it is often difficult to obtain two truly independent primary sources, the label of "fact" is also applied to information in which reputable primary and secondary sources agree, without any source disagreeing. In short, to consider a piece of historical data as fact we must have three elements: (1) corroboration from two independent sources; (2) one independent source a primary source; and (3) we must also have no reputable sources who hold a contradictory view of events.

If any of these three elements is lacking we cannot aspire to referring to fact, but must limit our aspirations to referring to probability. We can establish a probable historical event when we have one reliable primary source without corroboration but also without contradiction, or two independent secondary sources without any contradictory evidence. Finally, if we only have data from one primary source whose reliability we doubt, or if we have primary sources who disagree with each other, we have the difficult research decision of judging relative truth from our perspective at some distant point in time. In this instance we utilize all of the techniques referred to in evaluating the source and the data, and also attempt to consider the possible biases in the contradictory sources. In this effort, the researcher compares the data reported by each source to the known bias of the source, giving greater weight to information a source reports which runs counter to his known bias than to information he reports which supports that bias. Despite these efforts, when sources disagree the researcher must apply his own professional knowledge and judgment to make the final evaluations. No rules of thumb can spare him this responsibility.

THE PROCESS OF HISTORICAL RESEARCH

The actual process of historical research can be summarized into the nine major steps listed below.

1. Determination that the problem selected is appropriate for study through the historical approach
2. Specification of the population of data needed
3. Initial determination that sufficient data are available
4. Begin data collection through:
   (a) consideration of known data
   (b) seeking new data from known sources
       (1) primary sources
       (2) secondary sources
   (c) seeking new and previously unknown data
       (1) in the form of data
       (2) in the form of sources
5. Begin to write report
6. Interaction of writing and additional search for data or examination of data.
7. Completion of descriptive phase of research
8. Completion of interpretative phase of research
9. Application of data to present and hypotheses for future

The first step is to determine that the researcher has selected a problem for which the historical approach is relevant. The largest group of these problems are relatively easy to identify since stating them always involves the past tense of the critical verbs. Consider the problem we referred to in Chapter 3 in the consideration of pure and applied research: What *were* Pestalozzi's motivations for moving into education? Or consider other historical projects conducted by recent students of the author's: How *did* the school health requirements in New York City originate? What attempts *were* made in the nineteenth century to simplify English spelling? How well educated *have* American Presidents *been?* Notice that in stating all of these research questions, the past tense must be used, and this in and of itself is usually enough to make it clear that we are dealing with a problem for which the historical approach will be appropriate.

Not all problems for which the historical approach is appropriate need to be stated in the past. A problem stated in the present tense can be tested with the historical approach provided that it is a current expression of a situation which has happened before. We need go no further for an example than the problem discussed in Chapter 1: finding the best method of teaching English as a second language to newly arrived Puerto Rican children. Here the research question is stated in the present. Yet, as we discussed in that first chapter, we knew that similar problems had been faced by successive generations of teachers in the New York City schools, some of whom obviously had solved the problem creatively. This type of recurring problem, then, is also appropriate for the historical approach.

The second step is for the researcher to develop a statement of the specific population of data he needs for the study of the problem. In most areas of historic interest a wide variety of data exist, only some of which have direct relevance for the problem. In the Language Study, for example, the directly relevant data would have been descriptions of methodology, the school populations who were taught, and the degrees of success achieved with the varied methods. Data on the folklore or living conditions or social functioning of previous migrant groups, while interesting, would have been irrelevant to the problem being studied, and so excluded from the population of data.

As we noted earlier in this discussion, it is in this delineation of the population of information that the historical researcher can offer fresh perceptions and insights into how events came about. It is interesting to conjecture what educational historians will consider the relevant population of information when they write the history of the American urban educational scene in the period 1950 to 1970. The extent to which sociological, psychological, political, economic, and cultural values will dominate the educational policies and issues is hard to estimate, but it seems obvious that the population of data for such a history will be far broader than we imagine now, as we live in the midst of that period.

Given this description of the required population of data, the researcher can move on to the third step, the initial overview of the data through which he can decide if sufficient data exist for the historical approach to be successfully implemented.[3] It did not take long in the Language Study for it to become clear that there were totally insufficient data on previous methods employed and their relative success for the historical approach to be used. In other instances this determination may be more difficult, but it must be made early in the process if the researcher is to avoid the risk of investing large amounts of time and energy only to end with insufficient data.

Of course, there are instances in which the researcher's entire interest in the historical approach is motivated by the belief that previously unknown data *do* exist. The archeological literature has many instances of such researchers. For example, most knowledgeable people of his time, asked to estimate the success potential of Schliemann as he set out to uncover the ruins of Troy, would have said that there was no such potential at all.

Similarly, there seemed little likelihood that Howard Carter would uncover any significant new tombs when he began digging in the already well-worked Valley of the Kings. Yet within two years he uncovered the most fabulous find of all: the tomb of Tutankhamen. But data of educational significance are seldom buried beneath the sands of time. As a matter of fact, there are no examples in educational research which parallel the discoveries of Troy or of Tutankhamen's tomb, or which are even approximations.

Thus, it is sound, if the success potential of a possible historical project is poor, to conclude that some alternative approach or problem is a wiser course. Hoping that we will discover the Tutankhamen's tomb of educational data has a significance probability well below any accepted level of significance!

Assuming that the judgment is made that there is reasonable hope for success, then the fourth step in the process of historical research is to begin the collection of data. As the list above indicates, this involves the consideration of three major aspects. The first is the obvious aspect, the researcher's responsibility to become familiar with all the data already known to exist. The second aspect involves his review of sources which are known to exist, in the hope that these sources might provide him with new data. Finally, the third aspect involves the search either for previously unknown sources or previously unknown data.

[3]This stage in historical research is analogous to the stage in the review of the literature in which the researcher estimates the success potential of his research.

Often these three aspects are entirely different in terms of richness for a particular project. For the Language Study, for example, the first aspect was all but nonexistent: There were no data on previous efforts to teach English as a second language in New York City, but there were possible untapped sources which might have provided new data. Some of the thousands of adults who had gone through the schools as children and been taught English might have kept records or notebooks, just as there might be plans and materials in the possession of the hundreds of teachers of those years who were still alive.[4] For our selection of a "best" method to recommend for use in a school system, these sources were not appropriately precise, and so we made no effort to tap them. But had our historical problem been to write "The History of Efforts to Teach English as a Second Language in the New York City Schools," these sources would have been tremendously fruitful. Thus once again we see how the research problem and research process interact to make each research project a unique entity.

The third aspect of the data collection phase is to search for new and previously unknown elements of the historical record. In the sampling terms used earlier, the researcher seeks to enlarge the sample by finding previously unknown elements of the population. Thus in the Language Study we might have searched newspapers, magazines, and educational books of these earlier periods to see if they contained articles on methodology which had been forgotten. Of course, the same rules of sampling discussed in the chapter on sampling apply here as well. Adding more elements to the sample is of research significance only if they are elements which either are new and so alter the composition of the sample or else are of such a nature that they alter the previously existing proportions in the sample. Thus if we were studying the history of how educators received the plan for the first nursery school established in London in 1907, assume we lacked the plan but had available to us letters from several contemporary educators who knew the plan, a majority of which indicated that they approved it. If the historical researcher then discovered a draft of the original plan, this would dramatically alter the elements of the sample of information, since this was not known before. But he might also find additional letters and articles by contemporary educators who commented upon the plan. Now we already have letters, so this is not in and of itself an exciting or significant discovery. Moreover, if the newly discovered letters and articles were also from educators who had

[4]In the next chapter we shall discuss the retrospective survey, a second research approach concerned with the past. Where historical research seeks data created in the past, the retrospective survey seeks data from the present about the past. Thus, using these notebooks or planbooks would be considered historical research since they were created in the period under study. Interviewing these students or teachers would be a retrospective survey because the data would be created in the present.

supported the plan, we have learned only that support was even more widespread than we had known. However, if the material was from educators who opposed the plan, and particularly if this new cache meant that now the majority of educators whose position was known opposed it, this would be an important contribution to the sample of known material.

After certain amounts of data have been collected, it is often advisable to move on to the fifth step and make the first effort to write the project report. This is suggested at this intermediate stage before the data collection phase is terminated because it maximizes the interaction between the data collection and the written report at a time when additional data can still be collected. In essence this phase becomes a trial run to see if the data collected tie together usefully and completely or if there is a need for more. Then, if the decision is that there *is* a need for more, it is the tentative written report which structures that "more." This process of writing and searching continues (the sixth step in the list above) in much the same way as was discussed in Chapter 4 on reviewing the literature, and it ends at a similar point: when the researcher has sufficient data to answer the set of question words. Like the review of literature phase of any research, historical research too seeks to answer, "who," "what," "where," and "when."

At this stage some historical research stops. This historical research is concerned with the purely descriptive approach (step seven) exemplified in these four words. It is concerned only with understanding what happened to whom, in what place, and at what time. This descriptive branch of historical research has played a dominant role in a discipline like archeology. In contrast, in the social disciplines, including education, an eighth step in historical research writing is added and is often the dominant one. This is the step which adds a fifth question word to the previous four, the word "why." It is this concern with why events happened in the way that they did which distinguishes historical research from a massive review of the literature, if "literature" is used in the broadest possible sense. In the social disciplines sound historical research must seek not only to describe but to understand the forces which have shaped events and determined policies.

The process of interaction between writing, collection of additional data, and/or additional interpretations continues then until, looking back, the researcher feels that he had achieved satisfactory answers to all five of the question words. At this point if he is correct he has satisfactorily completed the historical phase of the research. He may then, if he wishes to move it into the present, consider what the implications for the present are of this increased knowledge of the past. If the research has been concerned with a relatively "pure problem," then there may be no immediate application. But if it has been at the practical end of the spectrum, then he should consider what the project means for, and says to, the present.

Moreover, given sufficient information and insight into the past to understand why events happened as they did, and sufficient insight to apply them to the present, the historical researcher can move to step nine and even pose sensible hypotheses about the future.

PRACTICAL CONSIDERATIONS

For students at all levels, but particularly at the graduate level, where time becomes more critical, the historical approach has one severe practical limitation: It is not possible to estimate the length of time it will require to complete any specific project. This is particularly true if the research problem demands a search for new data, for obviously there is no way of determining how long it will require for new data to be found. But even in the simpler historical problems based on a reworking or reintegration of existing data, it is difficult to predict a completion date. This is because of the complex interaction between data and idea, which is unique to the historical approach. For it is not the data which structure the historical project, but rather the ideas and insights of the researcher. And since it is impossible to place insight within a time-table, the historical researcher may well spend unexpected weeks, months, and, in some instances, even years contemplating masses of data, seeking in vain the insight that will tie everything together and enable him to produce a valid historical study which can be defended both in terms of soundness of design and structure and in terms of meaningfulness of the contribution to knowledge.

Undoubtedly, this practical limitation explains the relative paucity of historical research in education, as compared to other disciplines within the liberal arts like English, philosophy, economics, and, of course, history itself. The educator has been a practical student, oriented to completion of degree requirements but also to projects with a more applied approach than pure orientation. Most institutions have been willing to orient their doctoral programs in this way as well. Thus in most programs leading to the Ed.D. degree, projects are applied rather than pure research, and this too has limited the incidence of historical research in education.

THE TONE OF HISTORICAL RESEARCH

All research strives for a tone of dispassionate inquiry, a tone in which the researcher communicates his willingness to see the truth as it is, whether or not it corresponds with his individual point of view. But in survey and experimental research projects the design of the study establishes the kind of data which will be available, and these data are the foundation upon which interpretations are made and conclusions drawn. For this reason survey and experimental research typically are based upon the researcher's hypothetical expectations of the results. Historical research has a different problem in these areas. Typically the kinds of data are not structured by the research problem other than in the vaguest way, and so the reader of the historical project has little choice but to assume that the researcher has fully presented all of the possible data relevant to the problem.

This means that the historical researcher must establish this tone of thorough inquiry throughout the design, execution, and reporting of his project. It means that stating his hypotheses or expectations has a greater importance than is generally recognized. For just as the researcher evaluates a piece of data by considering the possible pressures operating on the source which might bias the data, so does the reader of historical research wish to be able to evaluate the report by knowing of the possible biases operating on the researcher. It also means that in deciding which data to include in the historical report the historical researcher, like all researchers, should include all relevant data and not limit his report to those data which support his particular interpretation. This is particularly critical in the consideration of cause, where the temptation is great to report only those aspects of the situation which support a specific causal explanation and ignore those which cannot be included within that explanation or which contradict it. Nothing can destroy the value of historical research more quickly than giving in to that temptation. The tone communicated must be of the researcher first seeking to identify, consider, and report all of the data relevant to the problem, and then offering his interpretation of this total set of data.

Chapter 15

THE SURVEY APPROACH

The second research approach, the survey, is present-oriented research, and therefore suitable for problems in which the researcher believes that although the data needed to resolve his research question do not exist, the settings in which those data could be generated *do* exist. The research approach then is to go to those settings, administer appropriate data-collection devices and analyze the data. In the sense that the settings are known and the data required reasonably well defined by the statement of the research problem, the survey approach is more structured for the researcher than the historical approach. However, surveys have their own problems: the difficult problems of instrument development.

In contrast to the lack of historical research, education has had large numbers of studies using the survey approach. Nevertheless, there are whole areas within education where needed survey data are all but nonexistent. The paradox stems from the fact that there are many kinds of surveys, and some types have been popular in educational research whereas others have been consistently ignored. This will be clarified as we consider the three main types, and the variations within each. The three major types, as noted in Chapter 2, stem from the researcher's intent to describe, compare, or evaluate. These types are the *descriptive survey,* concerned with describing a specific set of phenomena at one point in time; the *comparative survey,* intended to compare two or more research situations in terms of some preselected criteria; and the *evaluative survey,* planned to evaluate some aspect of a research situation, again in terms of preselected criteria.

THE DESCRIPTIVE SURVEY

A descriptive survey is intended to describe a specific set of phenomena in and of themselves. The rationale for the purely descriptive survey is the fact that the information provided is in itself the answer to the research question posed. The most familiar example of the descriptive survey is the United States Census, which seeks information designed to answer a wide variety of research questions beginning with "how many people. . . ." Many descriptive surveys have this census type head-counting aspect beginning with "how many," "what," or "where." For example, a descriptive survey would be appropriate to seek answers to questions like the following. "How many classroom seats are there for retarded children in the Northeastern states?" "How many Negro children attend classes with white children in the schools in the Southeast?" "How many teachers currently teaching grades 4 through 8 have less than a baccalaureate education?" "What is the median salary for full professors in fully accredited colleges?" "Where are the colleges and universities that offer advanced preparation in educational research?"

Thus, in educational research there are two conditions which occurring together suggest and justify the descriptive survey: First, that there is an absence of information about a problem of educational significance, and second, that the situations which could generate that information do exist and are accessible to the researcher.

There is, as this is written, a need for descriptive research in education. The beginning researcher or graduate student is often surprised at the variety of phenomena in education about which we know relatively little. What are the socioeducational characteristics of the high school seniors who consider a career in teaching? What changes take place in in-class behaviors of teachers undergoing psychoanalysis? What is the relationship of selected psychosocial characteristics to success in school? Success as a teacher? Administrator? What were the childhood experiences of "disadvantaged" youth who graduate from college with academic honors? What are current practices in use in secondary schools for teaching content to the child reading below the fifth-grade level? To what extent are school plants fully utilized? For what kinds of activities are they used? We could continue on and on, listing topics of interest for which no, or only limited, data exist. And yet the situations needed to provide the data exist for each of these problems. All of these, then, by definition, would be appropriate problems for a descriptive survey.

Read back over the first several questions. Notice that while all involve a descriptive survey in the sense that they could be answered through a set of data collected at a specific point in time, nevertheless they differ in other significant aspects. The first problem, involving defining the characteristics of high school seniors who consider a career in teaching, is the census-type survey we mentioned earlier. The end product we would seek here is a thorough survey of high school seniors in different regions of the

United States so that all relevant sociological and educational variation was included and so that the incidence of the several different such characteristics could accurately be estimated. The level of data sought is what we referred to in Chapter 13 as surface or subsurface, and so this type of survey would require large numbers of respondents to be done with any degree of accuracy. Therefore we shall call it a *mass survey*.

The problem concerned with in-class behavior change of teachers undergoing psychoanalysis poses entirely different problems of data collection. First, there would be relatively few respondents available and willing to participate. Second, the level of data required is the description of behavior, and undoubtedly would also involve the subtle areas of attitude, mood, and reaction by teacher and child. To be done successfully, it would have to be done at the depth level, and the sophisticated researcher would even wish to make some attempt to work at the nonconscious level. Moreover, each teacher would have to be considered as a separate unit for the research, since group data would have little meaning. The final analysis of the data would be built up respondent by respondent, and so this type of descriptive survey is called a *case-study survey*.

The next three examples all involve estimating the magnitude of relationships, in one case between psychosocial characteristics and success in school; in the other two cases, success in professional functioning. Because these research questions can be answered through collecting appropriate data at one specific point in time, the descriptive survey approach is applicable. The problems involved all call for estimating the relationship between two sets of data, and so this type of survey is called a *correlational survey*. The level of data involved is similar to the surface or subsurface levels employed in the mass survey. However, since relationships are relatively stable phenomena and since they can meaningfully be studied for specific strata of a larger population, the numbers involved in these correlational surveys are usually smaller than in mass surveys.

The sixth question, involving childhood experiences of disadvantaged youth who have graduated from college, may seem like a strange problem to include under the survey approach, which has so often been referred to as "present-oriented." But in this problem too, the data would be collected in the present, for we would have to identify these youth and ask them to recall their childhood experiences. This type of survey which involves inquiry into the past from the present is called a *retrospective survey*.

Mass Surveys

The mass survey usually functions at the surface level to provide relatively superficial information, typically of a demographic nature. This information should definitely and precisely characterize the population and universe. For example, a census is intended not only to delineate how many different ethnic backgrounds are represented in a population surveyed, but also to estimate precisely what proportion each specific ethnic group is of the population. For this reason, it requires large numbers of subjects, and is often conducted with entire populations or universes rather than samples. Also for this reason, the mass survey is usually inappropriate for the resources students have available unless there is a population of educational significance which is finite and limited and available to the researcher. For example, in one phase of the Language Study we were concerned with the methods of teaching English as a second language then in use in the New York City schools. The problem defined a finite, if large, population and one that would be accessible. Thus, a student might have attempted this survey. If a student can also define a research problem in which a relevant local population can be defined, then he can plan a mass survey within those limits.

Mass surveys do not need to include entire populations, particularly if the research question being asked is a simple one and/or if there is a great deal of information available on the basis of which the researcher can meaningfully stratify the universe or population. We are all familiar with the phenomenon of the computer each November predicting the outcome of an election while the television screen is showing 1 percent or less of the total vote cast. This attempt to predict the action taken by the population, even though only an infinitesimal proportion has been surveyed, is sensible because of two factors. First, there is so much known about voting behavior that it is possible to stratify the population in terms of several variables known to be related to voting behavior. Second, the survey question is typically a dichotomous one: We usually have only two candidates who are serious contenders for any one political office.

Typically, in educational surveys we do not have such simple dichotomous questions nor do we have the amount of information possessed by the political scientist about voting behavior. What is necessary to compensate for these two lacks is to increase the size of the sample so that it accounts for larger proportions of the population. There is no simple answer to how large this increase should be, and no mathematical basis for determining minimum sample size other than the procedure discussed in Chapter 11. That procedure required the researcher to state an estimate of the value he is seeking to learn, the risks of both Type I and Type II errors he is willing to run, and the level of precision he wishes to attain in making his estimate. Few researchers know enough about the situation in survey research to fulfill all these conditions, and so the mathematical basis for sample size is unavailable. It is the author's experience that for the level of complexity of most educational survey questions, and taking into account the relatively little we know about the educational process, surveys require a data-producing sample of at least 20 percent if the proportions in various categories within the population are to be accurately represented. If we have reason to believe that there will be attrition in the course of data collection, then of course, we should seek a larger selected sample in excess of the 20 percent we wish to have in the data-producing sample.

The Case-Study Survey

At quite the opposite end of the number scale to the mass survey is the *case-study survey*. Here the research unit is one, that is, a case-study survey can be based on a single case, and in fact if it involves more than one, it nevertheless is made up of analyses of individual cases. In contrast to the mass survey which is content with relatively superficial description of groups or masses of people, the case-study survey seeks to achieve a deep and involved understanding and description of individuals. The basic rationale for the case study is that there are processes and interactions, such as aspects of personality and social functioning, which cannot be studied except as they interact and operate within an individual. Moreover, this argument runs, the probability is that if we learn how these processes interact in some few individuals we shall also learn much about the processes in the abstract, and ultimately learn all there is to know about them.

For example, there are many mass surveys as to the sociopsychological characteristics of children who ultimately become sufficiently anti-social as to be legally classified as juvenile delinquents. We know that most often they come from broken homes, that, except for sex offenses, they are more likely to be boys than girls, that their social malfunctioning is accompanied, and usually preceded, by academic malfunctioning, and so on. Yet we still have not learned from this mass survey approach how the different deprivations and difficulties interact so that some children become serious delinquents and others, who exhibit the same characteristics identified by the mass survey, do not. The answer lies in other characteristics yet to be identified, and/or in the pattern of interaction of the characteristics in the individual. It is at this level that the case-study survey approach would function, studying the characteristics as they exist in company with each other within the person and life space of individuals.

Because the case study uses the individual as its basic unit, it is particularly suitable to student research, provided that the student is sufficiently knowledgeable to carry on the studies in the depth that the case study approach demands. In other words the student must be sufficiently expert in the area under study to be able to collect the wide variety of data needed for the case study. Moreover, he must also be expert enough in the field under study to be able to recognize relationships, and particularly to know when the relationships being revealed are consonant with existing theory and research and when they contradict it. Finally he must be trained in the methods and techniques needed to function at the depth and nonconscious level. In short, the case study is not an approach for the beginner but rather for the advanced student, who knows enough to be dissatisfied with the generalizations available in the field and with the discussion of human characteristics removed from their functioning in the human individual. This level of dissatisfaction can almost be considered a prerequisite for the case-study approach.

The Correlational Survey

We have had relatively few case-study surveys in educational research. Instead our concern with relationships and interactions among characteristics has been expressed in correlational surveys.

The correlational survey is exactly what its name implies: a survey designed to estimate the extent to which different variables are related to each other in the population of interest. The critical distinguishing characteristic is the effort to estimate a relationship, as distinguished from simple description. The correlational survey thus moves the researcher one long step away from the consideration of characteristics in isolation to the study of them in company with each other in operation within people. Nevertheless, in its orientation to groups rather than individuals, it is still a long step from the study of interactions possible with the case-study survey.

The correlational survey had a remarkable increase in popularity in the 1960s, stimulated by the development of computer oriented statistical techniques for the study of multiple interrelationships and underlying dynamics through factor analysis. In all candor, as this is written in the late 1960s one would have to summarize that all of the relationship surveys conducted have added little to our knowledge of human functioning. In large part this has been due to the problem of weak instrumentation discussed at several points earlier in this book. About all we have learned to date is what we should have known earlier: Relationship surveys conducted with instruments of weak reliability and dubious validity will not produce evidence of meaningful relationships. The approach is nevertheless a sensible one, provided that instruments are available to obtain reliable and valid data for the characteristics to be related.

If the instrument is reliable and valid, relationship studies do not require large samples, and so are appealing for students. The argument for the relatively small sample size (typically between 50 and 100 subjects) is that *if* the relationship exists it will be evidenced in a sample of any reasonable size. But the italicized "if" in the preceding sentence is intended to highlight one major precaution for the student contemplating a correlational survey: He must be certain that his study will make a meaningful contribution even if the data produce little or no evidence of the relationship under study. The risk of this finding of no relationship is still high. Thus the student must think ahead and imagine how he would treat the data and defend the study's value if no significant relationship was indicated. He must also realize that he cannot, at that point, explain the finding of no relationship by pointing an accusing finger at the instrument as inadequate to test for the relationship. In other words, he must be willing to defend the study as a valid search for the relationship, and so if none is found to defend the point that *none exists*. Too often students complete a relationship study which produces inconclusive results and then ponder for long hours and weeks how to reconcile this finding with currently accepted theory. Their dilemma is that they do not feel confident enough in their own findings to challenge current theory, and yet cannot reconcile the nonsignificant finding with the theory. A researcher should not plan a study which could place him in that dilemma. We should undertake a relationship survey only if we feel we can explain both the finding of a relationship and the finding that there is no relationship.

A final point to which to be alert if we are planning a correlational survey is that the actual amount of data we will have is extremely limited. Each semester the author sees students who ignore this caution and who are stunned at the end of a correlational survey by the realization that the total amount of data they have collected can be summarized in a few two-digit decimals. This means that it is wise to have a second aspect to a correlational survey if the reseacher is conducting one for a major paper or dissertation. The correlations themselves seldom make for a sufficiently complex study for this type of assignment.

Retrospective Surveys

The retrospective survey is an effort to learn about the antecedents of some current situation by illuminating aspects of the past. At first glance the retrospective survey may seem like historical research, because it is concerned with illuminating some past period. But there is a basic and extremely significant difference. The historical approach is concerned with a question in the past, but is based upon the premise that data needed to answer the question already exist. The researcher's task then is to find these data. The retrospective survey, like all surveys, is based upon the premise that the needed data do not exist, but the research situation needed to generate them does. Although like historical research the retrospective survey involves a research question oriented to the past, its basic premise is that this is a question about the past for which no data are known to exist. Therefore the researcher seeks out persons who were alive during the period in which he is interested, and asks them to recall the specific circumstances he wishes to study. Note then that historical research is based upon the analysis of data which were actually created in the period under study. In contrast the retrospective survey is based upon the analysis of data collected at some time *after* the period or event under study.

The Sample of Respondents

While the historical researcher must seek and find his data, the researcher undertaking a retrospective survey must seek and find his respondents. In historical research, the basic task is to identify potential sources, for once a potential source of data is found it can usually be tapped. However, in the retrospective survey once a potential respondent is found, his cooperation is necessary before he can be "tapped." An equally serious concern in developing the sample of respondents is to verify that they represent as a group the range of different human roles in the original situation. For example, if the survey is of a teaching situation, we would want students, teachers, and administrators represented among the respondents.

Thus an early task for the researcher planning a retrospective survey is to identify the types of persons originally involved in the research situation he wishes to study, so that he can develop a stratification plan indicating what the desirable sample of respondents would be like. With this in hand, he has some basis for knowing what kinds of respondents to seek. Moreover, he also has a basis for evaluating the representativeness of his final sample. Given this, if some particular role is not represented or is underrepresented, this can be stated as a limitation to the conclusions and taken into account in the report of the research.

The Sample of Information

Both historical research and the retrospective survey face the problem peculiar to studies of the past: the extent and nature of the sample of information which has survived, and the extent to which the researcher is aware of this sample. In fact, in Figure 14-1 we sketched out this concern. A similar concern troubles the researcher who conducts a retrospective survey. The variation of this basic problem of a data sample, as it applies to retrospective surveys, is shown in Figure 15-1. Again we begin with

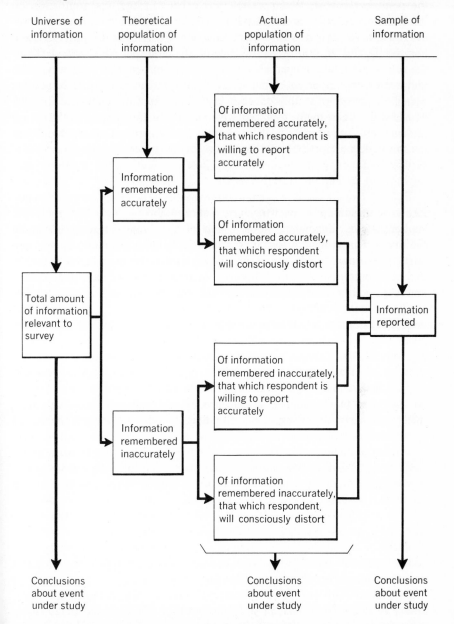

Figure 15-1   Conceptualization of sampling process in retrospective survey.

the universe of information. In this case it is the universe which would have been available had the researcher conducted a descriptive survey at the point in the past. When we reach the second stage, the population of information, the issue is not physical survival of information as in historical research. Rather it is the extent to which this information has survived completely and accurately in the memories of the people involved. Thus the researcher's first concern is how much information has been forgotten, and even more important, what kinds of information have been forgotten. Stated the other way, this concern is if the information recalled can be considered a reasonably representative sample of the original universe of information. Unfortunately, there is little the researcher can do to alleviate this concern short of applying his professional judgment to the research problem and the respondents in the effort to identify the pressures that might operate to create selective recall.

But the two theoretical populations of information remembered, accurately or inaccurately, must each be conceptualized as consisting of two subpopulations, depending upon which of the remembered information the respondent is willing to impart. Thus, each subpopulation consists not only of information the respondent is willing to impart as he remembers it, but also consists of information he wishes to impart in a deliberately and consciously distorted manner. The researcher must recognize this aspect of a retrospective survey, that the respondent may seek to create what he considers a desirable picture of the past or what he did in the past.

Thus, the final sample of information is selected from four subpopulations of information: (1) information remembered and reported accurately; (2) that remembered accurately but deliberately reported in a distorted way; (3) that remembered inaccurately but reported accurately; and, finally and most confusing of all, (4) that information remembered inaccurately and reported in a deliberately distorted way! It is from this composite population of information that the researcher draws his conclusions as to what the situation in the past was like. As in historical research, the value of the description of the past which is obtained in the retrospective survey is directly related to the extent to which the different sets of conclusions at the bottom of the figure can be considered to be homogeneous. To estimate this homogeneity involves extremely complex problems of the evaluation of sources and of the data obtained from these sources. For this reason, the retrospective survey is an approach which the beginning researcher should not attempt.

It is never fully possible to parcel out those pieces of the sample data which do come from each of the subpopulations of potential data. However, there are some things which can be done, and as might be expected they parallel the techniques used to evaluate the merits of any piece of historical data. First, we examine the internal consistency of the information provided by any single source. In fact, instruments for data gathering developed for retrospective surveys should have built into them regular provisions for seeking the same information in several ways so that some estimate of internal consistency can be obtained. In addition we seek external corroboration, that ' , seek information about the same event from many people involved in it so that we can identify those aspects of the event on which they all agree and those aspects on which they disagree. We also take into account the probable motivations of the respondents in discussing the event, trying to estimate the pressures operating on them to distort information, and so estimate those data provided in which we see no reason to distort and those which we would consider with suspicion unless verified. One important way to verify those data where we fear distortion is to select respondents with different pressures to distort. If we are able to do this we can compare the sensitive areas each reports, and those aspects on which they agree can be considered reasonably reliable. Those aspects of the same event on which they disagree must be reported with caution.

A final aspect of this evaluation is to compare the findings obtained through the retrospective survey with any contemporary data available from the period under study. Of course, the very rationale for the retrospective survey is that such historical data either are not available or so limited as to be of little use in answering the research question. But there might be sufficient data available to provide some estimate of the extent to which the universe of information has been tapped and the extent to which the remembered information can be considered accurate.

Despite all of those efforts the researcher who attempts the retrospective survey must be aware of the nature of his data. At best he has a picture of the past *as people remember it and are willing to report it*. This picture *may* also accurately reflect the way it really was. But to some extent, it almost certainly will not.

The Descriptive Survey as a Test of Theory

One particularly fascinating application of the descriptive survey is to test whether a situation described by some theory exists in reality. As this book is written, for example, there has been widespread interest in the developmental theories of the Swiss psychologist, Jean Piaget. He has offered a wide variety of theoretical statements about the development of children's mental abilities in areas like language, the formation of concepts like life, or God, or mathematical concepts like probability or the conservation of substance. In each of these areas Piaget offers both a statement of the different sequential stages in development in the area and his hypotheses of the ages at which each stage occurs. What makes his work particularly fruitful for the student or professional contemplating a descriptive survey is that Piaget offers these theoretical statements without supporting data and based on his observations in a middle European culture.

Immediately then we face several research questions. Do children indeed develop in the way he says? Are the specific stages of development he identifies empirically demonstrable? If they are, do they occur in the sequence he suggests? Or at the ages he notes? Finally, do these stages cut across culture, in the sense that they can be identified by researchers working with children of varied sociocultural backgrounds? Note that all of these questions are questions for which we lack data but for which the research situations exist, that is, there are accessible children at different ages and levels of development from backgrounds different from those Piaget has observed. These then are all research questions for which the descriptive survey is a perfectly appropriate research approach.

THE EVALUATIVE SURVEY

The evaluative survey can be understood most simply as a descriptive survey with at least one criterion measure available so that, in addition to description, some evaluative judgment can be made about the research situation. Since evaluation is tied to a criterion measure, the evaluative survey can be conducted with only one group and need not have any group-to-group comparison at all. Because of this, however, the validity of such a survey rests in large part on the validity of the criterion measure or measures used. These measures not only must be valid in the technical measurement sense, but also must be valid in the sense that the practitioners involved will accept them as relevant criteria against which to evaluate the research situation.

Education offers innumerable opportunities for meaningful evaluative surveys. Ironically, for a field which offers so many opportunities and which in some respects like grading is firmly committed to evaluation, startlingly few evaluative surveys were conducted before 1965. Consider evaluative questions like the effectiveness of programs of teacher preparation, or of high school programs of college preparation, or the effectiveness of programs for teaching social studies in the middle elementary grades. None of these have been evaluated.

In part this has been because teacher and administrator alike have equated evaluation of program with evaluation of staff. They have seen evaluation as a personal threat, and have argued that evaluative data are too easily taken out of the context of pupil ability and misinterpreted as reflecting only teacher and administrative functioning. These blocks to evaluate surveys were partially eliminated in the mid-1960s, when as part of the Elementary and Secondary Education Act the Congress included provision for evaluation of the programs funded under the act.

Selecting Criteria for Evaluation

In evaluative surveys once we state the evaluative question, "how effective is . . . ," we come to the criterion issue: "effective" in terms of what? Over the years in education we have generally begged the question of identifying meaningful criteria and developing reliable and valid measures of them. Moreover, we have been hindered in our efforts to develop these criteria by the comparable lacks in psychological and sociological measurement. For example, many programs for school integration under way as this book is being written have among their objectives the improvement of psychological aspects of functioning like self-concept and aspirational level, or sociological aspects like social acceptance of others. But these criteria are difficult, even treacherous, to employ for at present no measures of them exist of demonstrated reliability, validity, and sufficient precision.

Thus, over the years we have found a stereotyped reliance on achievement as the basic source for evaluative criteria, for this is the one area in which existing measures meet professional standards of reliability and validity. For many years there was not even any significant amount of instrument-development activity in the other areas. In the late 1960s, however, stimulated by the vast demands for evaluation within the federally funded programs under Titles I and III of the Elementary and Secondary Education Act, there were increased efforts to develop new instruments to measure psychological and social functioning. As this book is written it is too soon to know if these efforts will be sufficiently successful to make it more feasible to include psychological and social criteria in comparative and evaluative surveys.

Stating Criteria in Advance and Adhering to Them

Note that throughout this discussion of the evaluative survey we have considered that the criteria are stated before the survey. This implies that the researcher knows the problem sufficiently well in advance of the survey to enable him to state the criteria. Not only should the criteria be stated, but the standards by which evaluative judgments about the program or programs will be made should also be stated in advance. In this way the researcher surrenders the ability to decide how many respondents will meet his criteria, an ability possessed by the researcher who does not state his criteria in advance.[1] A simple illustration of this would be an accrediting agency which set out to evaluate the extent to which junior colleges meet acceptable standards as institutions of higher learning. The proper procedure for this evaluative survey would be for the researcher to state in advance of his study not only the characteristics which distinguish an institution of higher learning but also the specific levels or standards within each characteristic. Thus if one characteristic is size of library, we would also want him to state how large a library it must be for it to be acceptable. If it was faculty-student ratio, again we would want him to state what the minimum acceptable ratio is. If this were not done, the possibility is open for the researcher to collect data on all characteristics, and then for the friendly researcher to set standards sufficiently low to assure that all or most programs meet them or for the hostile researcher to set them high enough to assure that few programs meet them.

Before moving on beyond this discussion of criteria, there is one more point to be made. Once a researcher plans an evaluative survey using specific criteria as the basis for evaluation, he is committed to accepting and defending these as the relevant and valid criteria for the problem under study, *no matter how the data come out.*[2] Thus, if the data come out negative, contrary to the aims of the program being evaluated, the researcher has no right to undermine his criteria in an effort to explain away the data. The time to question criteria is *before* an evaluative survey is undertaken, and if insufficiently valid or reliable criteria exist, then the plans for an evaluative survey may need to be changed to a purely descriptive survey. Once he begins the evaluative process, the researcher is subtly saying to his public that he believes he has criteria upon which to make a sound judgment of "better" or "how effective."

Evaluation of Change over Time

One popular and critical aspect of evaluation is the evaluation designed to identify change, learning, or development over a period of time. This is possibly the single most frequent application of a research method to education, for in almost every class in almost every school data collected

[1]This argument for the desirability of prestated criteria is similar to the argument for insisting that researchers state their level of significance in advance.

[2]In this sense he has the same kind of commitment to criteria as the researcher doing a correlational survey has to his instruments.

at the end of the school year are compared to data collected at the beginning of the school year to evaluate the extent to which learning has taken place.[3]

Considered in its more general sense, there are two entirely different ways of designing an evaluative survey to estimate the extent of change over time: the *longitudinal approach* and the *cross-sectional approach*.

Longitudinal Surveys

The longitudinal approach to designing a survey of change over time is the obvious one: The same situations or persons are studied at the two points in time. This is relatively simple to implement if our interest in change involves a relatively brief period, in other words, one school year.[4] It is these *short-term longitudinal surveys* which exist in such abundance in education. The longitudinal approach is more difficult to implement if the period of time involved is a long one such as the elementary school years, or the high school sequence, or from childhood to the early adult years. To accomplish a long-term longitudinal study, the researcher must wait several years between his initial and final data collections.

It was noted above that the short-term longitudinal survey is the single most frequently employed research approach in education. It might also successfully be argued that one of the greatest single lacks in educational research is the relative absence of *long-term longitudinal studies*. We seem to be an impatient people in the United States, far too impatient to wait five, ten, or twenty years for research results, except in isolated instances like Terman's twenty-year study of genius[5] and Bayley's[6] twelve-year study of the relationship of intelligence and aging. Instead when we do longitudinal studies most often they are of the short-term type, involving following the respondents for a year or less.

The most dramatic example of this in the 1960s was the short-term longitudinal approach to the evaluation of the Head Start programs to provide preschool experience for educationally disadvantaged children. The clearly stated objective of the program was to better prepare these

---

[3]In some few radical institutions this comparison is even used to evaluate the extent to which teaching has taken place!

[4]It is recognized that for the student facing a deadline even one academic year may seem like a long time to have to wait to complete data collection.

[5]L. M. Terman and M. H. Oden, *The Gifted Child Grows Up* (Vol. IV of *Genetic Studies of Families*, L. M. Terman, ed.) (Stanford, Calif.: Stanford University Press, 1947).

[6]Nancy Bayley, "On the Growth of Intelligence," *The American Psychologist*, no. 10, (December 1955), p. 815.

children to function when they entered the regular school program. It was particularly hoped that these preschool experiences would better prepare children to handle the materials and symbolic processes involved in learning to read and perform arithmetic computations when they reached the third and fourth grades. To evaluate how much children profited from this instruction obviously required a long-term longitudinal study following the children at least through the early grades in elementary school, and ideally into secondary school. Instead we had the shortest possible short-term studies, some comparing the children at the beginning and end of a summer's instruction!

The severest problem for the short-term longitudinal study is the relevance of this period of time which elapses between the initial and final measures. On the one hand the researcher is concerned that not enough time will have elapsed for measurable change to have taken place, or for slowly developing changes to have appeared. If this happens, it leads to spurious conclusions as to the failure of the program. The contradictory possibility is that over a short period of time temporary changes induced by enthusiasm and excitement of participation in something new will take place which would lead to spurious conclusions as to the success of the program.[7]

Because of this, it is wise to plan any longitudinal study which is concerned with change and development so that data collection takes place in at least two different stages of the particular developmental process under study. In the Head Start example above, this would mean continuing this study long enough for measures to be available of the children's performance both at the end of kindergarten or first grade and again in the third or fourth grade. In this way the researcher is able to verify any changes and development he has detected at the end of the elementary grades preceding formal instruction. He is also able to determine if there are any changes appearing later which did not appear initially.

The fallacy in most short-term longitudinal studies of course is that the goals of the educational process are not short-term goals. For example, the basic aim of elementary and secondary education is to enable the child to grow into an adult who can function successfully in society as a literate, enlightened, and self-supporting citizen. How can the success of this effort be evaluated other than by considering the extent to which the end product of the educational enterprise *is* that successfully functioning adult? Are reading grades at the end of second or fifth grade, or performance on statewide examinations in senior high school relevant intermediate criteria

[7]This is the widely cited "Hawthorne Effect," which is discussed in Chapter 16.

for this ultimate aim? Or must we wait until the child becomes an adult to learn how successful any particular program was?

Notice that stating these questions highlights one of the basic difficulties with long-term longitudinal studies. This problem is the realistic one that in a long-term longitudinal study involving several years the final data may become available too late to serve any useful purpose. For while our goals in education are long-term goals, our decision-making periods are short-term periods. This is particularly true about decisions in continuing new or innovative programs. We can seldom wait for longitudinal evaluations. It would not have helped the Congressman in 1967 who had to vote on a bill to provide additional funds for Head Start programs to know that in 1972 data would be available to provide a reasonably solid basis for evaluating the success of the program. He needed a basis for action in 1967, and so the pressure for short-term evaluations is created. Unfortunately as federally financed programs proliferated in the 1960s, this pressure for data available annually oriented almost all of the evaluation designs to short-term longitudinal studies. Innumerable opportunities for beginning significant long-term longitudinal studies were lost in these years, as researchers responded to the need for immediate data.

The obsolescence of data is a perfectly valid objection to long-term longitudinal studies. However, in recognizing this problem, the research fraternity seems to have concluded that the only alternative is the one semester or one year short-term study. A simple compromise would have been to design and plan long-term studies with intermediate data collections providing the tentative reports needed for action.[8]

A second problem with long-term longitudinal surveys is the practical problem of maintaining contact with the same individuals over the period of years required to complete the study. Remember, the longitudinal study is conducted by collecting data from the same individuals at the various points in time involved.[9] Obviously the longer the survey runs, the more attrition occurs, and the more difficult it is to maintain researcher-respondent contact.

Despite these practical problems there is no substitute for truly long-term longitudinal studies. However, the fact is also that the graduate

[8]One objection to this kind of compromise, and one raised about longitudinal studies in general, is that frequent collection of data makes the respondents such sophisticated data producers as to make the data spurious. To this author, this problem is vastly overrated, since few longitudinal studies collect data with a frequency for this to be a realistic concern.

[9]This point is often forgotten in educational research studies involving comparisons from the beginning to the end of an academic year. For it to be a thoroughly longitudinal study data should be analyzed only for those children who were present for the entire school year and who took both the data-collection devices administered at the beginning and at the end of the year.

students for whom this book is written are not the researchers who can be expected to assume the burden of doing these studies. Pressures of time and money and desire to complete programs of instruction effectively rule this out. Hopefully the system of regional laboratories established by the United States Office of Education in the mid-1960s will stimulate more long-term longitudinal research. The hope is there because these laboratories have the stability in staff and funding which are prerequisites for longitudinal studies.

Cross-sectional Surveys

An entirely different approach to evaluating change over time is to use the cross-sectional survey, which evaluates change over time by comparing at the same point in time different people representing different stages of development. During the research project of which the Language Study was one phase, another research question of significance was the extent to which Puerto Rican children improved their language fluency with longer residence in the United States. The longitudinal way to evaluate this improvement would have been to select a sample of newly arrived Puerto Rican children and test them soon after they arrived. Then they would be tested periodically over the next several years, so that ultimately data would be available on the basis of which their improvement could be evaluated. However, the cross-sectional approach would be to select schools with large numbers of Puerto Rican children, and identify those children who were recently arrived, and those here one, two, three, and more years. Then to each of the subgroups, in terms of length of time here, we would administer some tests in whatever language modality was of interest to us. To evaluate improvement over time we would compare the scores of the children here for different periods of time.

The virtue of the cross-sectional approach is obvious. The complete set of data needed for conclusions about change are available simultaneously, without the three-and-four-year delay of the longitudinal approach. This is a major advantage which for students can often make the difference between being able to contemplate a study of change or rejecting it as not feasible. In fact the virtue is so overwhelming in terms of practicality that the immediate question which comes to mind is why all studies seeking to evaluate change do not utilize the cross-sectional approach.

The answer to this lies in identifying the assumptions involved in the cross-sectional design. When we take our subsample of children here less than six months and compare their scores to the children here two years, we are assuming the existence of all of the conditions necessary to make the two-year data a valid prediction of what the six-month children would score were we to wait until *they* were here two years, that is, if we were to do a longitudinal study. Figure 15-2 sketches out this kind of projection, as well as another way of considering the data. This would be to turn the time orientation around and to say that the data obtained from the children here six months or less are a reasonable approximation to the data we would have obtained from the children here two years or more had we tested them when they had only been here six months.

However we conceptualize it, the basic assumptions involved are similar: that the two groups are comparable, and that over a two-year period, nothing will happen (projecting forward) or has happened (projecting backwards) in the area under study to invalidate the comparison of the two groups of children as the basis for evaluating what changes take place over time. Over a period like two years most researchers would have few qualms about accepting the assumptions. Over a period of ten years, most would hesitate. It is hard to pin down the dividing line with any precision other than to suggest that natural units sometimes can guide the researcher. For example, in studies of elementary school children a cross-sectional study utilizing children in first and sixth grade would be more likely to be

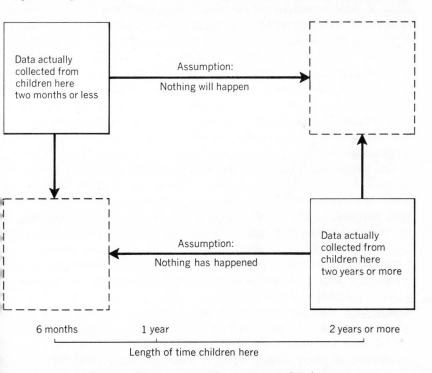

Figure 15-2   Conceptualization of cross-sectional survey.

accepted without argument than one cutting across the elementary and junior high school years to compare first and seventh graders.

But in planning our own studies, we should remember that it is not the period of time which is the critical issue in defending a cross-sectional study, but rather what happened during that period of time which might possibly have had some impact on the research results. For example, had a researcher picked two groups of children for a study to evaluate the impact of a remedial reading program in the upper elementary grades, he might select a fourth- and sixth-grade group. But had he done this in 1965 when the Elementary and Secondary Education Act was first feeding vast sums of money into school systems throughout the nation, he would have to face the fact that because of this the world of the schools had changed dramatically. Even the short two-year period now would be suspect as a basis for identifying two groups which could be considered to have had a comparable educational experience.

Comparing Longitudinal and Cross-sectional Surveys

Each of these approaches to studying change over time has strengths and weaknesses. The overriding strengths of the cross-sectional design are that it provides the researcher with his data quickly, eliminates the problem of obtaining the same respondents at different points in time, and by using different people to represent the different time intervals avoids any possibility that the data, in part, reflect the test-wiseness of the respondents. Its great weakness is that it rests on the assumption (untestable, like all assumptions) that each element at an advanced point in time provides us with the same data that earlier elements would if we waited and did a longitudinal study.

The major strength of the longitudinal design is that it avoids the assumption of comparability of different groups by using the same respondents at every data-collection interval. Its weaknesses are the length of time required to obtain the complete set of data and the difficulty in maintaining contact with, and reassembling, the respondents throughout the length of the study. Some researchers also add the weakness that continued exposure to the data-collection instruments and the research produces a degree of sophistication or test-wiseness in the respondents which is reflected in the data.

The data currently available indicate that the cross-sectional design functions well as an approximation to the short-term longitudinal study. Unless there has been some dramatic shift in the research situation, the assumption of group comparability is a sensible assumption over a short time period of up to five years. However, data recently reported from long-term longitudinal studies begun during the 1930s have indicated that the cross-sectional design does not function well as an approximation to the long-term longitudinal study. One striking example of this involves research on the change, if any, which takes place in intelligence as measured by intelligence test scores as a person ages. Generalizations on this were originally based on cross-sectional data, until some longitudinal data became available in the 1950s. The cross-sectional data indicated a decline in intelligence functioning as older age groups were tested. Thus 40-year-olds achieved lower scores than 30-year-olds, who in turn achieved lower scores than 20-year-olds. Accepting these data, texts in psychology and in maturity and aging noted this generalization, as in this quotation from Commins and Fagin in *Principles of Educational Psychology:* "The findings from tests administered to adults show that test performance not only stops gaining with age, but that it actually goes downhill steadily past a certain age range of 'peak' performance."[10]

For many years this was generally accepted, although a controversial point. However, it was first seriously challenged in the 1950s by W. A. Owens,[11] who reported the results of a 30-year follow-up study of 127 individuals who were tested at age 50 after an initial test at age 19. He found that scores improved. The more widely known challenge came from Nancy Bayley who reported similar longitudinal findings from the Berkeley Growth Study. In this study the two tests were only 12 years apart, but more than a thousand respondents were tested, ranging in age from 20 to 50. Bayley reports "when they were grouped into 5-year age intervals, the test-retest scores of all age groups increased."[12]

The consideration of these two sets of data, with a basic contradictory finding, highlights all of the problems in choosing between the cross-sectional and longitudinal approaches. If we accept the Bayley finding, we can easily explain the cross-sectional results by pointing out that these studies violated the basic assumption of sound cross-sectional sampling: It was fallacious to think of a 20-year-old producing a test result which would accurately represent the test result 20 years before of a person tested at 40 years of age. The educational system and the utilization of tests had changed too drastically every generation for the assumption to make sense. Therefore, the cross-sectional results would be explained as a reflection of the changes in education and the quality of schooling and not changes in age.

[10]W. D. Commins and Barry Fagin, *Principles of Educational Psychology* (New York: The Ronald Press Company, 1954), p. 200.

[11]W. A. Owens, "Age and Mental Abilities: A Longitudinal Study," *Genetic Psychological Monograph,* no. 48, 1953, pp. 3–54.

[12]Nancy Bayley, "On the Growth of Intelligence."

However, a contrary interpretation of the Bayley data could argue that these data do not reflect the true state of the effects of aging on performance on intelligence tests. This point of view would say that her respondents were tested often enough to become a highly sophisticated group of test takers, and her data reflect the fact that people can be taught to take intelligence tests and do not demonstrate the effect of age on intelligence.[13]

Of course, with the present data neither point can be answered. What this conflict does indicate is that definitive answers to this type of question involving change over time cannot definitely be answered by either design. What is needed is a combination of them, which at this point has not been utilized in research in the social sciences. This design would create a large initial sample, which would be broken up into equivalent units. The number of units to be created would be determined by the number of longitudinal data collections. At each interval a randomly selected proportion of the original group would be tested. In this way, no one group would be tested more than once, and the issue of test sophistication never would arise. This type of longitudinal plan is sketched in Figure 15-3, for five data collection intervals.

While we should be alert to the difficulty of both cross-sectional and longitudinal designs, the author believes that the advantages of the longitudinal study, even allowing for test sophistication, far outweigh the

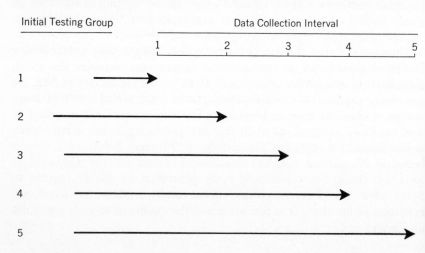

Figure 15-3   Plan for longitudinal study with nonrepetitive participation.

[13]On this point, Bayley, referring to Owen's and her own study has said: "One can hardly claim practice effects after a lapse of 31 years. Even the 12-year interval of the Terman study is rather long for any such claim."

disadvantages, whereas whenever the time interval goes beyond four or five years the assumptions of the cross-sectional approach become too tenuous.

THE COMPARATIVE SURVEY

The third major type of survey is the comparative survey, in which the researcher wishes to obtain data to enable him to decide which of two or more research situations is superior—again, in terms of specific prestated criteria. In other words, a study is a comparative survey if the researcher takes at least two entities *now in existence*[14] and establishes a formal procedure for obtaining criterion data, on the basis of which he can compare the entities and come to some conclusions as to which is best. For example, a comparison of three different teacher education programs in terms of retention, that is, the proportion of graduates who are still in the field ten years after graduation, would be a simple comparative survey using one criterion for comparison.

The comparative survey, based as it is on the study of two or more different research situations, obviously must be justifiable in terms of the educational significance of learning about the similarity or difference of those research situations. In other words, a comparative survey is a sensible research approach only when there are worthwhile things to compare. Moreover, it is sensible only when the comparison will be complete in the sense of comparing all the research situations of professional significance. If the survey comparing three different teacher education programs ignored a fourth variation on how to prepare teachers, it would be incomplete. How serious a drawback the incompleteness would be would depend on the importance of the omitted research situation. To avoid this problem, the initial planning of the comparative survey should include a thorough review of all potential research situations, and verification by experts in the field that those selected for comparison represent a complete set of the important situations.

Isolating the Comparative Variable

The first major problem in a comparative survey is establishing the extent to which the situations being compared differ on variables other than the one of research interest. Ideally the comparative survey is conducted in several research settings which are comparable on all critical characteris-

---

[14]If one or more of the entities did not currently exist, but was created for the purposes of the study, then it would no longer be a comparative survey but an experiment, as will be discussed in the next chapter.

tics other than the one the researcher wishes to study. In reality this never happens, of course, for two or three different educational settings inevitably differ on a wide variety of factors. Thus the example above, in which three different teacher preparation programs are being compared, may have stemmed initially from research interest in the fact that the programs differ widely at the point in the undergraduate program at which students are first placed in classes for practice teaching. However, the researcher could not stop with establishing this one difference. He would have to explore the extent to which the student populations were comparable, and do the same for faculty and administration. He would be concerned with the comparability of the school settings in which the practice teaching was done. He would be concerned with knowing the length of the practice teaching period and the frequency of supervisory visits. In short, he would need to do a thorough descriptive survey of the several research settings on all other characteristics which could affect his criterion variables.[15]

Since he would almost certainly find that the settings being compared differed on some of these other variables as well, the conclusions from a comparative survey are necessarily tentative and limited. They remain tentative until supported by experimental studies of the comparative variable. This leads to an important point about comparative surveys: They do not provide evidence for an inference of cause and effect any more than the correlational study does. They are only suggestive and are most effectively used as a means for generating hypotheses for future experimentation.

Delineating the Criterion Variables

The second critical element in the comparative survey is the delineation of criterion variables which are reasonable for all of the different research situations being surveyed, yet are sufficiently meaningful for the original research problem. The danger is that by eliminating variables which might favor one particular setting or be unfair to another, the researcher may be left with a set of bland and innocuous variables which are fair to all but which will not serve any real research purpose. The researcher contemplating a comparative survey must have the courage to select the critical variables, using the ultimate research goal to provide the rationale for selecting the variables on which the settings are to be compared. However, in fairness to the various settings, the researcher should include the

[15]The student contemplating a comparative survey should read the sections on bias and intervening variables in Chapter 16 on the experimental approach, since the parallels are extensive between the approaches.

information he has on the relative emphasis each setting has placed on developing the skill or knowledge or attitude being evaluated.

The final concern in the comparative survey is the translation of these variables into specific criterion measures. It is one thing to agree that attitude toward school is an important variable in comparing different educational programs. How to measure attitude toward school is quite another problem. However, this problem is the same criterion problem just considered in the discussion of the evaluative survey and, to avoid redundancy, let us simply note that the researcher contemplating a comparative survey should recognize that all said earlier about the nature of criteria in the evaluative survey applies to him as well.

Combining Types of Surveys

Considering the three major types of surveys separately as was done here is not intended to suggest that these are mutually exclusive types. It is perfectly possible in fact to combine types and even to have all three major types within one study. An example of this is the well-known survey of the American educational scene which resulted in the report entitled "Equality of Educational Opportunity."[16] This project had within it a descriptive phase, a comparative phase, and an evaluative phase. Moreover, the descriptive phase involved simple description, correlational studies, case studies, and mass surveys. One descriptive phase involved determining the nature of the school plants and facilities available in the United States, describing selected characteristics of the teaching and administrative staff, and the family backgrounds, home settings, and a wide variety of academic and sociopsychological characteristics of the pupil population. The correlational phase involved determining the relationships between these variables, that is, the extent to which pupil achievement was related to school characteristics or to teacher background or to pupil background. Moreover, while most of the survey was done on a mass basis involving the total American educational community, the study also involved case studies of school integration in different communities. Thus, within this one study appeared all the variants of the descriptive survey.

But the study involved a comparative survey as well, for many of the analyses involved comparisons of the educational settings available for Negro and white children in the United States. Finally, one of the major foci of the study was to evaluate the extent to which Negro and white children had comparable educational opportunities in terms of criteria like

[16]James Coleman and others, "Equality of Educational Opportunity," (Washington, D. C.: Government Printing Office, 1966), 737 pp.

school plant, or teacher preparation and ability. The study also sought to evaluate the extent of segregation in the nation's schools, using as the criterion whether or not children attended schools "where almost all of the fellow students are of the same racial background as they are."[17]

"Equality of Educational Opportunity" is also an excellent refutation of the argument sometimes advanced that surveys are bland and uninteresting and of little significance. Few studies have stimulated more discussion than this one, and few research findings in recent educational history have provoked more debate than the finding from the correlational phase that school quality and teacher quality had only small relationships to the quality of pupil functioning. While not all researchers can aspire to conducting a survey of the scope and significance of this, many can aspire to conducting surveys whose findings will be provocative and meaningful. Let us turn then to the steps in actually conducting a survey.

THE PROCESS OF SURVEY RESEARCH

The several steps in the survey approach are outlined in the list below.

1. Statement of the research problem
2. Determination that the problem is appropriate for the survey approach
3. Selection of the appropriate type of survey
4. Identification of the objectives of the survey and the translation of these into criterion variables
5. Determination for which of the variables identified:
    (a) adequate techniques for data collection exist
    (b) adequate techniques can be developed in time
    (c) adequate techniques neither exist nor can be developed in time
6. Interim determination of success potential of proposed survey
8. Initial determination of the availability of a representative sample
7. Identification of the population of research situations or respondents needed
9. Decision as to those aspects of survey for which representative sample can be obtained
10. Final evaluation of success potential of survey in view of availability of adequate data-collection instruments and required sample, and *all* potential results
    Then if success potential seems reasonable:
11. Design of data collection
12. Collection of data
13. Analysis of data

[17]Coleman, "Equality of Educational Opportunity," p. 3.

14. Preparation of report:
   (a)   descriptive phase
   (b)   comparative or evaluative phase
   (c)   conclusions

As in any research approach, the first steps involve the *statement of the research problem* and the *determination that the problem selected is appropriate for study* through the approach under consideration, in this case the survey approach. For all surveys, the research problem must be one for which needed data do not exist but the situations or respondents needed to generate the data do. This is the basic characteristic which guides the researcher to the survey approach in general. The third step is to determine which of the specific types of survey is most appropriate. The special aspects of a research problem which suggest each of the specific types of survey have been discussed earlier in this chapter and those discussions will not be repeated here. To review them we shall note that these several types differ in their orientation in four dimensions, and once the researcher has placed his problem and need for data in these dimensions, he has selected his type. The basic dimension is the intent of the researcher, as dictated by the research problem, to describe, compare, or evaluate. It is this intent which guides the selection of the major survey type. Once this is selected, he can consider the second dimension, orientation in time. Although all survey data are collected in the present, and are usually concerned with the present, we have also noted that the referent for these data may be some point in the past (retrospective) or may be change over a period of time (longitudinal and cross-sectional). A third dimension involves the orientation to the nature of the sample, for we noted that the surveys can run the gamut from concern with samples built on units of one (case study) to studies of large samples and populations (mass survey). Finally, we have noted a fourth dimension, the orientation of the survey to describing the research situation in terms of independent characteristics or to the study of relationships (correlational survey). Most important of all, we have concluded that it is simple and sensible to plan a survey which includes many of these types within it, if that is what the research problem requires.

The next stage, *identification of objectives and their translation into criteria,* is a particularly complex phase in view of the current development of measurement in the social disciplines. In this phase, the researcher must identify each specific aspect of the survey in which he has some interest, which is an intellectually challenging task requiring knowledge of the situation to be surveyed. In fact, the wise researcher will involve representative practitioners at this point to be certain that, when completed, the survey will be accepted as having studied the correct objectives. Some objectives are directly translatable into criteria, as for example, the objective of improving children's ability to read is easily translatable into the criterion of gain in score on a standardized test of reading achievement. In contrast, an objective like improving children's aspirational level is difficult to translate into a specific variable which can be expected to change. What variable reflects aspirational level? Is it a long-term goal like the highest educational level which the child expects to reach, or the job he expects to hold as an adult? Or is it a short-term goal like whether he expects to complete this specific assignment or this current term with considerable success?

If we read projects in educational planning, we note that it is far simpler to state objectives in the area of psychosocial functioning than it is to translate those objectives into specific variables which the researcher can be expected to study. Thus, in planning a survey, do not equate stating objectives with selecting the variables. Stating a set of objectives on which researcher and practitioner can agree is a significant part of this fourth stage, but only part. They must also agree on the translation of these into behavioral or attitudinal components, so that the researcher can turn to the next stage, estimating his ability to obtain the data needed to complete the survey successfully.

With the objectives translated into criteria, the researcher's next task is *survey the data-gathering instruments* available so that he can divide his criteria into three subgroups: (1) those for which instruments exist which are both relevant and technically adequate (that is, sufficiently reliable and valid); (2) those for which no instrument exists which is both relevant and technically adequate, but for which the researcher believes he can construct one within the time available for instrument development; and (3) those for which no instrument exists and for which the researcher does *not* believe he can construct one in time. This classification and evaluation of instrumentation is one of the most critical stages in survey planning because a glance at Stage 6 indicates that it is an interim basis for the researcher to *initially estimate the success potential* of the proposed survey.

We have noted at many points in this book the necessity for the researcher at some appropriate interim point in his research planning to be willing to revise or even abandon his proposed research. In the survey approach this point comes for the first time just after the overview of instrumentation is completed. For now the researcher knows those criteria (and objectives) which can adequately be evaluated through proper instruments, and those which cannot. Obviously he is then able to decide if he can successfully capture enough of the important criteria to merit going on with the survey. The meaning of "enough" in the preceding sentence will vary from survey type to type. The most leeway comes in the descriptive survey, in which the researcher may decide that while he cannot obtain data on some important variables he will be able to obtain sufficient data on other variables to conclude with a significant set of data. For comparative surveys, and particularly for evaluative surveys, there is no such leeway. The researcher must be able to obtain data on the basic variables needed to compare or evaluate. He cannot justify these two types by saying that while he could not compare or evaluate on the critical variables, he did obtain a great deal of other information on the research situations. Success potential at this stage must be evaluated with absolute candor if innocuous and meaningless results are to be avoided.

Assuming that instrumentation is considered adequate, the researcher moves on to the next stage, in which he *identifies the population* of research situations or respondents needed for the particular survey and then goes on to *estimate the extent to which a representative sample* of this population *will be available* to him. Here, too, candid appraisal of possibilities is essential in developing an ultimately successful survey. At this stage the researcher must be ready to abandon aspects of the proposed survey if he concludes a representative sample will not be available for it. For example, in a recent evaluative survey conducted by the author, one objective of an innovative educational program was to improve parental attitude about the school. It was agreed by researcher and practitioner that this objective could be translated into a series of direct questions about the school program asked of parents. It was further agreed that an instrument to obtain these answers could be developed within the time required. But as we considered the problem of obtaining a representative sample of the parental population, we also agreed that within the time and resources available we could not accomplish this. Previous such studies with parental populations like those involved indicated that mailing the survey instrument to the parents or sending it home with children would result in less than a 25 percent return. More important, it was felt that the return was a biased one, being limited to the more interested and vocal parents. Since there was neither time nor money to use alternative techniques like home interviews to improve the representativeness of the sample, this phase of the survey was eliminated. In short, we decided that no data were preferred to potentially spurious data. The researcher contemplating a survey must be ready to make this decision at this stage.

Then comes the point where the researcher takes one final look across these several stages for his *final evaluation of the success potential* of the proposed survey. Again, he candidly appraises the nature of his instrumentation and the samples available, but he also considers all possible results to make certain that no matter how the data come out he will have a sensible and significant statement to make in his research report. Note that the concern with results here is not to avoid data it might be unpleasant to learn. It is to avoid data that are so limited and so far from the meaningful objectives and criteria as to have no interest to the profession involved.

This must not be a stage passed by casually. It must be done with the researcher ready to alter or even abandon a potential survey if he believes that the lacks in instrumentation, sample, or certain potential results will severely limit the significance of his result.

Assuming the happier instance in which the instrumentation, sample, and potential results are judged as adequate and the decision is made to go on, the next three stages are common not only to the three types of survey but to all research approaches. These are the phases in which *research is designed* and the *data are collected and analyzed*. As noted in the model in Chapter 2, these stages in the research process are implementation stages involving little of the decision making and judgments which characterize the earlier phases.

Finally, assuming that the data are collected and analyzed, comes the phase in which the data from the research situation surveyed are reported and conclusions relative to that situation and the research problem are drawn and stated. In this stage the three types of survey differ considerably. The researcher committed to a descriptive survey will be more concerned with a rich and full description than with conclusions. In fact, in some descriptive surveys, like the United States Census, description is the only task the researchers attempt. They see their function as providing descriptive data for others to study and interpret and draw conclusions. In contrast, the researcher doing a comparative survey is concerned primarily with the conclusions he draws as to the relative merits of the different research situations he is comparing. In fact, one often reads reports of studies comparing several methods of instruction in which one learns which method was best, but never learns what each method accomplished. In these studies the researcher has become so preoccupied with the comparative conclusion that he has ignored the descriptive function. In the evaluative survey, too, the researcher is concerned primarily with the conclusions rather than with description. However, he is less likely to ignore the descriptive function because his conclusions must be supported by reference to the data.

For the student preparing a paper or dissertation, all of these phases should be included, where relevant. Thus, the descriptive survey includes both description and conclusions. The comparative and evaluative surveys include description, comparison or evaluation, and conclusions. The student, in short, does not have the luxury of the census taker to avoid dealing with the meaning of the data. He must conclude his survey with his interpretation of the data in the context of the original research problem.

THE COMPARATIVE SURVEY AND QUASI-EXPERIMENTAL RESEARCH

What we are calling the comparative survey in this book is referred to in some books as *quasi-experimental research*[18] and in others as *naturalistic research.*[19] All three terms refer to instances in which the researcher takes natural settings, already established and functioning, and adds a data-collection dimension so that he can come to some conclusion about relative effectiveness. Thus Campbell and Stanley define quasi-experimental research as that done in "natural social settings in which the research person can introduce something like experimental design into his scheduling of data collection procedures."[20] McCandless defines what he calls naturalistic research as that done when the organism is "studied under real life natural conditions."[21] The author of this book has chosen to treat this kind of study as a survey rather than a quasi-experiment for two reasons. The first reason for applying the label comparative survey is that it *is* a survey, that is, a study of existing research situations with the research component limited to data collection. Second, it is *not* an experiment, whether an experiment is defined in terms of the fact that it is focused on the study of something new or in terms of the researcher's ability to manipulate the variables of major interest. To label it quasi-experimental research seems to confuse an issue unnecessarily by implying that it belongs to the family of experiments. Particularly dangerous is the misconception that as a member of the family of experiments, this type of research will test for cause and effect. It will not, no matter how we label it.

The rationale for this distinction will be further illustrated as we move on to the experimental approach. But whatever it is called, the process whereby the researcher studies existing settings in as formal a way as possible is a fruitful source of information about educational programs and processes. It is the author's hope that seeing these studies as rigorous surveys rather than weak attempts to simulate experimentation will encourage researchers to attempt them, for they are needed.

[18]Donald T. Campbell and Julian C. Stanley, *Experimental and Quasi-Experimental Designs for Research.* Skokie, Ill.: Rand McNally & Company, 1963, 84 pp.
[19]Boyd R. McCandless, *Children's Behavior and Development.* Second Edition (New York: Holt, Rinehart and Winston, Inc., 1967), 671 pp.
[20]Campbell and Stanley, *Experimental and Quasi-Experimental Designs,* p. 34.
[21]McCandless, *Children's Behavior and Development,* p. 60.

Chapter 16

THE EXPERIMENTAL APPROACH

The third major research approach, the experimental approach, has been described earlier in this book as oriented to the future in the sense that the researcher is seeking to evaluate something new. Thus, the experimenter operates under the basic assumption that the research situation he wishes to evaluate has never existed and does not now exist. He, therefore, must create it to be able to study it. We are using the term *research situation* here in its broadest sense. It would include both a "situation" in the sense of a new program, or curriculum, or method for organizing classes, as well as a "situation" created to test for the presence of a psychological dynamic to be expected from a specific theory.

If experimentation is defined as involving some new and untried element, or condition, then experimentation involves the evaluation of the effects of this condition or element. The condition or element being evaluated is referred to as the *independent variable* in the experiment, while the criteria by which it is to be evaluated are referred to as the *dependent variables*. Ideally, an experiment is so designed that there is a direct relationship between the independent and dependent variables— direct in the sense that it is reasonable to believe that whatever differences exist on the dependent variables after the experiment can be attributed to the independent variable. In most educational research this ideal design is not realizable, for other variables come between the independent and dependent variables. These other variables, referred to as *intervening variables,* can, in the simplest sense, be defined as all conditions which impede attributing all differences in dependent variables to the independent variable. Note that this definition does not require that the independent variables necessarily precede the intervening variables in time. A difference in intelligence between two groups being compared in a learning experiment would make intelligence an intervening variable, as it is defined here. Why? Because that initial difference in intelligence would

454

impede attributing final differences on the dependent measures to the different learning processes studied.

CAUSE AND EFFECT

Since at least one of the situational elements in the experiment is created by the researcher, many authors who write about experiments define the process in terms of the researcher's ability to manipulate the research situation. Thus, Good notes that "in experimentation the investigator controls (manipulates or changes) certain independent variables and observes the changes which take place in the form of dependent variables."[1] The researcher's manipulation of at least some aspects of the research situation does indeed characterize experimentation, but it is characterized even more by his ability to attribute whatever changes he sees in the dependent variables to the manipulation of the independent variable. Experiments, in other words, deal with cause and effect. In an ideally designed experiment the researcher concludes with an understanding not only of what happened but why it happened.

What makes the attribution of cause possible is eliminating all factors other than the independent variables as possible explanations of differences in the dependent variables. This is basically a theoretical statement, for in reality in the social disciplines we seldom have the ability to completely eliminate all other relevant factors.

In fact, we have considerable difficulty even knowing what the relevant factors are for many research problems. The discussion in Chapter 11 on sampling, in which the difficulties in achieving representativeness were cataloged, could be repeated here with but slight variation. For when we speak of asking the experimenter to control relevant factors we are often paying lip service to an ideal and ignoring reality, which is that there are four basic obstacles to sound control in experimentation in the social disciplines. Two of these factors are unique to the experimenter in the social disciplines, while two are shared by the experimenter in the physical sciences.

The first difficulty, and a shared one, is knowing what to control. The sparcity of correlational studies in the social disciplines, which we referred to earlier in discussing the survey approach, haunts us here for it means that we simply do not know what characteristics are related to each other. It also means that the experimenter must often rely on theory to suggest

[1]Carter V. Good, *Introduction to Educational Research*. Second Edition (New York: Appleton-Century-Crofts, 1963), p. 444.

the critical characteristics on which he should depend for control. In fields like teaching, where theory is insufficiently developed, he must even go back one further step, and rely on intuition or hunch. In contrast, the physical scientist, when faced with the same problem, has available a much richer repertoire of both correlational data and theory to help him decide the characteristics over which to seek control.

Even assuming that the social experimenter does know the characteristics which he should control, he faces the second shared difficulty: developing the ability to measure those characteristics. Consider a researcher desiring to experimentally evaluate a new organizational pattern for disadvantaged children in early elementary grades. He may realize that to compare learning rates between the experimental and the traditional organizations he must control characteristics like the children's desire to learn, the teaching staff's role perceptions and attitudes to children, and so on through the area of attitude, interest, and perception. It is quite another thing for this experimenter to achieve any significant ability to control these characteristics when he has almost no ability to measure any of them with precision sufficient enough to speak of control.

Even if he achieves the measurement ability he faces the third and perhaps most critical obstacle, and the one that differs most dramatically from the situation of the physical scientist: the ability to manipulate the research situation sufficiently to implement the proper degree of control. This particular aspect of the problem of control involves having the proper range of respondents available, having them available in sufficient numbers, being able to move them from situation to situation, and other practical difficulties. In the example above, let us assume that the experimenter developed a reliable and valid measure of teacher attitude toward disadvantaged children which he could give to the teaching staff available for the study. For him to be able to use these data to achieve control on this characteristic, he must have sufficient numbers of teachers at each gradation in attitude so that some can be assigned to the new experimental classes and comparable numbers to the classes to be organized under the old pattern. Moreover, he must have the administrative authority and teacher cooperation so that these shifts in assignment can be made.

The final aspect of control, also unique to experimentation in the social disciplines, is the researcher's ability to maintain control after he has established his experimental conditions and the study is under way. For now he is faced with the problem of maintaining "control" over the people involved in each of the separate conditions of the experiment, so that he can be assured that nothing but the desired variations of procedure are operating and, moreover, that they are operating as he wished. For example, if the study involves variation in program or of teaching method, how does a researcher guarantee that no one involved in program A communicates subtly or directly with one of the teachers involved in B? If they share their experimental secrets, either unintentionally or intentionally, then instead of having an experimental comparison of methods A and B the experimenter has a comparison of A mixed with an unknown quantity of B, and, conversely, the other way around.

DRAWBACKS OF EXPERIMENTAL APPROACH

Over the years, it has proven to be tremendously difficult to avoid this type of leakage or contamination and to keep each experimental variation pure. Thus, unlike his colleagues who study learning and behavior with animals, the educational researcher cannot be certain his subjects come from identical genetic backgrounds, cannot control their experiences before, after, or even during the experiment, and cannot control the variables extraneous to the experiment which will intervene. In this sense, experimentation in education is qualitatively a different research approach than it is in psychological experimentation with animals or in most of the physical sciences. In fact, it is impossible to fully counter the argument that experimentation, in the sense in which the physical scientist uses the term, cannot be achieved in education, or for that matter, in any of the social disciplines.

This detailed introduction is not intended to discourage attempts at experimentation, but rather to alert the reader to the difficulties faced by the experimenter in the social disciplines. Moreover, understanding these problems, one can better understand the low repute in which experimentation is held in education. In the index of the Handbook of Research on Teaching there is an entry for "experimentation in education." The first specific under this entry refers to the "history of" experimentation, and the second to "disillusionment with" experimentation.[2] In their article on experimental design in the Handbook,[3] Campbell and Stanley spell out further how a "wave of enthusiasm for experimentation" dominated education in the 1920s, turning into what they describe as "apathy and rejection"[4] in the 1930s, so that Monroe can be quoted in 1938 as concluding that the direct contributions of controlled experimentation

[2]N. L. Gage, ed., *Handbook of Research on Teaching* (Skokie, Ill.: Rand McNally & Company, 1963), p. 1184.
[3]Donald T. Campbell and Julian C. Stanley, "Experimental and Quasi-Experimental Designs for Research on Teaching." In N. L. Gage, ed., *Handbook of Research on Teaching,* pp. 171–246.
[4]Campbell and Stanley, "Experimental and Quasi-Experimental Designs," p. 172.

have been disappointing.[5] Since Monroe made that statement 30 years ago, the direct contributions of controlled experimentation to education, if anything, are even more disappointing than they seemed to Monroe.

Nevertheless, we cannot avoid the hard fact that experimental evidence is the most solid evidence we can obtain as to the functioning validity of a new program or plan, just as experimental data supporting a theory are the most convincing data that the theory has validity and relevance for educational practice. Thus, the educator and educational researcher do not have the luxury of ignoring the experimental approach simply because past efforts to use it in education have been notably unsuccessful. Rather, we need more rigorously designed experiments based on a fuller understanding of the questions and issues involved in designing and implementing an experiment in the social disciplines. Moreover, if we are to have more meaningful experiments in education, researchers must be rigorous and candid in the identification of those settings and problems for which the experimental approach is appropriate. Finally, the same rigor and candor must be applied in the stage of research in which the success potential of the study is estimated. For it is during this evaluation of the success potential that the researcher contemplating the experimental approach must be able to argue that he has identified all of the relevant intervening variables and will be able to handle each sufficiently well so as to be able to attribute any differences in the dependent variables to the established differences in the independent variables. Once he begins on an experiment, in other words, the researcher must be willing to defend the fact that he has been able to create experimental conditions which represent a fair test of the independent variable.

Speaking personally for a moment, this author has little patience with the researcher who designs and conducts an experiment and then, when the results come out contrary to what he believed, points an accusing finger at the intervening variables. If the feeling is that the intervening variables are insufficiently controlled to make the experiment a valid test of the independent variable, then *do not go on with the experimental approach.* This is far preferable to proceeding with it, with the expectation that if things do not work out, we can always blame the intervening variables. The only exception to this after-the-fact highlighting of intervening variables would be those instances in which, during the course of an experiment, a researcher gains insight into the operation of an intervening variable which there was no reason for him to anticipate. When this happens, however, the researcher must note this and not consider the

[5]W. S. Monroe, "General Methods: Classroom Experimentation." In G. M. Whipple, ed., *Yearbook of the National Society for the Study of Education,* vol. 37, part 2, 1938, pp. 319–327.

experiment a valid test of the independent variable, no matter *how* the results come out.

Obviously, then, the key element in planning a sound experiment is the identification of the independent, intervening, and dependent variables.

THE INDEPENDENT VARIABLE

The identification of the independent variable is seldom a problem, for the statement of the research usually identifies it readily. However, the identification of the elements or variations of that independent variable can be a difficult chore. Thus, in the Language Study, once the problem was stated as finding the best method of teaching English as a second language to non–English-speaking Puerto Rican children, the independent variable was clearly identified: method of teaching English as a second language. However, to specifically identify which methods would be those experimented with involved an extensive review of the literature to identify those methods used in the past, or only existing on paper. This was followed by a survey to identify other methods currently in use, but not in the literature. This suggests, and properly, that no researcher can sit down and spell out the variations within his independent variable without first conducting a thorough review of the literature in the problem area and also conducting whatever survey is necessary to verify that the proposed experiment contains relevant variations of the independent variable.[6]

The fact that references in this chapter have been to the independent variable, in the singular, does not mean that the researcher is limited to one independent variable. In Chapter 10 we noted how the complex analysis of variance makes it possible to mathematically attribute portions of the data obtained to the several sources which might have contributed to those data. This is easily translatable to experimental terms. It means that through the analysis of variance technique it is possible to attribute portions of the final data from each dependent variable to each of several independent variables which might have contributed to these data.

The availability of the complex analysis of variance means that we can begin to approach reality in social experiments. For, in reality, variables do not exist in simple, isolated units but rather in conjunction with other variables. Ideally, to truly study reality an experimental design considers the appropriate multiplicity of independent variables. In a sense, the experiment with a single independent variable is as far from reality as the

---

[6]This review of literature and survey will also verify that the experimental approach is necessary, that is, that data do not already exist on the basis of which the research question can be answered.

simple correlational survey is from the multidimensional reality considered in the case-study survey. But while we can design an experiment with multiple independent variables, as we have already noted so often, we are simply not far enough advanced in our understanding of human behavior or in our ability to measure human characteristics to properly establish such experiments in practice.

THE DEPENDENT VARIABLE(S)

The basic referents for the identification of the dependent variables are the original research problem and the hypotheses the researcher wishes to test. The problem guides the researcher in knowing the general areas of interest within which he should seek dependent measures. The hypotheses, particularly if they originate in theory, structure the need for dependent variables more specifically, since measures to test each hypothesis will be needed.

Developing the dependent variables involves identically the same process and problems as identifying criteria does in the comparative and evaluative survey. As in these types of survey, the researcher in experimental research must first identify those dependent variables which will, taken together, make a reasonable test of the independent variable. Then each dependent variable must be translated into a measure of some kind, either by using or adapting an existing measure or developing a new one for purposes of the experiment. Thus, in the Language Study, a consideration of the objectives of the second-language teaching led to the relatively simple identification of the four modalities of reading, writing, speaking, and understanding spoken English as four relevant dependent variables for the study. But there were others which were also relevant. For example this set of dependent variables was completely achievement-oriented and ignored the whole realm of attitudes such as attitude toward English, school, or education. It ignored appraisals of in-class functioning by teachers, or the friendship patterns established by the children, and a dozen other potential dependent variables. Perhaps even more critical, all of these dependent variables were short-term rather than long-term, and so told us nothing about the effects of these different language methods in the years beyond the one year studied.

The researcher in education is always faced with these two problems: the necessity to select from among the vast number of potential relevant dependent variables, and the difficulty of securing the funds and cooperation needed to employ any but short-term dependent variables. The first problem is more conceptual than actual, however, for the number of potential variables is rapidly cut down at the stage in which the researcher determines the availability of measuring devices for each dependent variable. It is typically at this stage when potential dependent variables in areas like attitudes, interests, ratings, and sociometric concerns lose out in favor of dependent variables in the achievement area, for it is in the achievement areas where the most solidly developed instruments exist. This lure of existing instruments is difficult for the researcher to resist, particularly for the student pressed for time and with limited opportunities for instrument development. Unfortunately, not every experiment is sensibly evaluated by achievement tests, and so the researcher is well advised, when he evaluates the success potential of his research, to consider whether these variables in and of themselves will be sufficient to provide a meaningful test of the independent variable.

In the Language Study, although we limited the dependent variables to the area of achievement, we did not limit them to the one modality for which standardized tests already existed: reading English. We felt that a reading test would simply not be a full and fair test for these different approaches to teaching English as a second language, particularly when each of the three emphases with which we were experimenting had a strong aural-oral component. Therefore, we took the year necessary to develop our own measures in the other modalities, for without these we felt that the success potential of the experiment was poor. In terms of the present state of development of measurement in the social disciplines, a researcher contemplating experimental research must be willing to develop his own instruments if he is to have a relevant set of dependent variables.

THE INTERVENING VARIABLES

The identification of the major groups of intervening variables is a relatively simple task for the researcher familiar with the significant elements of the educational process. The general areas of family, child, neighborhood, school, teacher, method, material, and content, work well to structure the identification of the variables that might intervene. Within each of these areas, of course, the list of possible specific variables is all but endless, and it is in the process of winnowing these down to those which will be seriously treated that experience and knowledge in the problem area become of paramount importance. The comment made in the chapter on sampling applies here as well: the traditional variables of age, sex, socioeconomic status as measured by father's occupation, and highest educational level of parents are not the relevant intervening variables for all educational studies—any more than they are for all stratification.

But once they are identified, the researcher's concern with intervening variables is not with measuring them but rather with making certain that they do not affect the data obtained on the dependent variables. In other words, he must stop them from intervening. A more precise way of stating this would be to say he must stop them from intervening *inconsistently*. In other words, the researcher does not mind an intervening variable operating, provided that he can estimate its effects and that it operates in the same fashion, and to the same degree, on all of the groups in the experiment. He does mind when the variable operates differently on some groups within the experiment than it does on others. For in the instance of differential effect, the independent variable can affect the data in ways difficult to estimate.

Techniques for Handling Intervening Variables

This leads to the immediate question of how the researcher can establish conditions so that the intervening variables cannot affect data differentially. He has five techniques readily available, four connected with the design of his study and the fifth tied to the statistical analysis of the data. The most direct way of handling a potential intervening variable is to *hold it constant,* in the sense of limiting all experimental groups to one gradation of the variable. Thus, if we wish to control for the potential intervention of age in an experiment, the most direct way is to use children of one age group. Similarly, to control the effect of size of community on a curriculum experiment, we would only use communities of one specific size. This technique for handling intervention, while direct, has one important drawback. The study being conducted is obviously then limited to that aspect of the variable which is represented in the experiment.

Therefore, researchers are reluctant to use this technique unless the limitation it brings with it is perfectly consistent with the purpose of the experiment. However, for the graduate student considering an experiment it has genuine merit in that it is one way to solve some of the problems of intervening variables while simultaneously reducing the scope of the proposed project. In fact, student experimentation for a thesis or dissertation can successfully be designed with a few of the major potential intervening variables held constant. The resulting project has relevance then for a limited section of the total experimental field, but it will be a reasonable contribution to that limited section.

A second way of handling the intervening variables, which does not limit the experiment as severely as does holding a variable constant, is *systematic variation*. This involves using more than one gradation of the potential intervening variable, but holding the gradations comparable from group to group[7] within the experiment. Thus, in handling age as an intervening variable a researcher might use children of three different age levels but would use these same levels in each of the experimental groups. Similarly, the curriculum study could be done in communities of different sizes, provided that each variation in curriculum could be placed in the schools of communities of each specific size involved.

The third technique for handling a possible intervening variable is to assume we have *correlated variation,* that is, that the variation of the new variable has already been accounted for by its relationship to a variable already held constant or being permitted to vary systematically. This makes sense when two variables being handled in this way are correlated sufficiently well. In quantitative terms, a reasonable standard to employ is a correlation at least at the .80 level so that there is a shared variance of at least 64 percent.

The fourth technique is not a technique in the same sense as the other three, because it involves the researcher doing nothing about the potential intervening variable other than to assume that whatever effect it will have will be *randomly distributed* throughout the groups in the experiment and so have no consistent effect on the data. It is listed here as a technique to indicate that it must be deliberately selected by the researcher as the way he will handle a specific variable or variables. It is not a solution which can be employed without thought and care. It, like the assumption of a correlation, can only be employed with variables where such an assumption makes common sense.

The fifth technique is the one mentioned in Chapter 10, the *analysis of covariance.* This is a statistical procedure which combines regression and analysis of variance to allow for differences between experimental groups which existed prior to an experiment on one or more intervening variables. This is particularly useful in two instances. The first instance is when the researcher knows that the groups within his experiment differ on one or two critical variables but cannot do anything about it. This often happens if the researcher is using existing groups like classes in a school, which have been made available on the proviso that they be kept intact. Therefore, the researcher may know they differ in reading level but still have to use them. The second time analysis of covariance is particularly

[7]Specific techniques for achieving this comparability will be discussed later in this chapter.

useful is when the researcher learns about the inequality on a variable or variables from data collected during the course of the experiment and not available prior to it. In both instances, the analysis of covariance enables the researcher to move on with an experiment which otherwise would be damaged or even destroyed by these inequalities.

While it is unusual for all five of these techniques to appear in one experiment several are often applied in designing complex experiments, as illustrated during the Language Study. Within each unit of the study, grade in school was held constant. In other words, in the elementary level phase of the study all classes were fourth grade. This control of grade also meant that a variable like age, highly correlated with grade in school, was also reasonably well controlled for the purpose of the experiment.

Other variables were permitted to vary systematically. The most important of these was the proportion of Puerto Rican pupils in the school. To do this, schools were selected with different proportions of Puerto Rican children. Thus, schools with four different proportions of Puerto Rican pupils were used in the study (those with less than 20 percent, 33 percent, 50 percent, and 75 percent or more). Then, within each school, three fourth-grade classes were used for the three variations of the independent variable (the three methods of teaching English). Since the different experimental conditions were implemented in all schools, we could argue that the proportion of Puerto Rican children varied systematically. Interestingly enough, this procedure also enabled us to assume that a wide variety of variables highly correlated with school itself were also varying systematically. For example, we assumed that all of the factors involved in neighborhood differences such as language spoken, facilities, socialization opportunities, recreational opportunities, and culture conflicts were sufficiently related to the location of the school so that they would have no differential effect on the data because each methodological variation was now housed in each school.[8] By this same reasoning the potential intervention of general school factors like the physical facilities of a school, or the quality or caliber of the administration could now be assumed to vary systematically. While these factors could operate, and could account for differences from school to school, we had no reason to

[8]The reader aware of how the concept of the neighborhood school changed in the period from 1950 to 1970 will recognize that current studies could not make this assumption about the neighborhood school. In a society with flexible concepts of district lines, busing children, paired schools, and other administrative techniques to aid the integration of schools, a researcher could not assume that all children in a school live in the same neighborhood, which we could do in 1952 when district lines were rigid and children attended the school in the district in which they lived. This illustrates well how research assumptions are tied to the larger society in which the research is to be conducted.

believe they would differentially affect the data. A good principal should be a stimulant to school functioning, but he should stimulate all three fourth-grade classes involved, and so would not *differentially* affect the data.

Notice that the knowledge a researcher has available is quite different from those potential intervening variables he (1) holds constant; (2) systematically varies; (3) assumes are correlated to other variables he holds constant or systematically varies; or (4) leaves to chance. Those variables he holds constant or assumes to be highly correlated to those he holds constant are known to him, and comprise what are usually called the *delimitations* of the experiment. They define the boundaries within the problem area within which the experiment will be done, and the populations of people, animals, or situations to which the findings will apply. Thus the fact that the Language Study in the elementary school was conducted only in the fourth grade defined the population to which these findings might apply,[9] not only in terms of grade but also in terms of the highly correlated variable of age.

The variables being permitted to systematically vary further define the delimitations of the study, as for example, we delimited the proportions of Puerto Rican children in the schools to be studied. However, when we consider the variables correlated with those permitted to vary systematically, we find that these do not specify any additional delimitations. This is because all the researcher knows is that he has minimized the likelihood of their differential effect. He does not know what specific values he has. For example, we have noted earlier the belief that permitting the proportion of Puerto Rican children to vary systematically by placing each experimental variation of method in every school in the experiment also minimized the possible effect of correlated clusters of variables connected with neighborhood as well as with the general characteristics of schools, like administrative caliber. If we were asked what *gradations* of principal caliber had been employed in the study, we would not know, any more than we would know the kinds of neighborhoods. Obviously the researcher may learn this information from other data. We are noting here that he does not learn it from the fact that he can argue that these variables are correlated to others he is systematically varying.

There are two other aspects about the handling of potential intervening variables which are important to consider. First is the fact that the researcher does not have a free choice as to which of the several tech-

[9]The reader is reminded of the discussion in Chapter 1 on the assumptions connected with deciding precisely how severe this delimitation was. It was noted at that point that the researchers agreed that the findings obtained from the fourth grade could also be *assumed* to apply to the fifth grade as well.

niques he will employ for every variable. Some *must* be held constant or else no meaningful experiment can be established. For example, in the Language Study, the amount of time spent on direct language instruction, and the content of the lessons used to give that instruction, had to be held constant across all the method groups and from school to school. There simply would have been no experiment had some teachers been permitted to teach for an hour, and others for 25 minutes. Therefore, the researcher must identify these potentially critical intervening variables and make certain that he can hold them constant before moving on with planning the experiment.

The second aspect is at the opposite end of the scale from the "must hold constant" point. It involves those about which nothing can be done. In terms of the current state of measurement in the social disciplines, and in view of the fortunate fact that researchers lack the authority to manipulate people and systems, some potential intervening variables cannot be handled adequately in any of the ways described. These variables survive the experiment with their potential for intervention undiminished. All the researcher can do is identify them and evaluate their potential impact. If this impact is sufficiently serious to rule out any sensible study of the independent variable, the experiment should be abandoned. If it is not considered that serious, then the researcher should keep the possible intervention in mind, for it will be one of the factors that limit his conclusions.

ADDITIONAL SOURCES OF BIAS

Lest the experimenter not have enough difficulties in identifying the elements of the experiment, and in achieving the needed stages of control, he must also be concerned with additional factors which might bias the experiment. These are factors external to the elements of the experiment but involved with the process by which it is implemented.

In identifying sources of bias in experimental data we shall consider five areas of interest: the experimenter or his agents; the measuring devices employed; the research situations, particularly during data collection; the implementation of the experiment; and the impact of experimentation itself.

The experimenter or his agents know the nature and purpose of the experiment. If the research situation is such that they can, as individuals, have any effect on it, they may bias the results. They may do this completely innocently and unconsciously, yet do it nevertheless. An experimenter may communicate cues to children being tested by the interest and/or anxiety he displays at some times during testing, rather than at others. He may unconsciously motivate his experimental groups more thoroughly than his control groups, or his hopes and enthusiasm about the experiment may serve as a differential motivating device. To eliminate this potential source of bias it is often wise for the experimenter to have nothing to do with the data-collection phase of the research. Unfortunately for students, this advice, while sound, is seldom realistic, for the cost of hiring and training replacements would be prohibitive. Therefore, an effective compromise is to have some portion of data collection done by a disinterested, but trained, second person, so that some estimate can be obtained of the effect that the experimenter had as an individual. If the second party is truly disinterested, and still achieves the same effects as the experimenter, it is safe to conclude that the experimenter did not bias the results.

A second set of factors involves the measuring devices employed. In an experiment, innovation exists. Something new is being tried out and compared to something old. How then do we measure comparative accomplishment? If we limit ourselves to the traditional measures which have probably been developed for the old or control research situations, we may bias the data against the innovative experimental research situation. If we develop new measures specifically applicable for the experimental research situation, we may be biasing the data against the control situations. In short, it may be difficult to find or develop data-gathering instruments which will have comparable content validity for both experimental and control research situations. If, after evaluating the objectives of the experimental and control settings this seems like a realistic problem, there is little choice but to use two sets of measures, one appropriate for the traditional aspects of both control and experimental situations, the other for the innovative aspects of the experimental situation.

A third source of bias is the problem of leakage or dilution of the independent variable. Unique to the social sciences, the potential for this bias comes from the fact that people's natural curiosity to learn about the actions of others seems to be magnified many times over if some of the people are designated controls, and others experimental, groups. Motivated by this curiosity, the different groups often seek each other out and seek to learn directly or surreptitiously what the others are doing. If they succeed, the result may be that both control and experimental conditions become a hybrid dilution of what the experimenter intended. The experimenter must attempt to avoid this happening, but should also plan during the experiment on verifying periodically that the discrete variations of the independent variables are being implemented as discrete variations. One way in which experimenters have attempted to avoid the bias of leakage is to deal with the problem indirectly. These experimenters meet with each group separately, never tell one about the other, and hope that they never get together on their own. The more sensible approach, in the author's experience, is to face the problem directly. In this approach you explain the total experiment to all the respondents, identify their separate roles, and make clear how leakage would destroy the experimental test of the independent variable. At that point, they must decide if their interest in the research question and in collecting data which might ultimately help answer that question is sufficient to make them want to participate. It also helps if we can randomly designate the control and experimental classes, or schools or teachers. This helps eliminate another force which makes people seek out the role of others in the experiment—the fear that experimentation means evaluation and that the results they produce will be attributed to their individual functioning rather than to the experimental variable. Equally important as the fact that it is a defense against leakage is the fact that this level of discussion with potential respondents and participants is compatible with the proper ethical standards for research in the social disciplines. It treats respondents with the dignity they deserve and provides for obtaining their informed consent before they participate in the experiment.

It is not difficult to understand the motivation for contamination in the social disciplines and education in particular. That motivation is professional involvement. Every experiment in methodology involves a new procedure, program, or method which someone believes to be better than anything which now exists. This is true by definition, since such experiments are conducted to evaluate the belief that the experimental variable is better. But in the course of each such comparative experiment, one or more conditions are implemented which someone believes to be inferior. These may be conditions with long histories of use, and may be in use at a wide variety of sites other than the experimental one. Nevertheless, there is a variation being implemented which may be better. What then of the practitioners asked to function in the research situation, under conditions which it is hoped will prove to be inferior? Theirs is a difficult role. They are now involved in a role which in some experiments they have perceived as involving less than their best possible performance. This belief has led to deliberate efforts to seek out the key to the experimental variable and implement it in the control groups. As noted above, this is a perfectly understandable motivation, but one which has disastrous experimental effects.

The fourth source of bias is connected to the implementation of the experiment. The most carefully matched groups and the most thoroughly developed materials can be severely damaged by the differential implementation of an experiment, such as collecting data at different times of day from experimental and control groups of children. To avoid this potential type of bias the researcher must exert every effort throughout the life of the experiment to make certain that everything goes off on schedule with rigid comparability for experimental and control groups. In other words, the experimenter's task does not cease with the establishment of the experimental conditions. He must continue to exert constant vigilance throughout, until data from the dependent variables have been safely collected. In fact, he may even wish to collect data during the course of the study to verify that it went off on schedule. The reader who recalls the full details of the Language Study will remember that we collected data throughout the study to verify that the study was being implemented as designed.

The fifth area from which bias can stem involves the experimental process itself. For example, in an experiment which involves data collection before the independent variables are applied, the pretest itself may be a source of bias. It is possible (though less probable than some texts in experimental design imply) that the pretest itself is a profound enough experience to affect functioning throughout the experiment. First of all simply taking most instruments a second time results in somewhat different performance, usually higher in the area of achievement. While these changes are not usually dramatic, they do occur and may have some meaning, particularly in short-term experiments. Because the overall changes expected are usually not large, the small practice effect would have greater impact on a short-term study. There is also the possibility that to some extent the experience of taking the pretest may precipitate a period of self-study and inquiry which is ultimately reflected in the posttest performance. If this happens with the experimental group, the researcher may confuse this change with the effect of the independent variable. If it happens with the control group, the researcher may obtain a spurious estimate of the kinds of changes and developments which take place simply through the passage of time. For this reason one of the key issues in designing an experiment is to obtain some estimate of change during the experimental period free of this possible bias. Design principles to achieve this will be discussed later in this chapter.

A more subtle kind of bias in this area of the pretest is the bias which stems from the interaction of the pretest and the independent variable for the experimental group. Consider a study in the area of creativity, where some initial estimates of the respondents' creativity is obtained through a pretesting session. It may be that this exposure triggers a set of responses which make the children in the experimental group uniquely receptive to the experimental teaching procedures applied. The pretest, in short, serves a motivating or conditioning function, so that the response to the initial set of materials is different than it would have been without that initial experience.

Another aspect of bias introduced by the experimental process itself is the simple fact that experimentation is exciting and intriguing. Excitement and intrigue motivate people, and so affect functioning. This kind of bias is usually called the *Hawthorne effect*, named after the studies conducted at the Hawthorne plant of the Western Electric company. These studies, conducted in the 1920s and 1930s, indicated that sheer involvement in a study, with the accompanying interest and attention, can produce responses from people like those to be expected from the independent variable. It is difficult for the researcher to distinguish change which is a function of his independent variable from change which is a function of the response to experimentation. The best defense against this kind of bias is to permit the experimental period to run a long time, or to be replicated often. The rationale here is that the Hawthorne effect, if it is operative, will not be maintained for a long period of time, whereas the genuine response to the independent variable will be.

In some few instances, the nature of the study permits the researcher to establish a group which is the equivalent of the placebo group in medical research. This group receives all of the attention that other groups in the experiment do, but does not receive the independent treatment. Any change which is reflected in this group then can be attributed to the Hawthorne response to participation. The opportunities for this are limited, both by the difficulty of creating an experimental illusion, and by the ethical implications of doing it. When it is both feasible and ethical, it does help estimate the Hawthorne effect.

THE NATURE OF THE EXPERIMENTAL GROUPS REQUIRED

The definition in this book of an experiment as involving the creation of some new condition implies that the basic purpose of an experiment is evaluation of the new. One way to accomplish this is similar to the evaluative survey, in which the experimental results are compared to some existing set of data obtained from the already existing method or procedure or program. We shall call these *evaluative experiments*. Thus the effectiveness of a new procedure for remedial reading can be evaluated, provided that data are available from gains achieved under the old procedure. Similarly, the effectiveness of an experimental guidance program for entering freshmen can be evaluated in terms of criteria like retention, or the kinds and number of problems students encountered in school prior to the program. The second approach to experimental evaluation is the *comparative experiment*. This type parallels the comparative survey in that the experimental method is introduced but so are one or more variations of the current or traditional method. Then, under as nearly similar conditions as possible, both the experimental and nonexperimental conditions are allowed to run their course. After they have been completed, data are collected on the criterion variables, and the evaluation of the effectiveness of the experiment is in terms of these comparative data.

Thus there are two major types of experimental evaluation: one in which the experimental condition alone is created and studied and evaluation is in terms of already available criterion data; and second, the comparative experiment in which both the experimental and comparison conditions are established and data collected on all conditions. Notice that we are dismissing, as not worth serious consideration in a chapter on experimentation, a study without some second set of data, either from previous evaluation in the same setting or from comparison groups within the experiment. No serious estimate of an experimental effect can be made with any pretension of scientific precision unless some scientifically obtained data are available to provide a basis for evaluation or comparison.

Thus the problems of designing an evaluative experiment are different from the problems of designing a comparative experiment. In the evaluative experiment the researcher is concerned with obtaining an estimate of the change or learning or development which takes place in the experimental situation alone. He is willing to evaluate that change in terms of already existing and accepted normative referents. In contrast, in the comparative experiment the researcher must not only generate the same estimate of experimentally induced change or development, but must also generate an estimate of the change or development which takes place in the traditional or nonexperimental settings. In their chapter in the *Handbook of Research on Teaching,* Campbell and Stanley distinguish between the nature of these designs, calling the evaluative experiments "preexperimental designs" and the comparative "true experimental designs."[10] This distinction implies a qualitative difference between the two types of experiment from the standpoint of technical experimentation. The evaluative experiment *is* less stable and less complete as a scientific entity, for the two sets of data were obtained at different times under different conditions. However, evaluative experimentation may be the only choice the researcher has if he is to provide even a tentative experimental answer

[10]Campbell and Stanley, "Experimental and Quasi-Experimental Designs, p. 176.

to a valid research question. Nevertheless in an evaluative experiment the researcher must recognize that he is conducting an experiment which may well produce spurious results and lead, therefore, to spurious interpretations and conclusions. The two frequently encountered normative designs will be noted here briefly, so that they can be recognized if considered.

Evaluative Experimental Designs: One Group

DATA COLLECTED POST-EXPOSURE ONLY   This design is for a research setting from which no data will be available prior to exposure to the independent variable. Evaluation is done on the basis of previous data available from presumably similar groups who have gone through the same situations without the independent variable. This might occur if an experimenter was given access to a class of fourth-grade children with whom he was to try out a new method of instruction in fourth-grade arithmetic. For reasons of availability or feasibility he is able to test only at the end of the semester. If data are available from end-of-semester tests given in previous years in this same school setting, and if he can argue that children this year are substantially the same as in the previous years, then he can use these old data as the basis for a weak evaluation of the experimental method. Notice that this design for an evaluative experiment rests on all of the assumptions of the cross-sectional approach for survey research, and is susceptible to many of the effects of intervention and the sources of bias we have discussed in experimental research. Thus the experimenter may be generating sufficient interest and excitement to create differences. Or it may be that this year's class is brighter than the classes of the previous years which produced the comparative data. Or they might be older, or have larger proportions of students interested in careers in science and mathematics. It is because of this susceptibility to intervention and bias that the estimate of the experimental effect can only be described as weak, at best.

DATA COLLECTED PRE- AND POST-EXPOSURE   The second evaluative design is the one-group *pre–post-design*. This involves the same single experimental group and the same use of previous data for the estimate of experimental effectiveness, but it adds the dimension of two data collections from the experimental group. One data collection takes place prior to exposure to the independent variable, and one takes place after that exposure. This design is most likely to be sensible if the evaluative data available from previous years were also obtained from both pre- and post-testing. This is because the potential bias from exposure to the pretest is minimized in this way.

Note that in these two evaluative designs, we are assuming that data from previous years will be available to the researcher from settings and students who can reasonably be accepted as like those to be involved in the experiment. Only with such data can the researcher truly argue that he has a sensible evaluative experiment. A common fallacy is to use norms for standardized tests of achievement as the data on which to evaluate the experimental effects. The researcher argues that if the class exposed to his experimental method achieves beyond the normal progress expected on the standardized test, this is evidence that the independent variable has functioned effectively. Two immediate problems with that argument are the fact that the researcher would be hard put to complete his thought and answer the question: "Effective in comparison to what settings and what methods?" The norms for any standardized test are derived from many settings, and so stem originally from a multiplicity of methods. Thus they provide no basis for an evaluative statement about the effectiveness of a new method or procedure. The other problem is that these norms may be a relevant standard for evaluation for some children, in some school, in some systems. For others they are too high a standard, and for still others too low a standard. Thus the only data relevant for the evaluative experiment are data obtained from similar research settings to those employed in the experiment.

Comparative Experimental Designs

The general approach to experimental design in a comparative situation has been to establish the experimental condition and the comparative condition under as nearly identical circumstances as possible, measuring the dependent variables either at the end of the study or both at the beginning and the end of the study. Inferential statistical procedures are then used to determine if the experimental and control groups differed, and so determine if the independent variable had any significant effect.

POST-EXPOSURE   In its simplest form the post-exposure design becomes the *after-only design with one control group.* Here the researcher establishes both an experimental and a control group but collects data from them only at the end of the period of experimentation. He is forced therefore to assume comparability of the groups at the beginning of the study. This type of design is useful in research in school settings where only limited opportunities are made available for data collection by the researcher. It can also be useful if the nature of the data to be collected is considered too likely to have an effect on those who respond to it, or if it is such that it can be administered only once. This would be true of a unique instrument in which part of the phenomena being measured is the response to the new material. For example, studies seeking to estimate creativity, by offering unusual pictorial or verbal stimulus materials, might prefer the after-only approach to data collection.

The statistical analysis of the data obtained in the after-only design with one control group are those inferential procedures applicable to the comparison of two groups. Thus the *t* test can be used provided the data are at least at the interval level. If they are only at the ordinal level, then the Mann-Whitney test can be applied.

The soundness of the design rests on the soundness of the assumption of comparability of groups. This assumption is reasonably sensible when the researcher has been able to form the groups (as contrasted to being asked to use existing classes), and particularly when he has been able to form them using the process of random assignment discussed in the next section. Under these conditions, a pretest may serve no useful research function and, as we noted earlier, may introduce a potential source of bias.

PRE- AND POST-EXPOSURE   The *pretest, posttest design with one control group* remains the single most popular experimental design in education. This design is the same as the previous one, except that a pretest is administered to experimental and control groups prior to the introduction of the independent variable to the experimental group. In educational research, this pretest has been used as a means of verifying the comparability of the control and experimental groups at the beginning of the study and also to provide a basis for determining if change took place in the control and experimental groups. More properly it is used as a basis for deriving a change score for each participant so that inferential statistical procedures (usually a *t* test) can be applied comparing the mean gains in experimental and control groups. The availability of pretest data also makes it possible to utilize the analysis of covariance for these change scores, which adds considerably to the potential precision of the analysis.

MULTIPLE-CONTROL GROUPS   However, the pretest, posttest one control-group design contains the potential bias of the pretest itself as well as the bias from the interaction of pretest and independent variable. To counter these, Solomon[11] suggested an extension of the design into four groups, adding a second experimental and control group who are not exposed to the pretest. This design then is a *pretest, posttest, multiple-group design,* as sketched out in Table 16-1. The doubling of the experimental and control groups means that the researcher now has a wide variety of bases for

[11]R. L. Solomon, "An extension of control group design." *Psychological Bulletin*, no. 46, 1949, pp. 137–50.

Table 16-1 Comparative Experimental Design with Four Groups

Group	Pretest	Experimental Condition	Posttest
Experimental A	X	X	X
Control A	X		X
Experimental B		X	X
Control B			X

estimating the effect of his independent variable. He can compare each of the two experimental groups to its control for a direct estimate of the effectiveness of the independent variable with and without the pretest and the possibility of pretest interacting with the independent variable. He can also obtain a direct estimate of the extent of these potential sources of bias by comparing the posttest results for the two experimental groups.

Analysis of the data involves some decisions as to the appropriateness of specific tests of significance. The arguments involved are beyond the scope of this discussion, but the student planning such a design should know that Campbell and Stanley question Solomon's suggestions for using an analysis of variance of gain scores, noting that "Solomon's suggestions concerning these are judged unacceptable." They go on to suggest alternative statistical solutions.[12]

DESIGNS FOR MULTIPLE INDEPENDENT VARIABLES

Throughout most of the chapter we have spoken of the independent variable in the singular. In the classical sense of experimentation, there is one independent variable which is the only characteristic that differentiates the experimental and control groups. However, there is no reason why experiments cannot be designed with more than one independent variable, and, in fact, in the social disciplines it is far more real to design experiments this way. The number of variables and the number of gradations of each variable determine how complex the design problem becomes, and to fully consider the variety of designs and issues involved an entire book, devoted to nothing else,[13] is needed. Here we shall consider

---

[12]Campbell and Stanley, "Experimental and Quasi-Experimental Designs," p. 195.

[13]Two thorough texts are: Walter T. Federer, *Experimental Design, Theory and Application* (New York: Crowell-Collier and Macmillan, Inc., 1963), 544 pp.; E. F. Lindquist, *Design and Analysis of Experiments in Psychology and Education* (Boston: Houghton Mifflin Company, 1953), 391 pp.

the situations when such designs are needed, and the basic principles involved.

Factorial Designs

In any instance when the researcher wishes to study the effect of more than one variable and has at least two gradations of each variable, he has an example of what is called a *factorial design*. The simplest such design would be two variables with only two levels for each variable. This might occur if the researcher was conducting an experimental study of a new instructional method and wished to estimate its effectiveness in comparison to the traditional method when a text was used and when lectures only were used. The design for the study is illustrated in Table 16-2.

We have already noted, in the discussion of the complex analysis of variance in Chapter 10, that one of the major advantages of the factorial design is that it provides the researcher with a statistical basis for estimating the effect of the interaction of the two independent variables. Referring to Table 16-2, we can see that to describe group 1 we must refer to both independent variables: In other words, these are children taught by the experimental method with the use of a text. The design also provides an estimate of the independent or main effects of each of the independent variable. For example, studying the variation around the overall mean of the two combined means labeled 1 + 2 and 3 + 4 provides an estimate of the main effect of the two methods.

The factorial design should be based on a logical need for studying the two independent variables in each other's presence. In the example above, once we saw that a factorial design was employed we would

Table 16–2 Illustrative Layout for Two-Variable, Two-Level Complete Factorial Design

Use of Text	Experimental	Traditional	*Totals across Method*
	Method		
Used	Group 1	Group 3	Groups 1 + 3
Omitted	Group 2	Group 4	Groups 2 + 4
Total across use of text	Groups 1 + 2	Groups 3 + 4	

assume that it was the researcher's judgment that the experimental and traditional methods could not be meaningfully compared using one of the simple comparative designs previously discussed. Instead, he is arguing that a critical element in that comparison is the operation of the experimental method with and without the use of the text. The factorial design, in short, is one which is used only in instances when the researcher can support the logic of studying the independent variables together.

When we move beyond two factors and two levels of each factor, the complexity of implementing the design and of analyzing the data increases tremendously. Consider the layout in Table 16-3 for a three-factor experiment with three levels for each factor. In this illustration we have used three levels of method, three levels of supplementary materials, and three levels of teacher experience. Even to establish such a study under the complete application of the factorial principal would involve 27 different groups of children. This is because the complete factorial design calls for establishing at least one experimental group which will reflect the operation of each level of each variable in conjunction with each level of each other variable, that is, a group for all possible combinations. For this reason, the complete factorial design, although popular in the physical sciences, is seldom seen in educational research for complex studies with more than two variables.

Table 16–3   Illustrative Layout for Three-Variable, Three-Level Complete Factorial Design

Method	Experience Level of Teacher	Nature of Illustrative Material		
		Text	Film Strips	None
Experimental A	Less than 3 years	Group 1	Group 2	Group 3
	3–5 years	Group 4	Group 5	Group 6
	More than 5 years	Group 7	Group 8	Group 9
Experimental B	Less than 3 years	Group 10	Group 11	Group 12
	3–5 years	Group 13	Group 14	Group 15
	More than 5 years	Group 16	Group 17	Group 18
Experimental C	Less than 3 years	Group 19	Group 20	Group 21
	3–5 years	Group 22	Group 23	Group 24
	More than 5 years	Group 25	Group 26	Group 27

Whichever of the preceding designs is used, ultimately the researcher must turn to the problem of peopling the groups within the experiment.

CREATING THE EXPERIMENTAL GROUPS

With the decision made as to the number and nature of the groups required for the experiment, the researcher faces the problem of creating those groups. The problem is different if the researcher must work with already established groups, such as existing classes, or if he has a pool of potential respondents available from whom he can develop his groups. We shall consider the situation with an available pool first.

The aim here is to develop experimental and control groups which will be as comparable as possible on critical variables through a process as free of bias as possible. The desire to be free from bias rules out the use of the researcher's judgment, or anyone else's judgment, as the means of assigning respondents to groups. We also want a system which would be free of the bias that would be introduced were we to permit the potential respondents to volunteer for participation in experimental or control groups. This concern with bias in the selection process should remind the reader of a similar discussion in Chapter 11 on sampling, where we pointed out the virtues of random-selection methods in sampling. The analogy in assigning respondents to experimental groups is a technique called *random assignment*. But just as we noted in the chapter on sampling that random selection does not assure that representativeness will have been achieved on any one variable, so random assignment does not assure the researcher that comparability will have been achieved for the groups in his experiment. It is reasonable to assume that given large numbers, and many replications of the experiment, there will be no consistent biasing effect in favor of one level of the experiment. But for any one study the researcher may emerge with noncomparable groups from the use of random assignment. Therefore, we shall also discuss methods of developing the experimental groups which parallel the sampling concept of stratification and deliberate assignment. These methods can be used when the researcher has information available on selected variables which he wishes to use in forming his groups to assure maximum comparability on these variables.

Random Assignment

In random assignment, the researcher places all of the subjects available to him in one pool, and then divides them into the number of subgroups required by the design of the experiment. Had we used random assignment to assign children to the classes in the three experimental variations in the Language Study, we would have pooled all fourth graders in any one school and assigned each a number. Then we could decide that the first child selected would be in the vocabulary class, the second in the structure class, and the third in the experiential class (or any other order we had arbitrarily selected). Using a table of random numbers we would then select our first child, assign him to the vocabulary class; select the second child, assign him to the structure class; assign the third to the experiential; and then begin the cycle all over again by assigning the fourth child to the vocabulary class. We would continue this until all three classes had been formed from the pool of children.

As is always true of the process of random selection, we could be assured that no systematic bias entered into the assignment of children to language emphasis. This would enable us to analyze the data using those parametric statistical procedures which assume a normal distribution in a bias-free set of data. Again note the caution that with small numbers this would *not* assure us that the three groups were *comparable* on all essential intervening variables relating to children. Table 16-4 illustrates this phenomenon. Presented are the data for 21 children, listed in order of ascending IQ, with sex of the child also indicated. The Table also shows how these 21 children would have been divided into three classes of seven each, using a table of random numbers. The first number selected was 06 and so Phil was assigned to class A. The second number selected was 09, and so Clara was assigned to class B, and so on until the 21st number selected, 16, resulted in Mary's being assigned to class C. Notice how each of the three classes is reasonably representative in terms of IQ, but how class B is predominantly male whereas class C is predominantly female, and class A is divided into males and females in the same way as the pool of 21 children. This illustrates the dangers of random assignment with small numbers of respondents, and shows why researchers in this situation should consider the deliberate techniques for stratifying or matching to be discussed later.

Deliberate Assignment

If a researcher has been able to identify some critical variables for his study, he may prefer to use deliberate methods for assigning respondents to groups. The simplest of the deliberate methods involves creating *matched sets* of respondents, and randomly assigning one member of each set to each of the groups in the experiment. If there is only one experimental and one control group, this method of assignment is known as a *matched*

Table 16–4   Illustration of Random Assignment in Experimental Design

		Assigned to Experimental Group					
		A		B		C	
No.	Name	IQ	Sex	IQ	Sex	IQ	Sex
01	Albert			93	M		
02	Martin					95	M
03	Abby	96	F				
04	Lucy					98	F
05	Barbara			98	F		
06	Phil	100	M				
07	Polly					101	F
08	Harry	104	M				
09	Clara			106	F		
10	Bob			108	M		
11	William			110	M		
12	Fran					110	F
13	Adam	112	M				
14	Laura	115	F				
15	Jonathan			118	M		
16	Mary					118	F
17	Charles					125	M
18	Wanda	128	F				
19	Oscar			132	M		
20	Frank	135	M				
21	Betty					138	F

pair design, but the thinking involved is easily extended to trios and quartets. To go beyond this (that is, matched quintets) usually involves such heterogeneity within the set that the matching concept is endangered. The method involved can be illustrated with the pair. What the researcher does is to seek within the pool of subjects that pair most closely matched on the characteristics with which he is concerned. Thus, if a researcher had identified intelligence, sex, and age as three variables on which he wishes to match, he would select from the pool pairs of boys, ideally of the same age and measured IQ, and do the same for the girls. With his pairs identified, he then would revert to random assignment as the basis for deciding which member of each pair was to be in the experimental, and which in the control, group.

Another method of deliberate assignment is a *matched group design.* Here the researcher assigns respondents to the different groups on the basis of the characteristics with which he is concerned, but his basis of deciding if comparability has been achieved is the group, rather than the individual. Thus, if he is concerned about comparability in measured intelligence, he will compare the potential experimental and control groups in terms of their mean IQ and their standard deviation in IQ.

There are two things to note about the argument that groups are matched. First, the comparison is in terms of a measure of central tendency *and* a measure of variability. As noted in Chapter 6, these are two different characteristics of a set of data, and it is important that the groups be comparable on both. In fact, for many educational problems the comparability on variability is as critical as the comparability on central tendency, for it is variability which might pose the problems of teaching a specific set of material to the group within the time the experiment will run. Second, note that we have said here that the groups must be comparable, although we have noted in the earlier chapters on inferential statistical concepts and procedures that we have no statistical test for comparability. In practice this means that the researcher goes through a two-stage check to determine comparability. First, he uses the inferential procedure appropriate to the particular variable to verify that there are no statistically significant differences between the groups. If there are, he must reassign children until he creates groups which do not differ significantly.

If the statistical analysis indicates that the groups do not differ significantly on the variables tested, then the researcher has one more step. He must verify that they will be accepted as comparable by professionals functioning in the problem area of the study. This is obviously a matter of professional judgment, and a delicate judgment. It is based upon the realities of research in education, in which the mass of practitioners do not live by the same gods of statistical significance as researchers do. If we wish our experiment to be accepted as a reasonable test of the independent variable with comparable groups, we must consider this aspect of comparability as well as the issue of statistical significance.

Deficiencies in Pool of Respondents

One problem which random and deliberate assignment share is that neither technique can remedy a deficiency or bias (from a research point of view) in the original pool of respondents to be assigned. Consider the assignment of teachers to the classes for the Language Study. Assume that in studying the backgrounds of six potential teachers we notice that one has many years of experience in general, and specifically in teaching

English as a second language. The other five teachers have had relatively limited amounts of experience, no more than a year of which has been devoted to teaching English as a second language. No matter which method of assignment is used, once the experienced teacher is assigned to a method she will provide that method with all of the concomitant advantages (or disadvantages) that accompany experience.

Faced with this problem a researcher has but two choices open to him. He can live with this bias, recognize it, and consider it in the course of the discussion of his results. The other choice is to eliminate that teacher from the pool of teachers subject to assignment, assuming that sufficient numbers of teachers are otherwise available. This elimination would solve this problem of bias, but of course would also eliminate the possibility of learning how an experienced teacher would function in the experiment. In terms of principles of experimental design, however, there would be no choice. The basic goal is to eliminate or minimize the probability of each intervening variable differentially affecting the data obtained from the dependent variables. Eliminating this experienced teacher from the pool to be assigned would achieve that goal; retaining her would not. If she was eliminated, we could then argue that experience, in itself, would not seem to be a factor which differentiated the teachers and therefore would not seem to be a factor in the data from the dependent variables. This is what we are always striving to achieve.

WORKING WITH EXISTING GROUPS

If the researcher has no opportunity to create groups, but instead must use already existing groups if he is to do his experiment, he is severely limited in his ability to function. In fact, he must seriously consider whether he will be able to achieve a reasonable degree of control to provide a meaningful test of the independent variable.

If he is to work with existing groups, the researcher minimally must collect sufficient data on the important potentially intervening variables so that he can know how the groups compare on these. A simple way to select those variables for this data collection is to identify those which would be used for deliberate assignment if it were possible. These data should be collected before the experiment for those variables that will be susceptible to the experimental conditions, but can be collected during the experiment for variables like background data, which are not susceptible to change.

With the data collected, the researcher then can apply appropriate inferential procedures to determine whether or not the groups did in fact differ on each variable. Through happy chance, he may find some on which there were no significant differences. Inevitably he will find others on which there will be statistically significant differences. If he has obtained the data in advance of actually beginning the experiment, he has three choices open to him. He can decide to abandon his plans and not use these groups for the experiment; he can plan on using the analysis of covariance to statistically eliminate this known difference if he has interval or ratio data; or he can plan on going ahead and treating the difference as a limitation to the conclusions of the study. "Choice" is perhaps a misleading term to use in the preceding sentence, because demands of the experiment and the particular variable involved interact to determine which of these three paths is truly available to the researcher. In the Language Study, for example, if one class offered was predominantly male and the other predominantly female we have a variable too closely related to language learning for us to ignore. Yet it is also a variable providing only nominal data, and so the analysis of covariance route is not available. We would have no choice then but to abandon these classes if we could not reorganize them. In contrast, if the classes differed significantly in IQ, while this too is a critical variable for language learning, it is one which we could handle with the analysis of covariance. If we found that the only variable on which the groups differed was the proportion of unskilled and semi-skilled fathers, we would probably decide that this variable was not sufficiently related to language learning to make us eliminate these classes, even though we could not handle the nominal data provided through analysis of covariance. Thus we would plan on noting this difference in the report of the research, considering it one of the limitations to the conclusions. It is this level of deliberate decision making which the researcher must achieve in working with existing groups.

Same Respondents for Multiple Treatments

One of the most effective techniques for assuring that the groups responding to different experimental treatments are comparable is to have the same people make up the successive experimental groups. This obvious solution to the problem of comparability is not used more often because of the equally obvious danger it contains that after being exposed to one experimental situation the respondent can no longer be assumed to be a naive subject for further experimental situations. In those instances when this can be assumed, however, the use of the same respondents for each of the treatments within the experiment does eliminate the problems of comparability. Note that once again we face the necessity for the researcher to be an expert in the educational practice involved, or have an expert available for consultation. This is because the judgment that the experimental treatments will have no cumulative effect, and so can be administered to the same subjects in succession, is a complex professional judgment. Moreover, it must be made in terms acceptable to the practitioner if the experiment is to be accepted beyond the research fraternity.

One technical problem in using the same respondents for the several experimental treatments is to randomize the order of presentation. To do this properly, the researcher needs as many experimental subjects or groups as he has experimental treatments. To assist him in assigning treatments to respondents, techniques based upon mathematical principles of combination and randomization are available. The simplest such technique is the *Latin square*. The Latin square is simply a layout of the same number of rows and columns. The rows correspond to the separate subjects or groups of subjects. The columns correspond to the order in which the experimental treatments will be presented to the subjects. In the cells appear letters from the Latin alphabet, one letter corresponding to each experimental treatment. Thus the number of letters used corresponds to the number of rows and columns.

As an illustration, Table 16-5 presents three of the 12 possible[14] 3 × 3 Latin squares, with the first one labeled as the researcher intending to use it would label it. To use the square, the researcher lets each row represent one individual or group. He then assigns each of the letters in the square to one of the levels of the independent variable. Thus if we were to use Latin square number 1, in Table 16-5, group 1 (the first row) would first receive the level of the independent variable we had labeled C, then the level labeled A, and finally the level labeled B. Group 2, in contrast, would receive the levels in the order B, C, A, with group 3 receiving the third variation: A, B, C. Note that this arrangement places each level of the independent variable in each of the possible ordinal positions, but places it there once only. Thus, in this upper left-hand square that we have used as an illustration, the level designated A was given second to the first group, then third, and finally first.

The advantage of the use of the same respondents is *only* in the virtue of comparability of the groups used for the separate treatments. It does not save groups. The randomization of order achieved through the Latin square procedure requires the same three groups as a matched group design would, and so there is no saving there.

If the researcher is using two independent variables and wishes to randomly assign the order of treatments, he uses the *Greco-Latin square*

[14]To determine the maximum number of Latin squares for X levels of an experimental variable, we use the formula $(X$ factorial$) \times (X - 1$ factorial$)$.

Table 16–5 Three Illustrative 3 × 3 Latin Squares

	First Treatment	Second Treatment	Third Treatment		First Treatment	Second Treatment	Third Treatment
Group 1	C	A	B	Group 1	A	C	B
Group 2	B	C	A	Group 2	B	A	C
Group 3	A	B	C	Group 3	C	B	A

No. 1   No. 2

	First Treatment	Second Treatment	Third Treatment
Group 1	A	B	C
Group 2	B	C	A
Group 3	C	A	B

No. 3

principles. In principle this involves two superimposed squares, one using Latin letters for the levels of the first variable, the second using Greek letters to designate the levels of the second variable. The applications on the Greco-Latin square and its varieties are beyond the scope of this book. The reader interested in a full treatment of this topic should consult Federer[15] or Lindquist.[16]

STEPS IN EXPERIMENTAL APPROACH

Listed below are the several steps in the experimental approach.

1. Statement of the research problem
2. Determination that the experimental approach is appropriate
3. Specification of the independent variable
4. Specification of the levels of the independent variable
5. Specification of full range of potential dependent variables
6. Initial statement of hypotheses

[15]Federer, *Experimental Design, Theory and Application.*
[16]Lindquist, *Design and Analysis of Experiments in Psychology and Education.*

7. Determining the availability of measures for the potential dependent variables, identifying variables for which:
   (a) sufficiently reliable and valid measures exist
   (b) measures do not exist but researcher believes that they can be developed in time
   (c) measures neither exist nor can be developed
8. Initial estimate of the success potential of the research in terms of:
   (a) the possibility for establishing the levels of the independent variable, realistically and ethically
   (b) the availability of measures for the dependent variables
9. Identification of full range of potential intervening variables, and categorization into those which:
   (a) should be controlled
   (b) can be permitted to vary systematically
   (c) can be ignored because of their relationship to variables in (a) or (b)
   (d) can be left alone
10. Formal statement of the research hypotheses
11. Design of the experiment to test hypotheses by establishing:
    (a) comparable experimental and control situations
    (b) the levels of the independent variable(s)
    (c) the needed conditions to handle the intervening variables
    (d) the needed conditions to handle other sources of bias
    (e) the needed data collection(s) for the dependent variable(s)
12. Statement of limitations to the potential conclusions and the assumptions of the experiment
13. Final estimate of the success potential of the proposed experiment in terms of:
    (a) the extent to which the design of the experiment will produce a valid test of the independent variable with reasonable control of intervention
    (b) the determination that all possible outcomes will meet the researcher's needs and goals
14. Implementation of experiment through collection of any pre-experimental measures and beginning of experimental and control conditions
15. Periodic verification that intergity of experiment is being maintained
16. Collection of any intermediate measures
17. Termination of experiment through collection of post-experimental measures
18. Analysis of data to test hypotheses
19. Preparation of report

   More so than the other approaches to research, the early steps may in themselves involve considerable effort and study by the researcher—a fact which was illustrated with the Language Study in Chapter 1. The first two steps in the experimental approach, as in every research approach, are the *statement of the research problem* and the *determination that the approach being contemplated is appropriate*. Some few problem statements clearly call for an experimental approach; most others do not. For example, if the research problem calls for estimation of the effectiveness of a concept the researcher knows to be new, then the experimental approach is immediately indicated. However, if the problem involves concepts which might exist, then the researcher must do sufficient study to be able to determine whether the comparative survey might be a more appropriate research approach. In some few instances, and the Language Study was one of those, the researcher must also consider the possibility that the historical approach would be most appropriate.

The reader may recall that the problem of the Language Study was stated originally as: "What is the best method of teaching English as a second language to newly arrived non–English-speaking Puerto Rican children?" A review of literature and available sources quickly indicated that the historical approach was inappropriate because of the absence of material. This was followed by a thorough survey of sites where the problem or a related problem in second-language teaching existed. This eliminated the possibility of a comparative survey because one of the major methods advocated, the vocabulary emphasis, was not in existence in any school setting. It was at that point that the appropriateness of the experimental approach was established. The problem required data about a research situation which did not exist.

Once it is recognized that the experimental approach is appropriate, the researcher turns to the next two steps, which involve the *specification of the independent variable or variables* and the *specification of the levels within each independent variable*. The purpose of the research, the literature review, and the prior surveys of the first stages interact with the realities of the current settings to guide the researcher at this stage. In the Language Study, the research purpose and problem clearly identified the independent variable as "method of teaching English as a second language." The review of literature identified two potential levels of that variable (vocabulary and structure emphasis). A third level (experiential emphasis) was identified during the same survey of existing situations which ruled out the comparative survey as a possible research approach. Other potential levels involved combinations of emphases, but these were ruled out on the grounds of our inability to select from among the infinite number of possible combinations. The other potential level considered was a control group not exposed to any formal instruction. This was ruled out since it was ethically impossible. And so we concluded with the identification of three levels of the independent variable "method of teaching. . . ."

The next stage involves the *specification of the full range of potential dependent variables* and the *initial statement of the hypotheses of the experiment.* This may seem like a strange pair to treat in one stage, except that, as noted earlier, these two aspects interact so closely that it is impossible to state categorically which is developed from which. If an experiment is being developed from some theory, then the hypotheses will be structured by the theory. In this instance they should be stated and used as a basis for identifying the kinds of dependent measures required to test them. In other instances, like the Language Study, the problem stems from a situational need rather than theory, and so no natural hypotheses exist. In that instance the researcher typically will identify his dependent variables on the basis of professional consideration of aspects of the problem. It was this kind of consideration which led to the identification of the four language modalities of reading, writing, speaking, and understanding, and the potential dependent variables in the area of children's and teachers' attitudes and reactions. Note that if the hypotheses do not precede the statement of the dependent variables the researcher is concerned with identifying the full range of potential dependent variables that might have relevance for the experiment. He is not concerned at this stage with deciding which can and which cannot be employed in the ultimate experiment. In this instance, too, the statement of hypotheses are delayed until a later stage, after the actual dependent variables to be employed are selected.

The next stage, *determining the availability of measures for the potential dependent variables,* is a particularly critical one. As in the survey, the researcher now considers the extent to which sufficiently reliable and valid measures already exist or can be developed. In this way he identifies those variables for which adequate measures neither exist nor can be developed in time, and which therefore will have to be omitted from the experiment. The critical importance of the stage is that adding this information to that previously obtained about the independent variable provides the researcher with the basis for his *initial estimate of the success potential of the experiment* (step 8).

This estimate is made in terms of his ability to create the situations needed to establish the desired levels of the independent variable and to obtain measures of the essential dependent variables. The first criterion, establishing the required levels of the independent variable, is not the automatic stage that some naive researchers expect. This stage may involve reorganization of classes, the training of participating teachers, or the development of experimental materials for lessons and units. All of this takes time, and much of it also takes a high level of cooperation by schools and staff who may not share the experimenter's enthusiasm for the study proposed. Some experiments, like the Language Study, require all of the items listed above to implement the independent variable. If many items are required, then the experimenter must also consider the time factor. Developing units and other experimental materials takes time, as does the training of teachers or other participants. The experimenter must decide if he has the time to prepare these adequately or if he will be pressured into beginning the experiment with inadequately prepared materials and without fully trained staff. This would not be a full and fair test of the independent variable, and so the success potential would be low.

Similarly, if he faces the unhappy prospect that for several important dependent variables measures are not available and there is no reason to expect that they can be developed in time, the success potential is low. Instrument development, too, takes time. Even worse, where we can reasonably estimate how long it will take to develop materials, we cannot accurately estimate how long it will take to develop an instrument to a sufficient level of reliability. At this stage the researcher must candidly appraise his ability to produce a meaningful experiment, when this is defined as an honest test of the independent variable measured with reliable, valid estimates of the critical dependent variables. Note that we are referring here only to an honest test of the independent variable. Thus productive failure, in which data come out contrary to what the researcher hypothesized, will be perfectly meaningful provided the experiment can be considered an honest test of the independent variable.

In some instances the researcher is faced with an embarrassment of riches, that is, he finds measures available for more dependent variables than he believes he can encompass within the experiment. In that case, of course, he must select those most relevant to the original research problem. He may also wish to use the initial set of hypotheses to further guide cutting down the number of dependent variables.

In all cases it is important before making final commitments to consider the dependent variables as a total set, identifying the areas of educational, psychological, and sociological concern represented within that set. The effort here can almost be considered an effort to estimate the content validity of the set of dependent variables.

Assuming that the researcher can candidly conclude that the success potential of the experiment is reasonable, he moves on to the ninth stage: the *identification and categorization of the potential intervening variables.* Here the effort is to first identify all of the potential sources of intervention, and second to place each of them into one of the three categories of "hold constant," "systematic variation," and "leave alone." This categorization is done with the research problem and independent variables as referent. The researcher asks himself what he must achieve with each potential intervening variable to properly study *this* individual problem and *these* independent variables. Not only must the problem and the independent variables be considered now, but so must the realities of the research situation in which the experiment is to be done. The issue in this stage is to come out with decisions as to how to dispose of the potential sources of intervention in terms which can be implemented in that research situation.

If they have not been stated in the previous stages of the research, then this is the point for the formal *statement of the research hypotheses.* With the independent variable specified in terms of its levels, and with the dependent variables selected and translated into specific measures, it is appropriate for the researcher to state his expectations for the experiment. Moreover, it is critical for this to be done at this point, because the hypotheses are necessary to guide the design of the data-gathering plan and to evaluate the utility of that plan. With the hypotheses stated the researcher moves immediately to stage 11, the *design of the experiment.*

As the list above notes, this design involves several stages, each of which has previously been discussed in this chapter. We shall not repeat what was said earlier, but we shall note that the design must achieve more than the conditions necessary to control the intervening variables and eliminate other sources of bias. We stress this because so many books on experimental design are almost exclusively oriented to the negative: that is, to designing a study to avoid the bias of the pretest, or the intervention of teacher ability. Comparable attention is not given to the positive aspects of what a design must achieve and produce. As step 11 notes, the design must provide a test of the hypotheses by providing for the establishment of the levels of the independent variables and for the collection of data on the dependent variables.

With the experiment designed, the researcher is now in a position to look back over what he has been able to accomplish, and thereby identify what he was not able to accomplish. With the "not accomplished" items in hand, he can *state the limitations to his potential conclusions.* These are based upon aspects of the intervening variables which have not been handled or aspects of the design which admit some potential bias, or even aspects of the independent variable which could not be implemented as desired. In other words, he identifies all those specific aspects of the experiment as designed which keep it from being the perfect experimental study of the specific research problem. At this stage, in addition to identifying and listing the limitations, the researcher also *identifies* and lists *the assumptions* implicit in his design.

The reason that the assumptions and limitations need to be identified at this point is that in the succeeding stage 13 the researcher makes his final estimate of the success potential of the proposed experiment. He now knows what he will do if he proceeds and how he will do it. He can therefore weigh what the professional and intellectual contribution of the study will be if it is successful, and once again consider the contribution if it is not successful. The student, particularly, in this evaluation must be certain that however the data come out, the experiment will meet his goals and purposes.

If he is satisfied that the success potential is there, he proceeds to *implement the experiment*. Depending upon the design, this may mean the administration of pretest measures, or it may mean simply beginning the experimental and control condition. But notice that there are two more stages which involve the researcher's activities during the life of the experiment: *periodic verification that the integrity of the experiment is being maintained* and *administration of any intermediate measures*. The reference to integrity involves the discussion earlier in this chapter to leakage as well as to the experimenter's desire to know that his paper plans are being turned into educational practice in the ways in which they were originally envisioned.

When the experiment has run its course, the final stage in the data-collection phase occurs, *the termination of the experiment through the administration of the posttest measures*. This is immediately followed *by the analysis of the data to test the hypotheses,* and the final stage, *the writing of the research report*. The experimental report should contain the basic descriptive findings of the experiment as well as any evaluative or comparative conclusions appropriate to the experiment.

Chapter 17

THE OBSERVATION METHOD
AND TECHNIQUES FOR OBSERVING

The five-step method of observation is the classic method of scientific investigation. The investigator (1) observes natural phenomena; (2) draws conclusions as to what is happening; (3) uses the conclusion to generate hypotheses or predictions of what result is a consequence of what act; (4) tests the hypotheses over time; and (5) attempts to develop theories to explain why it is happening. Undoubtedly this was the method of investigation which led to the great advances of prehistoric and preliterate man. Lacking the ability to measure or question the physical world, he nevertheless observed phenomena like plant growth, drew conclusions, and made predictions about the effect of planting seeds and the relationship between planting and subsequent growth and harvest. Similarly, archeologists and anthropologists speculate that the controlled use of fire came into man's repertoire through acute observation over the ages as men noticed the warmth available from natural fires and tasted the meat of animals, who had accidently been burned, and gradually came to conclude that this phenomena could be used for warmth and for cooking under controlled conditions.

Over the centuries, observation of natural phenomena continued and continues to be a dominant method of inquiry in the physical sciences. However it has developed from the original method which had as its basic technique simply watching sufficient phenomena until some hunch or insight was achieved. The first advance came when systematic classification was added to simple observation. At this stage man developed a system whereby the natural phenomena being observed could be organized and classified by some criterion. Man's first understanding of seasonal variation was an early classification system, with the distinction between night and day undoubtedly preceding it. More complex systems of classification were developed by the early astronomers and biologists with elements of the systems still in use such as the distinction between

492

planets and other heavenly bodies. A second significant change in the use of the observational method came when it was combined with the measurement method, and thus man not only observed but measured. This added to the precision of observational data, and each major advance in the ability to measure natural phenomena has significantly advanced the disciplines involved. Thus, as this book is written, the astronomers are rethinking basic aspects of theoretical systems as they develop the ability to measure radio wave activity. Theoretical systems had little need to account for sources of radio waves from other solar systems as long as they were not measureable, and so were only hypothesized. Now that they can be measured, and obviously do exist, they must be accounted for.

Two other major changes in observation as a method have come as man's ability to observe has improved and expanded. This happened long ago in the physical sciences but only recently in the social sciences. The telescope and microscope opened up worlds otherwise invisible to the physical scientist. But in the social sciences man's eye was the basic tool for observation until the relatively recent invention of the camera, and particularly the television camera, offered the researcher useful supplementary observational devices.

A final change, also far more utilized in the physical than the social sciences, has been the gradual change in the locale of observations from the natural world to the artificial world of the laboratory. This change in locale has come about because in the laboratory observations can be made under more controlled (and convenient) conditions, and replication of studies becomes a simpler matter. This change from the real world to the laboratory has occurred in the physical sciences in direct proportion to the extent to which the laboratory can meaningfully be made to simulate reality. Thus, the virologist works largely in the laboratory, the biologist works in both the real world and laboratory, whereas the astronomer still works almost exclusively in the real world.

Except for psychology, however, we have seen no comparable shift from the real world to the laboratory in the social disciplines. In education, we have seen some effort to make observation of the real world more convenient by building schools with observation rooms, usually with one-way vision glass, and sometimes with built in motion picture and television cameras as well. But basically we seem to believe that the teaching-learning process cannot meaningfully be simulated in the laboratory or even in the laboratory school. The interesting paradox is that the psychologists during this same period seem convinced that the learning process *can* be studied in the laboratory under artificial conditions. What seems true is that some of the processes basic to education, like learning or motivation, can usefully be studied in the laboratory as processes but must be observed in the school or a school-type situation if the social aspects of education are to be included within the study.

In this chapter we shall consider the types of research for which observation is an appropriate method, the elements of the method, the techniques available within the method, and conclude with an overview of the steps in implementing the observation method.

RESEARCH FOR WHICH OBSERVATION IS APPROPRIATE

Observation, which involves the researcher watching the research situation, can be used in survey or experimental research, but not in historical research. It has its most obvious applicability in survey research, particularly simple descriptive surveys. In this approach the researcher is basically concerned with straightforward description of the research situation, and one of the best ways to achieve this is to watch it. But as we noted in the introduction to this chapter, observation can also be done using systems to classify or measure the phenomena being observed, and this makes the method applicable to comparative and evaluative surveys and to experiments as well.

For example, a study recently conducted by the author[1] had as its purpose a comparison of the educational process in a set of schools with a newly developed special program and a set of schools with a regular program. To accomplish this purpose we sent observers into randomly selected classrooms in each set of schools to watch the educational process. The observers were asked both to describe what they saw and to rate the quality of teacher and pupil functioning. Based on these data we were able to conclude that the experimental organization of schools did not result in any observable changes in what teachers did, although there was some evidence that the quality of teacher functioning was better in the experimental schools.[2]

It is important to note at the outset of this consideration of observation as a method that it is a slow and expensive way of accumulating research data. Moreover these data, once accumulated, are also often slow and

[1] *Expansion of the More Effective Schools Program* (New York: Center for Urban Education, September 1967).

[2] This study also illustrates the "Hawthorne effect" we discussed in Chapter 16 on the experimental approach. We had to consider the possibility that this indication of higher quality of teacher functioning was not due to the independent variable (the new program) but rather to teacher interest in and response to the process of experimentation itself.

expensive to analyze. This is stated here not to discourage, but simply to establish the fact that while we say of each method that it is to be used when it is most appropriate, we add that the observation method is used only when questioning and measuring are inappropriate. But having noted the negative side, let us also note that when it is appropriate, the observation method will produce a kind of data which the other two methods cannot, for the raw material of observation is reality itself.

Levels of Observation

In terms of the levels of research,[3] observation is most appropriate for the subsurface and depth levels. It can function at the surface level as well, but is an expensive method (in terms of time and personnel cost) to obtain surface data, since these can usually be obtained with equal effectiveness, and far less cost, by the questioning method. When used at the surface, subsurface, or depth level observation is concerned with the overt aspects of the research situation. The observer in these instances is asked to deal with the phenomena he sees in front of him. This is not a simple task, for at the depth level we are asking the observer to observe what the respondent does and decide if this action reflects his (the respondent's) true reaction to the situation or if it is a response he has produced for any of a variety of social and personal pressures. Because the observer has seen the response he is asked to evaluate and has also seen the social setting in which it was made, he is functioning at the *manifest level of observation.* If we ask the observer to move to the non-conscious level of research, we ask him to "observe" dynamics, such as hostility or motivations. Since these are not overt, they must be inferred from overt actions, and so we are asking him to function at the *latent level of observation,* that is, to interpret phenomena beneath the surface of what he is actually watching. This is a far more complex task than observation at the manifest level, and a task which even the most expert observer has difficulty performing with satisfactory reliability for research purposes.

The manifest level of observation is to record, without evaluation or feeling tone, who says what to whom, or who does what. Thus the observer might note that the teacher asks a question, that five hands go up, and that she calls on Fred, who gives an answer she accepts as correct. The latent level interpretation of this same act might note that she asks the question *in an angry tone,* that five hands go up *hesitatingly,* and

[3]These levels are discussed in Chapter 13.

that she calls on Fred, who gives an answer which she accepts as correct, but in a way which *suggests she does not think it fully satisfactory but has no hope of receiving a better answer.* The difference between these levels lies in the italicized interpretations; the relative difficulty of the latent level should be obvious. A dozen competent researchers, watching this classroom, should all agree on the manifest level description of what happened and who participated. They would not all necessarily agree on the latent level interpretation. Where the one observer quoted above saw "anger," "hesitation," and "no hope of receiving a better answer," another observer might have seen a teacher trying to "motivate by the force of her own interest and drive," children "beginning to become aware that they had information and could respond" and so hands slowly going up, and a teacher "accepting a less than perfect response so as to encourage" Fred and his classmates to continue to respond.

As always when we work at the nonconscious level of research we cannot know if we are correct or not when we make our inferences. From a single set of observational data alone we would never know if the inference that the teacher was angry and had given up on achieving high standards was correct or if the alternate inference, that she was driving hard to motivate and willing to accept imperfect responses to encourage, made more sense. The key point for the researcher contemplating observation as a data-collection method is to recognize that the attribution of motivation or interest or hostility at the latent level cannot be done reliably unless there is a sound theoretical system in which dynamics like motivation can be translated into behavior, tone, and gesture which he can teach to his observers. We have few such systems available as this book is written, and so when observers are asked to function at the latent level, they are forced to use their own background and experience to develop individual theoretical systems to unite behavior with motivation and other dynamics. It is this forced reliance on personal rationales for interpretation which makes it difficult to achieve reliability in latent observation at the nonconscious level.

Nevertheless, while difficult, it should be recognized that reliable judgment is possible provided the distinctions required of the observers are not excessively precise. For example, work with instruments designed to measure teacher behavior[4] indicates the observers can reliably distinguish unsympathetic from understanding behavior in terms of a seven-point scale about a neutral midpoint and can make similar distinctions for characteristics like "apathetic–alert," or "inflexible–adaptable."

[4]D. G. Ryan, *Characteristics of Teachers* (Washington, D.C.: American Council on Education, 1960), 414 pp.

ELEMENTS OF OBSERVATION METHOD

There are four elements in observation, as we shall structure this discussion. First, and most basic, are the decisions concerned with specifying the outcomes and content of the observation itself. This element is concerned with establishing a foundation for the observation in terms of what the researcher wishes to be able to do with the data (the outcomes) and what and whom he wishes to observe (the content). The second element is the development of the observational guide, which is the researcher's operational statement as to the content he has decided to watch, and the instrument through which the observational data will be recorded. The third element involves the observers, specifically their identification, recruitment, and training. The fourth element is the respondent–observer interaction, which shall include the issues as to whether or not the respondent knows he is being watched, whether the observer is watching the actual research situation as it develops, or watching some indirect version of it, and who the respondent believes the observer to be.

Specifying Outcomes and Content

In all three data-gathering methods the researcher must begin with a clear translation of the research question and hypothesis into the kinds of data he requires. Of the three methods, this is particularly critical in observation because the potential phenomena which the observer might watch are so vast and often so amorphous that whatever structure can be supplied should be supplied. Therefore, the first element in the application of the observation method is a clear statement of the expected outcomes of the observation, and the content of the observation. By "outcome," we mean simply whether the researcher wishes to use the data to describe the research situation or whether he wishes to be able to evaluate the situation, or aspects of it. By "content," we mean those variables within the situation which we shall ask the observer to watch.

The researcher can begin with a consideration either of content or of outcome, but ultimately must consider both if he is to use the observational method. In other words he can decide that his primary research interest is to study teacher functioning in the classroom (the content) and that he wishes to be able to evaluate (the outcome) how well the teachers observed function. In contrast, he might have decided that he wishes to evaluate the adequacy of current programs (the outcome) and so will send observers into the schools to observe teacher functioning (the content).

The researcher determines his outcomes and content by beginning with his research question and/or hypothesis and asking what kinds of data would be needed to answer the question or test the hypothesis. In some instances the process is simple and the answer obvious. For example, in Chapter 1 we noted how, in planning the Language Study, we became concerned that teachers might not remain methodologically "pure" in the sense that they would begin to share methods and techniques. We concluded that we could not simply assume that they would be, nor could we accept the possibility that they were not consistent as a limitation to the conclusions. Therefore we decided to obtain data on this point. Observation of their performance in class was the preferable method. Moving from research question to outcome and content was simple. The data we needed were descriptions by observers as to the method employed by each teacher.[5]

More often, the research question does not immediately lead to such a specific statement of the data required, but rather leads to a statement of the areas in which data will be required. The researcher must then take the next step and specify the content of the observation on the basis of the literature, and his own experience and insight. For example, in the late 1960s the author directed a study[6] designed to evaluate the effects of busing nonwhite children from their neighborhood schools to previously all-white schools. The general research question posed was to identify the effects of the program on the children involved. It was simple to translate that question into the need for evaluation in areas of concern like academic achievement, pupil perception of self, school, education and society, teacher morale, and in-class interactions. It was equally simple to note that observation was the preferred method[7] to obtain data relevant to evaluating an area like "in-class interactions." But saying that did not specify the kinds of data to be obtained in the same sense as our previous translation did, that is, that "we needed descriptions by the observer as to the method employed by each teacher."

When all the research question does is identify an area in which data are needed, the researcher must further specify his content if his observers

[5]We shall see, later in this chapter, how the statement of the research question also structures the specific observational technique employed. In this instance it was clear to us that to obtain a valid insight into the consistency of method we had to watch teachers when they were unaware of the specific time an observer would arrive, although they were entitled to know that they would be observed. Thus, we used the technique called *direct observation, known, but not scheduled.*

[6]*Expansion of the Free Choice Open Enrollment Program.* (New York: Center for Urban Education, 1967), 63 pp.

[7]Indicative of how the methods interact, in some areas we might have used the questioning method to supplement these observational data, in other words, by simply asking the children to give us their impressions of the in-class interactions.

are to function. To do this rationally, the researcher must develop a model of the research situation. To assist in selecting content, this model must specify in detail all the variables within the research situation so that the researcher may ultimately distinguish those he wishes his observers to watch from those he wishes them to ignore. The model for selecting content moves far beyond the initial statement of the areas of interest. It is one thing to decide that for research purposes we need an evaluation of in-class interactions. It is quite another to develop a model of the separate variables which comprise in-class interaction, in other words, "conversation among children," "selecting partners for a shared activity," "seating patterns when seating is voluntary," "verbal challenges," "physical challenges," and so on. Similarly, the decision that one outcome of the observation is to be a description of teacher functioning must be developed at this content stage into a model of teacher functioning which would spell out its elements like "how the teacher introduces her material," "her use of aids," "how she asks questions of children," "how she responds when they offer a wrong answer," "how she reacts when children ask a spontaneous question," and so on throughout all of the behavioral aspects of which the researcher subsumes under "teacher functioning."

Given this complete model, the researcher can then return to his research question and hypotheses and use these as the basis for initially selecting those variables within the model which he wishes to include in the content for the observation. In some limited observational situations, the researcher may aspire to observing everything which happens. For this to be a sensible level of aspiration in any situation involving people there must be at least as many observers as there are respondents to observe. Even under these conditions, in complex interpersonal situations, it may well be that some aspects of the situation involving the overall tone or mood of the situation will be lost. And obviously, in any complex situation, there are feasible limits to the number of observers who can be provided. Thus, in almost all instances in which observation can be used, the researcher faces the necessity to select those aspects which he wishes to observe and record. The basic references for this selection are the research problem and hypotheses, if any, for these structure the kinds of information required.

For every variable which is to be included within the content of the observation the researcher ultimately must decide between describing it in operational terms for his observers, or leaving it undefined, and so assuming that all observers will define it in the same way. For example, a variable like the teacher's use of aids might be left undefined as we decide (or discover through pilot studies) that every observer we consider expert enough to use for the project knows what we mean by teaching aids, and moreover all of them understand the term the same way. A different researcher might note that in the literature teacher-made instructional worksheets are not always included in discussions of instructional aids, and so decide that, since he wishes to include them, he had better specify carefully what he is including within this term.

Similarly, the researcher considers each variable which he wishes to include and decides which lend themselves to specific definition, which he can safely leave undefined but assume that his observers understand, and which he can neither define nor assume understanding. These last, obviously, cannot be included within the content of the observation. For example, continuing with the illustration of teacher functioning, the researcher might decide that simply stating the variable "how teacher introduces material" is sufficient because all observers he will use will understand what he means by the statement. In contrast he might recognize that simply stating the variable "how a teacher reacts when a child asks a spontaneous question" is not sufficient, for all observers might not recognize that he (the researcher) is concerned with identifying the extent to which the teacher is accepting and supportive of questioning, and actively encourages the process. Illustrative of the third possibility is the variable "teacher's interest in teaching," for which the researcher might decide that he can neither assume common understanding nor satisfactorily define in any operational sense so that his observers could "see" it. This, then, would be an aspect of the possible content which would be omitted.[8]

In deciding how to handle each specific variable within the possible content of the observation, the researcher uses his own (or his staff's or consultant's) knowledge of the development in thinking and understanding in the area under study. If he has reason to believe that sufficient knowledge of the area is already available he can immediately decide which variables to include within the observation. If sufficient knowledge is not available then he should plan a series of pilot observations designed to determine which variables can, and which cannot, reliably be observed in the field.

Once the variables to be observed are selected and defined, the researcher must decide if he wishes to state a dimension through which the observer will communicate what he saw. Consider, as an example, the decision that we wish to use the observational data to describe the teacher's use of instructional aids. This statement provides us with both a statement about content and outcome. We could decide to go no further, and simply ask the observer to watch this aspect of teacher functioning and after completing the observation to write his impressions of what use the teacher made of aids.

[8]These variables which can neither be defined nor assumed to be understood are excellent clues to needed research.

In most research instances the researcher wishes to provide his observers with more structure than this. The simplest level of structure is to ask whether the aspect was seen or not, that is, "Did the teacher use instructional aids?" Once we move in the direction of structure, however, we usually move past this simple level to more complex distinctions asking the observer to make some quantitative and/or qualitative distinctions. In this illustration we might decide that a simple "yes" from the observer was not as valuable for our descriptive purposes as asking the observer to record which specific aids were used so that we might obtain an estimate of how many were used and how many different ones were used. We might move even further and ask him to indicate the teaching purpose for which they were used, and could then move beyond simple description and ask him to rate the "effectiveness" with which they were used, or the "creativity" involved in their use, or the "children's responses" to them.

As we proliferate the distinctions we might ask the observer to make in reference to the teacher's use of aids we cannot ignore the fact that each successive distinction requires that the observer devote more and more of his attention to the teacher's use of aids. Thus, it may well be that by the time we have exhaustively listed all of the distinctions we can ask him to make, we have tied up a disproportionate share of his time, *in terms of our research purpose.*

This means that this stage of selecting content is usually another one of those decision stages in which the researcher must winnow down a list of what he would like to do, until he has a feasible list of what it will be possible to do. As always, the criteria for winnowing are the research question and hypotheses. The researcher must resist the temptation to have the observer collect data because "they would be interesting," or because "we so seldom get permission to put observers in that school, it seems a shame not to find out," or any other rationale for collecting data other than the fact that the data are needed to answer the research question or test the research hypotheses.

If the researcher has many more variables which he might study than will be possible, it often helps at this stage to actually lay out the total possible set of variables and all possible dimensions of each variable in a kind of blueprint for the observation. Given this blueprint, cutting the list to feasible size can be done with a constant view of the total observation. For it is the total amount of data to be derived which will determine whether or not the content is adequate to answer the research question.

PARTICIPATION, INTERACTION, AND PROCESS   A different way of considering the potential content of an observation is to focus on the fact of participation itself rather than the behavior of the participants. In this orientation to the content, the observer watches and records who says what to whom, and how specific individuals react and interact. Research at the extreme of this orientation may pay no attention to identifying the topic of a particular discussion or lesson but instead may be totally immersed in the interpersonal aspects of that discussion.

This orientation to what constitutes the content of an observation has enjoyed greater popularity in social psychology, particularly in group dynamics, than in education. However, in the late 1960s, as this book is written, there is increasing interest in the area of classroom interactions, with emphasis both on teacher–child and child–child interaction. Of course, the researcher does not have to choose between observing interaction and observing behaviors. It is perfectly feasible to attempt to combine both within one research project. What must be made clear is that the observation of participation, interaction, or process must be developed as a clearly separate part of the content, and the attention of the observers specifically directed toward this aspect of the observation.

The researcher who moves in this direction should also recognize that almost invariably observing participation and interaction is more complex than it seems at first. For example, on first consideration identifying who participates in a situation would seem to be a simple surface level piece of data, at the manifest level of observation. This simple surface level of information can become more complex if "participate" is defined as more than overt actions or words indicating the respondent's involvement. Is the child who listens attentively to what the teacher and children say "participating" in the lesson, even if she never says a word herself? Is the teacher who sits silently throughout a faculty meeting, but who smiles, grimaces, and otherwise reacts to statements made by others, "participating"? Each researcher must decide for himself, in the context of his research problem and hypotheses, the most sensible definition of participation. But the range of possible definition is large, and the more broadly defined the deeper the level of observation required.

Similarly, the researcher who wishes to move into the observation of interaction and process must define these terms with the same care required in the specification of behaviors to be observed. In both of these areas, however, there is an ever-increasing literature suggesting categories which can be used in structuring the observation.[9]

The Observation Guide

Another element in the application of the observational method is the instrument or *observation guide* through which the data will be recorded.

[9]One basic reference is Robert Freed Bales, *Interaction Process Analysis; A Method for the Study of Small Groups* (Reading, Mass.: Addison-Wesley Publishing Company, Inc., 1950), 203 pp.

The purpose of the guide is to provide whatever structure the researcher wishes the observer to have as he watches. We have already discussed how the researcher has the responsibility to determine the outcome and content of the observation. In a sense the instrument becomes the researcher's operational statement both as to what he expects the observer to watch and what he expects from the observation. For this reason instrument development must be preceded by the stage in which outcome and content are selected.

Of course, in some observations there may be no formal guide at all. This occurs when the observers are instructed to watch the research situation and write a description of it. In this extreme of unstructured observation the researcher does not even specify the dimensions along which he wants this report written, but is content to let the observer's impressions structure the selection of the report.

More usually the researcher identifies in the guide the dimensions he wishes watched. He may tell this to the observer or he may provide him with a written statement of the dimensions to guide the observations, which the observer takes with him into the research situation. As the researcher develops a more structured view of what he wishes, the observation guide becomes more structured and more complex, until we reach the opposite extreme from the absence of an observation guide. This is the totally structured observation guide in which every aspect of the situation to be watched is identified for the observer, and every response he makes is selected from options predetermined by the researcher and placed on the observation guide.[10]

There is no "right" amount of structure, but rather an appropriate amount for each research purpose. However, it is a useful rule of thumb to remember that we are reasonably certain to have relevant data for those dimensions and distinctions that actually are on the guide. We may or may not have relevant data for those dimensions not spelled out on the guide. Thus, the author believes that the basic rule to follow is: "If in doubt, spell it out."

Like all other instruments, observation guides are subject to the requirement that they be sufficiently reliable for the research purpose, valid, sensitive, and objective, and function within ethical limits. As a general rule, the greater the degree of structure, the simpler it is to achieve satisfactory reliability. But like so many generalizations in research, this one cannot be stated without qualifying it, in this case by noting that excessive structure, which requires distinctions more precise than those the observer can make, will damage reliability.

[10]The technical aspects of developing these structured guides are discussed in Chapter 19, under the section devoted to rating scales.

This means that an observation guide should never be used without a period of pilot testing during which both reliability and validity can be estimated. This is true even in the apparently simple instance in which the observer is asked to write a descriptive report. In this instance the pilot phase can be used to estimate the reliability with which observers select the same dynamics for their report and report those dynamics they select in the same terms.

The Observers

The next element in observation, and one which often gets less attention than it deserves, is the observer. When observation is conducted by human observers, as opposed to mechanical or electrical devices like motion picture or television cameras, all of the planning and objectification of process can be no better than the quality of observation that the human being performs. As we noted in considering the historical approach, no person can record an "objective" record of an event, in the sense that we have defined objective as referring to data which are determined only by the research situation. To obtain such an objective record would mean that the observer's record of the event was completely a function of the event, and not at all affected by the observer himself. No person can look at human interactions completely freed of his personality, background, and experience. The more experienced the person is with the area and content of the observation and the phenomena or material to be observed, the more fully developed is the cognitive structure within which he "sees" events.

Because of this, the selection and training of observers is a critical stage in every project using the observation method. To move into this stage the researcher must be well along in delineating the outcome and content of the observation. For considering questions about observers is sensible only within the context of a general understanding of what it is they are to observe and what kinds of judgments and distinctions are expected of them. Given this information, the researcher can make the first decision in relation to his observers: whether he wishes to use persons with specific experience in the research situation or whether he wishes to use persons without such experience. If the observers are being sent into the situation for purely descriptive observation, they are simply the eyes and ears of the researcher; they do not require experience in the problem area. In fact, the person without experience in the problem area may be a more objective observer than the person with experience. This is because the inexperienced person has no pre-set convictions as to the meaning of behavior in the problem area, has no experiences by which he can "interpret" or "understand" what is "really happening." In short, he has a far greater probability of observing and recording the event as it transpired. However, if the observer is being sent into the situation to evaluate as well as to describe, then he must have sufficient experience to make these evaluative tasks sensible.

For example, in the Language Study when observers were sent into classes to judge which emphasis the teachers were using, the observers had to be experts in the teaching of English as a second language. It would have been pointless to send in persons who were not extremely knowledgeable in this area, for the judgment we were asking them to make was highly technical. Similarly, had we decided that we wished the outcome to be an overall evaluation of interaction in the class seen in comparison to the interaction in some hypothetical average class, this would have placed a heavy responsibility on the shoulders of the observer who had to provide the referent of interaction in "some hypothetical average class." This would have called for observers expert in their knowledge of what kinds and degrees of interaction took place among children in the grade level in which they would observe.

In contrast, had we decided on descriptive data as to the pattern of interactions, we could have selected less experienced observers. For here the observer's task is more straightforward recording of what happens, with the required skill a compulsive "stick-to-itiveness" in capturing every interaction which takes place. Most experts, in fact, would not be willing to work at this task, and so we would recruit some suitably compulsive graduate students.

Whether experienced or not, observers must be oriented and trained to function reliably within each specific project. The orientation involves acquainting them with the purpose of the research, the goals of the observation, and the content which has been selected to be observed. The training involves their learning to observe this content reliably, so that all look at the same aspects of the research situation and see the same thing when something happens. Moreover, the training includes learning to use whatever guides and instruments have been developed to record their observations.

One specific technique which greatly aids the reliability of observational data is to bring those who are to observe into the research process as early as possible. Once the general idea of content has been decided, the kind of observer needed can be determined. If these observers are recruited early, they can at least listen to, and may also participate in, the discussions which lead to the selection of the aspects to be observed and the development of the specific dimensions of each aspect. Given this participation, it is a simpler task for them to apply these criteria reliably in the actual research situation. Unfortunately, most researchers delay the recruiting of observers until well along into the process, so that their orientation and training comes after all discussion on the content of the observation has been concluded.

The process of training will vary from project to project but will typically involve some variant of the following procedure. First, pilot settings are selected or developed which simulate the actual research settings in which observation is to be done. Second, the observers who are to be trained are thoroughly oriented to the desired outcomes, the content to be observed, including the specific aspects to be studied, and to the observation guide through which the observational data are to be recorded. Third, the observers are given the opportunity to raise all questions related to their understanding of the variables to be observed and the distinctions required by the observation guide. Fourth, the observers are sent into the pilot settings for their initial attempt to observe and use the guide. Fifth, the data are analyzed to provide an estimate of the extent to which the observers have been able to observe reliably. Sixth, opportunity is provided for discussion of all instances in which the observer's views are discrepant, the purpose of this discussion being to identify the sources of the discrepancies. Steps five and six are repeated until such time as the observers, individually and collectively, have reached a reliability level appropriate for the project.[11] When this has happened, the actual observations for the purposes of data gathering are ready to begin.

Thus the selection of observers is a three-stage process in which the researcher first decides the kind of observer who will provide him with the most objective set of data, then recruits a set of those observers, and finally orients and trains them until he has reason to believe that the data they will provide will be reliable.

A final aspect which must be taken into account is the effect of observers of different kinds on the research situation. For example, whether the observer is male or female or will be perceived as young or old by those functioning in the situation can make a critical difference in the effect that the observer will have. The ideal observer fits so easily into the research situation that nothing about him is obtrusive or disruptive. Thus, any disruption is because an observer is present, and not because of who

[11]While there is some flexibility possible in how an appropriate standard for reliability is defined, the author believes that no project should begin until the observers have achieved an agreement on 85 percent of their independent observations. Even for the more complex educational variables this standard is realizable provided the dimensions of the variable have been thought through sufficiently and expressed in clear behavioral terms. If the standard is not realizable, this fact is telling the researcher that he is posing an impossible task for the observers, and thus that greater clarification is needed of the variables to be observed.

the observer is or what the observer looks like. A beautiful girl in a short skirt would not be a good observer to send to watch a group of teen-age boys in school, no matter how well qualified she might be for the observation task by other criteria.

Because the observer plays such a central role in observation, and because even the most extensive period of orientation and training cannot totally eliminate the personal aspect of observation, no research should be planned unless more than one observer will and can be used. Ideally several observers are used, and the data-gathering plan is designed so that about 10 percent of the observations are joint observations by two observers. In this way a continuous check on the reliability of the data is available. This is particularly useful if the project involved is one in which observation will be carried on over a long period of time. For it then becomes difficult to maintain the initial precision with which the observation guide can be used, and one way to keep all observers alert is to establish this on-going check of reliability.

Respondent-Observer Interaction

Another element of the observation method involves the observers, but is sufficiently important in its own right to be considered separately, and that is the interaction between respondents and observers. The variety of possible interactions is complex and involves the simultaneous operation of three different dimensions: whether the observation is direct or indirect, whether the presence of the observer is known or unknown to the respondent, and, if known, what role the respondent believes the observer to be playing.

Let us consider the simplest dimension first: whether the observational data shall be collected in a *direct* or *indirect* manner. In all research using the observation method, a human observer ultimately watches the research situation and provides the basis for analyzing the data. He may do this directly, by watching the actual situation as it unfolds, or he may do this indirectly by watching a motion picture or television transmission (either live or on tape) of the research situation. In both of the indirect observation procedures the direct observer is a camera, and the human observer's view of the event is limited to the field of the camera, his hearing to the sensitivity of the microphone, and thus the observation is considered indirect.

Each of these interactions has advantages and disadvantages and therefore each has research situations for which it is preferable. What the observer can supply that the camera and recorder cannot is the ability to react to, and report, the feeling tone and subtle socioemotional context of a classroom or a group meeting or any human interaction. This level of interaction is often lost even in the most complete motion picture record, and is the reason the human observer cannot be completely replaced by the machine. Unfortunately, to function reliably at this level places an excessive demand on our knowledge of psychosocial processes and particularly on the behavioral manifestation of these processes in both action and word. The current state of knowledge in these areas cannot meet the demand completely enough to produce reliable observational data, and so this advantage cannot fully be realized at present.

The second advantage is fully realizable, and that is the flexibility, in direct observation, as to what is watched. Being present, the observer can watch aspects of the situation at different places, can change the focus of his observation, and if sufficiently alert can watch unexpected aspects of the research situation if they develop. In contrast, the disadvantage of indirect observation is that it typically involves cameras in relatively fixed positions and so lacks this flexibility. This means that direct observation is preferable if the research situation is one which is expected to flow back and forth over a large area (that is, a classroom), and/or is one in which it is difficult to fully anticipate where important aspects are likely to occur or even to anticipate what all of the important aspects are likely to be.

The disadvantage of direct observation is that it is liable to all of the weaknesses and fallacies and idiosyncrasies of the human perceptual system. Stated simply, the researcher is provided only with what the observer saw and reported. Moreover, the research situation is not reproducible, for what the observer saw literally disappeared before his eyes. Thus, if later analysis of the situation reveals the need for additional review of what happened, the researcher must rely on the memory of the observer.

Because of the fallacies in the human perceptual system, indirect observation has become increasingly popular. When appropriate, the maximum combination of naturalness, ethics, and research efficiency is obtained when the researcher makes known to the participants the fact that he intends to observe them, but uses some mechanical device as the eyes and ears for observation. One advantage of this technique is in producing a permanent record of the situation, available for repeated and detailed study. In fact, this advantage provides the technique with virtues beyond research, for it is an effective technique for improving the insights of the participants themselves. Seeing themselves in action usually affects people more thoroughly than hours of description of what they did by a second party. For research purposes, however, the advantages lie in the reproducibility and the thoroughness with which these techniques record what the camera is aimed at and the microphone directed toward. The researcher need have no fears of selective perception on the part of a camera, nor no concern that because of its personality structure the camera will see but not record a particular event or interaction. Similarly he need not be concerned that as the observer looked down to record the nature of the interaction between Fred and Jean he missed the reaction of Harry. For with the scene on film or tape, it can be re-run as often as necessary to fully record all of the significant elements in the situation.

A final advantage to indirect observation is the ease with which the reliability of the observations can be determined. With the scene on film, multiple observations can be obtained even should only one observer be able to view the material at any one time. Indeed, not only can reliability be estimated, but the specific events on which the observers differ can be identified and studied in detail. This kind of diagnosis can tell a researcher much about the situations he is studying, for it clarifies for him the dynamics in the situation on which competent observers cannot agree. Presumably these are the constructs for which the behavioral statements are too ambiguous, or the attitudes or motivations which cannot be inferred from reaction and expression. In a practical sense, this kind of analysis of a situation also identifies those aspects of the data about which the researcher can have confidence and those he must consider limited and doubtful.

But these advantages only outweigh the disadvantage of inflexibility if the research situation is sufficiently limited in both physical space and movement of the participants to be meaningfully recorded by a camera or cameras. A counseling session would lend itself to indirect observation, as would a case study of the responses of a child (whom the camera could follow in and out of class, occasionally recording the actions of others related to the situation).[12] It would also be appropriate for studies of teacher behavior or of the activities that take place around the teacher's desk, or in the science corner, or in the fourth and fifth laboratory benches in the second row.

A significant advance in indirect observation came in the late 1960s with the introduction of the inexpensive television camera and video-tape recorder. With such a setup available, the researcher can transmit a live picture of the research situation to a distant location where it can be watched by one or more observers. If flexible operation of the camera is employed, this gives the researcher the opportunity to ask to see specific aspects of the situation as needed. If, for example, he is curious to know

[12]A superb example of the use of the camera for this kind of case study is the film *The Quiet One*, which follows a young child through the crises leading to an antisocial outburst, his subsequent commitment to the Wiltwyck School, and to his first step toward accepting help.

how two particular children are responding, he can have the camera move to those children, or have a close-up of their facial expressions. Moreover, if he records the television picture on video-tape, he has the ability to review the situation endlessly.

Thus the mid-1960s brought opportunities for indirect observation, with flexible camera operation combined with permanent records of the events. As this book is written, school systems and universities are using these technical advances to establish television observation laboratories for use both in research and teacher training. It can be expected that, with these facilities, the observation method will make as significant contributions to educational practice and theory as it already has to the physical sciences.

KNOWN AND UNKNOWN OBSERVATION   The second dimension of researcher-respondent interaction varies in terms of whether the presence of the observer is known or unknown to the respondent, and if it is known, whom the respondent believes the observer to be. Because of this dimension the nature of the observer-respondent interaction is one of the most delicate and difficult aspects of research in the social disciplines. One might argue that the basic virtue of the observational method is its ability to provide the researcher with a view of human behavior in a natural setting. To fully achieve that end the respondent must be functioning in the situation with nothing operating to affect his behavior other then the normal elements of the situation.

What happens if the respondent knows that he is being watched? This occurs in its most serious form when the researcher uses the observation technique which we shall call *known and scheduled observation*.[13] This is a technique in which the respondent not only knows he is about to be observed, but is also told the precise time at which the observation will begin. Think of the school which learns that a research team is coming the following Tuesday to observe class 4–1 at ten o'clock. The administrative and teaching staff will respond in varied ways. In some instances they will plan and even rehearse everything class 4–1 will do that day, in essence putting on a show for the observers. In this instance the observers do not see the natural situation, but rather see a situation as close to what the respondents think is expected as they are capable of producing. In other instances the administrators and teachers may decide to go on about their business "as they always do" but in reality may be subtly affected both in their planning and functioning by the fact that observers will be present. Even if we assume the unlikely possibility that the knowledge that observers are coming has no effect on administrators and teachers, we must

[13]This and the other techniques for observing are discussed later in this chapter.

allow for the probability that the children's behaviors will be affected once a strange adult or two sets foot in their room.

While the risk of excessive and atypical planning and the distraction of the observer are implicit whenever the respondent knows that he will be observed, the researcher can minimize both disadvantages by having the observers remain in the situation for a sufficiently long period of time, or sufficiently often, for the respondents to revert to their normal behavior. In this author's experience with observation, the reversion to a normal state occurs within a few observations involving no more than a few hours of actual observation time.[14] If the actual collection of data is delayed until the observers have been in the research situation for this initial period of time, then the researcher can argue that, at least in part, he has eliminated the disadvantages of over-planning and distraction.

Nevertheless, the techniques which are based upon the respondent being aware of the presence of the observer are open to the danger that this fact will produce some distortions in normal behavior. This is true of the indirect interactions as well as of the direct interactions. The various techniques for direct and indirect observation vary in their susceptibility to this weakness (as we shall discuss later in this chapter), but all of them are subject to it to some extent. Thus, techniques have been developed in which the presence of the observer is not known to the respondents. These techniques include direct observation through a one-way vision glass, the research equivalent of "bugging" by placing cameras and microphones unknown to the respondent, or the introduction of the observer into a group without informing the group that he is an observer. All of these share the fact that the presence of the observer is unknown to the respondent or respondents.

It is obvious that the *unknown* interaction solves the problem of distortion of the natural situation implicit in the known researcher-respondent relationship. If the respondent has no knowledge that he is being observed, he is under no pressure to distort the natural situation. It should be equally obvious that the use of an unknown relationship brings with it severe ethical problems. The researcher must find a satisfactory answer to the question as to what gives him the right to invade the privacy of the respondents in this way, and must be willing to live within an ethical system in which a research purpose justifies what dynamically comes out to be spying. That researchers have been able to do this, or else have been

[14]Additional evidence in support of the argument that only brief periods of time are required in educational settings to become acclimated to the presence of an outsider is provided by the ease with which student teachers are accepted and the speed with which they become part of the normal routine.

able to ignore the question, is indicated by the number of studies that have used the unknown researcher-respondent interaction.[15] This author is not able to do so, and is pleased to note increasing evidence, as this is written, that society as a whole is developing considerable antipathy to such invasions of privacy both in research and in lay circles.

OUTSIDE OBSERVER AND PARTICIPANT OBSERVER   The third dimension of the respondent-observer interaction, the role in which the respondent sees the observer, is not totally independent of the dimension of known and unknown observation. It is considered as a separate dimension here because it has important characteristics which are best discussed in the context of roles and which cut across this other dimension of known or unknown.

There are three widely used roles which observers assume in the social sciences, only two of which have been popular in education. The first role is the traditional role of outside observer. The observer is introduced as an outsider who will enter the research situation as a stranger, and who, while physically present to watch, will remain outside of the situation in a behavioral sense. He will not say anything or do anything nor will he react. Hopefully, no one will react to him. In this role his presence is known, he is clearly superfluous to the situation, and his every move must be seen as irrelevant and therefore potentially distracting to the situation.

To avoid this, the other two roles which have developed both place the observer into the situation as participant as well as observer. These roles are both referred to by the term *participant observer,* a term coined by E. C. Lindeman in 1924.[16] He argued that an event can only be fully understood if two points of view are considered, what he called the inside point of view of the person participating in the event and the outside point of view of the person not involved. He felt that the best way to synthesize these two views was by placing the observer into the situation as participant.

There are at least two clearly distinct approaches to participant observation. One is the approach made famous by anthropologists like Margaret Mead and Colin Turnbull who studied a primitive culture by moving into that culture to live among the people. Less dramatic instances of this same approach to participant observation occur in the work of William

---

[15]It is further indicated by the publication of a book devoted to this and similar techniques: Eugene J. Webb, Donald T. Campbell, Richard D. Schwartz, and Lee Seechrest, *Unobtrusive Measures: Non-Reactive Research in the Social Sciences.* (Skokie, Ill.: Rand McNally & Company, 1966), 225 pp.

[16]Eduard C. Lindeman, *Social Discovery* (New York: Republic Publishing Co., 1924), 375 pp.

Whyte who studied gang behavior[17] by convincing a street gang of his interest and sincerity, so that they permitted him to attend their meetings and participate in some of their activities. In this approach to participant observation, the observation is still known, for the observer is initially clearly identified as an outsider who is coming into the situation to learn about it as thoroughly as possible. Depending upon his own individual personality he succeeds to varying degrees in being accepted as a genuine participant as time goes on. This approach has not been widely used in education.

The second approach to participant observation, which has enjoyed some popularity in education, is to introduce the observer into the group as a new participant without informing the regular members of the group that this new member has any research responsibilities at all. In brief, ideally no one other than the researcher considers the observer as anything but a participant, and so we have unknown observation. The observer does his observations unknown to the others and records his information when he is alone, often at the end of the observational period when he has left the research situation. This procedure has been used in the social disciplines not only for research purposes but for other investigative purposes as well.[18] An example of this is the book *The Blackboard Jungle* which resulted from a few weeks of teaching by the author in the school which was the prototype for the one portrayed in the book. During this period the author told no one he was a writer, but played the part of a new teacher in the school.

Before discussing the advantages and disadvantages of participant observation, let us note that this last version brings with it all of the ethical problems attendant to unknown observation, plus some unique to the use of this role. For now, in addition to the invasion of privacy of unknown observation, we have the introduction of false and hypocritical interpersonal relationships between the actual participants and the participant observers.

There are two major advantages claimed for participant observation. First is the argument originally advanced by Lindeman that, as a participant, the observer has firsthand experiences which provide him with insights into what the situation is like that he can never obtain as a nonparticipating observer. Only as a participant does the observer feel the pressures operating in the situation, and only with a feeling for those

[17]William Foote Whyte, *Street Corner Society* (Chicago: University of Chicago Press, 1955), 366 pp.
[18]In fact, the best known application of participant observation in education is not in research but in student teaching, where it is the primary role for the learner.

pressures can he understand how and why the other participants respond as they do. Thus, the proponent of participant observation would say that only by standing in front of a class, with responsibility for teaching that class, can an outsider learn what teaching is like in any specific school.

While the argument has merit, it fails to allow for the generalizability of experience. Thus, it is perfectly true that someone who has never taught cannot fully know the responses and reactions of the teacher standing before 30 children. But that totally inexperienced person would not be a suitable observer if the task was to observe teacher reaction and response. The more relevant question is whether someone who has taught in situations X and Y must be a participant observer in situation Z to fully understand it. The author believes that it is not necessary unless situation Z is so totally unique that for all practical purposes it is an entirely different situation than X and Y. The other point to note is that if participant observation is designed primarily to obtain first-hand experience for the participant observer, then there is no reason why other participants cannot be informed who the observer is.

The reason they are not informed is so that the technique can also capitalize on the second advantage of this version of participant observation: the ability to see the other participants at work and to talk with them as a colleague rather than as an outsider. If there is a unique advantage to the technique it is the presumed frankness and honesty with which others will approach the participant-observer and the accurate picture he will obtain of the research situation, since it remains normal, undistorted by an outside observer present or known to be watching. If we contemplate using participant observation because of this advantage, we should be alert to the fact that while an outside observer has not been introduced into the situation, a stranger has been. Anyone who has had the real experience of entering a situation with established relationships knows that it is a long time before the experienced people open up and take the newcomer into their confidence. The participant-observer is no exception to this rule, and so his role is the complex one of the stranger. It is complex because the pressures which operate on the actual participants to conceal or distort the truth from a stranger they believe is becoming one of them may be far more difficult to estimate than the pressures on them to conceal or distort the truth from a clearly identified outside observer.

Other than the ethical problem involved, the major disadvantage to participant observation is the dual role which the observer must play. He has responsibilities as a participant, and he must discharge these. Inevitably these responsibilities take time and energy away from his role as observer, and, in complex situations like teaching may actually eliminate most of that role. In fact one might hypothesize that the more the participant part of the role is successfully filled, the less the observer role is. At some point, in short, the participant observer becomes another participant, and the researcher is as much in need of an observer as before!

A second and often unrecognized disadvantage is the physical inflexibility which participant responsibilities impose upon the observer. As a participant he not only has things to do, but he also must be in certain places at certain times, and these places are not necessarily the places in which the researcher would like him to be for the purposes of data collection. This forces the researcher to accept the relative immobility of the observer as a limitation to the desired plan for data gathering.

For these reasons, those researchers who can reconcile unknown observation with their ethical system are far wiser to use unknown direct or indirect observation in which the researcher watches from some vantage point like a one-way mirror, or the research situation to be observed is recorded on cameras which are hidden and whose presence is unknown to the participants. Of all the research techniques, the latter is one of the best known to the lay public, since "Candid Camera," a television program popular in the 1950s and 1960s, used it as a means for gathering the content of the program.

Both known and unknown observation will be facilitated by the fact that new schools are now almost always constructed with rooms specifically designed for observational purposes. Available for research and demonstration, these rooms not only have the facilities to expedite watching but also are wired so that verbal interactions can be heard and recorded as well. This author's hope is that these facilities will be used for known observation, but he is not so naive as to ignore the probability that they will facilitate a far greater use of unknown observation in future research.

TECHNIQUES WITHIN THE OBSERVATION METHOD

The various techniques for observation can all be identified by considering the interaction of the dimensions we have already discussed: whether the respondent knows he is being observed or not, whether the observer is functioning as an outsider or as a participant, and whether the observer will have a direct or indirect view of the research situation. The three dimensions interact to make nine techniques which will be discussed in this section, without repeating what has already been said about each of the three dimensions.

As we have noted before, the original interaction for observation in social situations was to introduce an outside observer into the situation, with no responsibilities in the situation other than his research responsibilities. Depending upon what those to be observed know about the time or nature of the observation leads to three possible techniques: direct outside observation which is (1) known and scheduled, (2) known but not scheduled, and (3) unknown.

The most formal is one mentioned earlier, *direct observation, known and scheduled*. This is observation by appointment, with the researcher scheduling an observation for a specific time. The technique has two advantages. It is proper and courteous, and it enables the respondent to prepare to whatever extent he wishes. It is particularly appropriate in instances when the researcher wants the observation to take place under optimum rather than average conditions. Thus, this is the traditional technique employed on evaluation visits to teachers, when the supervisor comes in to see a class on the basis of which he can write a formal report.

But where known and scheduled observation works well if the research purpose is to see the best the respondent can produce, it is not useful if the research purpose is to see typical behavior. For then the basic disadvantage of direct observation, that it will often produce more than usual planning and preparation, becomes a dominant factor, and the researcher will turn to the *known but not scheduled* technique.

In this technique, the researcher informs the respondents that at some point in the future observers will arrive to collect the research data, but he does not make a specific appointment or schedule. Under this arrangement the researcher is usually reasonably secure that he will walk into a situation no different than a typical situation, for the respondent cannot plan an endless series of "performances." In fact, the researcher can even argue that should the respondent succeed in planning such an endless series, then this has become his typical pattern of functioning.

Given some research purposes, known but not scheduled observation is essential. For example, in the analysis of the Language Study presented in Chapter 1 we noted how we used known but not scheduled observation to obtain the data as to the methods teachers in the experiment were actually using. Had they known our observer was coming on Wednesday at 1:40, it would have been simple for them to be using the proper method and materials at that time. But told only that they would be observed periodically, without ever knowing when the observer was coming, meant that they either had to adhere to the experimental plans or risk being seen when they deviated.

During the discussion of this procedure in Chapter 1 we also noted how maintaining the element of surprise, which is the critical characteristic of known but not scheduled observation, can be complex and expensive for the researcher. In a school, for example, you can introduce an observer into the school and instruct him to walk directly to room 203, enter and observe. That observation can be considered to have been conducted totally without warning. Such is the power of school grapevines, however, that no succeeding observations in that school can be so considered. In reality, this means that the researcher must be willing to go to the expense of having the observer make only one observation in any one site on any one day if he wishes to be able to argue that he has fully achieved known observation without warning. This adds considerably to the expense and time involved.

As to *direct outside observation, unknown* to the persons being observed, this author has already given his opinion that unknown observation is unethical, unprofessional, and unbecoming to any discipline which purports to search for truth in the social sciences. Moreover, the author is convinced that in large part the measures are also unnecessary! For sustained known observations seems to be a perfectly sensible alternative in most situations in which unknown observation has been employed. In those few instances in which sustained known observation would not work, then the ethical researcher may very well have to accept the difficult alternative that the research he contemplates cannot be done. Every researcher must develop his own ethical system, but this author finds it difficult to imagine one in which any research purpose is sufficiently critical to justify unknown observation. National security may justify spying, but research does not.

A second set of three techniques is available when the researcher turns to indirect observation which can be combined with the three variations in scheduling just discussed to make techniques to be called: (4) *indirect observation, known and scheduled,* (5) *indirect observation, known but not scheduled,* and (6) *indirect, unknown observation.* All three techniques physically remove the observer from the research situation and so eliminate him as a direct distractor. This is their primary unique advantage, for they vary along the same dimension of what the respondent knows which we have just discussed.

The final three techniques involve the use of a participant rather than an outside observer with the three variations of the knowledgeability dimension, leading to: (7) *participant observation, known and scheduled,* (8) *participant observation, known, but not scheduled,* and (9) *unknown participant observation.* The participant observation techniques are effective in minimizing the disadvantages of preplanning and of distraction, but are limited by the dual responsibilities of the participant and his relative inflexibility.

DESIGN OF THE OBSERVATIONS

The final aspect of the observational method is designing the data-gathering plan for the observations. This includes two separate decisions related to timing: first, the determination of the length of the basic observational unit, and second, the determination of the specific time periods to be observed.

While there is no need for all observations to be conducted for a standard length of time, the researcher should have a rational basis for selecting the time period or periods he does use. Brief periods of observation can be used whenever the behavior to be observed is itself brief, particularly when it is repetitive. Thus a researcher seeking to observe teacher response to children's questions would be able to argue that any one question and the following response take little time, and moreover the behavior occurs dozens of times during the school day. Therefore, brief periods of observation would be appropriate for any one visit to a class. Longer periods of observation are needed when the behavior to be observed is complex, and particularly if it is difficult to understand out of context. In these instances the observer needs to be in the situation before the behavior occurs so that he can also see the circumstances which precede it and, often, which precipitate it.

One additional aspect of the length of an observation is the public relations aspect. Even when the behavior to be observed is brief and recurring, and could be seen in five-minute observational periods, the researcher may be wise to have his observers remain in the research situation for longer periods. The purpose of the longer visit is simply to avoid having the respondents feel that they were not seen sufficiently long for anyone to form a coherent view of what they did and how they did it. This is particularly true when observing professional functioning, such as watching a teacher in a classroom. The five- or ten-minute observation is tactless in this instance, no matter how well it serves the research purpose.

Time Sampling

The issue of which specific time periods to observe is the other aspect of timing the observations. While human behavior is complex and variable, it is not so variable that we must observe 60 minutes of every hour for every hour that the research situation runs. It is perfectly sensible to sample the time period. The process of *time sampling* is conceptually no different than the process of sampling to obtain respondents. In time sampling, all possible replications of the research situation represent the universe, with those replications available to the researcher representing the population. The time intervals during which observers actually watch the research situation represent the selected sample, and in this instance the selected sample is usually identical to the data-producing sample. The same processes used to select a sample of respondents are used to select a sample of time intervals for observation, and the goal is the same: to achieve a representative sample which will simulate the population in all significant characteristics. Thus we can stratify, use random-selection or deliberate selection procedures, and even use proportional selection, although this is rarely necessary in time sampling.

For example, if we set out to observe teacher-child interaction in classes for disadvantaged children, the several days of the school year in the school systems accessible to us would represent the population of time intervals.[19] Obviously we would not need to watch every day of the year, nor even every hour of the days we do select. We develop the time sampling plan in the same way we do any sampling plan, beginning with a delineation of the critical characteristics of the population. We may begin by noting that the school year consists of some different periods for our research variable. The first day of school, for example, is a unique day in terms of teacher-pupil interaction. In fact, we might argue that the first hour is a unique hour for this variable. As the first days turn into the first weeks we would expect that teacher-pupil interactions begin to develop a stable pattern and that the interactions during the tenth and eleventh week would not differ much. We might consider the pre-Christmas period with its special activities and feelings a period that might affect teacher-pupil interactions.

Note that what we have already discussed would provide the basis for stratifying the first four months of the school year. We have broken it down into four strata: (1) the first interactions between teacher and child (the first hour); (2) the foundational interactions (the remainder of the first day or first few days); (3) the stable period beyond the first week until the pre-Christmas period; and (4) the pre-Christmas period. Now the researcher might wish to apply proportional thinking here and seek to sample for the entire first hour (the first stratum), for 15 minutes of each hour for the rest of the first day (the second stratum), for 15 minutes of three randomly selected hours for each day during the rest of the first week (the third stratum), for one hour on each of three randomly selected mornings and afternoons after the first week until pre-Christmas (the fourth), and so on through the other strata which could be identified during the school year.

[19]The universe would consist of the several days in the school year of all such school systems.

The example above illustrates the common conventions for time sampling. We can use a few large units like an hour, or many small units like 15-minute periods. Which we choose is a function of the content of the observation—what we wish to see. Actually in this illustration, a 15-minute period would be questionable for there may be insufficient teacher-pupil interactions in that brief a period for any significant observation to be made. The researcher has also recognized in his sampling plan that the morning and afternoon are different research situations in most schools and so need to be sampled separately. However, he has assumed that the several days of the week are similar, for he has made no provision for sampling these separately. If this were a school system with weekly quizzes on Friday, or with high teacher absenteeism on Monday, or with released time for religious instruction on Thursday afternoon, then the time sampling plan could not sensibly be based on the assumption that any one day is like any other day.

The complexities of research situations in education are such that sequential sampling[20] provides the most sensible basis for time sampling. If the researcher is uncertain if more than one weekday is needed, he can initially sample two separate days and analyze the data to determine if any significant new dimension has been uncovered by the second set of data. He can continue this until he is satisfied that he has achieved the goal of time sampling: to have seen everything significant without unnecessary duplication.

A different, and historically the original, perception of time sampling was developed in the 1920s by Olson.[21] He defined time sampling as ". . . the systematic recording of a definitely delimited unit of behavior described in terms of action over a stated time interval yielding quantitative individual scores by means of repeated time units." In short, Olson used the concept as a means of both data collection and analysis. In his perception, the researcher defines specific categories or aspects of behavior which he wishes to observe, selects a brief period of time for the sampling unit, and has the observer record whether or not each behavior occurs in each time period. Thus, a researcher may decide to break the morning of the school day into 10-minute intervals, and asks his observers to record whether or not the teacher praises specific children in the class during each 10-minute period of observation. The periods can be sequential, or they can be scattered over different days. In either event, this plan yields a score for each child which is simply the number of intervals in which he is praised. Over the years, researchers using the Olson technique in

[20]This technique is discussed in Chapter 11.
[21]Willard C. Olson and Elizabeth Mechem Cunningham, "Time-Sampling Techniques," *Child Development*, vol. 5 (1934), pp. 41–58.

addition to counting the number of intervals counted the total number of times the behavior occurred and also generated an average occurrence per time period.

STEPS IN THE OBSERVATIONAL METHOD

Listed below are the several steps, in order, which are followed in applying the method of observation to a research problem.

1. Statement of research problem and hypotheses sufficient for delineation of data required
2. Determination that observation is appropriate and required
3. Specification of outcomes and content of the observation
4. Identification of the selected sample of research situations
5. Consideration of characteristics of research situation in conjunction with the content, to guide decision on the elements of the observation:
   (a) direct versus indirect observation
   (b) known versus unknown observation
   (c) role of observer
6. Consideration of content of observation and desired interaction to guide choice of experienced versus inexperienced observer
7. Selection of technique for observation
8. Recruitment of observers
9. Development of observation guide (based on experienced–inexperienced decision)
10. Training of observers to sufficient reliability
11. Pilot studies to:
    (a) provide observers with field experience in use of guide
    (b) provide data to provide estimate of reliability of the guide
    (c) provide test of data analysis plan
    (d) verify that data will answer research questions and test research hypotheses
12. Design of the observation data-gathering plan
13. Invitation to selected sample to participate
14. Implementation of data-gathering plan
15. Analysis of data
16. Preparation of report

The first step is one which will apply to all methods. Before making a decision on method, the researcher must have *a statement of the research problem and hypotheses sufficient to delineate the data which will be required.* Given this statement, he can weigh the needed data against the data-producing proclivities of each method. If he concludes that he needs descriptive or evaluative data which can best be obtained by watching the research situation, then he has arrived at the second step, the *determination that observation is appropriate and required.*

Given that determination, the researcher moves into the process itself, beginning by translating the research problem and hypotheses into *a specification of the outcomes and content of the observation.* This is the foundational step upon which all else will rest, and so all the time necessary to build it thoroughly and well must be given. At this step, the researcher must keep in mind a basic rule enunciated at several places in this book: For research to be a rational process the researcher must be aware of what he does *not* do as well as what he does do, and must have a rationale for distinguishing between the two. This applies with special force to the creation of the model of the research situation from which the content of the observation is selected, for it is relatively simple for the researcher to sit down and identify some things he wishes the observers to watch. But these things may not represent the research situation in a valid way. The only way to know if they do is to build up the complete model of the research situation and use it as the basis for selecting the content for the observation.

To move into the next series of steps, the researcher must know the situations in which the observations will be done, although these settings need not be invited to participate as yet. Step 4 is the *identification of the selected sample of research situations* which will ultimately be asked to provide the settings for the observations.

With content selected, identified, and the sample of research situations selected, the researcher can consider the *characteristics of the research situations,* which, *in conjunction with the content will guide his decisions as to the respondent-observer interaction.* At this step the researcher considers things like where the observation is to be done (that is, in schools, in play situations, or in social situations), the physical setting and facilities available, and the age and backgrounds of the respondents to come to a decision as to the kinds of interaction which will most expeditiously produce the data required for the research and still be consistent with the researcher's ethical principles. With this step completed, the researcher can now combine content and interaction to *guide the choice of experienced or inexperienced observers.*

Now that he knows his content, the interaction to be established between observer and respondent, and the experience level of the observers, the researcher is in a position to *select the technique for observation.* As we have just discussed, this choice is basically made for him through the decisions already arrived at as to the three subaspects of the interaction, but he will also verify it against the decisions on content. On the experience level he will seek in the choice of observers to be certain that all of these decisions are homogeneous.

In the list above it is suggested that the next step is to *recruit the observers*. This is suggested at this point so that, if possible, the observers can participate in the eighth step, the *development of the observation guide*. While we have described the guide as the researcher's operational statement of what it is he wishes the observers to watch and how he wishes them to record their observations, this guide must also be fully comprehended by the observers. The most efficient procedure for assuring that it expresses the researcher's intent in words which the observers understand is for both researcher and observers to participate in its construction. If for some reason (such as a budget which limits the amount of time observers can be on the payroll) this sequence is not possible, then step 9, *training the observers,* should begin with an extensive orientation of the observers to the purposes of the research in general, and to the observation guide in particular. Once this orientation is completed the formal training of the observers in the use of the guide can begin. This can be done through simulated research situations or more efficiently by *pilot studies* in sites other than those to be used for data collection. The pilot-study approach is more efficient in that it provides field experience for the observers but also provides data to estimate the reliability of the observation guide and to test data-analysis plans.

If all has gone well to this point, the researcher can feel he is able to *design the observation data-gathering plan.* It is in this stage at which he will decide specifically which situations will be seen and the time-sampling plan he will use. With this complete he now knows what kind of a commitment he needs from his sample and so is ready to *invite the selected sample to participate.* Of course, if unknown observation is employed, this stage is simplified considerably, for no invitations need to be extended to those who will not know they are being watched!

The observational method concludes with a repetition of the three steps which conclude the research process, whether we are considering research approach or research method: the *implementation of the data-gathering plan,* the *data-analysis plan,* and the *preparation of the research report.*

Chapter 18

THE QUESTIONING METHOD
AND TECHNIQUES FOR QUESTIONING

The questioning method for data collection, in which the researcher obtains his data by posing a verbal question for the respondent, is obviously a method unique to the social disciplines. Verbal interactions must involve people. Questioning as a method of inquiry is recorded as early as the Lord inquiring of Cain, "Where is Abel, thy brother?" As a method of thinking it flourished in antiquity through the teachings of Socrates, and as a method of data collection it flourished in the 1950s, 1960s, and will continue to flourish in the 1970s as public opinion polls of all kinds seek information.

This last phrase highlights the difference between questioning as a process and as a *data-collection method;* as a method the essential purpose is information seeking. In short, when he uses the questioning method the researcher poses a question because he does not know the answer. Thus, when a pollster asks a person his choice for President, the questioner does not know the respondent's choice and needs to if he is to achieve his research purpose. In contrast, questioning as a process is also used in the measurement method discussed in the next chapter. But here the researcher's interest is not in the answer in itself (which he often knows) but rather in using the answer obtained to provide a basis for some estimate of, or inference about, a personal characteristic of the respondent. Thus, if a questioner asks who Lenin was, he already knows the answer, but may be asking the question to estimate the respondent's knowledge of Russian history. Similarly, if as part of a measure of job satisfaction a respondent is asked if he is satisfied with his current salary on a job, the researcher is not interested in the answer in itself, but rather in what the answer implies about job satisfaction.

In this chapter on the questioning method we are concerned with those research problems in which the intent is information seeking and the questions are posed to elicit responses which are themselves of direct interest.

RESEARCH FOR WHICH QUESTIONING
IS APPROPRIATE METHOD

More than 40 years ago the psychologist Floyd Allport noted that if we wanted to know what someone thought, the best way to find out was to ask him. This is still true. Translated into research terms, this means that whenever we wish to obtain some information we believe a person has, or to learn his opinion on a specific issue, the best way to find out is to ask him a direct question. We often seem to have forgotten this idea in research in recent years, or if we have not forgotten it we have ceased to believe it, for we have evolved complex indirect processes to get at truths which simple questioning could reveal. Direct questioning is particularly appropriate at the surface and subsurface levels of research, for here the researcher seeks information for which there is an immediate association between question and answer. Provided he can convince the respondent that he would respect his confidence and use the material appropriately the researcher should be able to obtain his answer.

Questioning is appropriate as well at the depth level, but somewhat more difficult to implement, because the researcher must establish a closer bond with the respondent if the respondent is to reveal the personal and threatening material involved at the depth level. However, when questioning is defined as information seeking, as it has been for this chapter, it cannot be used at the nonconscious level, for information obtained at that level is not of direct concern but is used as a basis for an inference about the respondent.

In terms of the approaches we have discussed, the questioning method is most effectively used in the survey approach. For the descriptive survey, it is the most appropriate method for obtaining specific information about the research situations or the respondents who function in them. For the comparative and evaluative surveys, too, it can be a useful method for the generation of information on the basis of which comparative or evaluative conclusions can be made. But whereas in descriptive surveys the questioning method may, in itself, provide sufficient information to answer the research question, in comparative and evaluative surveys there is usually need for some kind of observation or measurement to supplement the questions.

For the retrospective survey, questioning is the only method available because observation or measurement of the past is obviously impossible. In this instance, the researcher can only question those who participated in the experience or situation he is seeking to study. For the same reason, the inability to question retroactively, the questioning method is ruled out of the historical approach. It can function in the experimental approach, but typically is not adequate by itself as the data-collection method in experiments. Rather, as in the comparative and evaluative surveys, questioning must be supplemented by measurement or observation.

Questioning, then, is most appropriate when the researcher's research purpose is to seek information at the surface or subsurface level. In this instance, well-chosen and well-worded questions represent the most efficient and effective data-gathering method.

ELEMENTS OF QUESTIONING METHOD

In using the questioning method, there are six elements to consider: (1) the context of the questioning, which includes both why the researcher is asking the questions and why the respondent believes they are being asked, since these are not necessarily the same; (2) the content of the questioning; (3) the question, which can be defined as the verbal stimulus to which the respondent will be exposed; (4) the provision for answering, which refers to the response the respondent will be expected (or in some techniques, what the respondent will be permitted) to produce; (5) the way in which the response will be recorded, which refers to variations like writing or speaking or recording; and (6) the nature of the researcher-respondent interaction, which considers whether researcher and respondent actually meet face-to-face or whether they communicate impersonally.

Context of Questioning

At any level of research, the researcher must allow for the fact that questioning involves a unique social relationship between researcher and respondent. The first element in implementing the method is to consider the context of the questions, as the respondent sees them. In the questioning method, context includes why the respondent believes the question is being asked, what he believes will be done with the data, and, a subtle but real aspect, the researcher's orientation as it is communicated by the content, tone, and form of each question.

Context is particularly critical when questioning moves beyond the surface level to subsurface or depth levels. For at these levels the researcher must recognize that while the respondent will think through to the correct answer he will hesitate before answering and consider alternative answers he might give, and also consider the possibility of not answering at all. The basis for his decision are those factors in the situation which we have called the context of the questions. The context a researcher seeks to develop is one of dispassionate inquiry of an important topic. He tries to communicate to the respondent that he, the researcher, is in search of information which will serve a useful social purpose, that he is competent to analyze the information properly, ethical enough to present it thoroughly and fairly, and finally that the respondent is a logical and important source of the information sought. A researcher communicates this through the personal impression that he and his staff make on the respondents but also by the impersonal impression that the questions make. Nothing will antagonize a respondent quicker than being asked a question of the "when did you stop beating your wife" variety. For he then sees the questions as loaded, intended to produce a set of data oriented in a particular direction. Once he sees this, the likelihood of his refusing to respond is increased. Even worse from the viewpoint of securing rational data is the possibility that the respondent will then accept what he perceives as the researcher's challenge and set out to outwit him by providing spurious answers.

Equally offensive is the impression a series of questions sometimes conveys that the researcher is not fully informed about the research situation. If questions ask for information the respondent believes any knowledgeable person should know without asking, and/or if other questions ask for distinctions the respondent believes cannot be made, he begins to conclude that the researcher is not sufficiently competent to merit his, the respondent's, cooperation and information. Similarly, questions which seek information which is readily available to the researcher without taking the respondent's time will offend the respondent. He must be convinced that the researcher is willing to do his share of the work and is coming to the respondent only for that information he can obtain in no other way or from no other source.

Any of these errors will damage the context necessary for the frank interchange of information, for this context depends on the respondent being convinced of the knowledgeability of the researcher, the willingness of the researcher to assume the proper burden of work and responsibility, and the researcher's commitment to ethical and sensitive use of the information provided by the respondent.

Content of Questioning

Questioning, like all research methods, involves sampling. Rare indeed is the research situation in which the researcher is able to ask every question he would like to ask. Instead he can only ask some, generally because there is just so much of the respondent's time available to him. To decide what to ask, however, the researcher must put the issue of content into the same model we have developed for all other instances in which sampling is the research concern: The sample must be either randomly or deliberately selected from a known population. There is seldom any reason for random selection in the questioning method. Every student who has sat through a class which totally perplexed him without asking questions knows we must know something about a situation to ask questions. In research this means that the researcher intending to use the questioning method should know enough to establish the bounds of the population of information he seeks, and also should be able to delineate the significant strata within that population. He should be able to spell out the areas of information needed, and the specifics within areas. For example, in the Language Study, one of the early stages was a survey of current methods of teaching English as a second language. As we considered this problem area, we were able to identify the major components within it, such as the sources of new vocabulary words and how they were introduced, the sequence in which language patterns were introduced and the rationale for the sequence, the nature of language experiences provided, and so on.

In the preceding chapter it was noted that in identifying the various aspects of a research situation which might be observed it is useful to develop some overall outline or blueprint of the situation; in questioning it is useful to fully develop a blueprint of the various aspects of the situation about which questions might be asked.[1] With the areas sketched out to this extent, the researcher can turn to the sampling process, particularly to deciding what proportion of his questioning time will be allocated to each aspect of the content.

The identification of all possible areas for questioning and the consideration of proportional allocation of time are often ignored by the researcher, and yet they form the foundations upon which he can build the argument for the content validity of the instrument for questioning. For this reason, the stages in selecting content should be based not only upon the researcher's knowledge of the research situation but upon the literature in the problem area as well. The literature reviewed for these purposes should be both the research and nonresearch literature, for this blueprint, and the decisions made from it as to content, should reflect both what others have studied and what others have thought about what constitutes the problem area.

[1] A more specific discussion of the process by which this is done appears in this chapter under the heading "Instruments for Information-Seeking Questioning."

The Question

In this chapter, we shall consider the stimulus used in the questioning method as made up of two parts—the question and the provision for responding—and shall consider these separately.

The heart of the questioning method and its most significant element is the question itself. For research purposes there is only one standard a question must meet: It must make the researcher's intent clear to the respondent. For this to be true, the question must have a clarity and singleness of purpose and interpretation which is far more difficult to achieve than the researcher who has never tried it can believe. At the surface and subsurface levels of research, the question functions as a stimulus to which we expect the respondent to make an immediate associative response. If this response is to be the relevant one, then the question must function perfectly in this stimulus role. This perfect functioning would be damaged, if not destroyed, if the question were ambiguous and so led to more than one association, for the respondent would have to decide which was the meaning and therefore the association the researcher sought. This need for clarity is even more critical when questioning is used at the depth level, for now we expect the respondent to use the question as a point of departure while he searches his thoughts and feelings to identify the answer which is true for him. We have noted how difficult it is to motivate respondents to function at this depth level under the best of circumstances. In questioning, the best of circumstances demands clear, specific questions, for if the respondent must wrestle with a confusing stimulus in addition to the search for the answer already implicit in the depth level, he is likely to abandon the entire enterprise and either refuse to respond or else respond with some immediate surface or subsurface association.

For a question to serve as an effective stimulus it must possess characteristics which are discussed below.

1. *Clarity of language.*   This characteristic means that the intent of the question and the nature of the information sought is clear *to the respondent*. The italics are intended to emphasize that it is the respondent about whom the issue of clarity revolves. This means that the researcher must relate the vocabulary, the language structure, the conceptual level, and the sophistication of the information subsumed in his questions to the abilities, levels, and background of his respondents. Questions which may be perfectly clear to the researcher and his staff may be confusing and even incomprehensible to respondents, as in the obvious instances when

the respondents are children, or when English is not their native language. Clarity is also a potential problem in the less obvious instance when the respondents are less well educated than the researcher, or do not have some specific educational or technical experiences which some questions assume, or have not all had the same sequences of life experiences which other questions assume.

The best protection for assuring clarity is to write questions in simple, uncomplex language, with vocabulary of everyday speech, eliminating as much as possible the jargon of particular fields, and avoiding the tendency to use the questions to demonstrate one's prowess in language. Another help in achieving clarity is giving the respondent an example of the type of response the question is meant to elicit.

But clarity can not be fully established by the researcher or his staff unless they verify the clarity of the questions in pilot studies with respondents of comparable educational level, experiences, and sophistication as the respondents ultimately to be questioned. Only in this way can they be certain that the questions they have written do communicate effectively.

2. *Specificity of content and time period.* This criterion is allied to the first criterion of clarity of language, for it too is concerned with the researcher's ability to communicate his intent effectively. It is listed here separately because it is equally critical and because clarity of language and of content are so often erroneously equated. A question may be stated in perfectly clear language and yet leave the researcher's intent ambiguous and confusing to the respondent. For example, consider the researcher concerned with identifying what teachers perceive as their most interesting experience in teaching formal lessons to children. He first considers the question: "What has been your most interesting experience since you became a teacher?"

Now the language here is clear and simple. Yet the question is not fully specific. The time interval to be used in identifying the answer is reasonably clear (". . . since you became a teacher") but the question is vague as to what limits, if any, the researcher wishes placed on the frame of reference for selecting the content of the response. Is the teacher who, since she became a teacher, met her fiancé on a blind date, free to relate that as her "most interesting experience"? If not, the researcher should rule out such social and personal experiences by asking, "What has been your most interesting teaching experience since you became a teacher?" The researcher who wanted to rule out teaching activities like field trips, plays, and other out-of-class activities might go further and ask, "What has been the most interesting experience you have had in teaching a formal lesson to children since you became a teacher?"

Notice how more structured this question is, and how much more likely it is to be answered with the kind of information the researcher is seeking. Good research questions must achieve this level of structure and specificity in terms both of the content and time period from which the respondent is to select his answer.

3. *Singleness of purpose.*   This characteristic is intended to assure that each question seeks one, and only one, piece or bit of information. A frequent error in questioning is to seek more than one piece of information within a single question unit. This not only poses an impossible task for the respondent but provides an uninterpretable piece of data for the researcher. For example, let us suppose we were concerned with teachers' opinions about the attractiveness of the phonics materials and with the frequency with which they have used them. Posed correctly, these are two separate questions—the first question dealing with the opinion of the attractiveness of the materials, the second question dealing with the frequency of use. Incorrectly, they might be combined in one question, for example: "Do you think the phonics materials are attractive and have you used them frequently?" The double question, of course, is possible to answer only in the instance in which the response to both parts is the same—the teacher who finds them attractive and used them frequently could say "yes." The teacher who neither finds them attractive nor has used them frequently could say "no." The teacher who, although she finds the materials attractive, did not use them has the same problem of not being able to respond to the double question as does the teacher who, although she finds the materials unattractive, nevertheless did use them frequently. Furthermore, the researcher who gets back a "no," would be at a loss to know if the teacher is saying: "No, I didn't find them attractive," "No, I didn't use them frequently," or "No, I neither found them attractive, nor used them frequently," or any of the other possible combinations of responses. It is for this reason that the third criterion for good questions is that each question seek a single piece of information, and so serve as a single stimulus.

4. *Freedom from assumption.*   This characteristic is intended to make certain that to respond to a question the respondent does not have to respond to a prior, unasked question. For example, asking a teacher to "give an example of an instance in which you believed you have failed as a teacher" forces the teacher to say "yes" to the unasked question: "Have you ever experienced failure as a teacher?" Most readers will react to these statements by saying: "How can anyone teach for any period of time and not experience failure?" Researchers, too, will typically offer this defense when criticized for phrasing questions that make this type of

assumption. But the issue is not whether or not everyone experiences failure, or whether everyone gets angry at a supervisor, or every child has a fight with his father. The issue is that some respondents may respond "no," that they have never experienced failure or anger or had a fight, and not only are they entitled to make this response (whether it is a distortion of life or not) but that they make the response is important for the researcher to know, and that is why the prior direct and open question should be asked. It should then be followed by a question beginning: "If you have had such experiences, please give an example."

5. *Freedom from suggestion.* There should be nothing in the language or phrasing of the question which, in any way, suggests to the respondent that some answers are expected, or that some are more desirable or acceptable than others. This criterion is particularly critical with children, or in a situation with adults when someone in authority is questioning respondents of lower status, but it should be adhered to in all questioning. Introductory phrases—like "don't you agree that . . . ?" or "isn't it surprising that . . . ?"—make obvious suggestions of the answer desired, as does a less obvious phrase like: "Can you think of any justification for . . . ?" Similarly introductory phrases to establish a context will also work to suggest answers; that is: "In view of the number of obsolete school buildings in the community do you think school taxes should be raised?" is a different question from: "Should school taxes be raised to replace obsolete school buildings?" Each is different from: "Should school taxes be raised?" The researcher will wish to say enough in the question to provide the respondent with the context in which he (the researcher) wants the question answered, in other words, the taxes would be raised to finance new buildings. But he must write this with great care, because the researcher sincerely interested in discovering the respondent's beliefs deliberately avoids any wording or references in the questions that would directly or subtly suggest the answer.

6. *Linguistic completeness and grammatical consistency.* The preceding are all research criteria. But it should be remembered that the questioning method is essentially a verbal interaction between researcher and respondent, and care should be paid to the linguistic quality of the question unit. There are two different aspects to developing questions of linguistic quality: making certain that the question unit provides a complete cue to the linguistic nature of the response, and writing questions such that the answer desired is grammatically consistent with the question.

Linguistic completeness should be considered in company with the criterion of freedom from suggestion just noted, for while the question should *not* suggest the content of the answer, it should suggest the linguistic form of the answer. For example, if you intend to ask your respondents to indicate their opinion about the effectiveness of the vocabulary method by selecting from among three options which read, "more effective than the structure method," "equal in effectiveness to the structure method," and "less effective than the structure method," the incomplete question might read: "What do you think of the vocabulary method?" The linguistically complete question would ask: "How does the effectiveness of the vocabulary method compare to the effectiveness of the structure method?"—indicating to the respondent that the researcher desires him to think, and answer, in terms of a comparison of the vocabulary and structure method.

The second aspect of this criterion, grammatical consistency, simply means that the question and response should form a grammatically correct unit. This aspect is most apparent in techniques of questioning which use questions and predetermined responses such as the structured questionnaire, for here the respondent sees both question and possible answer before him. A simple example of what is meant is to consider two questions for the three options above. One question reads, "Was the vocabulary method as effective as the structure method?" The second question reads, "How effective was the vocabulary method in comparison to the structure method?" Note that the three options offered are grammatically consistent with the second question but not with the first. This level of concern may seem like a matter of interest only to the purist in language, but the willingness of a respondent to take the time to answer questions can hinge on such simple matters as his reaction to the linguistic character of the questions. A thorough researcher does not risk losing any potential respondents by ignoring this criterion.

Provision for Answering

The next significant element of the questioning method is the way in which the respondent will be permitted to respond. To one who does not know research that phrase in itself would seem strange. Obviously, they would expect, when we ask a question, we permit the respondent to "respond" as he wishes. But equally "obviously," in many applications of the questioning method we do not. Instead, researchers often proffer a question and follow it up with a finite list of possible answers. Thus, instead of asking the respondent to answer the question, they ask him to select an answer from among those offered to him.

In a sense there are only these two major types of responses to research questions. One is the free-response type in which the researcher after asking the question, gives the respondent the freedom to determine the response. The second is the structured type in which the researcher both asks the questions and suggests some or all of the potential answers. There are obvious research implications in the difference between asking a question without suggesting the answer, and both asking the question and providing some idea as to the answer. In the first instance the question serves as a stimulus only, with the data provided by the respondent's associations to the question. In other words, all of the data emerge from the respondent and his associations and reactions to the *research question.* In the second instance the data are provided by the respondent's reactions and associations to the combination of research question and the *researcher's* associations and reactions to that question. Thus, the entire frame of reference for the data is different under the two conditions.

Within these two major response types, researchers have available four different kinds of response formats: (1) the *totally free response,* in which the researcher does nothing more than pose the stimulus question, placing no limits to the response and offering no suggestions as to the areas of content to be considered or the form of the response; (2) the *limited free response,* in which the researcher places some limits as to the response, most often a limit of time, or else limits the boundaries of the response by suggesting areas of content for the response and/or the form of the response which he desires; (3) *the structured response with a free option,* in which the researcher actually suggests certain answers from among which the respondent can select those which apply to him, but also offers a free option which permits the respondent to add additional responses or additional comments which are not on the list; and, finally, (4) the *totally structured response,* in which the researcher states his question and offers a list of potential answers requiring that the respondent choose from among them without the opportunity to add any of his own.

TOTALLY FREE RESPONSE   The *totally free response* is a theoretical, but seldom realized extreme in which the researcher sets no limits and provides no structure. In the Language Study we might have sought insight into teachers' feelings about Puerto Rican children by asking them to "talk to us about Puerto Rican children." This question[2] places no restrictions on the response, and suggests nothing about the content or form of the answer. Thus it would be reasonable for the respondent to discuss her observations of the in-class behavior of Puerto Rican children, or to comment on their sociopsychological characteristics, or to note how she feels about them, or the advantages and difficulties of having children of another culture and language background in her class.

[2]This example typifies the fact that when we use "question" in the questioning method, we are not necessarily referring to a question, grammatically. The label "question" is applied to all verbal stimuli to which a verbal response is sought.

This kind of question worked exceptionally well for Kahlil Gibran as a means of introducing the sections of *The Prophet,* but it seldom works well in research because it gives too much freedom to, and imposes too much responsibility upon, the respondent. The freedom is excessive because it gives each respondent the opportunity to select the form, the length, and the content areas which will comprise his response. And because the respondent has these freedoms he also has responsibility which is not properly his. As a consequence, he is forced to devote a disproportionate share of his interest and attention to deciding what to say and how to say it. This level of responsibility is not appropriate if questioning is being conducted for research at any of the conscious levels, for we wish our respondent to associate to an answer, not to the form or length of the answer. Moreover, even at the nonconscious level the responsibility may be excessive, for the stimulus question is intended to get the respondent to begin talking, and if it is too vague he is at a loss to know where or how to begin.

LIMITED FREE RESPONSE   For these reasons, researchers interested in using a free response turn to the *limited free response* format in which they establish limits or a structure to assist the respondent. Perhaps the most ubiquitous guidelines provided are clues as to the length of the response expected and the general content areas of the response. One limited free-response version of the question to the teachers in the Language Study would be: "In the next five minutes, will you tell us about your feelings about Puerto Rican children?" Notice that this question not only provides a clue to the length of the response, it also makes it clear that comments about methodology or the sociopsychological and educational characteristics of the children are not desired, but rather the researcher wishes the respondent to discuss his or her own feelings.

Within this type of response, the researcher can, of course, provide varying degrees of structure going beyond what little we have used in the example above. We shall see later in this chapter in one of the techniques for questioning called the *critical incident technique,* the respondent asked to think of a recent experience of a highly specific type and asked not only to describe the incident but also to describe who was involved, and what led up to the incident. Similarly in the Thematic Apperception Test, a technique using questioning at the nonconscious level, a respondent is shown a vague and ambiguous picture and asked to tell a story about the picture, including in his story what is presently going on, what led up to the present situation, and what will happen in the future.

TOTALLY STRUCTURED RESPONSE   Once we move in the direction of providing structure for the response, we can move in this direction until we reach the *totally structured response,* the end of the continuum opposite from the totally free response. In our example the question with the totally structured response would appear in a form somewhat like this: "Listed below are feelings which teachers have reported about Puerto Rican children. Circle all of these feelings which you have had."[3]

Note that in this totally structured response the respondent has neither the ability to determine the form nor the content of his response. He can only select from among those possible responses which the researcher offers. If, for example, he experiences a feeling not on the researcher's list, he cannot express this feeling. Thus, this kind of an option is feasible only if the researcher can have confidence that he has the ability to identify *fully* all relevant specifics which should be considered and offered to the respondents. This need is deceptively critical, for if one or two relevant options are forgotten and therefore omitted, this not only affects the data for these options but for all other options as well. This is because if the omitted ones had been included, the respondent might have chosen them and not chosen others.

STRUCTURED RESPONSE WITH FREE OPTION   Because the totally structured format requires such advance knowledgeableness on the part of the researcher, and so severely restricts the respondent, researchers often take a step back from the totally structured end of the response continuum to the *structured response with a free option,* that is, they add an unstructured option at the end of the structured list. Typically this option simply says "other . . . ," in other words, the option would be entitled "other feelings" in our example. Although in this format he is no longer using a totally structured response, the researcher has taken but one short step back toward the free response end of the continuum, since realistically, most respondents answer within the list offered and do not exercise the "other" option.

Perhaps even more important a restriction than the limitation of possible responses is the fact that the structured response with or without the free-response option suggests answers to the respondent. Thus, it is possible, indeed probable, that at least some of the answers he actually circles might not have been produced had the initiative been totally his. This is a critical limitation since this means the researcher is now in that part of the questioning process which is not properly his province: producing the answer to his own questions.

WHEN STRUCTURE IS APPROPRIATE   The totally structured format is most appropriate when the range of possible responses is limited and known.

---

[3] In the section of this chapter on the questionnaire technique, we shall discuss alternative ways of stating these response options to obtain different levels of precision.

This is exemplified in research by the variety of surface level questions seeking descriptive data about respondents such as age, gender, education, or marital status, or by simple opinion questions which can be answered yes or no. For questions like these the researcher should provide the possible answers for the respondents, for he can then capitalize on the advantages of the structured response: Most obvious is the fact that it simplifies the respondent's task, minimizes the amount of time and energy he must invest to respond, and so maximizes the likelihood that he will respond. Similarly, it simplifies the researcher's task of data analysis, for the data come to him neatly packaged in predetermined categories which can be counted directly.

The interaction of data collection, data analysis, and data reporting is exemplified again in this last point, for to fully capitalize on this advantage, the researcher should offer his structured options as he intends to analyze and report them. If he intends to combine all respondents who are either "divorced" or "separated," he should offer these as one option. Similarly, if he intends to use age only to analyze data separately for those respondents under and over thirty years of age, he should ask for age in terms of these two gradations and not in five-year intervals from twenty to seventy. But this simplification is possible only if, at the instrument development stage, the researcher has thought through what he ultimately wishes to do with his data.

Once we move beyond the surface level questions to subsurface or depth questions we can state as a general rule of questioning that the free-response rather than the structured answer formats should be used for the first studies into a problem area. Once researchers have identified the range of responses, as the *respondents* see them and as the respondents phrase them, then subsequent researchers may use these initial studies to develop structured response formats. As a minimum step in this direction, if we are planning an early study in a problem area and wish to use a structured answer format, we should conduct sufficient pilot studies using the free-response format to enable us to feel confident that we have identified the relevant range of potential responses.

Researcher-Respondent Interaction

Basically there are only two different researcher-respondent interactions within the questioning method: the *personal interaction* in which researcher (or his agent) and respondent meet face-to-face, and the questions are posed by the researcher actually asking them of the respondent, and the *impersonal interaction* in which the researcher is represented by a piece of paper upon which the questions are printed and upon which the respondent puts his answers. In an effort to capture the advantages of each interaction and eliminate some of the disadvantages, a third interaction has come into use in recent years in which the researcher or his agent meets face-to-face with the respondents, usually in groups, to introduce the research and to answer their questions as to research purposes and procedures. Having done this, he proceeds to distribute the questions and the answer forms which have been printed as in the impersonal interaction. This hybrid interaction is one we shall call a *mixed interaction.*

PERSONAL INTERACTION   The personal interaction generally involves a one-to-one relationship between researcher and respondent, and in this fact lie two pairs of advantages and disadvantages. The first advantage and disadvantage stem from the simple fact that a face-to-face, one-to-one relationship is a much more basic human relationship than mailing someone a piece of paper. If this relationship is an empathic one in which the respondent feels relaxed, confident, and accepted, the relationship itself will help motivate him to respond fully and frankly to the research questions. However, as elements of distance, anxiety, suspicion, hostility, and any other negative aspect of human interrelationships enter the picture, the willingness to respond frankly breaks down until ultimately the motivation to respond in any fashion is dissipated. The sensitivity of the personal interaction has been demonstrated in a wide variety of studies[4] which have shown that the interaction will be affected by the match-up of researcher and respondent in terms of such characteristics as age, sex, skin color, style and quality of dress, and language fluency and regional accent.

Therefore the researcher contemplating the use of the personal interaction must be convinced that he and his agents will be able to establish a relationship which will be productive. As we have noted in comparable instances, the only sensible way of achieving this conviction is through the collection of pilot data, in this instance pilot data collected through both personal and impersonal techniques to provide a basis for estimating the effect, if any, of the personal presence of the researcher.

---

[4]Typical studies are: Eugene C. Bryant, Isaac Gardner, Jr., and Morton Goldman, "Responses on Racial Attitudes as Affected by Interviewers of Different Ethnic Groups," *Journal of Social Psychology,* vol. 70, no. 1 (1966), pp. 95–100; R. F. Berdie, "Psychological Processes in the Interview," *Journal of Social Psychology,* vol. 18 (1943), pp. 3–31; Benjamin Pope and Siegman Pope: "Interviewer warmth and Verbal Communication in Initial Interview," *Proceedings of the 75th Annual Convention of the American Psychological Association,* vol. 2 (1967), pp. 245–246; William M. Womack, and Wagner Womack, "Negro Interviewers and White Patients: The Question of Confidentiality and Trust," *Archives of General Psychiatry,* vol. 16, no. 6 (1967), pp. 685–692; Robert R. Carkhuff, and Richard Pierce, "Differential Effects of Therapist Race and Social Class Upon Patient Depth of Self-Exploration in Initial Clinical Interview," *Journal of Consulting Psychology,* vol. 31, no. 6 (1967), pp. 632–634.

The second advantage-disadvantage pair of the personal interaction is based on the fact that questions are verbally transmitted to the respondent by the researcher. The advantage lies in the ability this provides for the researcher to repeat a question if necessary, to explain it if not understood, and to ask a follow-up question or two if the initial answer the respondent provides is insufficiently clear. Moreover, if the researcher is present to ask the questions he can move into areas of questioning not fully anticipated in advance, can go off onto tangents when some intriguing response is made, and can decide to explore in depth some area of the content of the questioning which seems worthy of exploration in view of some of the responses made. This is the unique advantage of personal interaction, and one can state as a guiding principle that unless the researcher wishes to make use of this advantage, he is ill-advised to use this interaction. This means that it is best used in those instances when the researcher only knows the general areas which he wishes to study and knows the people he wishes to question, but is not able to delineate in advance all of the questions he might wish to ask.

For example, let us assume in the Language Study we decided that it would be useful to know which aspects of the guides to methods and materials the teachers found helpful and which they did not. Now this identifies the areas of questioning and the people to be questioned. We can even write the basic four questions:[5]

1. Which aspects of the guide to methods did you find helpful?
2. Which aspects of the guide to methods were not helpful?
3. Which aspects of the guide to materials did you find helpful?
4. Which aspects of the guide to materials were not helpful?

But if we think to what questions we would ask second, we are left with the vague question "why?" or equally vague requests to "explain your answer." Given this problem we might well decide that the most sensible thing to do would be to recruit a team of sophisticated interviewers to ask the teachers the basic questions about likes and dislikes, giving the interviewers the responsibility for following up with subsidiary questions, depending upon the initial responses.

This statement highlights a basic disadvantage however: the responsibility it places on the questioner, who must be skilled in the art of questioning and knowledgeable in the area of the project, to successfully carry out the responsibility.[6] Moreover, the flexibility in questioning means that the researcher cannot claim that each respondent has reacted to identically the same stimulus circumstance. Some have responded to the

[5]Note that we adhere to the principle of single specific questions and so separate the like–dislike dimension and the method–material dimension into separate questions.

[6]This problem is discussed in greater detail in the section of this chapter on the interviewing technique.

initial question only, some after a second repetition, and others only after a follow-up explanation. If standardization is important to the researcher, as it would be in any project involving the study of a sensitive area (such as the evaluation of a new or controversial program or project) then this loss of standardization is a serious disadvantage. Equally serious is a third disadvantage: The possibility always present in a verbally posed question that something in the tone, intonation, emphasis, or expression of the questioner will suggest the content or at least the direction of the answer expected or desired. The damage this would do the data is obvious. For some respondents it will determine their answer, either because they are sufficiently suggestible to say what they think is desired, or sufficiently strong-willed to deliberately avoid it even if true.

The third advantage-disadvantage pair is based on the fact that the personal interaction assures both a high proportion of returns and responses,[7] that is, a higher proportion of the sample questioned will answer the questions than in the impersonal interaction. This may sound like an unmixed blessing, but when one says that the response rate is high because in a face-to-face relationship it is difficult to decline to answer, the disadvantage should become clear. This pressure to respond means that to some extent the answers obtained in the personal interaction represent answers which the respondent might have preferred not giving, but which he produced under social pressure. In this circumstance he may give some answer other than the true answer, or some response which is partial rather than complete. What is worse, the researcher usually has no basis for estimating the extent to which this kind of pressure is operating to produce data. This pair of advantages-disadvantages means that the researcher contemplating using the personal interaction must weigh the gains in proportion of responses against the potential distortion, in the context of his research problem and the content of his questioning. In other words, for some research questions (that is, questions about controversial or personal matters) it may well be more useful to learn what proportion of the selected sample will freely respond to the questions than to apply the social pressure of the personal interaction and elicit a misleadingly high rate of responses, some or many of which are spurious.

We must conclude by noting the single major disadvantage of the personal interaction: the cost, considering expenditure of time as well as money required, of acquiring data through a one-to-one relationship between researcher and respondent. Each bit of data acquired demands the full amount of time it requires to run through the questions and record the

---

[7]The distinction being made here is that any instrument a respondent gives back is a return, even if it is not completed fully. He must answer the question for us to have a response as well as a return.

answers. This means that the interaction is feasible only if the research problem is one in which limited amounts of data will satisfy the research purpose. It is not an appropriate interaction for problems in which large amounts of data will be required, as in the mass survey.

MIXED INTERACTION   In an effort to capitalize on the high returns, verbal flexibility, and personal human touch of the personal interaction, yet cut costs, the mixed interaction has been developed. In this interaction, the researcher meets with a group of respondents, explains the purpose of the research, the intent of the instrument, and answers all questions from the respondents. He then distributes the printed questions and may even answer questions again at this point in the process. When all questions have been answered the respondents answer the questionnaire. Thus the mixed interaction retains some of the personal flavor and involvement and some of the clarification ability of the personal interaction, although it loses the spontaneous flexibility and the ability to inject additional questions for purposes of clarification, detail, and specificity. To compensate for these losses, the mixed interaction does provide the researcher with the ability to argue for standardization, in other words, to assure that each respondent has answered the same set of questions in the same order.[8]

The mixed interaction will usually work as well as the personal in assuring a high proportion of returns, but the higher ratio of respondents to researcher and the use of a paper-and-pencil instrument means that a respondent who wishes to avoid answering a question may easily do so without the embarrassment of a face-to-face refusal. Thus, the researcher has retained the high proportion of returns, and even though the proportion of response is lower, this may be a more valid set of data than a personal interaction would have provided.

The mixed interaction is reasonable when masses of data are desired, for one researcher can meet with large groups of respondents and still maintain a reasonable personal relationship[9] in the sense of motivating and answering questions.

IMPERSONAL INTERACTION   If the researcher is confident that his questions are so clear as to require no explanation, and if he also has some basis for believing that a reasonable proportion of respondents will answer

[8]This argument is strongest when there has been no discussion and no further questions once the papers have been distributed. Therefore, typically, researchers prefer to limit questions from the respondents to the period before they see the actual questions to which they will respond.

[9]In the nursing research project directed by the author, we conducted one series of pilot studies intended to identify the size of the group with which one researcher could effectively meet. We found no differences in the data produced by groups as small as five and as large as 40.

his questions if they receive them on a piece of paper, he has the two conditions necessary to consider using the impersonal interaction. If these two conditions are met, the researcher is in a position to capture the major advantage of this interaction, the massive coverage of respondents which can be achieved quickly and relatively inexpensively. But note that all the interaction makes possible is massive *coverage*. It will not provide masses of intelligible data unless the first two necessary conditions have been met, that is, unless the researcher is certain that the questions will be clear and that the respondents will answer them.

Whether the questions are mailed to the respondents, handed out to them individually, or distributed to them as a group when they assemble, if the interaction is impersonal, then no words are exchanged between researcher and respondent, but instead whatever directions, explanations, and instructions have been printed with the questions speak for the researcher.

Since this is so, this interaction assures the maximum standardization we can achieve. While we cannot guarantee that every respondent will read the introductory material with the same interest or even with the same understanding, we are certain that each was exposed to identical instructions, and that is all which we can ever guarantee.[10]

The major disadvantage to the impersonal interaction is that the returns are usually low, seldom rising above 50 percent, and in social research typically running in the low 30 percent range. In fact, in one report by a firm which does commercial mailed surveys using the impersonal interaction, they note that the typical return runs about 3 percent.[11] In view of this, the researcher planning to use the impersonal interaction must be certain that he will have a useable set of data despite a low return. Put into the sampling concepts developed in Chapter 11, the researcher must be certain that even if his data-producing sample of respondents is less than half of his accepting sample he will nevertheless have a set of data which he can defend as meaningful and informative. This defense can best be established in instances when the research sample and population can be considered to be one reasonably homogeneous mass. If this is so, then any one-third or one-fourth of that mass can be considered to be providing some insight into the views of the mass. If instead, the research population was conceptualized as consisting of several strata, each of which was sampled, then the impersonal interaction is particularly treacherous for

---

[10]Realistically, a similar limitation exists when instructions are read aloud to respondents, for we can not guarantee that every respondent hears them to the same extent or understands them similarly.

[11]*Problems and Dangers in the New York City Public Schools* (New York: Trend Finders, 1963).

the returns, as likely as not, will be unevenly distributed through the several strata. In this event, the data are difficult to interpret and conclusions about the circumstances in the population are severely limited.

TECHNIQUES FOR QUESTIONING

We shall discuss four different techniques for questioning, but because two of them have one internal variation each, Table 18-1 lists six techniques. A glance at the table indicates that these techniques vary in terms of the researcher-respondent interaction which we have just discussed, and the type of response permitted the respondent which we discussed earlier in this chapter.

When personal interaction is used, the technique available is the *interview*. Table 18-1 indicates that two kinds of interviews are available: the *unstructured interview* in which the questions are posed in a face-to-face situation, and either a totally free or limited free response is permitted, and the *structured interview*, in which the questions are posed and some or a complete list of potential answers is offered.

When the impersonal interaction or the mixed interaction is used the questions are "asked" by being printed on paper, and "answered" by the respondents in writing. Under these circumstances, Table 18-1 indicates that four techniques are available: the *unstructured questionnaire,* the *critical incident technique,* the *structured questionnaire,* and the *check list.*

Table 18-1 Conceptualization of the Techniques for Questioning as a Function of the Researcher-Respondent Interaction and the Response Format

Type of Response Format	*Nature of Researcher-Respondent Interaction*		
	Impersonal or Mixed		Personal
Totally free		Unstructured questionnaire	Unstructured interview
Limited free	Critical incident	Unstructured questionnaire	Unstructured interview
Structured, with free option		Structured questionnaire	Structured interview
Totally structured	Check list	Structured questionnaire	Structured interview

When one considers these various techniques for questioning, it is useful to distinguish two kinds. The first kind consists of those techniques which are intended to provide a wide variety of information and in which the researcher has the opportunity to ask many questions. This group includes both kinds of interview, the questionnaire, and the check list. The second kind, the critical incident technique, is intended to provide a deeper, more thorough set of information about a few dynamics and is more concerned with the description of behavior than it is with providing specific information. Since the process of instrument development is different in these two instances, we shall discuss the two kinds of questioning techniques separately.

Questioning for Varied Information

THE INTERVIEW   When the researcher wishes to question at the conscious level and intends to use the personal interaction, he is employing the technique for questioning called the *interview*. As we have just noted, in employing this technique the researcher may offer the respondent any of the four formats for answering, ranging from the totally free response to the totally structured response.

As would be expected, everything we have said earlier about the advantages and disadvantages of the personal interaction between research-er and respondent applies to the interview, and we shall not repeat it here. Similarly, the earlier comments on the free-response or guided response format apply to the unstructured interview as do the comments on the structured response format to the structured interview.

We do wish to note here some additional comments which are uniquely applicable when these interactions and formats intersect into the technique for questioning called the interview.[12]

Perhaps the single critical element in achieving success with the interview technique is the interviewer's ability to establish sufficient rapport with the respondent to elicit honest and complete responses without himself influencing the nature of these responses through his (the interviewer's) sociopersonal characteristics or manner of questioning. This means that the researcher contemplating the use of this technique for questioning should pay particular attention to the sociopersonal characteristics of respondents and use these as the basis for selecting his interviewers. For example, in one of the evaluation studies referred to earlier, the author wished to interview two parent groups, one black, one white. Since

---

[12]There are two major types of interviews in the social disciplines: the data-gathering interview and the personal evaluation interview used in job placement and clinical diagnosis. In this section we are considering only the data-gathering interview.

these interviews were to be conducted during a time of intense community agitation and unrest, much of it focused upon the schools and the question of parental involvement, it was decided that not only was skin color an important characteristic to consider in selecting interviewers but the fact of being a parent of a child in the schools under study also was. It was these considerations which led to the decision to recruit teams of black and of white parents to interview other parents of the same skin color.

THE STRUCTURED INTERVIEW   The kinds of skills needed by the interviewer over and beyond his basic characteristics depend upon whether the interview is to be structured or unstructured. In the structured interview the questions are stated specifically in a fixed list (called the *interview guide*) and the interviewer is instructed to ask these verbatim in the order in which they are listed. When complete standardization is desired, he is told not to repeat a question, not to deviate from the order, not to ask additional questions, and to ask all questions even if, for example, the answer to question five has already been learned through an overly complete response to question three.[13]

Moreover, the answers expected from the respondent are also predetermined and listed on the interview guide in the structured interview. Given this degree of structure, the interviewer needs interpersonal skills but does not need to be particularly knowledgeable in terms of the research project. One might even argue that the less he knows about the content of the research, the less likely he is to inject any bias into the interview through intonation, emphasis, or gesture. This is a widely used and familiar technique of questioning, for it is the one used by all of the public opinion polling services. Typically the services use the totally structured response format, that is, they ask a question, and then offer a finite list of responses permitting the respondent only the additional option of not responding. When the possible responses are so specific and so clearly identifiable in advance of data collection, the only justification for using the interview rather than the most appropriate impersonal questioning technique is the fact that a high proportion of responses is desired as in polling. Otherwise, this is a wastefully expensive way to acquire highly specific data.

THE UNSTRUCTURED INTERVIEW   However, in the unstructured interview, the interview guide serves as a reminder to the interviewer of the areas which should be covered. Even if it also lists specific questions, the interviewer is not restricted to this list and is free to ask additional questions, to repeat questions, and to move off onto tangents which show

---

[13]The motivation for this repetition is the possibility that the response to question 6 (and even later questions) may be affected by the fact that question 5 was stated and answered before them.

promise of providing information useful to the purposes of the research and likely to help answer the research question. But of course this means that in addition to the same interpersonal skills needed in the structured interview, in the unstructured interview the interviewer also must be knowledgeable and sufficiently sophisticated in research to make the variety of judgments this type of interview demands.

RECORDING DATA DURING INTERVIEW   One problem faced in the unstructured interview is how to record the data. The choices available narrow down to the interviewer himself writing down the responses or recording them on a tape recorder. If a thoroughly verbatim record of what the respondent says is needed, the recorder is required, and it is preferable even if a less than verbatim record is desired. This is because it frees the interviewer to concentrate on his basic role of questioner. It also frees him while the respondent is answering to pay attention to nonverbal aspects of the response such as body position, facial expression, and hand movements. Moreover, freeing the respondent from the necessity of writing incessantly as the respondent speaks makes it more likely that the interviewer can establish the natural human interrelationship so critical to success in the personal interaction. The negative side to the use of the recorder is the possibility that the presence of the machine will make the respondent uneasy, but the danger of this grows less likely each day as tape recorders come into wider use in schools, business, and at home.[14]

If because equipment is unavailable or is not feasible to use and the interviewer does write down the responses, the researcher should do all that is possible to simplify his task and minimize exactly what he must record. This can best be accomplished by thinking past the point of data collection to the analyses which are to be done with the data. If the structure of these analyses can be developed before the interviews are conducted, then an interview guide can be developed in which the question to be asked is listed and actually followed on the guide by the response expected. Given this type of guide, when the respondent makes one of the expected responses all the interviewer need do is circle that response. Below is a section of such an interview guide used to interview the principal in a project the author directed in 1968.[15]

[14]Developments during the 1960s in the miniaturization of equipment made it possible to record interviews without the respondent being aware that his words were being recorded. An innocent-looking attaché case, book, or pack of cigarettes in a breast pocket all are capable of recording interviews. Like unknown observation, unknown recording is obviously unethical and unworthy of any researcher in the social disciplines.

[15]*The More Effective Schools Evaluation* (New York: The Center for Urban Education, October 1968).

Question 1. How do you feel about the MES program now?
  (a) Enthusiastic
  (b) Strongly positive, but not enthusiastic
  (c) Slightly positive
  (d) Slightly negative
  (e) Strongly negative
Question 2. Do your teachers discuss the program with you?
  (a) Yes
  (b) No
Question 3. If yes, ask: Under what circumstances do they discuss the program with you?
  (a) At conferences
  (b) At staff meetings
  (c) In private conversations
  (d) Other. Specify: _____

The questions indicate that when the principal was asked his feelings about the program when it began, his response would be categorizable in one of the five options offered the interviewer in question 1, and so we listed these on the guide to minimize the actual writing the interviewer would have to do. This process also enabled us to have the interviewer categorize the feeling tone of the principal's response. In question 3, the listed options did not involve categorization, but rather were simply the most frequent answers we expected to obtain. In this instance, they were listed only to minimize the writing required of the interviewers. In both questions, of course, we included additional space on the interview guide for the interviewer to record any response which had not been anticipated. This particular problem is avoided in the structured interview, for then the respondent is not only asked a question but offered a specific set of choices from which he may select one. These responses can be preprinted onto the guide and the interviewer can so easily indicate the response given that tape recording is unnecessary.

WHEN INTERVIEW IS APPROPRIATE   Basically the interview technique is most sensible in those research situations in which the unstructured interview is required. For the expense of the technique, and the slow pace at which data are acquired, can best be justified by the need to have the flexibility and freedom and access to information provided by the combination of a knowledgeable skilled interviewer talking to a potential respondent in possession of information important for the research. The structured interview can be defended best in two instances. First, as we noted in discussing the personal interaction, there are times when some aspect of the respondents requires a face-to-face exchange of question and answer by word-of-mouth, as when the respondent cannot read. The second instance is when the researcher is determined to achieve a high proportion of returns and responses, and so wants each individual respondent seen as an individual. If one or both of these conditions is not present, the specific questions and structured answers that characterize the structured interview can usually be replaced by the less expensive technique, the questionnaire, to which we shall turn now.

The Questionnaire

If the researcher believes an impersonal interaction will suffice, he puts his questions on paper, submits these to the respondents, and asks them to place their answers on paper. This technique, called the *questionnaire,* exists (Table 18-1) in both a structured and unstructured version, but in essence can be employed in the full range of response formats. In fact, any one questionnaire can include all four response formats.

Since the questions are on paper and the interaction impersonal, the questionnaire technique brings with it both advantages of that interaction: relatively inexpensive mass coverage of potential respondents and complete standardization of the instructions to which the respondents are exposed. Moreover, the ability to include all response formats provides the researcher with great flexibility in the nature of the information sought. The disadvantages are also those of the impersonal interaction: The necessity to be able to state the questions in advance so that their intent is clear without additional interpretation and explanation, and the real danger that only a small proportion of respondents will return the questionnaire.

This means that in using this technique the researcher must take two general procedural paths. First, he must be completely satisfied that the questions can be stated with sufficient clarity to function in the impersonal interaction which characterizes the questionnaire. Second, he must take all possible steps to maximize the likelihood that a respondent will answer and return the questions. The first procedure generally requires some field testing, either through informal testing of the questions with respondents like those to be used in the study or through a formal pilot study.

The second procedural path involves four steps: (1) limiting the length of the questionnaire so that respondents need to devote as little time as possible to the chore of responding; (2) structuring the response format to as great an extent as possible so that the actual amount of writing the respondents must do is minimized; (3) writing the introductory material eloquently and frankly so that respondents know the purpose of the research and the use to be made of the data and are convinced that the purpose is worthwhile and professionally desirable; and, finally, (4) making some provision for the respondents to learn about the results of the research, if they wish, so that the exchange of information becomes a two-way rather than one-way street.[16]

As can be seen from the above paragraphs, the researcher using the questionnaire technique needs to devote as much thought and care to the issue of getting the questionnaires returned as he does to the content, for brilliant questions unanswered and unreturned serve no research purpose.

Researchers generally structure the questionnaire to as great an extent as possible, for this both minimizes the time and effort required to respond and expedites the analysis of the data. Thus the researcher planning a questionnaire should devote some significant proportion of his time to selecting, for each question, that answer format which will best combine the structure needed for ease of response and analysis with the freedom needed to obtain the research data. The goal in setting up these questions and answers is a clear one: to provide every respondent with a means of responding which reasonably approximates the answer he wishes to provide to the question. No respondent should be forced either to select an inappropriate option or to omit the question for lack of an option he can accept.

SEEKING DESCRIPTIVE INFORMATION   When the researcher is seeking specific descriptive information such as the demographic data sought in a census, it is a simple matter to use the totally structured format, since the full range of each variable is known. Thus, listed below is a section of a questionnaire in which the questions asking for gender, age, marital status, size of hometown, and sources of support in college have been printed with fully structured answers.

1. *Gender*
     (a)   Male
     (b)   Female
2. *Age*
     (a)   20–24
     (b)   25–34
     (c)   35–44
     (d)   45–49
     (e)   50 or older
     (f)   I prefer not to answer.
3. *Marital Status*
     (a)   Single

---

[16]We shall repeat this point again in Chapter 20 on the major principles of data gathering, but it is noted here since it is a prime technique for maximizing returns for a questionnaire.

    (b)   Married
    (c)   Divorced, Separated
    (d)   Widowed
4. *Size of Hometown*
    (a)   Smaller than 10,000
    (b)   10,000 to 50,000
    (c)   50,001 to 250,000
    (d)   Larger than 250,000
    (e)   I do not know.
5. *How were you supported while in college?* (Circle all that apply.)
    (a)   Personal funds   (d)   Part-time work
    (b)   Family funds   (e)   Scholarship
    (c)   Full-time work   (f)   Loan
                   (g)   Other—Please specify: _____

Note two things in this procedure. First, note that the choices offered represent decisions by the researcher as to the distinctions he wishes to make within each variable. Once the age options are listed the researcher has lost any ability to distinguish between those respondents included within any of the options, that is, to distinguish between those under thirty and over thirty, since the second age option spans that year. This means that the actual options offered should be carefully thought through in terms of the needs of the research problem and the data analyses planned. In planning his options the researcher is striving to achieve a balance which will provide all the precision and make all of the distinctions he will ultimately require and which will simultaneously simplify the respondent's task as much as possible.

Second, note that the options have been written so that they provide a means of answering for *every* respondent, even those who do not wish to provide certain data or who do not know other data. This has been done by utilizing four specific procedures:

1. The *open-end option.* This has been used in the options for age, indicating that the researcher is not interested in analyzing the data separately for those respondents older than fifty, no matter how old they might be. This option is most effectively used at the point in the variable where the researcher believes he will no longer have many respondents, or else has no further interest in distinguishing among respondents. The fact that the researcher did not use the open-end option at the other end of the age scale indicates that he is *certain* that none of his respondents are younger than twenty.

2. The *other option.* In asking for source of support in college, the researcher has listed the most frequent possible responses, but has also

given the respondents the opportunity to specify any other. This procedure is advisable when in addition to common responses there are many possible responses, no one of which is considered frequent enough to merit specification by itself.

3. The *I do not know* option.   In asking for size of hometown, the researcher has offered four options which reflect the kinds of distinctions he wishes to be able to make, and has also offered the respondents the opportunity to indicate that they "do not know" the size of their hometown. The purpose of such an option is to make clear to the respondents that not knowing this information is an acceptable response, and that the researcher would prefer that they candidly indicate that they do not know instead of guessing. This option should be offered in any question where there is some likelihood that some of the respondents will not know the information requested.

4. The *I prefer not to answer* option.   Consistent with the principle of offering all respondents an option which reflects their view on the variable, the researcher has recognized that some respondents are reluctant to reveal their age. To provide these respondents with a means of answering, he has added an option that enables them to express their reluctance. Some researchers prefer to avoid this option, believing it will suggest to the respondents that they can avoid answering. The author's belief is that the respondent who wishes to avoid answering can so easily omit the item in the questionnaire technique that there is no loss involved in providing him with a specific means of indicating his reluctance.

SEEKING QUALITATIVE INFORMATION   If the researcher is seeking information more qualitative than descriptive the structured question must both identify the continuum within which he shall seek the response and the options to be offered the respondent. The continuum to be used can usually be identified from the research question posed. For example let us assume that after the Phonics Study we wanted some indication of how often teachers used specific materials. This need for data identifies a continuum of frequency of use, which can be simply translated into a question stem such as: "How often did you use . . . ?"

In stating options for questions seeking qualitative information, the researcher's goal is the same as for descriptive information: to provide a response for every respondent which reasonably approximates that respondent's association to the question. The danger in stating options to substantive questions is that the researcher will force the respondent to over-generalize typically by offering too few options. For example, consider the following questions.

1. Did you use the film strips available?
   (a) Yes
   (b) No
2. How often did you use the film strips available?
   (a) Frequently
   (b) Sometimes
   (c) Once in a while
   (d) Never
3. How often did you use the film strips available?
   (a) At least four times a week
   (b) Two or three times a week
   (c) Once a week
   (d) Sometimes, but less often than once a week
   (e) Never

All the questions seek to determine whether or not the respondents used the film strips available to them. In the first question the researcher has made the use of the film strips a "yes-no" question. This means that the respondent who used them once, and the respondent who used them every day, and all the respondents in between must select the "yes" option. This extreme generalization would be justifiable if the researcher intended to use this question only to divide the respondents into two groups, those who did, and those who did not, use the film strips. Even with this research purpose, however, the use of only these two options would be poor public relations because it would leave the sensitive respondent feeling that he had no accurate opportunity to indicate his use of these particular materials.

The two-option answer need not be restricted to "yes," "no," questions but can include questions which ask the respondent to "agree" or "disagree," to indicate whether he is "satisfied" or "dissatisfied," or any two-dimensional response. The great advantage of the two-option answer is that it does force the respondent to take a position at one end of the dimension or the other. This advantage, of course, is its own drawback, in that the approach is usable and sensible only in those instances when the choice offered is truly a two-dimensional choice and only two-dimensional, that is, in which the respondent really must hold one opinion or the other and there is no opportunity to have an intermediate feeling or opinion.

Since few questions involving opinion or feeling are so simply structured, researchers are wiser to offer respondents a set of several alternatives, and so avoid the disadvantage of forcing a choice between two extremes. This more closely simulates reality by providing the respondent with different positions along the response continuum. In a sense, this takes cognizance of the fact that few issues of opinion are "yes," and "no," kinds of issues and that people generally will occupy different positions along the dimension of the study or positions which are different in degree, rather than extremely opposite.

Thus, in the second version of the question in the list above the researcher has approached the problem by offering four options, three providing some gradation of use, the fourth indicating no use. The problem in this version is that the researcher has stated these options in terms of the ambiguous words "frequently," "sometimes," and "once in a while." He now forces the respondent to translate his actual use of the materials into one of these terms, and the researcher is forced to assume that all of the respondents will use the same basis for these translations. To avoid this assumption, the third version states the options in terms of specific time periods with no ambiguity possible. Now every respondent who selects the first option is making the same statement: He has used the film strips at least four times a week.

No aspect of the questionnaire is more critical than the selection and development of the answer formats to be used. It was noted earlier in this discussion that any one questionnaire may employ one, all, or any combination of answer formats. In fact, within one question it is possible to have a series of structured options followed by an unstructured option asking "why," or "please explain your answer," or "please give an example of your answer." However it is done, the researcher must be certain that his answer formats meet the double goal of the questionnaire: providing every respondent with the ability to answer in a way which reasonably reflects his answer and providing the researcher with the data he needs, in the form in which he needs them, to answer the research question.

THE CHECK LIST   When one uses the extremely structured format above exclusively on an instrument for questioning, although it is still a questionnaire, the practice has developed of calling the technique the *check list.* By definition then the check list is simply a questionnaire in which the totally structured format is used exclusively or with some use of the free-response option. Its advantages are those of the totally structured format: ease of response and of data analysis. Therefore, if the researcher knows the full range of possible responses to all of his questions, and believes that the respondents will be willing to accept this relatively passive role of indicating which of the potential answers apply to him, the check list is a sensible technique for questioning.

WHEN QUESTIONNAIRE OR CHECK LIST IS APPROPRIATE   The questionnaire or check list techniques are appropriate only for those research problems in which the information sought is sufficiently structured so that it can be explained by means of a printed question, and for the researcher to be content to abandon any possibility of follow-up or tangential questions. The research population must be sufficiently literate for the impersonal interaction with its communication through reading and writing to be feasible. These two conditions must be met for either technique to be appropriate, but in addition the researcher should consider the nature of the selected sample. If it is in excess of 100, and/or is widely scattered geographically, these characteristics, too, will suggest the use of the questionnaire or check list. Finally, as we have noted earlier the selected sample must be sufficiently homogeneous for the researcher to believe that he will have a useful and usable set of data even if the proportion of responses drops below 50 percent.

Instruments for Information-Seeking Questioning

The first step in developing an instrument for information-seeking questioning is for the researcher to draw a blueprint for the instrument. This blueprint simply defines the several aspects of the problem area about which information is needed, and indicates the relative importance of each aspect *to the problem under study*. The italicized words are intended to emphasize the basic point that the specification of aspects and particularly the indication of relative importance is unique to each specific research problem. A simple way of handling the indication of relative importance is to jot down a percent which reflects the relative importance of the area. It is suggested that this blueprint be developed at the beginning, before any specific questions are written, for it can then serve as an estimate of what the instrument should contain and how the questions should be allocated completely independent of the estimate which comes later from the number of questions which can be thought of in each area.

The blueprint also serves as the foundation for the content validity of the instrument, the strongest validity argument possible in questioning. For the content validity argument to have strength, the blueprint must be based on a thorough understanding both of current practice in the field and of both the research and nonresearch literature in the problem area. In short the blueprint is a summary statement expressing the researcher's and others' feelings as to the specific aspects of the problem area and their relative importance.

A final aspect of the blueprint is to relate it to the research situation by estimating how much of the respondent's time can be asked for by the researcher to ask his questions. Some rough estimate of this time should be in the researcher's thinking from the beginning of his work on the instrument.

The next step in the approach to constructing any instrument for any of the techniques involving questioning for information is to get onto paper all possible information which might be sought. In this second stage the researcher should not be concerned with niceties of language like wording, grammar, or parts of speech. Nor should he be concerned with repeating a question or whether he ultimately can ask certain questions nor whether he can possibly ask all of the questions on the list. These are all proper concerns for later stages in the instrument development, but at this stage it is more important to brainstorm and free associate so that the maximum number of questions get onto paper.

It will expedite later stages considerably if the "paper" used in this second stage consists of 3×5 cards, with a separate question on each card. The reason for the use of cards is that the third stage of the instrument development is to try to group the several questions which were written down into major areas within the content area of the instrument. This process of grouping is considerably simplified if the separate questions are physically on separate cards, for then the researcher can shuffle and reshuffle them at will.

With the questions written, we must now consider each area separately. Our aim is to study the questions in each area and sort them into four packs to identify four kinds of questions: (1) questions based on aspects of the problem area which *must* be asked if the area is to be thoroughly covered; (2) questions based on aspects which are both important and relevant even if not critical in the same sense or to the same degree as the first set; (3) questions which are relevant and/or interesting but neither critical nor important; and (4) questions which emerged during the brainstorming and free-association session but which on second look are either not relevant or are covered in some other and better question. Put aside the third and fourth packs and work seriously with the first and second packs.

It is at this point that the researcher can make his initial research estimate of the length required for the instrument by totaling the number of questions in categories one and two. This initial content estimate is compared to the estimate in the blueprint of the length to be desired in terms of access to the respondents. If they are reasonably close together the researcher is in the happy but rare position of being able to include almost all of the questions he would like to include. In the more usual instance when the researcher finds that he has more questions than the blueprint will allow, he enters the critical and difficult phase of instrument development in questioning in which he must eliminate information he has already classified as either critical or important. There is no easy guideline for this editing operation other than to begin with the second category of less critical items, and to scan all of the items for repetition and redundancy.

We should not be surprised if, at the end of this thorough examination of the two major categories, we have not saved very much in the way of items, for what typically happens is that during the examination of the items new items come to mind, some of which we believe belong in this first or second category. Hopefully we come through the operation somewhat ahead, that is, we cut more than we add! However, all researchers ultimately experience a situation in which, on this initial run-through, they actually save no items and even lose ground. When this happens, of course, we simply must repeat the operation with more rigorous standards for retaining a question.

At this point, with a set of questions which successive editing has convinced him are critical to obtaining the needed information to answer the research question, the researcher considers the ways in which he will ask his respondents to answer the questions, for the answer format is the third element (together with the respondent's time available and the number of questions) which will determine the ultimate length of the instrument.

This blueprint establishes the approximate length desired in the final instrument, in terms of number of separate items. The final decision as to length is a complex professional decision involving the researcher's initial estimate of how much of the respondent's time he will have available, how many questions will be required to cover the content areas thoroughly and properly, and the nature of the response the instrument will require, that is, how long it will take the respondents to answer each question. If all the respondent need do is circle an option ("yes," "no," or "don't know"), the time required to respond is basically only the time that the respondent needs to read the question and think through his opinion so that he is ready to respond. The actual time needed to produce the response is negligible, thus many such questions can be answered in a brief period of time, with four or five questions a minute a reasonable estimate for literate adults interested in and willing to respond to the instrument. In contrast, for questions which require that the respondent not only read the question and think through to the response but also that he write out his response in some detail, as in any free-response question, the researcher must not only allow for the time needed to read and understand the question and think through to the answer, but also for the time required to write the response. Obviously, there can be no guideline given as to how many questions of the free-response type can be answered. This depends upon the complexity of the written response which is required and upon the respondents themselves, particularly their literacy and fluency. If time is an important consideration, and it almost always is, then we should be certain that at some point in the instrument-development process we try out a reasonably accurate prototype of the final instrument so that we can obtain some estimate of how much time it takes for the respondents to complete it.

In the questionnaire technique, length is an issue not only in terms of the number of separate questions to be asked, but also in terms of the sheer physical bulk of the instrument. With experience we learn that every page added to the questionnaire lessens the proportion of respondents who will complete it. Therefore, the thorough researcher not only considers how many questions he can eliminate and still retain the integrity of his research, but also considers ways of physically reducing the bulk of the instrument. One effective procedure we can follow to cut length while retaining information is to see if there are several questions which seek a common kind of information and in which the answer format is the same. If so, these can often be consolidated in a check list which will retain their separate identities yet eliminate the space-consuming redundant answers. For example, consider the researcher in the Phonics Study who might wish to ask teachers who participated to indicate how often they used workbooks, film strips, readers, study guides, and teacher guides which were provided. Initially he decides to ask for each piece of information in a separate question and so writes the first question as: "How often did you use the workbooks provided?" He then intends to provide six options: "every day," "three or four times a week," "once or twice a week," "no more than once every two or three weeks," "only once or twice during the experiment," and "never." After he has written these six options to each of the five different instructional aids, he has devoted two pages to obtaining these five simple pieces of information. The fact that the same answer options are repeated should clue him to the fact that these five questions can easily be consolidated by using a two-dimensional check list as below. In this format, the questions are placed vertically and the answers horizontally, so that all five questions can now be stated in the space that previously was required for one. The question now becomes a more general question and includes specific instructions on how to respond. For example, it might read like this:

Listed below are five instructional aids provided for the experiment. Indicate, by placing a check in the appropriate column, how often you used *each* of these five aids. You should place a check next to each of the five aids.

Frequency of Use

Aid	Every Day	3 or 4 Times a Week	Once or Twice a Week	No More than Once Every 2 or 3 Weeks	Only Once or Twice during the Experiment	Never
Workbooks						
Film strips						
Readers						
Study guides						
Teacher guides						

We continue repeating these editing and consolidating operations as often as necessary until the instrument has been whittled down to the minimum length possible. This obviously means that we must eliminate some questions we would like to ask and even some we believe to be important. This is all but inevitable in developing a set of questions, for a researcher can seldom ask all that he would like to ask.

What we must keep in mind at all times are the purposes of the research and the basic blueprint of the total instrument. These must be maintained, and so these intermediate stages of development always involve shuttling back and forth from area to area, trying to balance the elimination of two questions in one area by the addition of one question in a related area. It is also wise at this stage to return to the discards in the original set of questions to determine whether or not some of the original questions since eliminated now have a different importance or usefulness. To be certain that the content validity has been maintained, once the final version of this draft is ready, we go back to the original blueprint to make certain that the areas derived from the literature and our experience are present as intended and reasonably close to the proportions intended.

Given a draft of reasonable length, the researcher may then move on to the pilot-testing phase in which he will verify the clarity of the language and the intent of the questions.

Questioning for Behavioral Description

THE INCIDENT TECHNIQUE   The techniques just discussed—the interview, questionnaire, and check list—are appropriate when the researcher's purpose is to obtain a broad range of information. A quite different technique of questioning is available when the researcher is interested in questioning for the purpose of behavioral description of a relatively specific nature. For example, in the nursing project mentioned earlier in this book, directed by the author, we were interested in questioning nursing students and female college undergraduates to obtain insight into situations they had recently experienced which they had found satisfying and others which they had found stressful. In a sense we wanted only these two pieces of information from any one student. But we wanted the questions to elicit a reasonably detailed description of one satisfying and one stressful situation. Given this circumstance, the need for a few, but detailed, descriptions of situations, the technique for questioning which is particularly appropriate is the *critical incident technique,* developed by John Flanagan[17] in the 1950s. Its unique usefulness lies in the fact that it combines some of the advantages of the impersonal interaction (particularly its applicability to large groups of respondents) with the fact that the respondents themselves select events or incidents of significance to them. Thus, as opposed to observational techniques for recording behavior, the critical incident technique avoids the problem of the perception of the outside observer reading motives into the behavior of the respondent.

As Table 18-1 indicated, the incident technique is used with the impersonal or mixed interaction and the limited free-response answer format. Specifically, what the critical incident technique involves is the researcher posing a highly structured question for the respondent in which he, the respondent, is asked to recall an actual incident of a specific type and describe that incident in detail. He may also be asked to describe specific auxiliary circumstances such as what led up to the incident, who was involved, and what happened after the incident. In other words, he puts on paper a transcription of a specific behavioral situation and such other circumstances as the researcher requests.

The "critical" dimension in the technique involves asking the respondent to think of an extreme illustration of the behavior under study. In our nursing example the continuum being studied involves identifying examples of satisfying or stressful situations. To identify the critical ends of the continuum we would ask the student to describe "the most satisfying" or "most stressful" situation she had experienced recently. Similarly, were we studying effective and ineffective teaching behaviors, the respondent would be asked to identify examples of the "most effective" and "least effective" instances of teaching he had observed. Many researchers, including this author, have used the technique without the "critical"

[17]John C. Flanagan, "The Critical Incident Technique," *Psychological Bulletin,* vol. 131, no. 4 (July 1954), p. 327.

dimension and it seems to work fully as well, producing incidents as detailed and as deep in concept and language as those produced when the critical dimension is added. In this instance, the respondent is asking to identify a "satisfying situation" or an "effective instance of teaching."

The major problem with the critical incident technique is the analysis of the data. The basic unit for data analysis consists of the description of the situations which may run from a few words, or a few dozen words, to several hundred words. If the intent of the research is only to learn about the frequency of occurrence of certain specific aspects of situations, such as how often teachers of different subject areas are named in the incidents describing successful and unsuccessful teaching experiences, data analysis is not a major problem. Here the basic piece of data to be derived from the analysis is identified in advance, is specific, and therefore can be counted directly from the incidents themselves. The only problem is the time involved in reading through all of the material until the subject field of the teacher is noted.[18] However, if the aim of the analysis is to extract from the situations some synthesis of the kinds of teaching situations the respondents consider effective and ineffective, then the problem of data analysis falls into the realm of content analysis, a technique for analyzing verbal data, discussed in Chapter 22. Content analysis is intellectually challenging but also tremendously time consuming. Furthermore content analysis requires masses of data to provide a basis for the data analysis, and therefore Flanagan suggests that the critical incident technique not be employed unless at least 2000 incidents will be available to form the basis for the content analysis.[19]

Whatever the difficulties of analysis, the general experience of researchers who work with incident data (with or without the critical dimension) is extremely positive. It is the one questioning technique which inevitably moves to the depth level and which yields data so rich that we feel we are dealing with reality and are learning about real people functioning as individuals rather than faceless numbers or a circled response to a structured question. If behavioral description is the research goal, and we also wish to obtain masses of data, this is the technique to consider.

CRITICAL INCIDENT INSTRUMENT   The instrument used in a critical incident study may appear deceptively simple, for it can consist of a single question at the head of a blank sheet of paper on which the respondents can describe the incident. Yet this simple instrument has within it four components each of which is significant in the development of the instru-

---

[18]If this were the intent, the researcher should have added to the directions a notation that the respondent should be certain to spell out the subject field or content area of the teachers involved.

[19]Flanagan, "The Critical Incident Technique," p. 343.

ment: (1) the criterion continuum from which the respondents are to select incidents; (2) the selection of the referent from which the respondent shall write; (3) the direct stimulus question; and (4) the auxiliary circumstances which the respondent will be specifically asked to identify.

IDENTIFYING THE CRITERION CONTINUUM   Developing the instrument for use in the critical incident technique begins by identifying the types of behaviors about which we wish to learn and then identifying the criterion continuum by which we wish the respondents to select the incidents which they are to report.

For example, had a researcher decided that he wished to learn about teaching behavior, this would identify the content area for the incident. But he then must go on to decide the criterion continuum. Does he want his respondents to report successful and unsuccessful teaching behavior? Is he more interested in learning about what the respondents consider creative and stereotyped teaching behavior? Is his interest more for the continuum of effective and ineffective teaching behaviors?

The decision as to the specific criterion continuum to be employed is of course determined by the research question and the researcher's specific interests and curiosities. However, since few questions are asked in studies using the incident technique, considerable thought and care must go into selecting the few continua which can be studied. It is often useful to conduct some pilot studies using various continua so that some data are available to help the researcher decide which continua do provide different types of incidents and which do not. In our illustrations in the paragraph above, the researcher might discover that whether he asks for "effective-ineffective" or "successful-unsuccessful" teaching incidents makes little difference, for in both instances he obtains descriptions of situations which are defined by how much children learned. In contrast he might find that the "creative-stereotyped" continuum yields a different kind of incident, defined more in terms of what the teacher does. Thus the pilot data would have provided insight into some redundancy among the contemplated criteria, as well as into the kinds of incidents each elicits.

Unless the research question is so specific as to directly state the criterion continuum, some pilot efforts like these are in order to help narrow down the list of potential continua to those eventually to be employed. The author's own research has indicated that as many as 12 incident questions can be completed in an hour of respondent time when the respondents are extremely involved and willing to write for that long. However, in most research projects three or four incident questions are the most which can be expected of respondents, and so some choice is usually necessary to select the three or four most critical continua from among all those which might be studied.

SELECTING THE REFERENT   In the incident technique a person is asked to describe only situations he has experienced firsthand. However, these may be either incidents in which he actually participated or incidents which he observed. It is the researcher who selects the referent by indicating in the directions to the respondent whether he is asked to report an incident in which he participated or one which he observed. In some research problems the problem itself establishes the referent. For example, in a study comparing teacher and principal perceptions of effective and ineffective administrative practices, the teachers must be asked to write impersonal incidents, that is, practices which they have observed principals perform. However, the principals could be asked to write about their own practices which they considered effective and ineffective or else asked to write about practices they have observed in other principals. The researcher must make this decision.

There are two schools of thought about these two different kinds of referents. One school argues that people will write more freely and candidly about situations in which they did not participate. This school also argues that since the criterion continuum in the incident technique frequently is an evaluative one (that is, effective-ineffective, creative-stereotyped) the researcher is more likely to obtain incidents based on dispassionate evaluations if the respondent was not personally involved.

The other school of thought argues that one of the unique qualities of the technique is that it makes available to the researcher a self-evaluation and appraisal which is available through no other technique. But this advantage can only be fully realized if the respondent is asked to describe situations in which he participated.

There is no clear evidence, as this book is written, that the use of the personal referent results in any loss of freedom or frankness. In fact, in the author's own experience with the technique, when this point was tested there was no discernible difference in the kinds of incidents which were written by those respondents who were writing about their own experiences and those who were writing about experiences they had observed. Thus, the author recommends that when a choice is possible the personal referent be used to capitalize on the self-evaluation features of the technique.

WRITING STIMULUS QUESTION   Once the dynamic to be studied and the referent have been selected, the researcher can write the stimulus questions. This is not always as simple a procedure as it would seem, since the English language is particularly ambiguous in words that describe dynamic aspects of human functioning. For example, the mid-1960s saw a proliferation of research and discussion on creativity, a good portion of which was devoted to arguments as to what kinds of acts were creative acts. The researcher who wishes to ask teachers to describe for him "their most creative lesson" must be concerned with whether or not all of his respondents will interpret "creative" in the same way or whether some will try to recall the most vivid example of divergent thinking, others will try to think of a way in which they used old materials in a new way, and still others will try to remember a new and different lesson which they had never done before. Similar problems would be faced by researchers seeking to study dynamics like "effective teaching" (where the respondents would have to decide the criteria by which to evaluate a lesson as effective) or "democratic administrative practices" (where the concept of democratic would have to be translated into behavioral terms).

The researcher can handle this problem in three different ways. The simplest, but most treacherous, is to assume that respondents will all interpret the stimulus words in the same way. The critical incident elicited is too much a function of the association to the stimulus word or words for the thorough researcher to ignore the possibility of multiple interpretations. The second thing the researcher can do is to add supplementary words or phrases which will seek to make clear to the respondents precisely what he (the researcher) means by the words. If this sounds like the research equivalent of the scene in *Through the Looking Glass,*[20] when Humpty Dumpty says to Alice in rather a scornful tone, "When I use a word it means just what I choose it to mean—neither more nor less," in a sense it is, for that is what the researcher is seeking to accomplish. In this instance, the researcher who wanted to elicit examples of creative teaching characterized by divergent use of classroom materials would phrase his stimulus question so that it began: "Think of the most creative lesson you have taught in the last month, a creative lesson being one in which regular classroom materials are used in different or unusual ways."

This approach of defining the stimulus concept to maximize the likelihood that the respondent will understand the kinds of behaviors which the researcher is seeking to elicit is preferable to the first approach of simply assuming everyone will understand. The words and concepts used in the definition can come from the researcher's own thinking, from the literature, or even from people like the respondents themselves. For example, in the author's study of stressful situations, the question asking for a stressful incident was phrased this way:

> Sometimes things happen which are stressful to us. We may feel nervous, tense, fearful, rushed, anxious, confused, excited or tired. Of course all people feel and react differently and, when you are in stressful situations, you may

---

[20]Lewis Carroll, *Through the Looking Glass.* In *The Complete Works of Lewis Carroll* (New York: Modern Library, 1936).

experience one or more of these feelings or you may experience other feelings. Recall an incident that occurred during the past three months that was stressful to you. Describe the incident. Please be specific and tell exactly what happened.

The supplementary words used all came from a separate pilot study in which students like those to be studied, but not in schools in the selected sample, were given a sheet of paper and asked to list words which "describe how people feel or react when they are in a stressful situation." A simple frequency count of the words most often listed was then done, and the most frequent words were used in the stimulus question to define stressful for the respondents. It should be obvious that the quality and validity of the data obtained is directly related to the effectiveness with which the stimulus question communicates the researcher's intent, and so any effort, including a pilot study for definitional purposes, is well worth the expense and effort entailed.

The third thing the researcher can do to make his intent clear is to provide an example of the kind of incident he is seeking. While this will help in communicating his intent, it brings the obvious and serious risk that the particular example included will serve as a part of the stimulus as well. Should this happen then the researcher will find that his respondents will write incidents similar to the example in greater proportions than they would otherwise. Therefore the second way, of adding supplementary words or phrases to help avoid ambiguity, is preferred, particularly if these words and phrases have been selected on the basis of pilot data obtained from respondents like those used in the actual study.

DECIDING ON AUXILIARY INFORMATION   With the stimulus questions written the researcher can turn to the last aspect of instrument development: selecting which specific auxiliary information he will ask the respondents to supply. It is at this point that he must think ahead to the data-analysis stage and try to identify all those aspects of the situation that he wishes to use in the analysis of the data. For example, if he wishes to compare and contrast the kinds of teaching behaviors reported by teachers in different grades, then he must ask the teacher to record the grade about which she is writing if it was a personal incident, or the grade of the teacher about whom she is writing if it was impersonal. Similarly, the respondent should specifically be asked to refer to any variable for which analyses are to be done, such as the kind of class, the level of ability of the children, and so on. Moreover, any aspects of the situation which are required for the data analysis, such as what circumstances led up to the situation, who was involved, and what happened after the situation, should be specifically requested of all respondents.

However, we should only ask for those aspects which we must know, because asking a respondent to note a specific characteristic of the situation or people involved in the incident may also bias the selection of incidents. For example, an instruction asking for specification of the ethnic status of the children involved in the class may make the respondents take this variable into consideration as they consider what incident they should select and write down. To this extent, then, certain incidents will be written which might not have been had not this particular characteristic been asked for. But, as usual, the alternative also poses a problem: Not asking that ethnic status be specified means that it will be omitted in a large proportion of the incidents, and so these will have to be omitted from this phase of the data analysis.[21]

Thus, once again the basic responsibility of the researcher is to decide between two difficult alternatives, seeking to select that which will best help him realize his research purpose.

STEPS IN THE QUESTIONING METHOD

1. Determination that the questioning method is appropriate
2. Identification of the areas of content for questioning
3. Identification of the full range of specific questions which might be asked
4. Initial classification of potential questions into those considered critical for the research and those not critical
5. Identification of demands of research problem for a researcher-respondent interaction
6. Identification of the limits in respondent contacts
7. Selection of researcher-respondent interaction
8. Determination of the kinds of questions to be used and the format of the answers
9. Selection of the technique for questioning
10. Development of the instrument for questioning
11. Pilot studies to determine the characteristics of the instrument
12. Implementation of the data-gathering plan
13. Implementation of the data analysis plan
14. Preparation of the research report

As with all methods, the questioning method begins with a verification that the method is *appropriate* for the research problem or question. As we have noted at the beginning of this chapter, the questioning method is appropriate for any problem in which information is sought. Thus, in the Language Study when we were concerned with identifying the methods

---

[21]A further discussion of the problems in handling omits appears in Chapter 20.

teachers were currently using to teach English as a second language, once we had identified the need for this information we had identified a problem for which questioning was appropriate.

The next steps then are the *identification of the areas of content* for the questioning, and the *identification of the full range of specific questions which might be asked*. This is what we have previously referred to as preparing the blueprint for questioning. It needs to be done whether the study will involve a multiplicity of questions, as in studies using the questionnaire technique, or will involve a few questions, as in studies involving the critical incident technique. In fact, it is the multiplicity of potential questions identified at this early stage which provides the researcher with his first clue to the most appropriate technique for this specific research problem. It is suggested that this series of early steps conclude with the researcher making an initial *classification of these potential questions into those considered critical for the research and those* which, while useful and/or interesting, are *not critical* to the research. This, too, will structure the specific needs for information which ultimately will be translated into researcher-respondent interaction and data-gathering technique.

When this first concern with content is completed, the researcher next turns to the researcher-respondent interaction, so that the fifth step is to *identify the demands of the research problem for researcher-respondent interactions*. It is at this stage that the researcher considers whether the kinds of information he seeks can be stated with sufficient clarity and precision to make impersonal interactions possible, or whether they require the flexibility of explanation and/or the potential for asking unexpected questions of the personal interactions. At this stage he is not concerned with the limits of reality, for that will be considered later. Instead he is considering only what would be ideal in terms of the research problem.

Having done this, he then injects reality into the planning by the *identification of the limits in respondent contacts*. It is here that the researcher considers questions like how much of the respondent's time is likely to be available to him, the circumstances under which he will have access to the respondents, the literacy level of the respondents (particularly critical in research with school children), the knowledgeability of the respondents in the area to be studied, and any other variable that would have some bearing on the specific study which is being planned. This is a vital stage, for it will not only have bearing on the immediately sequent stage but on the later stages as well.

Having identified these limits, the researcher then integrates stage five, where he identified the kinds of interaction the research problem demanded, and stage six, where he identified the limits to the interaction set by the nature of, and circumstances surrounding, his respondents. This integration leads to the *selection of the researcher-respondent interaction* to be used. As we have noted so often, research planning is a matter of compromise. While the researcher would like to achieve the ideal he delineated in stage five, he must be willing to modify that ideal in terms of the realities identified in stage six. For example, no matter how sensible an impersonal interaction may be in terms of a research problem, if the respondents cannot read then some other interaction will be necessary!

With this decision made, the researcher returns to the direct matters of questioning, to *determine the kinds of questions he will use and the format of the answers.* Note that this stage follows the stage in which content is identified as well as the stage in which the researcher-respondent interaction is selected. This sequence is suggested because both question type and response format are considered tools which can be adjusted and adapted so that the needed information is realized in each of the possible researcher-respondent interactions. In contrast, as we have just noted in the last sentence of the paragraph above, there are some interactions which are totally unfeasible, and similarly there is some content which must be achieved. Because these two stages have these inflexible elements, decisions about them precede the decisions about the more flexible issue of format for question and response.

With the formats and researcher-respondent interaction selected, it is a relatively simple matter to *select the technique for questioning,* because in most instances all of the elements which have been considered in the preceding stages combine to one and only one technique. If more than one technique is possible, the deciding criterion is, as always, the research question and the data needed to answer that question.

With the technique selected, the researcher moves on to *develop the instrument for questioning.* As we have noted, the complexity of this stage depends upon the technique for questioning to be employed. In the critical incident technique, instrument development is relatively simple, as it is a matter of finding the best wording for the one or two stimulus questions. In other instances, like the interview or questionnaire, instrument development involves the long process of winnowing the list of all possible questions that might be asked down to the actual set of questions that can be asked. But no matter whether this stage is short or long, in all applications of the questioning method the instrument development stage should be followed by *pilot studies to estimate the characteristics of the instrument.* In fact, in some instances, the pilot studies are conducted during the instrument-development stage to guide decision making in this stage.

It is easy for the researcher to delude himself that there is no need for pilot studies in the questioning method. After the work involved in selecting question and answer formats, and particularly after the lengthy process of rewriting and editing which typifies instrument development for the questionnaire or interview techniques, the researcher may decide that every question is clear and every answer appropriately provided for. But until the questions are asked of persons like those to be in the data-producing sample, no researcher can be certain that he has eliminated all possible ambiguity[22] and has provided for all possible relevant responses. As noted above, the researcher may prefer to begin pilot studies midway through the instrument-development stage. If so, he may use these studies to try out different wordings for the stimulus questions and different response formats. In this event he actually has some data available to guide his choices and decisions as he completes the instrument-development stage.

While all of the techniques for questioning are forced to rely on content validity, in the longer techniques like the questionnaire it is possible to obtain some statistical element of reliability. This is done by seeking the same information through different questions or through different question and answer formats. If this is done, the researcher can obtain an estimate of reliability by computing the percentage of times he obtains the identical information from these deliberately redundant questions. Of course, the instrument must be sufficiently long and complex for the researcher to be able to argue that the respondent was actually responding twice and not simply repeating a remembered response to a recognized repeated question. There is no general way to define "sufficiently long" in the preceding sentence. Each researcher must decide whether or not his instrument provides this kind of test for the respondent, but he can use the pilot study itself to help him by simply asking the participants if, when they answered question 38, they were aware that the same information was sought as they had already provided in question 5.

In questioning as in observation or measurement, the pilot-study stage may produce positive or negative results. If positive, the researcher moves on to the implementation stages that follow. If negative, he returns to those stages that have caused trouble. One of the delights of the questioning method is that almost any of the stages can be troublesome! The researcher may find that his decision on needed content was wrong and that his questions did not provide the needed data. He may find that the researcher-respondent interaction which he selected did not work as antic-

---

[22]The word "possible" is deliberately used here to indicate that there are some ambiguities in the language itself which even the most ingenious use of language will not eliminate.

ipated, or he may find that the question and answer formats did not function successfully. It is because of this multiplicity of potentially troublesome stages that the pilot-study stage is so critical in the questioning method.

Assuming that at some point the pilot-study stage is successfully completed, the researcher is ready to move into the three implementation stages involving the *data-gathering and data-analysis plans* and the *preparation of the research report.*

Chapter 19

THE MEASUREMENT METHOD
AND TECHNIQUES FOR MEASURING

Measuring is a method of inquiry which in the physical sciences goes back into antiquity. In the behavioral sciences it has a much younger heritage, beginning with the first psychological laboratory by Wundt in Leipzig, in 1879. But these first efforts to measure, although conducted in the name of psychology, were heavily physical in nature. It was only in the twentieth century that measurement moved into educational, psychological, and sociological areas like attitudes, achievement, intelligence, aptitude, personality characteristics, interests, and motivations. But it has been a slow movement, with progress limited, as these aspects of human functioning have proven to be difficult to measure. Therefore, the general caution in planning research involving measurement of the nonphysical attributes of human functioning is that many of the measures available at present are relatively primitive prototypes of what we must ultimately develop if we are to move significantly forward in the use of this method.

The process of measurement involves a four-step process: (1) the delineation of what needs to be measured in terms of the research problem; (2) the selection of the appropriate technique for measurement; (3) the selection or development of an instrument; and (4) the collection and analysis of the data. Historically, the social disciplines have differed in that stage of the process where they have had difficulty. For example, psychoanalytic research has had its greatest difficulty in the analysis of the data. There has been general agreement in this field that the motivational structure of the individual is what needs to be measured. There has also been agreement, although to a lesser extent, that projective techniques do measure motivational structure, and a variety of such instruments have been developed. The difficulty has been in achieving any real ability to meaningfully and consistently interpret the data obtained. In contrast, researchers in social psychology and sociology have also known what they

570

need to measure, that is, social processes, but have been bogged down in the efforts to develop sound measuring techniques and instruments.

Education has exemplified a third variation, where the difficulty lies in determining what needs to be measured. What are the characteristics of an educational situation which, if measured, would delineate good teaching? What phenomena would identify the entering freshman who will be functioning in teaching ten years hence? What do we measure to predict the reaction when teacher X works with child Y? What characteristics would provide data to meaningfully explain the nonresponse of child Z to his school and teacher, in contrast to the vigorous response of child B? All of these questions exemplify the basic difficulty faced in educational research in utilizing measurement as a data-gathering method: knowing what to measure. In large part this stems from the lack of any clear theoretical formulations in education or its allied disciplines which would guide the search for measures. For it is those disciplines that have developed theories which have most successfully gone past this first stage of knowing what to measure.

This lack of knowing what to measure was dramatically illustrated during the mid-1960s when the focus of educational research and practice turned to the disadvantaged child. Innumerable programs and projects foundered on their inability to define the child with whom they were concerned in sufficiently specific terms so that any meaningful effort could be made to measure the characteristics of the children. And so educators and psychologists who began with a belief that disadvantaged children were disadvantaged in areas like cognitive processes, levels of symbolic thinking, richness of visual and auditory stimulation, self-concept, and level of aspiration had by the end of the decade fallen back to defining the children in terms of income and father's occupation. Why? Because one set of characteristics could be translated into measurable terms and the other could not.

This particular series of events also exemplified one other trait which has characterized the history of measurement in the social disciplines: a willingness to define problems in terms of easily measurable constructs and to settle for existing measures rather than grapple with the more difficult problems involved in developing operational definitions of new constructs and new measures for these constructs.

This is stressed at this point in the belief that the single most important point for the researcher contemplating the use of the measurement method to recognize is that using inapplicable constructs or inappropriate measures only because they are readily available dooms a study to failure. While this is true of all methods, the history of research in education and the other social disciplines indicates that it is most likely to happen in studies involving measurement, probably because the difficulty of blazing a new trail in measurement is so much greater than in observation or questioning.

This increased difficulty is attributable to the fact that while, unhappily, we have been willing to ignore criteria such as reliability and validity in studies that use observation or questioning, we have applied them to studies that use measurement. Thus the researcher who plans on using a newly created measure must develop this to a reasonable level of reliability and validity before his measure, and therefore his study, will be seriously considered.

In Chapter 12 we discussed the process required to develop a new measure which satisfactorily meets the standards for research. It is a long and difficult process, and one which may end in failure as readily as in success. Nevertheless, the author believes that a researcher must be willing to face this process if the only available alternative is the distorted use of an inapplicable construct.

MEASUREMENT AS A DATA-GATHERING METHOD

Of the three methods considered in this book, the measurement method is the most confusing to discuss. This is because while the method has some unique processes, it relies heavily on the processes of questioning and observation previously discussed as discrete methods in their own right. But while this similarity of process may be confusing, the method can be clarified by recognizing that the purpose and goal of the process is different in each method. When a question is asked as part of the measurement method it is not because the answer is required or unknown (as in the questioning method) but rather because that answer, particularly when combined with several other answers, provides an estimate or measure of some aspect or characteristic of the respondent, such as his knowledge-ableness, attitude, or personality structure. Similarly, when for measurement purposes we observe a respondent as he performs some sample of a complex work task, we are not interested in learning about or recording the specific behaviors, but rather in obtaining an estimate or measure of some component of his repertoire of skills and abilities.

Because measurement uses the processes of observation and questioning, all that has been said in the preceding two chapters about the elements of these processes applies with equal force when they are used to measure. This point is noted to alert the reader that this chapter on measurement presupposes his familiarity with the preceding two chapters on observation and questioning and will refer to, rather than repeat, those chapters.

When Measurement Is Appropriate

Measurement as a data-gathering method is appropriate for all the four levels of research discussed in Chapter 13. One can measure at any of the three conscious levels, with the measurements of physical characteristics an example of the surface level, the measurement of interests on the subsurface level, and the measurement of attitudes on the depth level. But unlike questioning, measurement is also possible at the nonconscious level as we seek to estimate characteristics such as motivational or personality structure.

Table 19-1 presents a summary of the kinds of variables for which measurement is an appropriate data-gathering method in the social disciplines. A glance at the table will indicate that to consider whether or not measurement is the appropriate method one must take into account two characteristics: the kind of variable about which information is being sought and the social unit which is being studied. There are three social units outlined in the figure: individuals, groups of individuals, and institutions. Then vertically are listed five categories of characteristics which can be measured, ranging from physical characteristics through cognitive, attitudinal, and psychological characteristics to the effort to estimate how the individual, group, or institution functions. Finally, examples of variables appropriate for measurement are indicated in the cells of the table.[1]

This conceptualization of measurement can be exemplified by considering a class of 29 third-grade children sitting in a room while a teacher conducts an arithmetic lesson. A researcher could seek to measure characteristics of the children, such as their height and weight, interest in arithmetic, motivation for learning, or extroversion-introversion. He could also seek to measure some characteristic of the group, such as the sense of group identification the children feel or he senses, the climate of the classroom, or whom the children would prefer to sit next to. Or he might consider the teacher, seeking to measure aspects of her physical, cognitive, or attitudinal characteristics, or the quality of her teaching. Finally, he could move beyond the class to consider the institution of the school and measure aspects of its physical or attitudinal structure or organizational pattern.

[1]The entries in the cells are examples only and are not an all-inclusive list of characteristics which might be measured in the social disciplines.

Table 19-1 Visualization of the Types of Variables and Social Units Appropriate for Measurement, with Examples

Type of Variable	Individuals	Social Unit — Group	Institution
Physical characteristics	Height Weight Hearing acuity	Size Ethnic composition Gender composition	Size Facilities
Cognitive characteristics	Intelligence Academic achievement Cognitive style	Distribution of abilities, achievement, and so on	Intellectual climate
Attitudinal characteristics	Likes Interests Opinions	Social climate Sociometric pattern	Social climate Reputation
Psychological characteristics	Motivation Self-concept Personality structure	Leadership pattern Group pressure	Psychological orientation (permissive versus authoritarian)
Functioning processes	Ability to perform specific task	Interaction pattern Quality of decisions and problem solutions	Quality of functioning Organizational pattern

THE ELEMENTS OF MEASUREMENT

In applying the measurement method the researcher must consider five elements: (1) the variable about which information is desired; (2) the operational statement of the variable; (3) the measuring instrument; (4) the researcher-respondent interaction; and (5) the possibility of intervening variables.

Variable about Which Information Is Desired

All measurement begins with the identification of some variable or variables about which information is desired. The cells in Table 19-1 include some of the variables about which we seek information in the social disciplines. For the measurement process to get under way, the researcher must begin at the level of specificity represented by the entries in the cells, that is, he must be able to state that he wishes to obtain information about the "interests" of the individual students in the classes in the Language Study or about the "sense of group identification" of the children in the classes studied. But often this is an insufficient level of specificity, and to really move into the process the researcher must go further. For example, it would not be sufficient to refer to "interests" without stating some specification of the kinds of interests to be studied. Is the researcher interested in reading interests, in out-of-school interests in general, or in school subjects in which the child is interested? He would need to make this decision before he could move on to the next element in the method.

Operational Statement

For measurement purposes it is often not sufficient to simply identify the variable about which information is to be sought, for that variable may not be measurable directly. Thus, while information about the height of the children can be secured through direct measurement, information about their out-of-school interests or the sense of group climate in a class can not. For variables like these the researcher must develop an operational statement expressing some physical or verbal behavior in which the variable might be expressed and which *can* be measured. For example, the researcher might decide that out-of-school interests would be expressed in the number of activities in which a child would say he wanted to participate, if offered a list of possible activities. He might also decide that the sense of group identification would be expressed in the extent to which the children in the class remain together in a free-play situation at recess or in the lunchroom. Note that he has expressed one variable, out-of-school interests, in a verbal operational statement, whereas he has expressed the other, sense of group identification, in terms of physical behavior.

In reality, both variables involve physical behavior because out-of-school interests too are ultimately reflected in the activities in which the child actually does participate. But as so often happens in social research, the researcher in this example has decided that he would prefer to seek the verbal statement about activities rather than the actual physical behavior, because the verbal statement is so much simpler to acquire.

In fact, in considering this aspect of measurement it is possible to posit two kinds of reality, the *behavioral reality,* which consists of the person's actual behavior in real-life situations, and *verbal reality,* which consists of the person's verbal responses to operational verbal approximations of the real-life situation. Our concern in educational research and, in fact, in all of the social disciplines, is with human behavior. We do research to enable us to better understand human behavior, to better know what motivates it, ultimately to enable us to better predict it. In any event, the ultimate criteria through which we evaluate the usefulness of research data is their relationship to reality and the insights they provide into reality. Unlike the physical scientist who works with material phenomena, the social scientist has a problem in studying reality. He often finds it difficult, if not impossible, to reach what we have called behavioral reality, that is, what really does happen, how the respondent really does behave, how children do relate one to the other—their actual preferences, likes, and dislikes, their actual feelings and attitudes. Instead, he may have to do his research with verbal reality. The distinction essentially would be this: A child may dislike reading intensely and avoid it whenever possible. This is action reality. This is his true feeling. However, when asked by his teacher if he enjoys reading, because of the pressures stemming from relationships with the teacher, he may say "yes." This is the verbal reality, the reality at which the question functions. His response of "yes" to the question about his liking is not unreal. It is a real verbal response. However, as an estimator or measure of his true feeling, the action reality which governs his behavior, it is wrong, for in this instance the two realities are different.

In a sense, much of the history of research in education and in the social disciplines is the attempt to bridge these two realities and to bring them closer together, such that our research at the verbal level is truly related to and indicative of what will happen or what has happened at the action level. At present, it must be recognized that a gap, and a serious gap, still does exist between these two kinds of realities. While we may function effectively at the verbal level, this does not necessarily mean our data can be applied immediately and in a one-to-one relationship at the action level.

In developing his operational statements the researcher should take into account his own personal views and orientations as well as the views and orientations he has abstracted from the literature. Because the operational statements should be a synthesis of his own and others' thinking, it is often useful at this stage of the measurement method to return to the literature and selectively review those articles and studies which have treated the same variables under consideration in the current study.

The Measuring Instrument

Once the researcher has made what he considers a satisfactory operational statement of the variable or variables to be measured he can turn to the selection of the measuring instrument. Essentially he must end this stage with an instrument of satisfactory reliability which he considers valid for his research purpose and consistent with his operational statement of the variable.[2] If he is fortunate, during his review of the research literature he will find that such an instrument exists. If so, his only problem is to secure whatever permission is required to use this instrument.[3] Researchers are thus fortunate in some areas of educational research, such as the measurement of cognitive skills like the ability to read, or do arithmetic computations, or in the measurement of a wide variety of aptitudes and some aspects of interests. If he does not find an instrument he can use directly, the researcher may discover an existing instrument which he can adapt to his particular research needs and operational statement. Here again he requires permission, but in addition, once the adaptation is completed, he must obtain new data to demonstrate the reliability of the adapted instrument. He might also decide to estimate the validity or sensitivity.

In many areas of social research the researcher, despite the most thorough and exhaustive review of the literature, finds no instrument which fully meets acceptable standards of reliability and which looks to be valid for his research purpose and consistent with his operational statement of his variable. If there were absolutely no instruments at all, then the researcher would have no choice but to develop his own if he is to proceed with the research study. But in many instances he faces a more

[2]The reader is reminded that Chapter 12 might profitably be reviewed at this point, for it contains a detailed description of the characteristics which are desired in a measuring instrument.

[3]Minimally, the original author's permission is required. In addition, some payment may be involved for copyrighted or published instruments.

difficult dilemma, for what he has found during his review of literature are one or more instruments which are possibilities, but have one or more undesirable characteristics. Perhaps the reliability is low, or the instrument purports to measure something akin to but not quite what needs to be measured in the current study, and so its validity is doubtful. Or perhaps the instrument seems to have been developed by someone who had a somewhat different operational statement of the variable. The temptation to use this "almost" measure is difficult to resist, as almost any issue of any research journal will indicate. Realistically, instrument development *is* difficult and, perhaps even more serious for the student, requires extensive time and field testing. Therefore, when one horn of the dilemma is the process of developing a new instrument, and the other horn is using an existing instrument which is not quite what the researcher would have wanted, researchers have developed the ability to overlook the shortcomings of the existing instrument. They begin to think thoughts like "maybe the reliability will be higher this time," or "maybe my research purpose can be restated so that the instrument fits more sensibly into the purpose," or "maybe the other researcher's operational statement of the variable makes as much, or even more sense."

The author believes that many a promising research project has ended when thoughts like these are accepted and the decision made to use the existing instrument. If sufficient attention has been paid to the preceding steps in the research process, the research purpose and problem represent our best thinking about what we have wanted to study. Our operational statement about the variables, too, should represent our best efforts to synthesize our own thinking and experience and the thinking and experience of those others who have previously studied in our problem area. The products of this thinking, the research purpose and operational statements of the variables, should not be abandoned easily, and certainly not simply to avoid the effort which accompanies the process of instrument development. If these intellectual reasons do not suffice to convince us to resist the lure of the inadequate instrument, there are practical reasons as well. The reliability generally is *not* any better for us than it was for the original users of the instrument, the dubious validity is usually *not* strengthened by our revised research problem, and the data from the measure with a different operational statement of the variable will usually *not* be adequate.

Therefore, if we conclude our view of available instruments with the conclusion that none exist which we can use or adapt, we must accept the difficult fact that either we develop one or abandon the effort to measure this particular variable. Research using the measurement method is worth the time and effort required *only* if the measuring instruments meet all of the requirements for sound research instruments.

The Researcher-Respondent Interaction

As we noted in the beginning of this chapter, most measuring instruments involve some verbal interaction between researcher and respondent which fits within the models we developed in Chapter 18 for the questioning method or Chapter 17 for the observation method. Therefore, here we shall simply review these processes in the context of measurement, then consider other aspects of this interaction relevant for the measurement method.

INTERACTIONS WHEN OBSERVATION IS THE PROCESS   When observation is the process through which the measurement method is implemented, all three aspects of the researcher-respondent interaction discussed in Chapter 17 apply: (1) whether the observation is direct or indirect; (2) whether the fact of being observed is known or unknown to the respondent; and (3) whether the observer is perceived by the respondent as an outsider or participant. In Chapter 17 we discussed how the simple fact of being observed often induces sufficient concern and anxiety in respondents to considerably distort what the observer sees. We shall discuss below how the simple fact of being measured also induces anxiety and concern. Therefore, in a research process in which measurement is conducted by observation the researcher must pay considerable attention to techniques for maximizing the validity of respondent behavior. We discussed the advantages and disadvantages and ethical issues involved in the different interactions in observation in Chapter 17, but it is useful to repeat here that impersonality of the indirect interaction, with the researcher watching at a distance through television or motion picture, may be particularly useful for measurement purposes. It is also worth repeating that as serious as the ethical issues posed by unknown observation are in general, to the author they seem particularly critical in measurement. If a person is to be watched as he functions so that some estimate can be made of his functioning ability or personal characteristics, simple respect for the dignity of the individual would demand that he be told when, and by whom, the observation is to be made.

INTERACTIONS WHEN QUESTIONING IS THE PROCESS   In the discussion of the researcher-respondent interaction in questioning, in Chapter 18, three different interactions were noted: (1) the personal interaction in which the researcher and respondent meet in a one-to-one, face-to-face situation and exchange question and answer by word of mouth; (2) the impersonal interaction in which the researcher poses his questions on a piece of paper to a respondent he never sees who writes his answers on paper; and (3) the mixed interaction in which the researcher meets with groups of respondents to explain the research and/or the instrument, after which they answer questions written on paper as in the impersonal interaction.

All three of these interactions are possible when the questions are asked for purposes of measurement, with the mixed most frequent and the impersonal relatively infrequent. The mixed interaction occurs every time a researcher (or teacher) administers a test to a group of children or adults by explaining the purpose of the test and reading the directions, after which the group goes on to respond to the test questions as printed. The personal interaction occurs in instances in which individuals are measured as individuals, as in a test of visual acuity, or measurement of height, or in the administration of an individual test of intelligence such as the Wechsler Intelligence Scale for Children.

The impersonal interaction is rare for it would involve the researcher's mailing or otherwise delivering a self-explanatory measuring instrument to respondents who would answer the questions and return it. One well-known example of this interaction in measurement was the effort to measure verbal facility of teachers for the study "Equality of Educational Opportunity,"[4] better known as the Coleman Report.

In this study a test of verbal facility was sent to teachers by mail within a battery of questionnaires and attitude scales. They took the test at their leisure and returned it to the researcher with the rest of the battery by mail. The study by Coleman, as all studies which use the impersonal interaction in measurement, was open to the criticism that there was no way of knowing the extent to which the respondents used reference materials or consulted other persons before responding. The researcher has no response to this charge, other than to note the techniques he used to motivate the respondents to provide valid responses and, in some instances, to indicate that the distribution of scores suggests honest rather than dishonest responses.

ANXIETY AND MOTIVATION   In the discussion above on the researcher-respondent interaction when observation or questioning are the processes used for measurement, two constructs were mentioned which have not yet been discussed: *anxiety* and *motivation*.

The researcher contemplating the measurement method must understand that in many measurement situations, indeed some argue in all, there is a component of respondent anxiety to be considered. Whether the respondent is a child taking an achievement test, a student teacher teaching a sample lesson, a group of executives participating in a group interview as part of the selection process for higher office, or an adult

---

[4]James Coleman and others, *Equality of Educational Opportunity* (Washington, D.C.: Department of Health, Education and Welfare, 1966).

answering a questionnaire on his interests and aptitudes, to some extent all feel the implicit pressure which accompanies the measurement process in a test-oriented culture such as ours. This is because we have come to see measurement as synonymous with evaluation, and most individuals feel pressured when being evaluated. The researcher faces a particularly frustrating aspect of this pressure in that he may argue there should be no pressure when measurement is done for research purposes because the individual is not being evaluated but rather information is being gathered about characteristics of individuals or, more often, groups. The naive researcher may even decide that he can eliminate this pressure by assuring his respondents that he is not interested in them as individuals and does not even want to know their names. The realistic researcher knows that such verbal assurances may diminish but will not eliminate the pressure, and so throughout the measurement method he should be aware of the potential for anxiety.

Only if the researcher understands the potential pressures in the situation can he take measures to minimize anxiety and take the pressures into account both in his data analysis and writing of the research report. The basic techniques to minimize anxiety in measurement all involve persuading the respondent that he is not being studied as an individual, but rather as a representative of a role or as a member of a group. The most frequent way in which researchers seek to communicate this is to permit the respondent to remain anonymous. But this effort exemplifies a particularly troublesome aspect of handling respondent anxiety: Efforts to anticipate and diminish anxiety may very well have an interlocking and opposite effect on the respondent's motivation.

Thus, the researcher who takes strenuous efforts to convince a class of children that the material he is distributing is "a game we are about to play" and "is not a test, and will not count toward your work in school," and who may even add, "your teacher will never see what you write or know how well you have done," may have done an excellent job of alleviating much of the anxiety which the children might have experienced had they considered the task a test which their teacher *would* see and which *would* count toward progress in school. But this same effort may also have considerably diminished the motivation to work at the task for those children for whom the anxiety would have been a stimulating force.[5] Similarly, the adult whom the researcher has convinced he is not studying as an individual, and who is not asked to identify himself in any way, may so disassociate himself from the research that he fails to respond

---

[5]The literature on anxiety indicates that for some respondents it serves to stimulate and motivate and so elevate performance, while for other respondents it inhibits and depresses performance.

at all, or else responds with some half-hearted surface answers to what the researcher hoped would be subsurface or depth questions.

For these two factors not to interact and intertwine in a kind of reciprocal relationship so that each cancels the other, the researcher must find that thin line so that what he says to the respondents will serve to alleviate any inhibiting anxiety they may feel but which will simultaneously convince them of the necessity to respond seriously to the research instruments. With children it is the author's experience that the researcher should be more concerned with maintaining the motivational level than with anxiety, for children can accept the fact of measurement without crippling anxiety. With adults, in contrast, measurement can bring such a degree of anxiety that the researcher must deal with it. Moreover, once anxiety is relieved, adults can understand and generally will respond to explanations of the importance and significance of the research and the need for the data to be collected.

The Possibility of Intervening Variables

In the discussion of the experimental approach to research in Chapter 16, we discussed how the researcher had to consider the possibility that some variables would intrude or intervene in the ideally direct relationship between the independent variable being manipulated experimentally and the dependent variables being used as criteria for the experiment. A similar danger exists in measurement, in that a variable or variables may intervene in the relationship between respondent and measuring instrument. These intervening variables are the skills or abilities which are required to understand, and/or respond to, the measuring instrument. For example, many measuring instruments require a respondent to read before he can respond, even though there is no intent to measure his ability to read through the instrument. A paper-and-pencil test of social studies achievement would be a simple illustration of how this factor might operate. If the test were for children in grade 9, and the authors of the test assumed a reading level of at least grade 8, any child reading at grade 5 or 6 would be severely handicapped in reading the questions or the potential answers, and so his score would be a function both of his social studies information and his ability to read.

This problem was widely discussed in the educational literature in the late 1960s, generally in the context of measuring various cognitive skills of disadvantaged children. But it is a factor with wider applicability than one group or even one kind of measure. It affects any measure which involves reading and writing, such as interest inventories, opinionnaires, sociometric devices, or attitude scales. It operates with particular force in the impersonal interaction where the respondent has no ability to raise questions. One favorite counter-measure is to use the mixed interaction, in which the researcher meets with groups of respondents and paces them through the measuring instrument by reading all questions and potential answers. This helps if the intervening variable is ability to read. It does not help if the intervening variable is the ability to write, and so if that is a problem the researcher must revert to the personal, one-to-one interaction and permit the respondent to speak his answer while the researcher either transcribes it on tape or writes it down.

TECHNIQUES WITHIN THE MEASUREMENT METHOD

No method has the multiplicity of techniques the measurement method does, for in addition to techniques developed primarily for research use, one can use the wide variety of measurement techniques developed for evaluation and assessment, the wide variety developed for studies of attitudes, opinions, and interests, and the measures at the nonconscious level developed for clinical and diagnostic purposes.

At a general level of classification, there are six different kinds of measuring techniques used in the social disciplines: (1) *testing techniques* in which a question, problem, or task is posed for the respondent at the conscious level, and the accuracy of his responses or the efficacy of his performance used to generate some measure of his knowledge or skill; (2) *projective techniques,* which function at the nonconscious level, and in which a stimulus is presented to the respondent and his association to that stimulus recorded and interpreted in terms of some psychological dynamic; (3) *inventory techniques,* in which a multiplicity of questions are asked of or about the respondent so that the total amount of information amassed can be used to measure some characteristic of the individual or institution; (4) *sociometric techniques,* in which the members of a group or class are asked to indicate individual preferences by some social criterion; (5) *scaling techniques* in which a finite sample of concepts is ordered along a continuum in some instances with, in other instances without, quantitative measurement of the variable represented by the continuum; and (6) *physical measures* of the physical attributes or characteristics of respondents.

The last of these areas of measurement has received little attention in the literature on social research and will not be considered here because both the variables and the measures are clearly defined and present no problems of selection or use. Each of the other five areas deserves, and has, books specifically devoted to the area, and here space is not available to consider these techniques in comparable detail. Some detailed references are listed below.

1. Testing techniques: H. Gulliksen, *Theory of Mental Tests* (New York: John Wiley & Sons, Inc., 1950); Anne Anastasi, ed., *Testing Problems in Perspective* (Washington, D.C.: American Council on Education, 1966); Lee J. Cronbach, *Essentials of Psychological Testing* (New York: Harper & Row, Publishers, 1960).

2. Projective techniques: H. H. and G. L. Anderson, *An Introduction to Projective Techniques* (Englewood Cliffs, N.J.: Prentice-Hall, Inc., 1951); G. G. Stern, M. I. Stein, and B. S. Bloom, *Methods of Personality Assessment* (New York: The Free Press, 1956); A. C. Carr, et al., *The Prediction of Overt Behavior through the Use of Projective Techniques* (Springfield, Ill.: Charles C Thomas, Publisher, 1960).

3. Inventory techniques: Anne Anastasi, *Psychological Testing* (New York: Crowell-Collier and Macmillan, Inc., 1961); L. L. Thurstone and E. J. Chave, *The Measurement of Attitude* (Chicago: University of Chicago Press, 1929).

4. Sociometric techniques: J. Moreno, *Who Shall Survive?* (Washington, D.C.: Nervous and Mental Disease Publishing Co., 1934); Gardner Lindzey and Edgar F. Borgatta, "Sociometric Measurement," in Gardner Lindzey, ed., *Handbook of Social Psychology,* Vol. 1 (Reading, Mass.: Addison-Wesley Publishing Company, Inc., 1954).

5. Scaling techniques: Warren S. Torgerson, *Theory and Methods of Scaling* (New York: John Wiley & Sons, Inc., 1958); Charles E. Osgood, George J. Suci, and Percy H. Tannenbaum, *The Measurement of Meaning* (Urbana, Ill.: University of Illinois Press, 1957); William Stephenson, *The Study of Behavior: Q-Technique and Its Methodology* (Chicago: University of Chicago Press, 1953).

For the first four areas we shall develop an overview of the techniques available, then concentrate on the fifth area, scaling techniques, since these are relatively unique to research and are not generally treated in detail in books on the other areas.

Testing Techniques

The widest variety of measurement techniques available to the researcher are those which we shall group under the general heading of tests. Within this general heading come specific techniques as widely varied as paper-and-pencil objective tests, performance tests, and situational or work-sample tests. All of them are conducted at the conscious level, and all can be seen as involving the same dynamic situation: A problem is posed for the respondent and his response is evaluated by some value criterion, that is, "right–wrong," "well done–poorly done," "creative-stereotyped." The different tests differ basically in the nature of the problems they pose, the criteria they employ, the kinds of researcher-respondent interactions they require or permit, and the availability of measures.

OBJECTIVE TESTS   Objective tests typically pose a series of brief, specific problems or questions which have answers that can be defended as right or correct. Thus, they yield two kinds of measures for the researcher, the total number of correct responses each respondent obtains and whether or not each respondent knows the right answer to each question. If groups rather than, or as well as, individuals are the focus of the researcher's interests, he can translate this information into summary statistics about the group in these same two terms: the distribution of right answers within the group and the proportion of the group who knew the right answer to each question.

The rich variety of achievement and intelligence tests falls within this type, as do many of the tests of aptitude.[6] In almost every content area at the elementary and secondary level, there exist well-developed tests available to the researcher, so that test development is seldom necessary. For research with adults, fewer tests exist, and so researchers either adapt tests developed for the secondary level or develop their own, using one of the existing ones as a model.

The decade of the 1960s saw two important developments in the efforts to measure cognitive processes. One was research into cognitive style, which led to the development of instruments intended to measure this aspect of human functioning. The most widely used measure as the decade closed was the Embedded Figures Test[7] developed by Witkin. This measure bases the estimate of cognitive style on the ability of the respondent to extract a hidden figure from a confusing and distracting surrounding ground. While on first glance it may seem more a physical measure of some aspect of visual acuity or precision, research completed by Witkin,[8] Gardner,[9] and others[10] supports the argument that this test and similar visual tasks provide at least a gross classification of the

[6]Summaries of available measures in these areas appear in Robert L. Thorndike and Elizabeth Hagen, *Measurement and Evaluation in Psychology and Education* (New York: John Wiley & Sons, Inc., 1955). Also, Anne Anastasi, *Psychological Testing* (New York: Crowell-Collier and Macmillan, Inc., 1961).

[7]H. A. Witkin and others, *Psychological Differentiation* (New York: John Wiley & Sons, Inc., 1962).

[8]Witkin, *Psychological Differentiation.*

[9]R. W. Gardner and others, "Cognitive Control," *Psychological Issues,* monograph, 1959, p. 1.

[10]J. Kagan, H. A. Moss, and I. E. Sigel, "The Psychological Significance of Styles of Conceptualization." In J. C. Wright and J. Kagan, eds., *Basic Cognitive Processes in Children.* Monographs of the Society for Research in Child Development, vol. 28, no. 2 (1963), pp. 73–112. Also, S. Messick and F. J. Fritzky, "Dimensions of Analytic Attitude in Cognition and Personality," *Journal of Personality,* vol. 31 (1963), pp. 346–370.

respondent's cognitive style as field dependent or field independent, the terms coined by Witkin, or as a leveler or sharpener, the terms developed by Gardner and his associates.

The second development in the 1960s was the interest in using less structured forms of objective testing in research into creativity. Stimulated in part by criticism of the limitations of the objective test with its "right" answer, researchers such as Torrance[11] and Barron[12] began to develop objective tests with a limited free-response answer. In the verbal form of these tests, a respondent is presented with a problem in the traditional way, but the problem has no right answer, instead permitting a wide range of answers. A favorite problem in research in the area in the 1960s was to ask the respondent to list all the uses he could think of for a brick or a piece of paper. As with the objective test with a structured answer, data from the less structured instruments can be analyzed to yield information about individuals or groups. The data can be derived in terms of sheer number of different responses, different types of responses, or distinguishing between possible and impossible uses, reinjecting the notion of "correctness," to some extent. In the nonverbal forms, the respondent is presented with some lines or a partial design and asked to make a drawing based on them. The data can be analyzed to reflect criteria such as originality or complexity, or artistic criteria such as composition, balance, or use of space.

There is a growing research literature on these instruments, which has the advantage of making available to the researcher data on the basis of which he can identify usual or unusual responses from his own respondents. However, the tests used cannot be considered standardized or normed in the sense that the structured objective tests have been. Moreover, they typically consist of nothing more than a few stimulus problems. In view of this, a researcher contemplating using one of the less structured techniques in a comparative survey or experiment can easily develop his own stimulus concepts and analyze his data in terms of the responses obtained from his own groups.

Whether structured or unstructured answer formats are used, all objective tests come under the questioning process. They all lend themselves to the mixed interaction in which they are administered to groups, such as a class, with the function of the researcher to explain and proctor while the actual tests are completed by the respondents. Tests intended for use in this way are referred to as *group tests,* and are exemplified by tests of

[11]E. P. Torrance, *Guiding Creative Talent* (Englewood Cliffs, N.J.: Prentice-Hall, Inc., 1962).

[12]F. Barron, "The Psychology of Imagination," *Scientific American,* no. 199 (1958), pp. 150–166.

achievement and aptitude such as the Metropolitan Achievement Tests or the Stanford Achievement Tests. The researcher should be aware that in addition to the obvious intervening variable of reading and possibly writing, when tests are administered with the mixed interaction, testing becomes a social situation. Any one respondent becomes susceptible to the pressures which come from working in a group setting, and whether these stimulate his competitive tendencies or inhibit him, they will have some effect on the measure obtained. Thus, the researcher should only use the objective test in the mixed interaction if he is seeking to obtain measures of characteristics of the respondent in social settings.

If the researcher is concerned with eliminating the possibility that social pressures will intervene, he can use the objective test in the personal interaction, in which the researcher and respondent meet in a one-to-one situation. Tests designed for use in this way are referred to as *individual tests*, with two intelligence tests, the Wechsler Intelligence Scale for Children and the Stanford-Binet Intelligence Scale, the two most widely used such measures. Of course, the reader will recognize that the personal interaction injects pressure of its own, and the researcher must decide which pressure is the more reasonable approximation to the life situation he is seeking to simulate.

The researcher planning a study in which an objective test is required will generally find one of the already published tests is appropriate for his use. If he is doing a study involving children, he must determine what tests and even what forms of tests the children may have already taken. This should be done not only to avoid inadvertently administering a test already administered, but also to be certain that the norms for the tests to be given can be compared to those for the test already given.

PERFORMANCE AND WORK-SAMPLE TESTS   When the task posed by the test is for the respondent to do something rather than answer a question or solve a problem on paper, the test is called a *performance test* or *work-sample test*. The tasks used in the test are the basis for differentiating these two kinds of tests. In performance tests, the task are general tasks selected because they require some motor skill, such as copying designs, or manipulating weights to achieve a balance, or assembling objects. In work-sample testing, the task is selected because it requires some specific skill or combinations of skills which will be required to function in a particular setting. The task may even be a complete prototype of the ultimate situation in miniature, such as the tests some school systems use to select new teachers, in which the candidate is taken to a school, assigned a topic, and given a period of time to prepare a lesson which he is then asked to teach to a class.

The performance test uses the process of questioning as the objective tests did, but the work-sample test uses observation. Both kinds of tests are individually administered and so require a personal interaction between researcher and respondent. The consequent costs in time as well as money have limited their use in research. The particular appeal of the performance test is that the possible intervention of the ability to read and write is eliminated, as is the possible intervention of the social aspects of the testing situation. The price paid for this is the unhappy fact that scores on performance tests are not as highly correlated to many of the aspects of the educational process studied in educational research as are scores on the objective tests. This is undoubtedly because our schools are heavily oriented to learning situations which are both verbal and social rather than motor and individual.

The work-sample testing notion is implicitly popular, because the parallel between the real situation and testing situation is so great and so overt. For that reason, it has an immense positive public relations aspect, for respondents leave the testing session with the conviction that they have had a more relevant trial than would have been furnished by an objective test. For research purposes the work-sample tests are difficult to use, not only because of the time and expense but because of the difficulty of replicating a testing session so that it has the stability needed for research. If a teaching performance test is given to decide which candidates meet acceptable standards, the fact that the candidates are placed in different classes is not critical, for the judgment to be made is simply whether their performance is acceptable or not. However, if the tests were given to decide if there were differences in the teaching ability of graduates of two different teacher-training programs, then the comparability of the performance situation would be critical. This level of comparability is difficult to achieve with real situations, and researchers have also tried to develop prototypes of situations which they re-enact for each respondent. This can succeed in creating a common situation in which the respondents function, but it increases costs and loses a considerable degree of the reality flavor, which is perhaps the strongest virtue of the technique. It is this complex of problems which has limited the use of the technique.

Projective Techniques

When the researcher chooses to test at the nonconscious level, he moves into the realm of projective techniques.[13] We shall distinguish two kinds,

---

[13]Unlike the other techniques we have been considering, the projective techniques should only be administered by psychologists trained specifically in this aspect of test administration. Thus, a prerequisite for any project planning to use these techniques is the availability of sufficient well-trained staff for test administration.

visual projective techniques, in which the stimulus offered the respondent is a design or ambiguous picture, and *verbal projective techniques,* in which the stimulus is an incomplete verbal thought. In both of these instances the researcher is presenting a less than fully structured stimulus as a means of eliciting responses, on the basis of which he can obtain some estimate or measure of an aspect of the respondent's psychological structure.

The most frequent pictorial techniques used in social research are the Rorschach Inkblot Test[14] and the Thematic Apperception Test,[15] usually referred to as the T.A.T. The Rorschach Test presents bilaterally symmetrical inkblots to the respondent, who is asked to tell what he sees in them. Extensively used in clinical measurement, there exist several scoring schema and bases for interpreting the total set of responses.[16]

The T.A.T. presents the respondent with a picture of a scene involving people, which is sufficiently ambiguous to be subject to multiple interpretations. The respondent is asked to tell a story about the picture, including the events which led up to the picture and what will happen afterward. As with the Rorschach, alternative procedures have been developed for the analysis of the stories and for the interpretation of the psychological dynamics revealed.[17]

The major verbal projective techniques employed in social research have been the *word association technique,* the *incomplete sentence technique,* and the *story completion technique.* Each of these is based on the same principle: that the association a respondent has to a word or to a sentence or story fragment is a meaningful projection of some dynamic aspect of his personality structure. Thus, some interpretable generalization can be made when several associations are obtained from the same individual to a set of words or fragments preselected to reflect a particular personality dynamic.

The principle is generally accepted. The difficulty, as in all projective techniques, is to implement the principle so that an interpretable set of data result. This is sufficiently difficult in clinical diagnosis and research,

[14]H. Rorschach (trans. P. Lemkau and B. Kronenburg), *Psychodiagnostics: A Diagnostic Test Based on Perception* (Berne: Huber, 1942).

[15]H. A. Murray, *Thematic Apperception Test* (Cambridge, Mass.: Harvard University Press, 1943).

[16]B. Klopfer and D. M. Kelley, *The Rorschach Technique* (New York: Harcourt, Brace & World, Inc., 1942); S. J. Beck, *Rorschach's Test* (New York: Grune & Stratton, Inc., 1952), 3 vols.; Z. A. Piotrowski, *Percept-Analysis: A Fundamentally Reworked, Expanded and Systematized Rorschach Method* (New York: Crowell-Collier and Macmillan, Inc., 1957).

[17]J. W. Atkinson, ed., *Motives in Fantasy, Action and Society* (Princeton, N.J.: D. Van Nostrand Company, Inc., 1958); W. E. Henry, *The Analysis of Fantasy: The Thematic Apperception Technique in the Study of Personality* (New York: John Wiley & Sons, Inc., 1956).

but in educational research the difficulty is even greater, for the research data are usually obtained out of the context of the additional data available to the clinician. The problem in interpreting the data is the simple lack of sufficient theoretical structure and empirical information to provide a basis for establishing a necessary connection between a response and an interpretation. This, coupled with the limited normative data available from populations of nondisturbed respondents, limits the use of these techniques in educational research.

The one instance in which the lack of theory or norms is not a totally crippling handicap to the researcher is in a comparative survey or experiment. In these instances the researcher's aim is simply to provide some basis for determining if two or more groups are comparable or different. Then one of the projective techniques may be useful if comparisons at the nonconscious level are relevant to the research. An example of this use of the techniques is the Davidson-Greenberg study[18] in which a group of achieving children attending elementary schools in Harlem in New York City were compared to a group of nonachieving children attending the same schools. One basis for comparing the groups was the Rorschach Inkblot Test. For the purposes of this study, the relevance or even validity of the clinical insights the Rorschach permits was not as important as the basic fact that it enabled the researchers to conclude that at the nonconscious level the groups were significantly different.[19]

The researcher contemplating the use of the projective techniques in research should plan to use one of the established pictorial techniques, and unless he is planning a massive data collection (in excess of 500) should also plan on using one of the previously developed verbal techniques.[20] To develop his own for use at the nonconscious level[21] involves

---

[18]Helen H. Davidson and Judith W. Greenberg, *School Achievers from a Deprived Background* (New York: Associated Educational Services Corporation, 1967).

[19]Davidson and Greenberg, *School Achievers from a Deprived Background*, p. 49.

[20]Word association instruments are presented in Grace H. Kent and A. J. Rosanoff, "A Study of Association in Insanity," *American Journal of Insanity*, no. 67 (1910), pp. 37–96, 317–390; D. Rapaport, M. Gill, and R. Schafer, *Diagnostic Psychological Testing.* (Chicago: Year Book Medical Publishers, Inc., 1946), vol. II. Incomplete sentence instruments are presented in J. B. Rotter and Janet E. Rafferty, *The Rotter Incomplete Sentences Blank* (New York: Psychological Corporation, 1950). Also, Amenda R. Rohde, *Sentence Completion Test* (Los Angeles: Psychological Services, 1953–1957). Story completion instruments are presented in S. Rosenzweig, *Rosenzweig Picture Frustration Study* (St. Louis, Mo.: The Author, 1947–1949); Helen D. Sargent, *The Insight Test: A Verbal Projective Test for Personality* (New York: Grune & Stratton, Inc., 1953).

[21]The reader should recognize that the same techniques discussed here could be used at the conscious level by simply analyzing and reporting what it is the respondents said, with no attempt to interpret the unconscious dynamics reflected. If this is done, however, the researcher is not measuring, but is simply questioning his respondents using an unstructured stimulus question with an unstructured answer format.

perhaps the most complex aspect of instrument development in the social disciplines and is not suggested unless the researcher has the time, resources, and experience to have some reasonable basis for expecting either success or a meaningful failure.

The pictorial techniques are generally individually administered, and the word association techniques usually are as well. However, the Rorschach and word association tests can be administered to groups using the mixed interaction, and the incomplete sentence or story techniques can also be effectively administered this way. The impersonal interaction, with the researcher not present, is inappropriate for any of the projective techniques.

Inventory Techniques

A popular technique for measurement in the social disciplines is the *inventory*. In a sense, the inventory is the application of the check list to measurement, for the inventory typically is a lengthy list of possibilities presented to a respondent with the request that he indicate those which apply to him. The technique has been used in efforts to measure characteristics of individuals such as interests (for example, the Vocational Interest Blank developed by Strong[22] or the Kuder Preference Record[23]); personal problems (the Mooney Problem Check List[4]); or personality (the Minnesota Multiphasic Personality Inventory[25]); and has also been used to measure characteristics of institutions such as climate (the Stern-Steinhoff Organizational Climate Index[26]).

All inventories are based on the questioning process, usually with totally structured response patterns, and so they are sufficiently structured to permit impersonal as well as mixed interactions. The key element in obtaining valid data from them is the motivation of the respondents, because they must be sufficiently motivated to provide honest answers and also to work through the lengthy response task the inventory technique often involves. For example, the Strong Vocational Interest Blank contains 400 items, one form of the MMPI contains 550 items, and the

[22]E. K. Strong, Jr., *Strong Vocational Interest Blanks*. Revised (Palo Alto, Calif.: Consulting Psychologists Press, 1938–1959).

[23]G. F. Kuder, *Kuder Preference Record—Vocational* (Chicago: Science Research Associates, Inc., 1934–1956).

[24]R. L. Mooney and L. V. Gordon, *Mooney Problem Check List*. 1950 Revision (New York: Psychological Corporation, 1950).

[25]W. G. Dahlstrom and G. S. Welsh, *An MMPI Handbook: A Guide To Use in Clinical Practice and Research* (Minneapolis: University of Minnesota Press, 1960).

[26]George Stern and Carl Steinhoff, *Organizational Climate Index* (Syracuse, N.Y.: George Stern, 1963).

Stern-Steinhoff inventory to measure institutional climate contains 300 items.

There is a reasonable variety of developed inventories available to the researcher, and this variety covers many of the areas of social research.[27] They are easily adaptable in the sense that sections can be used without using the entire inventory, recognizing that this adaptation diminishes the applicability of any statistical data or other arguments advanced to support the reliability and validity of the inventory. The technique's use is further broadened because this type of measure is also among the simplest to develop. If carefully founded in the literature, a new inventory can be defended as valid by the content validity argument, provided that pilot work has satisfactorily demonstrated the reliability.

Sociometric Techniques

One basic aspect of research in the social disciplines is to consider the nature of social interaction itself. A researcher may be concerned with the friendship patterns within a class or whom the adults in a group perceive as leaders. This kind of research became particularly important in the last years of the 1960s when many communities began programs of busing, pairing, and rezoning designed to achieve greater racial integration in the public schools. An immediate research interest was the extent to which restructuring the racial composition of a school population achieved any meaningful social interaction between children. One study of a school busing program, conducted by the author,[28] used a simple sociometric technique in which children were given a list of the names of all the children in the class and asked to place a number 1 next to the names of their "very good friends," a 2 next to the names of their "good" friends, a 3 next to the names of the children who were "okay," and a 4 next to those whom they "didn't know well enough to rate."

In addition to the instructions we used, the original instrument asked the child to place a number 5 next to the names of those children he "does not like." We felt such an instruction would arouse ill feeling within the classes we were studying, and so chose to omit it, and performed our data analysis in terms of the liking patterns only. The alternative would have been to assume that any child without a number next to his name was disliked, and while this seemed to be a reasonable assumption, we chose to present the data on friendship patterns only.[29]

---

[27]These inventories are fully discussed in Anne Anastasi, *Psychological Testing*.

[28]D. J. Fox, *Free-Choice Open Enrollment—Elementary Schools* (New York: Center for Urban Education, 1966).

[29]The data indicated that every child being bused selected at least one resident child as a friend, and was in turn selected by at least one resident child as a friend.

This type of sociometric technique, in which the members of a group indicate by name those other members who are friends, can be expanded to questions asking which members exhibit specific behaviors of particular interest in a specific research project, such as aggression or high aspirations. Any of these variations can be administered to groups, using the mixed interaction. One caution to remember: The respondents must be sufficiently well spaced so that they feel that the numbers or names they record are totally private and cannot be seen by other members of the group. They must also be assured and convinced that the data will be held in confidence and that no member of the group will be told his own, or any one else's, ratings. If no relevant existing instrument can be found, these instruments are simple to adapt or develop, and with minimal effort instruments specially adapted to the needs of a specific research project can be made.

The more widely known use of sociometric techniques is the original work in the area by Moreno.[30] In his technique, each member of the group being studied indicates the names of one or more members with whom they would prefer to share some kind of social interaction, that is, work, play, visit at home, or invitation to dinner. The data can be analyzed to yield the number of times each child is chosen, or, as in the school busing study above, the number of times subgroups of children are chosen from within and without the subgroup and themselves stay within the subgroup or move out for their choices. The data can also be analyzed in pictorial terms in the widely known *sociogram* developed by Moreno and his associates. In this representation of the data, each child is represented on the chart by a circle containing his name, and lines are drawn from his circle to the circles of the children he chooses. When completed, the sociogram looks like Figure 19-1, based on hypothetical data. For comparison, the figure also presents a tabulation of the same data, so that the reader can see how these two forms of sociometric analysis compare. Both versions of the data make clear that Sam is the most popular choice (a star in the sociometric literature), and that Tom is never chosen (an isolate). Both also indicate the other levels of popularity. However, unique to the sociogram are two aspects of the data: the perception of the two subgroups within the major group and the specific interaction of the reciprocal choices. Thus, at a glance we see the two groups, the one consisting of Alan, Lou, Fred, and Mark, and the other consisting of Sam, Charles, Jack, Bill, and Phil. Equally apparent is the reciprocal pattern of choice between Alan and Lou or between Sam and Jack, and the other pairs as well. It is this unique ability to identify the interaction patterns

[30] J. L. Moreno, *Who Shall Survive? Foundations of Sociometry, Group Psychotherapy, and Socio-drama.* Second Edition (Beacon, N.Y.: Beacon House, 1953), Sociometry Monograph, no. 29.

Sociogram of Data

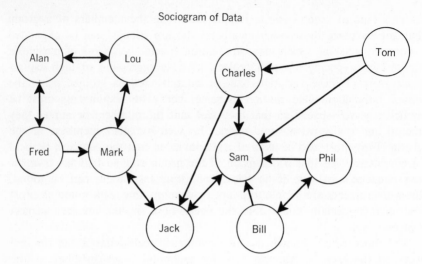

Table of Data

Child	Number of Times Chosen	Number of Times in Reciprocal Choices
Sam	5	2
Jack	3	2
Mark	3	2
Lou	2	2
Alan	2	2
Charles	2	1
Fred	1	1
Bill	1	1
Phil	1	1
Tom	0	0

Figure 19-1 Example of sociogram and corresponding tabular form of the data.

which makes sociogramatic analysis so useful in research concerned with this level of social functioning.[31]

The basic procedure is simple to adapt to any particular group situation and to any stimulus question for which a rational basis exists for making choices. As with the selection techniques discussed above, the researcher must take care that the data are collected under conditions so that the

[31]Other analyses are suggested in Moreno, *Who Shall Survive?* as well as in Helen H. Jennings, *Sociometry in Group Relations: A Work Guide for Teachers* (Washington, D.C.: American Council on Education, 1948).

respondents feel their choices will be known to them and the researcher, but not each other.

Scaling Techniques

One of the aspects of measurement in which considerable success has been achieved in research in the social disciplines is in measuring how people order a universe of concepts. For example, let us assume several discussions with staff members of a school have indicated specific areas of staff satisfaction and dissatisfaction. Research interest then turns to learning which of these specifics is considered by staff to be the most important area of satisfaction, which second in importance, which third, and so on to the least important of the universe identified. This typifies the research purpose of ordering, a purpose for which there are four different scaling techniques. These are *rating scales, rank-order scales, the Q-sort, and the paired-comparison scales.*

All four of the techniques have the same three components: a finite sample[32] of specific concepts or items that the researcher wishes to order; a criterion continuum along which they are to be ordered; and a procedure by which the respondent indicates his placement of each specific item on the continuum. While all four techniques have these same components, and may be used with the same criterion continuum, they do differ in the size of the sample of items for which they can be used appropriately, and in the type of task they pose for the respondent. From the researcher's point of view, they also differ in the nature of the data they return and therefore in the nature of the generalizations they permit, as we shall discuss below.

RATING SCALES   In the rating scale, the task posed for the respondent is to rate each element separately in terms of a criterion by selecting a verbal or numerical rating from among those offered. Thus, for the hypothetical study of staff dissatisfaction, Table 19-2 presents a possible *verbal scale* and Table 19-3 a *numerical scale*. In Table 19-2 the respondent is provided with a list of ten causes of staff dissatisfaction and a criterion (importance) and also with five gradations within the criterion. Notice that this technique uses the totally structured answer format, as the respondent has no ability to add other causes or to respond with a rating other than these five gradations. The second kind of rating scale, the *numerical scale,* offers the respondents somewhat more flexibility in assigning a rating. Table 19-3 presents the numerical form of the scale for the

---

[32]If the researcher does not know the universe of possible items, then he should use one of the questioning techniques, with free response questions.

Table 19–2 Example of Verbal Rating Scale

Some possible causes of staff dissatisfaction are listed below. On the basis of *your own experiences,* to the right of each cause place a check mark in the column that most closely describes how important it has been as a cause of staff dissatisfaction.

Rating

Cause	No Importance	Slight Importance	Moderate Importance	Very Important	One of Most Important Causes
Equipment and supplies					
Interpersonal relations between teachers and administration					
Lines of communication among staff					
Personnel practices					
Quality of teaching					
Quantity of personnel					
Salary scale					
Teaching schedules					
In-service staff education programs					
Status of teachers					

first two of the items presented in Table 19-2. Note that the continuum is the same: from a rating of "no importance" at one extreme to a rating of "one of the most important causes" at the other. Where the verbal scale defined three specific intermediate points in verbal terms, the numerical

Table 19-3 Example of Numerical Rating Scale

Some possible causes of staff dissatisfaction are listed below. On the basis of *your own experiences,* place a check mark next to each cause indicating how important it has been as a cause of staff dissatisfaction. Place your check along the continuum from "0" indicating "No importance" to "10" indicating "One of the most important causes."

Rating

Cause	No Impor- tance 0					Moderate Impor- tance 5					One of Most Important Causes 10
Equipment and supplies	0	1	2	3	4	5	6	7	8	9	10
Interpersonal relations between teachers and administration	0	1	2	3	4	5	6	7	8	9	10

scale delineates nine intermediate points, defining only the point in the center of the scale.

In each instance, the task posed for the respondent is identical. He is to consider each separate item and place it somewhere along the continuum. Each item to be rated is considered separately, and since the respondent is permitted to use each rating as often as he wishes, or avoid certain ratings entirely, the rating assigned any one item need have no carryover effect on the ratings assigned other items.[33]

Each type of rating scale involves a basic assumption. In using the totally defined verbal scale, the researcher must find meaningful verbal labels which will make clear his perception of each scale point and must assume these labels communicate the same qualitative meaning to all respondents. For example, the researcher using a scale such as the one in Table 19-2 must assume that all of his respondents interpret the words "very important" as meaning the same degree of importance. The numerical scale avoids this assumption in part, because it visually communicates to the respondent that the researcher is asking him to place each item on a continuum with only the end and midpoints defined. But the numerical

[33]The possibility that position on the list may affect the rating is discussed in the section of this chapter entitled "Developing the Instrument for Scaling."

scale, too, has an implicit assumption: that each respondent defines the numbered scale points as meaning the same degree of importance, so that it makes sense to assume that three respondents, each of whom circles the number "3," are referring to the same importance.

In a sense each of the assumptions involved is both tenable and questionable at the general level of this discussion. It is only in the context of a specific research problem and a specific research population that one can decide between them. The simplest rule would be that where the qualitative rating is important and the potential scale points can be defined in terms that are unambiguous to the population (which can only be verified through pilot studies) the verbal scale is preferable, for it elicits a clear statement of position on the continuum from each respondent.

The researcher obtains two kinds of data from the rating scale: the qualitative rating assigned each item and a basis for ordering the entire set of items. The qualitative rating obtained is more thorough and specific for the verbal than the numerical scale, with the basis for ordering more precise for the numerical scale. This then, is another basis for deciding between them: whether the primary research need is the rating of each item or the ordering of the entire set of items.

The qualitative rating of each item is obtainable for any individual respondent directly from his rating. For a group of respondents it is available from the distribution of ratings assigned the item. The researcher's perception of ordering, that is, which item the respondent or group of respondents considered most important, which second, and so on, comes from the summary frequency distribution of ratings. The rating scale often yields only a gross kind of ordering, for two or three items may have similarly positively oriented distributions, another few centrally oriented distributions, and so on. Therefore, in the effort to obtain a more precise distinction from rating scales than that provided by the summary frequency distribution, researchers seek some measure of central tendency. This can be done directly from the numerical scale, and is done with the verbal scale by applying a series of digits to the several verbal points. The research literature indicates that, inevitably, the digits used come out in consecutive order (in other words, 1, 2, 3, 4, and 5, or -2, -1, 0, +1, and +2 for a five-point scale).[34]

The computation of the median for a rating scale can be defended since the ratings are, by definition, ordered. The computation of the mean is harder to defend, because it assumes that the scale is an interval scale

[34]The disadvantages and increased potential for error in processing negative numbers far outweighs the advantage in assigning "0" as the midpoint of a positive–negative scale.

with the several scale points equally distributed. As we discussed at length in Chapter 5, the simple assignment of consecutive digits does not transform either the verbal or numerical rating scale into an interval scale. What is required is a long and difficult procedure designed to empirically determine and define the several intervals and substantiate that they can be considered to be equally far from each other on the continuum.[35]

THE SEMANTIC DIFFERENTIAL SCALE   One version of the numerical scale, which attracted considerable interest in the social disciplines during the 1960s, is the *semantic differential scale,* developed by Osgood.[36] This technique uses the same components as the rating scale we have been discussing (a criterion and items to be rated) but inverts them, in a sense. The rating scale, as it has been discussed so far, consists of a single criterion (importance, in our example) and several concepts to be rated in terms of that criterion. The semantic differential technique takes one concept and asks the respondent to rate that concept in terms of several criteria. Each criterion is stated as a pair of bipolar adjectives (good–bad), and the respondent is asked to indicate his perception of the concept to be rated somewhere on the continuum from "good" to "bad."

As an example, let us assume that the researcher in the Language Study had hypothesized that the different methods of teaching English to Puerto Rican children might lead to different attitudes toward English, toward school, and language in general. To test this he could use the semantic differential scale illustrated in Table 19-4.[37] At the top of the page appears one of the concepts to be rated, in this case "English." Identical pages would be prepared for the other concepts. Below the concept appear the criterion scales, each presented as a verbal scale, with only the end points described, and with the number of intervals on the scale indicated by the series of boxes. The respondent is asked to indicate, by placing a check in one of the boxes, his perception of English on the continuum from "good" to "bad," then on the continuum from "hot" to "cold," and so on through the 12 pairs of adjectives on this particular instrument.

In his work on the development of the technique, Osgood has worked with three major scaling concepts and developed his adjective pairs within

[35]This procedure was first developed by Thurstone in a series of articles in 1927 (*Psychological Review,* no. 34, pp. 273–286, 415–423, 424–432; *American Journal of Psychology,* no. 38, pp. 368–389). His work is summarized and expanded in Warren S. Torgerson, *Theory and Methods of Scaling* (New York: John Wiley, Inc., 1958).

[36]C. Osgood, G. Suci, and P. Tannenbaum, *The Measurement of Meaning* (Urbana, Ill.: University of Illinois Press, 1957).

[37]This scale was used in the study of Helen H. Davidson and Judith W. Greenberg, *School Achievers from a Deprived Background* (New York: Associated Educational Services Corporation, 1967).

Table 19–4   Example of Semantic Differential Scale

ENGLISH

good	☐	☐	☐	☐	☐	☐	☐	bad
hot	☐	☐	☐	☐	☐	☐	☐	cold
soft	☐	☐	☐	☐	☐	☐	☐	hard
red	☐	☐	☐	☐	☐	☐	☐	green
small	☐	☐	☐	☐	☐	☐	☐	large
quiet	☐	☐	☐	☐	☐	☐	☐	lively
strong	☐	☐	☐	☐	☐	☐	☐	weak
dirty	☐	☐	☐	☐	☐	☐	☐	clean
brave	☐	☐	☐	☐	☐	☐	☐	scared
ugly	☐	☐	☐	☐	☐	☐	☐	beautiful
slow	☐	☐	☐	☐	☐	☐	☐	fast
kind	☐	☐	☐	☐	☐	☐	☐	mean

them. The three are what he has called *evaluative, potency,* and *activity* scales. The labels are basically self-explanatory and can be illustrated from the pairs in Table 19-4. The pairs of adjectives considered to be evaluative are: good–bad, dirty–clean, ugly–beautiful, and kind–mean. Those considered to reflect potency are soft–hard, small–large, strong–weak, and brave–scared. The four pairs left (hot–cold, red–green, quiet–lively, and slow–fast) are considered to reflect activity.

Thus any semantic differential instrument is considered to be a series of separate scales (each pair is one specific verbal rating scale) but can also be considered to consist of subscales, either the three which Osgood has developed or others the researcher has developed.

A glance at Table 19-4 indicates that some adjective pairs have an obvious and overt relevance to the concept being evaluated, such as "good–bad" or "ugly–beautiful." Others, such as "red–green" or "brave–scared," have no overt relevance at all. However, the original work of Osgood, and subsequent research done with the technique, empirically demonstrates that adjective pairs such as "red–green" can have meaning in delineating the perception of a concept. Therefore adjective pairs like these, taken from Osgood's original list of 50 pairs, have continued to be used meaningfully. Researchers have also developed their own pairs, borrowing from Osgood only the basic idea of presenting the scales to respondents in the semantic differential format. In this event, considerable developmental work is needed to demonstrate that the new pairs do yield a good distribution of responses, in contrast to the piling of responses in the middle of the scale which characterizes the data from respondents completely puzzled by a particular adjective pair.

The semantic differential technique can be used in any of the interactions in questioning, but is often sufficiently confusing to respondents so that the mixed interaction is advisable. The researcher should anticipate some confusion and even objection as the respondents struggle with their feeling that some of the pairs are totally irrelevant.

The analysis of semantic differential data has consistently accepted the seven scale points as providing interval data, and so the basis for analysis is the assignment of the numbers one through seven to each point. The numbers are assigned so that one always has the same connotation, that is, is always assigned to the positive or negative end of the continuum.[38] Given the assignment of values, data analysis can then be done at the individual and group level. At the individual level, the values assigned different concepts can be compared on specific scales, overall scales (by computing an overall mean), or on the basis of whatever subscales have been built into the instrument (by computing subscale means). These same three levels of comparison can be made on the group level. Since the data are perceived as interval data, the semantic differential technique can also be analyzed through analysis of variance and is particularly appropriate for factor analysis.

[38]The reader will note that in the scale reproduced in Table 19–4, half of the scales have the positive end on the respondent's left and half on his right. This is to avoid any consistent position set in responding, a point discussed further in the section of this chapter on instrument development.

RANK-ORDER PROCEDURES   When the researcher has no concern whatsoever with the qualitative aspects of rating, but is totally concerned with
ordering, he uses one of the ranking procedures available, generally either
the *rank-order scale* or the *Q-technique,* or as it is commonly called, the
Q-sort.[39] Both techniques offer the respondent a set of concepts or items
to be ranked, and both state a criterion continuum along which they are to
be ranked. In the rank-order technique the respondent is asked to rank
the items consecutively, so that one item is assigned to each of the possible
ordinal positions. Thus, if 15 items were to be ranked for importance in
creating staff dissatisfaction, the respondent would be asked to assign one
to each of the positions from 1 through 15, with "1" assigned to the item
considered most important in creating staff dissatisfaction, "2" to the item
next most important and so on down to the "15" assigned to the item
considered least important. In contrast, the *Q*-sort technique asks the
respondents to rank the items in clusters, usually clusters of different sizes.
Thus a *Q*-sort approach to the same problem would be to offer the
respondent 50 or more[40] items related to staff dissatisfaction and ask him
to read the list and identify the two extremes, that is the single most
important item and the single least important. This is comparable to
ranking the first and last item. But then the respondent might be asked to
consider the items still unranked and identify two clusters: the three most
important and the three least important. He would identify each of the
items in these clusters as belonging to the cluster but would not be asked
to order them within the clusters.

The difference between the two procedures can be seen directly by
considering the sample following which presents, side-by-side, instructions
for ranking a hypothetical set of 25 items by the rank-order procedure
and the *Q*-sort procedure (recognizing that this is fewer items than would
be used in a *Q*-sort). Note that the rank-order procedure asks the respondent to consider the entire sample of items as a total set and to order
within that sample, making equally precise distinctions at every point in
the ranking, that is, distinguishing the item ranked "12" from the item
ranked "13," just as he distinguished the item ranked "1" from the item
ranked "2." In contrast, the *Q*-sort asks the respondent to make steadily
grosser distinctions, asking for precision comparable to the rank-order

---

[39]The *Q*-technique was developed by William Stephenson, who offers it as useful in
a wide variety of social research situations, and who has developed an extensive and
complex methodology for its use, in *The Study of Behavior* (Chicago: University of
Chicago Press, 1953). We shall consider it here only in its role as a technique for
ordering concepts, the role most relevant for education, and not in the varied ways
developed by Stephenson.

[40]*Q*-sort are generally done with between 50 and 120 items.

Instructions for Rank-Order Procedure	Instructions for Q-sort Procedure
Twenty-five possible causes of staff dissatisfaction are listed below. Read the entire list of these causes and rank them in the order of how important you believe them to be as a cause of staff dissatisfaction. Use "1" for the most important cause, "2" the next important cause, and so on, with "25" assigned the least important cause.	Twenty-five possible causes of staff dissatisfaction are listed on these cards. Read the entire set of these causes and place in pile 1 the card containing the single most important cause, and in pile 7 the card containing the single least important cause. This leaves 23 cards. Read these over, and place in pile 2 the three cards containing the most important causes and in pile 6 the three containing the least important causes. This leaves 17 cards unsorted. Read these and place in pile 3 the five containing the most important causes, and in pile 5 the five containing the least important causes. This leaves 7 cards. Place these in pile 4.

scale only once, when the respondent makes his initial selection of the two extreme points.

Obviously, the rank-order procedure provides a set of data which appears more precise, since each item has a specific rank. The precision is in part an illusion, because every researcher who uses the procedure soon learns that as the respondents move toward the middle of the scale, they begin to differ most from each other. If a test-retest effort to establish the reliability of the instrument is made, the researcher also learns that his individual respondents will seldom change their ranking at the extremes but will often vary on how they assign the middle and intermediate ranks from one data collection to the next. Thus the precision of the rank-order procedure is often deceptive, for it does not necessarily reflect precise perceptions by the respondent, but rather is an artifact of the procedure itself.

The Q-sort procedure avoids some of this by seeking clusters of ranks, but is not an unmixed blessing, for the clusters into which the respondent sorts are also arbitrarily imposed upon him by the researcher. The respondent who works with the Q-sort referred to in the sample above may not see the 25 concepts as consisting of one "most important" followed by three "next most important," but rather as consisting of two equally "most important" and four equally "next most important." But he has no more opportunity to express this perception in the Q-sort than he does when asked to rank these six items from one to six. And of course, should a respondent genuinely see the 25 items as 25 clearly distinguishable concepts, the Q-sort forces him to a grosser level than his perceptions.

This is the basic limitation to recognize in any use of the ranking procedures: The leeway allowed the respondent is set by the researcher, and this may mean that the data obtained are considerably distorted from the perceptions held by the respondent. Not only is this a problem in data analysis and write-up, but it may also cause considerable resentment in the respondents, particularly if they feel strongly about the research and want their views expressed validly. Therefore, basic to the use of these procedures is sufficient pilot testing to determine that the ranking task being imposed is a feasible one for the respondents, is appropriate for the distinctions they can make reliably, and that the items presented within the scale are rankable, that is, represent different positions along the criterion continuum.

These two approaches to ordering also differ in the size of the samples they can order, and in the researcher-respondent interaction they require. The rank-order scale is most effective when 10 to 15 items are being ranked but can work with up to 20 to 25 items. Beyond that it becomes an almost unmanageable task for the respondent. In contrast, the Q-sort can function with 100 or more items, and most authors believe the procedure should not be used with fewer than 50 items, with the range between 50 and 100 a popular one in the literature. This minimum limit on the Q-sort has been set in terms of the more complex statistical analyses possible with the procedure. When it is used as a simple ranking procedure as discussed here, it can be used with as few as 25 items with reliable and useful results.

However many concepts are employed, the researcher using the Q-sort must select the clusters to be used. Most often, researchers select the number of items to be placed in a cluster so that if graphed the clusters would assume the shape of the normal curve. This is essential only if some of the more complex statistical procedures suggested by Stephenson and others who have used the procedure are used in the analysis of the data.[41] If the procedure is being used as a simple form of ranking, distributions of clusters which assume shapes other than the normal curve may be employed, even a series of equal clusters.

The rank-order scale can be used with any of the interactions possible in questioning, although it is usually used with the impersonal or mixed rather than the personal interaction. It is easily used with large numbers of respondents, and the data can be simply processed by machine to yield

[41]An overview of some of these procedures appears in Fred N. Kerlinger, *Foundations of Behavioral Research* (New York: Holt, Rinehart and Winston, Inc., 1964, pp. 581–599).

the distribution of ranks assigned each item. From this the researcher can move to the descriptive statistics appropriate for ordinal data, computing the median rank for each item as well as the interquartile range. The total set of items can then be ordered by the use of the medians, that is, the lowest median is assigned a rank of one, the second lowest a rank of two, and so on.

The Q-sort, based as it is on the sorting of a pack of cards by the respondent, requires either the personal or mixed interaction. This means that amassing data from large numbers of respondents is difficult and expensive. The data are processed by assigning a number to each pile, in much the same way as in the analysis of the verbal rating scale. If the normal curve has been used as the basis of the development of clusters, then the numbers assigned are treated as interval data, and the mean cluster value assigned each item can be computed and used as the basis of the final ordering. If some other basis for developing the clusters has been used, then the numbers assigned should be treated as ordinal numbers and the final ordering developed on the basis of the median cluster value of each item.

THE PAIRED-COMPARISON SCALE   When the researcher is concerned with the ordering of a small sample of concepts (that is, ten or fewer) and is anxious to achieve the maximum precision in developing this order, he is advised to consider the *paired-comparison scale.* In this procedure, the respondent is presented with all possible pairs of the items and asked to indicate which of each pair he would rate higher in terms of the criterion continuum. Below are the instructions and some of the items from the paired-comparison version of the causes of staff dissatisfaction we have been using as an example in this discussion of scaling.

Each item below lists two causes of staff dissatisfaction. Read the item and circle the letter of the cause you believe is the more important.
Continue through the list, judging each pair separately.
1. (a) communication
   (b) teachers' status
2. (a) quantity of staff
   (b) equipment and supplies

.   .   .

23. (a) teachers' status
    (b) communication

.   .   .

41. (a) equipment and supplies
    (b) quantity of staff

Notice that each pair appears twice, with the order of items reversed. This will eliminate any biasing effect of order, that is, respondents consistently preferring the first cause listed. Notice also, that unlike the rank-order scale and the *Q*-sort, where the researcher *hopes* the respondent is comparing each item to each other, in the paired-comparison scale the respondent *must* compare each to each other. Therefore, if these direct comparisons are critical, the paired-comparison scale does it best.

The necessity to present all possible pairs and to present each pair twice so that the order can be reversed means that even small samples of items involve large numbers of comparisons. The number of pairs involved in a paired-comparison scale is the number of items to be scaled multiplied by one less than the number of items. Thus to use seven items in a paired-comparison scale involves 42 pairs (7×6), and to raise this to ten items involves 90 pairs. For this reason, the technique is best used with the small samples of items.

The paired-comparison scale can be used with any of the interactions involved in questioning but is most effective with the mixed interaction. This is because at some point in the scale, most respondents will become aware that the items are repeated and will be tempted to look back over their responses to see if they have been consistent. In the mixed interaction, with groups of respondents answering the instrument while the researcher is present, he can serve as proctor and control this rewriting of history. In the impersonal interaction he cannot.

The data can be analyzed at two levels: to yield a measure of consistency and to yield a basis for ordering the concepts. These analyses can be done for individuals and for groups. First, they can be analyzed at the individual level to yield the extent to which the individual has been consistent in selecting the same concept in each pair. An example of how one individual's response can be so tallied appears in Table 19-5, based on the data obtained from one response to a paired comparison scale for seven of the causes of staff dissatisfactions. The individual's first choice has been tallied in the columns, so that the circled double tally in the lower left-hand cell means that when offered the choice between "equipment and supplies" (the column heading of that cell) and "teachers' status" (the row heading of that cell) as a cause of staff dissatisfaction, this respondent selected "equipment and supplies" both times. Note that every cell in which only a single tally appears means that the respondent has been inconsistent for that pair, selecting one item the first time the pair appeared and the other item the second time.

The number of tallies in each column has been added to provide the sums in the eighth row. These can be used as a basis for ordering the items. These data indicate, for example, that this respondent considered "quality

Figure ... Paired Comparison Data for One Respondent

Item Rejected in Pair	Item Selected in Pair						
	Equipment and Supplies	Quality of Teaching	Salary Scale	Interpersonal Relationships	Quantity of Staff	Teachers' Status	Lines of Communication
Equipment and supplies	x	//	//	//	/	/	
Quality of teaching		x	x				
Salary scale		//	x	/			
Interpersonal relationships between teachers and administration	/	//	/	x	/		/
Quantity of staff	/	//	//	/	x	//	
Lines of communication	/	//	//	//		x	/
Teachers' status	(//)	//	//	/	//	/	x
Total number of times item selected	4	12	9	7	4	4	2
Rank on the basis of times selected	5[a]	1	2	3	5	5	7

[a] Note that when more than two or more concepts are tied for a rank, they each are assigned the mean of the rank for which they are tied. The three ties here involve ranks 4, 5, and 6, which sum to 15 for a mean of 5.

of teaching" the single most important cause of staff dissatisfaction, selecting it every time in comparison to every other item. His second choice was "salary scale," his third "interpersonal relationships," and so on.

At the group level, a series of these individual analyses can be simply summed across individual to provide the same two pieces of data: the extent to which the group held consistent views and the overall order in which the items were perceived.

Interpreting Scaling Data

The techniques just discussed differ in terms of the kinds of information they provide the researcher and, therefore, in terms of the kinds of generalizations they permit. Only rating scales provide two kinds of information, a qualitative evaluation and a basis for ordering, through the use of the median rating. Thus, a researcher can draw conclusions not only that his respondents perceive "quantity of staff" as most important of the ten causes rated, but can also make the qualitative interpretation that "more than half of the respondents rated it 'very important' or 'one of the most important' " causes. This second conclusion, the qualitative evaluation, is unique to the rating scale of the techniques for ordering. The others provide data on ordering only and therefore permit conclusions only about ordering. Thus, if a researcher has data available from a rank-order scale he can report which of the 25 items achieved the highest median rank and therefore conclude which one his respondents considered most important *of those 25 items.* He cannot draw any qualitative conclusions since he does not know whether or not the respondents considered three, ten, or none of the items important, *in the abstract,* This same limitation holds for the *Q*-sort and paired-comparison scales as well. They enable the researcher only to draw conclusions as to the relative position of each item within the sample offered the respondents.

Developing the Instrument for Scaling

Despite the diversity of the specific procedures for scaling which we have discussed, it is possible to discuss the general process of instrument development cutting across procedure. The process can be described in terms of three steps: (1) the identification of the concepts to be scaled; (2) the identification of the criterion continua by which these concepts are to be scaled; (3) the selection of the role or roles the respondent will be asked to assume.

Each of the techniques discussed enables the researcher to obtain scaling information on several concepts. Since they differ in the number of concepts they can involve, they place different pressure on the researcher to be economical in his selection of concepts. While it is true that a large number of concepts can be included with a simple rating scale, and that the Q-sort can involve one hundred or more concepts, this should not suggest that the process of selecting content should be any less rigorous than it is for the paired-comparison scale with ten or fewer concepts, or a semantic differential scale with even fewer. In all instances of scaling, the researcher should proceed through the same thorough process of literature review and consultation with content experts to guide the selection of content, for the basic defense of the validity of a scale is its content validity.[42] In fact, it might be argued that the larger the list of concepts to be included within the scale, the more rigorous the selection process need be. The half-dozen critical concepts which might be included in a paired comparison scale should be obvious once the research problem is stated. The 90 most significant to be included within a Q-sort are far more difficult to identify fully and state, since one must drop to lower levels of "criticalness."

The basic criterion by which the researcher must evaluate his final selection of content is his ability to test his hypotheses and answer his research questions. This he must achieve, and his need to achieve it will determine the limits he can place on the scope of the content to be covered within the scaling procedure he adopts. A researcher whose problem commits him to learn the respondent's perceptions about a wide variety of concepts must move to those scaling techniques such as the Q-sort which permit varied concepts. He can use limited content techniques such as the paired-comparison scale only if his problem is so specific as to be illuminated with the limited content information returned.

The different techniques also make different demands on the content included within them. All of them demand that the content be relevant to the rating or ranking task, that is, that a range of opinion and perception be possible for each item. In the ranking procedures, an additional limit is imposed. Within the total range of content on the instrument, there are concepts which can reasonably be expected to fall at different places along the criterion continuum to be used.

The criterion continua require equally careful selection. In all techniques other than the semantic differential, there are few criteria, often only one. This means that they must be selected in terms of the research problem, and often are directly taken from the statement of the problem or an hypothesis. In the semantic differential, in contrast, there are varied criteria represented in the adjective pairs. These can either be selected

---

[42]The process of content selection, discussed in detail in Chapter 17, can profitably be reviewed here, for it is fully relevant.

from those already studied by Osgood, or from among others developed by the researcher, and do not bear the same direct relevance to the research problem.

A different aspect of the criterion continuum in rating scales and the semantic differential is the question of how many scale points to offer the respondents. The researcher is striving to achieve a balance between so few points that the data are too gross and the distinctions meaningless, and so many that there is no consistency in response and the distinctions requested are artificial. For most social variables, five- or seven-point scales work as good balance points. Because respondents do consistently avoid extreme ratings, it is advisable to begin the process of instrument development with a more detailed scale than ultimately expected, until pilot data are available. Thus if a five-point scale is considered adequate, at the planning stage the researcher should work with a seven-point scale until he has some data on the basis of which he can determine if his respondents will actually use points one and seven.

The other tendency in respondents to which the researcher must be alert in developing instruments for scaling is what is usually referred to as *position set,* the tendency to respond to the same side of a scale, or to respond more positively to the items first presented. For this reason, the items in the paired-comparison scale appear twice, with the order reversed. But this same dynamic should be considered in the other techniques as well. It is well to develop two forms of a rating scale or rank-order scale, with the order of the items reversed, so that the researcher can analyze the data from two forms to estimate the extent to which order, in and of itself, made a difference in the respondent's rating or ranking. It means that in a semantic differential scale, half of the adjective pairs should be presented with the positive adjective at the left, while a randomly selected half is presented with the positive adjective at the right, as was done on Table 19-4. In short, the researcher should scan his final instrument to be certain that he has either eliminated the possibility of position set affecting the data or, if this is not possible, that he has a basis for estimating what effect it did have.

The final element in the scaling techniques is the selection of the role the respondent shall assume as he rates or ranks. All of the procedures permit the researcher to ask the respondent to answer in terms of his own opinion or in terms of some other person in the process or hierarchy under study. Thus teachers can be asked to rate, or complete a Q-sort, or do a semantic differential as they, themselves, feel. Then they can be asked to respond again as they believe their principal would respond, or as they think their principal would like them to respond, or in any other role that is relevant for the research. Although all of the techniques discussed lend themselves to this variation in role assumption, the Q-sort and semantic differential have been particularly useful.

STEPS IN THE MEASUREMENT METHOD

The steps in the measurement method are listed below.

1. Determination that the measurement method is appropriate
2. Delineation of the specific variables to be measured, in terms both of characteristic and social unit
3. Translation of each variable into an operational statement of the behavior or verbalization through which it is to be measured
4. Search of the research and nonresearch literature for suggestions of measuring instruments which might be adopted or adapted for use
5. For those variables for which no satisfactory measure exists, the consideration of the probabilities of developing one
6. The decisions as to which variables to retain in the research and the instruments through which they shall be measured
7. The development of the new instruments required by Steps 5 and 6 above
8. The final decision as to the variables to be included in the research (based on the success achieved in the instrument development stage in Step 7)
9. The selection of the researcher-respondent interaction
10. Implementation of the data-gathering plan
11. Implementation of the data-analysis plan
12. Preparation of the research report

The method begins with the *determination that the measurement method is appropriate,* a determination based on the need for data on one or more characteristics of individuals, groups, or institutions. As we have noted, the data needed may be within any of four categories or groups of characteristics which can be measured, and may range from the relative precision possible in the measurement of specific knowledge to the relatively gross measurement obtained through a three-point rating scale. Whatever the characteristic of social unit or level of precision, it is this need for some measure or estimate which dictates the use of the measurement method.

Once the method is deemed appropriate, the next step is the *delineation of the specific variables to be measured.* This step is in part a by-product of the first step, for in the course of determining appropriateness, some initial delineation of variable had to be accomplished. Now the researcher moves on to delineate them all, guided, as always, by the research problem. He proceeds through this step until the variables to be studied are spelled out, in terms of both specific characteristic and social unit. But simply stating the variables is not sufficient; the researcher must *translate each variable into an operational statement.* For this step to be successfully concluded, each variable must be translated into the specific behaviors or statements through which the variable can be measured. Only if this level of specificity is achieved can the researcher hope to have any success in Step 4, as he begins his *search of the research and nonresearch literature for suggestions of measuring instruments.* We have noted earlier in this chapter that he is seeking either instruments that can be used in their original form, with permission, or can be adapted for the specific purposes of the current research. Ideally he finds them for each variable to be studied. However, Step 5, reflecting the reality of the state of measurement in the social disciplines, indicates that *for those variables for which no satisfactory measure exists,* the researcher must *consider the probabilities of developing one* of satisfactory reliability and validity within the timetable established for the research. This is a complex professional decision, and is one which should be made with the help of expert consultation unless the researcher has had extensive experience in instrument development in the problem area of the research.

When the selection of existing instruments has been completed and the decision made as to the success probability of any new instruments contemplated, the researcher can make the *decisions as to which variables to retain in the research and the instruments through which they shall be measured.* If instrument development has been decided upon, he then immediately moves to the *development of the new instruments required.* This stage may well be a tangential stage, conducted simultaneously with other stages of research, such as the identification of the population and selection and recruitment of the sample. There is one more decision stage related to instrumentation. When the instrument-development stage has been completed, the researcher can make the *final decision as to the variables to be included in the research.*

Now that he knows his variables and his instruments and has selected his sample, he is in a position to *select the researcher-respondent interaction.* In doing so he considers the requirements of the instrument, but also the necessity to minimize anxiety, maintain the motivation of the respondents at a high level, and eliminate as fully as possible the effects of any intervening variables.

Given all of the above steps successfully completed, the research can now move through the *implementation of* his *data-gathering* and *data-analysis plans* to the *preparation of the research report.*

PART IV

The Process of Data Analysis and Data Presentation

Chapter 20

THE DATA-ANALYSIS
AND DATA-GATHERING PLANS

The final two steps in research planning are to develop the plans for gathering and analyzing the data. We shall consider them here in the order opposite to that in which they are implemented, for the data-analysis plan may have implications for data gathering and so should be developed first.

THE DATA-ANALYSIS PLAN

With the method and technique selected and the data-gathering instrument in hand, the researcher turns to the question of how he shall analyze the data. While this is a projection into the future, it must be done before the data are collected if the researcher is to be certain that he will emerge from the project with the ability to fully test his hypotheses and illuminate the motivating research problem.

Developing the data-analysis plan involves four phases: deciding the level at which the data will be treated, identifying the statistical procedures to be used, delineating and laying out the tables to be included in the research report, and identifying the assumptions and limitations of the research.

Selecting the Level of Data

We have discussed the levels of data in Chapter 5, and repeat here only so this basic decision will guide all statistical analysis and will be seen as an element in the extent to which knowledgeable readers accept the research findings. There is seldom any question in labeling nominal data, for these nonquantitative data are typically obvious to researcher and reader alike. However, for quantitative data, the distinction between ordinal and interval or ratio data is a critical one and, moreover, one which different

615

researchers see differently. This author advises as a general principle in planning data analysis that the researcher consider the data ordinal, unless he can specifically identify a rationale *other than the assignment of consecutive digits* to consider them interval data. This rationale may be purely intellectual and based on the processes involved in selecting the various points on a scale, or the rationale may be empirical and based on the data collected during pilot work from which the final instrument was derived. But there should be some specific set of reasons or data which can be cited when the researcher departs from treating his numerical data as ordinal data.[1]

Selecting the Statistics

As he plans the analysis of the data the researcher should consider two sections of the research report in which statistics will be relevant. The first of these is the section in which the data-producing sample is described and in which it may also be compared to the selected sample and to the population. In describing the sample, the basic descriptive statistics of the summary frequency distribution and the appropriate measures of central tendency and variability serve to provide the reader with some insight into the nature of the respondents. Readers are interested in the usual demographic characteristics such as gender, age, occupation, and educational level, but in addition any one project will suggest other descriptive variables about which data should be collected. For example, in the Language Study, whether or not the teachers had ever been in Puerto Rico was a useful descriptive characteristic, as was whether or not they had ever studied Spanish.

Provided data are available, the researcher should also employ inferential statistics such as chi square or the *t* test to determine whether or not his data-producing sample differs from his selected sample or population. By selecting which analyses he will prefer at this early stage, the researcher structures the kinds of data he will need to produce about the population and can incorporate the search for these data into his data-gathering plan.

The second section of the report in which statistical procedures play a role is in the reporting of research results. The selection of these procedures should be well structured by this point if the researcher has stated specific hypotheses and research questions. The necessity to test the hypotheses provides guidance to statistical procedures at the general level,

---

[1]The same need for a specific rationale is present for the researcher to move to the perfection of his ratio data, but here the question is simpler, since the fact of an absolute zero is a relatively clear-cut issue.

with the decision as to the level of data available providing the key to which specific procedures to employ. Thus, an hypothesis which refers to the expected "relationship between . . ." two variables, immediately indicates the need for a correlational analysis. Once the researcher decides that the two variables will yield ordinal data, for example, he can move directly to the specification of the rank-order correlation.

The specification of statistical analyses at this stage of the research also enables the researcher to estimate his data-analysis costs in both time and money and make whatever arrangements are necessary to reserve time on data-processing facilities.

Blocking Out the Tables

With the statistics selected, one additional step the researcher can take to avoid problems after the data have been collected is to block out the tables through which he will present his data.[2] The purpose in blocking out the tables is to provide a final check on the kinds of data which might be needed to develop a table and to verify that the levels of precision in the instruments will suffice to develop the tables. The tables to be developed include both those related to the sample and those related to the research results. Thus the researcher simply works through his hypotheses and research questions and blocks out in outline form the table or tables he intends to produce relevant to them. This should be an all-inclusive stage in which tables are blocked out whether or not they will ultimately be included in the final report.

In blocking out tables the researcher should pay particular attention to the size of the intervals he uses and relate these to the intervals used on the data-gathering instrument. If he develops a table which reports the respondents' ages with intervals such as "under twenty-five" and "twenty-five to twenty-nine," he may decide to replace the free-response question asking for age with a set of structured options paralleling the intervals developed for the table. In all such respects, the precision in the tables and the instruments should relate to each other.

Planning for Data Analysis

The next aspect of the data analysis plan is to scan the data-gathering instruments in the context of data analysis. During the process of selecting a method and technique and developing an instrument, the researcher is usually so oriented to content and procedure that he ignores the relatively

[2]Specific guidance in how to develop a table appears in Chapter 24.

minor issues in instrument development, such as whether or not there is a place for the respondent to indicate his name, age, class, or any other data that will be required for data analysis. After the data are collected and about to be analyzed it is often too late to capture this information. Thus, it is at this point of planning the data analysis that the researcher can profitably refer to the list below of characteristics of the data-gathering instrument that will expedite data analysis.

1. There should be a place for name, school, class, age, sex, or any other identifying information the researcher will need in data analysis.
2. Every item should be numbered, and every option within an item should be separately numbered or lettered, for ease of data analysis.
3. Options should not overlap on structured questions, that is, if one option is 5–10, the next should begin with 11.
4. It is preferable to have options circled rather than checked. This expedites the analysis of data and also eliminates the possibility that the check below means "high school" to some respondents rather than "college" as the researcher intended.

_____ high school __√__ college

5. The order in which items appear on an instrument reflects the priority of information sought. The researcher must recognize that respondents and observers tire, and if they do the items which appear late in the instrument are answered less carefully or omitted entirely.
6. The order of the items has been planned with the processing of data in mind. If two pieces of data are to be analyzed simultaneously, this analysis can be expedited considerably if they are physically close together on the instrument as opposed to appearing on page one and page five. Similarly, if some subanalyses within the instrument are planned, such as computing the number of items correct on a subtest or the number of positive responses on an interest inventory, the layout of the instrument should consider the placement of those items on each subtest.[3]
7. The instrument should provide the respondent with a way of indicating inability or unwillingness to answer a question, record an observation, or respond to a measure. This means giving observers a way of saying "I have no basis for making this observation" or giving respondents a chance to say "I don't want to answer this question" or "I don't know." The reason for these options is that it tells us the extent to which the nonresponders are simply not informed or are unwilling to answer. These two pieces of information are in themselves data, and part of the findings yielded by that question. It is possible to seek even more information of this type, by adding to

[3]This suggestion is critical only if data are to be processed by hand, as discussed in Chapter 21. If they are to be processed by computer (discussed in Chapter 23), physical location is unimportant.

the "I don't want to answer . . ." option the final word "because . . ." followed by a space in which the respondent can indicate his reason for not wanting to answer. To the extent that these spaces are filled in we have learned still another piece of information about the respondents in the area under study. None of this information would have been learned had the respondents left the answer space blank.

8. The possibility of precoding instruments, or printing them on different color paper as an aid to data analysis should be considered. Instruments used in the pre- and postadministration of any technique should be easily distinguishable and so impossible to confuse. Colored paper is one simple way to achieve this, as are preprinted devices like lines across the top of the post-instrument, or the preprinting of the word "posttest" on that instrument. This same concept can be extended to make it simple to distinguish the instruments administered to the several different groups in a comparative survey or a multiple-group experiment. Note that this piece of advice is not to be equated with precoding instruments to achieve pseudo-anonymity so that respondents can be individually identified without their knowledge. This author categorically rejects this procedure as unethical, as has been noted earlier in this book.

Reviewing Assumptions and Limitations

Then the final aspect of the data-analysis plan is for the researcher to look back over all of the decisions and choices that have been made to identify two things: the final set of assumptions required for the project to be sensible and the limitations to the conclusions which will hold if the current plans for the project are implemented. In identifying both assumptions and limitations the researcher is concerned with those aspects of the research process over which he has no control or about which he has no information. This includes aspects of the potential respondents, such as why some agreed to participate and others did not, or why after agreeing to participate some failed to complete the data-gathering instrument, as well as the frankness of those who did complete it. It may include aspects of the research approach, such as the availability of data in the historical approach, or the comparability of survey sites in the comparative survey, and often includes aspects of the research method, such as the relevance of the time periods selected for observation or whether or not rapport was established in an interview.

Any uncontrolled aspect which the researcher considers critical for the research to make sense must be stated as an assumption. Thus the frankness of the respondents, the comparability of survey sites, the relevance of observation time periods in most projects would be considered assumptions because it makes no sense to report data from respondents who cannot be considered frank, or to do a comparative study in sites not considered comparable, or to report observation data obtained during time periods which cannot be considered relevant for the problem under study.

Those uncontrolled aspects which are not critical may be stated as limitations to the conclusions. Thus a researcher may decide that he can live with the fact that his historical project is limited to sources available in English.

Having stated the assumptions and limitations, the researcher should scan them as a total set and review them with one thought in mind: the impact on the audience to whom his research is directed. He must candidly appraise the effect of his assumptions and limitations on the acceptance and implementation of his research findings and must be willing, even at this late stage, to revise or expand his research plans if one or more assumptions or limitations seems likely to damage the significance of the research too greatly. For example, instead of deciding to live with the limitation of his conclusions to sources available in English, the historical researcher may conclude that this is so severe a limitation that it will destroy the acceptance of his conclusions. If so, he must build into the research at least an overview of the materials of major significance in other languages. Or the researcher planning the comparative survey may conclude that simply saying he assumed that the several survey sites were comparable will not be a sufficiently strong argument, and so decide to incorporate into his data-gathering plan specific efforts to obtain data to verify comparability.

While these decisions could be made in earlier stages, they often are not, as the limiting factors or assumptions seem reasonable under the pressure of research planning and the desire to move through the planning stages as quickly as possible. That is why it is wise to review them after all decisions have been made, in the few moments of quiet before data gathering begins. But review without willingness to change is pointless, and so the researcher must have the flexibility to take whatever action seems dictated by this final consideration of the assumptions and limitations of the project. Once satisfied that the necessary assumptions and limitations will not damage the usefulness of the research, he can turn to planning the data gathering.

THE DATA-GATHERING PLAN

The entire research process has been created to reach one point in time: that point at which the researcher and respondent meet and interact, and the data are collected. Whether the data-gathering instrument is an observation guide completed by the researcher as he watches the respondent on television, or an interview guide completed by an interviewer as he talks to a respondent, or a questionnaire or rank-order scale completed by the respondent, the data-gathering plan must be successfully developed and implemented if the study is to have any hope of success.

The basic orientation the researcher must bring to this stage is that it is an implementation rather than a design stage. Before considering how he will gather his data he must have selected his research approach, method, and technique, decided the nature of the study he wishes to attempt, developed his instruments, and selected and recruited the sample. Thus, if he is conducting an experiment, the decision as to whether he will collect data before and after the independent variable is introduced or whether he will collect it only after that variable is introduced will have been made before he reaches this stage. Similarly, in a comparative survey, the number and nature of the settings to be surveyed and compared will have been selected. The stage in which the data-gathering plan is developed, in short, is not a decision-making stage but simply one in which the researcher establishes the most effective way of carrying out the research he has already designed.

The general principle that governs the development of the data-gathering plan is to expedite collecting the data needed for the research problem in a way which will simultaneously maximize the validity of the data and minimize any upset and inconvenience of the respondents (whether individual, group, or institution) before, during, and after the data-gathering process.

This perception of the data-gathering plan means that any such plan is a compromise between what the researcher would like to do ideally, and what the simplest level of participation would be for the respondents. In practical terms it means that some things the researcher would like to do cannot be done at all, and others must be done in some way other than he would prefer. It means the respondent, too, will be asked to do things he would prefer to avoid, but which are critical for the research. In brief, it means that in developing the data-gathering plan the researcher has a dual responsibility, his responsibility to the research and his responsibility to the respondent. We shall consider the responsibility to the respondent first, if for no other reason than because researchers so often consider it last!

Researcher's Responsibility to Respondent

The basic orientation a researcher needs to adopt if he is to understand his responsibility to the respondent is to recognize that he is an intrusion into the on-going life process of the respondent, and that when he departs that process will continue. Thus he must consider what participation means to the respondent and anticipate any confusion he might cause *before* the data are collected as well as afterward. He must design his data-gathering plan not only to minimize this but to include whatever follow-up activity is necessary to deal with post-research feelings.

BEFORE DATA GATHERING   Thus, before the moment of data collection a respondent is entitled to sufficient information about the nature of the research, the kinds of information and/or behaviors expected of him, and the use to be made of the results so that he can decide whether or not he wishes to participate. This rule is not limited to adult participants. Children are entitled to know these aspects of research, within the limits of their maturity and understanding, and their unwillingness to participate should be respected. This effort to inform and allow for a realistic opportunity to decide should be built into the data-gathering plan, which should allow for whatever time will be required to carry out these pre–data-collection activities.

Seeing research in the context of the life process also means designing a data-gathering plan which recognizes that the respondent does not function out of the context of other people. Thus, in his planning, the researcher should identify what might be considered the peripheral people who should be informed of the research, and whose permission may be required. This issue became a heated one in the mid-1960s as parents began to object to the administration of research instruments to their children without parental permission. While initially these objections centered on clinically oriented instruments used in psychological research, the objections quickly broadened to include studies of pupil opinion and attitude. In a study[4] the author directed involving school integration, parental objections were raised to the right of the research staff to have access to children as children, before the parents knew the instruments to be administered or the questions to be asked. The concept that there are people on the periphery of the research situation can be applied to adults as well. For example, research involving teachers should be known to the supervisors as well, and the data-gathering plan should allow for informing the supervisor of the purpose of the research and the plans for data gathering.

DURING DATA GATHERING   In Chapter 12 we discussed the researcher's responsibility to his respondents in terms of what happens during the process of data collection, and we shall not repeat that discussion here.

[4]D. J. Fox, *Free-Choice Open Enrollment—Elementary Schools* (New York: Center for Urban Education, 1966).

We shall only reiterate the basic point made: The researcher has the responsibility to make certain that no respondent is asked to provide information or is placed in a situation which calls for unethical or self-damaging behavior at either the action or verbal level. This is true when children are asked questions about their school, class, or each other, and it is true when adults are placed in competitive, or anxiety-inducing situations. The researcher must carefully consider, as he plans for the collection of his data, what meaning the data-gathering situation will have for the respondent; in other words, the researcher should anticipate the feeling and reactions with which the respondent will leave the research situation. If these can in any way be considered deleterious to anxiety-free human functioning, then the researcher must build into his data-gathering plan specific steps to counter those feelings.[5]

AFTER DATA GATHERING   Once the data are collected, the researcher has one last responsibility to the respondents: to inform them of the results of the study. For too long social research has been characterized by a one-way flow of information, *from* the respondent *to* the researcher. This author believes that much of the public and professional ill-feeling toward research participation is attributable to the limited extent to which participants in research projects have been informed of the results and of the effects on program or policy of the research in which they participated. Thus, they not only feel neglected, but they have no reason to feel that the research accomplished anything. Minimally the researcher should make a summary of the results available to those respondents who wish it. Maximally, he can establish an open channel of communication in which periodic reports and summaries are sent to the respondents, as well as notices of the publication of articles, reports, or books based on the study in which they participated, and the ways in which the research findings have been implemented. It is ironic that social researchers have generally not seen research as a social situation with a two-way channel of communication.

The reason this should be built into the data-gathering plan is that the researcher needs to consider how he will reach the respondents after the data have been collected. He may provide a place on the data-gathering instrument where the respondent can indicate whether or not he is interested in receiving summaries or reports of the research, and if so, where they should be sent. However, some respondents see this request as an underhand way to force them to identify themselves. Therefore, if the researcher has any reason to believe he is walking into a suspicious group

---

[5]This discussion assumes that at the earlier stage of selecting approach, method, and technique the researcher has convinced himself of the necessity to create these negative feelings and has reconciled creating them with his own belief system.

of respondents, he may prefer to provide separate postcards or another separate form on which those respondents who wish a summary of the research can indicate where they wish it sent.

Desirable Characteristics of a Research Situation

With his responsibilities to the respondent fulfilled, the researcher can consider his own interests in data gathering. He now tries to develop a data-gathering plan which will have two basic characteristics: the respondents will be functioning under as nearly normal conditions as possible and, if more than one data-gathering session is required, the several sessions will be as nearly identical as possible.

NATURALNESS   The basic aim in creating the research situation is to set up one in which the respondent is functioning as naturally as possible. While this is most critical when the observation method is used, this same aim is relevant for the questioning method (as in the interview) or the measurement method (as in testing). Once the basic situation is created, the researcher should plan to keep it natural and comfortable, and so should build into his data-gathering plans provision for breaks and rest periods, particularly if the respondents are school-age children. It means that he should have precise estimate of the time the respondents will be available for data collection, and should make clear to them the time required for participation, so that no pressure is added to the situation as respondents wonder if they will be able to complete this inventory in time to get to their next class, or if the interview will go on beyond the period they have cleared.

The importance of naturalness also means that the researcher should build into his data-gathering plan deliberate provision for establishing the natural way in which strangers meet. He should specifically include instructions to his data gatherers to introduce themselves, to allow for a reasonable period for questions from the respondents and for whatever discussion may be needed to air their immediate and overt concerns. It also means that in a complex data-gathering plan, with many research situations and data-gatherers, the researcher tries to match the demographic characteristics of respondents and data-gatherers in making specific assignments. He should particularly consider the possible impact on the naturalness of the situation of characteristics such as age, sex, skin color, manner of dress, and implied experience. Sending a female examiner to collect data in an all-boys school will hurt the naturalness of the situation, as will sending a young and apparently inexperienced observer into a classroom to rate aspects of teacher behavior, and this will be true no matter how much experience the observer has in reality. For in considering naturalness of the situation, the researcher takes into account, and attempts to anticipate, the immediate reactions of the respondents when they *see* the data-gatherer. For purposes of maintaining naturalness, these reactions are real, whether they are justified or not, or consistent with the true characteristics of the data-gatherer.

Also important in the effort to create a natural research situation is the decision on the researcher-respondent interaction. We have discussed the various interactions possible within the three data-gathering methods, and suggested that the decision on this interaction be made as part of the choice of method and technique. It should be reviewed now, in the total context of the data-gathering effort, integrating the needs of the research, the nature of the respondents, and the practical realities such as personnel time and cost. The practical reality is clear: The best way to collect data is through inexpensive impersonal interaction. If we must meet the respondents face-to-face, then the best way is through large groups, followed by small groups, with the personal interaction and its one-to-one researcher-respondent ratio clearly the worst. But often the needs of the respondent and the research move in exactly the opposite direction, for the larger the group and the less personal the relationship, the lower the respondent's involvement and the less likely he is to complete the data-gathering instruments with diligence and care.

Since the decision as to researcher-respondent interaction was made during the selection of method and technique it is more likely to have considered research, rather than respondent, needs. Therefore, it should be reviewed primarily to determine if it will be consistent with the needs of the respondents. If not, some middle way can usually be found which will achieve both the needed data and the natural situation.

ANONYMITY VERSUS IDENTIFICATION   One specific aspect of naturalness which the researcher must consider in preparing his data-gathering plan is whether or not the respondents shall be identified. Here, once again, different research desiderata conflict. On the one hand, the desire for a normal, natural situation would call for identification of the respondents, since in life people are known to those with whom they interact. Some researchers believe that contrary goals are the desire to minimize the pressures operating on the respondent and to maximize the frankness and honesty of his response, whether that response is the answer to a question or the action in a situation in which he is being observed, and that these goals are best achieved when the respondent is anonymous.

No one answer can be given to reconcile these views. In certain situations all are correct, and all these dynamics may be operating. Here we can only outline the various views. What the researcher must do is to first develop sufficient insight into his own concepts of human relationships to decide what kinds of relationships he can abide and which he cannot. Given this understanding, he then develops a data-gathering plan consistent with his own beliefs and most likely to produce valid data.

For example, in his own research, the author acts in the belief that in research with people both researcher and respondent should function as fully identified human beings, known to each other by name. Thus, he always identifies himself and his staff and asks the respondent to indicate his name as well. Of course, no respondent is forced to do this, with each being free to omit his name. Asking for identification is based on the belief that data obtained from an identified respondent most closely approximate reality, because in the real world people *are* identified with their opinions and actions. The argument of other researchers is that the pressures in a data-gathering situation distort reality, and that permitting anonymity relieves some of that pressure so that the respondent can produce his natural response.

In deciding which of these approaches is most consistent with his own beliefs and research needs, a researcher should recognize that four choices are available, rather than the dichotomous choice implied in the heading for this section of "anonymity versus identification."

The most complete level of anonymity available is when the researcher not only does not ask the respondent to state his name but does not even know who is in the data-producing sample. This level, called *total anonymity,* is exemplified by the researcher who stands on a street corner and asks his research questions of every fifth passerby, or who enters a randomly selected classroom to observe children at play without ever knowing who the children being observed are. In total anonymity, the most the researcher can say about his respondents is to describe them as a group in terms of the distribution of their overt physical characteristics, that is, gender, skin color, apparent age, and so on. In this situation the respondent feels the least pressure or threat, but also the least involvement and identification with his response.

The next interaction is *partial anonymity,* in which the researcher has not asked the respondent to state his name but does know to whom the research instruments have been administered.[6] An example would be a questionnaire administered to the staff of a school which does not ask for

[6]In some instances it is useful to make a further distinction in the impersonal interaction in which the researcher mails his instruments to the respondents who return them by mail. When this is done, the researcher may only know to whom instruments were sent, with no ability to know who responded, much less to identify any single respondent.

the name of the respondent. Thus the researcher has no ability to relate a specific response to any one respondent, but he can describe the participants more fully. The respondents feel some degree of identification with the data, particularly if they are involved with what is being studied, that is, if the teachers are concerned with the impression the study conveys of their school.

In the third variation, *limited identification,* the respondents are asked to identify themselves by name, and so are known to the researcher who has the ability to relate a specific response to the individual who produced the response. The limitation to the identification is that in the reports of the research, data are reported for groups of respondents, or if by individual, without identifying the individual. In other words, while known to the researcher, no respondent is identified to the readers of the research report.[7] In this instance both pressure and involvement are significantly increased beyond the levels previously discussed.

Finally, there is what we shall call *total identification,* in which the respondent's identity is not only known to the researcher but is also told to the reader of the research report. This is clearly the maximum level of involvement and commitment as well as the maximum level of pressure on the respondent.

From among these four possibilities, there is one which will best integrate the researcher's personal beliefs and his research needs, and so will be incorporated into the data-gathering plan.

There is one more variation of this dimension, what can be called *pseudo-anonymity,* in which the respondent is led to believe that his identity is secret, when in fact it is not. In terms of the ethical code which has guided the discussions earlier in this book, this interaction is simply unethical. Whether it involves collecting tests from children in the order in which they are seated in a classroom (when the seating plan is available to the researcher) or the placing of commemorative stamps at fixed positions on return envelopes "enclosed for your convenience" so that each respondent is identifiable, the broken promise of anonymity is both a broken promise and a lie, and to this author is indefensible.

STANDARDIZATION   If the design of the study calls for more than one data-gathering session, it is desirable that the several sessions be identical. In a sense, this is saying that each research situation should be a replication of each other in every aspect other than the actual production of data by the respondent. If they are identical, then any differences in the data produced can be attributed to the independent variables under study.

---

[7] In some instances the reader is given the names of the data-producing sample, as in an appendix which lists the names of participating schools or teachers.

The need for standardization is most acute in the use of the experimental approach, where the intervention of any variable will diminish the certainty with which the researcher can draw conclusions about the independent variable. Standardization is also critical, however, in the comparative survey, where it is necessary to develop the basis for the comparative conclusions. It has no relevance for the historical approach. Of the methods we have discussed, standardization is most critical for the observation method, for the method deals with normal, uncontrolled, and unstaged behavior and many of the external circumstances such as day of the week or time of day which affect that behavior should be standardized. For the other methods it has differential importance for different techniques. Within questioning, standardization of the research situation is most critical for the interview, and within measurement it is most critical in testing. In both these techniques, the data are particularly sensitive to external characteristics and to the motivation and anxiety levels of the respondent, and so standardization is critical.

Even where not critical, standardization is desirable because eliminating the possibility of external or internal respondent factors affects data differently and improves the validity of any set of data. Therefore, in developing the data-gathering plan, the researcher should set replication as his ideal model for the several research situations. To maximize achieving his goal, he should first seek to identify that research situation he can most easily establish, asking, for example, if there is a particular day, time, or schedule which is most convenient for the respondents. Provided this is consistent with the needs of the research, he may then use this as the base[8] about which to develop the several replications of the research situations.

Another specific technique which aids standardization is to have all of the instructions for the data-gatherers written out in complete detail, with the words they are to say spelled out as in a script. If the data-gatherers adhere to the script, then an inadvertent off-the-cuff comment by one is not going to alter the mood or tone of the session. The researcher should also anticipate the questions that are likely to be asked by the respondents and build the responses he desires into the script. In fact, in those instances when standardization is most critical, as in experimentation, the data-gatherers should be rehearsed, and some staff member should role-play respondents, asking questions. With the easy availability of portable

---

[8]Obviously a research design which calls for sampling on different days or times should not be altered by this suggestion. We noted in the beginning of this chapter that the stage at which the data-gathering plan is developed is an implementation rather than a design or development stage, and nothing said in this section changes that basic perception.

tape recording and playback equipment, researchers can also consider recording the instructions to the respondents, which assures that every group hears identical instructions, spoken in the same way. In this instance, the data-gatherer is available to answer questions, but plays no direct role in instructing the respondents.

All of these efforts are directed toward one goal: eliminating as many extraneous variables as possible from having any differential effect on the data. Note that we are not arguing that these variables (for example, time of day) will not have an effect at all. We are only arguing that they will not affect the several research situations differently.

Anticipation

One of the basic truths every researcher learns about his data-gathering plan is that it will not be implemented exactly as he planned it. Social research involves people, and people get sick, plan schedules which conflict with data collection, confuse dates and directions, and consciously or unconsciously do a wide variety of things which infuriate the researcher and frustrate his realization of the data-gathering plan. Therefore to fully achieve standardization, the researcher must make alterations in a consistent way.

The researcher cannot know what will go wrong, but he can anticipate that something will. Thus when his research is fully designed and his data-gathering plan completed he should review it to establish priorities, that is, he should identify those aspects of the data-gathering plan which are relatively expendable, and those which must be implemented, so that sudden needs to change are consistently and rationally made. For example, if six classes are to be observed in a school, the researcher should decide in advance how he will reduce this number if on the morning of the visit, one or more observers calls in sick or fails to arrive. He may decide that the sixth grade is expendable, and so observers will be shifted to make certain that grades 3, 4, and 5 are covered. Or he may develop a list to randomize the cuts which may be needed, saying that the first grade to be cut will be the sixth, the second a fifth-grade class, and so on. The reason for trying to anticipate what changes and revisions will be made in the event something goes wrong is to avoid having to make this critical a decision under crisis conditions which may damage standardization.

This review of the data-gathering plan may also be the basis for the researcher building into the plan some degree of insurance against the unexpected. He may over-schedule, assuming that there will be some attrition, just as colleges admit more freshmen than they can house, secure in the statistics which show they will not all arrive. He may also decide to recruit one or two extra data-collectors to have available for emergency fill-in duty. Whatever he does, before considering his data-gathering plan finished, he should have anticipated all that might go wrong and have decided what he will do if it should.

Sufficient Time

One extraneous variable which deserves specific consideration is the time required for the administration of the research instruments. First, the researcher should recognize that he must obtain, through pilot studies, a reasonably reliable estimate of how long is required to complete the instruments. This estimate is necessary whether the instrument is being completed by the researcher himself as in an observation guide, or by the respondent completing a questionnaire. The estimate should identify not only the average amount of time, but the maximum amount of time.

Given this estimate, the researcher must then add to this the time required by the particular researcher-respondent interaction he is using. In the impersonal interaction, when the material is sent to the respondent, there is no additional time required. But in the personal and mixed interactions the researcher and respondent meet face-to-face, individually, or as groups. Under these circumstances the researcher must allow time for introducing himself, for explaining the purposes of the research, for accepting and responding to questions, as well as for the distribution and collection of the data-gathering instruments themselves. This too, can only be estimated accurately through pilot studies of the total process of data collection.

Other Aspects

In addition to the two major concerns, naturalness and standardization, researchers must recognize that there is a mundane aspect of the data-gathering plan: arranging the details which will make it possible to implement it. Thus, when the substantive aspects of the plan are complete, the researcher should develop the time schedule and clerical detail schedule which will be required. He must be particularly careful to identify, and allow sufficient time for, clerical details which must be completed prior to data collection, such as the receipt of letters of permission from parents allowing children to participate or the arrival and distribution of materials mailed to the research setting. His thinking in this phase of the data-gathering plan must reach the level of specificity so that he considers how his respondents will answer the research instruments, and allows time to obtain, sharpen, and deliver sufficient pencils if he decides he had best supply them. He considers the necessity for his respondents to be comfortable, and so investigates the physical surroundings under which the data will be collected, prior to data collection and arranges for any services (such as opening locked doors, light, heat) which must be available for reasonable comfort.

This often impresses beginning researchers as a level of concern too petty to merit any serious amount of time. However, the first time they lose half of a data-collection period frantically searching for the school custodian to unlock the door of the room assigned for their group interview with the ten parents milling about the hall, they recognize that this level of detail can damage a project far out of proportion to the significance of the specifics involved.

Chapter 21

TECHNIQUES FOR THE ANALYSIS OF QUANTITATIVE DATA

Let us now turn to the point in the research where the data have been collected and are ready to be analyzed. For the purposes of this discussion we shall consider data of two types: data which are essentially quantitative and data which are essentially qualitative. By quantitative data we mean simply data which can be directly analyzed, that is, counted, expressed in a number, and treated as a number. By qualitative data we mean data whose characteristics and qualities must first be abstracted before the data can be analyzed.

Quantitative data are most obviously seen in the numerical data obtained from a test score or the rankings obtained from a rank-order scale. But the data obtained by assigning numerical values to the points on a rating scale or semantic differential scale are also considered quantitative data, as are the data obtained from responses to a question such as:

Have you ever taught English as a second language?

    Yes   No   (Circle one)

Although the respondent's answer is a circled "Yes" or "No," we can easily count the number of circled "Yes" and "No" responses and so the responses to this question also yield what we are calling quantitative data.

In contrast, assume we had asked teachers this question: "List below your reaction to teaching during the Language Study," and had secured a variety of responses such as:

It was the most rewarding teaching I have done.
I enjoyed it.
I found it much like all other teaching.
It was boring.
The children were fine.
The curriculum was too elementary.

Now these responses can be transformed so that they can be expressed numerically but they are not capable of being directly analyzed as were the test scores or scaled data nor can they be counted in the same sense as the yes–no responses. To be counted they must first be processed through the procedure called content analysis which allows for the quality of the response, and so we shall call these data *qualitative*.

In this chapter we shall consider the process for analyzing quantitative data, including the techniques for hand tallying. While hand tallying may seem primitive in this age of mass data processing, for many student projects it is still the most feasible and fastest way to process a limited amount of quantitative data. Moreover, the basic concepts developed for hand tallying are directly applicable to machine processing as well. In Chapter 22 we shall discuss the process of content analysis, the basic technique for the analysis of qualitative data. The discussion of data analysis will conclude with the consideration in Chapter 23 of the techniques for electronic data processing, applicable to both quantitative and qualitative data.

By this point in the book, the reader should be aware that the author sees data analysis as an implementation stage of research. It is a stage in which the researcher carries out those analyses he has planned and for which he has prepared throughout all of the earlier stages of the process. Only in the event of a new insight, or a new association to a part of the analysis, does this stage involve the unexpected.

INITIAL PROCESSING OF DATA

Once data come in from the field the processing should, and often the analysis can, begin. Any classification or identifying information which will be needed for data analysis should be immediately verified before wrappings are destroyed or envelopes thrown out. For example, the researcher should check that school and class appear on individual tests before the folder with that information is thrown out, or that the date of an observation is on the observation guide before it is filed away. Once this has been verified, the data-gathering instruments should be sorted to as precise a level as possible. For example, assume that in the Language Study the researcher had observers complete an observation guide on a group of children before and after the experimental condition, and that the groups of children being studied represent both Puerto Rican- and mainland-born children and the three different language emphases. This statement identifies three variables (pre–post, birthplace, and emphases) which can be used for sorting and turned into the 12-category *basic sort* in Table 21-1. Each cell in that figure may be represented by a file drawer, a carton, or a folder, but it should be physically separate from each other cell so that as soon as an observation guide comes in from the pretest the

Table 21-1   The Twelve-Category Basic Sort for Language Study Involving Pre-Post Data Collection of Groups Separated by Birthplace and Language Emphasis

	Time of Data Collection			
	Pre		Post	
Language Emphasis	Born Puerto Rico	Born Mainland	Born Puerto Rico	Born Mainland
Vocabulary				
Structure				
Experiential				

research staff can verify the birthplace of the children and the language emphasis and file it into the appropriate place. This will expedite all further analyses of the data, ranging from knowing how many observation guides exist for each cell at any one moment, to gang punching information for these three variables during electronic data processing.

The researcher should also consider the possibility that additional initial sorting can be done. For instance, if the observational guide referred to above included a final item in which the observer gave his overall rating of the group he had just observed, the researcher may wish to sort the guides into a general positive-negative grouping, within each of the 12 cells of the basic sort. The point to note here is that the data should be moved along as far as possible during this initial processing stage.

Processing Incomplete Data

One perplexing problem in the analysis of data is what to do with respondents who refuse to answer. The answer differs depending upon the nature of the refusal. If the respondent totally refuses to participate, of course this simply means he is eliminated from the data-producing sample. In this instance he poses no problem in data analysis. Similarly, if the respondent agrees to participate but then turns in a completely blank paper, the researcher should consider him a nonrespondent and omit him completely from any data analysis.

The more usual problem is the respondent who completes most, but not all of the data-gathering instrument, that is, selectively omits certain items. Now the researcher is faced with the fact that different numbers of people responded to the different items, and for some respondents only an incomplete set of data is available. The problem posed, and ways of resolving it, differs for the different levels of data. For variables which yield nominal or verbal ordinal data, the basic descriptive statistic is the summary frequency distribution reporting the number and percent of the respondents in each category. For these levels of data, *omits*[1] can be handled in two ways. One way is to ignore the omits in the analysis of the data for each question and base the conversion to percents upon those respondents who actually provided an answer. In this instance, the number of respondents will be different for each question, but everybody who is counted and reported will have given a response. Also, percentages reported within each question in the substantive categories will always add to 100 percent and so can be compared across questions.

The alternative method is to add the category "omit" to the basic set of substantive responses and report the number and percentage of omits for each question. In this way, the total number of respondents for each question will always be the same, but will add to 100 percent only across all categories, including the omit category.

The preferred procedure is to use the omit category so that every respondent is fully accounted for in each question. Moreover, this provides the researcher and his reader with an estimate of the percentage of respondents who declined to answer each question, which is often an important piece of data. The big disadvantage to this procedure is that if the proportion of omits varies considerably from question to question it becomes difficult to compare the proportion of responses in comparable categories. For example let us suppose in one question of a survey given to teachers in the Language Study they were asked to indicate their feelings about the success of the language-teaching materials and the content units with which they were supplied. To answer, they were offered a three-point scale: "above average success," "average success," and "below average success."

The hypothetical data obtained are listed in Table 21-2. In the left-hand half of the table we notice that larger proportions of the teachers responded with one of the scale choices when asked about the language-teaching materials supplied than about the content units. Thus, the percentage who omitted an answer was 20 percent for the second question

[1] While this discussion concerns "omits," it also refers to those who say "I don't know" or "I prefer not to answer."

Table 21-2   Illustration of Effects of Omits on Data Analysis

Rating	Percentages Including Omits		Percentages Excluding Omits	
	Language-Teaching Materials	Content Unit Materials	Language-Teaching Materials	Content Unit Materials
Above average	30	30	31	38
Average	50	40	51	50
Below average	18	10	18	12
Omit	2	20	x	x
Number of cases	100	100	98	80

compared to only 2 percent for the first. The problem this poses is reflected in the comparison of the proportion who considered the materials "above average" in success. On the basis of the inspection of the data in the left-hand half of the table, in which the omits are included, the impression is that the same proportions of teachers rated the language materials provided as above average as assigned that rating to the content units. But this is because the omits deceive. Consider now the right-hand side of Table 21-2. Here the data are the same except that the percentages have been based only upon those who responded with a rating: that is, the 98 percent who rated the language materials provided and the 80 percent who rated the content units. And now the content unit materials have apparently received a higher[2] proportion of above average ratings.

This problem will occur whenever the proportion of omits varies considerably from question to question. This is why the convention has developed of using the actual *responders* as the basis for the computation of percentages. A compromise solution is possible, which is illustrated in Table 21-3. Here the researcher has based his percentages on the actual responders but has also told the reader the number and proportion who omitted the question. In this way the reader is provided with this important piece of information, yet the possible distortion introduced by using the omits in the computation of percentages is avoided.

With numerical ordinal or interval data an additional problem is how to treat the omits in any of the possible statistical computations. In numerical ordinal data they must be disregarded in the computation of the

[2]This reference to "higher" is based on the observed data only. A chi square would be required to substantiate a difference in the overall distributions.

Table 21-3 Illustration of Optional Method for Handling Omits

	Of Those Who Responded Number and Percent Giving Each Rating			
Rating	Language-Teaching Materials		Content Units	
	Number	Percent	Number	Percent
Above average	30	31	30	38
Average	50	51	40	50
Below average	18	18	10	12
Total of responders	98	100	80	100
Omit of total sample	2	2	20	20
Total sample	100	x	100	x

median or interquartile range, and these computations based only upon those respondents for whom the required piece of data is available. Similarly, in computing a rank-order correlation, only those respondents for whom both pieces of data are available can be included. With interval data, the same procedure can be followed in the computation of the mean and standard deviation and product-moment correlation. But in regression, factor analysis, and analysis of variance, the missing data pose more of a problem, for the omission of those respondents will result in unequal numbers of cases in different cells and will considerably complicate the statistical computations. Therefore, in these instances the mean for the responders is assigned to those for whom a particular piece of data is missing. This holds the number of cases to the original level and does not introduce any serious or significant distortion.

HAND ANALYSIS OF DATA

In many projects of limited scope and sample the simplest way of analyzing the data to develop frequency distributions, or of studying simple bivariate relationships, is to tally the data by hand. Even the second level of statistical complexity, the computation of measures of central tendency or variability, can quickly be derived from the distributions generated by the hand tally. Therefore, the researcher should consider this old, but still simple and effective, process for data analysis, provided four conditions characterize his study: (1) the sample is no larger than 150,[3] (2) he has studied only a few variables; (3) the descriptive statistics needed to test his hypotheses are few and simple such as means, standard deviations, or the intercorrelations of two or three variables; and (4) the inferential statistics required are at a level of complexity no greater than the t test or simple analysis of variance.

For samples in excess of 150, or for studies involving a multiplicity of variables, or for statistical analyses (with any size sample) at the level of complexity of regression, or factor analysis, or the intercorrelation of four or more variables, or for the complex analysis of variance, computer processing is suggested.

To illustrate the basic process of tallying, assume that we had asked the 150 teachers in a large replication of the Language Study whether or not they would like to participate in such a study again. Since the teachers represented three different methodological emphases (structure, vocabulary, and experiential), we should have initially sorted the responses from the teachers into three piles, representing these three methodological emphases. We would then turn to tallying the responses to the question "If the experiment were repeated, would you want to participate again?" by setting up a tally sheet as in Table 21-4.

Table 21–4 Illustration of Tally Sheet

	Emphasis			
Response	Vocabulary	Structure	Experiential	Total
Yes				
No				
I'm not certain				
I prefer not to answer				
Omit				
Total				

[3]Obviously this is no magic number, but is intended to indicate a general cutoff point above which hand tallying is too time-consuming.

Note that in addition to laying out the two substantive responses (yes, no) we have allowed for an "I'm not certain" and an "I prefer not to answer" as well as an omit category, and also made provision for a total row as well as a total column.

Now we take the group of data we wish to tally, that is, the pile for respondents who taught by the vocabulary emphasis, and proceed to record each response in the appropriate place using a diagonal line (/) to indicate one response. After we have tallied four responses //// we cross them for the fifth response 〢〢〢 so that they will be easier to count. Also for ease in counting, when our numbers are large we should line up every group of 25 separately so that 35 responses would look like this:

〢〢〢   〢〢〢   〢〢〢   〢〢〢   〢〢〢
〢〢〢   〢〢〢

or else separate them by a bracket like this.

〢〢〢 〢〢〢 〢〢〢 〢〢〢 〢〢〢│ 〢〢〢 〢〢〢

Now after we have tallied our 150 cases on question one our tally sheet may look like Table 21-5.

The tally provides several pieces of information, much of it provided visually even before considering the numbers. The fact that the teachers assigned to the different emphases held different opinions is clearly visible, with the teachers assigned to the vocabulary and structure emphases generally positive and the experiential emphasis teachers generally negative toward further participation. Greater positive feeling among the vocabulary as compared to structure teachers is also suggested, as is the small proportion of teachers who were not certain what they would want to do, with even this small proportion more frequent among the teachers assigned to the experiential emphasis. The double totals provide a convenient internal check on the work, for the total column and total row must add to the same sum.

This same procedure can be used to produce a simple or summary frequency distribution for ordinal, interval, or ratio data. For example, Table 21-6 presents the results of a hand tally for the same 150 respondents for the variable "years of teaching experience." In variables which provide quantitative data, the researcher must decide the level of precision at which he wishes to tally. In this illustration, he has established six intervals for the variable, distinguishing those teachers in their first year, those still in their probationary period (one to three years), and then used six-year intervals until he reached 22 years of experience which he used as the basis for an open-end, final interval.

Table 21–5   Completed Tally Sheet for Willingness To Participate in Study

Response	Emphasis			Total
	Vocabulary	Structure	Experiential	
Yes	┼┼┼ ┼┼┼ ┼┼┼ ┼┼┼ ┼┼┼ ┼┼┼ ┼┼┼ ‖ (37)	┼┼┼ ┼┼┼ ┼┼┼ ┼┼┼ ┼┼┼ ‖‖ (29)	┼┼┼ ┼┼┼ ┼┼┼ (15)	81
No	┼┼┼ ┼┼┼ (10)	┼┼┼ ┼┼┼ ┼┼┼ ‖ (17)	┼┼┼ ┼┼┼ ┼┼┼ ┼┼┼ ┼┼┼ ‖‖ (29)	56
I'm not certain	‖ (2)	‖‖ (3)	┼┼┼ ‖ (6)	11
I prefer not to answer	‖ (1)	‖ (1)	(0)	2
Omit	(0)	(0)	(0)	0
Total	50	50	50	150

The simple or summary frequency distribution for variables yielding ordinal or stronger data can be used as the basis for computing summary statistics of central tendency and variability. Table 21-6, for example, can be used to generate the median years of experience[4] for each group, as well as the interquartile range.

STUDYING RELATIONSHIPS BY CROSS-TALLYING

In addition to the generation of frequency distributions for descriptive purposes and/or as a basis for computing measures of central tendency and variability, the hand-tallying process can be used to study simple bivariate relationships. For example, assume that the researcher was interested in determining if years of experience were related to the teacher's willingness to participate in a similar study. Given this interest,

[4]The open-end upper interval eliminates the use of this frequency distribution to generate a mean and standard deviation, even if the researcher perceived these as ratio data. To compute these statistics, he would have to return to the original data for the actual experience of the eight cases in that interval.

Table 21–6   Completed Tally Sheet for Years of Experience

Years of Teaching Experience	Emphasis			
	Vocabulary	Structure	Experiential	Total
22 or more	I ⟨1⟩	III ⟨3⟩	IIII ⟨4⟩	8
16 – 21	++++ I ⟨6⟩	++++ IIII ⟨9⟩	++++ I ⟨6⟩	21
10 – 15	++++ ++++ III ⟨13⟩	++++ III ⟨8⟩	++++ ++++ ⟨10⟩	31
4–9	++++ ++++ IIII ⟨14⟩	++++ ++++ ++++ IIII ⟨19⟩	++++ ++++ ++++ I ⟨16⟩	49
1–3	++++ ++++ I ⟨11⟩	++++ III ⟨8⟩	++++ ++++ ⟨10⟩	29
First year	III ⟨3⟩	II ⟨2⟩	III ⟨3⟩	8
Omit	II ⟨2⟩	I ⟨1⟩	I ⟨1⟩	4
Total	50	50	50	150

instead of tallying the questions separately as we have done, he would plan a *cross-tally,* in which the responses to these two questions would be simultaneously tallied. The cross-tally will not only provide the insight into the nature of the relationship, but will also provide the same frequency distributions provided by the tallies of the separate questions.

To establish a cross-tally sheet we take one of our three groups of teachers whose responses have been sorted separately. Assume we begin with the 50 teachers assigned to the structure emphasis. We then consider the two variables we seek to relate. One, years of experience, has been set up with seven possible responses. The other variable, opinion, has five. We take the question with more choices, years of experience, and set it up vertically with a row for each option as before. However, we now set up the question on participation perpendicular to it, providing one column each for those who said "yes," those who said "no," those who said they were "not certain," preferred "not to answer," and those who omitted the question. The layout appears as in Table 21-7.

We now tally the pair of responses provided by each respondent, that is, we make *one* tally mark for the respondent's answer to *both* questions. Assume a respondent indicated that she had 11 years of experience and responded "no" she would not participate again. On the cross-tally sheet we go to enter her years of experience, as before, in the row for "10 to 15 years." But as we do we notice that we have a choice of five columns in that row in which the tally could be entered, the columns headed "Yes," "No," "Not Certain," "Prefer Not to Answer," and "Omit." Of course we place our tally in the column headed "No," since that was this teacher's response to the other question we're considering. And so in Table 21-7 the tally (/) was entered in the cell representing the interaction of the row for "10 to 15 years" and the column for "No."

Notice again that each *combination of responses* to the *two* questions is tallied with *one* mark. If we were to continue doing this for all 50 respondents we would make only 50 tallies for the 100 responses made to the two questions. Thus the number of tallies equals the number of respondents rather than responses.

The completed tally sheet might look like Table 21-8. Notice first that the column totals—29 "Yes," 17 "No," 3 "Not Certain," and 1 "Prefer Not to Answer"—tell us what happened with the question on participation and correspond to what we had obtained when we tallied this question separately (see column 2 of Table 21-5). The row totals give us the same data we had obtained with the separate tally for years of experience, as in column 2 of Table 21-6.

In addition to this information we could obtain from the tallying of the separate questions, we have the additional information unique to the cross-tally: how each "years of experience" group responded. We can see at a glance the important finding that the teachers willing to participate again were those with the fewer years of experience, whereas those with more than ten years of experience were almost unanimously unwilling to have a second round of participation. Thus, from the cross-tally we obtain an insight into what might be considered a second level of the data, the relationship between years of experience and willingness to participate.

Just as the summary frequency distribution from a simple tally can also be used to generate descriptive statistics, so can the bivariate distributions from a cross-tally. In addition, the distributions of the cross-tally can be used to generate the appropriate measures of association or correlation. In Table 21-8 some collapsing of categories would be necessary, but when done the data could be used as the basis for computing chi square to

Table 21-7 Layout for Cross-Tally of Years of Experience and Opinion on Participation

Years of Experience	Response to Question on Participation					
	Yes	No	Not Certain	Prefer Not To Answer	Omit	Total
22 or more						
16–21						
10–15		⟋				
4–9						
1–3						
First year						
Omit						
Total						

The tally indicating the double response "10–15 years experience" and "No"

Table 21-8   Completed Cross-Tally for Years of Experience and Opinion on Participation

Years of Experience	Response to Question on Participation					
	Yes	No	Not Certain	Prefer Not to Answer	Omit	Total
22 or more		///				3
16-21	/	++++ /	/	/		9
10-15	//	////	//			8
4-9	++++ ++++ ++++	////				19
1-3	++++ ///					8
First year	//					2
Omit	/					1
Total	29	17	3	1	0	50

verify the statistical significance of the observed association between the variables. Similarly, with two variables yielding interval data, the cross-tally can be used as the basis for computing the product-moment correlation. Used in this way, the cross-tally is generally referred to in statistics texts as a *scattergram*.

Since this double tally also provides the totals for each of the questions considered separately, it should be done instead of the two separate tallies in every instance when the researcher has interest in a relationship, either to test an hypothesis or provide some insight relevant to the research question. Of course, if he were interested in the relationships of any *one* question to *several* others, then successive cross-tallies for each pair would have to be done.

In setting up the cross-tally it is best to place the variable with the largest number of options on the left, using one row for each option. Then the variable with the lesser number of options is used for the columns using one column for each option. Remember to leave one row and one column for the nonresponse options such as "I don't know" or "omit" and one row and one column for "total."

The cross-tally procedure can handle two variables as in the example above. Because we had previously sorted the papers into three separate piles using language emphasis as a basic sort, if we repeated the cross-tally separately for each pile of responses we would actually have handled three variables at the same time. In this instance we would have ended the analysis with three tables, each one laid out as was Table 21-8.

Chapter 22

TECHNIQUES FOR THE ANALYSIS OF QUALITATIVE DATA

When the researcher has collected verbal or behavioral data through observational, measuring, or questioning techniques like open-end questions or critical incident questions, he is faced with a difficult problem of data analysis. Verbal responses and descriptions of behavior do not lend themselves to immediate analysis in the way that numbers or "yes-no" questions do. Therefore, to analyze such data we must apply an intermediate or transitional process called *content analysis*. Content analysis is defined as a procedure for the categorization of verbal or behavioral data, for purposes of classification, summarization, and tabulation. It is an intriguing process, probably the most intellectually demanding of all techniques of data analysis, and one of the few areas in the later stages of the research process in which the researcher plays a strong individual and creative role.

Content analysis was first used as a technique for the analysis and quantification of communication material, such as the contents of newspapers, magazines, and radio broadcasts. In recent years, the technique has been used in increasingly varied settings and for a wide variety of research purposes. In fact, the general model for content analysis that we will discuss in this chapter can be applied to data analysis in many of the techniques for questioning and observing.

The early studies using content analysis involved little more than word counting. For example, a typical such study might be one in which the researcher hypothesized that the morning and afternoon newspapers in his community had different interests in education. He decides to test this by counting the frequency with which stories appearing on page one of each paper for a 30-day period contained references to education. To do such a study he would make a list of relevant terms for this topic—education, school, teachers, pupils, school tax—read through the first page of each issue, and count the frequency with which each of the key concepts was noted. Notice that by the end of the study he would have quantitative data, in this case the frequency with which each of the two papers had used each of the key concepts.

He might also add a second dimension to this study by coding the feeling tone of each reference, that is, evaluating whether each reference was positive toward education, negative toward education, or neutral. The content analysis would then yield a quantitative estimate of the positiveness or negativeness of each of the papers as well as the absolute estimate of the amount of attention they pay to topics associated with education. It would then be possible to move one step further, and having these estimates of the frequency and tone of the references to make inferences about the intent of each paper, that is, to attempt to categorize them as pro-education, anti-education, or neutral toward education.

These two examples illustrate the three basic research purposes content analysis can be used to achieve: the specific analysis of *semantic content,* and/or the analysis of the *feeling tone* communicated by a set of data, and provision of a *basis for inference* about the intent of the source.

This last use of content analysis was perfected during World War II when the Experimental Division for the Study of Wartime Communication analyzed communication material for evidence of subversion. The contents of periodicals or newspapers suspected of subversion were analyzed in conjunction with German broadcasts and propaganda releases in an attempt to find a parallel in theme, approach, and emphasis. These parallels were then used as the basis for inferences about the intent of the writers and publishers. It is of interest that some of these analyses were used by the Justice Department in actual trials, and were accepted by the courts as evidence of the intent of the source.

THE LEVELS OF CONTENT ANALYSIS

Perhaps the most basic distinction to be made in content analysis is the distinction between content analysis done at the *manifest level* and at the *latent level*. Content analysis at the manifest level is content analysis of what the respondent *said,* strictly bound by the response, with nothing read into it and assumed about it. At this level the analysis is simply a direct transcription of the response in terms of some code. At the latent level, in contrast, the researcher attempts to code the meaning of the response or the underlying dynamics motivating the behavior described. In other words, he seeks to go beyond transcription of what was said directly and seeks to infer what was implied or meant.

There is ample evidence to indicate that content analysis at the manifest level can be accomplished reliably and validly but that this cannot be said of content analysis at the latent level. For example, consider data consisting of responses to the Thematic Apperception Test in which deliberately vague and ambiguous pictures involving interpersonal interactions are shown to people who are asked to make up a story accounting for the scene pictured. If the task is to do a content analysis of the themes in the stories, of the roles assigned each of the people, or of the kinds of endings to the stories in the sense of what ultimately happens to each participant, this task is content analysis at the manifest level. It can be done with the high reliability and with the face and content validity which characterizes all good content analysis. However, if the task is to do a content analysis of the quality of the endings (happy or unhappy), this moves us toward the latent level but it still should be accomplished with reasonable reliability and validity, since there are commonly accepted and understood concepts of what constitutes happy and unhappy resolutions to human interactions. However, if we are asked to analyze the psychological mechanisms involved in the situations described (for example, aggression, projection), or if we are asked to infer the nature of the personality of the respondent who told the story, then the reliability drops precipitously, and so limits the validity. For now we are deeply at the latent level and in areas where theory is developing but is not yet developed to the point where the behavioral concomitants of theoretical constructs are fully understood and agreed upon.

In short, if the data-collection methods being contemplated produce data requiring content analysis, the researcher must distinguish carefully between those analyses that can be performed at the manifest level and those requiring the latent level. It may well be that these latter analyses will not be able to be reliably performed, and so the success of the project cannot be permitted to rest upon them.

Need for Pilot Data and Trial-and-Error Period

Because satisfactory reliability cannot always be achieved, a pilot study is a critical "must" in any project in which content analysis is contemplated. Sufficient pilot data must be obtained to provide the researcher with some estimate of the success he will have if he sets out to develop a code and use content analysis to analyze the research data. To provide this estimate properly, the data obtained in the pilot study must present the same problems of analysis that the actual project data will present. The general rule on pilot studies, that the respondents must be like the ultimate respondents and the circumstances of data collection like those to be used, applies with particular force in this instance. This is because the basic purpose of the pilot data is to determine if the researcher can develop a reliable code at the level at which he wishes to work. Unless the pilot data have the same elements of clarity and ambiguity, certainty, and uncertainty as the final data, the researcher may come to a spurious conclusion as to his ability to handle these data through content-analysis procedures.

Even after this pilot period, the researcher should allow for a period of trial and error during which he continues to perfect his categories and develop the skills of his coders. Content analysis is a slow and time-consuming developmental process, and the researcher contemplating it must allow for both the pilot and trial periods if he is to complete it properly and successfully.

THE PROCESS OF CONTENT ANALYSIS

The process of content analysis is best understood with some data, and so Table 22-1 presents free verbal responses written by teachers to the question: "Have there been any changes in your school since the increase in the number of Puerto Rican pupils?"[1] The six responses listed are selected from several hundred responses obtained during the major study of which the Language Study was a part. We shall use these data to indicate three different ways data can be analyzed with content analysis as well as the three basic stages of the technique: (1) deciding what the unit of content to be analyzed will be; (2) developing the set of categories; and (3) developing a rationale to guide the placement of responses in categories. We shall begin with a consideration of content analysis for feeling tone, move on to a semantic content analysis, and conclude with the analysis of intent.

Content Analysis for Feeling Tone

Content analysis for feeling tone is employed when the researcher wishes to abstract some sense of the tone or attitude communicated by the response or behavior being analyzed. For the illustrative data in Table 22-1, this would mean abstracting some sense of the feeling of these several responses. The first decision is to select what is called the *unit of content,* or that material to be categorized. Generally this comes down to making one of two choices, either using the total response, or breaking down that response into the separate words or phrases which make it up. For example, if we were concerned with identifying the feeling tone of the

[1]This table also presents other material which will be referred to later in this chapter.

Table 22-1 Illustrative Data for Content Analysis Exercise

Response	*Column 1* Content Analysis for Feeling Tone	*Column 2*	*Column 3* Semantic Content Analysis	*Column 4*
	Using Total Response as Unit of Content	Using Words or Phrases as Unit of Content	Unweighted	Weighted
A. These children have lowered our academic standards, ruined the physical plant, and made for general chaos in the school.	5	5 5 5	510 520 530	-4.5 -1.1 -2.5 $\overline{-8.1}$
B. The Puerto Rican children have been a tremendous help in our art and music classes, enriched the general cultural and artistic level of the school, and their warmth and enthusiasm have made for a more pleasant school atmosphere.	1	1 1 1 1 1		
C. The Puerto Rican children who have come into our school have not been able to keep up with the work so that we have had to lower our academic standards somewhat. On the other hand, they have raised the level of the work done in the craft classes considerably.	3			-4.5 $+0.7$ $\overline{-3.8}$
D. These children had an effect on our academic standards, certainly, and also on things like pupil and staff relationships and school-community relationships.	7		710 741 742 744	
E. The children have made it necessary to alter our methods of teaching, make up many of our own materials, replace much of the equipment in the school, and, on the other hand, have been a strong factor in uplifting the level of creative response.	3			
F. It's much harder to teach, they don't know nearly as much, can't work as fast, but they are charming in a way,	3			

responses in Table 22-1, we might decide to use the total response as the unit of content. If we did, we would read each response completely and categorize it once on the basis of everything it contains. If we decided to use the separate words or phrases as the units of content, we would take each separate word or phrase that indicates some specific perception of a change, such as "lowered academic standards" in response A and categorize each such language element separately. For this illustration let us first illustrate content analysis with the total response as the unit of content.

To do the analysis we need a *set of categories.* As a guide in developing categories the researcher turns to the research purpose to be served by the analysis and also to the data. The research purpose is to abstract feeling tone, and so a continuum from *positive* to *negative* comes to mind suggesting the first two categories. Scanning the data, however, we note that all the responses do not seem to be one dimensional, and so we might add a third category to represent some intermediate point which we could call *mixed.*

To standardize the application of these categories, the researcher should define them. For example, we might set down the following definitions:

1. *Positive*—a response containing only perceptions of change representing gain, development, or improvement
3. *Mixed*—a response containing both positive and negative elements
5. *Negative*—a response containing only perceptions of change representing decline, retardation, or loss

For convenience in referring to the categories, we have numbered them. Note that we have assigned the numbers so that the numerical sequence follows the logical sequence, with the mixed category in the middle. Moreover, we have left an unassigned number between each of the ones assigned so that there is room for adding categories if we need them.

The third element required, the *rationale to guide the placement of responses,* is best developed during the trial-and-error period in which the researcher attempts to use his tentative set of categories. Therefore let us try to apply the three categories above to the data. In the actual process of content analysis, the researcher writes the category number assigned to the responses on the response itself or on some score sheet he has developed. In this example, these category numbers have been entered in column 1 of Table 22-1.

To begin the content analysis we read over the entire first response, response A, and decide in which category it might be placed. The answer is clear that response A belongs on the negative end of the continuum, and so should be placed in category 5. We have therefore placed a "5" in column 1, next to response A. Reading over response B, we see with similar clarity that it belongs in category 1. Response C, too, is clear, for it contains a reference to both a negative and a positive perception, which is how we defined the category *mixed*. Response D, however, stops us, for it does not immediately lend itself to placement in one of the three categories we have developed. What is the problem? Simply that the teacher who wrote it was unkind enough not to keep our categorization in mind! Note that she *has* answered the question and referred to the "changes" which have taken place in her school but has done so without providing us with a basis for deciding the feeling tone.

When faced with a response which cannot be appropriately placed into one of the existing categories, we must develop a new category, since every response must be categorized. In this case, we would call the new category *ambiguous*, defined as "a response which lacks the basis for classification in terms of the dynamic being studied." Note that the label ambiguous is applied to express the relationship of the response to the particular intent of the content analysis. This allows for the fact that the same response might be categorizable under a different content analysis, as we shall see later in this illustrative example. We have assigned number 7 to the ambiguous category to place it outside the numbers we have reserved for conceptual categories.

Since we have added a new category, we check back over the previous categorizations we have done and reconsider these in the light of the new category. It is always possible that we might have categorized these differently had we had the ambiguous category available. In this instance we would see no reason to change the categorizations of responses A, B, or C, and so we move on to response E.

Response E also should make us pause as we consider classifying it. On first glance it might seem like an obvious response to be placed in the *mixed* category. "Uplifting the level of creative response" is a perception of a positive change. But are altering methods of teaching, making up materials, and replacing equipment necessarily perceptions of negative change? Depending upon the school situation and the need for new methods, materials, and equipment it may or may not be negative. How then to categorize the response? The intermediate phrase ". . . on the other hand" provides us with a basis for categorization. We might argue that this phrase, which is followed by what we have agreed is a clear perception of a positive change, indicates that the *respondent* intended the preceding references to be negative. If we were to do this we could use this intervening phrase to develop a rationale which would guide the placement of response E into one of our categories. Suppose that we stated this first entry in our rationale as follows:

1. If a response contains one part without any implicit feeling tone, and one
    part which has feeling tone, and these parts are connected by a word or
    phrase indicating a reversal of feeling, that response shall be categorized as
    mixed.

This complex statement does settle the question of response E which
has one part without implicit feeling and one part which we agree is
positive and which has the words "on the other hand" connecting the two
parts. We therefore categorize the response as *mixed.*

The reason a rationale is stated on points like this is to assure that when
the same situation is faced, if it is recognized, it will be handled the same
way. For reliability is as critical an aspect of content analysis as it is of
any procedure for data analysis. For this reason, in stating the rationale,
the researcher tries to be as specific as possible. Ideally, he will be
sufficiently specific so that the coder who has to apply the rationale has
neither interpretation nor judgment to make. Every bit of judgment that
the coder must exert damages the reliability, and so we prefer that the
code and its accompanying rationale be sufficiently specific to eliminate
coder judgment. It is this aim which makes content analysis by computer,
discussed in Chapter 23, a perfectly feasible process.

The final response, F, indicates another difficulty with content analysis.
Students with whom this response is discussed often split in their classification of it, with some considering it mixed and others calling it negative.
Those who call it mixed argue that by the rationale above it must be
mixed, for the second part "they are charming in a way, I suppose" is
perceived as positive and it is preceded by a "but" which indicates that
the preceding material can be seen as negative. Those who argue for the
negative categorization point out that even the presumably positive phrase
"they are charming" seems to be begrudgingly stated and doubly qualified
by the phrase ". . . in a way, I suppose." This is true, but to begin to
reason this way places an interpretative responsibility which should not be
there on the shoulders of the coder. By the statement of the rationale
which was developed for response E we must code response F as *mixed*
unless we wished to restate the rationale. The restatement would have the
original rationale plus some involved addition, so that it would read like
this:

> If a response contains one part without any implicit feeling tone, and one
> part which has feeling tone, and these parts are connected by a word or phrase
> which indicates a reversal of feeling, that response shall be categorized as
> *mixed.* However, if that phrase expressing reversal of feeling tone is begrudg-
> ingly stated, or qualified by a subsequent phrase indicating doubt or uncer-

tainty, then the response is to be categorized on the basis of the part which has a clear feeling tone.

Not only is this phrasing ridiculously complex, but it violates the basic rule for the rationale: that it be clear and specific and not require interpretation on the part of the coder. Note that to apply the new rationale the coder must use his judgment to decide when a phrase indicates "doubt" or "uncertainty," or when a statement is made "begrudgingly." Therefore, with the unhappiness which characterizes a small proportion of the categorizations in any content analysis, we place response F in the *mixed* category.

We have now coded all six responses, and in so doing have added one category to the original three. Placing six responses into four categories is not a particularly effective summarization, but hopefully we could now code several more responses without the need for additional categories.

Changing the Unit of Content

Let us now consider these same data and the same research purpose and categories but use a different unit of content than the total response. We shall continue to seek a means for determining the feeling tone of the reaction of each teacher, but now let us use as the unit of content every word or phrase that refers to a specific component of the teacher's reaction. Instead of categorizing each response once, this time we shall categorize it as often as it has separate words or phrases describing change. Consider response A. How many separate words or phrases does it have? This teacher's response consists of references to three changes: (1) lowered academic standards; (2) ruined the physical plant; and (3) caused general chaos in the school. Thus we would code these three units of content separately, and in the case of response A, all three would be coded as negative. Therefore we have entered three "5's" in column 2 of Table 22-1.

Consider response B. In determining the number of units of content it contains we have a more complex task than we had in response A. Consider the first phrase, "tremendous help in art and music classes." Does that phrase contain one unit of content or two? A second element added to our rationale will answer that question. It is that:

2.   Any unit of content which would be coded if it appeared alone is coded if it appears in conjunction with another codeable unit of content.

Since we would have coded a reference to the children being a tremendous help in art classes or music classes, had either appeared alone, we therefore code both of them now that they appear together, and both are coded as positive. The same rationale serves to guide our decision on the number of units of content in the phrase "enriched the general cultural and artistic level of the school." We code two separate responses, for either phrase appearing alone would be coded. Note that the rationale does what it is supposed to do: It avoids the coder having to make a judgment as to whether cultural and artistic refer to the same or different dynamics. The last problem in response B is the last part: ". . . their warmth and enthusiasm have made for a more pleasant school atmosphere." This we consider one response since the grammatical structure of the response indicates that the reference to warmth and enthusiasm is intended to be the explanation of the more pleasant school atmosphere. Had the teacher said "they are warm and enthusiastic and we now have a more pleasant school atmosphere" we might argue for multiple coding, but she did not. The coder is always forced to code *what the respondent said, in the way that he said it,* and must resist the temptation to code some hypothetical alternative response. We conclude, then, having identified five units of content for response B, coding each of them as positive.

Responses C, D, E, and F have not been coded in Table 22-1, so that the reader may use them to test his understanding to this point. Try coding these four responses before reading on.

For response C we should have coded two units of content, one negative and one positive. The negative part is the entire first phrase referring to the children's inability to keep up with the work and the subsequent lowering of academic standards. The positive part is the raising of the level of work in the craft classes.

Response D should have been listed as containing four units of content, each of which was ambiguous in terms of feeling tone. Thus we should have entered four "7's" in column 2. There is one point of potential confusion in determining the numbers of units of content in response D, and that involves determining how many different relationships are listed. However, if we limit ourselves to coding on the basis of what the respondent said, in the way that she said it, we should have no trouble. We count pupil relationships and staff relationships as separate units, because they are separated by the word "and," but count school-community as one, since the respondent hyphenated it.

Response E should have been coded as having three units of content with ambiguous feeling tone and one with a positive feeling tone. Note that now that we have shifted the unit of content to the word or phrase, the rationale by which we decided the first part of the response was positive no longer applies.

Response F is troublesome, for the grammatical structure of the response makes us wonder if there are two units of content ("they're much harder to teach," and "they are charming") or if there are four. The problem involved is the possibility that the two phrases, "they don't know nearly as much" and "they can't work as fast," are intended to explain why they are harder to teach. Again we rigidly base the decision upon the language structure in the response and point 2 of our rationale. Since the phrases are connected by commas only and not by the word "because," and since each could be coded if it appeared alone, we would code four units, the first three as negative and the fourth as the one positive phrase.

The effect of changing the unit of content can be seen by considering responses C, E, and F. All three of these were originally placed in category 3, using the total response as the unit of content, but all three were coded differently when we changed the unit of content to the separate word or phrase. Moreover, the coding by separate word or phrase has resulted in response E no longer being perceived as containing both positive and negative elements, and in responses C and F having different balances of positive and negative elements. Obviously then, tabulation of the data based on the two different units of content would be different.

These differences illustrate perhaps the most important aspect of content analysis for the student to recognize: The data which emerge are extremely sensitive to the nature of the analysis attempted, to the unit of content selected, and to the researcher's expectations as reflected in the categories he develops. In a sense, content analysis is a personal statement by the researcher of his perceptions of the data. For example, another researcher who believed that changes in methods, materials, and equipment were all negative would have a basically different coding for response E than we have developed. Similar differences in perception at other points could have produced a different code, guided by different rationales, and producing different data. This personal aspect to content analysis will be illustrated even more graphically as we move on to the semantic content analysis.

SEMANTIC CONTENT ANALYSIS

Neither of the analyses of feeling tone grappled with the issue of actually coding what the teacher said. To do that the researcher would have to develop a *semantic content analysis,* which is the problem to which we shall now turn. A semantic content analysis involves the development of a set of categories intended to represent the dimensions and specifics of the actual content of the responses. To develop such a content analysis, we might argue that in the six responses we have been considering, there seem to be two dimensions or levels of content. Some aspects of the responses refer to general areas of the educational process like the academic area, physical plant, or the area of relationships. Other aspects of the content are quite specific, like the references to art and music classes, or the specific relationships spelled out in response D.

To develop a code for a semantic content analysis, the researcher first identifies the most general level at which he wishes to work and spells out the specifics within this level. For the data in Table 22-1 we have identified the process area as our most general level, and in the first column of Table 22-2 we have listed six specific areas which stem from the responses we have considered. In an actual project we would not limit the categories to those which stem from the data but would feel free to add other categories which are conceptually sound and likely to be needed for coding other responses. As an example of this, we have added area 7 with the most general level delineated. We then move to the first level of specificity, and so in the second column of Table 22-2 we have identified specifics within each area, using both the data and our knowledge of the areas.

To use such a code, we also need some means of expressing the quality of change referred to, as well as the area and specific noted. This means we have three different aspects to each semantic unit: the quality, the area, and the specific, if any. In general, we use as many digits as we have aspects to code, and so this semantic content analysis would involve a three-digit code. The first digit would refer to the quality of the response, the second to the area, and the third to the specific, if any. Since in multiple-digit coding, the position of the digit indicates the level of the code to which it refers, it must always be held constant. Therefore, if there was no specific indicated for our two-digit code we would indicate this with a zero in the third position. Let us see how this would work by coding the first few responses in Table 22-1, using as the unit of content the same separate word or phrase which gives a specific aspect of the teacher's reaction.

The reader will remember that we had decided response A contained three negative units of content. The first, "lowered academic standards," is easily located in the academic area and contains no specific information. It has therefore been coded as 510, meaning a negative general reference to the academic area. By this same thinking, "ruined the physical plant" is coded as 520, a negative general reference to plant, and "made for general chaos" as 530, a negative general reference to atmosphere.

Let us consider response D next. To this point, we have not been able

Table 22–2   Code for Semantic Content Analysis of Teacher Responses

First Digit = Quality of response

1 = Positive
5 = Negative
7 = Ambiguous
8 = No reaction, change

Second Digit Area	*Third Digit*	
	Specifics:	(0 to be used for references to area only, with no specifics)
1. Academic processes, including classes, courses and subjects	1 = art 2 = music 3 = craft 4 = social studies	5 = language-arts, reading 6 = science 7 = mathematics
2. Plant	1 = equipment	
3. Atmosphere, climate, creative level	1 = cultural 2 = artistic, creative	
4. Relationships	1 = pupil 2 = teacher, staff 3 = pupil-staff	4 = school-community 5 = teacher-administration
5. Teaching process	1 = methods 2 = materials 3 = difficulty of	
6. Characteristics of children	1 = knowledge 2 = intelligence	3 = work speed 4 = charm
7. Staff and administration	1 = turnover, stability 2 = morale 3 = quality	

to do anything with this response other than indicate that it has four units of content, none of which has any identifiable feeling tone. Now, however, while we continue to indicate ambiguity in feeling tone in the first digit, we can code the area and the specifics. The four code numbers entered in Table 22-1 reflect the general references to academic standards (710) and to the area of relationships involving pupils (741), staff (742), and school-community (744). This illustrates how a set of data can be ambiguous for one type of coding purpose, but codeable for another.

The coding spaces next to responses B, C, E, and F have been left blank for the reader's use in practicing coding. The coding the author suggests for these responses are explained in the footnote below.[2]

Personal Nature of Semantic Content Analysis

In discussing the content analysis for feeling tone, we noted how strong an element of personal statement was contained in that analysis. The semantic content analysis is even more personal, or arbitrary. Consider the code stated in Table 22-2. Another researcher, given this same research purpose and data, and same overall perception of what should be coded and how it should be coded, might have made several different decisions. For example, in area 1 he might have decided that art and music belong together as one set of classes devoted to the arts. He might have preferred pulling the references to creative and artistic level out of area 3 and made them into a separate area, arguing that "atmosphere and climate" refer to areas of the educational process quite different from the creative and artistic components. He might have argued that difficulty of teaching is more properly seen as a characteristic of children than as an aspect of the teaching process. All of these are sensible arguments which could be defended, just as the original placement of these concepts could be defended. It is this latitude for individual perception which makes content analysis uniquely personal as a technique for data analysis.

Not only might the other researcher have come up with these variations in area and specific within essentially the same code, he might also have come up with a radically different code. Table 22-3 illustrates this. Here the entire conceptualization of what constitutes an area, and what a

[2]The five positive units of content for response B should have been coded as follows: 111, for the positive reference in the academic area to art classes; 112, for the positive reference in the academic area to music classes; 131, for the positive reference in the area of atmosphere to cultural level; 132, for the positive reference in the area of atmosphere to artistic level; 130, for the positive general reference in the area of atmosphere.

In response C, the reference to lowered academic standards would be coded 510 just as it was in response A, and the positive reference to work in the craft classes would be coded 113.

In response E, the first two ambiguous units of content should have been coded in area 5, the teaching process. Specifically, the code numbers assigned would be 751 (methods of teaching) and 752 (making up materials). The third ambiguous unit on replacing equipment would be coded 721. The final positive unit of content, referring to uplifting the level of creative response, should have been coded in area 3 on atmosphere, as 132.

Response F has two of its three negative responses and one positive response all coded in area 6 since they all refer to characteristics of the children. The first negative response, on the difficulty of teaching, is coded 553. Then the responses in children's characteristics are coded 561 (don't know as much), 563 (can't work as fast), and 164 (charming).

Table 22-3   Alternate Code for Semantic Content Analysis of Teacher Responses

First Digit = Quality of response

1 = Positive
5 = Negative
7 = Ambiguous
8 = No reaction, change

Second Digit Area	*Third Digit* Specific: (0 to be used for reference to area only, with no specifics)
1. The School	1 = plant, equipment
	2 = atmosphere, climate
	3 = cultural, artistic, creative level
	4 = relationships with community
	5 = academic level of
2. The Teacher	1 = methods
	2 = materials
	3 = relationships among
	4 = difficulty of functioning
3. The Children	1 = knowledge
	2 = work speed
	3 = charm, wit, humor
	4 = relationships among
4. Classes and courses	1 = art, music
	2 = craft, physical education
	3 = social studies
	4 = mathematics, science
	5 = language-arts, reading

specific, is entirely different from the previous code. Some aspects which were areas in the first code are now specifics, that is, academic level, relationships, or physical plant. Other concepts which were separate specifics have now been combined (that is, music and art classes, cultural level, artistic level, and creative level). There would be no point in asking which code is right or even which code is better, for these are unanswerable questions. If they can be used reliably and if they produce relevant data for the research question, then they may both be right and equally good.

The point to note is that they are *different,* and thus the data they produce will be different. Consider as an example the perception each code will give of the importance teachers attached to changes with an academic component. In the first code where "academic" was an area within which specific classes were subsumed, we would find this an important aspect of teacher's concern. In the second code with "academic level" simply one of many specifics within the area of school, and with classes now a separate area, there would be relatively much less importance attached to the academic component in itself. This difference, one of several we could note even with the few responses considered here, illustrates the need for the researcher using content analysis (and anyone reading a study which used it) always to be aware that the data come out as they did at least in part because of the way the code was established. This author always reacts skeptically to reports based on content analysis which note that "10 percent of the responses fell into the category . . . ." Responses do not fall into categories; they are pushed into them! And the researcher should never forget that he did the pushing.

Weighting in Semantic Content Analysis

Even with this semantic content analysis completed we have not fully tapped all of the information in the data. Why this is so will become clear if we consider response C. The first time response C was coded, on the basis of total response it was placed in the mixed category, implying that the response was balanced in content. The second time it was coded, using the specific word or phrase as unit of content, it was coded as having one positive and one negative unit of content, again implying that it was a balanced response. The third time it was coded it was further indicated that both the positive and negative unit of content were in the academic area, once again implying balance.

Consider what those "balanced" units of content mentioned. The negative one involved a decline in the general level of academic performance. This was "balanced" by an improvement in the work done in the craft classes.

There are few educators who would agree that these are comparable phenomena by any criterion of educational significance. We face this problem because to this point we have assumed that the separate words and phrases were interval data, all with the same importance. Response C makes clear that this assumption makes little sense. Instead it is clear that the words and phrases have differential importance. The researcher's problem now is to capture this differential importance so that it can be utilized in the content analysis. The simplest way of doing this is with a weighting system in which the different possible responses are each assigned a weight commensurate with its educational importance.

The procedure for developing these weights can be summarized simply.

The actual content code would be submitted to at least three and ideally five or seven experts in the field relevant to the research. Each expert would be informed as to the purpose of the study and the nature of the responses to be coded. Then the continuum along which the experts are to weight the possible responses would be described in detail for the judges, as would the separate gradations along that continuum. When the continuum and the nature of the responses were both fully understood, the code would be given to the judges, who would be asked to assign a weight to each specific category in the code.

When this is completed the researcher will have the several weights for each item in the code assigned by the separate judges. He should scan these to estimate the nature of agreement among the judges. Assuming that the task was reasonable and the continuum accurately defined, the agreement should be good. In practice this means that the judges may differ a point or two from each other, but they should not differ in terms of the overall location of a response on the continuum. This means that one judge should not place a response at the low end of the continuum while another places it at the upper end. If this kind of extreme disagreement does occur, the researcher must return to the judges and attempt to clarify the disagreements.

Once they are clarified, the researcher takes the median of the different weights assigned by the several judges and this then becomes the weight for that response. It is a relatively simple matter to return to the original responses and rescore them so that these weights are reflected. Now instead of recording the response and stopping, the researcher records the weight as well. Thus when he is finished coding a response he can add the weights and obtain a total score for the response.

This process also makes it relatively simple for a researcher to distinguish between positive and negative responses, or between advantages and disadvantages attributed to a program. With data like those in our illustrative example, we have identical content, some of which is stated in a positive context, some negative. This system of weighting can easily be adapted to this situation by considering each positive response as a plus, each negative response as a minus, and each ambiguous response as a zero. Thus after they are coded and weighted, the negative and positive responses are added algebraically.

As an example, let us assume that we submitted the content analysis in Table 22-2 to five experts[3] in education. We explained the purpose of our study to each expert and gave them the following task:

[3]We are using expert here in the sense of professionally qualified and experienced rather than in the traditional student sense of "friend," "roommate," or "fellow student for whom I was an expert judge last week."

Table 22–4 Hypothetical Weights Assigned to Semantic Content Analysis of Teacher Responses

Area		Specific	Median of Weights Assigned by Judges
1. Academic	0	general	4.5[a]
	1	art	1.1
	2	music	0.8
	3	craft	0.7
	4	social studies	2.8
	5	language-arts, reading	4.1
	6	science	1.7
	7	mathematics	3.2
2. Plant	0	general	1.1
	1	equipment	1.2
3. Atmosphere, climate	0	general	2.5
	1	cultural	1.2
	2	artistic, creative	2.2
4. Relationships	0	general	0.9
	1	pupil	1.4
	2	teacher, staff	1.7
	3	pupil–staff	2.4
	4	school–community	3.3
	5	teacher–administration	2.5
5. Teaching process	0	general	2.7
	1	methods	2.1
	2	materials	0.9
	3	difficulty of	3.1
6. Characteristics of children	1	knowledge	2.8
	2	intelligence	3.7
	3	work speed	1.4
	4	charm	1.0

[a]To see how these weights were derived, let us assume that the five judges weighted "Academic–general" as 5.0, 4.6, 4.5, 4.3, and 4.2. The median of 4.5 is used as the average.

Read over the entire code. Then use the scale below the assign a value to each specific category reflecting the educational importance and impact of change in that specific category.

Use a 0 to indicate a change of absolutely no significance or impact and a 5 to indicate a change of extremely critical significance, one of the most important changes you can imagine. A 2.5 then would be a change of average importance. Ratings between 0 and 2.5 are changes of less than average importance. Ratings between 2.5 and 5 are above average, but less than critical.

Assume that we take the medians of the weights assigned by the five experts, and list the median weight next to each specific category, as in Table 22-4. Finally, assume we also decide to use the plus, minus, and zero system for handling positive, negative, and ambiguous responses. We could then return to the responses in Table 22-1 and next to each coding already completed place the corresponding weight in column 4. For response A, this would produce the weights of −4.5 (for 510), −1.1 (for 520), and −2.5 (for 530), adding to a score of −8.1. Let us move to response C, which stimulated our interest in weights, to see how it comes out now. The negative reference to academic standards (510) gets a weight of −4.5, whereas the positive reference to craft classes receives a +0.7. These add algebraically to −3.8. Thus, for the first time we communicate a feeling other than balance about response C. Now we see its negative component outweighs its positive component. The chart in the footnote below[4] lists the correct weighting of the other responses for students who wish practice.

Weighted Content Analysis in Measurement

An interesting point to note about this system of developing a weighted content analysis is that it is perfectly analogous to the process for scoring essay examinations. If we have before us 32 essay-type responses written by students to an examination question worth 30 points, we have two choices available for scoring. One is the traditional way of considering the

[4]Response	Coding	Weight	Total Score
B	111	+1.1	
	112	+0.8	
	131	+1.2	+7.8
	132	+2.2	
	130	+2.5	
D	710	0	
	741	0	
	742	0	0
	744	0	
E	751	0	
	752	0	+2.2
	721	0	
	132	+2.2	
F	553	−3.1	
	561	−2.8	−6.3
	563	−1.4	
	164	+1.0	

total response as our unit of analysis, that is, reading the answer and deciding how many points it is worth. Like the content analysis using total response as a unit of content, this is limited and superficial, and moreover is unreliable. The other choice is to consider the unit of content to be each separate point or suggestion made by the students. To do this we would develop a model answer (or code) containing all the possible answers which might be made and assigning a point value (or weight) to each of these answers. Scoring the examination under this procedure is then a matter of determining which answers the student has made, giving him the credit value for each, and adding these to obtain a total score. In fact, it is perfectly possible to use the plus–minus system as well, assigning a plus for each point correctly made, and a minus for each point touched upon but referred to incorrectly. The score in this case would be the algebraic sum of the weights. This system can be done with the same high reliability which characterizes the semantic content analysis.

ASSIGNING DIGITS TO LEVELS OF A CONTENT CODE

In any content analysis like the semantic content analysis in which the researcher is seeking to transcribe information at more than one level, he must decide how to handle the different levels. In the semantic codes we have used as illustrations, we have had three levels: feeling tone or quality of the unit of content, the area in which the response was located, and the specific response. We have handled these three levels with a three-digit code, assigning one digit to each level. But this cannot always be done. Assume a more complex set of data, such as data which were obtained from an adolescent reporting for us the most exciting example of teaching he had ever experienced. Such data might contain a wealth of descriptive information such as the grade level, the subject field, the sex of the teacher, the reported age of the teacher, or specific personal character-istics of the teacher. All five of these areas of characteristics may be important and worth coding, yet all are background to the semantic code we would need to develop for the actual teaching situation described. If we needed a one- or two-digit code for the teaching situations, we would have a seven-digit code if we assigned each of the five background characteristics its own digit.

Assigning the digits for a semantic content code is a task whose impor-tance is a function of the number of responses and the complexity of the analyses to be performed with the data. The intuitive response of the researcher new to content analysis is to treat each separate level with a separate digit. This is undoubtedly the simplest way of developing a code but also the most difficult to process and analyze. In fact, each separate digit multiplies the difficulties of data processing and data analysis so heavily that researchers prefer to make each digit in the code do as much work as possible.

One way to accomplish this is through *multiple coding,* that is, using one digit to code two related or compatible variables. For example, if we set out to code teacher characteristics, one digit might be used to code both the sex and grade level of the teacher. We do this by establishing a simple cross-tabulation grid, like that in Table 22-5 below. The digits in the cell now serve to code two pieces of information. The number "1," for example, tells us that the teacher was a male elementary school teacher, just as the number "6" tells us that the teacher was a female, but that the incident did not refer to her grade level. Note that this type of grid allows for the inevitable "omits" for each characteristic.

In such a double coding the researcher has ten digits readily available in the numbers 0 through 9. If he is planning to process the coded data by electronic data-processing equipment, he has twelve locations available for punching in each column, the numbers 0 through 9 and the letters X and Y.[5] This limitation to ten or twelve available code units, of course, forces the researcher to compress the variations in each variable and to work at the most general level, that is, not distinguishing between the lower and upper elementary grades or between junior and senior high school. But if the loss of specificity will not damage the data badly, it is more than balanced by the saving of one digit.

Another way to save digits is through a process called *geometric coding.* This is a process whereby numbers are assigned to consecutive categories beginning with 1 and successively multiplied by 2, that is, 1, 2, 4, 8, 16, 32, and so on. To illustrate this let us assume that the researcher sees that these descriptions of exciting teaching situations refer to the several as-

Table 22-5 Example of Cross-Grid for Multiple Coding

	Sex		
Grade Level	Male	Female	Omitted
Elementary	1	4	7
Secondary	2	5	8
Omitted	3	6	9

[5]A thirteenth possibility is to leave a column unpunched. However, for most statistical analysis it is preferable to use only the digits 0 to 9 in coding.

pects of the teacher's psychosocial structure, which he summarizes in six areas: personality, intelligence, knowledge of subject matter, interest in children, interest in or knowledge of fields other than subject, and creativity and ingenuity in teaching method. The coding problem is that these may appear in any combination, and the researcher cannot afford to use six digits, each of which would spell out the presence or absence of one of the characteristics. The geometric coding approach would allow him to code *all* possible combinations using only two digits.

He would assign numbers to the categories geometrically rather than consecutively so that the six categories were numbered as follows:

01[6]—teacher personality
02—intelligence
04—knowledge of subject matter
08—interest in children
16—knowledge, interest, in fields other than subject matter
32—creativity or ingenuity in teaching method

If there were no references to these characteristics of the teacher, the number zero would be used. If there were single references only, the numbers above would be used. Now assume that a response refers to *both* the teacher's personality and intelligence. These are categories 01 and 02. To code this combination we add the separate codes: that is, 01 plus 02 equals 03. Note now that the only combination which would add to 03 would be the 01 plus the 02. In short, the code number 03 always tells us that the response referred both to the teacher's personality and intelligence. Or consider the response which referred to the teacher's intelligence (02), knowledge of subject matter (04), and interest in children (08). The sum of these codes is 02 plus 04 plus 08 or 14. This is also a unique number, for the only way of achieving 14 from our code is to add 02, 04, and 08. Similarly, every number we obtain by adding any combination is a unique number obtainable in only one way.

For example, what were the characteristics of the teacher for whom we enter the number 44? The first thing to remember in solving that problem is to note that any geometric number other than the basic set above must include the first basic number below it. In this case the first basic number below 44 is 32, and so the response must have referred to the teacher's creativity or ingenuity in method. It could not have referred to her knowledge other than subject matter (16), because 32 and 16 add to 48. Her interest in children (08) could have been noted since 32 and 08 only add to 40, and the final reference must have been to her subject matter knowledge (04), since this is the only way we can reach 44.

[6]Note that we use the zero to hold the number of digits used at a constant two digits.

This process of geometric coding, although illustrated here with the relatively simple coding of descriptive data, can also be used to code aspects of responses in a semantic content analysis. It works provided the range of possible responses is limited. If the range of responses becomes larger than the six handled in the illustration above, the number of digits needed rises rapidly. For example, handling seven, eight, or nine levels requires three digits; handling 10 to 13 levels requires four digits; 14 levels requires five digits, and so on. Moreover, the work involved in adding many responses slows the coding process down so much that no real saving is involved.

CONTENT ANALYSIS FOR INFERENCE

The third function for which content analysis can be performed is to provide a basis for learning something about the intent or motivations of the respondent. This use of content analysis moves us to the latent level, where we are interested in what the response implies or infers rather than what it says. To function at this level with any hope of reliable and valid inferences the researcher must have a reliable and valid model from which to develop the code. For example, at the beginning of the chapter we noted that content analysis was used in World War II to make inferences about the underlying sympathies of writers and publishers suspected of pro-Nazi leanings. This was feasible because the writings and broadcasts of the Nazis provided a model from which one could develop a code to identify the orientation or point of view of the suspected materials.

In the absence of such a model, content analysis for inference is difficult to accomplish reliably. For example, consider the data we have been using, the teachers' responses in Table 22-1. What if we were asked now to apply the code categories of "positive" or "negative," or "hostile" or "friendly" to the *teacher,* rather than to the changes presented in the responses. The immediate temptation is to consider the teacher who wrote response A (about lowered academic standards, ruined plant, and chaos) as negative and hostile, and consider the teacher who wrote response B (help in art, music, enriched cultural and artistic level, and more pleasant atmosphere) as positive and friendly. But what if teacher A was expressing what she saw happen about her as a classic urban pattern reoccurred: Large numbers of non–English-speaking children entered a school while its older residents moved out. The sudden overcrowding of classrooms and school proved too much for an overtaxed and overage physical plant, and also made for a noise and activity level far beyond what had been true in previous years. Does the teacher's reporting this necessarily mean she is negative or hostile to children? We could argue that it does, for her response indicates no awareness of the true causes, rather she attributes them to, and blames them on, the children. Or we could argue that frankness and candor are not equivalent to hostility and negativeness.

The difficulty of resolving this to the satisfaction of both points of view stems from the lack of any model or theory by which we can clearly understand the relationship between dynamics like hostility and processes like perception. We know that people perceive and report selectively, but we also know that different motivations can result in the same end products in terms of what is selected and reported. Therefore, until we move much further along in our understanding of these functional social and psychological processes, content analysis for inference will continue to be difficult to do with adequate reliability and validity.

Let us turn to those characteristics now, and consider how they are estimated in content analysis.

DETERMINING RELIABILITY
OF CONTENT ANALYSIS CODE

It is critical, early in the development of a code for content analysis, to estimate the reliability with which the code can be used. In fact, reliability is the primary virtue a code must possess, just as it is the basic characteristic for data-collection instruments. In addition to estimating the reliability of the code, it is important to estimate the reliability with which each potential coder can use the code.

Procedurally, reliability in content analysis is estimated through computing the percent of time two independent coders agree when they each code the same material. As in most efforts to estimate reliability in data analysis, a sample of 100 units of data is enough to provide a good basis for estimating the reliability of the code, provided that the 100 units are selected randomly from the total mass of data and so can be considered to be an unbiased selection. In a one-digit content analysis code, the basis for estimating the percent of times the coders agree is a simple matter of applying the formula below:

$$\text{percent agreement} = 100 \times \frac{\text{numbers of units of data coded identically}}{\text{total number of units of data coded}}$$

At least 90 percent agreement should be reached for a one- or two-digit code before it is considered sufficiently reliable for use in research. With multiple-digit codes, like the three-digit semantic content code we used in the previous illustrations, 85 percent agreement is a more realistic expectation, because the possibility for disagreement exists at any level of the code.

Reliability of Coders

The reliability of the coder must be estimated as well, for the author's experience with content analysis on several projects is that many of a group of people, who otherwise would be considered perfectly sound research assisttants, cannot do coding. To code properly requires an unusual combination of verbal flexibility and task compulsivity. The verbal flexibility is required for the coder must be able to recognize that 100 different responses can all be included into the same category because they all represent different ways of saying essentially the same thing. The coder who lacks that verbal flexibility will conclude a day's coding with large proportions of the responses coded as "ambiguous," because he will not place a response in a category unless the respondent has written the category as stated.

The other characteristic needed in a good coder, task compulsivity, is required because to code properly the coder must often search through the several categories of a complex code (which may run to many pages) to find the single best category in which to place the response. The less compulsive worker will not do this, but instead will place each response in the first approximately appropriate category he comes to.

To estimate the reliability of any single coder, the researcher must develop a standard set of approximately 100 coded responses on which he and others involved agree. The coder whose reliability is to be estimated then codes this standard set of responses, and the percent agreement method is applied. The same standards applied to a code are applied to the coder, except that at least 90 percent agreement should be achieved even for codes more complex than one or two digits.

Handling Low Reliability

If we assume that the coders are fully competent, then low reliability estimates are telling the researcher that he is asking his coders to make finer discriminations than they can with their current training and understanding of the code, and with the code at its present stage of development. Whether the fault lies in the code or coders, the reliability estimate cannot tell us.

This means that during the developmental stages of a code it is critical for the researcher to identify the major sources of discrepant coding and to analyze these in sufficient detail so that he learns the reason for the discrepancy. The simple way to do this is to bring the two coders who differ together and in each other's presence have them each explain the rationale for their own coding of the data. Either we will learn about the problem from listening how the responses differed, or in listening to each other they will take issue with the alternate interpretations. Once we have identified the nature of the discrepancy, it is usually a matter of rewording a category to eliminate the possibility of alternate interpretations, adding a new category so that there is an appropriate place for coding the response which caused the trouble, or additional training for the coders so that they use the code more adequately.

Another way of handling the problem is to contrast those data which have been coded reliably with those which have not. In this way the researcher can learn if errors are concentrated in one section or sections of the code, or if they cut across the code to involve all areas and categories. Obviously if the entire code is involved, then a serious rethinking of the entire process is in order. If, instead, only some areas are the trouble spots, then the possibility of code revision or some alteration in the data-gathering instructions are likely possibilities.

If the problem of unreliability arises with many categories and the percent of agreement falls below 70 percent, then the researcher should rethink the entire operation, beginning with the basic premises on which he has constructed the code. He should also deal with the possibly unfortunate fact that the kinds of distinctions he is seeking to make from the data cannot be made reliably. If, for example, he is seeking to code at the latent level by coding the motivations of the person described in a critical incident type of description of a behavioral situation, he must often face the fact that this cannot be done with satisfactory reliability. At the manifest level of content analysis, it should always be possible to develop a reliable code of some kind. However, it may not be possible to code at the level of precision the researcher would prefer, making the precise distinctions he wishes. It is for this reason that obtaining a pilot set of data has been stressed as an absolute must if content analysis is planned. Before committing ourselves to this method for handling data, we must be certain that the data will lend themselves to the analysis and that a suitable and reliable code can be developed.

If it is discovered in the planning stage that content analysis will be either unsuitably imprecise or unreliable, there is still opportunity to alter the data-collecting instrument. Often a slight change in the instructions will sufficiently restructure the task for the respondent so that some additional element is specified by him. Given this additional information the coding may be improved significantly. In all of the questioning techniques, what is said to the respondent, and how the question is posed, plays an integral part in what he says and what he includes in his response. Thus, if we have trouble with the code in the pilot stage of development, we must consider, and experiment with, the possibility that revised instructions will help by altering the nature of the data.

Validity of Content Analysis

In the research literature the validity of content analysis codes has largely been ignored, even though it is a question which can be handled. Minimally, the code should have face validity, in that the areas or levels and the categories should bear an overt relationship to the purpose for which they have been created. This is as true of content analysis for feeling tone as for a semantic content analysis. The categories "positive" and "negative" for example appear, on the face of it, to be relevant and valid categories to extract feeling tone. Similarly, the two semantic codes presented in Tables 22-2 and 22-3 both are based on overtly valid perceptions of areas and specifics of school functioning.

The researcher can also aspire to what can be seen as a variant on content validity as well. Whether the code comes from the data, from his experience, or from the literature, or from all three, he should be able to argue that there is a rationale for what is in the code and what is not. Moreover, in a semantic content analysis he should be able to argue that there is some rationale to his organization of the different levels of the code. In other words, the researcher should be able to state what led him to designate some aspects of the potential data as areas of the code and other aspects as specifics within those areas. We noted earlier that there is no one "right" semantic code for a set of data. This does not mean that any code can be developed and defended. It does mean that many codes can be developed, each of which is organized on a logical, rational perception of the data and the research purpose.

One dramatic estimate of the validity of a semantic content analysis can be obtained by estimating the extent to which the original responses can be re-created using the code. For example, in Table 22-6 are data for two responses. In the second column, each response has been coded using the alternate semantic content code in Table 22-3. Try to re-create the originals of the two responses and write the re-creation in column 3. Having done this, in column 5 write the re-creation of the responses using the original semantic code of Table 22-2. What should have been done, and the actual original responses are presented in Table 22-7.

Both of the codes have enabled us to re-create the substance of the original response. We may have some feeling that one code has done it

Table 22-6   Work Sheet for Re-creating Responses from Codes

Response	Coding Using Table 22-3	Re-creation of Response	Coding Using Table 22-2	Re-creation of Response
1	511		510	
	512		520	
	515		530	
2	721		751	
	722		752	
	711		721	
	113		132	

better than the other. It is just that feeling which enables this re-creation technique to help us to decide which of two or more possible codes would be a more valid transcription of the data.

For the weighted semantic content analysis it is also possible to obtain an estimate of concurrent validity. In this instance, the researcher functions as in any effort to estimate concurrent validity: He obtains a second, and different estimate of whatever dimension he is scoring through the weighted content analysis and correlates the results from this second estimate with the results from the content analysis. Given a reliable content analysis, reassuring estimates of the validity are possible. In one study with which the author worked,[7] a weighted content analysis was used to estimate the quality of decisions written by Air Force staff officers

[7]Irving Lorge, Joel Davitz, David Fox, Kenneth Herrold, and Paula Weltz, *Evaluation of Instruction in Staff Action and Decision Making* (Maxwell Air Force Base, Ala.: Air Research and Development Command, Human Resources Research Institute), December 1963, Research Memorandum No. 20.

Table 22-7 Re-created Responses Compared to Actual Response

Response	Re-creation Using Alternate Semantic Code of Table 22-3	Re-creation Using Original Semantic Code of Table 22-2	Actual Response
1	Response contains three negative references in the area of the school, noting a decline in plant or equipment, in atmosphere or climate, and in academic level.	Response consists of three negative units of content, a general decline in academic area, a general negative change in the plant, and a general negative change in the area of atmosphere, climate, or creative level.	These children have lowered our academic standards, ruined the physical plant, and made for general chaos in the school.
2	Response begins with three units of content with ambiguous feeling tone: two in the area of the teacher, involving methods and materials, and one in the area of the school, involving the plant or equipment. It concludes with a (positive) reference to improvement in the cultural, artistic, or creative level of the school.	Response begins with three units of content with ambiguous feeling tone: references to methods and materials in the teaching process, and a reference to the equipment in the school plant. It concludes with a (positive) reference to improvement in the artistic or creative level.	The children have made it necessary to alter our methods of teaching, make up many of our own materials, replace much of the equipment in the school, and, on the other hand, have been a strong factor in uplifting the level of creative response.

attending courses of instruction at the Air University in Montgomery, Alabama. The validity of this content analysis was estimated by submitting sets of 25 decisions to 16 Air Force experts who were asked to rank these decisions from best to worst by whatever criteria they wished to use. These rankings were then averaged to obtain an overall estimate of the quality rankings. This overall estimate was then correlated with rankings obtained from the weighted content analysis. For two sets of decisions, the correlations were .84 and .87. These correlations are reasonably high and indicate that the weighted content analysis and the ranking by experts shared about 70 percent of their variance, that is, about 70 percent of the criterion factors they reflected were common to both methods.

ADDITIONAL ATTRIBUTES
OF A CONTENT ANALYSIS CODE

In Chapter 5 we considered two basic processes by which data can be obtained in the social disciplines: classification and measurement. Content analysis is the data-analysis equivalent of classification. Both processes are based on the placement of responses or fragments of responses in categories developed in the context of the research purpose. Thus, in addition to reliability and validity, the desirable attributes of a set of categories for classification (discussed in Chapter 5) are equally relevant for content analysis categories. These were the attributes of *homogeneity, inclusiveness, usefulness,* and *mutual exclusiveness.* We shall not repeat what was noted in Chapter 5 about these properties, but rather review them in the context of content analysis.

The homogeneity of categories in content analysis is desirable at all levels of a multilevel code, like the ones we have developed for semantic content analysis. One way of determining the quality of such a code is to see if each level is homogeneous in content and also in level of abstraction. The first code for semantic content analysis in Table 22-2, for example, lists seven areas for the code. All seven relate to each other, and to the research purpose as aspects of a school which might be affected by a change in the pupil population. Moreover, all seven are relative abstractions at much the same level, that is, academic processes, atmosphere, relationships, teaching process, children's characteristics, and plant. In the same way the second level of the code is homogeneous in the relationship of all the specific details it lists to the educational process, but also in their homogeneity in terms of specificity, that is, art or music classes, school-community relationships, or the intelligence of children. Thus in content analysis, homogeneity is desired not only of the relationships of the categories to each other and to the variable being studied, but also in the degree of abstraction of the various levels of the code.

A set of content analysis categories must be *inclusive,* since as we noted earlier, one basic rule of content analysis is that every response must be classified. Moreover, the research purpose is not served in content analysis any more than in classification, if inclusiveness is achieved by some catch-all category like "miscellaneous." A miscellaneous category is perfectly sensible as a way of categorizing a few responses, each of which is sufficiently unique so that it cannot be combined with another category, but so infrequent or unimportant that it does not deserve a separate category. But no more than 5 percent of any set of responses should be placed in a miscellaneous category. If more than 5 percent are, then the researcher should rethink the elements being placed in the miscellaneous category to attempt to extract some of them for placement into categories which provide more information.

Usefulness is even more critical in content analysis than in classification. This attribute was defined as reflecting the fact that each category serves a purpose and delineates a meaningful dimension of the variable under study. The critical nature of this attribute in content analysis is that it alerts the researcher to the great danger of proliferating categories so that several contain no responses other than the original response for which they were created. A content analysis category which, at the end of the data analysis, contains one or two responses serves no useful purpose. To keep a set of categories useful the researcher must be extremely reluctant to add categories once the basic set is established. Before adding one, he should check all existing categories to determine whether or not the proposed new category can logically be combined with an already existing category. If it can, it should be, particularly if the data analysis is well under way and the probability of the response occurring again is thereby diminished. But the criterion of usefulness also means that all meaningful dimensions of the data are independently delineated, and so this effort to combine categories should not be pushed to the extent that the combinations become so multidimensional as to cease to be useful. If this attribute is to be achieved the researcher must achieve a happy balance between the number of categories and the dimensions of his data.

The fourth attribute, mutual exclusiveness, is also a must for content analysis. There should be one place and only one place to code any one response. If there are more places, then the reliability of the code is damaged. During the development of the code, mutual exclusiveness is one of the major aspects the researcher seeks to estimate. We discussed earlier how reliability is estimated by having independent coders code material, and how they should discuss their disagreements. Often this discussion is focused on identifying aspects of the categories which are not mutually exclusive and which must be rewritten until they are. To some extent, with complex material, there may always be a residue of categories which cut across two dimensions of the code and so are not fully mutually exclusive and cannot be made so. For example, in our semantic code data the phrase that the children are "harder to teach" was seen as an aspect of the teaching process specifically involving the difficulty of teaching. But we also had a category "intelligence" in the area of characteristics of children, and some coders might want to put it there. Rewriting these categories would not help. But if the researcher has learned about these potential overlapping categories, he can alert his coders to what function each category was created to serve, and hopefully minimize any unreliability in the data.

The final attribute categories should possess is clarity and specificity. They should be stated in simple, direct terms so that their intent is clear. They must be sufficiently specific for the coder to have to make no inferences as to the function of the category, and no interpretations as to what type of responses should be placed in it. This ideal state is difficult to reach with complex behavioral and verbal data for which content analysis is used, but in the author's experience, it can be approximated sufficiently for content analysis to be performed reliably by staff with little formal research training, or experience.

Data Obtained through Content Analysis

Early in this chapter we noted that the purposes of content analysis were summarization and tabulation. Once the data are fully coded they can then be tabulated and summarized to achieve these purposes. In any complex content analysis, such as the semantic content analysis we developed in this chapter, electronic data processing is essential to fully tabulate the data. The full opportunities for analysis will be lost otherwise, for the complexities of the code far surpass the capacities of hand tallying and even simple sorting machines.

The first level of analysis which should be obtained is the frequency of occurrence of each specific complete category in the code. If a three-digit code has been developed, this means obtaining the frequency of every possible three-digit number. The researcher then should begin to summarize. Summarization begins with the most specific levels of the code and works backward to the most general levels. Thus, in the three-digit example, the researcher scans his third digits to see if there is some summarization desired. In the illustrative semantic code we first used (Table 22-2) we might have scanned the specific classes listed in the academic area and decided we wished to summarize the nonacademic classes (art, music, craft, physical education) separately from the social sciences and language arts, and from the sciences and mathematics.[8]

With these summaries completed, the researcher should then summarize at the next higher level of abstraction. In our example, we would find out how many responses occurred in each of the areas in the code, ignoring specifics within each area. Thus we now ask how many responses contained some reference to the academic area, no matter how general or what the class was. We could then move back to the first digit, asking how many positive, negative, or ambiguous responses there were.

One real virtue of content analysis is the variety of relationship questions it permits us to ask. We might analyze the data to see what the distribution of positive responses was across the different areas and how this compared to the distribution of the negative or the ambiguous responses. We might seek to analyze the relationship within response to determine what combinations of areas were most likely to occur. If we have background data on the respondents we can add these to the study of relationships with the content. For example, in the original study from which these responses were selected, this kind of analysis indicated that almost all of the responses categorized as negative came from teachers who were more than fifty years old.

In the midst of the fascination of this kind of analysis, however, the researcher must always remember that what he is obtaining is based on the way he structured the content analysis. The relationships between feeling tone and area reflect *his* perception of what should be the areas of the code, and *his* perception of which areas should be separate and which combined.

In terms of nature of the data, content analysis basically yields nominal data, although once frequency distributions are developed the relative frequency of the different categories can be treated as verbal ordinal data. Essentially though, the statistics involved are descriptive statistics appropriate for nominal and ordinal data, and that means essentially the mode and the simple or summary frequency distribution. It means that when the researcher wishes to test for differences between two sets of data from a content analysis, he is limited to the nonparametric techniques, principally chi square. The one exception to these statements is when the researcher has used the weighted semantic content analysis to develop a score of some sort for each response. Depending on the rigor with which he has developed the weights, these may be numerical ordinal data or

[8]Obviously this kind of summary can be obtained by simply adding the frequencies of the relevant three-digit numbers. But it generally saves time if the desire for these summaries is identified early enough to obtain them by machine.

interval data. In either case, he can now use measures of central tendency, external variability, and internal variability in describing the results. If he believes he can defend the weighting system as producing interval data, he can also use parametric inferential procedures like the t test or analysis of variance to test for differences between sets of data.

A FINAL CAUTION ON CONTENT ANALYSIS

Because content analysis is a developmental process, no one can predict how long it will require to reach an acceptable level of reliability. This is the one data-analysis technique in which an experienced researcher can-not tell a student approximately how long it will require to analyze a given set of data. For this reason, the student who plans a project in which the data analysis will require the development of a content analysis code should be alert to the fact that a considerable period of time may be required to develop this code. Therefore, if it is not to be developed until after the data have been collected, he should not plan to use the content analysis procedure unless he is certain that he will have sufficient time to do it properly. There is no way to speed up the process and no way in which the code can be sensibly used before it has been developed to a proper degree of reliability. Therefore, if we develop a study plan using content analysis, we double-check our plans and deadlines to be certain that there is sufficient time.

Chapter 23

ELECTRONIC DATA PROCESSING

by SIGMUND TOBIAS

The purpose of this chapter is to introduce the reader to electronic data-processing procedures and equipment. Specifically, the use, for research purposes, of various commonly available machines will be described, running all the way from the card sorter to the high-speed electronic computer. For the latter, an introduction to the important concepts in that area, some understanding of what is involved in computer programming, and the various programs that are available, and how they can be obtained will be provided.

Cadet training in the United States Air Force is supposed to have started with the flight instructor taking the new group of recruits out onto the airstrip, pointing to a plane ready to take off and saying: "This is an airplane." The present chapter will assume as little student familiarity with the data-processing equipment as the Air Force instructor did with planes.

AVAILABILITY OF EQUIPMENT

Electronic data-processing equipment is becoming available in schools, colleges, and universities to an ever-increasing degree. Beginning with the postwar period, card sorters, printers, accounting machines, and the ubiquitous herald of this invasion—the punch card—began to make their appearance in educational institutions throughout the United States. In the mid-1950s, electronic computers of various levels of complexity began to appear on college and university campuses. With the advent of the 1960s, any educational institution was capable of obtaining access to computers, even if the organization did not own or rent its own equipment. The introduction of computers into every phase of American life has generated a good deal of controversy regarding depersonalization, unemployment fostered by automation, and the like. Irrespective of what is said about automation in other areas, everyone agrees that it has been a boon for the analysis of research data.

In the social and behavioral sciences the availability of high-speed electronic data-processing equipment has made it possible to conduct statistical analyses previously impossible because of the time involved in the calculations. For example, it is rare to pick up a current research journal in education without finding at least one article using factor analysis. Prior to the availability of computers, journals seldom had such articles, for factor analyses were rarely computed. When factor analytic techniques were employed, they often reported estimates of more lengthy procedures, which were too time-consuming to conduct. The factor analysis which would have taken a team of researchers more than six months to compute can be conducted by modern equipment in five or ten *seconds*. The very brief periods of machine time needed to conduct even complex statistical analyses puts the cost well within the reach of most researchers, even if initial costs sound quite expensive. For example, as this is written, commercial rates on IBM 7090-type equipment are $1200 an hour. But this reduces to $20 a minute, and a minute is a long time on an IBM 7090! Moreover, in education it is generally possible to obtain machine time at much reduced rates for nonprofit research purposes. In such instances it is not uncommon for computer time on 7090-type equipment to cost as little as $150 an hour. The average researcher could thus conduct elaborate analyses of a vast amount of research data for from $10 to $20.

In order to make data accessible for processing by computer the data must be organized in a way so that they can be read into the computer. The data are then brought to the computation center where a program for the required analysis is prepared or selected from an existing library of programs. The program and data are then entered into the computer, the processing is performed, and the results become part of computer output. Each of these steps will be discussed in this chapter beginning with the computer system and program, and ending with a section on efficient organization of data for computer processing.

ELECTRONIC DIGITAL COMPUTERS

Computer systems range from relatively small and simple machines, such as the IBM 1620, to vast systems which simultaneously service a large number of installations, some or all of which may be several thousand miles away from one another. Despite this wide range, there are certain conceptions by which all systems can be characterized. An understanding

of these conceptions and usage of computers does not require any knowledge of how the computer is built, or of its internal operation. A widely
used analogy is to the operation of a car. Millions of motorists drive
automobiles of differing complexity, size, and cost while knowing little
about how they work mechanically. The same holds true for computers
and some of the equipment associated with them. A later section gives a
conceptual introduction to what computer programming involves and how
data analysis is accomplished.

Computer Systems

A computer differs from the conventional desk calculator in three major
respects: (1) it is very much faster; (2) it can store varying amounts of
information (though some desk-top calculators also allow for the storage
of a constant); and (3) it can make decisions based on previously
established criteria. These differences enable computers to perform more
elaborate and complex operations upon larger quantities of data at a
much faster speed than the old desk-top calculators.

A computer system is typically composed of the three elements depicted
in Figure 23-1: an Input/Output device, a central processing unit, and a
memory unit. Each of these parts of the system is available in many
versions which differ from one another in the complexity of their design,
the complexity of operations they can perform, and the speed with which
the operations can be performed. The role each of these components has
in the overall system is, however, fairly similar, irrespective of the sophistication of the particular version.

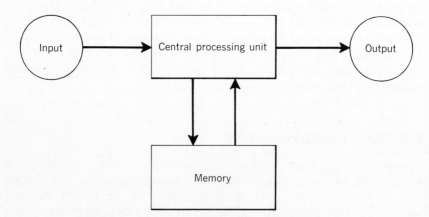

Figure 23-1   Elements of basic computer system.

INPUT/OUTPUT DEVICES   As their names imply, Input/Output devices involve equipment by which information is fed to the computer, and by which the computer transmits information and answers. The nature and number of these devices vary widely with the complexity of the computer, and the kind of Input/Output (abbreviated as I/O) equipment attached to it. These devices include the following: card reading and punching units, typewriters, printers of varying speeds, paper and magnetic tape, and magnetic discs. Generally, most computer systems have several types of I/O devices connected to a computer, and not infrequently include several machines of the same type.

Input/Output devices operate at much slower speeds than the central processing units. The difference in speeds is not due to the inefficiency of I/O equipment, but instead is testimony to the blinding speeds of the central processing units. For example, the IBM 7040 computer can perform calculations hundreds of times more rapidly than they can be printed or punched onto cards. This difference exists despite the fact that high-speed printers can operate at 1100 lines a minute, each line containing up to 130 characters. The discrepancy in printing and calculating speeds cuts down the efficiency of the computer because, while it is waiting for the results to be printed out, it could be processing one, or several, jobs. For these reasons, modern computing systems rarely accept data from cards directly, nor do they print results directly. Instead I/O operations are usually accomplished by magnetic tape or magnetic discs.

Magnetic tapes, or discs, are the fastest I/O channels available. However, they cannot be interpreted directly by humans, and most frequently serve as intermediate storage devices of I/O data. Figure 23-2 illustrates the typical sequence of operations for direct and indirect I/O from the computer. Typically, when data are brought to the computation center for processing, they are stored on punch cards. The punch card, illustrated in Figure 23-3, is a rectangular card on which 80 columns of information can be stored by punching one or more holes in each column. The information punched on the cards is transferred to magnetic tape or discs, and the tape or disc then becomes input to the computer.

After the data have been processed, the computer transmits the results, or output, onto another tape or disc. The output tape is then transferred to an intermediate device, the function of which is to print and/or punch the results stored on the tape. While the data are being transferred from cards to tape, or from tape to cards, the computer itself can process data fed to it from another input channel and transmit the results on still another tape. The gap between calculating speeds and I/O speeds is one of the reasons for the many whirring tape channels associated with data-processing equipment.

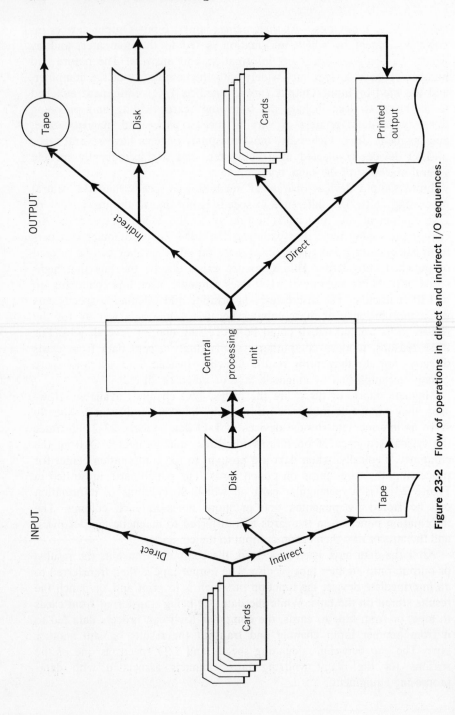

Figure 23-2 Flow of operations in direct and indirect I/O sequences.

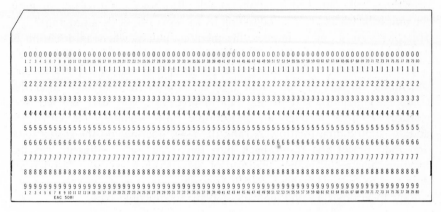

Figure 23-3   Punch card used to store information.

CENTRAL PROCESSING UNIT   The central processing unit (CPU) of a computer is the heart of the system; it is the place where the processing operations actually take place. The CPU is composed of two major parts: the *arithmetic and logical section* and the *control section*. The arithmetic and logical unit is built to accept and execute several kinds of instructions. Just as a desk calculator is built with the capacity to add, subtract, multiply, or divide by the suppression of the appropriate key, the CPU has an arithmetic and logical unit which will perform basic mathematical and logical operations through a specific instruction. The more complex mathematical operations are built upon these essentials, and elaborate computer systems may accept several hundred different instructions corresponding to different operations.

The second component of the CPU is the control section. The control section coordinates the various operations of the computer and arranges the sequence in which operations are carried out. These functions include: two-way transmission of data to and from memory, controlling the operation of the I/O units and the arithmetic-logical unit. In the typical operation the control unit scans a previously determined location in memory, copies the instruction in that location, and executes it. Execution of this instruction may involve, depending upon what the instruction is, going to a different location in memory for further instructions or data, activating an I/O device, or activating the arithmetic-logical unit for an operation. When this instruction is executed, the control section goes to the next location in memory, or to the address in memory to which it was directed by the previous instruction, and executes that instruction. These operations are continued indefinitely until all problems are solved, or until the unit is instructed to stop operation by the operator or by a program.[1]

MEMORY As its name implies, the memory unit is where information is stored in the computer. This information may consist of programs, which will be discussed below, or of data. A computer can not perform any operations on sets of data until they are stored in locations within the computer's memory unit. In the typical processing job, data are fed into storage locations through an appropriate input channel; the CPU, by adding, subtracting, multiplying, and dividing, operates on the stored data and then places the result back into the same, or a different, storage location. The result is then read out of these storage locations through an appropriate output channel. When new data are placed into these same storage locations, they automatically replace the previous data.

BINARY NOTATION Generally, data are stored inside the memory in binary rather than conventional decimal notation. In decimal notation there are ten symbols, 0–9. Quantities greater than the largest digit, that is, greater than 9, are represented by moving one place to the left and starting again with the smallest digit. Thus, the number 19 indicates that we have one unit of 10 and 9 ones. However, other notation systems are available which represent varying quantities with fewer than nine symbols. The binary mode, used by most computers, represents quantities by the use of only two digits: "0," representing the quantity zero, and "1," representing the quantity one. Quantities greater than one are designated by moving one place to the left. Thus, in binary notation the quantity two would be represented by 10, in other words, one unit in the two position, and no units of one. The quantity three would be written 11, or one unit of two, and one unit of one. Table 23-1 presents the binary notation for the numbers 0 to 10 and selected larger numbers.

Binary notation is critical to computer functioning because the memory location in which data are stored is physically made up of a magnetic core. Each core consists of a tiny ring of ferromagnetic material, a few hundredths of an inch in diameter. The cores are strung on a wire, much like beads on a string. When current is sent through the wire in one direction the core is polarized; reversing the direction of the current through the wire changes the polarization. The polarized and depolarized states stand for zero and one, thus conveniently accommodating data in

---

[1]Programs, discussed in detail later in this chapter, are simply a series of instructions to the computer. In order to fully utilize the speed of the computer and its ability to operate uninterruptedly, a special program called a *monitor program* is available, which supervises the sequence of problems, starts and ends jobs, records the time required for each job, and performs any of the other operations required to allow the computer to work without interruption.

Table 23–1 Decimal Numbers and Their Binary Equivalents

Decimal Number	Binary Equivalent	Decimal Number	Binary Equivalent
0	0	15	1111
1	1	16	10000
2	10	20	10100
3	11	25	11001
4	100	30	11110
5	101	32	100000
6	110	40	101000
7	111	60	111100
8	1000	64	1000000
9	1001	100	1110100
10	1010	128	10000000

binary notation. The polarization of a magnetic core takes only a few *millionths* of a second, which is one of the bases for the fantastic speeds of computers.

One final word about binary notation. Even though the data are stored internally in the computer in binary mode, this does *not* mean that the computer will accept only binary data for processing, nor does it mean that the results of computation are reported in binary form. When decimal data are read into the computer, they are automatically converted into binary mode by a series of instructions. After the computations have been performed, the binary data are converted back to decimal form prior to output. Should the user be interested, he can receive output in binary form, or in octal (base 8, utilizing numbers 0 to 7) mode, rather than in the conventional decimal notation.

AMOUNT OF MEMORY   The number of memory locations and their size varies widely with the kind of computer and the number of core storage locations with which it is equipped. For example, the IBM 1620 system can be ordered with 20,000 to 60,000 storage locations, in increments of 20,000, with each location accommodating one digit of information. In the IBM 7090 series of computers each storage location accommodates as many as six digits. The IBM 7040 computer system, for example, may be ordered with anywhere from 4000 to 32,000 locations, in increments of 4000. Obviously, the greater the number of storage locations and the number of digits accommodated in each location, the greater the capacity of the system, and therefore the greater its ability to accommodate large masses of data and longer problems.

Computers can process problems involving much larger quantities of data than would seem possible on the basis of their number of locations. For example, 32,000 locations can accommodate an immense quantity of data. An example may illustrate this point. Let us say we are interested in computing means and standard deviations for 1000 subjects on 50 different variables. It would appear that we would need $50 \times 1000 = 50,000$ locations to store all of the data in the computer prior to operating on it. In fact, only 151 locations would be required to store the data. The storage locations required will be indicated by the flow of operations in the computation of the 50 means and standard deviations: (1) raw data for the 50 variables is read into 50 locations; (2) the raw data are accumulated in order to obtain the sums—requiring another 50 locations for the storage of the sums for each variable; (3) the squares of the raw data are accumulated in yet another set of 50 locations, each containing the sums of the squared raw scores for each of the 50 variables; and (4) the total number of cases is read into one location. When all of the raw scores have been read in, the means and standard deviations are computed from the sums, and the sums squared. In this manner, an almost infinite amount of raw data can be processed in relatively few storage locations.

Large core storage units are needed whenever a large matrix of data is required to be in memory in order for computations to begin, such as in factor analysis where the matrix of intercorrelations between all the variables has to be computed and retained in memory before factor extraction begins. Large cross-tabulation problems also demand a great deal of storage. For example, if one were interested in analyzing the distribution of age groups (range one to one hundred) by sex (two dimensions, male and female) and by states (50), it would require at least 10,000 storage locations ($100 \times 2 \times 50$). The programs used to process the data are also stored and take up a variable number of locations depending on their size.

Programming

The computer performs any of the operations in its repertoire when it is directed to do so by an instruction. As indicated above, the CPU of a computer is wired to execute a number of operations when instructed to do so by a particular code number. Instructing the computer manually to perform one operation after another would obviously be tremendously wasteful, in view of its capacity for lightning-fast calculation. This problem is solved by preparing a *program*. The program contains all of the instructions required for the solution of a particular problem, arranged in a step-by-step sequence, according to the order in which the operations are scheduled to occur.

Typically, the first step in preparing a program is to break the problem down to the basic steps required for the solution of the problem and order these steps into a sequence. An instruction, or a series of them, are then written for each of the steps required in the problem's solution. All of these instructions together constitute a program. Prior to implementation, the program is read into the computer and stored in its memory. The control section of the CPU then locates the first instruction of the program, and begins the implementation. Succeeding instructions then determine the successive operations of the CPU.

MACHINE LANGUAGE   Instructions which are written in such a manner that they can be directly executed by the computer are referred to as being in *machine language*. Preparing a program in machine language is an extremely laborious process. An example will illustrate this point. Instructing the computer to perform this simple equation, $C = B + A$, first requires that the job be broken down into the seven logical steps listed below:

1. Ready the card reader for input.
2. Read one piece of data (A) into a storage location, location 100, for example.
3. Read one piece of data (B) into a storage location, location 101, for example.
4. Add the contents of location 100 to those of location 101.
5. Store the results in location 102.
6. Ready the printing unit.
7. Print the contents of location 102.

The first and last step would be particularly time-consuming, since detailed instructions about the synchronization of the units and the transfer of the data would have to be prepared. (Each of these operations is likely to take between 10 and 200 instructions.) The laboriousness of this process is increased by the fact that many computers accept instructions only in binary notation. Clearly, preparing a program in machine language would be an excessively detailed job, requiring a large amount of clerical activity to keep track of locations, sequence, and so on. The amount of activity required indicates that many errors would occur, and vast amounts of time would be needed to write a program.

PROBLEM-ORIENTED LANGUAGES   In order to reduce the tediousness, the potential for error, and to cut down on the amount of time needed to prepare a program, a number of problem-oriented languages have been developed. A program written in a problem-oriented language is referred to as a *source program,* and one written in machine language is called an *object program.* The problem-oriented languages, used for the processing of research data, have several decided advantages over machine languages. First, and most important, instructions can be written in a mixture of common words and mathematical symbols. The words IF, DO, and CONTINUE, in one of these languages, cause the computer to perform operations similar to those denoted by the words in everyday use. The mathematical symbols of −, +, and = also have pretty much the same meanings in the source programs as they do in mathematical applications. A second major advantage of source programs is that keeping track of

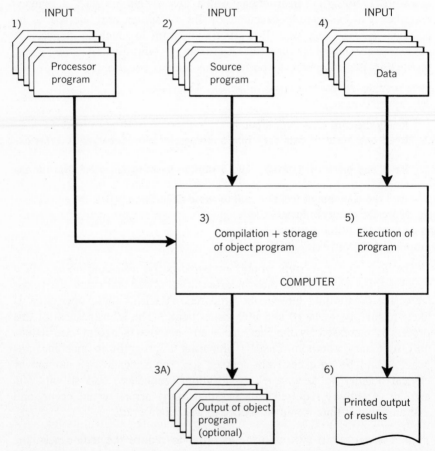

Figure 23-4   Flow of operations when the source program is compiled and executed.

locations is done automatically by the computer once the overall number of locations required is specified. Moreover, a source program written in a problem-oriented language can be converted into an object program by the computer itself. This conversion is made possible by a program, called a *processor program,* or just *processor,* or *compiler.*

The processor is analogous to a dictionary and grammar rule book which can be placed in the computer whenever needed. Figure 23-4 indicates the steps involved in compiling a source program and executing a data-processing operation. Step 1 involves storing the processor in the computer. In step 2, the source program is also read into the computer. The source program is translated into an object program by the processor within the computer in step 3, and is then stored in memory ready to process data. Step 3A is optional. It allows the user to obtain punched output of the object program generated by the computer so that the next time this particular program is required the user may submit the object program directly and save the time it took to compile the source program. The computer is now ready to execute the program, so in step 4 data are being read in, to be processed in step 5. The results of the processing are then reported in step 6.

A large number of processor programs are available. IBM supports a number of problem-oriented languages for a variety of different applications. Fortran (*for*mula-*trans*lation) is the language perhaps most widely used for the solution of research and scientific problems. Cobol (Common Business Oriented Language), as implied by the name, is most frequently used in business applications. Programs written in any of these source languages have one tremendous advantage over object programs. A source program written for one computer can generally be used on a different computer with only minor modification, whereas an object program can generally be used only on the one kind of computer for which it was written. This flexibility of source programs is achieved, of course, by virtue of having a processor program for each type of machine. To illustrate how much time is saved by programming in a symbolic language, look at Table 23-2 which describes the same problem discussed earlier. Column 1 repeats the seven steps needed to instruct the computer in machine language. In column 2, the instructions are in a source language developed at the University of Michigan, called Michigan Algorithm Decoder, or Mad for short.

The two most striking things about the Mad instructions are their brevity and their resemblance to conventional mathematical notation and to the English language. In fact, they look very little different from the kind of instructions one would give a clerk. This flexibility is achieved, of course, because the processor program converts the symbols into an object

Table 23–2 Instructions Required for Solution of Equation $C = B + A$

Machine Language	Mad
1. Ready the card reader for input. 2. Read one piece of data (A) into a storage location, location 100, for example. 3. Read one piece of data (B) into a storage location, location 101, for example.	1. READ DATA
4. Add the contents of location 100 to those of location 101. 5. Store the results in location 102.	2. $C = B + A$
6. Ready the printing unit. 7. Print the contents of location 102.	3. PRINT RESULTS C

program, keeps track of the locations involved and of the I/O units required by a particular program.

AVAILABILITY OF PROGRAMS   In the behavioral and social sciences it is rarely necessary for the researcher to do his own programming in order to get the data analyzed. To begin with, most computation centers have *general purpose programs* which can be used for data analysis. A general purpose program is not written for any specific application but is so designed that it can be used for a variety of purposes, providing a few simple instructions are followed. For example, assume that a researcher is interested in the intercorrelations between 12 variables. The computation center may have a general purpose program which computes intercorrelations for up to 50 variables. This program can be used for the problem involving only 12 variables if the user adds to the general purpose program the information on how many variables he wants analyzed and the number of cases in the analysis. With this supplementary information, the general purpose program can then be used to analyze this particular set of data or any other set of data with 50 or fewer variables.

In the event that a computation center has no appropriate general purpose programs, collections of programs which can be adapted for local use by computation center personnel are available from other sources. As this is written, a widely used collection of programs in the behavioral and social sciences is the BMD series.[2] A detailed manual of instructions for the use of these programs may be purchased through the University of California, Los Angeles, bookstore. The programs themselves are available free of charge from the UCLA computation center on magnetic tape, which must be provided by the requesting computation center. Another source of programs is a book by Cooley and Lohnes[3] which contains both a discussion of the rationale underlying many multivariate statistical techniques and a listing of the programs for their computation. Other collections are also becoming available, such as the one by Veldman.[4] An introduction to Fortran programming can also be found in Veldman's book, with special applications to data processing for the behavioral sciences. Other manuals on Fortran programming are those by McCracken[5] and Colman and Smallwood.[6]

COMPUTER RELATED EQUIPMENT

There are a variety of machines below the level of the computer which are of importance in data processing. These are referred to as EAM (Electronic Accounting Machines) and include such equipment as card sorters, reproducers, interpreters, and so on. This equipment is capable of minor data analysis; however, its major current usage is in facilitating the organization of input to computers. Since EAM equipment is much less expensive than a computer, organizing data on EAM machines, rather than on the computer itself, makes data processing more efficient and less expensive. The following section describes some of the procedures of greatest importance in research applications for which EAM equipment is available.

Transferring Data to Punch Cards

Computers can receive information from a number of sources—paper and magnetic tape, magnetic discs, electric typewriters, and a wide variety of

[2]W. J. Dixon, ed., *BMD. Biomedical Computer Programs* (Los Angeles: University of California Press, 1965).
[3]William W. Cooley and Paul R. Lohnes, *Multivariate Procedures of the Behavioral Sciences* (New York: John Wiley & Sons, Inc., 1962).
[4]Donald J. Veldman, *Fortran Programming for the Behavioral Sciences* (New York: Holt, Rinehart and Winston, Inc., 1967).
[5]Daniel D. McCracken, *A Guide to FORTRAN IV Programing* (New York: John Wiley & Sons, Inc., 1965).
[6]Harry L. Colman and Clarence Smallwood, *Computer Language. An Autoinstructional Introduction to Fortran* (New York: McGraw-Hill, Inc., 1962).

electronic scanners. But the most common method of addressing the computer is through the use of *punch cards*. Even when other input channels are utilized, the data are generally put onto punch cards first and then transferred to tape or discs, from which they are fed into the computer.

Information is transferred onto punch cards in a variety of ways. The most widely known means is to punch the information onto a card by means of a *key punch machine*. This machine has a keyboard similar to that of a typewriter. The depression of any of the keys causes the appropriate holes to be punched into the cards, and, for machines equipped with such an option, the identification to be printed on top of the column. More detailed information on the operation, and various options available, can be found by consulting the appropriate reference manual.[7]

Two other ways of transferring data to punch cards which are of some importance to the researcher are through the use of *mark sense cards* and *optical scanners*.

As the name implies, mark sense cards involve manually marking cards by pencil; these marks are then sensed by a machine which punches a hole in the desired field. A large variety of mark sense cards is available. These are the same size as the conventional punch card. The formats of some available mark sense cards include: cards with up to 27 fields, each of which can accommodate data ranging from zero through nine, cards accommodating responses to a multiple-choice test with up to 50 questions, and four choices per question. Cards with different formats can easily be constructed by consultation with a printer specializing in this area.

Mark sense cards require the user to mark the data or test responses with an electrographic pencil. The cards are then inserted into a machine like the IBM 519 (which will be described in more detail below) which senses each pencil mark and then records a punch for it. The punch does not have to be made in the same location where the card was marked. By appropriate wiring of the 519, the punch can be placed almost anywhere on the card.

Another method of transferring data to punch cards is by the use of an optical scanner. This machine scans an especially prepared answer sheet with a photo-electric cell which records the fields in which answers have been marked. Depending upon the needs of the researcher, these machines will then do any one or any combination of the following for each sheet: (1) score the answer sheet and print the number right as deter-

[7] IBM, *Reference Manual. IBM 24 Card Punch. IBM 26 Printing Card Punch,* No. A24-0520-3 (White Plains, N.Y.: IBM, 1965).

mined by comparison with a key; (2) punch each answer onto one or more cards; and (3) also punch the score onto the card. As with mark sense cards, there are many varieties of sheets available, such as test answer sheets accommodating up to 400 questions with five choices per question, or sheets with sufficient capacity to allow clerks to enter a student's entire high school record. Unlike mark sense cards, no special pencil has to be employed with these answer sheets, although a regular number two pencil does give best results.

A useful option available on optical scanners is the possibility of transferring data from answer sheets directly to magnetic tape. This can be a very great convenience where computer facilities exist which permit an input of data on tape, because one reel of magnetic tape will hold as much data as can be stored on a vast number of punched cards—a huge saving in storage space and cost. As this is written, the commercially available optical scanners are the Digitek 1500 and the IBM 1230. More information on either of these is available by consulting the appropriate manuals.[8,9]

Both the mark sense cards and the optical scanners have a tremendous advantage for the researcher. By using them it is possible to design data gathering in such a manner that the respondent records information directly on the card or answer sheet, obviating the necessity of having the information keypunched.

Reproducing Punch Cards

Once a researcher has his data on punch cards, he may want copies of his data deck or copies of a part of the deck. As a matter of fact, it is good practice to retain at least one copy of the data submitted for analysis in case of loss or damage to the cards. The machine used for a large variety of reproducing jobs is the reproducer, the IBM 519. This is an extremely versatile machine. In addition to the reproducing functions to be described below, the reproducer, by the operation of appropriate switches, can also perform the mark sense job described above.

The 519 will reproduce a punch card in a variety of different ways. In addition to making exact copies of the total card, the reproducer can be wired to pick up any part of a card which is of interest and reproduce it in

---

[8]IBM, *Functional Characteristics, Component Descriptions and Operating Procedures IBM 1230 Optical Mark Scoring Reader,* No. A21-9008-3 (White Plains, N.Y.: IBM, 1964).

[9]*Operating Manual. Digitek 100. Optical Scanning System* (Fairless Hills, Pa.: Optical Scanning Corporation).

any field of another card. It can also scan each column of a card and reproduce only some characters and not others. Thus, the machine may be wired to reproduce only numbers below five in all 80 columns, or to reproduce columns 10 to 20 on one set of cards in columns 30 to 40 on another set of cards. Or a researcher may have originally punched his data consecutively from column 1 to 38, and now wishes to have a blank space between each bit of data. Once it has been wired, the reproducer will handle any of these jobs at the rate of approximately 100 cards per minute.

Wiring EAM equipment is the process of specifically instructing the machine regarding which options are to be utilized in a particular operation. In the computer, this process is accomplished by a program, but for EAM equipment it involves plugging wires into appropriate holes on a wiring board. For the 519, this board has several banks of holes representing each of the 80 columns to be punched by the reproducer. Thus if data in columns 79–80 of the input card were to be repunched into columns 21 and 22 on the cards to be outputted, wires connecting positions 79–80 on the input bank to columns 21–22 on the output bank would be required. Banks of holes for verification and other functions are also present on the board. For large reproducing jobs this can become a laborious and time-consuming chore and should not be attempted by those without experience.

The IBM 519 is available with several options of interest to the researcher. The first of these is the *mark sense* attachment mentioned above. Another option is the *end printer*. This device will enable the machine to punch and print up to eight numbers at a time on the card, thus providing an option by which identifying numbers can be printed and then visually separated from one another. A *gangpunching* option enables the machine to punch a variety of common pieces of information onto all the cards of a set. A *comparing* option enables this machine to compare a number of punched fields to check whether the information in each is identical. This option is sometimes used to check the accuracy of key punching. A clerk is instructed to punch cards from data sheets twice in succession, and the separate stacks of cards are then fed into the 519 to check for differences. The theory behind this practice is, of course, that the clerk is unlikely to make the same error twice, and differently punched cards will be identified by the 519. More detailed explanations of any of these options are available in the 519 manual.

There is only one aspect of the punch card the 519 cannot reproduce— the printed information on top of the card. The 519 will punch a new card, but will not print all it has punched. If the machine is equipped with the appropriate option, up to eight numbers can be printed. Further information about this machine will be found in the manual.[10] In order to have a printed identification of the punch in every column of a card, an interpreting machine like the IBM 548 must be used. This machine scans the punches and identifies them by printing the appropriate character on top of the card. Similar to the reproducer, the machine may be wired to print information in any sequence desired; the printing thus does not have to correspond to the sequence in which the card is punched. The 548 operates at the rate of 60 cards per minute.[11]

Collating

The IBM 85 or 87 machines perform a variety of collating operations. By appropriate instructions this machine will take two separate stacks of cards and merge them into one, select out any cards with a particular characteristic, and any combination of selecting or merging operations, that is, merge some cards and not others. For example, suppose two sets of cards were available on each child in the Language Study, one of which summarized the teacher's ratings of his behavior, and another which summarized the pupil's test scores. These two stacks of cards could be merged so that the teacher's rating card for each subject precedes the test results card. Simultaneously, this machine could remove from the stack any card with an X in column 10, for example, which signified that the pupil moved in the middle of the school year. An additional feature of this machine is that it will check for and detect the presence of blank columns. The collators can process 240 cards per minute. Further information on this machine is available in the manual.[12]

Card Sorting

Another machine which is of some interest to the researcher is the card sorter. Basically, this machine will sort cards according to the punches they have in any one of the 80 columns into as many as 13 different categories. These categories correspond to the ten numbers 0 to 9, what are called the 11 and 12 punches at the top of each column, and leaving a column blank with no punch recorded. Sorters generally also have a

[10]IBM, *Reference Manual. IBM 519 Document-Originating Machine,* No. A21-1017-1 (White Plains, N.Y.: IBM, 1961).

[11]IBM, *Manual of Operations. 548, 552 Interpreters,* No. 224-6384-2 (White Plains, N.Y.: IBM, 1958).

[12]IBM, *Reference Manual. IBM 85 and 87 Collators,* No. A24-1005-2 (White Plains, N.Y.: IBM, 1960).

counter allowing one to determine the number of cards in each of the categories. This basic sorting function allows one to construct a frequency distribution on a variable simply by sorting the pack of cards to the column or columns in which the data for that variable have been punched. Another use of the sorter of interest to researchers is the possibility of separating the data according to a variety of categories and then analyzing each separately, for example, separating male and female subjects, or elementary from junior high-school students. Another use of the sorter which is of interest is that cards may be sorted into a particular sequence, low number to high, or high to low. The sorter may also be utilized to sort cards into an alphabetical sequence. This operation requires a good deal of experience with the sorter, for an alphabetical sort requires sorting each column twice, setting the machine to disregard certain kinds of punches each time.[13] Large sorting operations require a good deal of time when conducted on the sorters, and so analyses like these are generally conducted on computers in order to save time.

ORGANIZATION OF DATA FOR COMPUTER ANALYSIS

The computer can perform any statistical analysis done by any other machine, or carried out in one's head, providing a program for that analysis has been prepared. As indicated above, general purpose programs are available for a wide range of statistical routines ranging from the preparation of simple frequency distributions, to two- and three-way analysis of variance, a large variety of correlational techniques, and factor analysis. It is often faster to compute simple statistics, such as frequency distributions, means and standard deviations, and single correlations on a desk calculator, since preparing data for computer processing involves punching the data onto cards, getting them to the computation center, and waiting a day or so until the data are processed. In contrast, analyses of a number of variables or complex statistical procedures are invariably accomplished more efficiently by computer.

Another kind of analysis which can be performed by computer is content analysis. This can be accomplished either by storing the code numbers or by storing a number of words, their synonyms, and phrases in the computer, and then reading the text to be analyzed into the computer. The machine then tallies the number of times the preselected words and/or phrases have occurred. An elaborate program to accomplish quite

[13]IBM, *IBM 82, 83, and 84 Sorters*, No. A24-1034-2 (White Plains, N.Y.: IBM, 1965).

sophisticated content analyses is available under the name of *General Inquirer*.[14] Veldman's book[15] also contains programs for this purpose.

In order for a researcher to use data-processing equipment intelligently, it is critical for him to be able to organize his data efficiently for transfer onto punch cards. Once the data have been transferred onto punch cards, they can be reorganized in many ways by a variety of machines. Thus, this section is devoted to a discussion of the organization of data for computer analysis and to a brief description of the variety of machines that can make this process more efficient. We shall begin with a consideration of the punch card itself.

Punch Cards

The punch card is divided into 80 vertical areas, called columns, running from column 1 on the left to 80 on the right. Each column will hold only one piece of information such as a number, or letter, or a character such as a comma, parenthesis, or period. The nature of the information in a column is determined by the position of the hole punched in that column. Figure 23-5 presents a punch card with some information punched into it. For example, in columns 1–10, single-digit numbers have been designated by single punches running from the zero position near the top of the card, in column 1, to the 9 position at the bottom of the card, as shown in

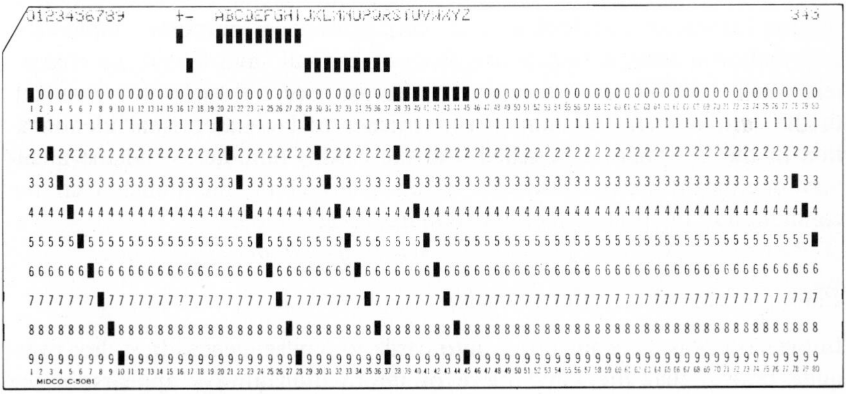

Figure 23-5   Punch card with information punched into it.

[14]P. J. Stone, R. F. Bales, J. Z. Namenwirth, and D. M. Ogilvie, "The General Inquirer, a Computer System for Content Analysis and Retrieval Based on the Sentence as a Unit of Information," *Behavioral Science.* Vol. 7 1962, pp. 484–498.

[15]Veldman, *Fortran Progamming for the Behavioral Sciences.*

column 10. Numbers greater than nine are designated by punches in adjacent columns with the number of columns needed identical to the number of digits in the bit of data. Thus, in Figure 23-5, the number 345 has been designated in columns 78, 79, and 80 by punching 3 in column 78, and the 4 and 5 in the two adjacent columns. Similarly, four- and five-digit numbers would require four and five columns respectively, and so on.

There are only two pieces of information, other than numbers, which can be designated with only one punch per column, the plus and minus signs. The plus sign $(+)$ is designated by a punch at the top of the card, as in column 16 of Figure 23-5, and is often referred to as a "12 punch." The minus sign $(-)$ is represented by a punch just below the 12 punch (column 17 of Figure 23-5), and is often referred to as an "11 punch." All other information, such as alphabetic characters and punctuation marks, is designated by multiple punches in the same column. In Figure 23-5 the 26 letters of the alphabet appear in columns 20 through 45. In columns 20–28 the letters A through I are designated. Each letter is designated by one 12 punch and a second punch in positions 1 (for A) through 9 (for I). The letters J through R are made up of one 11 punch plus a second punch of 1 to 9, as illustrated in columns 29 through 37, and the letters S through Z consist of punches in the zero position and in the 1 to 9 positions (columns 38 through 45).

Two aspects of the information printed on top of the card in Figure 23-5 deserve comment. First, note that all the alphabetic information is printed in uppercase letters. For data-processing purposes, alphabetic information is represented in the form of capitals, and lowercase characters can not be distinguished from uppercase. Second, the printing on top of the card is solely for human convenience to facilitate visual identification of the information punched into the card. Computers, and the ancillary equipment to be described below, sense only the punches in the columns, and the printed identification has no effect.

Planning Layout of Information

Information can be transferred onto cards in any sequence. It is, however, quite critical that the same piece of information always appears in the same columns for all individuals. For example, let us assume that the initial reading achievement scores for the children in the vocabulary group of the Language Study have been punched into columns 14–16. It then becomes vital that the reading achievement scores for all subjects in the study also be recorded in columns 14–16. In order to standardize this procedure for all individuals, it is useful to prepare a *layout sheet* with numbered spaces running from 1 through 80, representing the 80 columns of the punch card. The kind of information to be entered in each column of the punch card is then specified in the corresponding spaces on the layout sheet. Table 23-3 is an example of such a layout sheet for the Language Study.

In addition to standardizing location, the preparation of the layout sheet is a sensible precaution against the situation which has caused cold sweat to form on the brow of many a researcher: looking at data a year or two after they have been punched and seeing nothing but an endless jumble of now meaningless numbers. To have maximum protection from the layout sheet, prepare a number of copies of it. This practice is a painless way of avoiding that sinking feeling in the stomach when one manila folder after another fails to contain that one layout sheet which

Table 23-3   Example of Layout Sheet for Information To Be Entered on Tally Sheet in Table 23-4.

Column	Variable	Column	Variable	Column	Variable	Column	Variable
1.	School	21.		41.		61.	
2.		22.		42.		62.	
3.	Class	23.		43.		63.	
4.		24.		44.		64.	
5.		25.		45.		65.	
6.	Language emphasis	26.		46.		66.	
7.	ID	27.		47.		67.	
8.		28.		48.		68.	
9.		29.		49.		69.	
10.	Age	30.		50.		70.	
11.		31.		51.		71.	
12.		32.		52.		72.	
13.	Sex	33.		53.		73.	
14.	Pre-reading	34.		54.		74.	
15.		35.		55.		75.	
16.		36.		56.		76.	
17.	Post-reading	37.		57.		77.	
18.		38.		58.		78.	
19.		39.		59.		79.	
20.	Change	40.		60.		80.	

was placed there sometime or another. Preparing several copies of the layout sheet and placing one in each folder dealing with a particular study is an inexpensive way of warding off a computer-assisted coronary.

ARRANGING DATA ON TALLY SHEET The most effective way of organizing data for processing is to conceive of each individual, or subject, as representing a row on a tally sheet, and each piece of information about that subject as constituting one or a number of columns, depending on the number of digits or letters that the piece of data contains. The greater the amount of information to be processed for each subject, the more columns needed to represent it; in other words, the longer the row of data. Rows may be of infinite length. Operationally, each row becomes a punch card. Rows requiring more than 80 columns can readily be continued on another card, or on as many cards as necessary to record all the information about one individual. An example of the tally sheet for one of the classes in the Language Study appears in Table 23-4. Note that data which are to be repeated for each subject are entered only once. In Table 23-4 the code number 053071 is entered in the upper left-hand corner of the sheet, and represents school 5, class 307, and vocabulary emphasis (1). These numbers will eventually be gangpunched in columns 1 through 6 into the card for every child in this class. Consequently they do not have to be repeated on the line for each subject.

Once a layout sheet has been constructed, the information can then be transferred onto cards in accord with the plan represented by the layout sheet. The sequence by which various pieces of data are put onto cards can be determined at the convenience of the researcher. In most large computer facilities, general purpose programs are so arranged that the researcher can instruct the computer regarding which columns should be scanned for a particular data analysis and which should be omitted. This

Table 23-4 Example of Tally Sheet To Prepare Data for Electronic Data Processing

	053071 Name	Child's Identification	Age, Sex	Pre- reading	Post- reading	Change
1	Louis Adams	101	1041	037	051	+14
2	Mary Brown	102	0980	042	040	−02
3	Jim Park	103	1	039	045	+06
4						
5						
6						

instruction, called a *format statement,* is read into the computer just before the data, and allows the researcher to arrange the sequence of data on the card in the manner that would be most convenient and economical.[16]

If the data are to be analyzed by statistical techniques, it is, of course, vital to translate qualitative or alphabetic data into numeric information. For complex verbal or behavioral data this can be done by content analysis procedures discussed in Chapter 22. For simpler data a direct translation is made, that is, choices *A* to *D* on a multiple-choice test become the numbers 1 to 4. Similarly descriptive variables must be given numerical codes. See, for example, how the sex of the children in the Language Study is assigned to column 13 in Table 23-3, and is finally coded as 1 (male) and 0 (female) in Table 23-4. Some statistical programs are capable of accepting alphabetic information, but in these instances the computer can rarely perform anything more complex than a simple tabulation of the number of times a particular character, letter, or word appears.

There are some useful conventions which, if followed, facilitate transferring data to cards even though, as indicated above, data can be punched in any sequence. One of these conventions is to punch identifying information either at the beginning or at the end of the card. This practice allows the researcher to pick out particular subjects, groups, and so on readily by scanning only the first or last few columns of each card. Note that in Figure 23-6 the card begins with the data for school, class number, and vocabulary emphasis which were gangpunched into this card. Following these data comes each subject's individual code number. It may be useful to follow the sequence from the layout in Table 23-3, through the tally sheet (Table 23-4) showing the data tallied, to the actual punched card in Figure 23-6.

When follow-up data on particular subjects are expected it is sometimes useful to punch the actual name of the subject onto a card, in lieu of or in addition to a code number, since it will then be more convenient to enter the follow-up data. Entering names is a space-consuming process, because enough columns for the longest name have to be allocated, thus reducing the amount of data that can be entered onto any card. For example, while Jones takes up only five columns, Gloucester takes up ten, and if it were the longest name ten columns would have to be reserved for names. This would leave blank columns for all subjects named Friedman, Carter, Jones, Berk, or any name with less than ten letters. Assigning a code

---

[16]Some computation centers do not have the flexibility of reading in the format statement just before the data. Thus, it is wisest to contact the center you intend to use for instructions regarding the shape in which the data should be presented.

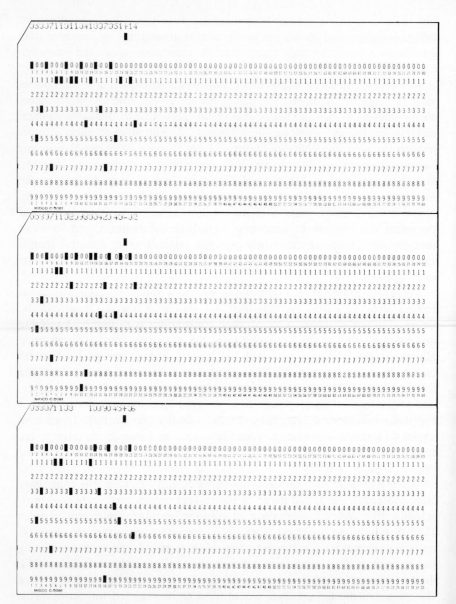

Figure 23-6   Three punch cards with data punched for individual students.

number is, therefore, more economical in terms of space than including the name of each subject. When more than one card is needed for all of the data on a subject, it is especially vital to include the code number on each card and reserve a column for the card number. The user can thus tell at a glance to which subject the data belong, and the card at which he is looking.

Another rule of thumb pertains to how much information on each subject should be coded. The best practice to follow in this respect is to code as much information as possible. When in doubt about whether or not to include a piece of data, include it. It is always easier to ignore excess information which has been punched than to go back and add information to a card. Furthermore, it is a rare research project which does not conduct some analyses not originally anticipated. Having all possible relevant data already on the cards makes such unanticipated analyses relatively simple. Finally, having all the information available makes it easier to go back and do follow-ups, or to reanalyze data to determine the effects of variables which originally were thought to be unimportant. This is particularly true when ideas re-emerge and information once thought unimportant becomes of interest. For example, as this is written, interest in the correlates of birth order frustrates a number of researchers not foresightful enough to have recorded the birth order of their subjects at the time they coded their data.

ASSIGNING SPACE TO VARIABLES   When the card layout is arranged, it is critical to allow as many columns for a piece of data as needed by the largest value that datum can take on. For example, leaving two columns for reading level is a shortsighted procedure, for sixth- and seventh-grade pupils can obtain grade equivalence scores of tenth grade and higher, which would require at least three columns to code. Incidentally, note that we leave columns for the numbers only; it is unnecessary to punch the decimal place onto a card. Why will be discussed more extensively below.

The position of a number in a set of columns, or data field, is also of critical importance. If three columns have been assigned as the data field for a variable, and a particular score on that variable requires only one column, it is vital that the number be placed in the last column of the data field, that is, in the rightmost position. This is referred to as *right justification*. For example, assume that three digits were allowed for a child's street number. The address of a child who lives on Eighth Street should then be punched in the last column on the right of that data field. In order to assure that this occurs, it is advisable to punch the leading zeroes. The number 8 then becomes 008, and can only be placed in the last column. The computer interprets blanks in any field as zeroes; therefore, an 8 in the second column of a data field will be interpreted as 80, and in the leftmost column (the first) it will be interpreted as 800. On the other hand, leading zeroes are disregarded by the computer, and 008 is thus correctly interpreted as 8. Punching the leading zero will thus insure that the data are right justified. For this reason the leading zeroes have been consistently coded for the data in Table 23-4, and punched as indicated in Figure 23-6.

Since the computer interprets a blank unpunched space as zero, the reader may wonder what advantage there is to including leading zeroes, rather than simply skipping the blank spaces. The advantage lies in reducing the possibility of confusing a blank column meaning "0" with a blank column signifying that the data were missing and could, therefore, not be punched. If leading zeroes are always punched for all available data, then a blank column always means missing data, and the danger of confusion between the two is minimized. Furthermore, such a policy facilitates a quick visual check of the cards for the missing data and enables the researcher to remove such cards from the deck, or to go back and collect the missing data. This policy is illustrated in Table 23-4 and Figure 23-6, where leading zeroes are punched for all the available data, and blanks are left for the third child's age, indicating that this piece of data is missing. The blanks stand out clearly, enabling the researcher to spot the missing data readily, and go back to record the child's exact age.

On the tally sheet depicted in Table 23-4 and in columns 20–22 of the cards shown in Figure 23-6, the plus and minus signs for the change scores have been coded and punched. When all data are positive, the plus sign need not be punched, for the computer assumes that all unsigned numbers are positive. However, whenever negative data are possible, a column should be allotted for the sign. This is especially important when change scores are being coded, as is the case in Table 23-4 and Figure 23-6. In such instances a negative score is possible, signifying a decline from pre to post. Therefore, one column should be allocated to accommodate the possible minus sign, and positive values should be designated with a plus sign.[17]

One final consideration which is of importance in planning for the transfer of data to punch cards involves the use of decimal numbers, which was alluded to previously. The decimal point need not be punched on the card, although it can be. Those data-processing systems allowing the researcher to read in the format statement just before his data, can specify where the decimal point ought to be, and the computer will automatically insert it. In such cases, decimal points which are punched onto the cards, and which are not in accord with the format instructions, will supersede the format instruction, and the data will be read in accord with the punched procedure. Omitting the decimal point can be useful,

[17]While this punch for the plus sign is not necessary, it is advised so that blank column always means missing data.

especially when correlations are being punched. It should, of course, be obvious that in cases where decimal points are omitted it is especially important to be careful about which columns contain what data, otherwise small fractional values can be read in as wholes, or hundreds. Decimals have been omitted for all the data in Figure 23-6. It may be useful for the reader to go back to Tables 23-3 and 23-4 to see how many more columns would have been needed had it been decided to punch all of the decimal places.

REVIEW EXERCISE

As a way of obtaining some supervised practice on setting up data for the computer, the following data are presented for four children in the Language Study. Assume we have been asked to set up the data. First answer each question below in Part A, and then in Part B set up the tally sheet for transmitting the data to the computer center.

Part A

The data below are for four of the twenty-five children in class 4-3 of School Three in the Study.

1. Robert was born in New York, has an IQ of 94, a vocabulary score of 27, and a standard score of −.03 in arithmetic.
2. Amy was born in Puerto Rico, has an IQ of 108, a vocabulary score of 35, and a standard score of .65 in arithmetic.
3. Mary was born in New York, has an IQ of 124, a vocabulary score of 49, and a standard score of 1.05 in arithmetic.
4. José was born in Puerto Rico, has an IQ of 91, a vocabulary score of 22, and a standard score of −1.33 in arithmetic.

Questions

1. In arranging the data for punching, what part of the data would be conceptualized as cards (rows), and what would constitute different columns on the cards?
2. Without adding any new variables, what numbers would it be useful to add?
3. Which set of data would have to be converted in order to be subjected to statistical analysis?
4. To record child, sex, birthplace, IQ, vocabulary score, and standard score in arithmetic, how many columns would be needed?

Now, verify your answers to Part A before moving to Part B.

Answers to Part A of Exercise

1. Each person represents a row, or card, and the information on him would be placed into columns on the card. A total of four cards would, therefore, be needed to punch all of the data about these four children.

2. A code number for each subject, that is, 01, 02, 03, 04. We use two digits because there are twenty-five children in all.

3. The data for sex and birthplace would have to be converted to numeric form, since alphabetic data can not be subjected to statistical analysis. Assigning "0" to females and "1" to males would code sex, and using "1" to stand for New York and "2" for Puerto Rico would conveniently accomplish this purpose for these four children. Other digits would be used as needed for other birthplaces.

4. A total of 16 columns, broken down as follows:

    (a) school and class   : 3 columns
    (b) child's code number: 2 columns
    (c) sex   : 1 column
    (d) birthplace   : 1 column
    (e) IQ   : 3 columns
    (f) vocabulary score : 2 columns
    (g) arithmetic standard
           scores   : 4 columns (1 for the sign, 3 for the score, none
                                        for the decimal place)

                —
                16

Part B

Set up the tally sheet for these data. The answer follows.

School and Class To Be Gangpunched

		343			
	Child	*Sex and Birth-place*	*IQ*	*Vocabulary Score*	*Arithmetic Score*
Robert	01	11	094	27	−003
Amy	02	02	108	35	+065
Mary	03	01	124	49	+105
José	04	12	091	22	−133

Chapter 24

WRITING THE RESEARCH REPORT

Writing a research report seems to be a unique writing task, in the sense that people who feel comfortable in other writing tasks do not feel comfortable when faced with the necessity to write a report of research data. University faculty all know well the phenomenon of the doctoral student who comes regularly for consultation and discussion throughout the planning phases of his project, and throughout the period of data collection and data analysis, and then disappears for weeks and months on end. Next seen at registration, he reports that he has not yet begun to write. In fact, seen at the next several registrations, he has not yet begun to write. Hopefully a full understanding of the nature of research writing, as well as knowledge of what belongs in the research report, will sufficiently structure the task so that it will become less forbidding.

THE BASIC PURPOSE OF THE RESEARCH REPORT

The basic purpose of the research report is to inform a relevant audience of the nature of the problem studied, the specifics of how the project was implemented, the results, and the researcher's interpretation of those results. This informing or communicating function can be stated more specifically in terms of the researcher's responsibility to communicate three kinds of information. First, the report is intended to communicate the nature of the study completed in sufficient detail so that another person could replicate the study exactly as it was done the first time. Second, it is intended to communicate the nature of the results of the study in sufficient detail so that the reader can judge for himself what the conclusions are. Third, it is intended to communicate the researcher's interpretation of the data, that is, his own conclusions and recommendations for further research and action. Notice that these three purposes all involve communication, and not entertainment. Thus in any decision situation about the writing process, the choice must be made in favor of the alternative which will expedite communication.

We must not lose sight of the fact that for information to be communicated through a research report, someone must both read it and understand it. Nothing said in the paragraphs above is intended to support or defend those research reports which are written in language so replete with personal vocabulary and professional jargon that no one but a handful of the professional "in-group" reads or understands them. Nor is this intended to excuse ponderously dull and deadly writing, because it is research. Communication means that the findings and processes of the research study are stated in language sufficiently clear and popular so that the relevant audience will understand it, and are written in a style sufficiently interesting and vivid so that this relevant audience will read it through to the end.

Finally, in this introduction to writing let us include a brief comment on the issue of a relevant audience. This author does not believe the purpose of research writing in education is to communicate the nature of a study and its findings solely to other researchers doing work in the same field or problem area. Equally important, and perhaps even more important, audiences are the practitioners in the classroom and behind the administrator's desk. If research is to result in some effect on educational policy and practice within a reasonable period of time after it is completed, then the results of that research must reach these practitioners soon after the study is completed. And they must reach the practitioners in language clear enough for them to understand not only the results of the research but the potential implications for classroom practice and school organization and administration. This responsibility is the researcher's, and it is a responsibility that researchers have clearly ignored in the social disciplines.

For the audience for whom this book is intended, the graduate student in education or another social discipline, this means that having completed a study there is still a professional responsibility to fulfill, and that is to report the findings of the study to the relevant audience of practitioners. This can be in the form of a report to a convention or an article in a professional journal which practitioners read, or both, but it should be done if we wish to feel that there is any flavor of reality to our research.

CONSIDERATIONS OF LANGUAGE AND STYLE

For those who have never written a report based on research data, the process of research writing is usually frustrating and confusing. It is frustrating because of the many strictures placed on the writer; there are rules governing form, the placement of tables, the order of topics, and several other aspects. It is confusing because stylistically it violates many of the rules for good writing which have been learned since elementary school. The use of imagination, creative free-association from idea to idea, and vivid, if somewhat ambiguous, language—all must be put aside for purposes of research writing. Even as specific a guide as varying language and avoiding redundancy by not using the same word over and over again is replaced in research writing by the advice to define a term and then proceed to use that term throughout the study, in a kind of deliberate and conscious effort to achieve redundancy. For these reasons, research writing can be considered a separate and distinct stage of the research process, no matter how much the researcher has written before. In fact, we might argue that there is a positive correlation between the amount of prior writing experience and the difficulty one will experience in writing the report of a set of research data.

Because it has some limiting rules and different stylistic considerations is not to say that research writing must be either dull or confusing or both. Expository writing can be just as interesting as literary writing and just as well written. It gains its strength, however, not by the fluency or the beauty of the language but by the strength of the basic ideas it is communicating. Thus, whenever a choice must be made between aesthetic appeal of language and precision in understanding, the obvious choice is understanding, for this is the basic goal.

Because research writing is expository writing, the primary virtues are simplicity, clarity, and directness. Avoid excess verbage. Decide what is to be said, say it in the most direct way possible, and stop. There is no place in research writing for a lot of words signifying little, since all they do is muddle up the meaning of what we are trying to say, confuse the reader, and distract from the clarity of our basic exposition. Stylistically also, the simpler, the better. We should make an effort to avoid jargon or terms which have a pseudo-sophisticated implication. Moreover, do not use a longer, unusual term when a shorter, more commonly used one is available. In the same vein, sentences should be brief. We should avoid run-on sentences and particularly avoid a sentence which contains several thoughts. A succession of brief sentences is preferred to one or two very long ones. In those instances when we decide that a complex sentence is preferable, then place the basic referent at the beginning of the sentence. For example, avoid a sentence beginning: "Although one might have expected it to be an important area, staff morale was seldom mentioned. . . ." Since the basic referent is "staff morale," place it at the beginning of the sentence and say, "Although staff morale might have been expected to be an important area . . . ." Suspense should play no role in research writing, so we should say what we mean as quickly as possible.

The Necessity for Precision in Writing

One major aspect of research writing which makes it differ from narrative writing is the precision required. Where narrative writing often deliberately leaves much unsaid or only suggested, so that the reader can use his imagination to complete the scene or action being described, research writing should leave nothing to the reader's imagination. Instead, everything which the researcher wants the reader to glean from the data should be stated directly and specifically and with sufficient clarity so as to eliminate any danger of misinterpretation. In terms of specific writing practice this means that there is no place in research writing for indefinite antecedents or incomplete comparisons.

For example, let us assume that in the report of the Language Study, the following sentences were to appear: "The children in the vocabulary group gained significantly over the period of instruction, while the children in the structure group did not change, and the children in the experiential group lost significantly. This indicates that . . . ." Notice that as we read through to the second sentence we must guess what the researcher had in mind as the antecedent of the first word, "this." Was it the overall pattern of the data? Was it the gain of the vocabulary group compared to the lack of change for the structure group? Compared to the loss for the experiential? It would be far better research writing to begin the second sentence with the precise reference the researcher has in mind when he writes "this," that is, to begin the second sentence like this: "That the vocabulary group gained significantly whereas the other groups either did not change or declined indicates that . . . ." The problem of indefinite antecedents usually occurs because the researcher, as he writes, knows precisely what his referent is, and so when he uses terms like "this indicates" there is no ambiguity in his mind. One of the keys to successful research writing, however, is to develop the habit of writing for the reader who does not know what we are going to say, making certain that sufficient information is provided for that reader to understand our referents.

It is for this reason that the incomplete comparison is to be avoided as well. Consider this sentence, reporting the gains made by boys and by girls in the third and fourth grades of the Language Study: "The data in Table 14 indicate that whereas children of both sexes in both grades gained significantly, in the fourth grade the boys gained more." The reader now is left with the problem of deciding, from the table, if this sentence is to be completed with the words "than the girls in the fourth grade," "than the boys in the fifth grade," or "than any other group studied." Avoiding such ambiguity is the researcher's responsibility, and so good research writing presents completed comparisons, painstakingly stating both parts of the data compared.

Another threat to proper precision is the use of indefinite terms of quantity, quality, or frequency. Some of these terms are obviously imprecise, like "many," "often," or "good." If ten of thirty-five children fail an examination, this may seem like "many children" if our experience had led us to expect no more than one or two children to fail. It may have seemed like a "normal" number to the observer who expected ten or eleven failures, but it may have seemed like a "few" children to the teacher who feared that twenty-five or more children would fail. But notice that all three terms used—"many," "normal," and "few"—are imprecise and reflect a personal orientation or expectation. The one precise way of stating what happened is to say that ten of thirty-five children failed the examination. This is the fact, and this is what should be communicated to the reader. If the researcher wishes to communicate his surprise or relief following the fact, he may do so, but the basic finding must always be reported without imprecision in language.

In addition to the terms which cause obvious imprecision in these three areas of quantity, quality, or frequency, there are terms which are less obvious but also cause problems. Consider sentences like the following:

1. A majority of the children in each of the three method groups in the Language Study reported that they enjoyed the periods for language instruction.
2. More than 70 percent of the teachers in the Language Study reported that the materials for orientation were helpful to them.

To many students the sentences sound precise, even statistical, with a reference to the "majority" in the first sentence and a bit of data, "more than 70 percent" in the second sentence. In fact, they are insufficiently precise. Consider the several columns of data below in Table 24-1. Everyone of them would be appropriate to subsume under the first sentence, for in every set, "a majority" of each of three groups is involved. Notice the dramatic differences between the sets of numbers. Set A consists of three percents all within six percentage points of 50 percent. Set B is widely scattered between 51 percent and 91 percent; sets D and E are homogeneous but one set is in the 70 percent range, the other in the 90 percent range. Yet the reader who is told only that "a majority of the children in each group . . ." has no way of knowing what the data actually look like from that statement. The same imprecision and consequent ambiguity applies to sentence 2 above; for columns D through G all could be included within the second sentence.

Table 24–1 Illustrative Data for Research Precision in Percent

Group	A	B	C	D	E	F	G
Vocabulary	51	51	51	71	91	71	73
Structure	55	71	80	73	95	87	95
Experiential	56	91	85	75	96	97	96

To achieve the proper level of verbal precision the researcher should state what the finding was, as in the several sentences below:

1. Between 51 percent and 56 percent of the children in each of the three method groups . . . (set A).
2. Between half and three-fifths of the children . . . (set A).
3. In the vocabulary group half, and in the other groups about four-fifths . . . (set C).

In each of these sentences the reader is given sufficient detail to obtain a reasonably precise picture of the actual set of data, and when he can do that the researcher can be satisfied that he has achieved a proper level of precision.

A final aspect of precision, and one that requires serious consideration, is the selection of a meaningful level of precision for data presentation. The level of precision employed in the data should be appropriate to the level of the data and not beyond. Moreover, the level of precision employed should be meaningful and not add decimal places for the sake of adding decimal places. For example, let us say we are reporting data on the mean scores for 21 children in the structure group in the Language Study on a 50-item test of vocabulary. Assume that we add up the scores for the 21 children and find that they add to 614 points. Dividing 614 by 21, we arrive at 29.23809, and could continue on for many more decimal places. Now at what place do we round off and report the data? The minimal level of precision would be to report the mean to the nearest whole number, in this example reporting the mean at 29. If we did, we would report the standard deviation to one place, for the rule is that the standard deviation is reported to one decimal more than the mean.

The more likely choice, judging by the literature, would be to report the mean to one decimal place (29.2) and the standard deviation to two places. But a problem occurs when this convention of reporting the mean to one decimal place and the standard deviation to two is followed slavishly, even if there is no rational basis for it and, more important, even if no significant gain in communication is achieved. For example, what significant piece of information do we tell our readers if we report the mean vocabulary score as 29.2 rather than 29?[1] It seems obvious that the added communication is nil. Nevertheless as we glance at the two numbers, note our own responses as to which is the more "scientific" piece of data. For most students, 29.2 sounds like a real piece of data, 29 like an approximation. It may well be that the real reason that this convention of reporting data to one and even two decimal places has persisted is because for many people it contributes to the illusion that the research is scientific.

In short, the suggestion here is that the data be reported to as many digits as are meaningful and not beyond. For most variables used in educational research this means using whole numbers or one decimal place at best.

The Necessity for Consistency

Allied to the characteristic of precision is a second major characteristic of research writing: consistency of terminology and style. We have noted at several points in this book the importance of definitions and the necessity to state these clearly and specifically. But once having stated them, and defined his terms, the expectation is that the researcher will use these terms. When we see a research report which includes a sentence like, "throughout this study the terms retarded, below grade, below normal, and below expectation will all be used to refer to children who were reading below grade level," we know that the writer of that report did not understand the necessity for consistency. What he should have done is select one term, define it, and use it throughout the study whenever he wished to refer to the children who were retarded, below grade, below normal, or below expectation.

The immediate reaction to this advice when given to students is that this will make the report terribly redundant or impossibly repetitious and dull. In most cases it will not, for the reader's attention should be on the data, not the labels applied to aspects of the research. It is for this reason that we suggest defining a term clearly so that it is established for the reader, who need thereafter devote none of his attention to reinterpreting the term. His attention then is free to interpret the data. But if we keep changing terms, then the reader must stop and wonder if the children now being called "below normal" are the same children who, in the preceding analysis, were called "below grade." This is wasted effort and a needless distraction. If the use of the same terms to mean the same things does

---

[1]The reader should note here we are discussing data *presentation*. We noted in Chapter 21 how for statistical analysis, particularly in tests of significance, the researcher will often work at a more precise level than he uses for reporting.

create some redundancy, this is a reasonable price to pay for avoiding the distraction caused by unnecessary variation in terms.

In addition to consistency in terminology, the researcher should strive for a consistency in style. For example, in discussing a series of tables he should decide the order in which he wants to present information. If he intends first to state an overall generalization—"All three groups in the Language Study showed statistically significant gains in ability to understand spoken English"—followed by specific references to each of the separate groups, he should plan on doing this for all of the tables. This is another way of standardizing the pattern of writing so that the reader's attention is free for the data.

Another way in which stylistic consistency should be maintained is at the level of the way in which data are handled. The researcher should decide how he wishes to handle each verbal situation and then handle it consistently. For example consider the question of the three percentages in data set B in Table 24-1 discussed above: 51 percent, 71 percent, and 91 percent. Assume that the researcher decides to refer to these in a sentence beginning: "In the vocabulary group, half of the children . . . ." Stylistic consistency would suggest that since he has begun referring to the data in terms of proportions (half) rather than percentages (51 percent) he should continue using proportions, referring to the next figure as "three-fourths" rather than 71 percent and the last as nine-tenths rather than 91 percent. This again has the effect of simplifying communication for the reader, for given this consistency, the reader is presented with comparable terms of reference.

A final aspect of consistency is consistency in the handling of numerical data. We noted earlier in this chapter that the researcher should devote some thought to selecting a meaningful level of precision for reporting his data. Once that level has been selected, the researcher should use it consistently. Assume, for example, he has decided to report means to one decimal place and standard deviations to two places. Then all means should be reported to one decimal place, and all standard deviations to two places. To thoroughly apply this rule of consistency, a mean of exactly six would be reported as 6.0, that is, to one decimal place.

The Feeling of Continuity

The good research report also has a continuous quality which is best described as a feeling of flowing from one section to the next. We should make an effort to use transitional sentences when we have jumped from one idea to another, when we go from one section to another, when we leave one aspect of the data analysis and proceed on to a second one, so that the reader does not get a feeling of a sudden jump without any preparation. The transitional sentence may be the last sentence of one section which establishes an introduction for the coming section— sentences like "after having considered the overall teaching experience of the sample, we shall now turn to the number of years they have been teaching in their current school." With this as a closing sentence the reader is prepared for the next analysis. Or the transitional sentence may be the first sentence of the new analysis. In which case we might say: "After having considered the years of overall teaching experience, we shall now consider the number of years teaching in the present school." What we should avoid is concluding a discussion of years of overall teaching and beginning a new section on current experience with a sentence like: "Of the teachers studied, 58 percent had been teaching in the present school less than two years."

Avoidance of First Person and Use of Passive Voice

One rule of research writing which students find difficult to accept is that it should be impersonal. The first person is never used, and so when we sit down to write research data we put aside the words "I," and "my." One way to avoid using the first person is to refer to oneself as "the investigator" or "researcher." We do not refer to "the writer," since that is not our primary role, and we refer to "the experimenter" only if we have used the experimental approach. If we combine these terms for self-reference with the passive voice we have a simple way to avoid using the first person. Instead of saying "I developed an instrument to measure attitude toward English," say, "an instrument to measure attitude toward English was developed by the researcher." Instead of saying "I assumed that . . ." say, "it was assumed that . . . ."

Throughout research writing the passive voice is a very useful device. For example, we noted how it should be used in reporting a content analysis. A phrase like "each response was categorized as either positive or negative" helps make it clear to the reader that the categorization schema was arbitrary: It was not that the response was either positive or negative but that the researcher categorized it that way.

CONSIDERATIONS OF RESEARCH FORM

The rules governing the form in which a research report is to be presented are so numerous that, quite literally, books have been written about them. The most useful, and most commonly consulted, of these books are listed below.[2] Almost every institution, in fact almost every faculty advisor, has a preferred guide for form. Therefore, the student should make a point of determining what that guide is and should obtain it at the earliest possible point. Moreover, he should consult it throughout the study, as hours can be saved if materials are prepared in proper form from the beginning.

Since books do exist to tell us how to cite a bibliographic reference, we shall not deal here with what to do when the reference we wish to cite was a chapter in a yearbook with three authors to the chapter and a board of editors for the yearbook. Instead, in this section we shall consider only those major considerations of grammar and report organization that are standard and which have direct implications for research writing.

Let us consider first a miscellany of the major aspects of grammar unique to the research report, beginning with the tenses to be used for verbs. There are relatively standard rules for tenses in research writing. When we sit down to write the report, remember that the study is over, so the basic verb tense to use is the past tense. All of our data analysis will be reported in the past tense, as will all of our references to the thinking and planning that preceded the data analysis. Everyone else's study is over too, so that our references to the literature should be in the past tense as well. The future tense is used only in two places: in stating the hypotheses of the study and in stating suggestions for further research. The present tense, in other words, is not used in research writing except in internal references to the data, that is, in phrases like "The data in Table 3 indicate that . . . ," where using the past tense would create clumsy grammatical constructions.

Speaking of data, they are plural, and so data should be accompanied by parts of speech (verbs) appropriate for a plural noun. "Data are," "data were," "the data indicate," and "these data" are all examples of the correct use of "data." Errors on this one point are so frequent that if a researcher has not written research reports before he should edit his report once just to verify that he has treated the word "data" correctly throughout.

There are a few rules on handling numbers which occur often enough to be worth mentioning here. In treating numbers the rule is that we spell out any number under ten and use digits for any number above ten. A second rule is to avoid beginning a sentence with a number, even one

[2]American Psychological Association Council of Editors, *Publication Manual of the American Psychological Association,* 1957 revision (Washington, D. C.: American Psychological Association, 1957); W. G. Campbell, *Form and Style in Thesis Writing* (Boston: Houghton Mifflin Company, 1954); Kathleen Dugdale, *A Manual of Form for Theses and Term Reports* (Bloomington, Ind.: Indiana University Press, 1955); *A Manual of Style,* revised and enlarged (Chicago: University of Chicago Press, 1949).

spelled out. Thus instead of writing, "Ten children in the structure group . . ." we should write: "In the structure group, ten children . . . ." Occasionally following the rule leads to clumsier sentences than we might otherwise have been able to develop, but it is a rule which should be followed if our report is expected to meet the criteria for good research form. A third aspect of handling numbers in research writing which often causes trouble is the use of percents. Either of two ways is acceptable, writing the number followed by the percent sign (42%) or writing the number followed by the word, "percent" (42 percent). Consistency is the key virtue here. Either adopt one procedure or the other. Do not use both in the same report. If the institution has no preference, the use of the number followed by the percent sign is somewhat easier when typing. A final note on numbers: the word "percentage" is never used in connection with a number but is only used in the absence of numbers. In other words, we might say: "In the Vocabulary group 28 percent responded yes and 72 percent responded no." Then in the succeeding sentence we might note that "the percentage responding no was significantly greater than the percentage responding yes. . . ." We would never say something like "the percentage responding no, 72. . . ."

Preparing Tables for Presentation of Data

One specific aspect of research form in which some guidance may be helpful is the preparation and placement of tables. As a matter of form there are some simple rules to remember in handling tables. First, the table should not appear physically until some reference is made to it in the text alerting the reader as to the nature of the data to be presented. This reference can be as simple as the statement: "Table 11 presents the mean grade equivalents of reading for the three experimental classes." Once that statement appears the researcher is free to insert the table. Moreover, tables should be integrated into the text[3] rather than appearing on separate pages, and should appear as soon as possible after they are first mentioned.

Finally, while not a rule, it is a matter of good practice not to make overly complex tables. Two simple tables are better than one complex table, for the purpose of the table, too, is communication. Nothing will more readily convince a reader to pass a table by without examination

[3]This rule does not hold if we are preparing articles for journals. In that instance we are best advised to consult the specific journal for its own guide and rules for preparing materials for publication. A good general guide is Helen M. Walker and W. N. Durost, *Statistical Tables: Their Structure and Use* (New York: Teachers College Press, Columbia University, 1936).

than the physical appearance of a complex table with columns, sub-columns, and sub-subcolumns. Do not attempt to place more than three variables in a table (that is, two variables in the vertical dimension and one in the horizontal, or the other way around). Remember that the visual impact of a table is important in determining whether or not the reader will stop to consider the data it contains.

In preparing a table, the basic criterion is that it must be able to stand alone and be fully understood by the reader who turns to it without reading the accompanying text. In practice this means that the researcher must exercise great care in preparing table titles and in labeling column headings. In the table title he must tell the reader four pieces of information: (1) the variable or variables for which data are being presented; (2) the groups on whom the data were collected; (3) the subgroups within the table; and (4) the nature of the statistic included within the table. Thus, had we decided to present reading grade equivalents for the groups in the Language Study separately for boys and girls, the title should tell the reader the following information:

Variable for which data are being presented	Reading grade equivalents
Groups on whom the data were collected	Fourth-grade children
Subgroups within the table	Boys and girls (by sex); language emphasis
Nature of the statistics included within the table	Means and standard deviations

The table title which would include all of this information would read as follows: "Grade Equivalents in Reading, Fourth Grade, by Language Emphasis and Sex, Means, and Standard Deviations." The order above presents the variables first, then the groups, then the subgroups and finally the nature of the data. Others prefer to place the nature of the data first, so that the table title would read: "Means and Standard Deviations for Grade Equivalents in Reading, Fourth Grade, by Language Emphasis and Sex." There is no right or wrong here, simply a matter of preference. In both orders the same amount of information is presented, so by the time the reader has completed the title he knows the nature of the data he will read in the table.

To make the table completely independent, the researcher must care-fully label his rows and columns so that the reader can easily identify the meaning of each number in the table. For example, in Table 24-2, the rows are clearly labeled as referring to the language emphasis. This is accom-plished by having the overall heading for the rows state "Language

Table 24–2 Example of Layout for Table To Be Entitled: Grade Equivalents in Reading, Fourth Grade, By Language Emphasis and Sex, Means, and Standard Deviations

	Reading Grade Equivalent			
	Boys		Girls	
Language Emphasis	Mean	S.D.	Mean	S.D.
Vocabulary Structure Experiential	3.6			

Emphasis" and then having separate headings for each row stating the emphasis for which data are presented in that row. Notice that the column headings are more complicated, for they must make clear to the reader two things: first, that the columns are organized according to sex, and second, that they present two kinds of data, means and standard deviations.[4] The labeling of the nature of the data is done below that for the organization by sex, so that the kind of data presented is as close as possible to the data themselves.

Once we have finished the draft of a table it is an excellent idea to test it for communication. There are two simple tests we can perform. First take any number within the body of the table and see what it would mean if we knew only the information at the top of the columns and side of the row in which that number appears. For example, let us assume we had done this with the number 3.6 in Table 24-2. Looking to the top of the column within which that number appears, we learn it is a mean, and furthermore that it refers to boys, and that it is a reading grade equivalent. Then looking to the left, at the row labeling, we learn that it refers to the experiential group. If we were uncertain what that means, the overall label for the rows tells us that this is some kind of a language emphasis. So we have learned that the number 3.6 is the mean grade equivalent in reading for the boys assigned to the experiential language emphasis group. Since this is all we could be expected to learn from the table, it is thoroughly and successfully labeled.

[4]Note that the table also has an overall heading, across all columns, reminding the reader of the nature of the data. Some schools of thought believe this is unnecessary, since this information has been provided in the title.

The second procedure we can use to test a table is to ask someone who knows nothing about our study what a specific number in the table means. This is usually a good insurance procedure, for we as the researchers know enough to read meaning into our data even if the table is less than thoroughly labeled.

THE SEPARATE SECTIONS OF THE RESEARCH REPORT

While there is no one way of organizing the survey or experimental research report, there are general conventions of what should be included and the order in which topics should appear. The grossest way to see a research report is to see it in two sections: one consisting of the thinking and action which occurred before the point at which the data were collected and the second reporting what happened after the data were collected. This dichotomous distinction must be maintained in any organization of a report. Before we report *any* of the data relevant to the hypotheses tested or questions studied, we must present all of the material on our thinking about the problem which structured the study, about the literature, about how we actually did the study, and any descriptive data about the people who comprised our sample. All of this must be out of the way so that the section reporting the data themselves can be free of this pre–data-collection information.

A somewhat more complex perception of a research report breaks each of the two gross sections into two subsections. Thus the pre-results section is divided into a section introducing the problem and reviewing the literature and a procedural section which includes all the information on how the study was done and who was involved. Then the second major section is also divided in two: one subsection in which the results are reported and a second subsection in which they are discussed and conclusions drawn as to the meaning of the study.

A still more specific breakdown divides the two major sections into four each, to make an eight-section report. The eight sections are: (1) introduction and problem statement; (2) review of the literature; (3) hypotheses; (4) design of the study and procedure for data gathering, including a description of the data-gathering instruments and the sample used; (5) the results of the study; (6) discussion of the results; (7) conclusions from the study and the limitations on these; and (8) suggestions for further research.

How we organize the report is a matter which practice at a specific college or university will determine in large part. However it is organized, the eight aspects above must be dealt with somewhere in every research report. In historical research these aspects, while considered, may not provide the structure for the organization of the report. Instead the different aspects of the content studied may be used to develop the report. But in survey or experimental research, these eight aspects not only are the topics which must be considered but also provide the structure for organization. Often, in fact, they provide the actual chapter titles. Therefore, let us consider each of them in turn, beginning with the introduction.

The Introduction

The purposes of the introductory materials are to inform the readers of the nature of the study about to be discussed, specifically: the problem to be investigated, the need for the study, the rationale for the study, and the scope of the study. All introductory chapters must include these four pieces of information. Stylistically, the introductory chapter should be forthright, direct, and brief. Usually these purposes can be achieved in less than five, and certainly less than ten, pages. Moreover, suspense should play no part in the introductory chapter. This means the problem to be investigated should be stated as early as possible, and that comes down to stating it in the first sentence. Unless there are extremely strong reasons not to, the first sentence should begin with some variation of the words, "This study was intended to . . . ."

This is one of the clearest differences in style between narrative writing and research writing. Where an introduction to a narrative piece may be carefully constructed to pique the reader's curiosity and interest and lead him into the story, the introduction to a research report is immediately intended to tell the reader the nature of the study. For it is his interest or lack of it in the problem under study which should determine the reader's desire to go on into the report.

Beyond this, the other elements should be handled briefly, specifically, and directly. The reader wants to know why the study is being done, in a general sense, and specifically why it is being done the way that it is with the sample being used. This is what is meant by the rationale of the study. This statement of the rationale may include one or two references to previous research or theories which were critical in structuring the current study. However, the literature should be referred to sparingly in the introduction, since the full review of the literature comes as the second section of the report. Therefore, the literature referred to here should be only the literature which is essential to understand the rationale for the present study. We are trying to convince the reader of the importance of the study at this early point, so that the orientation in writing the rationale is always with the following point in mind: What does the reader need to know to fully appreciate the need for the study and its educational significance? It is at this point that we would describe any aspects of our own professional experience which stimulated the study or which aroused our interest in the problem. This material, too, should be presented directly and briefly.

Some institutions prefer a separate statement of the need for the study, identified under such a subheading. If such a section is required, the basic point to be made in it is to demonstrate that the study will deal with valid questions of professional concern for which the proposed study will provide data leading to an answer. These questions may stem from simple lack of needed data, as in a survey or historical study, or they may stem from a point of theory the study is expected to resolve or clarify through experimentation. This is one point in the introduction at which a reference to the literature is both helpful and appropriate. If we have found a reference in which an accepted authority in the problem area has noted that a study such as ours is needed, this is the place to include that quotation. However, including it does not free us from the responsibility to develop the rationale for the study in the same way as noted above. It is not sufficient to say that we are doing this study because Professor X wrote an article a year ago in which he said this kind of study was needed. Professor X's article indicates that our judgment of the need for the study is professionally shared, and the reference to him should be written in that light.

Finally, it is relevant to include some reference to the scope of the study to be attempted. The simplest way to do this is to break the general research problem down into specific subproblems, if there are any, and there almost always are in a reasonably sound piece of research. For example, the general problem of the Language Study was to compare the effectiveness of three methods of teaching English as a second language to non–English-speaking Puerto Rican children. Yet within this general problem there were four subcomparisons involving the four language modalities of reading, writing, speaking, and understanding. Typically there should be homogeneity in the total research report between this section delineating the scope and subproblems and the later chapter on results. Here in the introduction the reader should be alerted to all of the major analyses of the data to which he will be exposed in the results chapter, with each of these major analyses specified as one of the subproblems.

For this reason it is a sound editorial technique in research writing to reread the introduction before beginning the results chapter, and again after completing the results chapter, to be certain that this homogeneity exists. We must be particularly alert for unexpected insights into the data during data analyses which produced unanticipated analyses of the data which were neither stated in the original introduction nor noted among the subproblems of the study. Therefore one of our last writing chores may be to amend the introduction to include these aspects of the study. In doing this, there is no need to feel we are rewriting history or to pretend we intended all along to do these analyses. We state frankly in the introduction that in the course of analyzing the data some previously unanticipated analyses were decided upon, which enabled us to study additional problems. We then specify the new problems.

The sequence for presenting the four topics in the introduction is the same as the sequence in which they have been discussed in this section. We begin with the statement of the problem. This is followed by the explanation of the rationale for the study and the defense of the need for the study. Finally we conclude with the delineation of the scope of the study, typically concluding with the specification of the subproblems.

The Review of Literature

The second element in the research report is the review of the literature. Practice seems to be relatively evenly divided between making this a separate chapter, as opposed to making it a second major section of the introduction. The decision basically should be made in terms of two criteria: the tightness of the introduction when it includes the several topics it should include, and the length of the review of literature. If the introduction makes a sensible and complete chapter itself, this author believes in making the review of literature a separate chapter. If the introduction is limited, with a brief rationale and statement of need and seems skimpy if left to stand alone, then the review of literature may sensibly be added to it.

In either case the structure of the review of literature is the same. Perhaps the major point to remember is that this section of the research report reviewing the literature must be sharply distinguished from the literature reviewed by the researcher in planning the study. The written review is highly selective, including only those aspects of the research and nonresearch literature that are relevant to developing the foundation of the current study. For this development of foundation is the critical function of this section of the written research report. It does not include everything the researcher has read and is not intended to demonstrate the scope of his reading nor the time he has spent among the library shelves. In short, every reference actually included in the written review of the literature must serve a specific study-oriented purpose.

It is generally good writing practice in this section to distinguish between the research literature based on data and the nonresearch literature including all the other types of written material. The reason for the distinction is because these two kinds of literature are presented in different levels of specificity. The previous relevant data obtained in the problem area is presented and discussed in sufficient detail for the reader to have the grasp of these data when he reads the results section of the current study. To accomplish this each *major* previous study is discussed in a separate paragraph or paragraphs, with the purpose of the study, the instruments and the sample used, and the results obtained specified. Less relevant studies are summarized without this much detail, typically by cutting or eliminating references to the instruments and sample. In fact when several researchers have studied similar aspects of the problem in similar ways, all of these studies can be consolidated into one paragraph beginning with a sentence like, "several researchers (Jones, Smith, Black, and Brown) have recently studied the effectiveness of remedial reading instruction using instructional techniques based on individualized reading." Following this introductory sentence the findings of these studies would be summarized as a group, rather than separately.

This same style of combining comparable sources typifies the treatment of the nonresearch literature. Except for references to major theorists in the problem area, the writings of authorities who hold similar views should be discussed together, within the same paragraph. For the review of the literature should read as a synthesis, written by someone who has read all of the literature and so is able to look across it all, select the highlights, and synthesize these into a totally integrated section. A review of literature is sharply different from an annotated bibliography, which consists of a series of independent references to single studies. If we read over our review of literature and each paragraph refers to a different specific study or reference, then we have not achieved this integration function sufficiently well. In that case we should rewrite, bringing together the separate references which logically can be combined.

Throughout the writing of the review of literature section we should always keep in mind that the goal is to review the literature in the context of our study. Thus each point made and each reference cited should be written in such a way that the reader sees its relevance to, and contribution in establishing, the foundation for the current study.

We should also recognize that we are writing the review of literature for our future use when we write the discussion of our results and conclusions from our study. In those later chapters we will want to refer to the findings of previous studies and the conclusions derived from them. The place to present those earlier findings and conclusions is in the review of literature. Thus we must write this chapter with some anticipation of what we might need in later chapters. This often means that just as we reread the introduction after finishing the results chapter, so we may wish to add to the review of literature when we write the discussion and conclusions.

Hypotheses

At some point prior to the presentation of the data, the hypotheses and the rationale for them should be stated. Since the hypotheses are derived from the researcher's experience and from the literature, the earliest point at which they can effectively be stated is at the conclusion of the review of literature. The review has presented the current study's foundation in previous research and theory, and the introduction has presented the researcher's perceptions. With all of this now before the reader it is sensible to state the expected outcomes of the study.

We noted in Chapter 2 that hypotheses can be stated in two different ways. One way is to indicate the expectation of difference, that is: "Children taught by the vocabulary emphasis will have significantly higher word knowledge scores than children taught by the experiential emphasis." The second way is to state an expectation of no difference: "There will be no difference in attitude toward school between children taught by the vocabulary and experiential emphases." Students are often confused as to the proper form in which to state hypotheses at this stage of the report, and the author believes that some of the confusion stems from the failure to distinguish between *research hypotheses* and *statistical hypotheses*. We discussed this distinction at length in Chapter 8, noting there that all inferential statistical procedures require a statement of the hypothesis specifying no difference, that is, in null form. But these statistical hypotheses of no difference are needed only for purposes of data analysis and in most instances are not formally "stated" at all. What should be formally stated in the report are the research hypotheses, that is, the researcher's actual expectations of the results. Thus in this section of the written report the researcher specifies each of his hypotheses, indicating those instances in which he expects a difference and those in which he does not.[5] Remember that the research hypothesis is defined as the researcher's prediction of a research outcome, and only when he states what he actually expects do the hypotheses meet this definition and communicate this information.

[5]The student should be aware that some colleges and universities persist in requiring that the student state his research hypotheses in null form. Obviously, if this is required, this is the way they should be stated.

A second point made in Chapter 2 about the hypotheses which should be remembered is that each comparison involved should be stated in a separate hypothesis. We noted in that early chapter that if the researcher in the Language Study expected no differences in attitude toward school among his three experimental groups, he would need to state three specific hypotheses, one for each expectation of no difference between: (1) structure and vocabulary groups; (2) structure and experiential groups; and (3) vocabulary and experiential groups. When we have a multiplicity of hypotheses about the same general point it can become dreadfully redundant to develop each fully, for this often means stating the same rationale several different times. It is a useful device therefore, in this instance, to develop a *general hypothesis* and state the rationale only for the general hypothesis. With this general hypothesis and its rationale stated, the researcher then presents the specific research hypotheses which have been subsumed under the general one. For example, the researcher in the Language Study could handle this area of attitude toward school by explaining the reasons he expects no differences in the area. He might do this by referring to studies he has discussed in the preceding review of literature, or to experts in the area who argue that method in itself will not affect attitude, or to his own experiences with non–English-speaking children. He might then note that these findings and opinions led him to the general hypothesis: "There will be no differences in attitude toward school between children taught English as a second language by emphasis on different components of language." Having stated this general hypothesis, he can then note that applied to his study, this leads to the following three specific hypotheses. There will be no differences in attitude toward school between children taught by: (1) vocabulary and structure emphases; (2) vocabulary and experiential emphases; (3) structure and experiential emphases.

Note what he has achieved. First of all he has stated, and defended, only one general hypothesis, eliminating the necessity to say the same things three times. Moreover, his general hypothesis would apply to any studies in the same problem area, and it should if his work is built upon previous work. With this done, he is able to state the three specific hypotheses unique to his study briefly and directly, placing the verbal material common to all three in the stem of the hypothesis. He will still be able to take specific action on each hypothesis, for the data will support or not support hypotheses 1, 2, and 3.

Hypotheses should be stated only for those analyses which were contemplated before the data were collected. There is no place in the research report for after-the-fact hypothesizing. Therefore, although we noted that unanticipated analyses should be indicated in the statement of the subproblems to the study, hypotheses should not be concocted and stated for them. Nor should hypotheses be rewritten once the data are known. The hypotheses should represent the researcher's best synthesis of thinking about the problem *before* he did his study. The fact that he is doing the study indicates that there is some room for movement or change in the thinking in the problem area, and so some possibility that the hypotheses will not be supported. Given this possibility for movement or change, should the data not support the hypotheses this result should stimulate reconsideration of previous data and rethinking of previous theory, but *not* rewriting of the hypotheses.

Procedure

With the hypotheses stated, the next major topic to which the researcher turns is the detailed statement of how the study was done. This section may be variously titled (Procedure, Method and Materials, Techniques for Data Collection and Analysis, and so on) and may be presented in one or several chapters. What it is called, and how it is presented is a function of the complexity of the material. No matter how it is structured, this section of the research report includes material selected from six areas: the definitions of the terms used in the study (if not already stated); the description of the sample used in the study; descriptive data about the instruments used; the design of the study, including the way in which the data were collected; the way in which the data were analyzed; and the assumptions and limitations of the study, identified through the point of data analysis.

Colleges and universities and even individual faculty advisors differ on which of the six areas they wish included, and so any individual reader is best advised to consult with his adviser on this point. Here we shall consider all six areas, briefly noting what should be included if it will be our responsibility to refer to the area.

DEFINITION OF TERMS   At some point in the early portions of the report, the researcher must state his definitions. Where the definitions are stated is determined by the uniqueness of the terms used. In some few studies the basic terminology is so individual that the researcher cannot intelligibly discuss the problem until the definitions have been stated. In this case the definitions appear early in the introduction. More generally an intelligent level of discourse can be established between researcher and reader without a formal statement of specific definitions until after the review of literature has been completed. The desirability of this should be obvious: The literature is the basic source of the functional definitions. Thus, once the literature has been reviewed, the researcher can then develop his functional definitions by reference to material he has already presented.

We have noted at several earlier points the distinction between these functional definitions and the conceptual definitions. Both should be included in the research report, that is, the researcher should indicate both the conceptual or dictionary definition of his terms and the functional definition; or how he is using the term in his own study. He should also deal briefly with the rationale for his functional definitions, indicating how each relates to previous research in the problem area. At times researchers seem to believe they have the right enunciated in *Through the Looking Glass* by Humpty Dumpty, that a word can mean anything they want it to mean. They do not, and so must indicate in this section the continuity between their own use and previous uses of comparable terms.

DESCRIPTION OF SAMPLE   The reader is entitled to know in considerable detail the nature of the sample used for data collection, as well as the process employed for sample selection. This material is incidental to the results and so should be placed in the chapter on procedure. In some instances it may be sufficiently critical to deserve a separate chapter. In any event data describing the sample are not properly considered results and so should precede the results. This is true even if chronologically these data were obtained at the same time (and even through the same data-gathering instruments) as the data used to test the hypotheses of the study.

The first aspect of sampling to be discussed is the identification of the population or universe of interest. Here the researcher briefly presents the rationale for considering this both a relevant and an educationally significant population or universe. Once this has been accomplished, the researcher then presents the plan he followed for selecting his data-producing sample. Included here are the efforts at stratification. If these were made, then it is necessary to present the rationale for selecting and using the stratifying variables actually employed. If some other variables which the nature of the problem and/or the population suggest as logical for stratifying purposes were not used, then the researcher should indicate why these were rejected. Here, as throughout the report, it is desirable to be frank. For example, if a variable could not be used because a measure was not available or because needed data were not available about the population, then the researcher should say so. Evasiveness at this point is no virtue and deceives no one.

Having discussed stratification, the researcher then presents his method of actual sample selection, and the rationale for the sample size used, if there was any. Random-selection methods need no defense, since they are accepted as preferable. Other methods of sample selection do need defense, and moreover, the implications of these for data analysis and generalization must be remembered throughout the study.

The last aspect of the discussion of sampling to be considered is to present the data available to describe the sample. Ideally, the researcher is able to present comparable data about the population so that the reader can form some judgment as to the representativeness of the sample. Remember, random-selection methods only assure that the sample selection process was bias-free. They do not assure representativeness, and the smaller the sample the less likely is representativeness. Therefore, the researcher presents what data he can to test the representativeness of his sample. Remember also that representativeness should be tested only with those variables relevant to the problem under study. It is not defended with any set of variables for which data are readily available.

Tables are often helpful in this section, particularly in establishing the basic characteristics of the samples. In these tables it is preferable to provide the reader with summary frequency distributions on critical variables, rather than only with group statistics like means and standard deviations. The basic purpose of presenting these data on the sample is to enable the reader to know exactly the nature of the respondents who provided data for the results chapter he is about to read. However, these data also serve purpose for future researchers who may wish to replicate or extend the research being reported. To do either of these things, they would need to know in reasonably precise detail the nature of the sample employed in the study being reported, and so summary frequency distributions are desirable.

INSTRUMENTS AND THEIR CHARACTERISTICS   Another aspect of the procedure section is the presentation of sufficient data on the data-gathering instruments employed so that the reader may evaluate them. Given the purpose, a sharp distinction in the nature of the materials presented in this section can be made between three kinds of instruments: (1) those widely used and recognized and considered standardized instruments; (2) less well-known instruments, not standardized but used previously in studies in the same problem area as the current study; and (3) those instruments constructed for the present study.

For the standardized instruments the researcher has available data on reliability and validity obtained during the standardization process. In most instances he can defend the use of these data for his own study, particularly in areas like achievement or intelligence testing. Seldom is one expected to obtain new reliability data on the Wechsler Intelligence Scale for Children or for the Stanford Achievement Tests, for example. In this instance, it is sufficient for the researcher to identify the instruments he has used and indicate why he believes the original reliability and validity data apply. Most colleges and universities do not require that these original data even be reported, but accept as sufficient a reference to the original manuals.

A word of caution is needed here: this easy adoption of previously obtained standardization data makes complete sense only if the sample used in the current study is reasonably approximate to the samples used in the standardization process. This latter information is readily available to the researcher in the manual which accompanies the instruments. If we are using instruments standardized on normal children with samples of severely retarded or educationally deprived children, for example, it may well be wise to obtain our own independent estimates of the reliability of the instruments. Few of the currently available standardized instruments included such children in the standardization sample.

If the instruments, while not considered standardized, have nevertheless been used in previous studies in the problem area, it is possible that the reliability and validity estimates previously obtained will be accepted for our study. But it is much wiser to obtain our own estimates. This is true because should our results not be consistent with the previous studies, one possible explanation is that the instrument functioned at different levels of reliability in the two studies. The only adequate way to deal with this possibility is to know the reliability of the instrument in our study. Whether we collect our own estimates or not, we should report the data originally collected about the instrument. If we do collect our own reliability data and it corroborates the original data, no comment need be made other than to note this. However, if our reliability estimates are lower than the original, we should report both estimates in our procedure chapter and deal with the effects of this in our discussion chapter. Typically this problem only occurs if we delay obtaining our own estimates of reliability until the time of our own data collection. When the problem does occur it is an excellent illustration of the reason reliability estimates should be obtained prior to any use of an instrument in data collection. If the instrument from previous research had been tested in advance and found to be inadequate, the researcher would have looked elsewhere rather than proceed with the inadequate instrument.

The most detailed discussion and presentation of rationale and data is required for "home-made" instruments, that is, those instruments constructed for the purpose of the current study. By definition, these are new and previously untried instruments, and so the researcher must establish their reliability and validity with reasonable strength. In considering reliability, there is no substitute for data. It is too basic a characteristic to be assumed, and so no matter how limited the study, some estimate should be obtained of the reliability of every "home-made" data-gathering instrument. Moreover, it is not enough to simply obtain the estimate; the estimate must be sufficiently high for the instrument to be accepted as sufficiently stable and precise for the research purposes intended.

For validity, the logical estimates are often accepted without requiring a statistical estimate. That is, depending upon the nature of the data-collection instrument, content validity may be sufficient for the new instrument to be accepted. If not, construct, congruent, or concurrent validity will serve, for only rarely are students expected to present evidence of the predictive validity of their home-made instrument.

There is no expectation that students will discuss the other characteristics referred to in Chapter 12 on characteristics of instrument. Concern with characteristics like sensitivity, appropriateness, and objectivity has been severely limited in education. Nevertheless it is suggested that the researcher consider them, however briefly, in the procedure section. This suggestion is based upon the fundamental principle of research writing that everything we wish to refer to in the results section and thereafter should have been referred to in the section prior to the results. Therefore, if we omit any consideration of these characteristics we must be certain that in our discussion we do not want to qualify or limit the findings by reference to one of these characteristics, like sensitivity. If we do wish to refer to them at a later point, we must refer to them at this early point as well.

DESIGN OF STUDY AND DATA-COLLECTION PLAN   One aspect of this section which all colleges and universities agree must be included is the detailed statement of the design of the study and the plan for collecting the data.

The importance of stating the design of the study varies widely among the different approaches to research. In historical research, it is an unimportant stage for there may be no formal design to the data collection. In the survey approach it is important, since the reader wishes to know how the researcher planned his study to obtain a representative set of data from the research situations surveyed. Although important in descriptive and evaluative surveys the section on design is usually simple to write, for it is a direct description of how the study was planned to yield the desired data. In the comparative survey, however, the description of the design of the study is more complex, and it reaches its peak of complexity in the experimental approach. The complexity in these instances stems from the necessity for the researcher to defend, as well as to explain his design. In the comparative survey he must defend the fact that he has sufficiently isolated the comparative variable for the survey to be a valid comparison of that variable. How detailed and deep a defense is required at this point depends upon the research problem and the situations being compared. The only general guide that can be stated is that after reading this section, the reader must be convinced, first, that there is sufficient reason to believe that the situations being compared did *differ* on the comparative variable, and second, that they were reasonably comparable on all other critical variables.

The additional complexity in experimental research is that the researcher should detail his efforts to control intervention and bias. We discussed these joint problems at length in the chapter on the experimental approach. Here let us note that in this section of the report the researcher is seeking to convince the reader that the design of the experiment was a rational process in which every decision taken was taken only after a full consideration of all alternatives, and that a research situation was created that was a reasonable test of the independent variable. Moreover he should do this in sufficient detail so that another researcher could design a comparable experiment, knowing how each potential intervening variable was handled.

The standard for evaluating the thoroughness of the statement of the design of the study is just this ability to replicate the study. And this same standard ties design to data collection, for as he moves on to describe his data-collection plan, the evaluation criterion is whether or not sufficient information is presented in sufficient detail for another researcher to replicate the current study. To meet this standard the researcher must identify every point in the data-collection process at which he might have proceeded in more than one way and make clear what he did. For example, if more than one instrument was used, he must specify the number of data-collection sessions involved, the instruments administered at each session, the order in which they were administered, and the time allowed for completing each. Moreover, he should include in the appendix to the report any instructions specifically developed for administering the instruments.

Students often find it painfully dull to write at the level of detail and specificity required in this section. This is particularly true if the section is written when the study is completed and the student is pressured by time. Then dullness is compounded by the frustration at having to deal with what is perceived as minutae of little importance when the student is anxious to turn to the data. Therefore it is wise to complete at least a draft of this section once the study is under way and the researcher is committed to a design and data-collection plan. Writing it then has the advantage of getting this material on paper before the pressure of data analysis hits. Moreover, it also has the advantage that the researcher is writing this section at that point in time when the details involved are fresh in his mind.

ASSUMPTIONS AND LIMITATIONS   Some colleges and universities prefer that within the procedure chapter the researcher formally list the assumptions and limitations involved in his research. If the researcher has identified these as he should have during the development of the study, this section then becomes a simple matter of developing two separate lists, one of assumptions and one of limitations. Both assumptions and limitations are stated in a series of numbered, declarative sentences, verbally sparse so that what is being assumed or recognized as a limit stands out clearly.

The usual differences among the research approaches occur here again: For this aspect is least important in historical research, important in survey research, but critical in experimental research. The difference in importance stems from the different degrees of control the three approaches demand. In experimental research so much of the control of the vast network of potential intervening variables depends upon assumptions, or else is reflected in limitations, that these separate lists should be developed by the researcher for his own use even if there is no insistence that he formally state them in his report. In the other approaches the researcher must know what he is assuming and what limits are operating, but he need not formally list them unless report writing practice demands it.

THE DATA-ANALYSIS PLAN   The procedure chapter concludes with an overview of how the researcher analyzed the data. Since techniques for data analysis, statistical analysis, and data presentation are all presented in detail in later chapters, they need not be detailed here. What this section of the procedure chapter does include are three specific points: (1) the type of data analyses that were done; (2) the statistical procedures completed, including the rationale for choosing these procedures and the level of significance that was used; and (3) how the researcher intends to present the data.

Not all of these points apply to all research approaches, of course. Historical research often has no statistical analyses, and so this section of the outline would include only a discussion of the nature of the data and the way in which they will be presented. In survey and experimental research, these two parts, plus the nature of the statistical analyses completed, should be included.

Presentation of the Results

With all of the prefatory material presented, the researcher turns to the chapter in which he states his results. This chapter must contain the data in sufficient detail for the reader to make his own interpretations. It may or may not contain the researcher's interpretations, for there are two different ways of structuring the results chapter. One way is to limit the chapter to the presentation of the data, leaving interpretation to a following chapter entitled "Discussion." The other approach is to integrate results and discussion into one chapter. The basis for choosing one of these two approaches[6] is the nature of the data and the research problem. If the problem and data are such that no one can fully understand all the ramifications until he has read, and been exposed to, all of the data, then the results chapter should be separate from the discussion chapter. If instead the study consists of several segments, each of which is relatively discrete, then there may be merit in integrating results and discussion for each segment. But for this procedure to make sense these must be conceptually discrete segments, referring to different aspects of the overall problem. Otherwise, it is preferable to have a straightforward presentation of all of the results in a chapter separate from the discussion.

If we should decide that ours are data which can best be presented in segments with an integrated discussion, then we must be careful that within each section we distinguish between the presentation of the data and the subsequent discussion. The reporting of data is an objective process, and several researchers writing about the same data should write essentially the same report. These several researchers might easily come to different interpretations, and so these interpretations should be clearly separate from the results.

To make data reporting completely objective, terms implying the researcher's orientation or expectations should not appear in the results sections, nor should value judgments. Expressions like "it was surprising to note that 20 percent of the group . . ." should play no part in data reporting, any more than a phrase like "only 20 percent . . . ." In either case, the fact being reported is that 20 percent of the group responded in a certain way, and that is what should be reported, unaccompanied by an expression indicating that the researcher did not expect this ("it was surprising . . .") or that he expected more than this ("only . . .").

This is not meant to imply that there is no place in research writing for the researcher to express his own opinion, response, or reaction to the data. It is meant to imply that the section reporting the results is not that place. The reason this is significant goes back to the statement earlier in this chapter that one basic function of research writing is to report the data with sufficient clarity and in sufficient detail so that the intelligent reader will be able to come to his own conclusions about the nature of the

---

[6]Note that the researcher should choose *one*. It is poor research writing to discuss some results but not others.

results. The reader is entitled to be able to read the report of the data without having to read about our biases and expectations, and so we say that the results section should be a dispassionate reporting of the facts.

The results section should convey a specific tone: that we, as researchers, are reporting the data fully and fairly. If we are reporting the results of a study with multiple possible interpretations, a good results section would leave proponents of all points of view completely convinced that they have read a fair and balanced presentation of the data. One side or the other may disagree with our interpretations whenever they appear, but all sides should be content with our presentation of the results. This means we pay as much attention to those aspects of the data which came out counter to our hypotheses and counter to what our personal expectations were as we do to those aspects of the data which came out in support of our hypotheses and in line with our expectations. It means we present those aspects of the results that will be hard to explain, provided they are important, in as full detail as they deserve, just as we present those aspects that are simple to explain.

STRUCTURAL ASPECTS   If the study has hypotheses, these offer the ideal structure for the chapter on results. The researcher takes each hypothesis in turn, presents the analysis of the data collected to test that hypothesis, and proceeds to come to some conclusion as to whether or not the hypothesis was supported or not by these data. He then proceeds on to the next hypothesis until each has been disposed of. If there are no hypotheses, then the sub-problems presented in the introduction may be used to structure the results section. The researcher uses these in the same way he would use hypotheses, taking each in turn and presenting the data relevant to it. If he has nothing more than an overall problem, with neither hypotheses nor subproblems, then the researcher must use the logical aspects of this one problem to help him decide the order in which to present the several aspects of the data. But in keeping with the homogeneity concept discussed earlier in this chapter, the way in which data are presented in the results chapter should be consistent with the way in which the problem was discussed and developed in the introduction.

Whether hypotheses, or subproblems, or aspects of the data determine the structure of the results chapter, the data must be presented. Moreover, the chapter should include both the descriptive and inferential aspects of the data. Typically, the descriptive data are presented in tables except for the unusual study in which the data are so limited that they can more efficiently be presented in the running text. This occasionally happens in a limited correlational survey when the results consists of one or two correlation coefficients. In that instance no function is served by a table, and the researcher is sometimes also reluctant to call attention to how little data there seem to be! But in most other instances, the data are best presented in tabular form.

Data which appear in the results chapter must serve a specific function, and generally should be summary data of some sort. Minimally these data should be in the form of a summary frequency distribution. More usually, data are presented through summary descriptive statistics for groups like means and standard deviations or medians and interquartile ranges. There is seldom any research purpose served by presenting data for each individual respondent, except when a case study survey has been done. In the usual research project where the group is the focus of interest and concern, if we would nevertheless like to provide the reader with some data on individuals, these properly belong in the appendix to the report. Placed there they are available to the reader should he wish to consult these data, but they do not impede the flow of the report itself.

Each piece of data we include must pass a simple test. The test is to ask ourselves what effect it would have on the report, and specifically on the reader's understanding of the report, if that piece of data were left out. If the answer to the question is "it would hurt the reader's understanding if this bit of data were left out," then we include it. If the answer is on the order of "it wouldn't hurt understanding to omit it, but it took me six hours to complete this analysis," then we should omit it.

Remember that any number of analyses can be performed with data, and the researcher will find a large number of these interesting. This does not mean he includes every one. He includes only those essential to the development of the major thesis, relevant to the hypotheses, and necessary to understand the study.

INTEGRATION OF TABLES   The complete research report is typically a mixture of text and table. The basic communication function is achieved by the text, with tables[7] serving a supplementary but independent function. This establishes the first rule in preparing tables: They must serve some function independent of the text. If the entire contents of a table are reported in the text, then there is little reason for the table. The primary independent function the tables serve is to report the data in detail which the researcher does not wish to put into the text. For example, in the Language Study we might wish to report the reading and arithmetic grade equivalents of the children in the three fourth-grade experimental groups. As we scan the data we notice that in all three groups the children were about four months behind grade in arithmetic and about six months

[7]A discussion on how to prepare a table begins on page 719.

behind in reading. We might decide that this is a sufficient statement to place in the text. It conveys the sense of moderate retardation on the average, somewhat more severe in reading than in arithmetic. Yet we also have an obligation to report the frequency distributions, means, and standard deviations for each of the classes in each of these two academic areas, and so we would include these data in two tables, to provide the specific data to support the general statement made in the text.

This perception of the table as supplementary and yet independent means that in preparing the research report the researcher can place *some* responsibility for the full understanding of the data upon the reader. But he cannot place all of it there. That is, he cannot go to the extreme of presenting a table with no comment other than an introductory sentence like: "The distributions and mean grade equivalents in reading and arithmetic were computed for each of the experimental classes, and these data appear in Table 1." This type of presentation places the entire burden of data analysis upon the reader, and this is bad research writing. The minimum comment the researcher must make upon a table is to note the generalization he feels is significant, that is, the generalization he feels justifies the inclusion of the data analysis reported in the table. If we have nothing to say about the table, the chances are excellent that there is no reason to include the table in the report.

Thus we have stated here that if the text includes everything that is in the table, the table need not appear. We have also noted that if the text includes no reference to it, the table should not appear. Obviously then the researcher's problem is to hit the appropriate middle way in which he reports, in the text, the highlights of the data in the table. While no rule which would apply to the variety of research studies can be stated for determining how much should be said, it may be helpful to remember the basic orientation of the results chapter: either hypothesis testing or subproblem description. This suggests that the text should include sufficient detail from the table for the reader to learn, from the text alone, the disposition of the hypothesis or subproblem.

In instances in which coding and content analysis have been employed for data analysis, the relationship of text and table is more complex. For now there are several levels at which the data have been analyzed, and the tables present the intermediate levels. For example, Table 24-3 reports some data from the content analysis for semantic content discussed in Chapter 22. Note that in this table the data are reported at the summary area level of the content analysis code. Thus the reader can see that data were grouped in six major areas. Moreover Table 24-4 indicates that there were specific categories used in area 1. Comparable data could be

Table 24–3   Illustrative Table for Presenting Data at Summary Level of Semantic Content Analysis

	Frequency of Appearance	
Area	Number	Percent
Academic processes	39	31
Plant	5	4
Atmosphere, climate, creative level	22	17
Relationships	30	24
Teaching process	19	15
Characteristics of children	5	4
Staff and administration	6	5
Total	126	100

prepared for the other areas. Even if this were done, the reader is still one level away from the actual responses written by the subjects. Thus, he still has no direct basis for understanding precisely what the responses were and how the researcher handled the data.

One way of providing this information would be to make a much more detailed table which would move to one level lower. But the good research writer does not behave like the young mother who launched into a 45-minute lecture when her five-year-old asked her where babies come from. When she concluded she asked him if he now knew, to which he responded: "Yes, but I know more than I really wanted to know." To avoid telling the reader more than he wants to know, the solution is to illustrate in the text the nature of the responses which were placed into each category. Thus in writing up the data in Table 24-3 the text might read something like this:

> Most, often, (31 percent) the responses were classified into the area of academic processes. Included within this area were responses which referred to language arts and reading (10 percent), mathematics (8 percent) and less frequently (4 percent or less) to social studies, science, and the arts.

In this way the reader obtains some insight into the specific kinds of responses placed into the various categories, without having to wade through excessively detailed tables.

HANDLING STATISTICS   In the results chapter, the researcher should specify which statistical processes were employed for each of the analyses

Table 24–4 Illustrative Section of Table Presenting Data at Detailed Level of Semantic Content Analysis

Area	Category	Frequency of Appearance	
		Number	Percent
Academic processes,	Art	4	3
including classes,	Music	3	2
courses, and subjects	Craft	1	1
	Social studies	5	4
	Language arts, reading	12	10
	Science	4	3
	Mathematics	10	8
Area total		39	31

reported. He is not expected to include computational material,[8] nor, if he has used standard statistical procedures, is he expected to present the computational formulas. If he has used unusual formulas or obscure statistical procedures, these should be presented in the appendix and mentioned in the results chapter. Whether or not a formula or process should be considered unusual or obscure can be settled by the basic criterion for all such decisions in research writing: the necessity to provide sufficient detail so that replication would be possible. Thus if the statistic used was found in a relatively rare journal, it should be included in the report.

Tests of significance should be reported and the values indicated in some way. The most direct way is to actually provide the numerical values of the statistics obtained, that is, stating the value of the specific t or χ^2. A second way is to indicate the significance probability, in other words, the maximum likelihood that chance could explain the obtained result. The third way is to simply indicate whether or not each result was statistically significant, using the level of significance selected for the study. For example, assume that in the Phonics Study, the researcher has obtained a t of 2.70 after testing the significance of the difference in mean

[8]The only exception to the rule that computational results are not reported is when the analysis of variance is used as the basis for a statistical inference. In this case the summary tables for the analysis of variance is included in the text so that the reader may see for himself the relative size of the sums of squares and the mean squares involved in the analysis of variance. Examples of how to lay out these tables were provided in the discussion of the analysis of variance in Chapter 9.

reading gain between the phonics and individualized readers groups. With the sample sizes in his study, a t of this size would only be expected to occur by chance one time in one hundred, and so the difference is statistically significant since the researcher was employing the 5 percent level of significance. He can report this finding in three ways. One is to simply note in his text that the difference was statistically significant. The reader would know then only that the obtained t was sufficient for significance at the 5 percent level. The second choice is to footnote the reference in the text that there was a statistically significant difference between the phonics and traditional instructional groups. The footnote in this case would read like this: $t = 2.70$, $df = 40$, $p < .01$. Note that the footnote provides the value of the statistic, the degree of freedom, and the significance probability. The final choice would be to present the data in a simple table like Table 24-5, in which the last column has an entry for the test of significance. Notice that in this instance, too, the researcher has indicated the significance probability, this time through a footnote in the table.

Discussion of the Results

The discussion is a much freer section than the results. Where the results are data-*bound,* the discussion is only data-*based.* This means that in the discussion the researcher is free to take off from the data and discuss what he believes they mean and how he believes they came about. Notice, however, that while the researcher has considerably more freedom in the

Table 24–5 Illustrative Table for Presenting Descriptive and Inferential Data for: Gains in Reading Grade Equivalents, Fourth Graders, By Method of Remedial Instruction, Means, Standard Deviations, and Test of Significance

| Method of Remedial Instruction | Gains in Reading Grade Equivalent | | | Test of Significance |
	Mean	Standard Deviation	N	
Phonics			21	
Individualized reading			21	$t = 2.70$[a]

[a]Statistically significant, $p < .01$.

discussion section, it is nevertheless based on the data. He is not free to interject interpretations and asides which come out of his experience and background unless they are a relevant departure from some aspect of the data. In all sections of the research report the basic referent is the study and the data, and comments beyond these must be built upon them. Personal experience and interpretations have a role in research writing, but that role is limited to their relevance for data interpretation.

In the discussion chapter, as in the results chapter, the researcher has the obligation to treat thoroughly all aspects of the data. In terms of the discussion specifically, this means that the researcher should consider all possible interpretations of the data, and not restrict his discussion to those interpretations he finds most sensible. The researcher should present those interpretations he has rejected as honestly as they would be presented by someone who accepted them. Having done this, the researcher is then free to indicate why he has rejected each such interpretation in favor of a different one. The purpose of the thorough presentation of all the possible interpretations is, as always, to provide the reader with all possible information so that he can form his own interpretations of the data.

There is a second important dimension to the discussion section other than the data, and that is the literature. For in the discussion the researcher interprets his data in the context of the previous research and theory he has reviewed in the introductory section of his report. This is the second purpose the review of literature serves. Where earlier the review established a foundation for the study, now it serves as the point of reference for the discussion of the new data. This is why in our earlier comments in this chapter we noted that all references presented and considered in the discussion section should have been presented in the review of literature. No references to the literature should appear for the first time in the discussion. To use the literature as a context, the researcher discusses those aspects of his results which are consistent with previous research and theory and those which are not. It is seldom necessary to point out to students that they should discuss those aspects of their data that are consistent with the literature, but it is usually necessary to insist that they also consider those aspects that are inconsistent, that is, that they accept all aspects of their data. In fact, this point is worth considering separately.

ACCEPTING THE DATA   If the data come out as expected, most students are delighted and excited and have no difficulty accepting the findings and going on to analyze and discuss them. In this event they generally feel good about their study, and while alert to its limitations in sampling or in instrumentation, they regard the limitations insignificant in the overall scheme of things. The study "worked," and that is the important thing.

Their theoretical orientation was sensible, for the hypotheses developed from that orientation were supported and there is an overall homogeneity between the rationale for the study and the data.

However, when the data do not come out as expected, this generally precipitates amazing insights into the weaknesses of the study! For most students the sample now seems so small and so unrepresentative of any meaningful population as to make the study totally inconclusive. The instruments seem of such dubious worth, so weak in reliability and validity that the findings can hardly be considered seriously as casting doubt upon the theoretical orientation from which the now unsupported hypotheses were derived. And so these students write a discussion chapter which assumes the air of a research confession. They point with devastating accuracy at every real and imagined weakness of their study and earnestly beseech the reader to ignore the negative finding and continue to believe, as the researcher has continued to believe, in the original theory and idea.

This is totally wrong. If we do a study in a certain way we are committed to defending that study and to accepting and interpreting the data derived from that study, *no matter how they come out.* While one of our responsibilities is to point out to the reader the limitations in the design of the research and the specific aspects of the research process like sampling and instrumentation, this does not free us of the responsibility for accepting and understanding our data. If the specific aspects of a research study are so bad as to make us, the researchers, disbelieve the data when they came out a certain way, then this is an excellent argument for us not to have done the study at all, and certainly not to report the results. This last insight is one we should have had *before* we did the study and saw the data, not after the data are known and perceived as negative and therefore "incorrect."

This means that a correctly written discussion section discusses the data as they came out. If they came out counter to the hypotheses and therefore counter to the theoretical rationale from which the hypotheses were established, then the discussion section should present the researcher's reconsideration of the theory and rethinking of the total area in the light of the new findings. To students it often seems presumptious to write a discussion based on the idea that their data are correct, and previously obtained, published data are incorrect. It may well be that this is presumptious, but the issue is not presumption nor whose data are correct and whose incorrect. When the findings of studies conflict and results are contradictory, it is likely that someone is correct and someone else incorrect. Only further research will permit us to know who is right. But it is also possible that some new insight into the situation being studied will reconcile what seem like conflicts under current perceptions. It is to this possibility that the researcher should direct his thinking and his discussion. In short, he should be stimulated by the "negative" data to some original thinking, rather than to a rejection of his study.

Conclusions and Implications

The third level at which the data are to be considered is reached in the sections of the report devoted to conclusions and implications of the study. In the results section the researcher has dispassionately presented his data. In the discussion he has presented his interpretation of what these data mean and how he believes they came about. Now he turns back to the original research problem or questions which motivated his study, and in this section he comes to some definitive conclusion about the original problem, that is, he states his final position as to the answer to the research question. This is the final statement the researcher will make as to the meaning of the data, and it should be clear, specific, and made without hedging. Professionally it should be relevant to the problem and leave no doubt about what the researcher feels the study has and has not demonstrated.

The implications are a different matter. Now the researcher turns to the question of what the data mean for educational program, practice, and theory, if there is a relevant theoretical issue. It sometimes helps in developing the implications to role-play a bit. Imagine that our study is completely correct, that others have corroborated whatever aspects needed corroboration. Further imagine that we are in a position to add to or change the current educational scene as we wish. Based upon our data, what would we change? What would we add? The things we identify as we role-play are the implications of our study for educational practice. Further imagine we have all the theorists relevant to our study assembled to hear our results and learn how these results affect the theoretical positions they have previously enunciated. What would we say to them? These are the theoretical implications of our study.

This section is one of the most intellectually challenging aspects of the research report. For it is here that the researcher ties his own study into the stream of previous research and current thinking. Thus it is perfectly appropriate and desirable to refer to the literature. However, these references should be briefer than the references in the discussion and should refer only to aspects of the literature we have already referred to and discussed there.

The final aspect of the conclusions chapter is usually a specification of the limitations to the conclusions. Here, for the last time, the researcher points out to the reader those aspects of the research process which he believes must be considered before fully accepting the study as definitive and proceeding to take action on the basis of the results. Typically these are limitations in areas like sampling which students have had to limit more than they would like. But note the placement of these limitations: They *follow* the statement of the conclusions and implications. In essence then the report presents a sequence of (1) the data themselves; (2) the discussion and interpretation of the data; (3) the conclusions and implications to be derived from the data; and, as a final note, (4) the limitations which should be kept in mind in deciding whether or not to take action on the basis of the data.

If he has thoroughly presented all four parts to that sequence, the researcher can feel that he has fulfilled his responsibility. It is now up to the reader to evaluate the total picture of results, interpretations, conclusions, and limitations and decide if the research has potential for action. That decision is the reader's. Providing the information so that decision can be made wisely is the researcher's responsibility.

Suggestions for Further Research

The last section of the research report for most student assignments is to identify areas of research suggested by the findings of the current project. Note that this section is data-based, in other words, it stems from the data. In practice this section is the weakest part of student reports. Students do not fully recognize that this should be one of the most creative sections in the entire report, for in this section they demonstrate the research thinking of which they are capable. It is in this section that we have the opportunity to demonstrate our ability to bring together our data, previous research, current thinking, and the full meaning of the limitations of the current study. For it is the synthesis of all of these which culminates in the suggestions for further research.

A favorite cliché in research is to say that every project raises more questions which need study than it answers. Like some clichés, this one is true. The educational process is so complex, and the varieties of human experience so diverse, that no one project can definitely answer all of the questions that might be raised in a problem area. But be aware that not all of these unanswered questions are relevant to include in the section. It too is data-based. As data become available in a problem area, certain aspects of the area are illuminated, and the light shed by this illumination typically also clarifies specific questions remaining unanswered. It is this relationship between finding and question that we mean when we say that the suggestions for further research are data-based. In short, they are research ideas which could not have been stated in quite the same way had the current study not been done, with the results which it actually obtained.

There are specific sources to which we should look for suggestions. Some come from the effort to explain the current results, in the course of which the researcher should have identified alternate explanations which only further research would test. This is particularly true if the current results in some significant way challenge existing theory and belief. Here, too, further research would be needed to determine if the current results or previous results make more sense. Another source for suggestions for further research lies in the limitations of the conclusions to the present study. But in considering the limitations as a source of suggestions, be aware that the stereotyped suggestion that the study needs replication, with additional samples or different grades or larger samples or better instruments, is not what is meant here. In a sense any study can use replication with a different kind of sample, or a larger sample, or with more reliable instruments. These are meaningful statements of needs for further research only if any one of these was a critical limitation in the current study. Critical in this sense means that full understanding of the data and interpretation of the results was limited by this aspect of the study, and so further research is needed.

A final note on these suggestions. In the atypical study it can sensibly be concluded that no further research directly in that problem area is in order. It may be that the research findings have reached a level of precision and completeness sufficient to draw this conclusion. Or the exactly opposite state may be true: The several studies done have been so inconclusive and so contradictory that it seems wisest to begin afresh with a different approach to method, technique, or research design. While this point of view is harder to defend, the student should consider suggesting this possibility if his is the latest in a line of inconclusive studies in a problem area. Thus, instead of suggesting further research would be more of the same, he suggests a new approach which might reconcile the conflicts and contradictions and possibly resolve the confusion in the problem area.

The Summary of the Study

Typically, the research report concludes with a summary of the study. In the summary of the report the researcher faces directly the fact of redundancy, which so often characterizes research writing. For now, having finally finished covering each aspect of the report and having gone through the successive levels of presentation of results, discussion, and conclusions, the researcher begins again in the summary with a statement of the problem.

The summary includes each of the significant aspects of the study, but in quite different detail. The statement of the problem, the rationale for the study, the hypotheses, the design for the study, the methods employed, and the results are all treated with sufficient care to be understood by someone reading the summary without the remainder of the study. The review of the literature, description of the sample, and description of the instruments are all omitted or treated extremely briefly, since it is believed that the summary can be read as an intelligent entity without these aspects repeated.

Practice differs in different colleges and universities as to the preferred placement of the summary. Some prefer it immediately after the results and discussion and before the conclusions and implications. In this instance, the summary is perceived of as a summary of the study only and does not include the researcher's overall interpretations reflected in the conclusions and implications. In other institutions the summary is the final section of the report, following the suggestions for further research. In this case it is obviously a summary of both results and conclusions and implications. In either case the tone is a straightforward descriptive tone spelling out in as few words as possible the key elements of the study.

GETTING STARTED ON THE RESEARCH REPORT

One of the world's more lonely feelings is that of sitting down at a typewriter with a blank sheet inserted and with a mass of data on a nearby desk. As noted at the beginning of this chapter, this feeling can be sufficiently dreadful to keep students away from the typewriter for months on end. How then to get started?

One technique many students find effective is to select some place other than the beginning for the first material to be written. Instead of beginning with the introduction, which may be conceptually complex and which is certainly relatively unstructured, begin with the procedure chapter, which is not conceptually complex and is relatively structured. But beginning at some point other than the first paragraph is simply a way of getting started. The full research report cannot be written effectively in bits and pieces which are then pasted together. If it is, it inevitably reads as a series of discrete units written by separate individuals, none of whom have read what the others have written.

The person who has not written a research report before may not fully appreciate that the kind of precision and consistency which typifies the good research report comes into being only after hours of editing and rewriting. No one can sit down and write initially at that level of precision. The student should recognize that what he first writes is not the final product, but only the first of several drafts. He should drive himself to get a complete draft on paper, rather than spend weeks endlessly perfecting the first four pages of the introduction. Moreover, he must constantly reassure himself that having an inadequately stated idea on paper is preferable to finer versions of that idea in his head. In short, the only way to get started on the research report is to sit down at the typewriter and write, paying little attention, at the beginning, to the fluency and eloquence of what comes through. Fluency and eloquence can be added, but only if a first draft is born.

A FINAL NOTE

At several points in this book we have commented on the amount of time required to prepare a research report properly. It seems appropriate to close both this chapter on research writing and the book itself with a reminder of that point. If it is to achieve the level of precision and consistency required, the research report must be written and rewritten with these goals in mind. Moreover, if the several sections are to build on each other and have the interactions of content which typify the good research report, then additional editing and rewriting is required. A kind of editorial chain reaction occurs in which, for example, a sudden insight in the discussion chapter may precipitate a rethinking and consequent rewriting of a piece of the review of literature chapter, as a reference not previously included suddenly becomes relevant. Similarly, an unanticipated analysis of some data will force a revision in the section of the procedure chapter which details the data analyses to be presented. All of this revision, editing, and rewriting takes time.

Research writing can be an intellectually challenging and satisfying task if time is available. Moreover, given that time, a readable, lively report can be created which also is consistent with the canons of research writing. If insufficient time is available the task is a grueling and frustrating one, and the report inevitably reflects this. Therefore, the final word of advice is to exert every effort in the planning of research to allow for enjoyment of the process, and this means allowing sufficient time for the proper preparation of the research report.

INDEX